THE CIVILIZATION OF THE AMERICAN INDIAN SERIES

The Toltecs

The Toltecs

Until the Fall of Tula

By Nigel Davies

NORMAN
UNIVERSITY OF OKLAHOMA PRESS

By Nigel Davies:

THE AZTECS, A History (London, 1973)

THE TOLTECS, UNTIL THE FALL OF TULA (Norman, 1977)

Library of Congress Cataloging in Publication Data

Davies, Nigel, 1920–
The Toltecs, until the fall of Tula.

(The Civilization of the American Indian series; v. 144)
Bibliography: p. 485
Includes index.
1. Toltecs. 2. Mexico—Antiquities. I. Title. II. Series.
F1219.D2783 972 76-62513
ISBN 0-8061-1394-4

 Manufactured in the U.S.A. First edition.

To José Manuel Bustamante

Contents

Foreword

Ever since I first studied the specifically historical aspects of ancient Mesoamerican civilization, I determined one day to try to write about the Toltecs. I soon realized that the subject was charged with controversy; I knew that the challenge would be severe, and my assumptions have indeed proved correct in that respect.

To tackle the Toltecs is very different from writing about the Aztecs, which I have already done at some length. For the latter, a plethora of information is available for which coherent conclusions are not too hard to draw. But the former stand upon the very threshold of recorded history. As we shall later see in much greater detail, contradictions abound in the written sources, and these in turn are often at variance with the archaeological record. In this volume, which deals with the Toltecs until the collapse of Tula, one of my main tasks has been to combine the two forms of information. In a later volume, which will concern the Toltec heritage after the fall of Tula, most of the material is to be derived from the written sources, and archaeology offers less supporting evidence.

It is time that someone grasped the nettle and recorded the available data on the Toltecs in book form. Toltec materials in this form offer the reader the possibility of studying the Early Postclassic Toltecs as one story, rather than in more fragmented form in a series of articles and papers, such as have previously appeared on the subject. In order to attain even a limited understanding of the problems involved, it is necessary to review the Toltec panorama as a whole rather than piecemeal.

If one studies only a part of the Toltec historical process, one may easily reach solutions which appear adequate purely for that portion of the whole, but which turn out to conflict with possible conclusions offered for other parts of the story.

It is rather like solving a jigsaw puzzle; one possesses many pieces which may appear to belong one to another, but he has to fit them all together into one picture. One may, for instance, find a number of gray pieces, obviously forming part of the same object; at first sight this may be taken to be a gray house. But it is only when the surrounding pieces are also accounted for that one may see whether his assumption is correct or whether the object in question is not really a gray elephant or, for that matter, a mouse.

I would like to emphasize that, if I had not had the privilege of studying under Professor Paul Kirchhoff and of drawing on his deep knowledge of the problems involved, I would never have been able to write this book. My indebtedness to Professor Wigberto Jiménez Moreno is as great; it was he who first aroused my interest, and only from such an incomparable teacher was I able to understand that the history of Mesoamerica is a living reality, quite as much as that of any other civilization or country. He has been most helpful in giving his time to the discussion of many chapters of this work; his generosity is all the more to be appreciated in view of the fact that we disagree on certain aspects of the subject, though much common ground also exists between us. In addition, I am most grateful to Dr. Ignacio Bernal, who has read almost all the book and given me much support and encouragement. My colleagues as a whole have been very helpful in advising on certain specialized facets, and I am particularly indebted to Professor Thelma Sullivan, whose continuous and unfailing aid in many knotty problems of Nahuatl etymology and interpretation has proved indispensable.

I would like to make only one further introductory comment. This book seeks to set out chapter by chapter the relevant facts as known today, but it usually also offers some kind of interpretation, that is to say, my personal view on the points at issue. I must stress, however, that I make no dogmatic claim that my opinions are necessarily always correct, more especially since in some respects I differ from more eminent authorities on the subject. I merely trust that my interpretations will be accepted as the best that I am able to offer on such a complex pattern of events; I would express the equal hope that they may provoke others to seek to improve upon my efforts.

I would feel that these had not been wasted if they helped in some small measure to convince students of the Institute Nacional de Antropología e Historia in Mexico, as well as elsewhere, of the need to familiarize themselves with both the archaeology *and* the written sources if they are to attain a full understanding of the development of Postclassic Mesoamerica.

I would like to express my gratitude to all those who have helped me in the preparation of this book, and in particular to Professor Jorge Acosta, Dr. Ignacio Bernal, Professor Beatriz Braniff, Dr. Richard Diehl, Dr. Lawrence Feldman, Professor Angel García Cook, Professor Doris Heydn, Professor Wigberto Jiménez Moreno, Professor Thomas Lee, Dr. Jaime Litvak, Professor Alfredo López Austin, Professor Florencia Muller, Professor Eduardo Matos, Professor Antoinette Nelken, Dr. Ramón Piña Chan, Professor Luis Reyes, Professor Thelma Sullivan, and the late Sir Eric Thompson. I am especially indebted to Max Clemente, whose fine photographs adorn this book.

NIGEL DAVIES

Mexico City, D.F.

Illustrations

Maps

The Toltecs

1. Fact and Legend

As HEIRS TO Teotihuacán and ancestors to the Aztecs, the Toltecs stand astride the history of Mesoamerica. They occupy a central or pivotal position; one might thus compare them with the creators of Tihuanaco in the northern Andes, with the Egyptian Middle Kingdom, or perhaps even with the European Middle Ages.

Archaeology and the Written Records

Accordingly, in surveying the whole Toltec panorama, we seek to bridge the gap that yawns between earlier Mesoamerican history, based on archaeological findings, and the final Aztec phase, known mainly through written sources. It is moreover intended that such a work, apart from its more specialized aspects, may interest any who seek those elusive rules that govern mankind's development, equally valid in the New World and in the Old.

Few approaches to universal history are undertaken nowadays, notwithstanding the formidable work of Arnold Toynbee, in unraveling the processes that accompany the rise and fall of empires. A hundred years ago it was generally believed, not only by historians but also by sociologists and anthropologists, that the stages of man's development were indeed governed by some such universal laws. Today the reaction against pure evolutionism has almost reached the point where the very existence of such norms is often denied. Julian Steward, for instance, points out that scientific evidence accumulated more recently suggests that cultures diverge significantly one from another and thus do not necessarily pass through unilinear stages.[1]

Even if absolute principles of human development cannot be laid down for all time, comparisons of New and Old World historical processes do surely offer a rewarding and almost virgin field for future research, to give deepened perspective to both. In order to draw attention to this need, the opportunity will be taken in this work to make certain such broader comparisons.

The Postclassic Toltecs were in a sense perennial frontiersmen, never too far removed from the marches of the preying nomads; in this they may offer a prototype for the problems facing sedentary civilizations when threatened by such groups, whether in Europe, Asia, or America. In one of the very few comparative studies of Mesoamerica and the ancient East, Robert McC. Adams fully treats this phenomenon as it affected Toltec Mesoamerica and early dynastic Mesopotamia.[2] Many parallels emerge between the two regions, both beset by similar perils; in each, the dominant culture tended in the long run to succumb to wilder peoples from border regions.

The pivotal role played by the Toltecs makes their history even harder to unravel, and its every facet cannot immediately be presented as simply as a children's tale. It would be idle to pretend that this task does not present a severe challenge. As Clavijero puts it in writing of the history of the earlier peoples of Anahuac, "Various of our historians have sought to penetrate this chaos, guided by the faint light of conjecture, of futile calculation and of uncertain codices. But they have lost themselves in the twilight of antiquity, and have been compelled to recount puerile and unsubstantial tales."[3] It is hoped that, through guidance by the lamps of modern archaeology and inspiration from the efforts of more recent investigators, at least some constructive light may be shed on the confused obscurity which the eighteenth-century historian justly describes.

In studying this Early Postclassic period, many complications admittedly arise because findings cannot be based solely on the work of the archaeologist, nor can reliance be exclusively placed upon the historical sources; the key to any solution must lie in an apt blend of both. Many investigators may have hesitated to adopt this combined approach, so hard to apply in practice. But however forbidding, it remains indispensable, and I shall try to show that it is not unattainable.

Much of the Toltec historical material is so confused and contradictory that one would be left baffled without the aid of the archaeologist. To take a simple example, the multifarious written reports of the departure of Topiltzin-Quetzalcoatl for Tlillan Tlapallan, the Maya land, could not be placed in any proper context if it were not for the physical remains of a Toltec presence there.

The reverse is just as true; the archaeological finds in Tula, Hidalgo, could not have been surely identified with the historic Tollan, as known to the Aztecs, had not Jiménez Moreno and others extracted clear evidence to that effect from the written sources.

Thus the Toltec saga in its broadest and most universal sense provides a field in which archaeology is admirably fitted to serve as the handmaiden of history, surely its ultimate purpose.

What has often impeded a more comprehensive approach to Mesoamerican history is a tendency of investigators to divide themselves into two camps: those who dig and ignore the writings, and those who read but ignore the diggings. Not infrequently excavators, particularly of Postclassic sites, may lack over-all perspective if they remain in happy oblivion of the relevant documentary evidence; the latter could often be used to pose the appropriate questions, even if unaided it cannot solve the riddles.

Equally, students of the chronicles may at times reach conclusions in blind contradiction to established archaeological facts. For instance, documentary accounts of the relatively late foundation of Culhuacán in the Valley of Mexico continue to be taken at their face value, notwithstanding the presence in that site of layer upon layer of pottery that is demonstrably far older.

To avoid such pitfalls, this work will examine at each phase both the archaeological evidence and the testimony of the documents. I believe that any attempt to solve Toltec problems is doomed to failure unless both are taken fully into account. If contradictions arise, then they must be squarely faced and somehow resolved or reconciled; they cannot simply be brushed under the historical carpet.

Archaeological Bypaths

Before embarking upon any detailed study of Tollan and the Toltecs, it is indispensable in this initial chapter to establish, as far as possible, a methodology, and to explain clearly how such a difficult theme can properly be tackled.

It must first be admitted that archaeological evidence, as well as the written word, has limitations, for archaeology itself is in danger of becoming lost in what Sir Eric Thompson has called "the bypaths of abracadabra."[4] Little purpose may be served in carefully marking and ordering innumerable sherds, unless it is done to serve a clear purpose, present or future. It is of rather limited interest to know that a greater proportion of red-on-buff pottery is to be found in one site and black-on-orange in another unless such data can eventually be linked to the course of history. In this respect it must be added that future possibilities should not be overlooked; the potentialities of the computer for the ordering of such data are almost unlimited, or even perhaps for the comprehension of written material on the Toltecs and other peoples.

Obviously one cannot hope for many solutions to the principal Toltec problems by the unaided assistance of excavation; apart from other considerations, the very questions themselves are posed by the contradictions apparent in the written sources. And, unlike its Old World counterparts, Mesoamerican archaeology cannot itself unearth the written evidence, in the form of decipherable texts graven in stone. An additional disadvantage derives from a New World tendency to abandon sites, particularly in the Postclassic era, after only a few centuries of occupation; to this Cholula and Monte Albán may be taken as partial exceptions. Rome, Athens, and even Ur spanned millennia; in contrast, the grandeur that was Tula begins late and ends early. Thus one cannot apply the surest mode of comparison: the tracing of successive eras of occupation through their manifestations in one single site.

Archaeology faces another limitation, of universal application but especially germane to Toltec questions. The work of the spade may uncover patterns of trade or cultural influences relating to a particular civilization, but if texts are lacking, it cannot demonstrate the extent of territory dominated, let alone the kind of rule that any conquerors might have imposed.

Similarities of style may indicate the maximum radius of cultural penetration, but cannot reveal its nature or cause. No exercise could be vainer than merely to delimit all points where Toltec-style remains appear, and then to denominate such a region as the "Toltec Empire." As John Paddock rightly insists, one is too apt to confuse a poor potter with an imperial army.

Examples of the fallacies of similar methods could be provided ad infinitum. To take one case: it might well be supposed that the future discovery in the ruins of eighteenth-century Europe of abundant pottery actually imported from China, together with many objects made in Europe but imitating Chinese styles (Chinoiserie), would intrigue future archaeologists. They would surely conclude not only that Chinese occupation had taken place, but also that the humble Europeans, not content with importing their products, showed such devotion to their Chinese overlords that they copied their styles after their own peculiar fashion (these very arguments have often been used as proof of Teotihuacán's physical domination of vast areas). Any notion that the Chinese never even came to Europe and that it was the Europeans who lorded it over the former would arouse ridicule. No European penetration of China at this time would be revealed by archaeology, since China was then paid in bullion for its exports and only much later imported European wares.

Furthermore, in this particular case, any superficial study of Chinese historical sources would admirably second such conclusions. In effect, in the eighteenth and far into the nineteenth century, the Chinese emperor refused to receive permanent European ambassadors; on the contrary, the absurd fiction was maintained, and even appeared in official writings, that all other sovereigns should regard themselves as the emperor's vassals, not his equals.

And in such a supposedly Chinese-dominated Europe, it might even be deduced that England constituted a kind of subprovince of the Republic of Venice, whose Palladian style of architecture became diffused to that country in the course of about one century; in the English mansion of Merreworth, the archaeologist would even discover an exact replica of La Rotonda, outside Venice.

By the same token, architectural styles and Toltec-type pottery designs recalling Tula, Hidalgo, do not automatically denote a Toltec military presence in any given place, any more than the wide diffusion of Teotihuacán culture in itself affords proof of physical domination.

Of course, the reverse is also often true when the extent of imperial rule is under study. The Aztecs did indeed conquer far and wide, but left relatively limited traces of their achievements except for occasional pyramids surmounted by twin temples; and even this particular style is not specifically Mexica in origin, being already present in Tenayuca. There is, for instance, little Aztec III and IV pottery in the Matlatzinca zone.[5] In coastal areas of the southern part of the state of Veracruz, Teotihuacán influences abound, but Aztec or Aztecoid are entirely lacking.[6] Paddock finds some signs of an Aztec presence in the Mixteca Alta, but no traces near Oaxaca itself.[7] He also points to the general failure of the Aztecs to proselytize outside the Huaxteca.

Thus some future scholar, attempting to map the extent of an Aztec empire with the sole aid of archaeology, would have drawn a virtual blank and might even have denied its existence on any scale. Clearly, excavations may establish stages or strata, but are ill equipped to define singlehanded the ultimate bounds of empire, Toltec or any other.

At best, one may be able to trace by such means a core or nuclear area, a kind of inner ring that surrounds the metropolis, and where the latter's culture has for the time being virtually superseded any local styles. Ignacio Bernal has attempted to define such a zone for Teotihuacán. Where the Aztecs are concerned, one may also recall the abundant physical manifestations of their influences in the nearby Valleys of Toluca and Morelos, even if in these latter cases distinct local patterns did also persist.

Confusing Sources

The written sources possess equally valid limitations. Moreover, while the pitfalls that beset archaeological interpretations are not always immediately apparent, the tendency of the records to prove unreliable, or merely allegorical, are all too patent. The unwary student, for example, scarcely needs to be cautioned not to believe that some people had ears so long that they could wrap themselves up at night, simply because "*L'Histoyre du Mechique*" says so!

At the same time, however, the sources offer traps of a more subtle kind. It is easy, for instance, to fall at first sight into the snare of supposing that all Chichimecs are wild hunters and all Toltecs urbane craftsmen. But in Mesoamerica paradox prevails, and the reverse may be equally true; as Paul Kirchhoff insisted, things often prove on closer examination to be the very opposite of what one thought at first.

One is faced with additional problems in dealing with Mesoamerican sources because contemporary records are often lacking, records actually written in the period when the events took place. Codices, except in the Mixteca, were habitually lost and possibly even deliberately destroyed.

Great attention was undoubtedly paid to the recording of the past: Out of deference to their special standing, singers, recorders, and writers were even exempt from taxation.[8] And as a corollary to such codical writings, much Mesoamerican history and legend was taught by those familiar with them, and their contents were thus handed down by word of mouth; naturally the farther back one goes, the more garbled such accounts become.

Such frustrations are the constant affliction of the investigator of the Toltecs. For they stand at the very limits of recorded and remembered fact; they are preceded in most sources by "giants" and other allegorical creatures. And while certain accounts dimly refer to events lying beyond the Postclassic horizon, material for the initial Toltec period is very scanty; most of the data on the Postclassic Tollan refers not to its rise, but to its fall. Kirchhoff in particular refers to the collapse of the Toltec empire as the great event with whose description the written history of ancient Mexico begins.[9]

In general terms, certain limitations of Mesoamerican historical sources, whether for the Toltecs or for later peoples, are obvious. Román Piña Chan aptly described the causes that give rise to the archaeologists' general distrust of the written records. These may be summed up as follows: sheer mistakes, due to human fallibility or errors of language; the overrich admixture of fable and legend; and, worst of all, continual contradictions between one account and another, together with a perpetual apparent confusion over chronology.[10]

Divergences occasionally deepen through the tendency of archaeologists and historians to use a different terminology. To take an example totally remote from Mesoamerica: the historian Bede writes of Jutish settlements in the County of Kent, whereas archaeologists deny the presence of any Jutish assemblages in that region. But what the latter mean by this is not at all what Bede intended to imply; he was clearly ready to apply the term "Jutish" to a group of heterogeneous North Germans, symbolized by a single Jutish princeling, who were not really Jutes at all.[11]

The Toltecs pose such problems of nomenclature in accentuated form. The term itself was used in many places at many times, and this in itself facilitates contradictions between the historian and the archaeologist, who seek different definitions for the same thing. One is continually faced with problems created by the very generalized application of the term "Toltec," employed even more loosely and universally than "Jutish."

In reality, perhaps the investigator of Toltec written sources is himself compelled to adopt techniques more reminiscent of archaeology, for the student of such writings must approach them rather in the spirit of a stratigraphic exploration, with a view to separating their rather jumbled data into appropriate layers or strata. One must first divide the period under investigation into its distinct phases, say, early, middle, and late; the material must then be analyzed and reordered according to such simple criteria.

To take one obvious example: the famous Chapter 29 of Sahagún's Book X, relating to the different peoples of Mesoamerica and their history, is at first sight most perplexing. Only after repeated reading and careful analysis can one even dimly discern which passages refer to the apogee of Teotihuacán, which to its decline, which to the interim pre-Tula period, and which to the rise and also to the fall of the latter. This account, like others, follows no particular chronological sequence, but switches with alarming rapidity from one era to another and then back again. Only by studying the context and subject matter can one judge where each paragraph properly belongs.

Problems of dating are all-pervading in Mesoamerican historical research. The compilers of chronicles did not themselves always understand the native system of counting the years; thus the tendency prevailed to pick year-dates and corresponding events from several different surviving records in order to concoct a new history; these are then combined in a *seemingly* logical chronological sequence, listing happenings for the year 1 Calli, 2 Tochtli, 3 Acatl, etc., in that order. But these reconstructions invariably overlook the fact that in such an arbitrary selection, an occurrence for the year 2 Tochtli that followed 1 Calli in the text may belong to quite a different year-cycle and thus really took place not one year after that listed for 1 Calli, but fifty-three years later, (i.e., 52 plus 1), or perhaps fifty-one years before (52 minus 1). Equally, as I have fully explained in another context, two such dates may also belong to completely distinct calendar systems, with different methods of naming the years.[12]

Thus, for instance, the above-mentioned 1 Calli might belong to the official Tencohca calendar, and the 2 Tochtli to what Jiménez Moreno has denominated the Mixtec year-count, differing from the former by roughly twelve years; in this case, the 2 Tochtli would follow not one or fifty-three years after 1 Calli, but thirteen years (1 plus 12) or sixty-five years later (1 plus 12 plus 52).

Such a situation is perhaps less surprising than might appear at first sight. Quite apart from the existence of the Islamic reckoning, one must not forget that in Europe itself the Orthodox calendar, based on the original Julian system and by then differing fourteen years from the Gregorian, was used in Russia until the end of the Czarist era, and continued in force in Greece for some years subsequent to this. Indeed, until as late as 1752, England and Spain counted the days differently, because England only adopted the Gregorian calendar in preference to the Julian in that year, when English dates were twelve days later than those in Spain.

If, as in Mesoamerica, England and Spain had named their years after the first or last day of each one, then they would also have recorded differently their *years* as well as their days.

When dealing with Mesoamerican dates, because of the uncertainties of diverse calendars and year-cycles, it is rather as if the first two digits in our own calendar were to be suppressed. Thus, instead of 1966, one would simply write 66. Aided by such records, one could well imagine that a future chronicler of our own civilization many centuries hence might compile a seemingly useful catalogue of events in England something like the following:

Year 65: Great plague of London (abbreviation of 1665).
Year 66: England occupied by William the Conqueror (1066); Fire of London (1666).
Year 67: Darnley assassinated; Mary Stuart marries Bothwell (1567).

To this might be added for the year 68 an event taken from the Islamic calendar.

Such a muddled sequence is literally no worse than some of the dates that face the Mesoamerican historian; by way of clarification, it could no doubt be explained in learned footnotes that it was quite logical to suppose that the Great Fire should occur after the upheavals of the Norman occupation. Equally, since the Great Fire and Mary Stuart's marriage both in different ways affected members of the House of Stuart, Charles II and Mary herself, it might seem quite natural to list them as following one another in successive years. The question of whether Charles II really reigned in the same century as Mary Queen of Scots or the one following might by then have become a matter of mere conjecture!

Thus, in any Mesoamerican source, the order in which events are reported to occur often represent little more than an arbitrary choice, arranged to suit the preconceived notions of the chronicler rather than the actual facts. Such a process is sometimes involuntary, due to mere human error, and at others deliberate, perhaps to enhance the antiquity of the dynasty from which the writer of the document claimed descent.

Of this problem modern investigators are, of course, generally fully aware. Notwithstanding this fact, however, misinterpretations continue to abound, based on an almost natural tendency to assume that, for instance, events listed on page 4 of a given edition of the *Anales de Cuauhtitlán* really did occur later than those events occurring on page 3, and that those of page 3 equally postdate happenings of page 2.

Much of what the sources tell us is therefore not only confused but positively misleading without careful reordering. The historian's task thus comes to resemble that of the archaeologist who seeks to establish his correct stratigraphy in a site confused by every kind of landslide or eruption and every other sort of distortion from the usual norm. He must base his deductions not so much upon the *level* at which his artifacts appear but on their associations with others of the same type or horizon.

Equally, it is only by the most minute examination of the evidence that it can be decided at which stratigraphic level of history much of the earlier material of the written sources belongs. The order in which events occur in the text often means little or nothing; thus, if one simply records facts in the same sequence in which they are related, the conclusions are likely to be abysmally negative. They will not serve to elucidate but only to confirm ancient misconceptions, and so to mislead.

It is really only by the aid of this horizontal method that one can even hope to disentangle the involved Toltec web. In dealing with each phase or aspect of the conundrum, one has to take from the texts all data that might apply to that particular facet or period, leaving the remainder for discussion in its due context. We shall find inextricably interwoven in various sources material concerning what one may call the three Tula stages: beginning, middle, and end. Such items of information are in their turn mixed up with semilegendary happenings of pre-Toltec times, together with certain stories of Chichimecs, who were not Toltec at all; they really followed after Tula, but their story is sometimes told as if they came before. To demonstrate the point, the events concerned are set out in tabular form in Table A, Appendix A, so that the reader may see at a glance what each source says upon the subject.

From such a medley it has proved necessary to choose carefully what correctly applies to each chapter of this work; it is of course necessary to show in its proper context why such a seemingly arbitrary selection of information has been made in each case. Above all, it has to be clearly demonstrated why events which the sources themselves associate with early and middle Toltec history are omitted until very near the end of the story. If one deduces, for instance, that personalities traditionally associated with the rise of Tollan really belong to its fall, the reader must exercise patience if their doings are not recounted till the end of the tale, where their presence will be duly justified.

Merely to recount what each document relates, and in the same order, is an easy but unrewarding task, which will only leave the hapless reader more confused than before. It is surely by this more analytical and eclectic method, breaking down the sources into strata, that a more meaningful picture may emerge. Such tactics may seem at first sight arbitrary, but they alone can offer results. In the course of this work, the full range of the extant material on the Toltecs will be taken into account, but assigned to its correct place in the story rather than introduced out of context.

The task rather resembles a game of patience. In this, one cannot succeed by simply taking the unshuffled cards and then piling them up in heaps of convenient size in the order in which they may come out of the pack. Instead, each card has to be examined as it is dealt and carefully put in its right place, according to its suit and number. Only thus can one evolve a coherent pattern and successfully conclude the game.

Fact and Legend Intertwined

The nature of such general and chronological difficulties confronting the Mesoamerican investigator may be relatively familiar. But the student of the Toltecs is faced with additional problems. The first of these arises because only certain records contain Toltec material, and this usually occurs at their very beginning. These versions are invariably confused by a rich admixture of underlying legend and myth.

It used to be the fashion all over the world to treat accounts of this type simply as confabulations on the part of priests and rulers, concocted as a soothing opiate for the people. However, starting with the discovery of the real Troy, which was followed by the triumphs of Cretan and Mycenaean archaeology and the scientific unearthing of the dwellings of heroes such as Nestor, previously relegated to mere legend, attitudes gradually changed. Mesmerized by these feats, historians tended toward the opposite extreme, regarding all myths as true in essence, if not in detail.

But such finds were isolated achievements in the context of world history. One has only to take the Greek legends as a whole to see that the alternative versions of the same set of events can differ radically; such divergent accounts cannot logically all be true and therefore equally verifiable by archaeology.

It must also be appreciated that many myths are not the product of a kind of spontaneous combustion but were deliberately devised and carefully nurtured to serve specific ends. To quote Malinowski: "The function of myth, briefly, is to strengthen tradition and endow it with a greater value and prestige by tracing it back to a higher, better, more supernatural reality of ancient events."[13]

Myth and legend in fact serve as a medium for presenting to the individual human conscience in intelligible form the more abstract conceptual structure of the prevailing socio-religious system. The rites and ceremonies that also form part of the complex often involve some manner of re-enactment of the myths. But unhappily in Mesoamerica, one is generally much better informed concerning such legends and ceremonies than about the actual concepts that underlie them.

As emphasized by Georges Dumézil in his examination of the common Indo-European heritage, every people has its own ancient or epic history, that is to say, an ensemble of narrations concerning their great ancestors and the heroes who supposedly lived in their land and gave form to their civilization. Such were Manu, Arjuna, and Rama as the sons of heaven, or Hercules, Theseus, and Lycurgus. The myths about these beings were often a more powerful influence than the divine myths and underlie the traditional philosophy of each nation.[14]

The same author goes on to say that this is equally true of a Central Australian clan and of the most remote Brazilian tribes, who have no recent history. The latter may barely know the facts of yesterday and the day before, but all of them possess their own "ancient story."

Such comments surely apply to the Toltecs, whose doings belong both to epic and to history in the more usual sense of the word, and whose era was portrayed as a kind of Golden Age by the mentors of the ancestor-conscious Mexicas. Toltec achievements thus do not reach us recorded in a straightforward manner, but often are subservient as much to divine ordainment as to human fallibility. As in the *Iliad*, mere episodes are sometimes told as if they were the whole story; in Tula as in Troy, the epic concentrates on the end of the tale.

But from such possible confabulations, the hard core of fact may be extracted by analysis and comparison. However, a further problem often arises; even after straining off the layers of legend, the residue of history is as ambiguous as the legend itself.

Forgetting such lessons, one may be tempted to take references to Mesoamerican native dates and place names as plain statements of fact, whose main purpose is to inform the reader. But the history of ancient peoples tended toward concepts different from our own, being devised to edify as much as to instruct. The real purpose of a story, as we have seen, might be its power to enhance the antiquity of a dynasty, the genius of its scion, or the magnitude of its conquests. Precise details, such as which ruler conquered which city, were often of lesser consequence. Such confusions are, of course, not peculiar to Mesoamerica; Ramses III enumerates his conquests in Asia, but his list is simply copied from that of the previous pharaoh, Ramses II, who in turn had used one that really originated with Tuthmosis III. In early Sumer, the same difficulty arises of collating dynastic lists for separate towns and areas and in bringing chronological dates together into an acceptable whole.[15]

The student of Mesoamerica is very familiar with such vexing problems, which are aggravated by a lack of contemporary versions of events and the limitations of pictorial codices. Consequently greater reliance must be placed on oral tradition. Moreover many of the surviving accounts were not complied in the sixteenth century or soon after contact with the Spaniards, but emanate from later chroniclers, more remote from true native traditions.

While much Toltec material comes from Sahagún, Muñóz Camargo, *La Historia de los Mexicanos*, Motolinía, the *Anales de Cuauhtitlán*, and the *Historia Tolteca-Chichimeca*, the story remains incomplete without extensive reference to later writers such as Ixtlilxóchitl and Torquemada, who provide some invaluable data, often based on ancient documents long since lost. At the same time they tend to add to the prevailing confusion by introducing a new mythology of their own to supplement the old. They insert, for instance, their views on early beginnings; Torquemada thus lists not merely the Romans and Carthaginians but even the Irish as possible ancestors of the Toltecs.

In ancient historical recording, a natural tendency exists to repeat the same story with only minor variations in a series of documents; each however may connect the tale in question with a totally distinct series of events. This applies especially to Mesoamerican sources, and in particular to the whole Ce Acatl-Topiltzin-Quetzalcoatl saga, of which one finds a plethora of conflicting accounts, some referring to the end of Tula and others to its beginning and even before. Certain of these emanate from Central Mexico, while others stem from Yucatán or even the distant highlands of Guatemala.

All over the world people tend to promote heroes into deities and perhaps occasionally to degrade gods into human heroes; thus, the story of an actual human being in one context becomes a generalized legend in another. The difficulty then arises of separating the deeds of the human being from the feats of the semimythical hero and even the god, often mentioned in almost the same paragraph of one text. To pinpoint in place and time the man or men called Topiltzin or Quetzalcoatl or merely Ce Acatl, as opposed to the divine counterpart, is sure to prove hard. The problem however cannot be avoided, if Toltec history is to be placed in its true perspective.

In view of such manifold ambiguities, one cannot at the outset automatically accept the existence of any human Topiltzin-Quetzalcoatl in Postclassic Tula, either in the first or last phase. The whole story might conceivably be related to the era of Teotihuacán or before, and not to Tula, Hidalgo, at all. One may not at this stage regard any of the conflicting stories of Topiltzin as strictly true or untrue.

And what concerns people also applies to places. Not merely are fact and legend inextricably interwoven into the same accounts, but an additional difficulty arises when Tollan, in most contexts a historical city such as Rome or Paris, in others becomes a kind of allegorical Garden of Eden.

As will later be seen in greater detail, in the *Annals of the Cakchiquels*, "Tulán" is no longer a locality in the state of Hidalgo but a place of fable, more to be compared with the paradise of Tlalocan. Actually, four "Tuláns" are mentioned in this text: one east, one west, one in the sky, and one probably intended as below the earth. For the Cakchiquels the four "Tuláns" played the same role as the Seven Caves in other cases as a common place of origin. Like Tula, Chicomoztoc undoubtedly was a perfectly identifiable locality for certain peoples, but it also tended to develop more into a concept, the universal Quinehuayan, the point of rising up or departing. Transformed into an abstraction, it could, like Tollan, be anywhere. The Mixtecs after all had their own Chicomoztoc, and Chimalpain even writes of a Tollan in Tlapallan Nonoalco, suggestive of the Tabasco region.

Borrowed Plumes

The second special problem facing the Toltec investigator arises out of the first; it concerns the particular need to separate material pertaining to Postclassic Tollan from records of events that went before and were connected more probably with Teotihuacán. For the early Postclassic Toltecs, conventionally known simply as the "Toltecs," undoubtedly borrowed from their predecessors, just as did the Aztecs in their turn from the Toltecs.

When one recalls that the Aztecs conjured up visions of a fabulous Golden Age, based ostensibly on the story of Tula, Hidalgo, a much more modest city than Tenochtitlán, the mind boggles at the thought of the incredible tales which the inhabitants of Tula must have told of the great Teotihuacán, many times larger than their own capital and of fairly recent memory in the early Postclassic era.

To separate events of one period from those of another is less simple than might appear at first sight. The story of the Mexica migration, as told in various sources, is a fairly straightforward tale of a definite period in the history of one tribe. It would be normal to take these accounts at their face value, making due allowance for a certain overlay of the supernatural in connection with such happenings as the birth of Huitzilopochtli or the death of Cópil.

When however one comes to examine matters more closely, it may be seen that the account does indeed relate certain episodes that could only have happened to the Mexicas and that belongs truly to their own particular story. On the other hand, it becomes equally clear that parts of the migration epic are little more than a kind of prototype tale, apt to be cited in the history of any itinerant group. In particular, certain main incidents may derive from the doings of early Toltec migrants, long before the Mexicas.

For instance, the two places regularly mentioned as lying on the Mexica route between Teoculhuacán and Tula are Coatlicamac and Cuextecatl-Ichocayan. But precisely the same localities were visited by the Toltecs before reaching Tula, according to the Anónimo Mexicano.[16] And, not content with this, Muñóz Camargo and Torquemada report that the Chichimecs of Xólotl passed by these localities on their way to the Valley of Mexico.[17] The Nonoalca Tlacochcalcas, coming from the opposite direction, also incidentally visited a place called Cuixtecatlycacan.[18]

To take a further point, not only do such names as Iztac Mixcoatl, and even Chimalma, dear to Toltec legend, also appear in connection with the Mexica migration, but equally the famous *teomamaque*, or bearers of the god, whom one inevitably associates with Huitzilopochtli, also appear in the *Codex Vindobonensis* in connection with Quetzalcoatl. In addition, Sahagún describes how, at a moment probably related to the end of Teotihuacán, the god Yohualli Ehécatl is carried off eastward by *teomamaque*. Even in the *Popol Vuh* there exists a certain parallel, as the tribal god is carried by his own bearers on the march, and like Huitzilopochtli, addresses his chosen people. Also according to the *Popol Vuh*, Zipacna kills four hundred *macehuales* with the help of ants, recalling Huitzilopochtli's feat in dispatching the four hundred Huitznahuas on his birth in Coatepec—or for that matter the story of the four hundred Mimixcoas, who met a similar fate as part of certain Quetzalcoatl legends.

But perhaps the famous Coatepec dam offers one of the more striking examples of the tendency to borrow legends. It was allegedly built by the Mexicas at Coatepec, described by various sources as situated near Tula, only later to be destroyed at the bidding of an angry Huitzilopochtli. It will later be argued that Tula, as the Toltec capital, situated in arid country, would develop some system of irrigation. Equally, one may allow that the itinerant Mexicas were less primitive than is sometimes supposed. But at this stage in their career, when still a wandering tribe, they could hardly have erected permanent dams or created an artificial lake, a major engineering feat. Clearly this story, dramatically told in Tezozómoc's *Crónica Mexicayotl* and by Durán, as well as the account of the rich fauna and flora that later vanished, describes certain events that might have accompanied the disintegration of Tula itself. But the original account, as connected with *Toltec* history, has disappeared. Thus, a perfectly good version of certain events that probably befell the inhabitants of Tula now only survives as a borrowed and colorful plume in the history of the Mexicas themselves.

By the same token we may discover that, just as the latter borrowed from the Toltecs, certain of the feats attributed to the Toltecs came from the history of their forerunners. Consequently, at each stage one must insistently ask whether any given happening really does refer to the Postclassic, or historic, Toltecs or is simply taken from the doings of their predecessors in Teotihuacán and other places.

A further kind of borrowing also deserves mention. The material of the sources was often recorded or handed down in a form molded to fit the Europeans' own notions of man's remote past. In particular, the Toltec section of certain documents, that is to say the early part, tended to be tailored to fit certain Spanish prejudices concerning peoples of the New World. Among the strongest of such preconceived notions was that of monogenesis; in other words, all mankind had a common origin, as told in the Book of Genesis. Thus, the different peoples of America, on their way from the Garden of Eden, must automatically have crossed the sea from east to west to reach their present abodes (the idea that they might have come the other way around across the Bering Strait had of course not yet arisen). The Spaniards for their part could not possibly envisage any independent development of the peoples of the New World, complete with an American Eden and their own Adam and Eve. From this dilemma arose curious attempts to provide a respectable pedigree for the American Indian, linking him with the lost tribes of Israel, the Egyptians, the Carthaginians, and even the Irish!

As related by Sahagún, the ancestors of the Mexicas crossed the sea to arrive at Panotlan, identified by him as Pánuco.[19] The constant references in this and other sources to Panotlan, Panohuayan, and even Pantlan (quite a different derivation) as a place of arrival or crossover of many different tribes in their early wanderings has accordingly led to the notion that Pánuco was a kind of universal point of entry, rather like New York for the nineteenth-century immigrants into the United States. Those who did not actually come through Pánuco at least visited Cuextecatl-Ichocayan, in certain contexts conceived as situated in the Huaxteca.

However Muñóz Camargo, an early source, casts distinct doubts on this notion of primeval sea crossings when he writes of the Mexicas, Tarascans, and other tribes who followed the same route, and all crossed either a stretch of sea or a biggish river which might, according to this author, have been the Río de Toluca; he confesses he is not clear as to what kind of water they crossed.[20]

Thus, according to one early source, these crossings may have concerned rivers rather than vast oceans. Maritime travel is at one time or another attributed to practically every tribe. In addition to reports to that effect concerning the Toltecs and Mexicas, Chimalpain states that the Nonoalca Tlacochcalcas made two sea crossings when they came from Tlapallan.[21] Veytia as well as Ixtlilxóchitl ascribes sea crossings to the Olmeca-Xicallancas.[22] The Chontales who eventually arrived in Nicaragua had the same experience.[23] The Quiche myths equally involve maritime journeys.[24] In the case of the crossing described in the *Annals of the Cakchiquels*, Eduard Seler draws attention to the obviously biblical origin of the whole story, related by Durán; as with the people of Israel in the Red Sea, the waters were made to divide with a stick.[25]

It must be conceded that sea travel had reached a certain stage of development in Pre-Hispanic times, as Thompson has particularly emphasized with reference to Yucatán. On the other hand, as the same author insists, the peoples of Central Mexico were relatively landlocked and were not mariners. It is a most unlikely supposition that they *all* arrived by sea, let alone that they all came along the Gulf Coast to Pánuco. If one ethnic group had perhaps done this, then the others presumably had simply *borrowed* the tale.

This in itself affords an excellent example of the perils of an overliteral interpretation of the texts, as regards both principles and places. Panotlan or Panohuayan, meaning simply a place of crossing, accordingly forms a concept that could be attached to any locality, particularly if situated on a river; it then however becomes transformed in tribal legend into Pánuco, lying on the Gulf Coast, and the journey in question involving that place becomes a sea crossing.

Working Hypotheses

We have already stated briefly the aims of this study and expounded at more length the purely general problems to be confronted and the pitfalls to be encountered. Such an over-all discussion constitutes an indispensable foundation on which to construct a more detailed study.

For the Toltecs, historical material exists in relative abundance, together with a considerable accumulation of archaeological data. But neither of these tell all that one wants to find out. The written sources are deeply impregnated with myth and legend; the archaeological information has other limitations and provides little guidance on personalities, dates, or conquests. But, as Paul Kirchhoff has pointed out, these are precisely the things which must be known, if history is to be written; what really count are the events to which date and locality can be assigned—the rest are mere mythology.

Were it not for such difficulties, it would be more normal in a work of this nature to leave the final denouement to its rightful place at the end, when more specific conclusions may be attempted. But in view of the complexities of Toltec history, it may be helpful to outline initially certain precepts likely to figure among our principal findings. This might seem at first sight to be little better than naming the killer in the first chapter of a detective story. But the Toltec plot is of necessity involved, and, before asking the reader to accompany us along paths as tortuous as those of a maze, it might prove useful to offer a few guidelines now as to where and how he may eventually hope to emerge.

Accordingly, general hypotheses may be presented as follows. These will be amply discussed and elaborated in due course, and more detailed conclusions then drawn.

1. "Tollan" and "Toltec" are concepts as much as proper names. Thus, one may on the one hand accept the thesis that when the Aztecs talked of Tollan or Tula, what they had in mind was Tula, Hidalgo; on the other hand, it will be shown that this was by no means the only place thus named, nor its inhabitants the only people to be called Toltecs.

2. By the same token, it will become clear that Quetzalcoatl is as much a symbol and office as a single person or deity. Without rejecting out of hand the plethora of historic reports from Central Mexico and the Maya area, it is very hard to single out one single individual called Ce Acatl-Topiltzin-Quetzalcoatl, who existed either at the beginning or the end of our history. It is impossible to clarify the general panorama without first accepting the existence of more than one being thus designated, and more probably a whole series. This problem will be discussed in Chapters 2 and 3, and to some extent later in the work. The appearance of a Quetzalcoatl in the Maya area belongs to Chapter 5, which deals with the Toltec-Maya question.

3. The Aztecs ascribed to the Toltecs a kind of universal "empire," such as they themselves were well on the way to achieving. In this they were seeking a precedent, in order to legitimize their own claim to a pan-Mesoamerican heritage. However, such claims for the Toltec achievement will be found to be rather exaggerated. The question is examined in Chapter 7, where a Toltec domain of more modest proportions will be proposed.

4. Practically all the names of rulers and the accompanying calendar dates (unfortunately) will be found to belong to the period of the decline and fall of Tula, to be discussed in Chapter 8. They will thus all appear upon the Toltec stage in due course, but perhaps not as early in the unfolding of the plot as the reader might normally anticipate.

2. Tollan as Name and Concept

Any study of Toltec problems is apt to end in greater confusion than it began without some initial appreciation of what the terms "Tollan" and "Toltec" really signify. Do they in the final analysis refer invariably to one people and one place only, or are they appellations of more general use, applicable to a greater or lesser extent throughout Mesoamerican history?

General Ambiguities

This question is ever present. Not only does a tendency exist in Mesoamerica for one people to use several different names as Kirchhoff has stressed, but the reverse is equally true; not uncommonly one appellation may be applied to a number of tribes. The name "Chichimec" is an obvious example.

And so interwoven with the whole Toltec saga are the manifold stories of Ce Acatl-Topiltzin-Quetzalcoatl, also known as Nacxitl, Meconetl, Kukulcan, Gucumatz, and so on, that before ending this chapter one must perforce ask the same question of the man as of the place: is Ce Acatl-Topiltzin-Quetzalcoatl one single personage, to whom a specific time and place in history can be assigned, or is the designation rather a more generic title, deriving from the god and applicable in different situations?

It is really impossible to embark on any detailed analysis of the subject without first examining such general and fundamental questions.

A basic difficulty soon arises; it becomes apparent that in fact "Tollan" and "Toltec" are not merely the names of one city and its people but are concepts, almost impossible to confine to one place, people, or period. Moreover, the blending of legend with history in all extant accounts makes it difficult to define the exact significance of the terms in any particular era.

Such a problem is of course not peculiar to Toltec studies. E. O. James, writing of the ancient Near East, states, "In legend and saga, the same theme may be repeated in association with similar phenomena. Historical situations may underlie such stories, and it becomes difficult to separate what is true from what is merely traditional; facts are the most unstable elements."[1] He further warns against any tendency to try to derive a whole complex of belief and practice from one single center. Such cautions are of universal application and will be ever present in our search for the true identity of Tollan. In this instance one is faced with an amalgam of legends, sagas, and stories of events which probably occurred at quite different times and places, but which, in surviving accounts, are all centered upon the one name "Tollan."

For in both the Old and New Worlds appellations and titles can easily pass from one people to another; a natural tendency exists for a newer group to seek associations with its forerunners and to adopt their name, in an attempt to establish traditions and achieve legitimacy. Thus the Hittite kings used other titles before they bore down upon the cities of Hattus and Nesa in Central Anatolia. But they subsequently took the names of those they conquered, assuming the dignity of "Kings of Hatti" and calling their kingdom the "Land of Hatti"—originally the name of indigenous occupants who were non-Indo-European and therefore of quite different extraction.[2] The Mexicas, who followed this example by adopting the name "Culhua," thus bestowed upon themselves the mantle of tradition and legitimacy that derived from Culhuacán.

At least the etymology of Tollan presents no special problem: it simply signifies "place of rushes," deriving from the Nahua word *tollin*, or *tullin*. It should perhaps first be stressed that *tol-*, the root of *tollin*, is commonly used in place names and that Tollan, Tula, and other part derivatives of the word such as Toltepec, Tulancingo, Toliman, and Tulapan are common Mesoamerican names. To cite only a few of many examples, even the neighborhood of the City of Mexico could boast of a Tula—Santa Isabel Tula near Tepeyacac, mentioned in a document of 1539.[3] San Andrés Tulpan is west of Tlalnepantla and Tolpetlac and southwest of Ecatepec. Near Cholula there exists a hill actually called Tolan. One of the three principal communities of the upper Teotihuacán Valley bears the name of Santiago Tolan.[4] Moreover the tendency to use this name in one form or another must have been enhanced by the greater prevalence in earlier times of expanses of water and of marshes, and hence of rushes and reeds.

The Nahuatl word for rush, *tullin*, or its modern counterpart *tule*, is a little hard in itself to define and embraces a fairly wide range of aquatic grasses with cylindrical stems that grow in moist land and that in English would be included within the term "rush." They are all members of the grasslike family "Juncaceae," counting over 250 species. Elizabeth Smith gives several illustrations of rushes as depicted in the Mixtec codices (for the purpose of illustrating names such as Tulancingo); these all have leaves and a kind of ovaloid bulbous growth near the top of their spike.[5] As such they are really bullrushes (Latin *Typha*), or in English, cattails. However, at times other varieties are depicted in Central Mexican documents, as for instance the *Codex Mendoza*, where leaves rather than spikes are shown in the Tollan glyph. The same place sign in the *Historia Tolteca-Chichimeca* follows the Mixtec pattern and depicts bullrushes.

Quite apart from the usefulness of the availability of water, inseparable in some form from rushes, the latter were in themselves an extremely important pre-Hispanic commodity, with a vast range of uses. The best form of container, whether for going to market or for bulk deliveries of tribute, was the basket made of rushes. Numerous bone implements have been unearthed in Mesoamerica that were used to make these baskets, but of course the articles manufactured with such tools did not normally survive, particularly in marshy soil. However, finds of such implements bear witness to a strong basketmaking industry.

Over and above this, Sahagún mentions that—somewhat naturally—the ubiquitous *petate* was made then, as today, of rushes. This versatile material served everyone from the ruler to his humblest subject; it would have been used to make the *teoicpalli*, or ruler's throne. It even served the gods; the image of Huitzilopochtli during the Mexica migration was carried in a case made of rushes, and the roofs of temples were probably often of this material rather than of straw.

Thus a "place of rushes" would be a city endowed with an especially useful asset. Furthermore, the presence of rivers or expanses of water, inseparable from rushes, were themselves of the greatest significance, offering such things as fish, fowl, animals that come to the brink, mosquito eggs, and perhaps salt—quite apart from the possibilities of some form of irrigation or hydraulic agriculture. In short, therefore, Tollan was synonymous with the ideal place and it is not surprising that Sahagún should refer to the name as signifying among other things "place of fertility and abundance."

Whatever the significance and importance of the original or basic meaning of Tollan, the name clearly came to be used in the more general sense of "metropolis." In Gabriel Rojas' "Descripción de Cholula," written in 1581, the city is referred to as Tullam Chulollan [*sic*], and the author states that many people claim that "Tullan," or "Tullam," means a multitude of people congregated together, recalling the way rushes grow.[6]

The same writer, however, questions whether even Cholula did not originally derive its title of Tollan from the initial meaning of the word; he states that there actually had existed a field of rushes adjacent to the hill where the Great Temple was situated. Furthermore, according to the same source, some people ascribed the use of the name "Tollan" in this instance not to any physical cause but mainly to the presence in the city of Toltecs, so-called because they had come from the original Tollan.

Vetancurt supports the implied suggestion of Gabriel Rojas that the notion of multitude and hence of metropolis derives from the way in which rushes grow: "Tollan signifies a congregation of people, based on the metaphor of the Tule, which grows with abundance wherever it is cultivated, and thus, as we said, in order to designate multitude as innumerable as the ocean sands, the natives use the parallel of the Tule."[7] The writer goes on to say that the Otomí word for the city of Tollan (in his context, Tula, Hidalgo) is Mahmeni, which also means "congregation of people." Wigberto Jiménez Moreno confirms that this name is still used today.

Eduard Seler toys with an additional possibility. Notwithstanding the apparently clear derivation mentioned above, Tollan could conceivably be derived from *toloa*, to bow the head or bow down, and would thus come to mean "the land where the sun goes down to the earth," i.e., the west. Seler backs this interpretation with the report in the *Chilam Balam* of ancestors of the tribe who came "from Zuiva, from Tollan Apan Chicnauhtlán"; he derives "Zuiva" from the Zapotec word *Zoo paa*, meaning "west."[8] Such arguments, however, may seem a little far-fetched. It has also often been suggested that Toluca might also come from *toloa*, but again, as in the case of Tollan, *tol*, the root of *tollin*, seems more acceptable as a basis.

In general the derivation of Tollan from *tullin*, or rush, is widely accepted. Chimalpain, for instance, confirms the obvious association not only of Tollan but of the name "Toltec" with this root, and writes of the Pyramid of the Toltecs, situated near water where great rushes grew.[9] The monument in question was situated in Texcalco Omemázac, near Amecameca.

For "Toltécatl" (plural Tolteca) a double significance is even more self-evident than for Tollan; apart from the stricter sense of "inhabitant of Tollan," it enjoys, as Jiménez Moreno points out, a general meaning of "metropolitan."[10]

Moreover, the name "Toltec" came to possess not merely these two meanings but also a third. In many contexts it simply implies the possession of certain skills or even at times the mere attainment of a high degree of sophistication. For "Toltécatl," Siméon gives the translation, "artisan, skilled worker, artist"; only after making this general definition does he additionally describe the Toltecs as a tribe inhabiting Tollan.

For the noun "Toltecayotl," Siméon gives in the first instance, "teaching of the mechanical arts, that which is relative to mechanics." He adds only as a secondary meaning, "state, land of the Toltecs." In point of fact the word "Toltecayotl" clearly attained a deeper significance, embodying the whole intellectual and spiritual force of the Toltec world, including its legacy to later generations. All this, however, seems to derive originally from the development of purely practical skills. Molina translates "Toltécatl" exclusively as "*oficial de arte mecánica*" and "Toltecayotl" as "*maestría de arte mecánica.*"

Thus, first as related to a place or places, Toltec refers essentially to the inhabitants of Tollan; from this derives the sense of "metropolitan." In addition, the name "Toltec" is at times employed by historical sources to describe people, after the fall of Tula, who had come from that city or who were ethnically related to its inhabitants. Equally, "Toltec" came to enjoy a quite independant meaning, associated with certain skills, and with a high degree of culture. Only from the individual context can it be determined which sense of the word is intended.

A Plethora of Tollans

If "Tollan" thus became applicable to more than one city, it must first be asked when and where the name initially arose?

Certain investigators have gone so far as to maintain that Tollan as such never existed. Brinton in 1887 wrote, "Why should we try to make an enlightened ruler of Quetzalcoatl, a cultured nation of the Toltecs, when the proof is of the strongest that they are a fiction of mythology?"[11] Such an extreme view now has few adherents, though in their emphatic rejection of a single and human Quetzalcoatl as a kind of saint in kingly robes, Brinton's rather sweeping assertions may contain a kernel of truth. While incorrectly denying the historic side of the Toltec story, he at least clearly perceives the other-worldly element sometimes overlooked by others.

At the opposite end of the spectrum are to be found the defenders *à l'outrance* of Tula, Hidalgo, as the one and only Tollan; such a view is indeed accurate in that this is the Tollan that is almost invariably implied when the sources use the name Tollan without mentioning another city, as occurs for instance in the case of "Tollan Chololllan" or "Tollan Teotihuacán."

It may be pointed out that the identification of Tula, Hidalgo, as the basic Tollan is not recent; on the contrary, it coincides with the earlier views of Mesoamerican investigators and was generally accepted until the first part of this century. Bishop Plancarte then proposed that Teotihuacán, not Tula, was the Tollan of the so-called dynastic lists. Following his excavations, Gamio was so inspired by the marvels he had unearthed as to insist upon Teotihuacán as the Tollan of tradition.

Notwithstanding the preference of Manuel Gamio and Bishop Plancarte for this site, Eduard Seler had already initiated a trend toward a compromise solution, making a distinction between the "historic Tula" on the one hand, meaning Tula, Hidalgo, and the Tula of ancient fable, referring primarily to Teotihuacán.[12] Such views were supported by other prominent investigators. Krickeberg refers to the "historic Toltecs"; S. Linné rightly stresses the clear distinction made by Sahagún between earlier and later Toltecs.[13]

As is well known, following the Round Table meeting of 1941, the wheel again took a full turn when the conference accepted Tula, Hidalgo, by then more extensively excavated, as the true Tollan of the principal historical sources of Mesoamerica. This decision was mainly inspired by Jiménez Moreno's identification of a series of place names referred to in such accounts of Tollan as clearly lying in the vicinity of Tula, Hidalgo.

It will later be noted that the conference resolution, while based on a correct assumption, was perhaps a little too sweeping in its insistence on Tula as the Tollan of the sources and in its hesitance to accept the parallel existence in certain accounts of other and more remote Tollans. Possibly Linné, who prefers to distinguish clearly between the Toltecs of history and those of legend, sums up the question aptly when he insists that by the name "Toltec" the Aztecs seem to have denoted *all* those highly cultured peoples who existed before their time and whose spiritual inheritors they considered themselves to be.[14] This well accords with our general premise that no absolute values can be assigned to "Tollan" or "Toltec," and that the intended sense can only be derived from the context.

Nevertheless, the notion that Tula, Hidalgo, is the basic Tollan of the "historical" Toltecs is widely though not universally accepted. Before discussing its full significance, however, it may be useful briefly to examine what other places have at times received historical mention as "Tollan"; most of such references were taken into account by the 1941 meeting.

CHOLULA

Apart from Tula, Hidalgo, the place most frequently referred to as "Tollan" is Cholula.

In addition to mentions of "Tullam Chololllan" [*sic*] in the "Descripción" of Gabriel Rojas, already quoted, the *Codex of Cholula* uses the same phrase.[15] Bente Bittmann Simons in her commentary suggests that Tollan here designates a particular ward or part of Cholula, or possibly even the whole city, the metropolis.[16] The same document incidentally also makes mention of "Tollan Tlacpac," i.e., "above Tollan." This might conceivably refer to the summit of the Great Pyramid, and thus give a sacred connotation to Tollan, particularly when applied to Cholula. The *Historia Tolteca-Chichimeca* mentions Cholula as "the place where the white tules divide."[17] The *Codex Vaticano-Ríos* contains the comment, "This tower was called Tulan Culula."[18] Torquemada remarks that in his day Cholula was called Tollan Chololllan, because Toltec refugees from Tula had gone there. The inhabitants of Cholula were held to be people of great distinction or special business acumen and were known as "*grandes Toltecas*."[19] He lays emphasis on the association of Toltec with artisans, silversmiths, and the like, and implies clearly that this was a *subsequent*, or *derivative*, meaning of Toltec, a term originally applied simply to the people of Tollan. Veytia also writes, following Torquemada, of "Tollan Chololllan"; he affirms that he found words written in Nahuatl on a painted codex or map stating that the Great Pyramid was a monument to the Toltec nation. Veytia, better informed than the document he quotes, points out that this edifice was really created long before; he attributes it to the Olmeca-Xicallancas.[20]

In general, the association of the name "Toltec" with "multitude," as opposed to its more literal meaning, may be perfectly correct, but does not seem to occur with great frequency or to be necessarily of very ancient origin, quite apart from its practical uses. The rush seems to have had a certain symbolic significance of its own in Mesoamerica; by their unusual form and their association with water, rushes have a certain universal appeal. Even in Ancient Egypt the dead had to pass through "the Field of Rushes" on the way to their last destination.[21]

TEOTIHUACÁN

In the "Mapa Quinatzin" a well-known glyph of tules, or rushes, occurs in association with Teotihuacán. The text gives as the full name "Teotihuacán Tlahtolovan," i.e., "tribunal of Teotihuacán." However, Alfonso Caso insists that, in the case of Teotihuacán as well as Tenochtitlan, Tollan implies "metropolis" more than "place of rushes."[22] Notwithstanding this, it must not be forgotten that in Classic times Lake Texcoco reached a point not far from Teotihuacán and that it may have been literally a "place of rushes."

TENOCHTITLAN

In the *Codex Sierra*, a glyph consisting of tules is located on a building denoted as Tenochtitlan. In addition, Caso mentions that in the *Relación del Origen de las Indias* it is stated that the Mexicas applied the term "Tula" to Tenochtitlan.[23] George Vaillant thought that the term "Tollan" might have been used also to denote Azcapotzalco, the immediate predecessor of Tenochtitlan.[24] This would seem very possible, even if the town no longer merited the title in its subsequent rather straitened circumstances.

Another possible reference to Tenochtitlan as Tollan is to be found in one of the *Cantares*, but it is really not clear from the context —the destruction of Chalco by Moctezuma I—whether "Tollan" in this case is Tenochtitlan or Chalco.[25]

In addition, the *Crónica Mexicayotl* sometimes refers to Tenochtitlan as "Toltzalan Acatzalan" ("among the rushes, or reeds"). Tenochtitlan is a lagoon city, and hence a place of reeds and rushes; while not normally thus named, the Mexica capital was par excellence the ultimate fulfillment of Tollan in a triple sense: the city among the rushes, the city filled with artisans, and above all the great metropolis.

Incidentally, the Mixtec equivalent of Tollan, as a town of rushes, would be Ñuu Co'yo. Beginning as early as the sixteenth century and continuing up to the present time, Ñuu Co'yo is the Mixtec name of the city of Mexico.

CHALCO

Apart from the above-cited reference from the *Cantares*, in the same text the following passage occurs: "*Tollan, Chalcon Dios ichan huiya quetzaltzanatlatoa, tlauhquecholtzanatl.*"[26] Leonhard Schultze-Jena translates the first four words as "At the house of the god of Tollan and Chalco." In view of the application of the name "Tollan" to other leading cities, there is no reason why this should not have applied just as much to Chalco; "the god of Tollan Chalco" could accordingly be a more apt reading than "the god of Tollan *and* Chalco." As already mentioned, references also occur in Chimalpain's *Relaciones* to the presence of rushes near the Pyramid of the Toltecs in Chalco; Chalco Atempan was of course a lakeside city, as its name implies.

Chimalpain refers to Chalco as "the father and mother of twenty-five cities" and thus a kind of sanctified metropolis somewhat like Tollan, which according to the *Historia Tolteca-Chichimeca* had twenty other cities as its confederates. Chalco moreover is described by some sources as maintaining certain Toltec connections after the fall of Tula.[27] One feels that the name "Tollan," in addition to implying metropolis, mere numbers gathered together, came to possess a certain aura of sanctity.

ACUCULCO ATZACALCO

Chimalpain also mentions the arrival of the Mexicas at Acuculco Atzacalco Tollan Anepantla, apparently situated between Culhuacán and Tizaapán.[28] Unless Culhuacán itself is intended, as could easily be the case, then Tollan would seem in this case to serve more as a kind of qualifying adjective, Tollan Anepantla, the place of rushes in the midst of the water.

THE MIXTECA

Apart from such relatively nearby Tollans, a glyph consisting of tules, or rushes, is to be noted fairly frequently in the Mixtec codices. The matter will be further discussed in connection with the possible extent of Toltec power and influence. For the meantime, it may suffice to mention a few examples of the occurrence of reedlike glyphs, often interpreted as denoting Tula or Tollan. Caso, in his commentary on the *Codex Bodley*, refers to 4 Tiger as "King of Tula" and describes his arrival at a place represented by a glyph of rushes; he does not however specifically say that he thereby implies Tula, Hidalgo, or any particular Tula.[29] Similarly, in interpreting the *Selden codex*, Caso writes of "II Snake as King of Tula," due to the presence of the tule glyph.[30] The author adds that the Lienzo Seler II states that II Snake was ruler of Tula Tenochtitlan, describing him as the ancestor of the Mexican monarchs—perhaps a rather uncertain contention.

Caso left the matter somewhat open, but the unwary reader might easily deduce that every glyph depicting rushes and every mention of "Tula" in interpretations of Mixtec codices must automatically refer to Tula, Hidalgo, particularly since Caso writes of "Tula," not "Tollan." This point has been admirably clarified by Elizabeth Smith. In the *Codex Colombino*, the important nose-perforating ceremony of Eight Deer takes place in a town with a compound sign representing the coastal town of San Pedro Jicayán, but with the addition of clearly illustrated tules, or rushes. The latter are identical to those to which Caso drew attention in his commentary on the *Codex Bodley* in connection with a possible "Tula." Smith has now irrefutably identified the place as Tulixtlahuaca, a dependency of Xicayán; as she mentions, in all likelihood Tulixtlahuaca was one of the principal pre-Conquest ceremonial sites in the coastal region of the Mixteca.[31]

The same author has further identified San Miguel Tulancingo, about eight miles west of Coixtlahuaca, with the same tule, or cattail, glyph. A similar sign of Tulancingo also appears in the Lienzo Antonio de León, where it is actually placed near the town of Coixtlahuaca.[32]

Smith points out, as already mentioned, that the Mixtec name of a town represented by a tule, or cattail, frieze should be *ñuu co'yo*. In the *Codex Bodley* a further frieze sign occurs that could possibly be interpreted as the Tulixtlahuaca near Jicayán, but could be some other local Tollan, whose Mixtec name is unknown but would originally have contained the word *co'yo* (rush). The Mixteca is comparatively well provided with Nahuatl names containing the root of *tollin*; among others, a Tula appears in colonial documents as a dependency of Yanhuitlán.

Robert Chadwick maintains that a certain parallelism may exist between the historical accounts of Tollan and of Quetzalcoatl in the *Anales de Cuauhtitlán* and other Central Mexican sources on the one hand and those of the Mixtec codices on the other—a suggestion which may not be entirely without foundation, though the same might be said with even greater insistence of Yucatec and Guatemalan legends. However, on purely chronological grounds if on no other, I do not accept his view that the long and detailed series of events described as occurring in the Valley of Mexico and nearby are simply copied from Mixtec codical accounts, with place names of one region substituted for those of another.[33]

THE MYSTERIOUS ZUIVA

The enigma of the Tollan Zuiva of the Yucatec and Highland Guatemalan chronicles remains unresolved. Perhaps because of its very ambiguity, the question has received relatively little attention since the days of Seler and his pupil Walter Lehmann. In general terms, Maya and Quiché sources mention Tulapan, Tollan, or Tullam as the place of origin of immigrants from Central Mexico who established themselves as a ruling class in their new surroundings. The accounts state that they had come through the land Nonoual, which F. V. Scholes and R. L. Roys identify with reasonable assurance as the land adjacent to the Laguna de Términos in southwestern Campeche.[34]

In particular, the *Popol Vuh* tells of the arrival of the Quiché tribes, after long travels, at "Tulán Zuiva, Vucub Pec, Vucub Ziván" (Tollan Zuiva, seven caves, seven ravines). The same text also refers to "Tulán Zuiva, from whence their god came." Gucumatz (Quetzalcoatl) is named as the tribal leader, and reference occurs to their veneration of the "great star," i.e., Venus, to be associated of course with Quetzalcoatl. From the expression "Vucub Pec" (seven caves), it is clear that this Tulán, or Tollan, was linked with a kind of mystical place of origin, or in fact a Chicomoztoc. The *Título C'oyoi*, recently translated by Robert Carmack, also writes of "Ciwan Tulán—Vukub Pec Vucub Siwan."[35] A parallel Quiché legend, occurring in the *Título Sacapulas*, writes of "seven caves and seven hills" as a place of origin of the tribe.[36]

According to Xiu legends, the mysterious Tulán Zuiva lay to the west: "For three score years they (the Tutul Xius) reigned at Siyan can, and they came down here (to Chichén)."[37] According to this version, Zuyva or Siyan was the pre-Chichén kingdom of the Xius; the same text states that the Tutul Xius came out of their home to Nonoual, from the west, from the land of Zuiva, from Tulapam Chiconauhtlan; these were the founders of the Mani dynasty of *Chilam Balam* fame.

From this passage, Seler finds it logical to seek Zuiva in Tabasco.[38] He suggests a location between Xicalanco and Coatzacoalcos. Such a contention regarding a Tollan in that region is supported by the *Toltec Elegy*, which refers to Tollan Nonoalco.[39] It is generally agreed, as will later be shown in detail, that Nonoalco in fact lay in the region of Tabasco.

Seler further writes of the puzzle of the word "Zuiva" itself. He draws attention to the mention on "Pa Tulán Pa Civan," i.e., "in or out of Tollan, out of Civan," to be found in the *Título de los Señores de Totonicapan*. This text in effect substitutes Civan (gorge) for Zuiva, as does the *Título C'oyoi*. He expresses uncertainty, however, that this provided the key to the correct meaning. In this he is probably right, in view of the above-cited phrase of the *Popol Vuh*, in which Zuiva and Zivan both follow the name Tulán. Seler suggests the possibility that "Zuiva" derives from *Zoo paa*, the Zapotec word for "west," and Lehmann supports this contention.

The objection may be offered that Tulán in these texts, though usually not in association with Zuiva, is sometimes situated in the east as well as the west. The *Annals of the Caḳchiquels* state that their forebears arrived from the west at Tulán, coming from across the sea.[40] The *Título de los Señores de Totonacapan* also affirms that Tulán lay over the sea, in the land where the sun rises. Moreover the word "*Zoo paa*" is not really so close to Zuiva. Incidentally, a place called Sivaca still exists to the southwest of Ococingo in Chiapas; Sivaca is perhaps nearer to Zuiva than is *Zoo paa*.

If indeed Zuiva is to be associated with the west as well as the east, it might more easily be just another Maya corruption of an originally Nahuatl word. Zuiva is the same as Çuiva; in transliteration from the Nahuatl, the semivowel *w* is sometimes given as *u*, sometimes *v* and sometimes *hu*. (Molina writes "*vey*," when nowadays we normally use the form "huey.") Thus Zuiva, or Çuiva (equivalent to

Çuihua), is not far removed from Cihua, which has a significantly western connotation deriving from the Cihuateteos, who resided in that region, in the place known as Cihuatlampa. Quetzalcoatl is himself connected with the notion of Cihuatlampa as Ehécatl, God of Wind; the west wind was known according to Sahagún as Cihuatlampa Ehécatl.[41] Siyan, another form of Zuiva, mentioned above, is quite close also to Cihua. Admittedly it is also close to Zivan (ravines), more favored by Jiménez Moreno as the correct derivation; he points out that Tepeji del Río, near Tula, implies "place of ravines" from *tepexite*, meaning "rock" or "precipice."[42] I feel, however, that the association of the Quichean peoples with Tula, Hidalgo, was indirect, as will later be explained.

Thompson lends certain support to the association of Zuiva with the west, but in a different context that simply suggests that it lay west of Chichén. He cites the *Chilam Balam of Chumayel*, which states that the Itzá came to Chichén in four divisions. The four (or possibly five) places from which they set forth are assigned to world directions. One, that to the west, is called Holtun Zuiva. "Holtun" appears to be a Putun word meaning "harbor";[43] it was in fact the Putun name for Puerto Escondido on the northern arm enclosing the Laguna de Términos. The same author, who considers the name "Zuiva" to be of Nahua derivation and closely associated with the Mexican invaders of Yucatán, suggests that Holtun Zuiva is a place in Chontalpa, the river delta area in Tabasco, where the Mexican Toltec and the Putun cultures met.

In the *Popol Vuh* text cited above, Tollan Zuiva has definite associations with Chicomoztoc, or "seven caves," as well as with seven ravines. But according to Roys, in Yucatec Maya, Chichén itself was probably still called Uucil Abnal (seven bushy places, or hollows) as late as Katun 4 Ahau, when Quetzalcoatl, or Kukulcan, is reported to have arrived.[44] In Maya prophesies, Uucil Abnal was actually a ritual name for Chichén, as it was subsequently called by the Itzá invaders who made it into their own sacred city.

Robert Carmack points out that this name, Uucil Abnal, recalls Vucub Zivan (seven ravines), a part of the description or appellation of Tulán Zuiva in the already quoted passage of the *Popol Vuh*. He thus raises the possibility of Tulán's being Chichén.[45] In addition he cites evidence from Yucatec documents also suggesting the possible identification of the Tulán of Maya and Guatemalan chronicles with Chichén. Nacxit, the name often coupled with that of Kukulcan as the ruler of the great Yucatán center, was known in Highland Guatemala as Ruler of the East, situated in Tulán, from whom the rulers of Guatemala received their investiture of authority.[46] Landa, in his *Relación de Las Cosas de Yucatán* also refers to visits made to the Lord of Chichén from Guatemala and Chiapas; tokens of peace and friendship were brought, thus again indirectly associating Chichén with the notion of Tollan as the universal center of power.

Accordingly, the possibility exists that the Maya Tollan could well be Chichén itself. If the texts contradict each other, either some are incorrect or they must be referring to more than one place in this context; some say that Tulán lay in the *west,* but we have equally clear references in the *Annals of the Cakchiquels* to people who went *east* to Tulán, across the sea. Chichén, the great center dominated by the Mexican invaders and permeated with the cult of Quetzalcoatl, becomes a *de facto* Tollan, both as metropolis, holy city, and home of the arts; it would have been only logical for the Nahua-speaking invaders themselves to have named it thus. Possibly even Sahagún's reference to Tollan Tlapallan might imply Chichén; the association of these two names by that author has at times been considered as a mere error, "Tollan" being substituted for "Tlillan," but Seler does not consider this likely.[47]

Last but not least comes the greatest enigma, the four Tuláns of the *Annals of the Cakchiquels.* The *Annals* tell in general terms of the arrival of the ancestors of the tribe at Tulán, on the other side of the sea (i.e., going from west to east). It then mentions the existence of four Tuláns, "one in the east, one in the west, one in Xibalbay, and one where god resides," that is to say, the sky. Taking Xibalbay as the underworld, these four points correspond to the daily trajectory of the sun; they are in fact the four sacred directions of the Quichean peoples.[48]

Recinos suggests that Xibalbay refers to the nether world, because of its association in the text with precious stones. This is surely correct, in view of the reference in the *Popol Vuh* to the *descent* of Gucumatz (Quetzalcoatl) to Xibalbay.[49] Seler also mentions the association of

Xibalbay with a figure dressed as a bat, a dweller in caves and other dark regions of the earth.[50]

The passage concerning the four Tuláns suggests a further possibility. Leaving aside the heavenly Tulán (where god resides) and the Tulán of the nether regions, there still remain the two Tuláns "across the sea," one lying in the east and the other in the west. One is thus faced not only with separate and independent references to one Tulán in the east and another in the west but with a simultaneous mention of Tuláns in east *and* west, not to mention one in heaven and one in the nether regions.

This might be partly accounted for by the fact that, for people coming from Central Mexico, a Tollan on the Laguna de Términos would lie to the east, whereas, seen from Chichén, it would lie to the west. As an alternative, it is not inconceivable that in this region "across the sea" at least two Tuláns actually existed, precisely as in the Mixteca more than one area had its Tula or Tulancingo. The first or easternmost one would be Chichén itself and the other, westward, Tulán Zuiva or Holtun Zuiva, lying in the river delta area of Tabasco, as suggested by Thompson. The word "Zuiva" normally accompanies a Tulán described as being in the west, rather than the east. If Zuiva is indeed to be associated with the west, whether with Central Mexico or with a Tabascan Tulán, a derivation from the Nahua "Cihua" seems more acceptable than the Zapotec "*Zoo paa*" (Nahuatl was also spoken as far east as Xicalango). Given the Maya propensity for abbreviating, as well as corrupting Nahua names (viz., "yolcat" for "yohualli Ehécatl"), it would be easy for Cihuatlampa to become simply Cihua and then Zuiva or something similar. A place called Cihuatecpa still exists in Yucatán.

There is thus probably no single and simple solution to the question of a Tollan situated in Yucatán or Tabasco. Here as elsewhere the name could mean more than one thing: at times the remote Tollan of the Central Plateau, at others some important intermediate site on the Laguna de Términos or nearby, and finally the great Chichén might naturally have been called "Tollan" by its Nahua-speaking invaders, just as Constantinople was conceived as New Rome.

The problem of the various Tuláns has been discussed in some detail because it throws light upon the very nature of the Tollan concept and illustrates a principle that cannot be overstressed: what may be a concrete and identifiable place for certain peoples, as was surely the Tollan of Tula, Hidalgo, for others may become more of a fable. Originally Chicomoztoc was probably also a real place, but in Maya legend it loses its physical identity and becomes a mere qualifying name for Tulán Zuiva "of the seven caves and seven ravines." Chicomoztoc thus becomes no more than a legendary Quinehuan, or "place of starting," for the seven Maya tribes and from which came their revered ancestors and rulers. (In this they are simply following a set Mesoamerican pattern; for instance, not merely in Central Mesoamerica but in certain Mixtec codices legends of seven tribes and the place of seven caves are to be found). Only subsequent to this does Tollan, thus converted from fixed place to mobile concept, again become a definite locality as Tulán Zuiva, or plain Tulán.

TOLLAN XICOCOTITLAN

Finally, having discussed the other Tollans, we broach the subject of the Postclassic Toltec capital, Tula, Hidalgo, or Tollan Xicocotitlan, as it may be preferable to call it.

In the first place one must ask: what is the literal claim, if any, of Tula to the title of Tollan, "the place of rushes"? The answer is not far to seek, apart from the obviously aquatic associations of the site, situated on the banks of a relatively large river. A marshy area replete with rushes and known as El Salitre is visible today in close proximity to the main pyramids, by which it is overlooked. Thus Tula still remains a "place of rushes." It is hardly necessary for us to recapitulate in detail the well-known results of Jiménez Moreno's investigations as to place names in the Tula vicinity, identifiable as belonging to Toltec history; these he communicated to the famous Round Table in 1941.

To name a few points, mostly taken from this report:

1. Xicócoc. Sahagún calls Tollan, where Quetzalcoatl resided, "Tollan Xicocotitlan," i.e., "the place nearby to Xicócoc."[51] The *Anales de Cuauhtitlán* also mention Xicócoc in connection with Quetzalcoatl.[52] In effect, Jiménez Moreno points to the famous hill called Xicuco near Tula and easily visible from the site.

2. Xippacoyan. Sahagún mentions this place in the same context,

referring clearly to the present-day village, also called San Lorenzo, in the immediate vicinity of Tula.

3. Texcalapan. Sahagún thus denotes the river Tula.[53] This same name is to be found in a text that accompanies an eighteenth-century map of Tula in the Archivo General de la Nación.

4. Sahagún's insistence that Tollan lay on a large river surely helps to identify it with Tula rather than certain other possible sites.

5. Xochitlán. Sahagún also mentions this place, to be located to the east of Tula.[54]

6. Cincoc. This hill is mentioned in the *Anales de Cuauhtitlán*.[55] It is situated to the north of Huehuetoca and is visible from Tula, as Jiménez Moreno stressed in his original report.

7. Huapalcalli. This, the "House of Beams," is also mentioned in Sahagún's Book III as lying near Tollan. Jorge Acosta refers to a locality of this name as still existing near to the principal ceremonial center of Tula.

8. Tlemaco. The *Historia de los Mexicanos* mentions, in the story of Huitzilopochtli's birth, Tlemaco "nearby Tula."[56] There exists today a Tlamaco, a village of the municipality of Atitalaquia, lying about two and one-half kilometers to the south of this and thus near to Tula.

9. Coatepec. The stay of the Mexicas during their migration at Coatepec and at Tula is a historical fact, as Kirchhoff has pointed out. Jiménez Moreno himself prefers a location for Coatepec farther to the east, in the Pachuca area; however, the sources do on the whole describe Coatepec as lying in the vicinity of Tula, Hidalgo, and the two are at times even taken to be synonymous.[57] In one of the Cantares, features normally associated with Tollan, such as turquoise-covered columns, the quetzal feather house, etc., are attributed to Coatepec.[58]

On the one hand, therefore, one has the undeniable physical identification of places near Tula, Hidalgo, which are associated in the sources with Tollan. Of almost equal consequence is the general attitude of the Aztecs to this place. Whatever the more remote associations in their subconscious mind, it is perfectly clear that when in Aztec times people wrote of Tollan or Tula, unassociated with any other name, they were referring to Tula, Hidalgo. It was still quite an important place in the Late Postclassic era, unlike Teotihuacán itself.

Perhaps it even enjoyed a privileged position, due to its sanctity and prestige, since it is not mentioned in the tribute lists of the *Codex Mendoza*.[59] One may cite two clear examples of this Aztec identification of Tollan with Tula. First, Torquemada writes of the great temple of Quetzalcoatl in the city of Tula.[60] By this he unquestionably means Tula, Hidalgo, for when he writes of Cholula, he uses the term "Tollan Chalollan." Secondly, when Cortés first sent presents of wine and biscuits to Moctezuma from his ships, they were taken to be gifts of the god Quetzalcoatl. Such sacred victuals were treated with great reverence and put into a new blue jar. After being presented as an offering in the Great Temple of Huitzilopochtli in Tenochtitlan, they were taken to the "ciudad de Tula" and given to the priests, who buried them in the Temple of Quetzalcoatl.[61] Durán's description mentions "the God Quetzalcoatl who stayed and resided with us in Tula." Mention is also made of how the god would return to reign in "Tullan," "Tula," or "Tulan"; in this instance these are unquestionably and indeed automatically to be taken as Tula, Hidalgo, a place often referred to by Durán in other contexts simply as Tula.

Should any doubts still remain as to whether in sixteenth-century texts Tula normally means Tula, Hidalgo, they may be further resolved by examining a passage of the *Crónica Mexicayotl* in which the third-mentioned grandson of the *tlatoani* Acamapichtli, Cuetlachtzin, went to reign in Tullan, having married Xiloxochtzin, the daughter of Cuitlaxihuitl, "*rey de Tullan*." From this pair, all the nobility of Tullan descended.[62] Periodic intermarriages between the dynasties of Tenochtitlan and Tullan, or Tula, continued. The *tlatoani* Axayácatl married Mizquixahuatzin, daughter of Aztauhyatzin, ruler of Tullan, and their son reigned in Tullan. It was the latter's daughter, thus a granddaughter of Axayáctl, who in turn married her second cousin, Don Pedro Tlacahuepan, eleventh son of Moctezuma II.[63] In case it could be conceivably supposed that such mentions of Tullan (and variants) could refer to Teotihuacán, Cholula, or any other place, it should be added that the descendants of this Don Pedro still survive and bear the title of Duque de Moctezuma de Tultengo (the latter lies adjacent to Tula, Hidalgo). Thus a title still extant actually links Tula with the Tullan of the *Crónica Mexicayotl*!

Notwithstanding such proofs of identity, certain doubts linger. It is sometimes thought that any discrepancies between conclusions of present-day investigators must take the form of an opposition between extreme views; the "historic" Tollan is to be sought either in Tula or in Teotihuacán, *to the exclusion of other places*. But this is surely no longer the case, since the work of Jiménez Moreno has achieved a certain concensus of opinion and indeed a general acceptance of the historic role of this later Tula, or Tollan Xicocotitlan. In particular one may cite Laurette Séjourné, an inveterate upholder of the claims of Teotihuacán as the true, or primordial, Tollan, but who does not hesitate to write of the "historic Toltecs who founded Tula," thus readily conceding the historic role of Tula, Hidalgo.[64] Chadwick offers a solitary exception to this rule; he still insists that "Tollan" refers mainly to Teotihuacán and subsequently to the dynasty of Tilantongo in the Mixteca.[65]

Tollan Teotihuacán

While accepting as a fact the historicity of Tollan Xicocotitlan, it remains very hard to determine to what extent this whole legend and concept of Tollan reposes upon Teotihuacán foundations.

On the one hand, certain claims are very hard to accept; for instance, Robert Chadwick goes so far as to write of Quetzalcoatl and Tezcatlipoca "dynasties" in Teotihuacán.[66] Of these the silent stones tell us nothing, and support for such a notion of a Quetzalcoatl dynasty seemingly derives from the presence in one fresco of two figures with bird's feet, together with other rather ill-defined attributes of the god. As to the existence of a Tezcatlipoca dynasty and the identification of the Ciudadela as the "palace" of that deity, evidence is based merely on the structure's proximity to the main river or canal and on the association of Tezcatlipoca-Huemac with Atecpanecatl, the latter name being assumed to signify "lord of the irrigation canal." But Atecpan is "water

* Atecpanecatl (lord of the water palace) and Atempanecatl (lord of the edge of the water) seem to have become confused and eventually interchangeable; the *Relación de la Genealogía* even uses "Atepanecatl." Chimalpain refers to Tecaélel as "Atempanecatl," whereas Tezozómoc calls him "Atecpanecatl." Chadwick cites Velázquez, the editor of the *Codex Chimalpopoca*, as saying that

palace," not "canal."* Moreover it will later be shown that the association of Huemac with Atecpanecatl is confined to one source.

However, when one comes to consider Séjourné's reasoning, it should fairly be admitted that, while not universally acceptable, it does possess a certain cogency. She maintains that there were two Toltec phases, that of the Teotihuacán priesthood, and the subsequent militaristic era initiated by Topiltzin.[68] She argues with some force that it is hard to identify in Tula, Hidalgo, the supreme expression of the genius of this great "civilizing people," the Toltecs. She goes so far as to insist that representations of Quetzalcoatl are not abundant in Tula —a point contradicted by Acosta, who excavated the site. Moreover, notwithstanding the fame of the Toltecs as the genial carvers of jade and outstanding metalworkers, no metal is to be found in Tula and only one piece of jade. It must be added that since this was written, Richard Diehl has found various green stone objects in Tula.[69] It should also be mentioned that no metal is to be found in Teotihuacán either.

Séjourné further insists that not a single one of the principal attributes of the Toltecs can conceivably be applied to the inhabitants of Tula, Hidalgo, even if certain stories can be historically situated in that site. Her contention is at least partly supported by Miguel León-Portilla; he finds that the deepest roots of the cultural creativity of the Nahuatl world, summed up by the word "Toltecayotl," must lie in Teotihuacán rather than Tula.[70]

Certainly a major problem presents itself. Descriptions abound of the Toltecs as the most fabulous of artists and craftsmen and of Tollan as a city resplendant in its art and luxury; one has only to read Sahagún's description of the place of worship of Quetzalcoatl, consisting of four abodes: one of gold, facing east; one of turquoise, facing west; one of shells or silver, facing south; and one of red shells, facing north.[71] A parallel version of this account occurs in the *Anales de Cuauhtitlán*.[72] Over and above such fulsome descriptions of the marvels of Tollan, the Toltecs themselves are constantly portrayed as

---

Atecpanecatl was the title of the first king of Teotihuacán, according to Chimalpain. In point of fact, the only ruler of Teotihuacán mentioned by this writer seems to be Quetzalmamalitzin, a contemporary of Axayácatl.[67]

erudite as well as artistic: to their genius is attributed the invention of the art of writing and the science of medicine in Mesoamerica. In fact, the catalogue of Toltec virtues and accomplishments is so unending as to offer the impression of a refinement worthy of Byzantium and an inventiveness recalling the classic Greeks.

Any student of the texts who allowed himself to be carried away by such descriptions would indeed be in for a sorry surprise when confronted with the actual ruins of Tollan Xicocotitlan. In spite of a marked grandeur of conception, one is inevitably struck by a certain coarseness of execution and a lack of artistic appeal. Moreover, the eye is not exactly dazzled by the average Mazapan pottery, so typical of Tula, and it is hardly a breathtaking aesthetic experience to examine the figurines in that style to be found in the Tula Museum. Even Toltec Chichén, notwithstanding its monumental scale, displays at times a degree of carelessness and a lack of refinement; it gives the impression of having been "executed rapidly and vigorously with forthright and not too subtle intention," to quote Proskouriakoff.[73] Similarly, Morris comments on the poor execution of the carving of the warriors in the Warriors' Temple.[74]

Accordingly, while not accepting certain of Séjourné's contentions, particularly her denial of the influence of Tula on Chichén, one is bound to concede that she makes an irrefutable point with respect to the disparity between the aesthetic limitations of the former and the descriptions provided by the sources.

Moreover, as Seler points out, the whole tenor and spirit of the mythical, as opposed to the historic, Tollan denotes "a place of peace and of bliss."[75] This is surely the very last way in which one could describe Tula, Hidalgo, or even Chichén, with their ubiquitous and fearsome warriors, armed to the teeth, and their constant reminders of bloody sacrifice.

Séjourné's openly declared intention is to lead us back to seek the real Tollan in Teotihuacán. As has already been stressed, this site, when first revealed to modern eyes in all its majesty and refinement, almost automatically evoked the true Tollan, capital of the genial Toltecs of tradition, in contrast to the less prepossessing ruins of Tollan Xicocotitlan, excavated somewhat later.

In addition to such aesthetic arguments, other points may be cited, some of which Séjourné mentions. Sahagún, for instance, writes of the Toltecs as the first who peopled the land; these surely cannot be the Postclassic inhabitants of Tollan Xicocotitlan. The same writer also mentions the Toltecs as the inventors of writing, suggesting very remote Toltec origins, if taken literally.

Ixtlilxóchitl also associates certain Toltecs with far earlier periods, stating that many of them died at the time of the destruction of the giants, or *Quinametin*, described by him as the original inhabitants of the land, and in certain contexts automatically to be identified with Teotihuacán and its gigantic proportions. The same author mentions in addition "Toltec" ruins both in Teotihuacán and Cholula.[76] He actually goes so far as to state that Teotihuacán was greater and more powerful than Tula. In addition, in a less frequently quoted text, Eulalia Guzmán finds an actual mention of the great Teotihuacán in association with Toltecs.[77]

To this it must be added that certain aspects of the saga of Quetzalcoatl and of Tollan, particularly those reported by Sahagún and in the *Anales de Cuauhtitlán*, are hardly applicable to the true Postclassic era, but fit more readily into the Classic pattern or into that intermediate period between the decline of Teotihuacán and the inception of the Postclassic era proper. This point will be illustrated in the following chapter, by means of a close analysis of the text of the famous Chapter 29 of Sahagún's Book X.

For now, let us take two general examples. The creation of the Fifth Sun is actually stated to have taken place in Teotihuacán, not Tollan or Tula, though it is generally considered to refer to a time when the former city was long past its apogee, if not actually in ruins. The Fifth Sun itself surely symbolized the new, or Postclassic, world, and is actually described as the sun of Topiltzin-Quetzalcoatl, god and hero of Tula.[78] However, the story of the creation of the Fifth Sun to which Sahagún also refers separately and in detail, has nothing to do with the site of Tollan Xicocotitlan.

Similarly, no one has ever suggested that Tamoanchan, which figures so prominently in such stories and to which Quetzalcoatl went after his visit to Mictlantecuhtli (lord of the underworld), is to be associated with the Postclassic Tollan Xicocotitlan and its period of greatness. Several investigators have indeed identified Tamoanchan with Xochicalco, possibly incorrectly; however, they perfectly rightly associate Tamoanchan with the final phase of Teotihuacán and with the immediate post-Teotihuacán era.

Finally, justification of quite a different sort could be offered for the association of Teotihuacán with the general concept of Tollan. It has already been mentioned that at the time of the apogee of that center, the lake of Texcoco extended farther toward Teotihuacán; the latter could thus at that time with much more reason lay a literal claim to the name of Tollan, the place of rushes.[79] It seems in fact probable that the lake level was higher at that time.[80] Moreover, there still exists a place called El Tular (*tular* means simply a place where reeds grow), a swampy area about three kilometers southwest of the springs of San Juan Teotihuacán. It contained no reeds in 1964, but presumably would have done so in earlier times. Reference has also been made to the existence of Santiago Tola, in the Upper Teotihuacán Valley.

The Toltecs of History and Fable

The reasons for identifying Tollan with Tula, Hidalgo, together with some of the objections, have now been outlined. By a supreme irony, some of the arguments for accepting and rejecting Tula as *the* Tollan are both drawn from the same Chapter 29 of Sahagún's Book X.

It has already been emphasized that by "Tollan" the Mexicas consciously denoted Tula, Hidalgo, and no other; there was certainly no confusion in their own minds between Tula and Teotihuacán. The latter still enjoyed a certain sanctity, and Moctezuma II was even reported to have visited the place; it was for them totally distinct from Tula, and in the *Coloquio de los Doce* Tollan and Teotihuacán are distinguished as quite separate holy places.

The grounds for identifying Tula as Tollan are valid, based as they are on the correct location near Tula of certain localities mentioned in the texts in association with Tollan. The only weakness is that, while they successfully link *part* of such accounts with Tula, they do not necessarily connect the whole.

On the other hand, the arguments against *normally* associating Tula with Sahagún's Tollan and with that of the *Anales de Cuauhtitlán* are less compelling. In particular, the whole basis of what might be termed the "aesthetic" case against Tula as Tollan, at first sight so well founded, appears somewhat fragile upon closer examination. Such arguments are based on a rather too literal interpretation of symbolic accounts of the wonders of Tollan.

In this respect, ample emphasis has already been laid upon the existence of a kind of heavenly Tollan, over and above the actual place which bore the name; Seler in particular drew attention to this point. These descriptions of exotic structures, together with the cacao bushes and the tropical birds, belong not to the earthly city but to the mythical or other-worldly Tollan, the source of all that is beautiful and perfect.

This is surely just another example of the frequent confusion of the material and the divine, so common to human thought. Not only did Rome, originally a city, later become in addition a symbol; this phenomenon presents itself in even more striking form where Jerusalem is concerned. In the early Middle Ages, men still envisaged Jerusalem as the town where Christ died. Over and above this material city, they conceived in their minds the new and heavenly Jerusalem. To quote the Book of Revelations, "And the building of the wall was of jasper; and the city was of pure gold, like unto clear glass. And the foundations of the wall of the city were garnished with all manner of precious stones. The first foundation was of jasper; the second sapphire; the third a chalcedony; and the fourth an emerald."[81]

In the descriptions of Tollan, both the "houses" of precious metals and those described as made of gorgeous feathers are associated with their respective cardinal points and with certain colors; the latter are themselves of course to be linked with the four directions, though the actual hues concerned may vary from one account to another. Quetzalcoatl by his nature as god of wind came to be connected with the four cardinal points. Moreover, as Seler has also pointed out, the Toltecs are par excellence the lords of the House of Turquoise, because as their name implies they are associated with water in which reeds grow and hence with the color turquoise or blue.

Fabulous edifices of this kind are by no means unique to Tollan. In Chimalpain's *Memorial Breve*, descriptions occur of similar wonders built to honor Nauhyotecuhtli, god of Teotenanco; in addition to "houses" of jade, turquoise, and so on, added refinements are mentioned, such as a house of red crystal and turquoise-colored mirrors.[82] No one is going to suggest that the modern Tenango del Valle is not after all the Teotenanco of Chimalpain simply because recent excavations in that place have not uncovered any such treasures. The house of jade in Chalco, described by the same author, has already been mentioned; in addition, in one of the *Cantares* reference is made to "houses" of jade, quetzal feathers, coral, turquoise, and the like, situated in Tenochtitlan.[83] Bernal Díaz, for all his enthusiasm for the marvels of the Aztec capital, never discovered anything approaching such splendor. At all events, even had they existed, the most optimistic of archaeologists could hardly expect to unearth houses of feathers, gold, or turquoise in Tula or elsewhere. The first would have succumbed to the ravages of time and the remainder to the predations of the Spaniards and others; Sahagún particularly insists that Tula was sacked of all its treasures when overcome by disaster.

If one considers the question carefully, he is hardly likely to take as a literal fact a house adorned entirely with quetzal feathers in Tula, or for that matter in Teotihuacán or Tenochtitlan. These descriptions may be purely symbolic, like those in the Bible of the New Jerusalem; it may be recalled that according to Sahagún's "Song of Tláloc," this deity possessed a turquoise house in his mythical paradise of Tlalocan.[84] If they existed at all, it is possible that such edifices were simply painted in certain colors and designs; the use of paint and frescoes was after all lavish in Mesoamerican architecture. Or, alternatively and more probably, these "houses" could have been of miniature size, more resembling portable altars. Sahagún describes them as "the place of worship of their priest," but this worship could have taken place in front of rather than inside such structures. It is most important to bear in mind that "*calli*" does not only mean "house"; Siméon also gives the additional meaning of "box" and even "basket."

These constructions were made of materials typically symbolic of tribute—turquoise, jade, feathers, and gold. It is probable that they were of miniature proportions if they existed at all. Further evidence for this may be cited. First, the *Anales de Tlatelolco* tell how the conqueror Tímal arrived and carried off "two houses made of quetzal feathers and two eagle vessels for his god."[85] Secondly, Henry Nicholson points to a scene in the *Vienna codex*, depicting Quetzalcoatl, in which four small "houses" figure, probably a Mixtec version of what this author aptly refers to as "oratories."[86] When in desperate straits, Topiltzin also sent a miniature ball court, studded with gems, to his enemies.[87]

The figurative nature of the whole of Sahagún's account becomes apparent in another way. Presumably no one believes that Quetzalcoatl at the collapse of Tula actually transformed cacao bushes (native of course to coastal Mexico) into mezquites, or that he actually sent away birds of gaudy plumage, never seen in those parts. If such deeds are not taken as a factual description, why should one interpret literally the tales of Toltec buildings of gold, turquoise, feathers, and the like, and then complain of their absence in that or any other archaeological site?

If indeed valid reservations exist concerning Tula, Hidalgo, as the true Tollan of the principal accounts, these should not be based upon any lack of exotic refinements in what is known of the site. More solid doubts might arise from the various references in Sahagún, the *Anales de Cuauhtitlán*, and elsewhere to events and achievements that are clearly pre-Tula and which will later be examined in more detail. In addition, objections may be put forward from a moral, or spiritual, rather than a merely aesthetic point of view. As Seler has pointed out, in Central Mexico the Toltec era came to be regarded in later times as a kind of Golden Age. Also in Yucatán, even after the imposition of Spanish rule, the time of the Toltec Mayas was regarded with similar nostalgia. Such visions of an idyllic past are hard to associate with the reality of the Postclassic Toltecs, who, like ourselves, appear to have lived in a changing and violent world.

To sum up, I think that the Round Table was correct in deciding that the historic data in the *Anales de Cuauhtitlán*, Sahagún, the *Relación de la Geneaología*, the *Origen de los Mexicanos*, the *Historia de los Mexicanos por sus Pinturas*, the *Leyenda de los Soles*, Chimalpain, Ixtlilxóchitl, and Torquemada refer to Tula, Hidalgo. Possibly the terms of the corresponding resolution were rather sweeping and it would be preferable to suggest that *most*, but not *all*, such references to Tollan do concern Tula, Hidalgo.

Black Is White

As with Tollan, so with the expression "Toltec" one is confronted with ambiguities. It has already been stressed that the term "Toltec" in the late Postclassic era came to denote principally an artist or craftsman, in addition to its basic meaning, i.e., an inhabitant of Tollan. Jiménez Moreno thinks, and I agree, that such skills were originally characteristic of the Nonoalca element of the population of Tollan rather than of other immigrants whose culture was less refined.[88]

The double meaning of the adjective "Toltec" is also to be encountered in Yucatán, where it may signify either a person originally from Tula or one skilled in jewelry making, silverwork, and the like.[89] A similar situation even exists to the northwest of Tula, and Jiménez Moreno interprets references to Toltecs in the *Lienzo de Jucutacato* as denoting either people originally from Tula *or* artisans.[90]

In certain contexts a contrary impression is conveyed of Toltecs being a rough and rude people who brought shameful things with them to Yucatán; in other words, far from being apostles of refined culture, they debased that which they found.[91] Ixtlilxóchitl also refers to them as great runners, implying athletic rather than intellectual qualities. Such an opposite meaning, denoting physical prowess and even a certain coarseness, is something to be attributed perhaps not to the Toltecs as such but to the Tolteca-Chichimeca element from the northwestern confines of middle America; it was these people who probably formed the sinews of the Toltec war effort. Their provenance, together with that of the Nonoalcas, will shortly be studied more closely. The latter were certainly in some way to be associated with the Olmeca-Xicallancas, of whom Sahagún writes, "These were also named Tenime, because they spoke a barbarous tongue. These, according to the tradition, were Tolteca, a branch, a remnant of the Tolteca."[92]

Kirchhoff goes so far as to suggest that the real Toltecs were the Olmecs of Cholula.[93] For Olmecs we would prefer to substitute the Nonoalcas, in a sense their kinsfolk, who came to Tollan Xicocotitlan, perhaps from the direction of Cholula and beyond, and who were indeed the standard-bearers of Mesoamerican high culture.

In contrast to the latter stood the other Toltecs who, according to

Sahagún, had gone forth far into the northwest and had lived in contact with the more barbarous Teochichimecs, or true Chichimecs. The people who later came to Tollan from this direction were called "Tolteca-Chichimeca"; thus the two opposite terms, "Toltec" and "Chichimec," become merged into one; as Kirchhoff puts it, having been taught that Toltec is white and Chichimec black, we learn that black is white.[94]

One is thus faced with the awkward paradox that "Toltec," meaning literally "inhabitant of Tula" when used alone without the additional epithet "Chichimec," is not usually employed to indicate the people who came to Tollan Xicocotitlan from the northwest and whose native language was Nahuatl. The truest Toltecs, the real *Kulturvolk*, are rather those who came from the opposite direction, the Nonoalcas.

Words Change Their Meanings

To sum up the rather complex issues so far discussed in this chapter, it is considered that Tula, Hidalgo, was probably the first city actually to be called Tollan and the one major center for which Tollan was the only name, instead of being a kind of qualifying or additional title, as for, say, Tollan Chollollan. Regarding previous Tollans, it can hardly be proved that, prior to the Postclassic Tula, either Cholula or Teotihuacán had actually been described as "Tollan," though this is certainly a possibility.

Regardless of whether it was used before, it is clearly demonstrable that subsequent to the era of Tula, Hidalgo, the name Tollan came to be applied to other centers, particularly Cholula, and probably retrospectively to Teotihuacán. The very significance of "Tollan" appears to change with the times; originating simply as "place of rushes," it acquired the additional sense not merely of "metropolis" but of a kind of holy city, with particular reference to the cult of Quetzalcoatl. Cholula in the Late Postclassic era takes on a special identity as Tollan Chollollan, the city of Quetzalcoatl and the spiritual heir of Tula, just as Tenochtitlan became its temporal successor.[95]

The Mexicas had assumed the name "Culhua," and through the medium of Culhuacán had claimed possession of the Toltec heritage emanating from Tollan Xicocotitlan. They thus came to idealize this Tollan, in order to enhance their historic importance and provide an aura of sanctity for their own culture. Mexica history was written (and expurgated from time to time as under Itzcoatl), as much to impress by its vision of greatness as to instruct by any precision of detail. A certain cult of forebears, if not attaining Chinese proportions, is apparent in ancient Mesoamerican thought; the Mexicas themselves were among the most ancestor-conscious and became sticklers for a legitimacy to which their claim was doubtful.

If Tenochtitlan was magnificent, then its predecessor Tollan Xicocotitlan had to be doubly splendid to enhance the glory of the Aztec capital. Accordingly, seemingly factual descriptions of this Tollan were in great measure symbolic. "Houses" of varying hues facing the cardinal points, and palaces of jade and turquoise formed part and parcel of ancient Mesoamerican lore, conjured up in particular as pertaining to the Golden Age of the fabulous Toltecs, whose glorious mantle the Aztecs had inherited. Only thus may one comprehend the differences in proportion between the dazzling Tollan of the sources and the more pedestrian remains which stand revealed. Such idealized accounts of Tollan were designed to serve as a backcloth to Aztec grandeur rather than as factual descriptions of a city and its people.

Moreover, perhaps as part of a deliberate oversimplification in the orthodox tradition, everything good or great from the past must perforce be linked with the known Tollan, rather than attributed to yet remoter peoples, of whom only confused reports survived. One may assume that any member of the upper hierarchy of priests, if closely interrogated, would have displayed at least an awareness that certain "Toltec" achievements, such as the art of writing and medicine or the invention of the calendar, must have first appeared much before the era of Tollan Xicocotitlan, to which they themselves attributed a limited life span. Such sages would have been aware that Teotihuacán, still visible to the beholder, had existed long before. If consciously or officially all the glories of the past were attributable to the known Tollan, still an important city in their time, subconsciously at least they must have realized that much of their own culture derived from remoter antecedents.

The same phenomenon occurs with the term "Toltecs." Originally it denoted simply an inhabitant of Tollan, but then took on an additional meaning as artist or craftsman. Of course it is possible that matters proceeded in a reverse order and that "Toltec" preceded Tollan, just as "Israelite," meaning "marauding soldier," preceded Israel as a place name. The Tepanecs and Acolhuas appear also to have existed before the names Tepanohuayan (often synonymous with Azcapotzalco) and Acolhuacan came to be used.

The alteration of the meaning of Toltec and Tollan thus came about in two ways. First, given the tendency of the Mexicas to place Tollan on a pedestal, all the finest and highest qualities became applicable to the Toltecs, regardless of prosaic and humble origins. Such virtues included not only skills of craftsmanship but universal wisdom and the invention of the original sciences. Second, a change in meaning occurred, not originally as part of a deliberate policy, but because the Toltecs did in actual fact become keenly refined with the passing of the centuries; from ruder antecedents, they and their descendants after Tula came to be the most highly civilized peoples of Mesoamerica. In this they recall the Dorian Greeks who bore down as savage destroyers upon the cultured cities of the Mycenaean world. These same people were to become the classic Greeks, and finally their tradition was to pass through Hellenism to Byzantium, where it inspired a Greek civilization no longer virile but exquisitely delicate in its artistic manifestations. Similarly, the rough Francs, fortified by a generous admixture of other blood, as occurred also in the case of the Toltecs, became the ancestors of the civilization of France.

So, from rude beginnings, the latter-day Toltecs in Cholula came into close contact with the peoples of the Mixteca, from where incidentally derives most of the turquoise and nearly all the goldwork found in Mesoamerica. The Toltecs really were by the end of the pre-Hispanic era what they had always been to the Aztecs, namely, the finest artisans and the true artists of their era; Cholula as a great merchant center was the very home of craftsmanship.[96] By a convenient transposition in time, the Aztecs fostered the legend that the Toltecs of Tollan Xicocotitlan had possessed from the outset identical skills and genius to those fervent adherents of the same deity, the "Toltecs" of Tollan Cholollan.

In this later period, the term "Toltec" did not altogether lose its earlier meaning of belonging to a specific ethnic community. Fairly frequent mentions occur in the sources concerning the inhabitants of Chalco, Xochimilco, certain sectors of Texcoco, and above all the people of Culhuacán as being of Toltec descent—clearly meant in an ethnic and not pure cultural sense.[97]

One is thus in effect confronted with three distinct layers of Toltecs. First, there are the legendary Toltecs, the inventors of all wisdom and science, sometimes named by Ixtlilxóchitl and Sahagún as "giants." In reality, but not in the conscious realization of the common people, such Toltec origins went back at least as far as Teotihuacán, not certainly in its own time known as Tollan.

Secondly, we have the actual inhabitants of Tollan Xicocotitlan, part Tolteca-Chichimeca from the northwest, and part Nonoalca from the southeast. These were the warriors and empire builders of the early Postclassic era and the people to whom most Toltec sagas refer.

Thirdly come the late Postclassic Toltecs, famous as great artificers and craftsmen, as typified by the Toltecs of Tollan Chololtlan, not infrequently thus named. The wisdom of the first, or legendary, Toltecs and the skills of the third, or latter-day survivors, then came to be equally attributed to the inhabitants of Tollan Xicocotitlan to produce a single composite, if confusing, picture.

Tollan and Toltec, ostensibly mere proper names, can only be comprehended as concepts, as something more than mere apellations, applicable to different places and peoples at different times—rather as the name Heliopolis, the city of the sun and of the sun god, was applied in various epochs to more than one leading center of ancient Egypt. Or for that matter as Rome, originally, like Tollan Xicocotitlan, the home of soldiers and conquerors, was reimbodied as the Holy Roman Empire, while the term "Roman" and "Rome" acquired a further connotation, almost entirely connected with spiritual rather than temporal power.

Universal Deity

It has seemed both useful and necessary for our study to analyze the general concepts, Tollan and Toltec. Similarly, before initiating any historical reconstruction, a brief examination of the bases of the Quetzalcoatl saga becomes desirable; for whether as symbol, god, or man, his image pervades our story.

The Plumed Serpent is a divine emblem of great universality in Mesoamerica. As expressed by Séjourné, "Quetzalcoatl springs from epoch to epoch, from city to city." This cult was indeed widespread, stretching on the one hand as far as Nicaragua; at the opposite extreme, among the Huicholes, rain clouds are considered as plumed serpents.[98]

The adoration of the Plumed Serpent enjoyed a long life span; starting in Teotihuacán and perhaps even earlier in rudimentary form, it outlived its apogee in Tollan Xicocotitlan and still flourished under the Aztecs. For the latter, one should view with a certain caution Spanish-inspired accounts tending to present Quetzalcoatl as a benign and respectable counterpart to the archfiends Huitzilopochtli and Tezcatlipoca. Nor can one believe all he is told of the opposition of a kindly Quetzalcoatl to the inception of human sacrifice. At least in the final pre-Hispanic phase, priests bearing his title were quite as dedicated to this practice as any others.

Because of its very timelessness, it is hard to reach the core of the Quetzalcoatl saga; just as occurs with the many tales of King Minos of Crete, one never quite knows who he really was or when he lived. Quetzalcoatl can be man, hero, or god, or as Plumed Serpent a mere symbol. Was there one or many human beings called Quetzalcoatl? When and where did he or they live?

Any answer must be complicated by probable mutations in the concept itself over the centuries. George Kubler rightly reminds us that in the Middle Ages in Europe, classic forms were used but with different meanings; Orpheus for instance becomes the Good Shepherd.[99] By the same token, the Plumed Serpent may well have evoked varying mental images in diverse periods and regions.

Whatever the subsequent development of the deity, its original basis remains beyond question; the word is derived from *coatl*, serpent, and *quetzalli*, green feather. It could equally be taken to mean "precious serpent." The whole notion of the bird-serpent has of course very special connotations, as symbolizing the combination of the celestial and terrestrial. The Aztec myth of the eagle on the cactus devouring a serpent may even be connected with this concept.

Investigators differ as to when and where the Plumed Serpent, a particularly Mesoamerican concept, really originated. Notwithstanding the tendency of Drucker, Heizer, and Squier to see the rattlesnake carved on Monument 19 of La Venta as a Plumed Serpent, Michael Coe finds such identifications hard to accept.[100] Bernal considers that the feathered serpent does not occur among the original Olmecs.[101] The only possible exception might be the stone sarcophagus of Tres Zapotes. Bernal points out, however, that the combination of man and animal is frequently to be found in Mesoamerica (and indeed elsewhere, as for instance in Egypt or India).

On the other hand, Miguel Covarrubias finds antecedents of the feathered serpent among the Olmecs.[102] Its development may have occurred in the same way that Tláloc, the Rain God, originated from the jaguar mask, as he so ably demonstrates. Piña Chan further recalls that the Plumed Serpent appears as an aquatic serpent in Tlatilco: its crest is symbolic of water.[103] Less obvious, but notwithstanding significant, is the incorporation of feline features in portraits of Maya rain gods.[104]

It hardly remains in doubt that the serpent cult, and hence that of the Plumed Serpent, grew out of that of the jaguar; among the Olmecs representations occur that combine the two animals. The jaguar represents the fertility that derives from the earth, and the serpent, that which comes from water. As Jiménez Moreno insists, in early times the serpent became associated with the jaguar, embodying perhaps partly this notion of cosmic earth and partly that of rain.[105] Thus the two derivatives of the jaguar cult, on the one hand the Plumed Serpent and on the other Tláloc (originally the more important of the two), seem like their jaguar prototype to have Olmec origins, even if their nature is somewhat embryonic. The twin concept survived in Mesoamerica to the very end; the actual phrase "jaguar serpent" is employed in the "Song to Tláloc," illustrating the still unbroken link between the two.[106] The joint notion is indeed to be associated with earth as much as water, two elements which are of course symbolically closely linked. Thelma Sullivan has concisely pointed out that the very name Tláloc derived from *tlalli* (earth) and not from *tlaloa* (to make sprout), as had previously been more generally accepted.[107] Armillas moreover stresses that the earth had two disguises, the *Quetzalcoanahualli* and the *Xiuhcoanahualli*.[108]

The Plumed Serpent in Teotihuacán

In Teotihuacán the Plumed Serpent is apparent but not omnipresent, and by no means all serpents are plumed; this is emphatically the city of Tláloc, not of Quetzalcoatl! The symbol occurs in this site as an adjunct of Tláloc and is thus closely associated with rain; indeed, Jiménez Moreno thinks that of the two the Quetzalcoatl of that era may be the representative of rain, while Tláloc is more the god of lightning.[109]

The views of Séjourné, an unflagging devotee of the cult of Quetzalcoatl, are well known and require little restatement. For her the real Tollan is Teotihuacán, and it is here in this early age that Quetzalcoatl, no mere vegetation deity or appanage of Tláloc, attains his full majesty; he remains no ordinary hero or god but stands forth as the inspirer of a new philosophy, or *Weltanschauung*.

Armillas, however, steering a more middle course sees this early Plumed Serpent as a kind of double of Tláloc. Florescano goes even further, maintaining that Quetzalcoatl was virtually nonexistent in Teotihuacán, where Tláloc reigned supreme. The Plumed Serpent as such, more symbol than god, enjoyed a brief vogue at the beginning of Teotihuacán II, and the temple in the Citadel thus named was later covered over. Neither murals nor architectural remains prove the existence of a fully fledged deity of that name; above all, no cult of the later Ce Acatl-Topiltzin-Quetzalcoatl is found. The feathered serpent at this stage is more to be associated with agriculture, the green plumes symbolizing vegetal regeneration.[110]

It is perhaps worthwhile to cite more fully the views of two principal commentators on this uncertain theme, Caso and Jiménez Moreno.

The latter, as already mentioned, sees the serpent as such emerge very early in the Olmec horizon, where the jaguar was the leading deity. Its position was reaffirmed in Teotihuacán, where it came to be associated basically with Tláloc. To this tiger-serpent was further added the owl, to indicate its nocturnal aspect; the composite deity was also to be identified with lightning, which had divine origins deriving from the old God of Fire, Xiuhtecuhtli.[111]

The role of this serpent double of Tláloc perhaps lay at the basis of the primordial Quetzalcoatl, originally a rain symbol and only later to be confused with the cultural hero who departed to Tlillan Tlapallan. Quetzalcoatl was never to lose entirely his association with water; apart from his connection with wind and therefore rain, he became, among other things, a fisherman's god.[112]

Caso for his part agrees that Tláloc is basically the tiger-serpent. Though the god's image is more tigerlike, he has serpent's fangs. The jaguar in Teotihuacán is fundamentally the animal of Tláloc.[113] Thus we find in this site:

1. Man–serpent–tiger = Tláloc
2. Man–bird–serpent = Quetzalcoatl.

Caso thinks that a Quetzalcoatl deity more or less independent of Tláloc already existed in Teotihuacán II. In both Caso's text and illustrations, however, the bird-butterfly rather than the bird-snake is predominant; few representations of the latter depict anything resembling a plumed serpent. Moreover, the profile and face on the "Quetzalpapálotl," or bird-butterfly figures, recall in certain details the owl as much as the quetzal and has owl's eyes. Caso affirms the presence in Teotihuacán of Tlahuizcalpantecuhtli, later to become an inseparable part of Quetzalcoatl, and of the merchant god Yacatecuhtli, also later to be associated with Quetzalcoatl in Cholula and elsewhere.

From such observations one may conclude:

First, the early Plumed Serpent was closely associated with the ubiquitous image of Tláloc. Both grew out of the jaguar; as such they were principally representative of rain and vegetation, but they also probably enjoyed an auxiliary association with earth and with fire—among the oldest Mesoamerican deities. Sullivan of course insists on the role of Tláloc as symbolizing the inseparable nature of earth and water, or rain.[114]

Caso does not admit the presence in Teotihuacán of the Xiuhcoatl, symbolic of the fire god. However, as Seler points out, the blue, or turquoise, snake, i.e., Xiuhcoatl, by its very color is linked with Tláloc and with water. It is thus also connected with Quetzalcoatl. In the "Song to Xipe" occurs the expression "*quetzalxiuhcoatl*."[115] Beyer also stresses connections between Quetzalcoatl and Xiuhcoatl.[116]

Secondly, the Plumed Serpent is clearly present in Teotihuacán in statuary rather than in mural painting; to judge by Caso's own illustrations, it is however not predominant. The bird-butterfly god is by contrast frequently represented, but the bird is not purely and simply a quetzal.

Thirdly, there is little evidence of the later Quetzalcoatl-Ehécatl-Tlahuizcalpantecuhtli, associated with wind and with the planet Venus; Séjourné sees a red Quetzalcoatl in Zacuala as equivalent to Tlahuizcalpantecuhtli, but it is not altogether apparent how she reaches this conclusion.[117] She also asserts that a "cult of man" permeates Teotihuacán and thus denotes the presence of Quetzalcoatl, as inspiring a kind of Mesoamerican humanism.

Any evidence as to the presence in Teotihuacán of the regenerated Morning Star-cum-Wind God Quetzalcoatl is somewhat scanty:

1. Caso speaks, but without much conviction, of "the raft of Quetzalcoatl" as mentioned by Séjourné.[118]

2. The same author is not assured that the central person in the fresco of Tetitla is Quetzalcoatl, simply because he bears a marine shell. He might be Tecciztecatl.[119]

3. Séjourné illustrates only one sherd that bears Quetzalcoatl's effigy (the Plumed Serpent, not Ce Acatl).[120] Moreover, her own work on Teotihuacán ceramics is noteworthy for the scarcity of illustrations surely identifiable as Quetzalcoatl; by contrast, even Xipe occurs frequently.

4. León-Portilla calls attention to various stylizations of the Plumed Serpent and of the bearded figure of Quetzalcoatl in Zacuala.[121]

5. Seler illustrates a full-face portrait on a *teponaztli* in the Paris Trocadero Museum, bearing the *epcololli* ear pendants. He says that the figure represents Quetzalcoatl and that it may be assumed to have come from Teotihuacán.[122]

6. Acosta draws attention to a symbol lightly scratched on the

back of a jaguar figure in Teotihuacán. It is difficult to decipher, but he believes it represents Ce Acatl.[123]

7. An incipient ehecailacalozcatl, a characteristic adornment of Quetzalcoatl, appears in a mural decoration on the molding of Portico I in Atetelco.[124]

So much for the somewhat meager traces of the presence of a more personalized deity, as opposed simply to the more anonymous Plumed Serpent effigy. Armillas perhaps best sums up the matter when he states that there is no true evidence of the cult of the god Quetzalcoatl before the Toltecs (meaning of course the historic Toltecs of Tollan Xicocotitlan). One might perhaps nowadays qualify this statement by adding Xochicalco to Tollan. Armillas expresses a justifiable uncertainty that all the plumed serpents of the last pre-Hispanic horizon actually represent the god Quetzalcoatl. He thinks that the "Temple of Quetzalcoatl" in Teotihuacán is really dedicated to the God of Rain; this monument also contains figures which Jiménez Moreno has identified as representations of the God of Fire (though Caso thinks they are Tláloc). Bearing in mind Kubler's insistence that emblems such as the Plumed Serpent could change their significance and associations over long periods of time, it may be recalled that the Xiuhcoatl, originally symbolic of Xiuhtecuhtli, also later became the emblem of Huitzilopochtli. Seler even suggests in his notes on the "Song of Xipe" that the Plumed Serpent, as a symbol of renewed vegetation, also came to be identified with Xipe Totec. Kubler cites Panofsky, whose life study has been the survival of classic iconography through the Middle Ages into the Renaissance. He insists that the same form repeated with frequency can acquire different meanings with the passing of time, and that one such meaning, or message, can be transmitted through differing visual forms.[125] As a very simple example of this, one might cite the tomb of Leonardo Bruni in Santa Croce in Florence; it is surmounted by two winged figures which one might call angels, since they are in a church, but they are in fact symbols of victory from a Roman triumphal arch.[126]

Certainly one must be on guard against assuming that what a plumed serpent meant to the people of Teotihuacán must be the same for those of Tollan or Tenochtitlan. The jaguar in particular underwent a whole series of symbolic metamorphoses in the course of Mesoamerican religious history.

From the available evidence, a true presence of the god Quetzalcoatl in Teotihuacán would appear questionable. It would rather seem that the Plumed Serpent in Teotihuacán enjoyed a somewhat restricted cult as an adjunct of Tláloc, and thus as a water, rain, and possibly earth god. Like the Xiuhcoatl in later times, it may even have served more as emblem than deity. More prevalent in the great metropolis was what Caso calls the Quetzalpapálotl, but that was not the same.

Moreover, the Plumed Serpent in Teotihuacán was only one of several plumed beasts. Quite apart from the Quetzalpapálotl, plumed coyotes are to be found, and in Tetitla frescoes of plumed jaguars and feathered snails appear.

If a personalized deity called Quetzalcoatl really figured prominently in Teotihuacán, one may ask why his gospel did not strike root among the Mayas of that period, considering their very close contacts with that city. Why did the propagation of this cult have to wait until the fall of Teotihuacán and the rise of the more distant and smaller center of Tollan Xicocotitlan? Seler professes to see plumed serpents in Copán, but the identification is questionable, and their occurrence is at best rare among the Classic Mayas.

The dynamic force with which the Quetzalcoatl cult went forth through central Mesoamerica, Yucatán, and the Mixteca in the Early Postclassic era logically suggests the diffusion of some new message; it could have hardly arisen out of the mere refurbishing of an already leading deity. It would seem most unlikely that a form of worship should have thrived in one great center for half a millennium and then suddenly should have burst its bounds with all the furore of a new and proselytizing faith.

It may be conceded that certain legends concerning the hero-god Quetzalcoatl, such as the invention of writing and of the sacred calendar, seem to go back to the era of Teotihuacán, if not beyond. But such stories are nebulous and imprecise, and it will subsequently be shown that they refer mainly to a reinvention or resuscitation of learned skills in the intermediate period following the decline and fall of the great center.

A Deity Reborn

The final decline of Teotihuacán to a certain extent spelled a temporary eclipse of Tláloc, leaving a kind of divine power vacuum. As Jiménez Moreno points out, the two contenders for the succession were Quetzalcoatl and Piltzintecuhtli; the latter displayed certain traits that were to become basic to Tezcatlipoca. The same author attributes to those Toltecs who came in from the north the introduction of this god rather than that of Quetzalcoatl.[127]

One should not exaggerate the degree to which Tláloc suffered a decline. He still figures quite prominently in Xochicalco and even in Chichén Itza; moreover, it is Tláloc rather than Quetzalcoatl who prevails in the designs of Plumbate pottery, the great trade ware of the Early Postclassic era.

The rise of Quetzalcoatl to new prominence was a notable development, but at the same time not out of keeping with the tendency for the fortunes of gods in Mesoamerica to fluctuate. Tláloc declined after Teotihuacán, but he certainly made a good recovery under the Aztecs; Quetzalcoatl was if anything less prominent in this late period, worshiped mainly as a god of Wind and somewhat overshadowed by Huitzilopochtli and Tezcatlipoca. If he figured so much in the stories of the Conquest, this may be due to the personal obsession of Moctezuma II, who deduced that since Quetzalcoatl had departed for the east, any divine being arriving from that quarter must *ipso facto* be the same god.

Such a variable situation was not confined to Mesoamerica. In Mesopotamia, which often offers striking parallels, unstable conditions caused the powers and functions of individual deities to wax and wane, leaving the pantheon in a constant state of flux.[128]

Quetzalcoatl was perhaps not alone among Mesoamerican deities in enjoying a limited status until revamped in spectacular fashion. Later, Huitzilopochtli, also seemingly connected with earth and water, was to undergo a similar transformation in Coatepec. As part of their new form, both gods assumed astral functions of a glamorous nature: Quetzalcoatl became the planet Venus and the Wind; Huitzilopochtli was identified with the southern sky and with the sun. In this they both reversed the career of the Hebrew Yahweh, who began life as a kind of weather or desert god and later settled down in Israel to a more sedentary role, with certain attributes of the Canaanite vegetation deities.

Of the radical nature of Quetzalcoatl's transformation ample evidence exists. In diverse parts of Postclassic Mesoamerica, representations of the god in the form of Ehécatl or as Tlahuizcalpantecuhtli, associated with Venus as Morning Star, occur more frequently than those of the established Plumed Serpent image. The change is sufficiently marked to reinforce any doubts as to the previous strength of the Quetzalcoatl cult in Teotihuacán; one's impressions are confirmed that the Classic Plumed Serpent was at best a muted deity, and that the real Quetzalcoatl was mainly a Postclassic phenomenon, with roots in the Late Classic era.

The first question therefore is: when and where did the new Quetzalcoatl cult arise? Did the refurbished deity appear first in one guise only, e.g., as Tlahuizcalpantecuhtli-Xólotl, the Morning and Evening Star—or simultaneously in all his new forms, including not only his role as Ehécatl, the Wind, but also his function as creator god, much emphasized by Sahagún?

Quetzalcoatl in new garb became associated with various attributes and gods, each linked with different regions of Mesoamerica. First, as Tlahuizcalpantecuhtli, the Morning Star, he was symbolically connected with the east, or with Tlillan Tlapallan. The adornments of this latter god are almost identical with those of Mixcoatl, the hunting god, mainly to be identified with the northern marches and with the land of the Chichimecs; such connections are to a certain extent shared by Xólotl, Quetzalcoatl's twin and God of the Evening Star. As Ehécatl, the Wind God, Quetzalcoatl is of course inseparable from the Huaxteca, the home of those round temples dedicated to the wind cult and of the Wind God's conical hat. The new Ehécatl Quetzalcoatl, complete with characteristic duckbill mask, is also ubiquitous in Mixtec codices from an early date that corresponds to the period of the apogee of Xochicalco.

The New God Made Manifest

Whatever the other regional associations of the refurbished

Quetzalcoatl, he is indissolubly linked by legend with the Toltecs and with Tollan Xicocotitlan. So deeply rooted are such traditions that his very transformation and emergence in new garb have at times come to be associated with that locality. Certain written sources actually tell us that a Ce Acatl-Topiltzin-Quetzalcoatl founded Tula, even if they do not insist that he was the first of that name. Thus it might at first sight be deduced that Tollan Xicocotitlan was founded by the legendary hero who afterwards inspired the renaissance of the cult of the god.

On purely chronological grounds, such a supposition is not easy to sustain. In the first place, a certain time lag ensued between the decline of Teotihuacán and the rise to importance of Tollan Xicocotitlan, as will later be explained. This interval, which may conveniently be called the Protopostclassic era, was marked by the apogee of El Tajín, as well as that of Xochicalco, whose greatest period coincides almost with Teotihuacán IV. These sites, together with Monte Albán, in its III b phase, have been called by Jiménez Moreno the "successor states" of Teotihuacán. The relationship between the two is fairly close; the Temple of the Plumed Serpents in Xochicalco displays certain trends recalling El Tajín.

It is highly significant that Xochicalco, if not El Tajín as well, already bears ample witness to the resurgent cult of Quetzalcoatl, at a time when Tollan Xicocotitlan either did not exist or was at best enjoying a very modest initial phase.

Notwithstanding the importance of Xochicalco, on which we shall dwell at greater length, one must not ignore the significance of El Tajín in this transitional period. If certain features of Xochicalco illustrate in clearer perspective new attributes of the god Quetzalcoatl, El Tajín is perhaps more symptomatic of certain traits that distinguish the Classic from the Postclassic era. In this site, the cult of death seems to emerge fully fledged for the first time, together with decapitation rites. There is thus something rather harsh and bellicose about this whole culture, not at all typical of the Classic era and of Teotihuacán.

El Tajín is notable for its long life span and the very wide diffusion of its culture. According to Proskouriakoff, the oldest El Tajín axes correspond chronologically to Teotihuacán II. At its peak, its influence spread far over Mesoamerica, to places as distant one from another as San Luis Potosí, Xochicalco, Palenque, and the coast of Guatemala.[129]

Regarding Xochicalco, César Sáenz has made a notable contribution not only by his useful monograph on Quetzalcoatl but by his discovery of the three Xochicalco stelae. These provide a connecting link between one cultural phase and another such as the archaeologist is rarely privileged to discover. They are so germane to our subject that it is worthwhile listing their salient points.

Stela 1

At the top of the main relief appears the reptile's eye glyph, frequently to be found in Structure B in Tula. The stela prominently displays a representation of Quetzalcoatl with human features, as Tlahuizcalpantecuhtli. This personage displays what Seler thought were rolled feathers in place of ears, but which Sáenz thinks represent the ehecailacalozcatl of Quetzalcoatl, though he is not sure of this. The whole figure of Quetzalcoatl is similar to one found in Structure B in Tula, depicting the god as Tlahuizcalpantecuhtli.[130] Below Quetzalcoatl, in the lower part of the stela, occurs a celestial band formed by glyphs which Sáenz believes to symbolize the planet Venus, similar to those of the Codices *Dresden* and *Pérez* and also to the pectoral of Tláloc in murals in Tetitla, Teotihuacán.[131]

Stela 2

The principal figure is Tláloc, with the sign of the year as head dress, just as in Teotihuacán. The figure of the god is surmounted by another glyph, also to be found in that site, as well as in certain Mixtec codices. A kind of leaf and stalk emerges from Tláloc's mouth, as in the Temple of Agriculture in Teotihuacán, and in Tepantitla. Also, on the reverse side of this stela, the planet Venus is depicted in the same way as in the Pyramid of Tlahuizcalpantecuhtli in Tula.

Stela 3

We again find the planet Venus represented just as in Tula. The principal personage of the reliefs also resembles the Quetzalcoatl Tlahuizcalpantecuhtli of that site. This figure is surmounted by the glyph 4 Ollin, the symbol of the Fifth Sun. Below comes another celestial band, formed of the integral elements of the Maya hieroglyph *Pop.* "Blood drops" are represented in this band, like those on three stones of Structure B of Tula. Thus, in the same celestial band are to be found elements typical of the Mayas, of Teotihuacán, and of Tula.

It is obvious that these three stelae constitute an invaluable connecting link, displaying in almost equal measure typical features of both Teotihuacán and Tula, together with certain Maya traits, as in the Temple of Quetzalcoatl in the same site.

As Sáenz puts it, they show, in general terms, strong Teotihuacán influences, but possess certain traits not present in that city. These include representations of the man-bird-serpent different from those of Teotihuacán and with certain characteristics that recall Tula and Chichén.[132]

Pottery found associated with the stelae provides added confirmation: Orange A, B, and B 3 predominate, together with other sherds, all corresponding to the Late Classic style.[133] Also present were fragments of Fine Orange Type Z, figurines of Teotihuacán type, others from Mezcala, and objects in El Tajín style. This assemblage corresponds to the Late Classic era of Teotihuacán IV or to Xochicalco III, in which Sáenz consequently places the whole find.

Piña Chan also emphasizes the importance of these stelae as providing early representations of Quetzalcoatl as the Morning Star (i.e., the new Quetzalcoatl). Above all, they are to be associated with the god as Tlahuizcalpantecuhtli and not as Ehécatl. Piña Chan aptly stresses that the base of the main temple of Xochicalco, with its huge plumed serpents, may suggest the arrival of new people at this site. He insists, moreover, that the major part of the associated offerings came from the Gulf Coast, principally from the Maya area. This point will be discussed later, in connection with the emigration of different peoples from Teotihuacán.

However, I am not able to concur with Piña Chan's identification of Xochicalco as Tamoanchan; I also have certain doubts concerning Jiménez Moreno's connection of Xochicalco with a human Quetzalcoatl. This hypothesis suggests that the latter was born in Tepoztlán and later conquered Xochicalco, as originally mooted by Lehmann. Such inferences appear to be based upon a report of "*L'Histoyre du Mechique*" to the effect that Ce Acatl-Topiltzin was born in Michatlauhco (a place of that name exists in eastern Morelos) and on a mention in one of the Tepoztlán legends concerning Tepoztecatl, in which the latter is referred to as "Topiltzin."[134] Such evidence constitutes a rather limited base for ascribing to Topiltzin-Quetzalcoatl the various local legends of Tepoztecatl's wars against Xochicalco, notwithstanding any associations of a rather generalized nature linking Quetzalcoatl with the gods of pulque, including of course Tepoztecatl.

Even if such specific identifications prove unacceptable, a measure of agreement exists as to the fundamental importance of Xochicalco as a link between Teotihuacán and Tollan Xicocotitlan and as a center prominently connected with the cult of the new Quetzalcoatl. In this respect, the discovery of the three stelae is of outstanding significance, without discounting the possibility that archaeology in the future might unearth yet further valuable clues as to the god's antecedents.

Because of their intrinsic traits and by virtue of associated finds, the stelae seem to lie midway between Teotihuacán and Tollan Xicocotitlan, at a time when the material development of Xochicalco was at its peak. Litvak states that in this Protopostclassic period the increase in density of settlements was resumed. On the other hand, by the early Postclassic era, i.e., the beginning of Tollan, the number of settled sites in the area had begun to decline (though not yet the total population).[135]

What one finds in Xochicalco—and what will also predominate in Tollan—is the god Quetzalcoatl in his identity as Tlahuizcalpantecuhtli, closely linked with the Morning Star. In such manifestations, there is less evidence of Quetzalcoatl as Ehécatl, god of Wind, complete with the duckbill mask and conical cap. One is really still confronted with two distinct aspects of the same deity; Henry Nicholson maintains that as Ehécatl he belongs to the Tláloc complex, whereas as Morning Star he is to be associated with that of Mixcoatl-Tlahuizcalpantecuhtli.[136]

On the other hand, it is precisely in the former of these two roles that Quetzalcoatl figures so prominently in the Mixtec codices. In these, one finds certain scenes interpreted by Caso as the actual introduction of the cult of Ehécatl-Quetzalcoatl.[137] The author cites the birth of Quetzalcoatl according to the *Codex Vindobonensis*, in the year 10 Calli, which he equates to A.D. 697. In the *Bodley codex* the date for the same event is 8 or 9 Acatl, or, according to Caso, A.D. 695 or 683.[138] Possibly the last word still remains to be said on Mixtec dates, but such interpretations certainly approximate more closely to the time of the Xochicalco stelae than of the rise of Tollan Xicocotitlan. An early Tlahuizcalpantecuhtli is also identified by Caso in Selden I as the god I Ollin.[139]

It would be a mistake to assume that the Morning Star element is totally absent where the Mixtec codices are concerned, as much as to think that in Tula Quetzalcoatl was bereft of all association with the Wind. For instance, in the *Codex Borgia*, fourteen representations of Tlahuizcalpantecuhtli appear, and only eight of Ehécatl, though admittedly the latter would be more closely linked with Quetzalcoatl.[140]

We are thus apparently faced with two parallel and contemporary developments of the new Quetzalcoatl both as Wind and Venus, possibly initiated in different places, but later merging into one dual deity. It would perhaps be more apt to speak of a triple rather than dual nature for the new god; his fundamental significance as creator must be constantly borne in mind; it goes to the very root of Toltec lore and legend. Seler goes so far as to link the creator role with that of wind god; he states that life (and therefore creation) was to be associated with the breath that emerged from the mouth, itself reminiscent of wind.[141] It seems conceivable that the creator role of the god might possibly have been developing in Teotihuacán itself in its latter stages, whereas other aspects of the new composite deity tended to come to maturity elsewhere. This particularly applies to the Ehécatl aspect, so intimately linked with the Huaxteca, where the curved element in architecture is indeed primordial.[142] The Huaxteca, moreover, has proved itself a fertile breeding ground for deities, including Tlazolteotl and Xipe Tótec. The final Quetzalcoatl gives every impression of being at least partly a Huaxtec product. Quite apart from the details of his special adornments, his association with marine shells, with exotic tropical birds, and with cacao suggests emphatically that he originated in the coastal regions rather than on the Altiplano. The ultimate deity, however, probably represents the fusion of a multitude of elements, not by any means all of coastal origin; David Kelley even sees certain aspects of the god, such as his jumping into the fire, transformation into the Morning Star, and drunkenness, as deriving from the opposite extreme of Mesoamerica and being of Yuto-Aztec origin.[143]

How Many Quetzalcoatls?

We are finally led toward a few preliminary points on one of the most crucial questions of our study. Doubts have persisted about whether the first man or hero called Ce Acatl-Topiltzin lived at the inception of Tollan Xicocotitlan, as a few sources suggest, or at its end, as others maintain. Either contention taken in isolation solves but few problems.

In the first place, if indeed a human hero was required to ignite the flame of the rekindled cult, such a person would have logically preceded Xochicalco III and probably also Teotihuacán IV, as has already been demonstrated. He would thus have been dead and buried, or more properly resurrected as Venus, long before Tollan rose to prominence.

One finds it very hard to see how one and the same hero could have founded Tollan and also constituted the human prototype for the reborn deity Quetzalcoatl, for the latter god was already manifest in his new form before such a person could have lived!

The situation would perhaps be explained by Piña Chan's proposition that matters could have proceeded in the reverse order; according to his view, the god would come first, then the myth, and finally the hero.[144] Any notion that a human hero could have initiated or inspired the cult of the new, or reborn, Quetzalcoatl is at variance with the views of López Austin as well as of Piña Chan. López Austin suggests a general, or prototype, format, applicable to this and other instances of the origins of gods.[145]

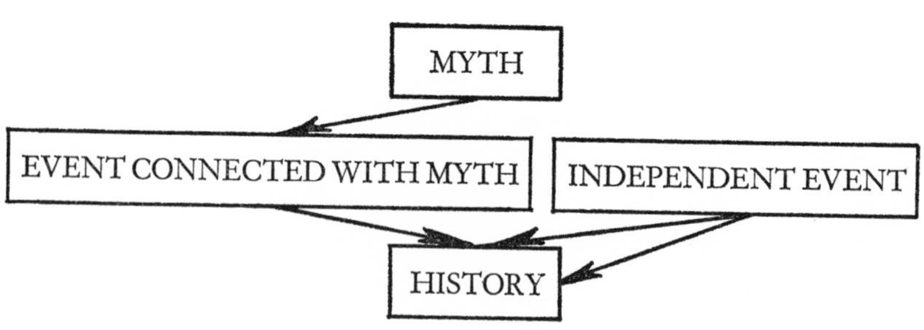

In other words, his interpretation of the most usual beginnings of Mesoamerican myths is that they were conceived independently of any historical fact or personage and that any real happenings related to these were in effect subsequent re-enactments by one or more human beings of the already spontaneously generated myths. This presupposes that the whole saga of Quetzalcoatl came into being in the first place as a figment of men's minds, including his going to Tlillan Tlapallan, being immolated by fire, and becoming the Morning Star, as well as the many other tales that form part and parcel of the rich store of legend that surrounds his name. These events thus never in fact took place as the spontaneous doings of one or more original heroes, but were simply enacted by subsequent priests or rulers who bore the god's name and title. The latter were of course historical personages, but part of their actions were performed according to the dictates of preordained legend. Such deeds, joined to those that they carried out according to the needs of the moment, were then joined together to become history.

López Austin sees the rulers concerned as a kind of vehicle for this superimposed pattern of life; the person in question is no longer a mere man, but the personification of the god. He behaves like the god, and thus makes history.[146]

This point of view, together with that of Kirchhoff as to the possibility of a kind of ritualized Toltec Empire symmetrically planned to contain the same number of dependencies in each direction, will be discussed fully in Chapter 7. For the present, I feel that in the militaristic Postclassic age, the struggle for power was too intense for such considerations to remain paramount, and Toltec policy would perforce have been based rather on a kind of *Realpolitik*. In the case of Tollan, which conquered a fair-sized domain, any officeholder bearing the title of Topiltzin-Quetzalcoatl would have been motivated more by the demands of the external political struggle than by the requirements of ritual conformity, whatever his theoretical obligations in that respect.

The whole question of whether leading deities had an original human counterpart is extremely far-reaching. It may well be argued that many principal gods, as for instance Tláloc, do not appear to have had an original human counterpart. But Tláloc as God of Rain and perhaps originally of Earth as well is a natural deity for settled Mesoamerican agriculturists; one might say that if Tláloc had not existed, one would have had to invent him!

One cannot help feeling that each case has to be taken rather on its merits. The legend of Quetzalcoatl (and to a certain extent that of Huitzilopochtli) is so personal and individual that one is left with an impression that it may have been basically inspired by the deeds of a living person or several persons rather than have come into being by a kind of spontaneous combustion. Of course, there are obviously mythical additions, such as his transformation into the planet Venus.

Any man called after an already existing Quetzalcoatl deity was not a cultural hero at all but simply a priest-ruler dedicated to the service of the god. To take an appropriate parallel, Egyptologists often presuppose that a human Horus really lived before the god came into being; they have never suggested that he could have existed after the god was born. Each successive Egyptian ruler was himself in life the god Horus and in death Osiris. But the pharaohs of Egypt were priest-rulers and in no respect cultural heroes. They were carrying on an old-established tradition, not creating a new mythology.

One could equally well turn the argument upside down and suggest that, on the one hand, the innumerable stories of Topiltzin-Quetzalcoatl and his deeds might have some concrete basis in historical actions; it could then however be suggested that the personages reported to have subsequently re-enacted such events were not real people at all but fictional characters, or alternatively that they merely filled the role as a sort of actor in a drama rather than as the controlling ruler or supreme pontiff. One must not forget Elizabeth Smith's insistence on the role of "deity impersonators" such as 4 Tiger in the Mixtec codices. She demonstrates that the latter is in effect a nonhistorical personage.[147] If such characters were depicted by the Mixtecs, it is quite feasible that they also existed in the records of Tollan, from which the surviving written accounts indirectly derive. It is always possible that the Toltec codices might later have been misread and certain fictitious characters taken for real ones.

To return to our main theme, it may be perfectly correct, as López Austin and Piña Chan suggest, that there simply was no original Topiltzin-Quetzalcoatl. All that one can say is that *if* the rich mythology surrounding the name was indeed attributable even in part to a human being, and *if* indeed an original hero Topiltzin or Quetzalcoatl existed whose life and deeds inspired the new cult which burst with such remarkable force upon Mesoamerica, such a person would have more possibly lived at the end of Teotihuacán III, rather than during Teotihuacán IV; the latter phase is practically contemporary with the Xochicalco stelae depicting the new god. Teotihuacán IV will be discussed in the next chapter, but in general terms the whole duration of Teotihuacán IV, say one century, would hardly have furnished more than the minimum necessary time interval for a living hero to become established as a fully fledged god. Accordingly, the man Quetzalcoatl as divine prototype, if indeed he existed, would have belonged more logically to the end of Teotihuacán III and the beginning of Phase IV, rather than to its end; by this latter date the image of the god was already being engraved upon stone in Xochicalco.

It will also be seen in Chapter 3 how, according to Sahagún, the *tlamatinime* (wise men) who departed eastward at the time of Teotihuacán's fall were ostensibly following in the wake of a god or hero who had already departed. His cult, it would thus seem, more probably grew to maturity in the coastal region of Tabasco rather than in Teotihuacán itself; from there it subsequently burst forth and emerged in such centers as Xochicalco and, later, Tollan Xicocotitlan. At some stage, as will later be explained, the Venus aspect, closely associated with Maya culture, became blended with certain Huaxtec traits that identified Quetzalcoatl as God of Wind.

After this cult had spread, priest-rulers, as opposed to gods or heroes, who bore the title of Topiltzin or Quetzalcoatl, seem to have lived from time to time, both in Central Mesoamerica and also in Yucatán, Highland Guatemala, and possibly the Mixteca. Such beings were the human representatives of a now flourishing deity.

Seen in this context, the arguments as to whether the real Ce Acatl-Topiltzin founded Tollan or led it to destruction become somewhat irrelevant. For the early Tollan, this work will put forward certain evidence of the possible pre-eminence of a Topiltzin or Quetzalcoatl; on the other hand, the Ce Acalt-Topiltzin who presided over the downfall of that city will be placed in historical and chronological perspective at the end of this work. These doings, however, were those of mortal men and not cultural heroes or gods, however much ancient legends may impose themselves upon the historical record, forcing them to comply with a preordained destiny. Like the *tlatoani* of Tenochtitlan, they were political and military leaders, even if they wore the mantle of the god.

We shall discover that the sources themselves often imply the existence of at least two persons who at different times bore the name or title of Topiltzin-Quetzalcoatl; notably such suggestions are to be found in Ixtlilxóchitl and the *Origen de los Mexicanos*. On closer examination it can also be seen that the Ce Acatl of the *Historia de los Mexicanos*, who reportedly founded Tollan, cannot possibly be the same person as he who later led away all the *macehuales* to destinations connected with the Toltec diaspora! Similarly, the Kukulcan who arrived in Chichén in Katún 4 Ahua can scarcely be identified with the personage of that name who, according to Landa, founded Mayapan.

One remains thus with the preliminary conclusion that any theory involving one single Topiltzin-Quetzalcoatl provides no viable working hypothesis. I prefer to believe that there was never one Quetzalcoatl, any more than there was ever a single Tollan. Like the name "Tollan," "Quetzalcoatl" in it various forms grew to be a concept of universal import. As a distinctive appellation or title it was then applied to men living in different places at diverse epochs.

3. The Last Days of Teotihuacán

WHATEVER may have been the significance of Xochicalco in the development of the new Quetzalcoatl, it is Teotihuacán that remains the true precursor of Tollan Xicocotitlan as the leading center of Central Mesoamerica, however notably the two societies may have differed. We would therefore only be building castles in the air if we sought to study the rise of Tollan without first giving due consideration to the fall of its mighty predecessor that for so long bestrode as a colossus the Classic world. It was indeed that city whose mantle Tollan was one day to assume.

The Crucial Questions

It is moreover in this general region of Teotihuacán that Sahagún situates the creation of the Fifth Sun, as part of those events which formed a kind of prelude to the Postclassic era. Later in this chapter, these happenings will be analyzed and situated in a context of time and space. Destiny had clearly dictated that only in the hallowed city of Teotihuacán, out of the dying embers of the Classic cosmos, should be kindled the flame that was to light the succeeding age.

Accordingly, one must now turn from problems relating to Xochicalco to the final phases of Teotihuacán. Though the two situations are almost contemporary, Teotihuacán IV may by definition be considered as Late Classic, whereas the prime period of Xochicalco and El Tajín at least borders on the Postclassic. For this time of transition, the term "Epiclassic" has been coined by Jiménez Moreno, though it is also more prosaically known as the "Protopostclassic."

This work cannot be concerned with every facet of latter-day Teotihuacán, let alone indulge in speculation about the causes of its decline. Questions of chronology are, however, important; in order to formulate ideas on the rise of Postclassic Tollan, it is first necessary to review the dating of what went before.

As a prelude to the story of Tollan, it seems appropriate to pose the following questions concerning Teotihuacán:

1. What dates are to be assigned to its later, or decadent, phases?
2. What happened to its inhabitants, who may still have exceeded one hundred thousand in the Teotihuacán IV phase, but were reduced to a few thousand at its end? Who were they and where did they go?
3. Do written sources or archaeology offer evidence as to the existence in latter-day Teotihuacán of any leader or hero who might have inspired the resurgent cult of a Quetzalcoatl deity?

In addition to such points, a few observations on the controversial question of a possible Teotihuacán empire may be useful; notions in this respect might offer some assistance when seeking to assess the performance of Tollan Xicocotitlan several centuries later. In addition, the economic structure of Teotihuacán may have a bearing on the ecological and environmental problems of its successor.

And lastly, Teotihuacán may even be said to form part of our theme in its own right, since in a limited and different sense, its inhabitants *were* Toltecs, as has already been seen. Not only did they possess in abundance those qualities which the Aztecs came to regard as specifically Toltec; they were also connected with certain events inseparable from "Toltec" legend.

Dates and Developments

The chronology of Teotihuacán is essentially an archaeological problem, on which no valid guidance can be sought from any written sources. The first part of this chapter must therefore be based on material evidence, including pottery sequences. The question is of undoubted importance to any study of the Toltecs, since one must perforce decide when Teotihuacán fell before forming any definite conclusions as to when Tollan rose. It is the last phase of Teotihuacán that really forms the point of departure for what follows.

Until recent years, the investigator had little to guide him on the final dates of Teotihuacán, save for some intelligent speculation as to the early chronology of Tollan Xicocotitlan, from which he could then work backwards. Such estimates have since been shown by more scientific methods to be far from inaccurate.

It is important to appreciate that the chronological scheme for Teotihuacán now currently accepted draws its conclusions from established *Maya* dating patterns, somewhat discarding certain radiocarbon data obtained in the site itself. Such deductions are based on the indissoluble links now established by the location of Teotihuacán objects in certain strata at Tikal and other Maya sites, thus firmly binding together the chronology of Early Xolalpan (Teotihuacán III) and Late Tzakol Maya. In Late Xolalpan (Teotihuacán III A) this close relationship with the Maya area already appears to have been on the wane.

The Goodman-Martínez-Thompson Long Count correlation places Late Tzakol as falling between A.D. 450 and 550. Such calculations are based on inscriptions and have nothing to do with radiocarbon. Taking Late Tzakol as a point of departure, early Xolalpan must *ipso facto* also fall approximately between A.D. 450 and 550, providing one accepts the Goodman-Martínez-Thompson Long Count correlation as correct in placing Late Tzakol between these two dates.

This general hypothesis gives the following chronological scheme for the final part of Teotihuacán's existence:

Early Xolalpan	(the latter phase of Teotihuacán III)	A.D. 450– 550
Late Xolalpan	(Teotihuacán III A)	A.D. 555– 650
Metepec	(Teotihuacán IV)	A.D. 650– 750
Oztotícpac	(Proto-Coyotlatelco)	A.D. 750– 800
Xometla	(Coyotlatelco, etc.)	A.D. 800–1150

The dates for the later phases are based on Florencia Muller's calculations, taken from her report on Teotihuacán pottery.[1] René Millon's figures are substantially the same, apart from an extra fifty years allowed for Oztotícpac, which he sees as ending in about A.D. 850.[2]

The whole problem might thus appear to be happily resolved, once and for all, were it not for one snag; while this tabulation is in perfect accord with the Goodman-Martínez-Thompson Maya correlation (and by and large with *Maya* radiocarbon dates), at first sight it is quite at variance with radiocarbon dating available from Teotihuacán itself.

Ignacio Bernal calls attention to fifteen samples from carbon produced by burnt ceilings and doors during Teotihuacán III and III A, giving figures from A.D. 50 to 370.[3] For the Quetzalpapálotl Palace, seven such dates range from A.D. 50 to 290. Leaving aside the earliest of these, all the remainder fall within a period from A.D. 160 to 290. Other dates from the Street of the Dead are as late as A.D. 370, but were taken from a building obviously reused *after* the great conflagration.

As Bernal points out, on the basis of such figures the dates for Teotihuacán III should fall between A.D. 160 and 290, or in round numbers A.D. 150 to 300; these would pertain to the construction of the monuments, not to their destruction. As he also stresses, temples built on platforms cannot normally be considered as very durable and may last in total between half a century and one century.

The gap is thus fairly wide between Teotihuacán's own radiocarbon data and the Maya-based chronology for the site, placing Early Xolalpan between A.D. 450 and 550. Millon insists that these radiocarbon figures are misleading, since the beams in question had been used more than once. It has indeed been observed that in certain instances this did occur, but of course Millon's contention presupposes that virtually all the beams tested had been reused, since the radiocarbon dates are moderately consistent. While making this point, Millon does not exclude the possibility that the sum of Teotihuacán II, III, and IV may in total years occupy less time than is now considered likely; but this does not modify his contention that Teotihuacán III cannot be dissociated from the generally accepted dates for late Tzakol.

In broad terms, the Mayan radiocarbon results tend to back the Goodman-Martínez-Thompson correlation, on which the above contention is based. They are less in accord with the Spinden calculation, even if this is more in line with the radiocarbon figures from Teotihuacán. Of a long list taken from Tikal, no less than twenty-three out of a total of sixty-three radiocarbon dates fall between A.D. 702 and 812.[4] These refer to the subsequent Tepeuh phase, not Tzakol, but fall far outside the end of the Classic Maya period, as given by Spinden's calculations.

Notwithstanding this general support for the Goodman-Martínez-Thompson correlation, E. Wyllys Andrews, basing his conclusions on data from Dzibilxaltun, continues to support the Spinden correlation, producing dates 260 years earlier. He backs his chronological contentions by insisting that Puuc and related styles do not in that site appear to be contemporary with the Late Classic Maya, as they must indeed be in great measure if the latter really survived till circa A.D. 850.

Andrews stresses that in Dzibilxaltun it can be demonstrated that Puuc in general terms postdates Tepeuh (this is one of the few places where the full sequence is present). He cites evidence to the effect that in this site the pure Classic period ended in about 10.0.0.0. (A.D. 570 or 830, according to the different correlations). He further notes that this phase is followed by a gradual transition to the new Puuc style; by the end of the period of change, the previous abundance of late Tepeuh trade pottery imported from the Petén is no longer in evidence.[5] Kubler, incidentally, upholds the same viewpoint as Andrews on purely stylistic grounds, which leads him to favor an earlier termination of the Classic Maya era. However, the concensus of opinion among archaeologists does tend to be that Puuc is more nearly contemporary with the Classic Tepeuh.

It lies outside the scope of this work to delve deeper into this particular question, except insofar as it affects Teotihuacán. Where the latter is concerned, it is likely that improved radiocarbon techniques may clarify the situation. In the meantime, it can only be emphasized that one cannot have it both ways. If the "orthodox" dating is right, then the present radiocarbon figures are misleading without further interpretation; either the great majority of the beams in question have been reused or some other explanation must be found.

The gap between A.D. 300 (as per radiocarbon) for the end of Xalalpan and 550 (as per Maya Long Count) is too long to be explained by any time lag necessary for diffusion from one place to another or by any possible interval between the inception and the destruction of the buildings from which the samples were taken. Perhaps these factors together might account for one century, but not for two or more.

Were it not for the respective insistence of such authorities as Millon and Thompson on the error of the radiocarbon figures and the correctness of the Long Count correlation, one might express a tentative hope that one day a compromise solution should emerge that would modify both the Teotihuacán radiocarbon dates and those calculated for Maya Tzakol and help to bridge the gap between the two.

It can be said very tentatively that supporting radiocarbon evidence from the Maya area is not totally lacking. William Coe, while emphasizing in general terms that Tikal dates support the Goodman-Martínez-Thompson correlation, does say that five samples from structure 5 D–52 in that site gave results of 625±30; this is almost a century earlier than had been predicated, using 9.15.0.0.0. as the dedicatory date supposed to be carved upon the lintel.[6]

Linton Satterthwaite also in general supports the orthodox correlation; however, he cites a figure of A.D. 621±36 for an average of seven dates taken from five beams in Temple IV at Tikal; the beams would have been difficult to reuse. The resulting readings are also about one hundred years earlier than Morley's interpretation of the accompanying Maya date glyphs, but admittedly these are not very clear and therefore open to doubt.[7]

However, notwithstanding any such lesser points of difference, the Goodman-Martínez-Thompson correlation rests upon sufficiently sure and solid foundations that it may be wiser to seek other explanations for any possible discrepancies in the Teotihuacán dates cited above.

Accordingly, it may be of use to mention certain doubts expressed in recent years regarding the general accuracy of radiocarbon dating and the attempts at calibration in order to attain a greater precision. While the margin of error naturally diminishes for later dates, Colin Renfew points out that the conventional radiocarbon figures for the Neolithic and Early Bronze ages in Europe are literally "wildly wrong."[8] Modifications now introduced in the method of calculation have virtually revolutionized our ideas of European prehistory.

There even exist certain divergences of opinion as to the correct C–14 half-life for the purpose of reckoning age; some continue to base their findings on the conventional half-life 5,568 years, while others prefer the allegedly improved but not definitive figure of 5,730. Apart from this, errors may stem from the following principal causes:

1. Lack of any standard laboratory procedure; for instance, some but not others pretreat with sodium hydroxide to remove humic acids, whose infiltration would tend to make the radiocarbon dates too young.

2. Apparent fluctuations occurring in atmospheric radiocarbon and deriving from causes not yet clearly established. Possibly they are produced by variations in the isotopic equilibrium of the earth's carbon-exchange reservoir (the seas, polar ice, and so on). Similarly, the atmospheric radiocarbon concentration could be affected by variations in the cosmic-ray flux.[9]

3. Difficulties in determining the age of wood converted into charcoal and in distinguishing between young and old samples of wood. This factor can to some extent be quantified, and Waterbolk demonstrates that the age of a tree is three times as great as the difference between that of the youngest wood and that of an average sample.[10]

Taking into account such divergences, it has been possible to establish calibration charts for the purpose of correcting the original, or "orthodox," radiocarbon dates. This has been done by comparing a whole series of readings with sets of figures firmly established by two other means: first, those calculated with far greater accuracy using dendrochronologically dated specimens of Sequoia and Bristlecone Pine in Pennsylvania and Arizona respectively; and second, by comparing orthodox radiocarbon dates with established Egyptian historic dates (at first it was thought that these Egyptian figures were incorrect, but it is now accepted that the error lay in the original radiocarbon method).

Such modifications to radiocarbon readings can be expressed in the form of a chart showing on the one hand the "true" dates, obtained by the above-mentioned methods, and on the other the orthodox, or original, radiocarbon figures.

As far as our study is concerned, it must again be stressed that whereas discrepancies around 5,000 B.P. are of course greater, those for dates in the Teotihuacán range are nevertheless appreciable. Moreover, the whole question is complicated by a peculiar fact; until as far back as about 300 B.C., the corrected dates are *younger* than the standard, or orthodox, figures. However, when one goes back beyond 300 B.C.—i.e., to dates earlier than presently concern us—then the corrected figures produce *older* dates than the standard procedure: at 7000 B.C. the gap already is a wide one and the original radiocarbon dates are now thought to be about seven hundred years too young.

Established dendrochronological dates are on an average seventy-six years younger than the mean of an orthodox radiocarbon reading of A.D. 400. Hultin's chart for the determination of true age from radiocarbon calculations gives a maximum deviation of as much as 150 years between a mean radiocarbon figure of A.D. 500 and wood from Groeningen, Sweden, dated by dendrochronology. In this case, also, the tree-ring dates are younger, though it is fair to add that dendrochronological specimens from Pennsylvania and Arizona diverged far less than those of Groeningen from the radiocarbon figure.[11]

The other matter strictly relevant to Teotihuacán is Waterbolk's point concerning the age of wood used for samples. In his correction table for dates from L'Anse aux Meadows, a Viking settlement in Newfoundland, he states that the mean age of the charcoal from which samples were taken would suggest a maximum age for the wood of 500 years.[12] He also draws attention to the fact that in Beidha and other preceramic settlements in the Near East, the variation between radiocarbon figures is very great; some of the wood must have been long in circulation.[13]

The above points are pertinent to Teotihuacán and to Mesoamerican dating in general. From figures quoted, it may be observed that in the time range of A.D. 1 to 1000 orthodox radiocarbon dates may in general terms be the best part of one hundred years older than the corrected figures, independently of the regular plus or minus factor that is always quoted. The age of the wood is only one of several causes of error to be taken into account. Notwithstanding the general usefulness of radiocarbon dating, it is clearly not possible, in the present state of knowledge, to use this method to prove or disprove written dating systems, whether those of the Maya Long Count or of the Central Mesoamerican written sources.

As far as the end of Teotihuacán is concerned, it is clear that the round figures of A.D. 150 to 300 given by radiocarbon for the duration of Xolalpan are thus open to adjustment and that anything up to one hundred years may be added by way of correction, in accordance with the factors mentioned above. If to this modification one then adds the average age of the buildings, say fifty years, and that of the wood used—a less-known factor—then from A.D. 300 for the end of Xolalpan one gets at least within striking distance of A.D. 550, the orthodox date, which fits with the dates of Tikal obtained from the Maya Long Count.

In order to account for any remaining discrepancy, an additional factor may be taken into account: the possibility of a certain time lag in diffusion from Teotihuacán to the Maya area. It will later be seen that pottery that recalls Teotihuacán IV, or Metepec, appears in Tollan Xicocotitlan at a date which is surely posterior to the ending of that phase in Teotihuacán itself. By the same token, it seems not impossible that Xolalpan did end say fifty to a hundred years before A.D. 550, even if its influences are still visible in Tikal until that date. If this supposition were correct, then logically the ending of Metepec and Oztotícpac would also be somewhat advanced.

Regarding Metepec itself, certain divergences of opinion also exist. In this respect, what one might again call the orthodox view suggests that the great ceremonial center of Teotihuacán was destroyed and at least partially abandoned at the end of Teotihuacán III A (Late Xolalpan). A catastrophe of such magnitude apparently did not profoundly alter the pattern of existence of the large population in the residential parts of the city; in spite of added insecurity, life went on much as before in the palaces and mansions that adorned these districts. Perhaps the scale of living was reduced and, as Bernal says, the creative spirit somewhat dimmed.

Millon, however, strongly questions whether it is realistic to believe that such a relatively serene and untroubled state of affairs could have persisted with the great ceremonial center merely a heap of ruins. He calls attention to the finding of Metepec pottery in the Street of the Dead, as well as in the outer suburbs; he also points to evidence of building construction in both areas during this phase, which he sees as one of considerable activity and some prosperity throughout all Teotihuacán and not merely on the periphery. Millon further stresses that the part of the city which suffered from the conflagration amounted to only two square kilometers, or less than one-tenth of the total urban area; in the remainder of the city, traces of fire have been found in only fifty instances. He mentions the interesting possibility that the priests themselves may have kindled the flames that consumed some of the principal buildings, so thorough was the destruction that it almost seems to be deliberate.[14]

One might observe that ancient peoples probably reacted differently from ourselves in the face of catastrophe; the urge to rebuild monuments ravaged by hostile hands may have been less compelling than in our own times. There is, for instance, ample evidence from close at hand that life in Knossos went on in much the same way even after the "final" destruction of the great palace.

Either point of view acknowledges the occurrence of some major upheaval as early as the end of Teotihuacán III A; this in some measure affected the lives of the inhabitants, even if the actual degree of subsequent recovery and reconstruction after the initial ravaging of the ceremonial center remains open to doubt.

Based on his excavations of apartment "compounds," Millon now estimates the population of Teotihuacán during the Xolalpan phase at a minimum of 75,000, with a more probable total of 125,000; it could even have been as high as 200,000.[15] During Metepec (Teotihuacán IV), after the initial disasters it probably fell somewhat, but the dramatic reduction came only at its end, when the population appears literally to have melted away. By Oztotícpac, Teotihuacán was reduced to a few scattered villages with 5,000 inhabitants or perhaps even less.

While it lies outside the scope of this work to speculate on the social organization of Teotihuacán or on its government, it may in general terms be said that evidence is ample of a complex organization, including a marked degree of military preparedness in the later phases.

Millon makes it clear that the city was not lacking in fixed defenses, as was previously thought. Nevertheless, concrete evidence of any Teotihuacán "empire" is still somewhat elusive, even if one concedes a reasonable probability of some control being exercised over contiguous areas that probably shared the same language and traditions.

A tendency may prevail to underestimate the ability of the city to supply at least part of its needs from local resources. (The same applies to Tula, but less surely to the island city of Tenochtitlan.) Millon, who himself somewhat discounts the importance of local agricultural production to the economy, nonetheless thinks that the highly concentrated chinampa system of food production may have been initiated in Teotihuacán.[16] Thomas Charlton suggests that the lower Teotihuacán Valley alone, using preconquest irrigation systems and aboriginal crops and techniques, had a potential output of basic grains sufficient for twenty-five to thirty thousand people. Adding the Upper Valley, the figure approaches forty thousand.[17] Sanders puts the food-producing capacity of the Valley even higher.[18] Surely a vast "empire" was not required to feed Teotihuacán; the Valley of Mexico, with the possible addition of the Puebla-Tlaxcala Valley, would have more than sufficed, even if allowance is made for the presence of a considerable rural population in those areas.

Commentators nurtured on Old World traditions are apt to conjure up visions of far-flung empires whenever they see an assembly of pyramids or an imposing group of monuments. In point of fact, it is not difficult to exaggerate the degree of organization and the population required to build such constructions. Cook suggests that the Pyramid of the Sun would have required three thousand laborers to build.[19]

Others are equally inclined to discover signs of political and military domination wherever they detect marked similarities of style between two areas. Such resemblances may reveal commercial and even cultural influences more than conquest. As Kaplan points out, inferences drawn from the archaeological record are uncertain by their very nature, and the leap from artistic styles to assertions about sociopolitical systems is a long and hazardous one.[20]

An exception may possibly be made in the case of Kaminaljuyu, where the people not merely copied styles and techniques but imitated a way of life to an extent suggestive of actual domination by some group of colonists from Teotihuacán, if only for a limited period—an association possibly not dissimilar from that which developed between Postclassic Tula and Chichén Itza, as will later be seen.

Obviously, it cannot be ascertained whether such possible migrants would have spoken Nahuatl. Notwithstanding this, they might perhaps be termed proto-Pipils, as precursors of the successive waves of Nahua speakers who followed later in their wake. The tendency for peoples from Central Mesoamerica to move in a southeasterly direction was both deep-rooted and ancient.

Compared with the more turbulent Postclassic period, Teotihuacán presents itself as the end product of peoples devoted more to the arts of peace than of war. Commerce may indeed be more fundamental than military force in the course of earlier Mesoamerican history; it would appear likely that, at least until the declining phases of Teotihuacán, relations between the different peoples were not primarily those of conquerors and conquered, but were rather based upon trade, often over very long distances. In such a complex, Teotihuacán undoubtedly played a supreme role over a long period, and Millon is at pains to emphasize its importance as a market as well as a ceremonial center.

The adage that each era of Mesoamerican history largely repeated the previous pattern becomes on closer examination less easy for us to accept, even though it commands wide support. On the contrary, as will be seen, the transformation from Classic Teotihuacán to Postclassic Tula may have been gradual, but none the less radical. Changes did occur, even if many forms and customs survived.

Nor for that matter did the Aztecs meekly copy what the Toltecs had already achieved; if in nothing else, by the very range and magnitude of their conquests they too seem to have been innovators.

The New Elements

Teotihuacán as a great center of trade and worship finally expired at the end of Metepec. Until then both population and palaces had continued *in situ*, having outlived the holocaust that marked the termination of Teotihuacán III A.

In the phase succeeding Metepec, Oztotícpac, the inhabitants were reduced to a few thousand living in scattered settlements clustered among the ruins, rather as did the shrunken population of Rome at the end of the first millennium. The remaining people had evidently departed or succumbed, and it will be possible to deduce from the testimony of Sahagún something of where they went and what befell them.

Judging purely by archaeological and linguistic evidence, it seems very possible that the first truly Pipil incursions into Central America resulted from the successive misfortunes of Teotihuacán, involving as they did limited destruction and, later, unlimited desertion. These migrations involved the southward movement of peoples, later found to be speaking a somewhat archaic form of Nahuatl, who finally settled in places as far distant as Panama.

Thompson, who originally regarded the Pipil influx into Guatemala as a Postclassic phenomenon, later saw the first waves as occurring in the Late Classic era. The arrival of the Pipils tends to be associated with the spread of the Cotzumalhuapa style of stone sculpture, as well as with San Juan Plumbate pottery.[21] Such a movement may well have taken an easterly as well as southeasterly direction; S. W. Miles sees Pipil groups as having established a hold over some of the coastal cacao lands as early as A.D. 600 to 650, i.e., the end of Teotihuacán III, according to the more generally accepted chronology.[22]

The Oztotícpac phase that in effect separates the fall of Teotihuacán from the rise of the new Tollan constitutes something of a cultural void in the Valley of Mexico and nearby territories, notwithstanding the efflorescence of other centers in El Tajín, Xochicalco, and, farther to the south, Monte Albán. Such apparently blank interludes tend to puzzle the investigators, who have tended to seek to narrow the gap.

However, if nature abhors a vacuum, history does not necessarily do so; Julian Steward, in seeking common ground between Old and New World civilizations, offers a comparative table of developmental stages through which both passed, after the more primitive initial phases. He lists them as follows:[23]

Formative
Regional Florescence
Initial Conquests

Dark Ages
Cyclical Conquests
Iron Age (or Spanish Conquest)

With respect to Mexico and Peru, he omits the third and fourth phases and implies that they passed directly from Regional Florescence (i.e., Mesoamerican Classic period) to the stage of Cyclical Conquests; on the other hand, he attributes to Egypt, China, and Mesopotamia those intermediate phases corresponding to Initial Conquests and Dark Ages.

One may perhaps leave aside the rather open question of whether an Initial Conquest phase is also applicable to Teotihuacán (as indeed it probably would be to Tihuanaco in the northern Andes); however, following the fall of Teotihuacán and of Classic Cholula, Central Mesoamerica seems to have passed through a brief Dark Age during Oztotícpac. While Teotihuacán faltered and Tollan Xicocotitlan had not yet risen to power, Xochicalco and El Tajín prospered, but rather on the periphery, just as the Byzantine and Arab civilizations shone splendidly outside the confines of Europe during the Dark Ages of the latter.

This interim period in the central region is artistically uninteresting but historically important; in effect, out of the resulting darkness was born a new world, metaphorically described as that of the Fifth Sun. During this time, the scanty settlers of Oztotícpac and other contemporary sites were the bearers or creators of the earliest pottery that savors of the Postclassic style, often referred to as Proto-Coyotlatelco.

To put Oztotícpac into its historic perspective, I fully agree with Piña Chan, who associates the period with the creation of the Fifth Sun, the significance of which will be discussed later. Jiménez Moreno, writing almost prophetically, anticipated the later and more precise archaeological identification of the Metepec and Oztotícpac phases, with their ensuing fall in population. He suggested that while some of the original Teotihuacán inhabitants stuck to their shattered homes, when faced ostensibly with invasion by Otomís or other disruptive elements, many dispersed, like the Jews after the fall of Jerusalem.[24]

The true identity of any such interlopers remains obscure, but it should first be mentioned that this Proto-Coyotlatelco pottery characteristic of their presence indicates a kind of resurgence of previous and more primitive forms used by the peoples who lived in the area before the Teotihuacán era. James Bennyhoff compares the early Coyotlatelco to the pottery of Tizayuca, predating Teotihuacán I, and states that the two share distinctive patterns.[25] Carmen Cook also sees possible antecedents to Coyotlatelco in Ticoman.[26] Cholulteca I, successor of the Teotihuacán-style pottery in Cholula, also displays traits that survive from Teotihuacán.[27]

Opinions, however, are divided concerning the basic derivation of this early Coyotlatelco and, consequently, the identity of its makers. The question remains so open that even the joint authors of a paper on "Classic to Postclassic," Muller and Drummond, plainly state that they are unable to reach agreement between themselves on this point. Drummond sees Oztotícpac pottery as a development from Teotihuacán, resulting from a resurgence of nonurban practices, after the elimination of the city as a politico-religious entity. Muller, on the other hand, regards it as an import from the north by way of recently excavated sites in Guanajuato that yield red-on-buff pottery in pre-Plumbate levels; he sees it therefore as contemporary with Classic Teotihuacán.[28]

The first point of view certainly enjoys considerable support. Bennyhoff, for instance, insists that Oztotícpac figurines are a direct derivation from Metepec.[29] Armillas, writing earlier, saw antecedents of Coyotlatelco in the later Teotihuacán phases.[30] Moreover, it is fairly generally conceded by investigators, with the exception perhaps of Paul Tolstoy, that Coyotlatelco constitutes a separate development from Mazapan, the typical pottery of Tollan, which undoubtedly started later and which does appear with more certainty to be a style with roots in the northwest.

Nevertheless, the balance of opinion tends to favor the view that Coyotlatelco was first brought into Teotihuacán by other peoples rather than being of local origin. Beatriz Braniff, basing her opinions on excavations in Guanajuato and neighboring territories, sees the people of that region as the bearers of the original pottery of that name, related to the earlier red-on-buff found in that area.[31] She also quotes Charles Kelly, who in Zacatecas and Durango found red-on-buff dating from Classic times, which embodied designs such as the *xicalcoliuhqui* and *xonecuilli*, falling very much within the Coyotlatelco tradition.

Jorge Acosta also argues the matter in some detail. He gives ample illustrations of Metepec and Oztotícpac designs and shows that they are really quite different one from another, though sometimes found in association. This Proto, or "Early," Coyotlatelco, as he prefers to call it, is far more closely related to the fully developed version of Coyotlatelco than it is to Metepec.[32]

Nicholson agrees that Proto-Coyotlatelco is not stylistically a direct derivation from the last Teotihuacán phase; he shares the view that the makers of Coyotlatelco were intruders from outside, but he insists on the other hand that at least *some* influence from Teotihuacán is apparent.[33] In Portezuelo, with a site assemblage not unlike Oztotícpac, Hicks and Nicholson perceive a *gradual* development displaying a degree of continuity from Classic to Postclassic.[34]

It may indeed be true that certain Coyotlatelco roots are to be identified in Teotihuacán; however, as Piña Chan suggests, far from being a kind of spontaneous local development, its inception must surely be attributed to the arrival of new groups from outside, bringing different traditions.[35] It seems highly probable that such a view is correct; it is difficult to see why Teotihuacán should have collapsed and its inhabitants dispersed of their own volition without so much as a skirmish with hostile raiders or the rattle of an *atlatl* discharged in anger.

Such intruders, perhaps in contrast to those who destroyed the ceremonial center at the beginning of Metepec, were not mere raiders but settlers, though seemingly few in number and bearing rather a limited culture. Of course the two disasters, probably a century apart, may have been caused by the same peoples, who acted differently on each occasion—rather as the Goths who first invaded and only much later settled in Italy as the sway of Rome ended. Jiménez Moreno, as already mentioned, thinks the intruders were probably of Otomí stock; Chadwick on the other hand suggests that the originators of Coyotlatelco were Olmeca-Xicallancas. Both may be at least partly correct.

As will shortly be seen, when we come to examine the written sources, the Olmeca-Xicallancas would seem in part to represent the remains of the people who were indigenous to the area, who had perhaps existed there for a very long time, even before the efflorescence of Teotihuacán, and who lingered on after the great dispersal. In the Oztotícpac phase these were quite possibly joined by Otomís or others, as Jiménez Moreno suggests. A blending of their joint traditions, thus combining both local and external elements, might have ignited a rather faint cultural spark and engendered the Early, or Proto-Coyotlatelco.

The period, clearly demonstrated by archaeology as a time of deep troubles accompanied by steep cultural and demographic decline, nonetheless heralds the inauguration of a new era: or in Mesoamerican terms, the birth of the Fifth Sun.

The Sources' Story

In Ixtlilxóchitl and Torquemada, passing references occur to "giants" and to Olmeca-Xicallancas who lived in the Teotihuacán period or just after. However, only in Sahagún's account do we find longer passages which seem to relate to the time of turbulence that followed Teotihuacán. It is therefore important to analyze very closely this one source of information on the matter and to relate its account where possible to the relevant archaeological data.

The passage occurs in the famous Chapter 29 of Sahagún's Book X, which describes the various peoples of Mesoamerica and their origins; the particular text in question forms part of what he writes of the story of the "Mexica or Mexiti." He does make it clear that the first portion of this account concerns the *ancestors* of the Mexicas, and only toward the end is told the traditional tale of the Mexicas themselves. Those Mexica forebears are described as "the grandfathers, the grandmothers, those called the ones who arrived [first], the ones who came sweeping the way, those who came with their hair bound, those who came to rule this land . . . came over the water in boats."[36]

The narrative then tells how they drew along the coast and landed at Panotla, meaning "where they crossed the water." Sahagún explains in another context that this is the same place as Pánuco (see page 21 for comments on this name); they then proceeded along the coast to Quautemallan.

Kirchhoff suggested that the place referred to is not the Guatemala that we know but a homonym. However, it is fair to say that certain sources, for instance Torquemada, Durán, and Tezozómoc, all refer to Quauhtemallan, Coatemallan, and so on in contexts which make it quite clear that they do indeed mean the modern Guatemala. Moreover, it may conveniently be recalled that the people of Teotihuacán did enjoy intimate cultural relations with Kaminaljuyu in the very heart of that territory. As has already been stressed, the Pipil movements toward Central America have quite early origins.

Presumably, however, the travelers to Quauhtemallan were a kind of splinter group, since the account continues by relating how a body of people, presumably the main group, next arrived at Tamoanchan, meaning, according to Sahagún, "we seek our home."

Certain salient points must be established concerning the text, our only extant account of such happenings, save for passing references in other sources. First, the story plainly refers at least in part to the closing phases of Teotihuacán; in this interpretation Jiménez Moreno, Piña Chan, and others are in full accord.

Secondly, it is clearly concerned with a period of abrupt change, involving continual comings and goings, both to and from Teotihuacán and other places.

Thirdly, continual reference is made to the abandonment of the area by different groups; those who lead the way are the wise men, the *tlamatinime*. Deprived of their esoteric lore, such a complex and refined civilization could scarcely hope to function and would be condemned to ultimate dissolution.

Sahagún's account of events is fairly long, covering five pages of the Anderson and Dibble translation. This text can only be correctly understood if interpreted as repetitions in different form of approximately the same series of events; the reader is on several different occasions brought back to Tamoanchan, the point of departure, and the tale obviously begins again.

This is not surprising; we are specifically told that existing documents were carried away by the wise men, or *tlamatinime*, to the east. Sullivan takes this to imply that they were really destroyed, and affirms that such was the established custom long before Itzcoatl's famous expurgation of the records, actually mentioned in this very section of the

Florentine codex. Such a supposition may appear reasonable when one recalls, for instance, the evidence of ritual destruction of inscribed Maya stelae, another form of written record. The version of events unfolded by Sahagún's informants could have thus only reached them by word of mouth, as a kind of spoken saga; it would presumably have formed part of the whole epic of the creation of the Fifth Sun. As often occurs in such recitals—and as can well be seen from the *Cantares* of the final pre-Hispanic period—every succeeding refrain tends to begin in the same way (in this case with people departing from Tamoanchan), and recounts in different words part of the subject matter of earlier refrains, but probably each time adding one or two new happenings to what has already been told.

The text in question, if read in any other manner, becomes confused and misleading. To take it as a *continuous* story, it would have to be supposed that the same or similar groups of people were constantly, on repeated occasions, starting out from Tamoanchan, and after a rather illogically planned peregrination, returning, only to set forth again from precisely the same point and then follow a somewhat similar route, once more ending up where they started.

Indeed, the story is told no less than four times of people departing from Tamoanchan; on each occasion it can be shown that part of the previous version of events is repeated.[37] Such a text can thus only be comprehended as constituting basically the same story, told in different ways. As to Tamoanchan itself, its possible location will be discussed later in this chapter. At this stage it may be suggested that in this context, but not necessarily in all others, the term appears to embrace not just one locality but the whole core region of the Teotihuacán-Cholula civilization.

Let us now examine the account incident by incident. The first departure from Tamoanchan one might properly regard as a kind of prelude to the epic, since it involves a parallel but distinct happening not repeated in the refrains that follow. However, this passage (from the middle of page 190 in the Anderson and Dibble translation to the last paragraph of page 191) does in itself constitute on initial refrain, since, like the three others, it first involves a departure from Tamoanchan.

As has previously been recounted, a group, stated to have come from Pánuco, had arrived at Tamoanchan. Shortly thereafter came the departure of the wise men—the *tlamatinime*, also called *amoxoaque*, (those versed in ancient paintings), as Sahagún himself describes them in the corresponding passage of his Spanish text. They carried away with them to the east the codical writings, together with their specialized knowledge of the principal crafts (the inclusion of metalworking among these being surely an anachronism taken from a different age).

The wise men left the remainder of the people behind; these they first addressed, saying that they, the *tlamatinime*, were following their lord and master, "Tloque Nahuaque, Yohualli Ehécatl." Seler suggests that Yohualli Ehécatl (Night and Wind) is a kind of universal deity, much as Tloque Nahuaque himself. In this particular context it might be more logical to consider that Quetzalcoatl is implied, though not specifically mentioned.

The wise men then went eastward, the image of their god being carried on the backs of *teomamaque* (bearers of the god), an office more commonly associated with the Mexica migration and the ministers of Huitzilopochtli, but which really existed long before that. In addition, they left behind four people referred to as *tlamatinime*: "Oxomoco, Cipactonal, Tlaltecui, and Xochicauaca."*

The latter took counsel, declaring, "The sun will shine, it will dawn," and went on to lament the departure of the god, asking how the common people will now live, after the writings had been carried away and their knowledge obliterated. They then proceeded to devise (i.e., redevise, or reconstitute) the book of days, the *tonalpoalli*, and the count of the years, the *xiuhamatl*: "And thus was time recorded during all the time the Tolteca, the Tepaneca, the Mexica, and all the Chichimeca reign endured." It is thus related in unmistakable terms that one is concerned with a kind of reconstruction of the world, prior to the era of Tollan Xicocotitlan, and perhaps with the formation of a new calendar count, of which many existed in different regions of Mesoamerica.

The account then tells how at least some of the remaining popu-

* Oxomoco and Cipactonal are a fairly familiar pair of sorcerers or magicians. They occur in Quiche legends as Xpiyacoc and Xmucane and among Nahua speakers of Nicaragua as Tamagastad and Cipattonal.[38] Tlaltecui might have something to do with Tlaltecuhtli.

lation also left Tamoanchan. This is, strictly speaking, the beginning of the first refrain of the epic, after the prelude already discussed. The people made offerings at Teotihuacán, where leaders were elected, and built the pyramids of the Sun and Moon (another anachronism, this time interpolated from an earlier rather than a later age). After a passing mention of Cholula, this part of the story ends with a second obvious reference to the creation of the Fifth Sun: "All were worshiped as gods when they died; some became the sun, some the moon." These events are of course described in greater detail in Sahagún's Book VII, as well as in the *Leyenda de los Soles,* but such accounts are more replete with magico-religious material than with historical.

The beginning of the second refrain of the epic occurs in the last paragraph of page 192, which in itself makes it perfectly clear that one is dealing, at least in part, with a repetition of what has already been told just previously.

Again certain people abandoned the land, after living in Tamoanchan; once more, certain others are left behind. This time, however, the identity is not given for those who depart but rather for those who stayed behind, now named as the Olmeca-Uixtotins, under their leader Olmecatl Uixtotli. Presumably referring to only a part of this whole group, it is told that they subsequently went off to the east, to become the Anauaca Mixtecas, i.e., the group of Mixtecs settled on a section of the Gulf Coast.

A new incident then follows, not to be found in the previous refrain, though this also mentioned Cholula. The story is told of how pulque was invented at Mount Chichinauhia, which Kirchhoff identified with Cholula, though Jiménez Moreno points to a Cerro Chichinauhtzin north of Tepoztlán.[39]

Again one must presuppose simply a reinvention or resumption of this and other rituals, rather than a true invention. Evidence of the use of pulque long predates this era, as the famous Cholula frescoes, attributed to Cholula II, bear witness. Going back even further, Muller cites evidence for the making of pulque in Tulancingo in the Late Preclassic era. However, in accounts of a semiallegorical nature, one should not be too disconcerted by descriptions of the introduction of metalworking long before this really occurred or of the invention of pulque long after the accepted date. This differs little, for instance, from the traditional boast of the Athenians that they were the first to receive from Demeter the gift of wheat cultivation, whereas, in point of fact, grain production is clearly not unknown to Homer.

Another new event is then added to this second refrain: the departure of the Huaxtecs after their ruler had become intoxicated in a manner exactly recalling, or rather anticipating, the inebriation of Ce Acatl-Topiltzin just before he abandoned Tollan—a good illustration of the tendency in Mesoamerica (and elsewhere) for legendary stories to be ascribed rather indiscriminately to one era or another. "And with shame the Huaxteca (Cuextecatl) abandoned the land; they took all his people with him. All who understood the language moved together; they moved in a body. They traveled there from whence they came, to Panotla, now called Pantla." Sahagún in a previous passage (page 185), actually refers to the Huaxteca as Panteca.

The third refrain of the saga follows (paragraph 3 of page 194). Returning once more to Tamoanchan as the point of departure, we are told: "And when the reign had endured a long time in the place named Tamoanchan, the seat of power was moved to Xomiltepec." This is a new detail and has often been taken to suggest that Tamoanchan must be Xochicalco, based on the location of a Jamiltepec in eastern Morelos, i.e., the direction of Xochicalco. The evidence does not seem to be altogether conclusive. The *Suma de Visitas* mentions a Xomiltepeque; its location is not given, but it occurs sandwiched in between Xocotitlán and Xiquipilco, which both lie southwest of Tula.[40] The name is fairly common and even occurs in two instances in Oaxaca.

After providing this added piece of information, an almost identical story is unfolded as in the first refrain, describing how at Teotihuacán the law was established (i.e. re-established) and new rulers installed; the same verb, "*netechcauhtlaliloc*," is now used for this re-enactment, as compared with "*unnetechcauhtlaliloia*" employed previously. Once again it is told how the people next departed from Teotihuacán; the members of the respective groups understood their own language and each had its leader and ruler. This time, additional peoples are mentioned as among those departing—no longer the

Huaxtecs, as in the second refrain, but the Toltecs: "And the Tolteca were the ones who took the very lead."

It is then told how the leader of the Otomís (not previously mentioned) left the others in Coatepec, presumably the place of that name near Tula. Following this, it is recounted how the "Nahua" peoples, including incidentally the Mexicas, went onward to Chicomoztoc. With the mention of Tulancingo and Tula, we are in effect suddenly transported from one era to another, a phenomenon one constantly encounters in these early accounts. With this break, the refrain ends, and the story of quite separate and subsequent events follows.

It now becomes necessary to comment on certain aspects of this saga and on its possible significance and chronology. The reader can hardly remain in any serious doubt that the saga is concerned with the abandonment by various groups of the general region of Cholula and Teotihuacán, repeatedly mentioned. It is logical to concur with other investigators and identify this as the period of exodus from those centers at the end of Teotihuacán IV and Cholula IV, as known from archaeological evidence, when the fall in population was so precipitous as to verge on total abandonment.

At the beginning, as might perhaps be expected, the intellectual elite are the first to foresee disaster and to abandon the sinking ship and go eastward, a process that reoccurs in different form toward the end of Tollan Xicocotitlan. It is worth mentioning that there are close archaeological connections between Teotihuacán and the area of the Tuxtlas in southern Veracruz, where an abundance of Teotihuacán objects have been found. It might not be illogical to suppose that the inspiration underlying the whole Teotihuacán civilization came from this region and beyond, the probable homeland of the first great culture of Mesoamerica, that of the Olmecs. One cannot avoid the impression that in many respects, particularly the abundance of shells and other coastal symbols, the entire Teotihuacán complex was in a sense what might be termed "Gulf oriented." Equally marked links with the civilization of that coast are to be found in Cholula, with particular reference to Cholula IV.[41]

That the original Quetzalcoatl legend involved his departure for the east, thus creating a precedent for his successors or namesakes, was surely a reaffirmation of such links, demonstrated by archaeology and recorded by Sahagún. For reasons fully explained in Chapter 2, we believe that any original man-hero Quetzalcoatl, if indeed he existed at all, would have left Teotihuacán for Tlillan Tlapallan after the first burning of the ceremonial center at the end of Teotihuacán III A rather than some hundred years later, at the point now under discussion, when the city finally collapsed. Oblique reference is to be found in Sahagún's description of these events when he writes, "He who died became a god."[42] Admittedly he goes on to say that this occurred on various occasions, but of course a precedent had to be set. Sahagún states that during the final exodus, occurring presumably at the end of Teotihuacán IV, the *tlamatinime* took with them not a man-hero but a *god*, identifiable as Quetzalcoatl, borne by *teomamaque*. No suggestion is made that any human being of that name presided over the city's final disasters.

The wise men left only after a new group had reportedly reached Tamoanchan from Pánuco. The account rather implies that the *tlamatinime* and the newcomers were the same people, but this is surely based on a misunderstanding. The wise men were the spiritual elite of Teotihuacán and the leaders of people who had been established in the region for many centuries; they could hardly have arrived recently by sea. In my opinion, importance should not be attached to the report that the newcomers came by sea. As already explained, the semimythical initial journey of each people is almost invariably maritime. The mention of Pánuco, lying on the "Mar del Norte," seems to imply that they came from the north. It may not be illogical to assume that these were the new elements who appear to have reached the region of Teotihuacán at the outset of the Oztotícpac phase, as its rather meager vestiges have been shown to suggest.

Equally to be noted are the other peoples who depart from the multiethnic metropolis. Specifically mentioned in the second refrain of Sahagún's account are the Olmeca-Uixtotins and the Huaxtecs; in the third refrain we hear of the emigration of "Toltecs," Nahuas, and Otomís, apparently in a northwesterly direction. Both in the second and third refrains we are specifically told that the departing groups constituted separate linguistic entities; we are also informed that part of the Olmeca-Uixtotins remained behind, a point to which later reference will be made.

One is thus clearly given to understand that Teotihuacán and the surrounding region were inhabited by various peoples, quite apart from the intellectual elite who went away first and whose ethnic affiliations are less easy to determine, notwithstanding their evident cultural links with the Gulf Coast, toward which they departed and which might perhaps be regarded as their spiritual home. Apart from those peoples mentioned above, archaeological evidence points to the presence in Teotihuacán of some kind of colony of people from the Oaxaca region.

On the basis of a single source, it would hardly be permissible to make hard and fast deductions; nevertheless, such a cosmopolitan picture of Teotihuacán would not appear exaggerated. A striking feature of the whole account of Sahagún is the repeated reference not only to dissolution and departure but to a kind of simultaneous re-creation, whether through the re-establishment of the *tonalpohualli* or the re-invention of writing.

Similarly, the tale is told and retold of the emergence of new leaders; references to rulers or gods who themselves became the sun and moon clearly concern the birth of the Fifth Sun. It would thus seem that this new creation must be interpreted in a highly allegorical sense; there is little in the archaeological evidence of what followed the final collapse to suggest any marked cultural regeneration in Teotihuacán itself. The birth of the Fifth Sun, supposedly in that place, is surely the mystical expression of the general spiritual resolve of Mesoamerica itself not to perish, but, Phoenixlike, to re-emerge from the immolation of the Classic world guided by new leaders, settled in new places, and comforted by new gods. Mesoamerican culture was to be reborn in forms that at times partly recall, but essentially differ from, past norms.

Paradise Lost

No study of the related problems could be complete without some further clarification concerning Tamoanchan, a name or concept open to such divergent interpretations that ample authority may be cited for practically any conceivable ubication or etymology.

Where later writers have tended to seek Tamoanchan toward the east, Seler unhesitatingly located it in the west. He writes of "Itzpapálotl, the goddess of the westward-lying Tamoanchan." He regards this deity as basically the equivalent of Cihuacoatl, representative of the Cihuateteo, the goddesses living in Cihuatlampa, i.e., the west.[43] In addition, he writes of Tamoanchan as "the house of going down, or the house of birth."[44] This passage might at first sight seem contradictory, birth being readily associable with the east, where the sun is daily re-created. But since the west, Cihuatlampa, is the home of the Cihuateteo, both east and west may equally at times be associated with birth. In a further passage, Seler refers to Tamoanchan as "the mythical west, the kingdom of darkness, where the sun sinks into the earth."[45]

Beyer also supported the view that Tamoanchan lay in the west, remarking that Xochiquetzal proceeded from Tamoanchan, "the region where the sun sets."[46] The same author cites another name of Tamoanchan as *Tlacapillichihuaualoya*, "the place where children are made," i.e., the land of birth.[47] Not content with an additional suggestion to the effect that Tamoanchan might even be the equivalent of the Milky Way, Beyer also cites evidence for a tentative association with the south, the land of growth and fertility, qualities with which the name is often associated. He explains that Xochicahuaca, "the place where the flowers stand erect," synonymous with Tamoanchan, is also a name for the south. Xochitlicacan, "where the flowers are," is another name associated with Tamoanchan by Muñóz Camargo.[48] Xochitlalpan is also used in this sense in the *Memorial Breve*.[49] This source adds Huitzlampa (south) as part of its description of Tamoanchan, by way of clarification.

Preuss on the other hand proposed that Tamoanchan was the center of the earth, a view which Seler roundly rejects.[50] Such a suggestion might be less at variance with the school of thought which seeks to equate Tamoanchan with Xochicalco. This notion was originally propounded by Bishop Plancarte of Cuernavaca, loyal to local traditions and apparently taking his cue from "L'Histoyre du Mechique," which actually describes Tamoanchan as situated in the province of Cuauhnáhuac.[51] Lehmann was also of this opinion;[52] it has had partial support from Jiménez Moreno and Nicholson; and more recently has been strongly upheld by Piña Chan.

Such views, however, tend to ignore the fact that in Sahagún's narrative Tamoanchan is constantly named as the point of departure, not the destination; the fact that Xochicalco was flourishing at the time would seem to argue against this identification, since it thus was not a place which people were tending to abandon. Moreover, there is little evidence of either Olmeca-Uixtotins or Huaxtecas having penetrated into these parts.

Sahagún's reference to the creation of a new year count has also been taken as evidence linking Tamoanchan with Xochicalco, in view of the material evidence of the occurrence of such an event contained in certain reliefs of the Pyramid of Quetzalcoatl. However, a plethora of year counts existed in latter-day Mesoamerica, and therefore happenings parallel to this must have taken place in many a site.

On the other hand, Kirchhoff, sticking more closely to Sahagún, who associates Tamoanchan with travelers from the Gulf Coast, seeks its identity in the region of Cholula—a point to which further reference will be made. For the moment one is left in the perplexing condition where, in whatever direction one may look—east, west, south, or even in the center—he may find Tamoanchan and cite ample authority for his choice. For that matter, Sahagún's implication of proximity to Pánuco could be taken as pointing to a northerly location of Tamoanchan, since the Gulf of Mexico was often referred to as "Mar del Norte."

Before examining further the question of its whereabouts, it may be useful to consider its etymology, a point which raises almost as many problems as its correct location. Sahagún himself gives its meaning as "we seek our home"; Seler and others, however, point out that the correct Nahuatl rendering of such a phrase would be "*quitemoa tochan*," and Sahagún's interpretation would thus appear to be mistaken.

Seler prefers the rendering of the annotations of the *Codex Telleriano-Remensis*, which gives its derivation as *temo* (to go down) and chan (home); he thus gives a translation of the Nahuatl components of the name as "the House of Descent." This would constitute a literal meaning and the true sense of the words thus remains, as in his original contention, "House of Birth," for the children who descended to earth from the thirteenth heaven.[53] He also relates Tamoanchan with the incident of the split tree in the Mexica migration, as described in the *Codex Boturini.* Beyer also points out that "Tamoanchan" generally figures in codices as a broken tree from whose stout trunk a number of short branches emerge, bearing a flower at each end.[54] Such additional associations, however, offer only rather general guidance in identifying the correct meaning or ubication.

Seler, in exploring such symbolic ties, also offers quite a different possibility concerning etymology. He links the symbol of Tamoanchan, the broken tree, and the man who comes down its trunk with that strange or mythical bird (*moan*, or *muan*) which for the Mayas probably symbolized the sky covered with clouds. *Moan-kin* had even preserved a modern meaning of "cloudy rainy day," and Seler thinks that it derives from the word for cloud, *muyal.*[55] In another context he points out that *moan*, the fifteenth feast of the Mayan annual calendar, signifies "cloud covering" (*Wolkenbedeckung*).[56]

Later writers have also tended to favor such non-Nahua derivations, pointing to *tam* as a frequent Huaxtec place-name prefix. Jiménez Moreno thinks "Tamoanchan" derives from the word *moan* (bird) and *chan* (place), i.e., "the Place of the Bird Serpent," which he in this instance identifies with Xochicalco.[57] Jiménez Moreno also draws attention to the presence of a bird in Maya glyphs depicting Tamoanchan. Quite apart from the fact, as stated by Seler, that *moan* also has other meanings, such a glyph could easily derive from the use by the Mayas of rebus writing to illustrate a Nahuatl name; Thompson has drawn attention on more than one occasion to the Mayan use of rebus writing.

It would seem that such views in general overlook not only the insistence of Sahagún's informants on a Nahuatl derivation (even if he himself confused the etymology) but the frequent mentions of the name "Tamoanchan," actually broken down into its component Nahua parts, in the *Cantares*, as well as in the *Memorial Breve* of Chimalpain.

For instance, one finds in the *Cantares*, "*Xochinquahuitl onicac in Tamoan ychan Dios yecha*" (the flowering tree stands in Tamoan, the home of the god).[58] This is followed by, "*Nappan tamo tamoa ychan yehuan Díos*" (four times in Tamo, Tamoa, the God's home). To take another example, "*Yn Tamoan, icha xochitl*" (Tamoan, the home of the flowers).[59] In the *Memorial Breve* occurs, "*Tictemoa yn tamoanchan yn axcan ye mihtohua tictemohua y huel nelli tochan*" (we seek Tamoanchan, which today signifies, "*tictemohua*"—"we seek it"—namely our real authentic home).[60]

This use of *tamo*, *tamoa*, or *tamoan ychan* as separate words gives the name an undeniably Nahuatl connotation in such texts. Moreover, it is hard enough to think of any other example of a place or person of great significance in Nahuatl mythology bearing a name deriving from another Mesoamerican language; for instance, all the other names of hallowed places cited together with Tamoanchan in Sahagún's "Coloquio de los Dioses" are specifically Nahuatl. It is even more difficult to envisage that in poetry such a name, of which the meaning unless of Nahuatl derivation would not be comprehensible to the author himself, should have been split up in several texts into its component parts, and arbitrary Nahuatl meanings then assigned to these. If the component syllables such as *tam* and *chan* were really of Huaxtec or Maya origin, such a process of splitting them into Nahuatl components could only be described as punning.

Of Nahuatl solutions mentioned, Seler's *temo-ichan* (the place of descent) is gramatically acceptable, but its meaning is rather puzzling, unless one also agrees with Seler that Tamoanchan lay in the west and was therefore truly the place of descent. Luis Reyes in a personal communication points out that *tamo* can also be seen as a root for words connected with maize, viz. *tamalli*, as well as *totomochtli*, meaning dried leaves or fibers from the dry maize plant. Accordingly, Reyes sees Tamoanchan as possibly signifying "the house of the lord or possessor of maize." As a possible alternative, a clue to the derivation might lie in the reference to "*Tamiyoanichan*" in the song in the *Primeros Memoriales*, dedicated to the eight-yearly feast of *Atamalqualoya*. *Temi*, with its impersonal form *temihua* (*i* and *e* are often interchangeable), means to lie down, to be full, to be replete. Sullivan points out that *if* Tamoanchan was indeed derived from *temihua* (impersonal form of *temi*), not *temoa* (impersonal form of *temo*), it might then be interpreted as "the place where one is full or replete," since *Tamiyoanichan* could then easily become corrupted into Tamoanchan.

Such a derivation would be much more in keeping with the ever present conception of Tamoanchan as the place of fullness and abundance; on numerous occasions it is associated in written texts with richness and water, or even with cloud and mist. Garibay identifies it with Tlalocan, essentially a place of water.[61] As he points out, Centeotl, born in Tamoanchan, is herself linked with rain and water. In the "Song of Xochiquetzal" one finds, "Out of the land of rain and mist come I, Xochiquetzal, out of Tamoanchan."[62] The *Memorial Breve* speaks of Tamoanchan as "where the jaguars dwell," suggestive of the coast rather than the altiplano.[63] Tlalocan, moreover, is probably to be associated more with the east and is described by Sahagún as the place from which the sun arose; this view is stressed by Nicholson.[64]

Notions persist of Xochicalco as Tamoanchan, but they hardly take into account the close association with water. Nor for that matter does the identification with any single locality allow for its essentially mythical nature as the dwelling place of gods as much as of men. The annotations of the *Codex Telleriano-Remensis* describe Tamoanchan as the home of the gods and as a kind of earthly paradise. Here the gods were nurtured; some even had the audacity to cut flowers and branches from the trees, and as a consequence, Tonacatecuhtli and Tonacacihuatl expelled them from their Eden. Xochiquetzal, as already mentioned, dwelled there; Nanahuatzin, who became the Fifth Sun, was born in the place, as also was Centeotl. Teoinnan also reportedly came from Tamoanchan.

In conclusion, it may be agreed that Jiménez Moreno is probably correct in supposing that two (or more) Tamoanchans existed: the first mythical in nature and associated with the Gulf Coast, while the second or later Tamoanchan could be identified more positively as a historical place. The same principle could possibly be applied to Culhuacán, Aztlan, Chicomoztoc, and almost to Tollan itself.

However, the arguments in favor of Xochicalco as the Proto-Postclassic Tamoanchan seem in some respects unconvincing. Xochiquetzal, to be associated with the place, may have been a leading goddess of the Valley of Morelos (a point seldom mentioned by the proponents of Xochicalco). However, the discovery of the stelae depicting Quetzalcoatl is hardly conclusive; he was after all only one of various gods associated in one way or another with Tamoanchan. Moreover, Sahagún's account is perfectly coherent, with its constant comings and goings between Tamoanchan, Teotihuacán, and Cholula, as if they enjoyed a certain proximity. Xochicalco hardly fits geographically into this category.

Kirchhoff identified Tamoanchan with the *region* of Cholula. I would prefer, if any exact location is to be assigned for this protohistoric version of the place—in itself an uncertain assumption—a territory embracing both Teotihuacán and Cholula, or the general area in which the greatest efflorescence of the Teotihuacán civilization took place.

The term "Tamoanchan" could possibly have embraced an even wider region. Jiménez Moreno believes that, because of the mention of Xomiltepec by Sahagún and of Amecameca by Chimalpain in connection with Tamoanchan, the concept in its fullest sense may include at least part of the Valley of Morelos and even a sector of the Valley of Mexico. He rightly insists that the eastern part of Morelos more nearly recalls the lush conditions of the coastal regions than any other part of the altiplano. The reverse is surely true of Xochicalco!

If on the other hand not an area but one fixed site were to be sought, then El Tajín would deserve as much attention as Xochicalco. First, it lies near the coast, though admittedly not very close to Teotihuacán; Sahagún says that from Tamoanchan some of the people actually re-embarked in their boats. Second, it answers more closely the repeated description of a verdant and lush paradise, a kind of Tlalocan. Even if Tamoanchan came later to be associated with an inland region, one can hardly deny that the basic connotation as a place of lushness seems to be mainly coastal.

It would seem logical that Tamoanchan did at one stage come to be identified with the Teotihuacán region in its very widest sense, though it may still remain as much a concept as a place and applicable to more than one locality. An identification with Teotihuacán would have formed part of a logical historical process. For the people of that site, Tamoanchan was the home of the gods. As such it might have been naturally associated by the people of Teotihuacán with the place of efflorescence of the Olmec civilization on the well-watered coast of southern Veracruz and Tabasco—from where the *tlamatinime* themselves may have derived, since it is there that they returned. This was surely the first and semilegendary Tamoanchan.

In the upheavals of the Proto-Postclassic period, Teotihuacán itself had in turn come to assume this very role, as the sanctified center that recalled a civilization whose lights were already extinguished. As the Classic culture dissolved, people no longer looked back on coastal Tabasco but on Teotihuacán or Cholula as endowed with a special aura of antiquity, a kind of Paradise Lost or cradle of the gods—a spiritually verdant Tamoanchan.

Olmec Riddles

At the expense of yet another digression, it is important before coming to the foundation of Tollan Xicocotitlan to consider the Olmeca-Xicallancas, as they are most frequently termed. As occupants of the Puebla-Tlaxcala Valley, they were by all accounts among the principal neighbors of the Toltec domain. Yet more significant, one of the two ethnic groups who joined in the formation of Tollan, the Nonoalcas, undoubtedly enjoyed Olmeca-Xicallanca affiliations.

The Olmeca-Xicallancas are known by a variety of additional names, the most basic of which is Olmeca-Uixtotins, used by Sahagún. Other appellations include Olmeca-Xochmecas, or Xochtecas; Quiahuiztecas; and Zacatecas. Muñóz Camargo even refers to them as "Olmecas y Chozamecas," probably deriving, as Jiménez Moreno suggests, from Chocaman, near Orizaba.[65]

As the more generalized name "Olmeca" implies, deriving of course from *ollin* (rubber), their original roots are firmly planted in the coastal regions of the Gulf of Mexico, regardless of any later associations. Sahagún, who incidentally groups them in his description with the Mixtecas, unmistakably defines their provenance; he specifically states that their home was the land of riches and flowers where grew the cacao bean and liquid rubber. These thrive in Tabasco and southern Veracruz rather than in the central and northern part of that state. Sahagún states that the old people actually gave this land the name of "Tlalocan" (place of wealth).[66] Any suggestions of Mixtec associations presumably derive from the Mixtequillas, situated on the Gulf Coast in southern Veracruz, in which is located the town of Mixtlan. Early colonial documents show that Mixtec was then still spoken in this area.

Jiménez Moreno and others appropriately identify the original Olmeca-Xicallanca territory as lying between the two Xicalangos, one situated on the Laguna de Términos and the other, near Boca del Río, south of the city of Veracruz. As confirmation of such a conclusion, Motolinía mentions that, in addition to Puebla and Totomihuacan, the Olmeca-Xicallancas populated "in the direction of Coatzacoalcos."[67] Ixtlilxóchitl also refers to their coastal origins and associates them with Coatzacoalcos, writing in the same context of "Coatzaqualcas, Nonoalcas, Xicalancas, Totonaques."[68]

Regarding the name "Xicalanco," or "Xicalango" in its modern form, Motolinía refers to this Xicalanco beyond Coatzacoalco as the *third* place of the same name, as if three in all were known on the same coast.[69] In the *Relaciones Geográficas*, we hear of a San Pedro Xicalan much farther to the north in Totonacapan.[70]

Guatemalan sources give added support to such origins for the Olmeca-Xicallancas; Oloman is mentioned in the *Anales de los Cakchiqueles* as situated near the coast in connection with the Nonoalcas.[71] Krickeberg points out that in the *Popul Vuh*, Quetzalcoatl-Gucumatz, specifically as god of the Gulf Coast, is called not only "*toltécatl*" but also "*Ah h' ol*" (the lord of rubber)—that is to say, the Olmec.[72]

It has already been seen that, over and above their basic links with southern Veracruz and Tabasco—and leaving aside for the moment later connections with the Puebla-Tlaxcala Valley—these Olmecs are at times to be associated not only with Tabasco but with coastal areas lying to the north of the second Xicalanco, which was situated near Boca del Río. Essentially it is the other name, that of Uixtotin, that is more precisely to be connected with Totonacapan or the Huaxteca.

Uixtocíhuatl is the goddess of salt, or, as Seler explains, of salt water.[73] In the *Codex Vaticanus A*, Ilhuicatl Uixtotlan is depicted as the lowest of the nine uppermost heavens. It is shown as having green fields, and the picture illustrates the Water Goddess Chalchiuhtlicue, or Uixtocíhuatl.[74] Krickeberg identifies the latter goddess with Tlazolteotl, par excellence a Huaxtec deity.[75]

"Olmeca-Uixtotins" may possibly be the earlier appellation of the people concerned; other forms such as "Xicallancas" would be intermediate, and perhaps "Zacatecas" was the more recently adopted name of this ubiquitous and enduring species. This term, deriving from Zacatlán in the state of Puebla, refers ostensibly to the days when the Olmecs had already sought new pastures inland, far removed from their native Tierra Caliente (hot land). Other Olmeca-Zacatecas, perhaps by definition latter-day Olmecs, are described by Muñoz Camargo as arriving from the *west* at Amecameca and Chalco. There might be some misunderstanding concerning the direction of their coming, but assuredly they are late arrivals upon the scene, dating seemingly from the time when the Olmecs were already in the process of being expelled from the Puebla-Tlaxcala Valley as a result of the Tolteca-Chichimeca diaspora.

On the other hand, when one comes to examine the linguistic and ethnic affinities of the Olmeca-Xicallancas, as opposed to their purely territorial associations, the picture becomes more blurred. It is quite clear that they ended by becoming profoundly Nahuatized, and by the time they were expelled from the Puebla–Tlaxcala Valley there is no suggestion that they spoke any other language. Sahagún indeed states that many Olmeca-Uixtotins spoke Nahuatl; Jiménez Moreno aptly stresses this aspect of their culture and even suggests that they may have been the forebears of the Nahuatl speakers of the Gulf Coast.[76]

Their progressive Nahuatization offers no clue as to their original linguistic affiliations; these present a more knotty problem. Jiménez Moreno in the above-mentioned context also draws attention to certain possibilities of Mixtec links. He cites Clavijero as saying that the Mixteca was called Xicallan; there are still two villages called Xicalango in that region. Further evidence might be cited, such as the above-mentioned presence on the coast of southern Veracruz—Olmec territory par excellence—of the Mixtec-speaking enclave known as the Mixtequilla. Sahagún in saying that the Olmeca-Uixtotins became Anahuaca Mixtecas may be taken as meaning that it was they who gave origin to this enclave (which could hardly have accommodated all the Olmeca-Uixtotins). Incidentally, the Mixtecs, like the Olmecs, used the name "Quiahuizteca."

The Mixteca has no monopoly of names denoting Olmeca-Xicallanca associations; moreover, it is hard to tell whether such appellations are of remoter origin or whether they derive purely from Late

Postclassic times. In the general region of Metztitlan there are also two Xicalangos, together with such names as Olotla, Olititla, and Los Hules.[77] These may date from the time of the known Olmeca-Xicallanca exodus from the Puebla-Tlaxcala Valley; equally, they may have existed earlier, since very possibly the Olmecs who had moved inland from the coast did not confine themselves to the Puebla-Tlaxcala Valley but simultaneously occupied a much wider region.[78]

It should not be overlooked, when considering possible Mixtec influences, that Motolinía and Mendieta, in listing the sons of Iztac Mixcoatl, give Olmecatl-Xicalancatl and Mixtecatl as the progenitors of two distinct tribes.

In addition to the possibility of Mixtec connections, Olmeca-Xicallanca ties with the Chocho-Popolocas have also been proposed by W. Lehmann and others. The latter belong to the linguistic group known as Mazateco but now more usually referred to as Popoloca; this term is possibly misleading, since, in a purely generic sense, it is sometime employed by Sahagún and others simply to denote peoples who spoke a "barbarous" tongue, unintelligible to Nahuatl speakers.

Moreover, there exist two distinct Popoloca groups: first, that of the state of Puebla and adjacent areas, where five languages in all are spoken—Popoloca, Chocho, Ixcatec, Mazateco, and Trique. The second is situated in southern Veracruz and speaks tongues affiliated with the Mixe-Zoquean languages.[79]

The Olmeca-Xicallancas have tended to be linked with the first of these two groups, seemingly because, after the fall of Tollan, the Nonoalcas, people who seemed to have enjoyed certain Olmeca-Xicallanca affiliation, went off to the region of Teotitlan del Camino, where the Popoloca languages are principally spoken. But again, the arguments are not wholly conclusive; the Nonoalcas were at most one of various affiliates of the Olmecs, and a rather separate one at that, as will become apparent. Whereas migrant peoples might sometimes return upon their own tracks, this does not necessarily mean that they usually went back to their precise place of origin or to the home of their blood relations. The Nonoalcas at the fall of Tollan were highly civilized, whereas the Popolocas who had already settled in the new Nonoalca habitat were nearer the aboriginal level of that region. From the cultural point of view, they were at best poor relations of the Nonoalcas.

Referring to their possible antecedents, Jiménez Moreno has at times referred to the historic Olmecs as a triethnic group consisting of Nahuas, Mixtecas and Chocho-Popolocas.[80] On the other hand, he has also affirmed that "Olmec" is a geographic more than a linguistic expression.[81] Kirchhoff does not consider them a really composite ethnic entity. These viewpoints seem to approach nearest to the truth; the term "Olmeca-Xicallanca" appears to be a somewhat generalized description or appellation, hard to relate exclusively with one or more ethnic groups. One cannot really specify what language or languages they originally spoke; the most that can be said is that, though later strongly Nahuatized, they probably originally belonged to the great Oto-Mangue family; but that is a very broad definition indeed and even of this there exists no actual proof.

In fact, the more one successively examines such terms as "Tollan," "Tamoanchan," and now "Olmeca-Xicallanca," the clearer it becomes that any attempt to define them once and for all in time and space is apt to end in a blind alley.

Like "Chichimec," "Olmec" was a seemingly generic term, applicable not to one tribe but to a whole multitude of peoples of differing cultural levels and probably speaking diverse languages. Whereas most of the peoples to the west of the Sierra Nevada could in one form or another be referred to at times as Chichimecs, the majority of those situated to the east of the Sierra, as far as the limits of Maya territory, could on occasion pass muster as Olmecs. As Sahagún puts it, "The peoples to the east are not called Chichimeca; they are called Olmeca, Uixtotin, Nonoualca."[82]

Having now examined the antecedents of the Olmeca-Xicallancas and sought to discover who they were and from where they came, it becomes necessary to investigate what they actually did that may concern our story. What first becomes apparent is that, whereas their origins are mainly to be sought on the Gulf Coast, their activities in the period in question were more specifically directed toward the Puebla-Tlaxcala Valley and adjacent territories.

As to their first appearance on the historic scene, Ixtlilxóchitl gives several accounts of the same series of events. These may vary in detail but concur in certain essentials. Basically, according to him, there existed three (not the usual four) worlds, or suns, before that of the Toltecs.[83] These were: Atonatiuh, the Sun of Water; Tlachitonatiuh, the Earth Sun; Ehecatonatiuh, the Sun of Wind. These three were followed by the fourth, Tletonatiuh, Sun of Fire, which marks the emergence of the Toltecs. The second world, Tlachitonatiuh, corresponds to the period of the giants, or *Quinametin*, who were then destroyed; various sources associate these with Teotihuacán and with its pyramids, ostensibly built by men of gigantic proportions. It is the third world, Ehecatonatiuh, which corresponds to the period of the Olmeca-Xicallancas, who had reportedly come in boats and were later also destroyed. Ehecatonatiuh is sometimes called by Ixtlilxóchitl the second world rather than the third.

This whole version is not in disharmony with Sahagún, who writes first of the existence of Teotihuacán, then of the Olmeca-Xicallancas, and finally of the Toltecs of Tollan Xicocotitlan. Other sources that at times coincide with Ixtlilxóchitl, such as Torquemada and Veytia, give the same general story, telling of the destruction of the giants by the Olmeca-Xicallancas.

However, it is difficult to determine whether the actual destruction by the Olmecs of the "giants," identified with Teotihuacán, can be taken as wholly historical, or whether this report was merely a deduction based upon their presence at the time in this area, where they remained after the holocaust.

Sahagún tells a different story of what happened. His actual words are, "*Auh in ye quexqujch cavitl onooac: in tamooancha, vncan eoaque tetlacaujque, vncan tecauhtiaque. Olmeca, vixtoti, in jtoca olmeca vixtoti.*" This is translated by Anderson and Dibble as: "And when they had lived at Tamoanchan a long time, they departed therefrom, they abandoned the land. There they left behind those named the Olmeca Uixtotin." The account goes on to state that the latter (i.e., the Olmecs) were *also* magicians and wise men (*tlamatinime*); they later followed those who had already gone to the east and they came to be called the Anahuaca Mixtecas.[84]

This passage is bewildering at first sight. In the first place, it tends to confuse the Olmeca-Uixtotins, some of whom reportedly stayed behind, with the *tlamatinime*, the intellectual aristocracy of Teotihuacán, all or nearly all of whom are said to have departed eastward, taking their books and paintings with them, as Teotihuacán lay at its last gasp.

Seler interprets this differently and states that the Olmecs were "taken off" (*fortgezogen*), not "left behind."[85] The problem lies in the rather ambivalent sense of the Nahuatl word *cahua*, which may mean "to leave, to abandon," but equally can signify "to remove" or even "to accompany."

The question of which interpretation is correct is crucial, as far as the Olmeca-Xicallancas are concerned. There is all the difference in the world, as any child will know, between being taken off on a journey and being left at home when the remainder of the family departs.

As often occurs, a fuller examination of the text provides the additional clue. As already explained, the same story is told differently several times over; if we turn back to an earlier passage, we find the report of how the wise men themselves went away, taking their writings, and so on. The account continues, "And when they departed, they summoned all those they left behind." The word translated as "left behind" is *quincauhtiaque*, and there is no doubt that on this occasion "left behind" is the correct meaning, and the wise men also say in their address to the people concerned, "But you shall dwell here; you shall stand guard here. Thereupon they departed to the east."[86]

This passage does not mention by name the Olmeca-Uixtotins, but from the similarity of the two successive quotations, both of which clearly refer to the same event—i.e., the departure of the *tlamatinime* to the east—one is left in no doubt that those people thus addressed on both occasions were indeed the Olmecs, even if this is specifically stated only in the second version. Only some remained, while others may have eventually followed the *tlamatinime*, as Sahagún himself implies when he writes of those who later became the Anahuaca Mixtecas. Possibly certain Mixtec-speaking Olmecs separated from their more Nahuatized kinsfolk, the former departing while the latter stayed in the area.

It may also be assumed that not even all the *tlamatinime* departed. Sahagún tells in another passage how Oxomoco and Cipactonal were among those who remained. He describes them as "Toltecs," but in this context, connected with Teotihuacán, that expression may be taken as meaning some of the wise men, or *tlamatinime*.

Added confirmation of such an interpretation may be sought in Sahagún's account in Spanish, the *Historia General*. He writes of the *amoxoaque*, whom he also describes as "*adivinos*" (wise men). "*Amoxoaque* means men who were versed in the ancient painted documents." He tells how these had left their companions behind in Tamoanchan (the Olmecs are not actually mentioned by name) and had gone off by boat to the east. It was the command of "*nuestro Señor Díos*" that the others should stay behind.[87]

It would seem that those who remained—only a very limited proportion of the original population—must be those very people whom, archaeologically speaking, we previously identified as staying in the area when the others left and who then combined with small numbers of new immigrants. These would together have been the initiators of the Oztotícpac and Cholulteca I phases, which show traces of both local and extraneous influences.

As far as any Olmeca-Xicallanca element was concerned, it would not therefore have consisted of immigrants but, in accordance with Sahagún, of people who had decided to stick where they belonged, among the scattered ruins of the metropolis. These Olmecs were perhaps among the less sophisticated of the various peoples of the former cosmopolitan community, but they would have tended to become the cultural leaders among the sparse settlers now occupying the region.

The Fate of Cholula

The Olmeca-Xicallancas have been discussed at some length, but so far relatively little has been said of the part they played in the history of Cholula in the Proto-Postclassic period, a topic that has attracted fairly widespread attention. As will have been seen, the city figures quite prominently in Sahagún's repeated descriptions of departures from Tamoanchan.

As in the case of Teotihuacán, ethnohistorians had already evolved a framework for Cholula's chronology and history well before the more recent archaeological findings. The account of what had occurred thus propounded had been almost universally accepted as the correct version. It was accordingly mooted that Classic Cholula, centered of course on the Great Pyramid, survived the collapse of Teotihuacán by some 150 years, and then, in approximately A.D. 800, succumbed to the assaults of the Olmeca-Xicallancas. With their arrival, a new phase commenced, seemingly corresponding to Cholulteca I, of which they were accordingly the bearers. Cholula thus enjoyed a continuous existence as a place of first importance and still stood forth as a thriving center of culture and power during the whole Toltec era. Lehmann first called attention to a passage in Torquemada which partly inspired such an interpretation of events; to this Jiménez Moreno has subsequently lent his authoritative support. Other leading investigators have also concurred; Armillas, for instance, writes of how, after the fall of Teotihuacán, Cholula became the capital of Central Mexico, a development linked with the accession to power of the "dynasty" of the Olmeca-Xicallancas.[88]

Such then is the "orthodox" version, but its widespread acceptance does not in itself make this interpretation correct. On closer scrutiny, the whole hypothesis displays certain weaknesses.

First, any notion that the Late Classic culture in Cholula long survived its Teotihuacán counterpart is no longer supported by archaeological evidence. While their architecture is far from identical, the equivalent phases in each center nevertheless follow one another closely, producing very similar ceramic forms and designs. Thus Teotihuacán III corresponds to Cholula III, Phase III A in the one is equivalent to Phase III A in the other, and Phase IV to Phase IV.

At first sight it might be just conceivable that one single phase in Cholula, say Cholula IV, could by some freak of history have fallen out of line and been prolonged a century or more beyond its equivalent in Teotihuacán, thus making Cholula IV contemporary not only with Teotihuacán IV but with the succeeding Oztotícpac phase as well. If it is to be suggested that Classic Cholula long survived Classic Teotihuacán, either it must be supposed that one later phase in Cholula lasted much longer than its Teotihuacán counterpart or that *every* phase in Cholula is later than its equivalent in Teotihuacán—Cholula III corresponding with Teotihuacán III A, Cholula III A with Teotihuacán IV, and so on. This surely is a far-fetched supposition;

diffusion of styles over such a limited distance could hardly require 150 years. Florencia Muller goes so far as to describe the Classic complex of Cholula as an impoverished version of that of Teotihuacán; as such it would hardly have been expected to show greater staying power and to have outlived the latter.

Moreover, the historical processes attending their fall seem to run parallel in both sites. This problem is well expounded by Drummond and Muller. According to their account of the more recent archaeological findings, it would seem that during Cholula IV, the Great Pyramid was largely deserted, just as occurred with the focal part of the great ceremonial center of Teotihuacán during Phase IV.[89] On the available archaeological evidence, the fate of the two cities seems to have been rather similar, since in each site Phase IV is found mainly outside the principal ceremonial center. Cholula IV pottery was recovered, not in the Great Pyramid, but in a pit nearby.[90] It is surely not unreasonable to suppose that the time interval between these processes in each site was not great.

The pottery of the succeeding phase, Cholulteca I, marks a fairly radical departure from Cholula IV. It is more abundant than Cholula IV in the Pyramid, now apparently partially reoccupied. It is however a very coarse product; the material that I examined (coming from Xochitécatl) has a strange and rudimentary aspect and is really difficult to relate to any people of high cultural attainments, ruled as suggested by a great Olmeca-Xicallanca "dynasty." Cholulteca polychrome, previously thought to be of earlier origin, really began not with Cholulteca II but with Cholulteca III, or probably not before the Tolteca-Chichimeca invasion, toward the fall of Tollan Xicocotitlan.

Therefore, Cholulteca I is the phase which seemingly corresponds to Oztotícpac in Teotihuacán; though related, its forms are somewhat different. In addition, the life of Cholulteca I may possibly have been rather more prolonged than Oztotícpac, even if they began at approximately the same time.[91]

Florencia Muller is of the opinion that, as in the case of Oztotícpac, Cholulteca I implies the arrival of new people, though probably different groups in the two cases, since Oztotícpac and Cholulteca I do not form part of a composite pattern of design.

As in the case of Teotihuacán, an impression persists that the rudimentary style was evolved from a combination of extraneous and indigenous elements. In addition to the Cholulteca pottery, contemporary figurines found in Xochitécatl actually possess Teotihuacán-type heads, but with the addition of almost grotesque bodies of a most primitive nature, vaguely recalling Coyotlatelco. In Xochitécatl, pottery of this period was found with designs also resembling in certain respects the Georgetown phase of Mogollon, together with Pueblo I.

Drummond and Muller thus place the end of Teotihuacán IV and the inception of Cholulteca I and of Oztotícpac as both taking place in about A.D. 800 (though I would prefer, as explained, a date of anything up to a century earlier). In Cholula, Coyotlatelco-type pottery, starts only with Cholulteca II strictly speaking—that is to say, with the presumed fusion or reuniting of the new inhabitants of Cholula with those of Teotihuacán (Xometla phase), corresponding to the commencement of the Tula-Mazapan horizon.

Thus Drummond and Muller do in fact accept the "orthodox" date of about 800 proposed by Jiménez Moreno and others for the fall of Classic Cholula; however, where they differ from his version is in insisting that Teotihuacán IV *also* continued until the same date and ended more or less at the same time as Cholula IV. From the available evidence, they see no possibility that Classic Cholula long continued on its own as the sole surviving bastion of a tottering civilization; nor do they make any suggestion that the Proto-Postclassic Cholula of Cholulteca I enjoyed a high cultural level, any more than the scanty survivals of Teotihuacán. Cholula was also for a limited period almost an abandoned city, at least as far as the Great Pyramid and its vicinity were concerned. Muller makes this same point in another paper published by the German Puebla-Tlaxcala project which includes detailed maps of the settled areas of Cholula in each phase.[92]

So much for the archaeological record. Quite apart from this, any hypothesis suggesting that Cholula suffered no cultural eclipse in its period of transition from Classic to Postclassic era encounters other objections, inherent in the written evidence put forward to support this proposition.

On examination, the Torquemada text on which such an interpretation is based is most ambiguous. What the writer actually says is, "Those of Nicoya [now part of Costa Rica] are descended from the

Cholultecas. They lived inland, toward the Sierra; and the Nicaraguas, who came from Anahuac, and are Mexicans, lived toward the Coast of the Pacific."[93] The account continues by suggesting that their migration to this area occurred "seven or eight ages—or lives of old men—ago."

In other sources one finds similar references to such "ages," meaning a double fifty-two-year cycle; accordingly, seven or eight of these become the equivalent of 728 or 832 years. Torquemada's work was published in 1615, but was probably written twenty-five years earlier, thus placing the occurrence in question about A.D. 800 in very round figures.

Torquemada continues, "In that time [i.e., some eight hundred years previously], they [the Nicaraguas] were attacked by a great force of people called Olmecs. These [the Olmecs] say that they came from the direction of Mexico and that formerly also they had been arch-enemies of the Nicaraguas, who were then settled in the uninhabited territory situated between Soconusco and Tehuantepec." The account then goes on to tell how the Olmecs, having attacked these unfortunate people, conquered them and imposed tribute. The Nicaraguas were so sorely afflicted that they could bear the situation no longer and left the region secretly.

The account quoted above mentions two distinct groups, though both were to settle in Nicoya and both had reportedly lived at least for a time on the coast of Chiapas. The first is that of the Cholultecas and the second that of the Nicaraguas, also referred to as "Mexicanos," i.e., Nahuatl-speaking people.

Paradoxical as it may seem, the group that supposedly came originally from Cholula obviously cannot be that of the Cholultecas (Cholulteca and Chorotega are versions of the same word, and Torquemada himself mentions a province alternatively called Cholulteca or Choroteca). Notwithstanding their name, those termed "Cholultecas," or "Chorotegas" have no connection with the city of Cholula in a direct sense; Jiménez Moreno emphasizes that such "Chorotegas" were from Xolotlan, a part of the coast of Chiapas which cannot in any way be identified with Cholula.[94] This is also the viewpoint of Seler.[95] He says that the Cholotla of the "Song of Yacatecuhtli," mentioned jointly with Pipitla (place of Pipils), could possibly be Xolotlan, a fairly common place name; one actually existed in Soconusco. This group, i.e., the Nicoyas whom Torquemada portrays as descended from the Cholultecas, or Chorotegas, were not described by the author as Nahuatl speakers; they might have been the forebears of the Chorotega-Mangues, whom the Spaniards were later to find in the Nicoya region. At the time of the Conquest, the Nahua-speaking Nicaraos inhabited a long coastal strip on each side of the present Nicaragua–Costa Rica frontier, whereas the Chorotega-Mangues were to be found to the north and south of the Nicarao group.

Since it cannot be these Chorotegas, it must therefore be the second group, the Nicaraos, whom investigators assume to have come from Cholula in about A.D. 800. Although they spoke Nahuatl, Torquemada, far from suggesting that they came from Cholula, specifically states that they are "from Anahuac"; this term is normally associated by chroniclers not with the Valley of Mexico but with the Gulf or Pacific littoral.[96] Torquemada states that they were living not in Cholula but in the area between Tehuantepec and Soconusco when they were attacked, possibly about the year 800. It was not they but their assailants, the Olmecs, who according to the author had originally come from "*acia Mexico*," but he does not say how long ago.

To make it clear that they were not then too far distant, Torquemada states that, following their departure, after twenty days' journey they passed "through the land of Quauhtemallan" and proceeded another hundred leagues to arrive at the province called Cholulteca or Choroteca. The account also mentions "those of Nicoya who went ahead"; that is to say, the two groups—the Nahua-speaking Nicaraos and the Chorotega-Mangue-speaking Chorotegas—formed part of the same migration from their previous home on the coast of Chiapas to the Nicoya region and the territory lying inland from there. From what then follows, it is even made to appear that some of the attacking Olmecs (themselves perhaps related to the Chorotegas, as speakers of an Oto-Mangue tongue) also went to that province.

Torquemada thus implies that the migrants reached Guatemala from their previous home in the space of twenty days, though the passage is not absolutely clear. At all events, no stopping place is mentioned between their former habitat and Guatemala.

The reasons that these people are believed to have been from Cholula rather than any other place remain unclear. Their victimization by Olmecs in itself means little; as has already been stressed, the latter were by no means confined to Cholula or to the Puebla-Tlaxcala Valley. Moreover, Torquemada states that the attack took place in Chiapas, and when assaulted the Nicaraos were living there and not in Cholula. It may well be that *before* going to settle in Chiapas, the Nahua-speaking Nicaraos had lived in one of the main centers of the Classic civilization in Central Mesoamerica; however, we have few clues as to which of these places might have been their home. They might conceivably have left Central Mesoamerica as part of one of the earlier Pipil migrations, which probably started before the fall of the Classic civilization. The antecedents of the Chorotegas, the other group, are also not clear. Spinden, incidentally, thinks that "Chorotega" means "displaced peoples." Stone insists that these migrants have left no trace of their existence in Chiapas.[97]

Torquemada describes the Nicaraguas as "those of Anahuac," probably in this context used to indicate the Gulf Coast. And it may well be that Pipil migrations of this type were responsible for spreading Tajín *yugos* and *hachas* throughout certain areas of Central America, as stressed by Jiménez Moreno. Such objects have also been located in the region of the Tuxtlas in southern Veracruz, as well as in Soconusco. Tajín implements may suggest the existence of links with El Tajín itself, but offer no proof of any connection with Classic Cholula, in spite of certain El Tajín influences present in that site. Modern research has tended to assign to the great El Tajín efflorescence dates rather earlier than those previously accepted, and these objects might thus have reached Central America before the end of Classic Cholula, rather than in the baggage of refugees after the fall of the city.

Lehmann based his notions as to possible Cholulan antecedents of the Nicaraos partly upon references by Fray Francisco de Bobadilla (who went to Nicoya in 1528) to "Ticomega and Maguatega" as places of origin, according to Nicarao traditions. Lehmann makes mention of a document connected with Cholula which contained place names that apparently could be identified with Ticomega and Maguatega. However, it is most significant that Lehmann placed the migration of the Nicaraos in A.D. 1000, not 800, and thus did not connect them with Classic Cholula.[98]

Samuel Lothrop, who thought that some relationship could be detected between certain ceramic designs of the Nicaraos and those of Cholula, also dates the departure of the Pipil-Nicaraos as having taken place during the Tula-Mazapan horizon, toward the end of the eleventh century.

I am therefore more inclined to agree with León-Portilla, who points to the general vagueness of Torquemada's chronology, and to concur with his suggestion that the Pipil Nicarao migration is more likely to belong to movements that coincided with the collapse of Tollan rather than with that of Teotihuacán or Cholula.[99]

Finally, one must add another objection to the hypothesis of a violent occupation of Cholula by the Olmeca-Xicallancas in about A.D. 800, namely, that they were probably already in possession of that region. It was already stressed above, on the basis of Sahagún's account, that when the Teotihuacán civilization fell, including of course Cholula, some of the Olmeca-Xicallancas stayed behind. If this is correct, they could not invade Cholula, since one cannot seize what one already possesses.

One is thus obliged for several reasons to reject the view that Cholula survived Teotihuacán for a considerable period, only itself to be later overrun by Olmec invaders. First, this is not what Torquemada says; secondly, the Olmecs were probably there already; and thirdly, on archaeological grounds one sees Cholula as having suffered a fate similar to that of Teotihuacán and at about the same time.

Muller believes, as already explained, that some new element was indeed present in the rather primitive and meager Cholulteca I phase. It seems likely that this was a small body of intruders from the south. It can hardly have required a massive invasion if, as Drummond and Muller maintain, Cholula was almost uninhabited at the time. Such a group might have fused with the Olmeca-Xicallancas, who far from being invaders constituted rather the remaining local inhabitants. Such contacts with the south may have been initiated at that time, even if the great efflorescence of the Puebla-Mixteca culture is to be ascribed to the succeeding era of Cholulteca III and IV.

New Horizons

In this chapter the dissolution of Teotihuacán has been reviewed, as well as the more temporary decline of Cholula. At the same time, problems presented by the Olmeca-Xicallancas and the emergence of Proto-Coyotlatelco pottery, which will be seen to bear directly on the ensuing rise of Tula, have been examined.

The question of the origins of the new Quetzalcoatl were discussed in Chapter 2. The conclusion was reached that *if* indeed there ever was a single individual whose existence preceded and inspired the rich efflorescence of the new cult, then such a person is likely to have lived in the closing stages of Teotihuacán III rather than during Teotihuacán IV.

The new Quetzalcoatl is graven in stone on Xochicalco's stelae, probably only marginally later in date than the end of Teotihuacán IV; as has been stressed, one must allow for a reasonable time lag before admiration of a hero's exploits can be transformed into worship of a god's image.

Moreover, Sahagún's account, so rich in other details, says absolutely nothing of any particular hero who led the final exodus from Teotihuacán. On the contrary, it was a collective move on the part of the wise men, and mention occurs of an already established god equivalent to Quetzalcoatl and whose image was borne by the eastward migrants; these are described as following someone who had gone before.

Certain details of the departure of Ce Acalt-Topiltzin from Tollan Xicocotitlan are suggestive of what might really have happened in Teotihuacán. Even the reported inebriation of Quetzalcoatl in Tollan corresponds exactly to Sahagún's story of what occurred to the Huaxtec leader when he and his people left Teotihuacán.

The end of Teotihuacán III A, when certain disasters befell the great ceremonial center, must have constituted a time of troubles, even if the city survived for a further period. It is often at such crucial moments that new religious beliefs arise, perhaps in this case the cult of a departing hero who went off to the east as initial disasters beset the city. Such a legend imprinted itself upon the mind of Mesoamerica and became part and parcel of its basic mythology. The story of the great being who departed eastward was later to attach itself to other leaders of a heroic stamp or at least of major importance and who lived long after the first Quetzalcoatl.

The birth of a new religion at precisely this stage is not at all hard to conceive; it must be remembered that the real development of Christianity as a world religion, as well as the appearance of Mithraism and other short-lived cults, may be said to have occurred at the beginning rather than at the end of Rome's period of decadence.

The new Quetzalcoatl may have emanated from Teotihuacán, but the development of his worship seems to have germinated outside that center, in Tabasco or in the Huaxteca. It subsequently spread to Xochicalco and the Mixteca and later to Tollan Xicocotitlan and to Chichén Itza.

Teotihuacán IV and Cholula IV ended more or less simultaneously, at the latest about A.D. 750 and possibly earlier. Sahagún and modern archaeological investigations concur in pointing to a great exodus at that time. The two sites were abandoned to what were little more than squatters in the Oztotícpac and Cholulteca I phases. New peoples appear to have arrived in small numbers, but evidence of their rather meager culture is more readily found in places outside the two abandoned ceremonial centers that had succumbed, as for instance in Portezuelo and Xochitécatl. The question is whether the early Coyotlatelco pottery owed its origin to people native to the region or to the intruders; I have suggested that it may have been both. Elements of the Olmeca-Xicallancas, whose original habitat has been defined as the Gulf Coast and more particularly the Tabasco region were probably among the people who remained after the great exodus.

During this age of upheaval the Fifth Sun was created, symbolizing the new Postclassic world; this took place in the area then designated as Tamoanchan, which I have defined as the general region of Teotihuacán-Cholula.

It was indeed a new world that was brought into being, and such dramatic events were the harbingers of great future changes. As sometimes occurs, the past was in part adapted and in part rejected, as the destinies of Mesoamerica came to be controlled by more violent peoples filled with the lust for war. The Fifth Sun rose upon a world differing as radically from its predecessor as our own twentieth century departs from the more ordered and serene patterns of the early eighteenth century.

In such a new order, Teotihuacán was never to recover. A slow and modest revival soon began in the Puebla-Tlaxcala Valley, but the real center of gravity became displaced with the rise of Tollan Xicocotitlan. This city was in many respects the successor of Teotihuacán, and it will now be our task to study its development.

4. The Approach to Tollan

WHEN FULLY DEVELOPED, the Postclassic differed markedly from the Classic era. However, it seems likely that the transformation from one to the other was more gradual than might be supposed. Notwithstanding the doom of certain cities, no dramatic changes occurred overnight. While Teotihuacán faltered, Xochicalco and El Tajín still bore aloft the banner of civilization. Perhaps, as Gordon Willey has pointed out, the single unifying characteristic of this third major stage in Mesoamerica—or for that matter in Peru—is the persistence of widespread social, political, and religious disturbances.[1] By such criteria, today we once more live in a Postclassic world.

General Problems

After discussing the great Teotihuacán diaspora and its epiclassic sequel, we now finally reach our central theme, the Early Postclassic period. One continues to use this term for want of a better, though Armillas prefers "historic."[2] The period is historic in the sense that some documentary evidence is available. It is of course limited to certain sources; others do not go back beyond the final, or Late Postclassic, era. Accordingly, at this point in our story, we stand upon the threshold of Mesoamerican history.

The initial phases of Tollan Xicocotitlan are ill-defined, both archaeologically and historically; neither its actual site nor the relevant texts offer precise information concerning its rise. One is thus forced in great measure to base his deductions concerning the beginning from what is known of the end.

From the purely archaeological point of view, the exact nature of the transition from Classic to Postclassic era is not always clearly discernible, and many questions still await an answer. The written sources likewise offer unsure guidance, and my own analysis has tended to further reduce the material genuinely applicable to Tollan's inception.

The first upheavals of the new age probably brought about no sudden or brusque transformation of the social or political scene, in Teotihuacán or elsewhere, but rather a general sense of disorientation. A gradual collapse of the established order probably reduced this deeply stratified society to a state of mental confusion, such as Frankfort attributes to the Egyptians following the irruption of the Hyksos at the end of the Middle Kingdom.[3] With the passing of the great center of Teotihuacán and the rise of other cities, we are in fact witnessing an increase in the power of the palace at the expense of the temple, precisely as occurred in Early Dynastic Mesopotamia. This process may well have begun before the final Teotihuacán debacle.

At first sight, it may seem paradoxical that a tendency toward secularization should develop at a moment of religious renaissance. But the new Quetzalcoatl cult initially perhaps presaged a transformation more social than political. There is little sign of any abrupt departure from previous patterns of rule at the inception of Tollan Xicocotitlan, or for that matter during its subsequent history. Certain evidence survives of plural kingship, as will later be explained; this mode of government even continued after Tollan's fall in Culhuacán, Xochimilco, and other cities that claimed Toltec descent.

Within this framework, emphasis may have shifted from the sacerdotal toward the secular. However, it should not be supposed that Mesoamerica turned militarist overnight. Indications exist of the presence of such tendencies in the closing phases of Teotihuacán; similarly, the surviving sculptural evidence of a martial and sanguinary spirit in Tollan belongs to the end rather than the beginning. One does not really know how things were at the outset, what decorative motifs then prevailed, or how far they diverged from previous patterns.

López Austin aptly writes that militarism need not be regarded as automatically following after theocracy.[4] As he suggests, the impulse to re-establish the glories of the past possibly engendered the concept of Tollan as a conquering city. This urge would have lent added luster to the warlike attributes of the new Quetzalcoatl, figuring as Tlahuizcalpantecuhtli, in contrast to his gentler role as Ehécatl, God of Wind; the latter element preceded the rain, and is therefore linked to the more pacific arts of cultivation and crops. Through a kind of amalgamation with Mixcoatl, the Hunting God from the north, Tlahuizcalpantecuhtli ceased to be merely the Morning Star and became instead the Warrior of the Dawn.

Whatever the pace of change from Classic to Postclassic era, the conviction remains that the transformation, when completed, was far-reaching; it may best be typified by the presence in Tollan and Chichén of the gruesome *tzompantli*, perhaps the starkest manifestation of the cult of war and death (in Tollan the actual *tzompantli* visible today may be of Aztec origin, but Toltec *tzompantli* altars also exist). It is difficult to imagine such structures in Teotihuacán or among the Classic Mayas, whatever the signs of incipient militarism.

The resuscitated Quetzalcoatl went accompanied in Tollan Xicocotitlan by emblems not present in Teotihuacán. On the one hand, the jaguar-bird-serpent, of such great antiquity, continued to be manifest. But Kubler suggests that in Tollan the jaguar now acquired a new meaning as representing the subterranean world. In Chichén it appears at the base of columns, surmounted by the sun's disk or by atlantids; in Tollan it is to be found between pairs of eagles and vultures or at the base of columns in the position of the underworld, under the feet of a priest or of warriors. Jaguars and eagles eating hearts became the emblem of the new warrior castes. As Kubler rightly insists, the jaguar had gained a new significance, as associated with the nether regions and also with war, in representations of the animal both seated and walking. Thus it gains entirely new undertones not previously visible in Teotihuacán or elsewhere.[5]

Tollan and Its Contemporaries

Before turning to the written sources, it may be fitting to examine any archaeological evidence applicable to the early days of Tollan Xicocotitlan and its contemporaries. Various sites provide useful data; none, alas, furnish exact dates!

For Tollan itself, regrettably little material can be directly ascribed to the first period after its establishment. Like many other cities, such as Tenayuca, Culhuacán, and perhaps even Tenochtitlan, Tollan appears to have come into existence well before its "official" foundation date. So far however, only rather meager remains of such an earlier Tollan have been unearthed.

Acosta insists that no Preclassic or Teotihuacán pottery is to be found in the area of the principal ceremonial center.[6] Recently, however, in Tula Chico pottery recalling Teotihuacán forms has been in the lowest levels in stratigraphic pits, together with a limited number of sherds that could be classified as belonging to Metepec (Teotihuacán IV). This Teotihuacán and Teotihuacanoid pottery was associated with Coyotlatelco; this does not occur in Teotihuacán itself, where Metepec and Coyotlatelco are found in separate strata, and these sherds may conceivably represent a carry-over, or survival, of older styles, rather than a stratigraphic level in Tula Chico truly contemporary with Teotihuacán. Such finds certainly show that Tollan was founded earlier than was thought likely at one time. But pending any further discoveries of Metepec remains in Tollan itself (a small Teotihuacán site exists to the north of Tollan, as previously mentioned), this Teotihuacanoid pottery in the early Tula Chico, associated with Coyotlatelco, seems more likely to be contemporary with the Oztotícpac phase in Teotihuacán. Therefore, according to present information, Tula Chico and perhaps other segments of Tollan were settled somewhere between A.D. 700 and 800. This early Tollan probably covers a limited part of the whole site and could hardly have been a leading center. In another work I have argued that Tenochtitlan was probably founded or settled well before the official date of 1325 or 1345; nevertheless, it is after this time that it begins to count, and the presence or otherwise of an earlier settlement of Chichimecs or Tepanecs is not of any profound significance.

What Acosta did find were certain interesting clues to the origins of Tollan's architecture, in the form of substructures with a big talud, surmounted by a plain *tablero* of about half its height. This cannot be considered as typically Toltec, nor does it exist in this particular form in Teotihuacán, but is to be found in Xochicalco and El Tajín, where this architectonic feature attains a distinctive character.

Acosta limits himself to distinguishing an "early" and "late" (or "recent") phase for the Tula-Mazapan period in general. He considers that Tollan attained its greatest splendor shortly before his suggested date of destruction of its ceremonial center. The Coatepantli (Wall of Serpents) and the Tlahuizcalpantecuhtli Temple belong to this last period, but reveal certain traces of earlier substructures.[7] Edifice Number 3 probably also belongs to the last period of the great Tollan.[8] No marked differences of style developed in this final epoch; up to a point, earlier variations are visible in substructures, but these are often hard to detect, due to the custom of using material from demolished buildings in new construction.

In contrast to Teotihuacán and other sites, neither by pottery classification nor by any other means has it yet been possible to make a precise definition of Tollan's development in terms of numbered periods or phases. The ceremonial center is rather all of one piece, and, notwithstanding the usual layer of superstructures, there is as yet no strict categorization such as Tula I, II, III, and IV to guide our studies.

Acosta insists that in very general terms Coyotlatelco pottery is earlier than Mazapan; as has already been stressed, it was already in use when Tollan was founded. By contrast, Mazapan, while perhaps not present at the outset, seems to span the whole period of Tollan's existence as a great center of power; it is to be found in all strata in the ceremonial centre, whereas Coyotlatelco appears only at the lower levels. Acosta thinks that Aztec II, which appears in the upper strata and whose distribution is more restricted, was used only after the partial destruction of the principal plaza and that the latter was ravaged by the makers of this pottery. Aztec II in effect comes to be viewed as a kind of additional period. One might accordingly distinguish in very broad and general terms four phases: Teotihuacanoid pottery with Coyotlatelco; Coyotlatelco with Mazapan; Mazapan alone; and Aztec II, with or without Mazapan.

The site seems therefore to be primarily a Postclassic phenomenon, with rather slender roots reaching down to epiclassic levels, i.e., to the interim pre-Mazapan period that followed Teotihuacán's debacle. It may be fair to add that Teotihuacanoid and also Chupicuaro-type pottery has been found in nearby Tepeji del Río. But in view of Tollan's rather limited associations with earlier epochs, it would seem desirable to examine other places that figure prominently in Toltec history and where closer links with the Classic era may be sought. A summary of the known data will first be given, followed by a few tentative deductions.

TULANCINGO

This one place figures in practically every account of early migrations of the Toltecs, before they reached Tollan. It occupies a key position, situated near the limits of the altiplano and on the natural route toward the northeast, before one begins the steep descent to the Huaxteca, a region intimately linked with the legend of Quetzalcoatl and the history of Tollan.

Tulancingo can boast of a very long past, reaching back into the Late Preclassic period in the lowest stratigraphic levels; we even have two radiocarbon dates, 1950 ± 200 B.P. and 1650 ± 200.[9] Pottery related to the Toltec period and more specifically to the Coyotlatelco complex was found between the top and second levels; Aztec III and IV was located on the surface.[10] Nor are traces of intermediate periods lacking; other investigators have found objects related to Teotihuacán.[11] In addition, rock paintings occur in Tulancingo that bear witness to both Teotihuacán and Toltec influences.[12] It may be worth adding that the neighboring archaeological site of Huapalcalco recalls by its very name Quetzalcoatl's own *huapalcalli* (house of beams), mentioned by Sahagún. Huapalcalco is actually mentioned in Sahagún's "Coloquio de los Doce" among those centers still regarded as most sacred at the time of the Conquest; one does not of course know if the place in question is that which lies near Tulancingo.

It is also of interest that Huaxtec pottery has been found near Tulancingo; in fact the Huaxtec Pánuco V has definite associations with the Aztec I-Mazapan horizon.[13]

CHOLULA

The importance of this city in relation to Toltecs, and in particular to Quetzalcoatl, hardly needs stressing. Here too, however, archaeological evidence of occupation in the early Tollan period is rather meager; admittedly, if the whole of the modern Cholula could be unearthed, a fuller tale could perhaps be told.

It has already been mentioned that the Great Pyramid appears to have been deserted in the period of Cholula IV—corresponding to Teotihuacán IV—after the catastrophe that apparently befell the city at the close of Cholula III. It is not until the succeeding phase of Cholulteca I that remains of pottery, absent during Cholula IV, are again to be found on the Great Pyramid.[14]

In the following phase, Cholulteca II, the early part of which probably more or less coincided with the inception of Mazapan, constructions of some kind were erected on the Great Pyramid; this level is rich in pottery similar to Aztec I (which is now thought to coincide more with Cholulteca II than with Cholulteca I, as Noguera originally thought). The notion is now rejected that Cholula polychrome began to be manufactured at this early date; its inception belongs to Cholulteca III, and it therefore postdates the era of Tollan Xicocotitlan.

Accordingly, it may be said in résumé that at the time of the rise to power of Tollan, Cholula at least existed; after a mighty fall, it was showing signs of resuscitation, but in rather circumscribed form.

CULHUACAN

The city in the Valley of Mexico, not to be confused with the semimythical Teoculhuacán in the remote northwest, is another site habitually linked with Tollan; in a sense, it was later even to become for a limited time its legitimate heir.

Notwithstanding reports of Culhuacán's "foundation" in Toltec Postclassic times, Teotihuacán III and IV pottery is to be found in the lower strata, as well as Coyotlatelco, and then—after a gap—Aztec I.

Séjourné has concluded that the original Culhuacán was contemporary with Teotihuacán, and indeed she has unearthed there much Teotihuacán material. She thinks that this early Culhuacán may have constituted a separate political entity to the city of the Aztec I horizon, contemporary with Tollan Xicocotitlan.[15] She fully supports opinions previously expressed by Boas and Gamio designating the site as the birthplace of Aztec I. (It was Tozzer who actually called this pottery "tipo Culhuacán," just as Aztec II was known as "tipo Pyramide," i.e., Tenayuca.)

It is of interest to note that Aztec I was found by Noguera in Cholula and displays motifs very similar to those of the equivalent period in that site. Aztec I has also been located in Chalco, another place mentioned by certain sources in connection with Tollan.[16]

TEOTENANGO

This imposing site has become much better known following recent excavations under the direction of Piña Chan. In Teotenango Phase I, Teotihuacán influences are manifest, as well as pottery related to Coyotlatelco forms; architectural styles (*tablero* with cornice) are present, recalling Calpulapan and other late Teotihuacán sites. Piña Chan dates this phase as lasting from A.D. 700 to 1000.[17] It may thus somewhat predate Tollan Xicocotitlan as a major center.

YUCATAN

Ranging much farther afield, one finds among the Mayas certain archaeological evidence relating to the early Tula-Mazapan period and that which immediately preceded it. It is now generally realized that the "Mexican," or "Toltec," invasion of Yucatán, ascribed traditionally to Kukulcan in Katun 4 Ahau, may be likened to a powerful new wave generated by a tide flowing well before this.

Even in Late Classic times, "Mexican" influences (the term conventionally used for traits emanating from what is now Central Mexico) are apparent in the Maya area. For instance, Tatiana Proskouriakoff points to Tláloc and Ehécatl masks on Stela 3 at Seibal. Stela 4 at Ucanel (with date glyph 10.1.0.0.0., i.e., A.D. 849 in the Goodman-Martínez-Thompson correlation) includes an individual bearing darts and *atlatl*, reminiscent of the Toltecs. The high-relief figures on columns of the Puuc period at Oxkintok, Dzecilna, and Xcochkax are very un-Maya in type.[18] Proskouriakoff also draws attention to Stela 12 at Oxkintok; the costume of the warriors is reminiscent of others from Tula and Chichén Itza. Toltec motifs are also to be found in Kabah; a lintel of about 10.0.0.0. (A.D. 830) shows incipient "Toltec" influences.[19]

Notwithstanding the examples quoted above, the association of Long Count Maya dates with incipient Toltec style is rare, but Proskouriakoff would put the beginning of the Toltec period at somewhere between 10.3.0.0.0. (A.D. 884) and 10.8.0.0.0. (A.D. 988). This would account for the close association of Late Classic and Toltec styles in Kabah.[20]

With such assumptions Thompson is in general agreement and he also came to favor this early appearance of marked "foreign" influence in Yucatán in general and Chichén in particular. At Kabah, a radiocarbon date of 870 ± 100 was taken from wood associated with Mexican-type vessels of Tláloc and Xipe.[21] Piña Chan also finds Mexican influences in Puuc, as well as others coming from Veracruz.[22]

Ceramic Patterns

Before examining the question of pottery styles, it is perhaps pertinent to define a little more clearly the period under study. To designate the great age of Tollan Xicocotitlan, the term "Toltec" is employed in rather general terms. But this in itself is a loose expression, since, as already demonstrated, "Toltec" can be at times applied to Classic Teotihuacán and even to Late Postclassic Cholula.

The most suitable term must surely be the "Tula-Mazapan horizon," to denote the era during which Mazapan pottery flourished; this period more or less coincides with Tollan's existence as a leading power, even if it came into being before Mazapan and survived long after. Even "Tula-Mazapan" may at times appear misleading, since it might imply that this pottery originated and was principally manufactured in Tollan. As will be seen, it was more a style than a ware and was made in many places throughout Mesoamerica.

The term "horizon" is essentially an over-all rather than a regional expression. As Litvak puts it, "Horizons are determined by the discovery, in various regions, of materials that are alike or which present similar diagnostic characteristics, in contexts which make it possible to establish their isochronism. This circumstance makes possible certain inferences about homotaxiality, sinchronology, contact, etc., which give the period so defined a wider context than that of region, and stamp it with a unity by which it is typified." The author defines phases as normally functioning on a regional level. With the wide dispersal of Tula-Mazapan, it surely fits the description of horizon in this and other ways. Litvak, while drawing attention to the limitations of the usefulness of the horizon concept, also emphasizes that a horizon (as surely in the case of Tollan) possesses common elements such as similar social, religious, and governmental systems.[23]

Retracing our steps from one extreme of Mesoamerica to the other, something must now be said of possible clues concerning any pre- or proto-Toltec styles or art forms to be found toward the outer confines of Mesoamerica, in the territory that lies, say, between Tollan itself and Nayarit. But whereas so far monuments have been cited, in these ruder regions pottery fragments alone provide the evidence.

For some time past, Jiménez Moreno has referred in rather general terms to the existence of a "pre-Toltec" culture, that is to say, basically pre-Mazapan in time, in the Bajío and beyond. Such suggestions have now proved to be reasonably well founded, even if they tell us little of the actual history of Tollan itself.

In particular, La Quemada has long been associated with the notion of "proto-Toltecs" who, it was suggested, lived in an area stretching from El Zape in Durango to San Miguel Allende, Guanajuato, with the great center of La Quemada as their capital.

The culture of the region is known as Chalchihuites, to be found at a number of sites in Durango and Zacatecas and extending southward toward La Quemada itself; its latter phases seem to have continued into the Tula-Mazapan period. Surprisingly, however, Charles Kelley finds that it apparently attained its maximum extension during Teotihuacán IV and was already declining—and the Mesoamerican frontier retreating—when Tollan Xicocotitlan first rose to prominence. For instance, during the Vesuvio phase in the Río Colorado Valley, the number of sites declined, and it seems that from that time onward the population slowly diminished.[24]

In the Calichal phase in the same area, a marked demographic decline had apparently already set in by about A.D. 500.[25] In the actual

Chalchihuites cultural region, Mexican influences diminished and seem to have disappeared by a date which Kelley gives as A.D. 1000, when Tollan was approaching its apogee.[26]

Looking even farther northwestward, to Sinaloa, the Chametla horizon is to be regarded as essentially contemporary with the Central Mesoamerican Classic, by which it was considerably influenced. Equally, in the Hohokam area in the American Southwest, it is during the Sacaton phase, in the Late Classic period, that Mesoamerican influence is at its strongest.[27] Chametla was followed by the Aztatlan complex, previously considered to be of later date but now regarded as principally belonging to the earliest Postclassic, beginning, say in A.D. 750. In its later Guasave phase, many elements recall the Puebla-Mixteca culture. Certain pottery of the Aztatlan complex, such as Sinaloa red-rimmed decorated, recalls Coyotlatelco.[28]

Moreover, the Mazapan style, in the form of figurines, itself achieved a wide distribution in the northwest; for instance, these figurines and local variations have been found in Nayarit. Such specimens however may be considered to be roughly contemporary with the period of Tollan, and therefore provide no real clues as to early migrations into the area of Tollan Xicocotitlan. It should be added that Mazapan and Coyotlatelco figurines, according to Braniff, are often so similar as to be hard to differentiate. She points out that the various red-on-buff variations of the northwest enjoy almost closer affinities with Coyotlatelco.[29]

As to any pre-Mazapan, or proto-Toltec, pottery, it is only recently that some concrete evidence has become available, since Braniff has established in more positive terms something already long mooted on a theoretical basis. She presupposes in general terms, in accordance with Sanders, a pre-Toltec culture, chronologically situated at the end of the Classic period; we may thus speak of a Toltec period in the marginal zones corresponding to the Late Classic of the rest of Mesoamerica, although the origins of such a culture are still debatable.[30]

Notwithstanding the presence of a Tula-Coyotlatelco horizon in Guanajuato, Zacatecas, and Durango, as mentioned above, she concurs that the frontier of Mesoamerica had already begun to retreat toward the end of the Classic period; she calls the abandoned zone Marginal Mesoamerica, i.e., the territory previously belonging to

Mesoamerica but not included within Kirchhoff's definition of the sixteenth-century frontier. In a later passage Braniff points out that the culture of Teotihuacán did not really penetrate to these regions, where no representations of Tláloc are to be found. Essentially, of course, archaeological sites in Marginal Mesoamerica are located in places where agriculture is possible.

Braniff gives details of what may be called pre-Toltec pottery in the site of Cerro El Cóporo, in the northwest of the state of Guanajuato; the intermediate phase, Cóporo Medio, may be contemporary with Teotihuacán IV rather than III. Together with local varieties of pottery, Blanco Levantado and Cloisonné were located. In the succeeding phase of Cóporo Tardío, Blanco Levantado, or Tula Watercolored, is also still present, along with Plumbate; both of course are also found in Tollan Xicocotitlan itself. Incidentally, in Carabino, in northern Guanajuato, Plumbate appeared, together with Mazapan and Mazapan figurines, but no Coyotlatelco or the other red-on-buffs present in the San Miguel Allende area.

Basically two types of pottery link the pre-Toltec culture of Guanajuato and beyond with the full Toltec of Tollan Xicocotitlan and the Valley of Mexico.

1. *Blanco Levantado*—This appears in Guanajuato as the ordinary domestic ware of the Classic period, though it may have originated in the Late Preclassic. It enjoyed, for example, great popularity in the San Miguel phase of the Agua Espinoza site. Also, it is very commonly found in Colima, Jalisco, and Sinaloa and is thus most widely diffused, although it makes its appearance much later in Tollan itself. As Braniff puts it, "The Blanco Levantado that appears in Tula has the form and texture of that of Guanajuato and Querétaro; it suggests to us that its presence in Tula may really represent the arrival of the great mass of these people from Guanajuato and Querétaro, since this is the popular and domestic type of pottery of that area."[31]

2. *Red-on-buff*—Braniff lists the different varieties and points out that, as with Blanco Levantado, the popularity of these forms and the corresponding decoration is confined to the Classic period, as far as the marginal northwestern zones are concerned: "Various elements are to be found distributed through the marginal zones of the west and

of Oasis America (that also reaches its apogee in the Late Classic), and that seem to originate in the Middle Preclassic of the Valley of Mexico."[32]

Some of these elements reappear in the Valley of Mexico in earliest times, migrate to the northwest in the Classic period, only reappearing in Central Mexico in the Early Postclassic, thus signaling the arrival there of these marginal groups. It would seem to me that Braniff's observations are thus in admirable accord with the reports of Sahagún and others regarding a tendency for people to depart from Central Mesoamerica into the western wilds and then *return* to the middle region.

As she interprets the situation, in the Late Classic period the initial groups of such "Toltecs" reached the area of Tollan and the Valley of Mexico, bringing with them pottery with internal red-on-buff decoration; this had been traditionally used in the marginal zones during the Classic period and shared the same general traditions as Coyotlatelco. (Conflicting opinions as to whether Coyotlatelco was a local or imported style were presented in Chapter 3.)

In the early Postclassic period, according to Braniff, larger groups arrived, also composed of these northern "Toltecs." They brought with them the more common and widely used Blanco Levantado. She suggests that, though she regards Mazapan as very generally part of the Coyotlatelco red-on-buff tradition, it does not appear to be directly connected. In Guanajuato, at the end of the Classic era, these red-on-buff types had already ceased to be used. Accordingly, Mazapan may well have developed from such pottery styles, not in these remoter parts where they had gone out of fashion, but rather in the Valley of Mexico itself or in that general region, where the newcomers had settled.

Thus Braniff provides valuable archaeological evidence for something already hypothetically proposed, namely, the penetration into Central Mesoamerica of cultural influences from the marginal regions at the end of the Classic period and thereafter.

On the other hand, for the second main group which converged upon Tollan, the Nonoalcas, we must rely on what we learn from written sources, since they are hard to link with any particular ceramic tradition. It has been suggested at times by supporters of a more local point of origin for the early Coyotlatelco of the Oztotícpac phase in Teotihuacán that this was the pottery of the Olmeca-Xicallancas, or even of the Nonoalcas. However, in view of their clear connections with the region of the Gulf Coast, associations of the Nonoalcas with Coyotlatelco rest on unsure foundations, since no one would suggest that this pottery came from Tabasco, or even from the Huaxteca, where they apparently sojourned.

Mazapan, par excellence the pottery of Tollan Xicocotitlan, enjoyed, like Aztec I, a wide distribution, but lacks a well-defined point of origin. It seems to have appeared at very much the same time in the Valley of Mexico, in Tollan itself, and in zones lying farther to the northwest.

It is generally assumed that, if not Mazapan itself, at least its formative influences came from Marginal Mesoamerica; Piña Chan sees in Coyotlatelco elements that later pass both to Aztec I and to Mazapan.[33] Thus, while the latter clearly exhibits traits suggestive of the northwest, it would seem that the style came to fruition only when such elements fused with the earlier Coyotlatelco, somewhere in Central rather than Marginal Mesoamerica; the actual birthplace would be hard to pinpoint. However, wherever it originated, it gives every sign, as Florencia Muller insists, of being not a tradeware but a style. It is essential to bear in mind the distinction between the two and to appreciate that at present it is *styles* that are under discussion. In Chapter 6, the early Postclassic tradewares, Plumbate and Fine Orange, will be considered.

Once engendered, Mazapan was diffused not only throughout the northwest, as well as to San Luis Potosí, but also to certain other parts of Mesoamerica. For instance, García Payón points to the interrelation between this style and Matlatzinca.[34] Sáenz finds examples of pottery similar to Mazapan in Xochicalco.[35]

But what occupies, geographically speaking, perhaps the more focal or central position in the Early Postclassic era is not Mazapan but the above-mentioned Aztec I, which Noguera finds to be closer to Mazapan than to Coyotlatelco. This is not altogether surprising if Aztec I and Mazapan are taken to be contemporary. Acosta sees in Aztec I (hardly present in Tollan itself) unmistakable Toltec traits;

he however thinks it may be derived from Tula-Mazapan and therefore be of somewhat later date.[36] Sejourné on the other hand sees Aztec I as developing out of Teotihuacán pottery.[37] Her conclusions are of course based on her work in Culhuacán, which contains Teotihuacán material.

Aztec I is abundant in Ahuizotla;[38] it is also to be found in Chalco and in Tenayuca.[39] But it is by no means confined to the Valley of Mexico. As Noguera also noted, it is stylistically as near to Cholulteca as to Mazapan and also abounds in Cholula itself. It has now come to be more closely associated with Cholulteca II than with Cholulteca I. Aztec I is also found in Tepoztlán.[40] Something resembling this pottery is reported also in El Tajín.[41]

Thus in some respects, while hardly a tradeware like Plumbate or Fine Orange, Aztec I occupies a central position as a kind of connecting link between the various styles of the altiplano during the Tula-Mazapan horizon. On the one hand, it is connected with Mazapan itself and equally with Cholulteca II and has even been found in association with Puuc material. The fact that Aztec I, whether or not it originated there, is superabundant in Culhuacán is surely of historic as well as purely ceramic significance; as will be seen, Culhuacán seems to have played a very major part in Toltec history.

Though Acosta sees Aztec I as later than Mazapan, one cannot help wondering whether it is not at least contemporary or perhaps even a little earlier. Thompson feels that the flat-based bowl with near-cylindrical tripod supports might derive from Maya Late Classic Tepeuh, via the Isla de Sacrificios Fine Orange. Braniff, unlike Noguera, finds that Aztec I has many more decorative elements derived from Coyotlatelco than from Mazapan. In the storerooms of the Museo Nacional in Mexico there exists an interesting vessel which in type belongs to Aztec I, but which is painted red-on-buff and has Coyotlatelco designs.

And finally, since, unlike Aztec I, it appears in quantity in Tollan itself, Aztec II must also be mentioned. Franco insists that this derives from Aztec I, though Muller suggests that the two might be contemporary. Aztec II is in fact something of a chronological mystery. On the one hand, Noguera maintains that in Tenayuca it is present in the same strata as Coyotlatelco. On the other hand, Acosta insists that in Tollan it is not merely post-Coyotlatelco but post-Mazapan and belongs not to the builders but to the destroyers of the city. As such, Aztec II will figure in the latter part of our story, where its possible chronology will be discussed.

So far, a brief account has been given of the pottery of Tollan Xicocotitlan and neighboring sites, leaving also for later discussion the question of Fine Orange and Plumbate, the standard tradewares of the Early Postclassic era, but not exactly typical of Tollan itself. What has been outlined in general terms is the basic complex of the Tollan period, Mazapan-Aztec I-Cholulteca II. Slightly prior to these, Coyotlatelco and Cholulteca I appear, and slightly after them, but also partly contemporary, comes Aztec II. Mazapan seems to have definite links with Marginal Mesoamerica; Aztec I on the other hand has roots that appear to stretch in the opposite direction, toward Cholula and beyond, bearing in mind the coastal influences present in Cholulteca I and II. Cholulteca I itself is principally a blend of Aztec I, Mazapan, and Coyotlatelco traits.

Three things are especially noteworthy:

1. Certain ceramic confirmation does exist of peoples who may have reached Tollan from the northwest at a time when this Mesoamerican frontier was already beginning to recede. However, archaeology offers no corresponding traces of others who may have come there from the southeast.

2. From the ceramic point of view, Tollan Xicocotitlan presents a scene of unwonted uniformity. Notwithstanding the presence of Coyotlatelco at the beginning and Aztec II at the end, Mazapan itself continues throughout the existence of the site; its separate phases, however, have not yet been discerned. Such a situation is not exactly helpful to the historian.

3. While the earlier Coyotlatelco enjoyed a more general pattern of distribution, Mazapan tends to abound more to the north and west of the Valley of Mexico, extending well into the area of Marginal Mesoamerica.

On the contrary, Aztec I (and equally Cholulteca I and II) appears almost entirely in the south of the Valley of Mexico and beyond, in a southerly and southeasterly direction. (Aztec II however is most frequent in the north of the Valley, as well as in the Tollan region.)

One is thus faced with what might almost be called a ceramic frontier; certain types of pottery are found in the north of the Valley of Mexico and far beyond, toward Marginal Mesoamerica, while others are located in its southern part and stretch toward the coast. This in itself is a curious phenomenon, and later it will be necessary to investigate whether it corresponded or not with some political dividing line. At this stage such conclusions would surely be premature.

The Sources' Version

Turning to the written evidence for enlightenment on the early Toltecs, one discovers more ample data than the archaeologist can as yet provide, but presented in the most confusing form. Archaeology, as we have already seen, provides clues as to those who came to Tollan from the northwest; but documents offer the only evidence of any who may have arrived from the opposite direction, the Gulf Coast of Mexico.

A double problem in fact arises. First, as explained in Chapter 1, this written material must be stratigraphically reordered, paragraph by paragraph, to determine whether it truly refers to the foundation of Tollan or is more properly to be associated with its end. Little data can even pretend to apply to the centuries that intervened between the two events. As a general rule, it is best to study Mesoamerican sources horizontally, not vertically; that is to say, incidents must be taken one by one and traced horizontally through the different documents where they are mentioned. To examine vertically the whole account of one source, before passing to the next, offers no proper basis of comparison and may even confuse.

In the case of some authors, such as Ixtlilxóchitl and Sahagún, the immediate problem is less vexed and the conclusions reasonably plain. But in other accounts, such as the *Anales de Cuauhtitlán*, *Leyenda de los Soles*, *Historia de los Mexicanos*, and so on, certain data, previously taken to belong to Tollan's foundation period, can be shown by our horizontal analysis in Appendix A to appertain in reality to its end.

In addition, one faces in the present instance an added problem:

that of deciding to which of two migrant bodies a particular account may refer. Sufficient evidence survives to establish clearly the existence of two distinct ethnic groups in Tollan, the Tolteca-Chichimecas and the Nonoalcas. The *Historia Tolteca-Chichimeca* states that they were in open conflict at the time of its fall and describes their departure to distinct destinations. Strong evidence emerges that they must initially have arrived from different directions, first converging upon Tulancingo before reaching Tollan. On the one hand, we have already examined Sahagún's account of the earlier departure from Tamoanchan of "Toltecs," or "Nahuas," in a northwesterly direction. What he writes about the return of these people, now described as Tolteca-Chichimecas, will shortly be seen.

On the other hand, in discussing the Nonoalcas later in this chapter it will become clear that their original home was centered upon the Tabasco region; accordingly, they came to Tollan from the opposite direction. Once it is evident that the Tolteca-Chichimecas came to Tollan from a westerly point of departure, as is widely agreed, and that the Nonoalcas derived from the Gulf Coast, the existence of two distinct migratory contingents no longer remains in doubt. For purposes of convenience, we prefer to call the first of these currents the *eastward* migration, though its precise direction was slightly south of due east, and the second the *westward* movement, though its general course was more northwesterly.

Initially, then, it must be decided which material truly belongs to the beginnings of Tollan and therefore merits discussion in the present chapter. Such data then requires further subdivision into accounts pertaining to the eastward movement of the Tolteca-Chichimecas and to the westward-moving Nonoalcas. The making of such a distinction is not entirely simple. To take a single instance, Kirchhoff and Jiménez Moreno have disagreed as to whether Ixtlilxóchitl's second *Relación* belongs mainly to one migration or to the other. Such doubts hinge largely on the correct identification of Huehuetlapallan, or Tlapallançonco, as the point of departure is sometimes called in this instance.

Just as archaeological information tells more of the eastward migration, we shall now discover that most of the sources' material seems to apply to the Nonoalcas. We will therefore begin our process of unraveling by examining accounts taken as referring to the westward migrants, the Nonoalcas. The question of their ultimate ethnic associations will be treated later in this chapter. Let it be sufficient at this stage to say that the place Nonoalco can be identified with reasonable assurance as the region of Tabasco and southern Veracruz; with this few investigators would disagree.

THE NONOALCAS, OR WESTWARD MIGRANTS

Ixtlilxóchitl gives alternative versions of "Toltec" migrations suggestive at first sight of the eastward march of the Tolteca-Chichimecas because of certain confusing references such as Tlaxicoliucan and Xalisco (taken as the modern Jalisco), coupled in one account with mentions of California and La Mar del Sur (i.e., the Pacific Ocean). It will be seen in his longer account of these events, however, that he is really describing the Nonoalca route from Tabasco to Tulancingo; his shorter version, added rather as an afterthought to the second *Relación*, probably, but not certainly, also concerns this group.

As a preface to his main description of the Toltec migration, he tells how the people changed languages and then went to different parts of the world. This passage offers initial confirmation that he is really concerned with the Nonoalcas; as will later be explained, Nonoalco is precisely the place where people traditionally "changed languages" and in this context is linked with Tabasco.

It must always be borne in mind that such chroniclers as Ixtlilxóchitl did not themselves appreciate that two migrations had occurred; that factor became apparent only from more recent and closer studies of the *Historia Tolteca-Chichimeca.* According to the original and accepted version, common in a vague way to different chroniclers, the Toltecs came from the northwest as one main group, proceeding from the wilds of Marginal Mesoamerica, and went to Pánuco or to the Huaxteca, then to Tulancingo, and ultimately to Tollan. The accounts, partly of the eastward and partly of the westward movement, were taken from the available documents, which really described the routes of two groups. These become merged in the surviving versions into one single account of the Toltec migration. Evidently, as sometimes happens, some codices still in part surviving illustrated glyphs of two series of places, situated in opposite directions, while others, probably more complete, related only to the Nonoalcas. But seventeenth-century chroniclers, acting on preconceived notions that all Toltecs came from one place, simply scrambled these into a composite version.

To those who came eastward, Pánuco tends to be added to the itinerary, though we consider it unlikely that these people really went there; for those who proceeded westward, confusing references such as California or the Mar de Cortés (between California and Baja California) are included. One can only suppose that these were appended by the editor or chronicler to the place names already contained in an earlier document; some were taken from a different list and others merely added for the benefit of the reader, to elucidate and confirm the account. For instance, when Ixtlilxóchitl mentions California, it is presumably by way of personal explanation; it is unlikely to have occurred in the original native account.

Ixtlilxóchitl's main version of events has been reasonably well clarified by Melgarejo as pertaining to a westward migration from southeastern Veracruz; he maps its itinerary in a form that seems generally well founded. His point of view is largely accepted by Jiménez Moreno, though not by Kirchoff. The latter always insisted that Huetlapallan or Tlapallan referred to the place of that name near Guadalajara, basing his conclusion on Ixtlilxóchitl's mention of Jalisco, the Mar de Cortés, and so on, in the same context.[42]

However, not only does the route mapped by Melgarejo from south Veracruz to the Huaxteca seem convincing, but evidence from Chimalpain tends to suggest that Tlapallan really is synonymous with Tlillan Tlapallan, lying in the east, to which Quetzalcoatl fled at the fall of Tollan. Chimalpain writes of "the direction in which the Sun rises, in which he holds his Pueblos, the Pueblos that worshiped Tonatiuh, a land called Tlapallan."[43] In another passage he actually refers to "Tlapallan Nonohualco," clearly lying to the east.[44] He repeats that Nonoalco is synonymous with Tlapallan.[45] In the *Memorial Breve*, Chimalpain tells how the Teotlixca Nonohualcas left their home, Huehuetlapallan.[46] These Teotlixcas are inseparably linked with the east, as well as the Nonoalcas, as will be seen. Walter Lehmann and Gerdt Kutscher actually translate Teotlixca as "easterners" in their version of the *Memorial Breve*. Various other sources, such as the *Leyenda de los Soles*, *Historia de los Mexicanos*, and *Relación de la*

Genealogía, state that after the fall of Tollan, Topiltzin-Quetzalcoatl departed, not to Tlillan Tlapallan, but simply to Tlapallan, meaning the "red land" and surely situated in the east. This is sometimes referred to as Huetlapallan or Huehuetlapallan.

It thus clearly emerges that Huetlapallan, or Tlapallan, was a kind of legendary place of origin in the east for those who came from that direction. It may have once been an actual locality, and Melgarejo offers a plausible geographic identification. It appears to fulfill a role equivalent to that of Teoculhuacán or Chicomoztoc as a point of departure for those who came from the west. The latter had probably originally existed as real places rather than symbols; the question is discussed in Appendix A, and the conclusion reached that there is a general tendency to confuse Teoculhuacán and the city of Culhuacán in the Valley of Mexico. By Toltec times the former tended to lose its geographical identity and become little more than a figurative starting place to those who began their journey somewhere in the west.

When considering Tollan itself, Chicomoztoc, or Huetlapallan, one must never lose sight of the dual concept, the real place on the one hand, and on the other, its etherial or other-worldly counterpart.

It would thus seem more correct to take Teoculhuacán and Huetlapallan as indicating the direction of the place of departure rather than its actual location. Inevitably, accounts of tribal migrations in Mesoamerica start from a specific place, whether Chicomoztoc, Teoculhuacán, or Aztlan. But in view of this dual vision, it is often vain to seek such names on a modern map; if they ever existed at all, their exact identity has long been blurred by legend. Mentions of Huetlapallan are simply indicative of a migration starting on the Gulf Coast, while those of Teoculhuacán suggest a point of departure in Marginal Mesoamerica.

To return to Melgarejo, the latter identifies the places named by Ixtlilxóchitl as visited by the "Toltecs."[47] He first of all emphasizes that the Huetlapallan mentioned by various sources as the ancient home of these people is simply Tlapallan, the prefix "hue" or "huehue" later being added, probably because of the existence of other places called Tlapallan. As an alternative explanation, it may be remembered that the Spaniards often changed "teo" appended to names for the prefix "hue"; thus Huetlapallan may have been Teotlapallan, as a kind of counterpart to Teoculhuacán. Since Ixtlilxóchitl starts his first narrative with Tlapallançonco, this would seem to be synonymous with Tlapallan, or Huetlapallan, which plays an identical role in other texts as the place of starting out.

The other places given in Ixtlilxóchitl's route in his second *Relación* are thus identified by Melgarejo as follows:

8 Acatl (given by Ixtlilxóchitl, certainly erroneously, as A.D. 551).

Tlapalançonco. Possibly Tlapalan, a "*congregación*" of Santiago Tuxtla, Veracruz. In a nearby place called Tula pottery of the Toltec period was found.

II Tochtli (554). *Hueyxalan.* Xalaco or Xaruco, today Mandinga, a ranchería belonging to Alvarado, Veracruz.

2 Tochtli (558). *Xalixco.* This was a rancho in Soledad de Doblado, Veracruz. Today a stud farm still keeps the name. An archaeological zone is to be found there, also with Toltec-type pottery, according to Melgarejo.

9 Calli (565). *Chimalhuacan Atenco.* There is still a spring called Atenco near Paso Manco, a rancho of Cotaxtla, Veracruz.

2 Acatl (571). *Tochpan.* There is still a hacienda called Toxpan near Cordoba, Veracruz. Jiménez Moreno prefers to identify this as the town of Tuxtepec, and on the whole I agree.

Quiyahuiztlan Anáhuac (no year given). This is the town of Quiahuiztlan that the Spaniards visited, north of the present Veracruz.

I Acatl (583). *Zacatlan.* Zacatlan de las Manzanas is in the state of Puebla.

8 Tochtli (590). *Tutzapa.* The archaeological remains of this place are still to be found in the direction of Chicualoque, Coyutla, Veracruz.

I Tecpatl (596). *Tepetla.* Not located by Melgarejo. (See my own identification below.)

8 Acatl (603). *Mazatepec.* Not located by Melgarejo.

3 Acatl (611). *Xiuhcoac.* This is San Isidro, also known as Dr. Montes de Oca. A *congregación* of Alamo-Temapache, Veracruz. (See note below.)

II Acatl (619). *Iztachuexuca.* From a route given in the third *Relación* of Ixtlilxóchitl, it is clear that this is the same as Huejutla Hidalgo, or came within its jurisdiction.

3 Calli (637). *Tulantzinco.* The modern Tulancingo in the state of Hidalgo.

I Calli (661). *Tula.* End of migration.

It may be added that, while in general terms I gratefully accept this topographical information provided by Melgarejo, I cannot accept Ixtlilxóchitl's equivalent dates in the Christian calendar, which Melgarejo seems to take literally. The question of the personages mentioned in the text as "discoverers" or leaders of each of the places on the above route will be dealt with later. It may also be added that Melgarejo apparently, like Ixtlilxóchitl himself, considers this route as the only Toltec migration, rather than as one of two. On the above list of place identifications a few comments may be added.

> *Chimalhuacan Atenco.* This seems to illustrate the typical tendency of chroniclers to embellish, by way of explanation, in order to reconfirm their own preconceived notions. Ixtlilxóchitl, himself thinking in terms of one single migration, presumably saw the name of glyph Atenco, and automatically took this to be Chimalhuacan Atenco, on the Lake of Chalco, and said so.
>
> *Tutzapa.* This is more likely to be the Tuzapan southwest of Tuxpan.
>
> *Mazatepec.* I have also been unable to identify this place.
>
> *Xiuhcoac.* I am not exactly in agreement with Melgarejo on this location, and prefer to situate Xiuhcoac between Tuxpan and Chicontepec.[48]

Accordingly, one possesses a reasonably plausible and well-defined route that can be plotted on a map for the westward Nonoalca migration as far as Tulancingo. It is further authenticated by the actual presence of these Nonoalcas in Tollan Xicocotitlan; the location of Nonoalco itself in the Tabasco region is a point to which later reference will be made.

This picture is admittedly slightly blurred by Ixtlilxóchitl's additional but shorter route, given as an afterthought at the end of the second *Relación* and also included in his *Historia Chichimeca.*[49] In these he states that the Toltecs, who represented the fourth age of mankind, left their homeland and came by boat to California, on the Sea of Huetlapallan, now known as the Sea of Cortés. The date of departure is again I Tecpatl. These Toltecs then sailed down past the land of Xalixco and along the Costa del Sur (i.e., the Pacific), and passed through Huatulco. From there they went to Tochtepec, later reaching Tulancingo.

It might be tempting to take this as Ixtlilxóchitl's version of the opposite, or eastward, migration of the Tolteca-Chichimecas, of which it certainly reflects certain echoes. However, the mention of Huetlapallan, the same starting point, links this version with his longer route, already discussed. It seems more logical to assume that in his second and abbreviated account the chronicler was so convinced that he was describing the eastward journey of the Tolteca-Chichimecas that he gratuitously added further refinements to that effect, such as the Mar del Sur, California, the Mar de Cortés, and so on. Incidentally, in a map included in the first volume of Torquemada's work, the Gulf of Mexico is also shown as El Golfo de Cortés.

In particular, references to Xalixco are suggestive of northwesterly regions, but an alternative identification has been given above of a place of this name in Veracruz. The "land of Xalixco," as Ixtlilxóchitl calls it, i.e., the modern state of Jalisco, derives its name from what was in pre-Columbian times a village of modest proportions in the Tepic Valley. Xalixco is a frequently recurring name, however, and the *Historia Tolteca-Chichimeca* lists another on the Nonoalca route, mentioned in the same paragraph as Ecatepec and Cencalco, i.e., Chapultepec. Also somewhat puzzling in Ixtlilxóchitl's abbreviated account is the mention of Huatulco, since a place of that name still exists on the coast of Oaxaca. However, Torquemada comes to our assistance by explaining that Guatulco, as the Spaniards called it, was the equivalent in native language of Cuauhtochco.[50] Thus Huatulco in this instance might well be the Cuauhtochco to the west of the city of Veracruz. This place, somewhat differently located, is now called Huatusco.

On first examination the place names of this shorter version, when added together, give the impression of a rather improbable sea journey, starting in California and ending at Huatulco on the coast of Oaxaca; it is then suddenly transformed into a land trail from there northeastward to Tochtepec (presumably the modern Tuxtepec in the northeast of Oaxaca). But on further consideration it seems much more likely that this is really the *same* route as in the longer account, also starting in Tlapallan, simply told again with many omissions and with such additions as Guatulco (Cuauhtochco) and Tuxtepec. The chronicler was perhaps vaguely aware that more than one migration had taken place and was thus prompted to give two versions, without explaining why he did this.

It should be added that Veytia gives exactly the same route and dates as those of Ixtlilxóchitl's longer description. Also, the Anónimo Mexicano gives the story of a Toltec journey beginning in I Tecpatl at Huehuehtlapal (i.e., the east) and ending at Tulancingo. The names of the leaders are similar to those in the above accounts.

In addition, before seeking written references to the eastward journey of the Tolteca-Chichimecas, it is necessary to mention Torquemada, who in effect makes two brief mentions of what is apparently the westward route. He, like the Anónimo Mexicano, refers briefly to this migration by stating that the Toltecs left their home in Huehuetlapallan in I Tecpatl and after 104 years' wandering reached Tulancingo.[51] This again is clearly equivalent to the abbreviated version of Ixtlilxóchitl, since the place of departure and the date are identical.

Torquemada also gives a second account of these events, entitled "*De la Poblacon de Tullan, y su Señorío.*"[52] In this, he provides a list of rulers of Tollan having much in common with that of Chimalpain's *Memorial Breve* for the kings of Culhuacán; this, in Appendix B, has been firmly associated with the end of Tollan, not its inception. The author next mentions the people who came to Tollan at the beginning —and then, as in so many other accounts, the story suddenly switches to a description of places to which refugees later went when they abandoned the city. Such are the confusions facing the student of Toltec history!

But the passage on early Tollan in Torquemada's description clearly refers to the Nonoalcas, or westward migrants, not on account of places mentioned but from certain other details. In the first place, the author states that the Toltecs came from the north, from Pánuco (the latter is commonly referred to as lying to the north because of its situation on the Mar del Norte). He further describes them as highly skilled craftsmen, though no one knew from where they came. He adds that they wore long tunics, a point also repeated by Ixtlilxóchitl concerning the same migrants. Such garments are hardly typical of the inhabitants of the wilder zones of Marginal Mesoamerica and appertain rather to peoples coming from the opposite direction and enjoying a high level of civilization.

By the emphasis that Torquemada places upon their skills, and by his mention of Pánuco, he leaves us in little doubt that his information derives from the documents that tell of the Nonoalca journey, not that of the Tolteca-Chichimecas. The story rather curiously relates that these people left almost immediately for Cholula, since the land was already overpopulated; this surely is just another example of the tendency to telescope Tollan's history and jump from its inception to a late incident, as if the middle passages had been deliberately removed from all accounts with the same pair of scissors.

Apart from the Toltec rulers mentioned above, Torquemada gives a list of seven *señores* whom he states to have led the early Toltec migration: Tzacatl, Chalcatzin, Ehecatzin, Cohuatzon, Tzihuac-Cohualt, Tlapalmatzin, and Metzotzin. These are almost identical to the "discoverers" of different places on the Nonoalca westward journey, as given by Ixtlilxóchitl. This latter author, in another version, gives as leaders Tlacomihua, "also called Acatl" (Zaca according to yet another list provided by the same writer), Chalchiuhmatzin, Ahuecatl, Coatzon, Tziuhcoatl, Tlapalhuitz, and Huitz.[53]

These lists may seem very confused, and it appears likely that the real number of leaders was less than seven, often regarded as a magic number, since several names are duplicated in each version; for instance, Tzihuac-Cohuatl and Cohuatzon in Torquemada's list and Tlapalmetzin and Metzotzin are probably the same individual; Tzacatl (Ce Acatl) and Ehecatzin of the same group may also be identical. The actual number thus might have been four or five; both figures were traditional where leaders were concerned, as can be seen from early Mexica history, where one finds four secular leaders and one priest, or sometimes four men and one woman (perhaps really a male representing a female deity).

Highly significant in this is the constant repetition of such names as Acatl and Tzacatl or even Ehécatl, suggestive of an early Ce Acatl-Topiltzin. This and other evidence which will be presented, far from refuting in their entirety the arguments of Jiménez Moreno, would suggest that there *was* indeed a Ce Acatl, probably also called Topiltzin or Quetzalcoatl, among the original leaders of the westward Nonoalca migration at the inception of Tollan. It is improbable however that he was a sole ruler, first, because these accounts join several other names together with his; second, because collective leadership, perhaps inherited from Teotihuacán, was probably the accepted norm for the Toltecs in general as well as for certain of their descendants after the decline of Tollan.[54] One must of course not overlook the fact that this leader was not necessarily in his lifetime called CeAcatl, but would have borne the equivalent name in whatever language the Nonoalcas may have spoken at the time.

Thus it is fair to state that for the westward, or Nonoalca, migration we do have not only a reasonably satisfactory itinerary but a somewhat garbled list of leaders in different sources, which include such names as Tzacatl, Acatl, and Ehécatl among the total. This person, a collective leader, would surely himself, unlike the later Topiltzin, son of Mixcoatl, have been a Nonoalca, strongly influenced by Huaxtec traditions; it will later be seen that he is linked in other sources with Pánuco.

THE TOLTECA-CHICHIMECA, OR EASTWARD, ROUTE

When one turns to the eastward migrants from marginal Mesoamerica, usually called Tolteca-Chichimecas, one finds on examination that the material is scantier than might perhaps be supposed. In fact, only one major informant, Sahagún, writes unquestionably of these people.

In Chapter 3 his account was analyzed, telling how, at the collapse of Teotihuacán, the Nahuas, or Toltecs, dispersed, in addition to the various other peoples. One learns that they wandered for a long time and were sorely afflicted. "They eventually went to settle at a place in the desert. At this place there were, or as one said, there are, seven caves. These different people made them [the caves] serve as their temples; they went to make their offerings there for a long time. No longer is it remembered how long they resided there. Then the one whom the Tolteca worshipped spoke to them; he said to them: 'Turn back. You shall go from whence you came.' Then they went to make offerings there in Chicomoztoc. Then they departed. First they came to arrive at a place called Tollantzinco. Then they passed over to Xicocotitlan, called Tollan."[55]

After this passage, which like so many other sources, suddenly switches literally in mid-paragraph, from the beginning of Tollan to its

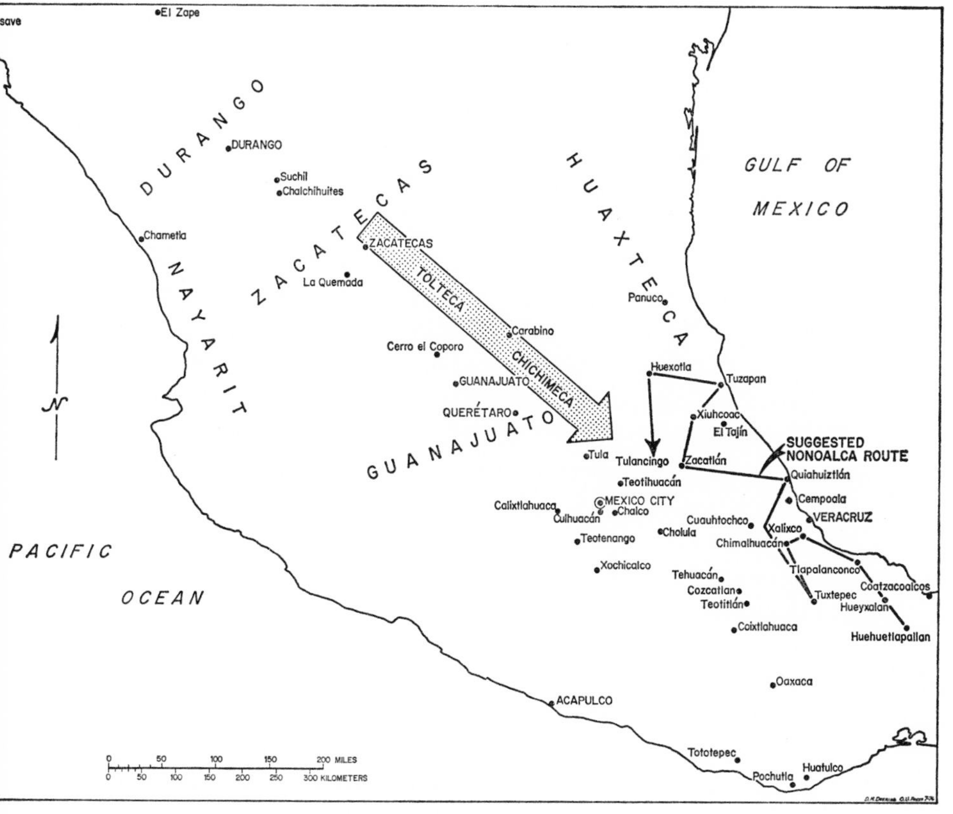

The Approach to Tollan

end, Sahagún writes briefly of an apparently *westward* migration of Chichimecs and Michoaques. This incident is then immediately followed by the unquestionably post-Toltec migrations of Tepanecs and Acolhuas.

From Sahagún's account one may note the following:

1. The story obviously covers a long stretch of time, extending from the earliest wanderings of these "Nahuas," after leaving Teotihuacán, until they finally reached Tollan Xicocotitlan.

2. In the author's words, they had "*returned*" to this place, after

venturing even farther into the outer marches of Mesoamerica. As Kirchhoff always insisted, many if not most of the peoples settled in Central Mexico in the Late Postclassic period are reported to have wandered forth into partly Chichimec territory and then come back.

3. Absolutely no information is provided as to the route to Tollan taken by these migrants, apart from the mention of Tulancingo.

In terms of mere methodology, the reader may be left asking why only this particular passage of Sahagún is here quoted, as pertaining to the Tolteca-Chichimecas. But in this instance, matters are clearer than usual, and interpretation of the text presents fewer complications. It is not hard to see that passages which preceded the words quoted by their very essence refer to the Teotihuacán diaspora; likewise, what follows these words concerns people such as the Acolhuas, whose entry upon the scene is indubitably post-Tollan. The mention of Tulancingo provides a further clue as to their identity.

When one comes to seek other accounts of this eastward migration to Tulancingo and Tollan Xicocotitlan, it soon becomes apparent that he confronts a mirage; much material when seen in distant outline appears to be applicable, but on closer inspection it always turns out to be something different.

On the face of it, it all appears perfectly simple; such valuable documents as the *Anales de Cuauhtitlán*, the *Leyenda de los Soles*, the *Historia de los Mexicanos por sus Pinturas*, and the like, obligingly start their story with a narrative of ostensibly pre-Tollan events. They make this abundantly clear by relating the birth or the early feats of a Ce Acatl-Topiltzin-Quetzalcoatl, or a garbled combination of such names, who is usually thereafter described as the first ruler of Tollan. Such accounts then mostly indulge in the universal trick of switching suddenly from the beginning of Tollan to its end, or at least to a period when this Ce Acatl-Topiltzin departed to Tlillan Tlapallan or to some equally remote destination, in certain cases accompanied by most of the population of Tollan. Part, though not all of this story is presented in each source.

So far, so good. And since certain documents say or imply that their initial passages concern the early Tollan period, they have somewhat naturally been taken at their face value. Accordingly, a reconstruction of early Tollan history has been put forward by Jiménez Moreno, which revolves around the personality of Mixcoatl and his son Ce Acatl-Topiltzin; the latter became first ruler of Tollan, after ranging far and wide in his youth, as a kind of incipient Alexander the Great, even conquering parts of the coast of Guerrero, which the Aztec armies were unable to subdue before the reign of Ahúitzotl. This interpretation of the beginnings of Tollan has received such wide acceptance that it now even appears in guidebooks of modern Mexico!

In all fairness, it should be added that Jiménez Moreno insists (personal communication) that one period cannot be integrally assessed by the use of data from another and that Aztec parallels are not always valid for Toltec times—a point with which I fully concur. In particular, he insists that in earlier periods many territories were less thickly populated and could be thus more quickly subjugated. It will be argued in Chapter 6 that Tollan's population was too limited even at the end, let alone at the beginning, for the subjugation and retention of vast areas. For the present, let it be sufficient to mention that lightning conquests in the Old World were made on horseback, and that Topiltzin's means of transport were his own legs, just as for Ahuitzotl!

In particular, two facts become apparent. First, these differing accounts in the various documents are really part of one and the same story, all possibly drawn from a single basic source of information. Secondly, the narrative itself seems clearly to be concerned in the main with the end of Tollan, not its beginning; it therefore, as far as we are concerned, falls outside the scope of the present chapter.

Kirchhoff has discussed the whole question in some detail, and his conclusions on the relationship between Huemac and Quetzalcoatl at the end of Tollan will be analyzed in our last chapter.

As he emphasizes, from the sixteenth century until the present day, two radically opposed attitudes have been adopted; one of these maintains that Quetzalcoatl was the first Toltec ruler and Huemac the last; the other viewpoint treats them as more or less contemporary with each other and with the fall of Tollan.

Kirchhoff mentions that Jiménez Moreno, the most distinguished investigator of ancient Mexican history of our times, has adopted the first stance: Kirchhoff himself bases his conclusions upon the second. He first comments that Jiménez Moreno builds his thesis upon the account of the *Anales de Cuauhtitlán*, which is partially supported by the *Relación de la Genealogía*. Kirchhoff then goes on to cite a number of sources, including Sahagún, Muñóz Camargo, Chimalpain, and Torquemada, who appear to give weight to the contrary point of view.[56] These questions will be fully reviewed in the last chapter. For the present, it may be sufficient to state that, having expressed opinions on the Nonoalca pilgrimage that concur with those of Jiménez Moreno rather than with Kirchhoff, on this occasion I basically support the latter, though not entirely, as will be seen later. In fact, by insisting that a Quetzalcoatl or Topiltzin was present at Tollan's inception, as well as at the end, we go at least some way toward meeting Jiménez Moreno's views. Where we differ is in maintaining, like Kirchhoff, that the Topiltzin described as son of Mixcoatl belongs to the period of Tollan's collapse, not of its foundation.

The sources that describe what one may call the Mixcoatl saga are the *Anales de Cuauhtitlán*, *Leyenda de los Soles*, *Historia de los Mexicanos*, "*L'Histoyre du Mechique*," Muñóz Camargo's *Historia de Tlaxcala*, and *Historia Tolteca-Chichimeca*. The Torquemada and Ixtlilxóchitl writings on early Tollan, as well as those by Veytia and the Anónimo Mexicano, already discussed, appear to concern the Nonoalca migrants from Pánuco, and omit Mixcoatl and his friends and relations.

The approximate relationship between the documents concerned can only be established by a close comparative analysis, as set out in the table and notes in Appendix A. In this horizontal study, each event or episode has been listed across the page as it occurs throughout the various documents, and the different versions (if any) can then be easily assimilated.

In Apppendix A, where the reader will find my reasoning fully set out, it will be seen that one is dealing basically with a series of events (fifteen are listed in Table A) of which each document includes some, but none contains all. The *Historia Tolteca-Chichimeca* differs from the rest in that Mixcoatl is not the principal chief, but only one among various leaders. From a cursory examination of Table A, it becomes obvious that the Mixcoatl story as told by the *Anales de Cuauhtitlán* and the *Leyenda de los Soles* is virtually the same, with certain alternative embellishments. Similarly, the versions of the *His-*

toria de los Mexicanos, the *Relación de la Genealogía* and the *Origen de los Mexicanos* are inseparably linked; at times even the very same words are used in the different works. Through the common inclusion of such strange incidents as the descent of the two-headed deer, to take a single example, it can be concluded that the accounts of this saga in these two above-mentioned groups of sources are beyond all doubt one single story told many times over.

Second, by the same token, one can see from Table A that the Muñóz Camargo account is unquestionably associated with that of the *Anales de Cuauhtitlán/Leyenda de los Soles*; the shooting of Itzpapálotl at the outset of the migration is only one of many striking similarities. To take another instance, the repeated mention in each of such people as Xiuhnel and Mimich and of place names such as Comallan and Mazatepec link these first-mentioned accounts with Muñóz Camargo.

Third and finally, a close parallel is apparent between names of leaders and of places given in the *Historia Tolteca-Chichimeca* and in the other sources, particularly Muñoz Camargo (*see* Appendix A, Notes 4 and 13). The *Historia Tolteca-Chichimeca* is of course indisputably post-Toltec and thus demonstrates the relatively late occurrence of this course of events described in the various other versions. Muñoz Camargo's account is also ostensibly post-Tollan and has absolutely nothing to do with the city's inception; according to the author, it concerns the later foundation of Tlaxcala.

Jiménez Moreno feels that, where these two latter sources are concerned, the incidents of the first part of their story are mere embellishments taken from historical events of the pre-Tollan period and tacked on to the Muñóz Camargo narrative; they are thus mere "borrowed plumes" such as are described in Chapter 1 in connection with the Mexicas. This view involves a difference in interpretation of the same data such as must inevitably arise in historical studies. However, I find the Muñóz Camargo account to be of a generally factual nature and prefer to take it at its face value, as a continuous narrative leading up to the conquest of Tlaxcala, in undeniably post-Tollan times. Moreover, the place names listed in Appendix A for the *Historia Tolteca-Chichimeca* figure in a long account of localities visited. If one rejects those that coincide with other accounts, such as Comallan, one must surely reject them all. These are only a few of the many reasons on which my interpretation is based, and which will be given more fully in Chapter 8.

In my view, therefore, by association and implication the other accounts mentioned above must perforce mainly concern the end of Tollan, not its beginning. The *Historia de los Mexicanos* and related sources say that Topiltzin was first ruler of Tollan, but then indulge in the switching trick, with which one is by now fully familiar, and proceed immediately to an account of decline and dissolution, in which Topiltzin leads away the *macehuales*. It should also be added that the *Anales de Cuauhtitlán* provide a long additional story of the end of Tollan, told after the Mixcoatl episode.

As Appendix A and Chapter 8 explain in much more detail, Mixcoatl, also referred to as Totepeuh and Camaxtli, is really a leader of Teochichimec origins, one of a group who came from Chicomoztoc at the end of the Toltec period, ostensibly to give support to those Tolteca-Chichimecas already installed in Cholula. No doubt, when their migration took place, Mixcoatl and his followers were no mere nomads, but a well-organized fighting body; they were in a sense what Kirchhoff called ex-Chichimecs, already to a considerable degree Toltecized. This Mixcoatl conquered Culhuacán and neighboring cities, and subsequently his son, the latter-day Ce Acatl-Topiltzin, was born of a local woman of noble birth. Their doings can safely thus be left to Chapter 8, which concerns not the rise of Tollan but its fall. The chronological study and table in Appendix B seek to provide dates for this Mixcoatl and Ce Acatl, and for the dynasty (mainly pertaining to Culhuacán rather than to Tollan) which I believe that they founded and which was still ruling in Culhuacán when the Mexicas arrived in Chapultepec. This reigning family will be shown to have been in conflict with Huemac, the rival of Ce Acatl-Topiltzin, who is sometimes also associated with the beginnings of Tollan, for instance by Ixtlilxóchitl; in nearly all accounts, however, he belongs to its fall, as Appendix B and Chapter 8 make clear.

What concerns us in this chapter is accordingly not the Mixcoatl saga but a curious interpolation, occurring in all sources except the *Historia Tolteca-Chichimeca*, which genuinely seems to refer to early Tollan. Perhaps the most significant of these passages comes in the

Anales de Cuauhtitlán. It tells how in the year 2 Tochtli, Quetzalcoatl arrived at Tulancingo, where he stayed for four years; he had come there from the Huaxteca. The text then relates that in 5 Calli the Toltecs brought this Quetzalcoatl to Tollan, to make him their ruler, and mentions that according to the original document from which the account was taken he was also a priest.[57]

This episode finds a faint and apparently not unrelated echo in the *Historia de los Mexicanos*, which says that Topiltzin was made first ruler of Tollan. The *Origen de los Mexicanos* has a similar passage; the latter source actually suggests the possibiilty of confusion and writes of "*el Toplice de los Mexicanos*," as it seemingly calls a latter-day Topiltzin. At this point the source is referring to the fall of Tollan, and for "*Mexicanos*" it might be correct to read "invaders" or even "Chichimecs."

In such instances one must seek to distinguish between what the chronicler gleans from other documents and what he himself adds by way of elucidation or comment. Just as Ixtlilóchitl and others thought in terms of one Toltec migration, so most of these account of the Mixcoatl saga envisaged one Topiltzin, when really two or more had existed and had been merged by the narrators into one person. The doings of one of the various original Toltec leaders, probably arriving with the Nonoalcas from the Pánuco area at the beginning of Tollan, are thus briefly interpolated into the story of the last Ce Acatl-Topiltzin, son of Mixcoatl, apparently coming from Marginal Mesoamerica. Into the story of the latter-day Ce Acatl are inserted small news items about the former bearer of that name, such as the reference to his becoming first ruler of Tollan. A similar interpolation to that effect occurs at more or less the same point in various accounts; this suggests that it was already present in the original source from which these versions were taken.

Muñóz Camargo, in a kind of insert, also comments pertinently on the puzzle of Quetzalcoatl's origin; as in the *Origen de los Mexicanos*, he differentiates between two Quetzalcoatls, or Topiltzins. He remarks that, although the latter was said to have come from Pánuco, and from there to Tulancingo, in point in fact all the people of whom he is writing (i.e., Xiuhnel, Mimich, Mixcoatl, and so on) came from the *west*.[58] He thus tacitly draws a clear distinction between any Quetzalcoatl arriving from Pánuco and the other Quetzalcoatl, whom he describes as the son of Mixcoatl Camaxtli, the Chichimec leader who proceeded from the opposite direction.

It would indeed seem that the references cited above to a Quetzalcoatl from the Huaxteca or Pánuco and to a Topiltzin who was the first ruler of Tollan are all to be associated with the westward-moving Nonoalcas rather than with the Tolteca-Chichimecas, let alone with the Teochichimecs of Mixcoatl. They also bear a resemblance to Torquemada's reported people of high cultural attainments who reached Tollan from Pánuco, led by Quetzalcoatl, and whom we have already identified with the Nonoalcas.[59]

It is not unreasonable to suppose that Pánuco or the Huaxteca was visited by the Nonoalcas but not by the Tolteca-Chichimecas. It must be borne in mind that comparatively close links existed between the various peoples of the lands of the Gulf Coast, which included the Nonoalcas and the Huaxtecas. Moreover, Ixtlilxóchitl's account, apparently of the Nonoalca journey, takes them, among other places, to Xiuhcoac, before reaching Tulancingo; for the Tolteca-Chichimecas, Sahagún mentions Tulancingo, but not Pánuco or the Huaxteca. This therefore confirms the impression, already stressed, that the Quetzalcoatl or Ce Acatl mentioned in connection with the foundation of Tollan would have been a Nonoalca rather than a Tolteca-Chichimeca. It has already been demonstrated that many manifestations of the cult of the new Quetzalcoatl are linked with the Huaxteca. Any human leader bearing that name (or Tzacatl, Zaca, and the like) would obviously be in some form a priest of the deity. It is therefore suggested that this Ce Acatl was one of several Nonoalca leaders who arrived from the Huaxteca, where they might have been settled for some time. They would probably have been adherents of the god Quetzalcoatl in their original Tabascan home, perhaps with greater emphasis upon his manifestation as the Morning Star rather than as the Wind. The Ehécatl aspect of the god is more to be associated with the Huaxteca. It may have been here that the Wind and the Morning Star first emerged into one deity.

Thus there occurs on the one hand in the *Anales de Cuauhtitlán* and the accounts of Torquemada and Muñóz Camargo mention of a Quetzalcoatl who came from the direction of Pánuco, together with references in certain sources to a first Toltec ruler also bearing that name, or called Topiltzin. On the other hand, the lists already quoted from Ixtlilxóchitl and Torquemada contain names such as Acatl, Tzacatl, Zaca, and Ehécatl among the early leaders *before* the Toltecs arrived at Tollan. These appellations and the Quetzalcoatl described as coming from Pánuco all seemingly refer to the same person, a Nonoalca chief.

Ixtlilxóchitl incidentally also makes mention, in a passage preceding those already quoted, of a Quetzalcoatl who came to Cholula, where a temple was erected in his honor on the ruins of the Great Pyramid destroyed at the end of the third age of man, which the author describes as that of the Olmeca-Xicallancas, before the Toltecs.[60] This reference may also be taken to apply to an early Toltec leader, though this cannot be certain.

Accordingly, to summarize what it has so far been possible to glean from the written sources in this chapter: There is on the one hand Ixtlilxóchitl's account of the Nonoalca migration westward from Huetlapallan. In addition, reports from eight sources can be cited ostensibly concerning the foundation of Tollan but which in Appendix A are shown to belong primarily to its end; they mostly contain short interpolated passages, similar in nature, concerning Tollan's inception and the arrival of Topiltzin from Pánuco. These references can also be seen on examination to refer, not to the eastward-moving Tolteca-Chichimecas, but to the Nonoalca migration from the Gulf Coast; substantial evidence has been quoted of the presence of a Ce Acatl-Topiltzin-Quetzalcoatl among the leaders of this movement. The *Anales de Cuauhtitlán* say that he was a priest of the god, and it might not be too rash a speculation to suggest that the leadership might have consisted of four secular chiefs and one priest, as in other Mesoamerican migrations.

As regards the eastward Tolteca-Chichimeca trek, one is thus left only with Sahagún's account of what happened to the "Nahuas" after they left Teotihuacán and of how they returned. Archaeology, as has been seen, offers certain clues as to the provenance of these people; documentary evidence on the contrary principally concerns the Nonoalcas. Sufficient let it be to say that a long drawn-out process may have been involved rather than any sudden happening. The Tolteca-

Chichimecas may have gradually moved into the region of Tollan and beyond over a period of many decades. Similarly the Nonoalcas, even if they originally came from Tabasco, may have settled in the Huaxteca for some time.

As to the manner and place of merging of these two migratory currents, a few suggestions will follow at the conclusion of this chapter, after consideration of the question of chronology and a more detailed study of the problem of Nonoalca origins.

Who Were They?

From certain archaeological evidence and from a few written sources, it has been possible to learn something respecting the actual provenance of the different founders of Tollan Xicocotitlan. But having studied their geographical origins, it still remains to ask in more precise terms: who were these peoples and what were their ethnic and linguistic affiliations?

Let us first take the Tolteca-Chichimecas, that is to say, the first known people of that appellation who came to Tollan, and not their successors of post-Tollan times. The very name presents something of a contradiction in terms and escapes exact definition. Taken at its face value, "Toltec" implies, as has been seen in Chapter 2, all that is oldest and most refined in Mesoamerica; "Chichimec," on the other hand, has opposite connotations, relating mainly to the new and barbarous!

It may be useful first to define the etymology of "Chichimec," which is not derived, as often thought, from *chichi-mecatl*, meaning "dog-cord"; this would give as the plural "Chichimecame," not "Chichimeca," the version always employed. The name comes notionally from the place name Chichimani, giving "Chichimecatl," plural "Chichimeca." This would mean "place of sucking," i.e., "place of the newly born," or thus "place of the young." Chichimecs are the young or new peoples, and "Tolteca-Chichimeca" implies a new people who have already become older and more civilized.

Perhaps the matter can be further clarified by first stating what the Tolteca-Chichimecas were not. To quote Sahagún, "The Tolteca are also called Chichimeca-Otonchichimeca. The Michoaque are also called Chichimeca. The people to the east are not called Chichimeca, they are called Olmeca, Uixtotin, Nonoalca."[61] That is to say, whatever their remoter origins, Tolteca-Chichimecas are *not* people who have come directly from the "east"; the latter term may be taken in this context to constitute the lands beyond the Sierra Nevada, from the Puebla-Tlaxcala Valley to the Gulf Coast, i.e., the territory occupied in particular by the Olmeca-Xicallancas, called by Sahagún "Olmeca, Uixtotin, Nonoalca."

Equally, the Tolteca-Chichimecas are most certainly not Teochichimecs, the true, or extreme, Chichimecs, depicted in codices as nomad hunters, dressed in skins and possessing neither agriculture nor fixed dwellings. Parenthetically, one should add that there are many differences of degree among these Teochichimecs themselves; notwithstanding their rusticity, Sahagún's informants describe them as excellent craftsmen, stonecutters, and feather workers.[62] Such skills were presumably learned from more settled peoples and would have hardly been practiced by the Teochichimecs in their pristine state but rather learned in order to satisfy the more fastidious tastes of other masters. Sahagún actually explains how the civilizing process took place, as the Teochichimec hunters came to learn a little Nahuatl, donned tattered garments, and sowed their own little plots of maize.[63] What Sahagún therefore really describes are Teochichimecs already in full process of assimilation.

The whole Chichimec question is complicated, and it will be examined at greater length in another volume. The term is generic, embracing many and diverse groups. There is, for instance, no specific Chichimec language. Even their geographic location was unstable. At the very time of the foundation of Tollan, as already mentioned, the frontier between settled Mesoamerica and the more nomad Teochichimecs was already fluid, and it receded during the Toltec era.

Our Tolteca-Chichimeca migrants to Tollan, for their part, were thus neither coastal peoples and easterners, like the Nonoalcas, nor were they nomad Teochichimecs. The possible presence of Otomís among these original inhabitants of Tollan should be borne in mind. They also occupied a rather intermediate cultural level, and it was they who remained in occupation of the Tollan region in the Late Postclassic period. People of Cascan affiliation and other pure Chichimecs may also have been included among the early migrants; the Tolteca-

Chichimecas were by no means necessarily a homogeneous body, any more than the Mexicas, who came from the same direction at a later stage in Mesoamerican history and were also in a sense Tolteca-Chichimecas, that as to say, half-nomad and half-civilized. Indeed, the term is sufficiently broad to include not only those who first created Tollan and those who later left for Cholula, but even certain others who apparently caused its ruin. Sahagún describes certain Tolteca-Chichimecas as Nahuas, who spoke in a manner less polished than the Mexicas, although they pronounced words similarly.

The Sahagún text continues, "These thus mentioned called themselves Chichimeca Mochanecatoca, that is to say Tolteca. It is these who caused the Toltecs to disperse when they went away, when Topiltzin Quetzalcoatl entered the water, when he went to settle in the place of the red colour, the place of burning."[64]

The equivalent Spanish text of his *Historia*, which often varies substantially from the *Florentine codex*, the product of his informants, runs as follows: "Although they were Nahuas, they were also called Chichimecs and were said to be of the generation of the Toltecs, who remained behind when the other Toltecs left their city and dispersed." It would seem from this account as if some Tolteca-Chichimecas stayed to the last, after the departure not only of those who went to Cholula but also of the Nonoalcas.

Like many others, the term "Tolteca-Chichimeca" thus tended to change its meaning. Originally it seems to have applied to the less civilized of the two groups who first came to Tollan. These were not pure Chichimec, but occupied an intermediate position in the cultural scale, rather as did the Otomís at the time of the Conquest. Later, toward the end of Tollan's great period, the name was applied to those who migrated to Cholula and there engendered one of the highest manifestations of Mesoamerican civilization. The term was also used at this stage or a little later to describe others, such as the Tepanecs and Acolhuas, who were not strictly speaking original Toltecs, but as vassals of the latter may have acquired much of their culture and learned their language.

Even the expression "Chichimec" itself later takes on new meanings, apart from those already mentioned. To the Mexicas, the appellation was something of which to be proud rather than the reverse, as denoting a measure of rugged manliness or hardiness, originally acquired in the northwestern marches; in other words, it represented the epitome of a warrior, as opposed to the more effete city dweller. The Mexicas sometimes called themselves Chichimecas, but could better be classified as latter-day Tolteca-Chichimecas. In fact, the original people of this name who founded Tollan may have been not unlike the Mexicas of the migration, that is to say, Nahuatl speakers, who were not altogether ignorant of agriculture or even simple building construction and who thus occupied an intermediate cultural level. The Mexicas and the pre-Tollan Tolteca-Chichimecas possessed other qualities in common, such as military valor and a Spartan endurance in face of adversity.

Documentary detail on the original Tolteca-Chichimecas is hard to find. No names of leaders survive which can with any assurance be ascribed to these people, nor can it be said precisely from where they came beyond a general region or direction being indicated. I shall later show that they were probably not worshipers of Quetzalcoatl and possessed no Ce Acatl-Topiltzin as leader. Reports of Tollan's collapse reveal their possible associations with Tezcatlipoca; Jiménez Moreno even regards this god's *tlachialoni* as a symbol imported from the northwest.

In addition, they were probably votaries of the Hunting God Mixcoatl, himself on occasion closely identified with Tezcatlipoca as well as with Quetzalcoatl. It was possibly only later that Mixcoatl became fused with Tlahuizcalpantecuhtli, an aspect of Quetzalcoatl whose adornments are at times almost indistinguishable from those of the Hunter God. This fusion may have been a gradual development; it must be borne in mind that the representations of Quetzalcoatl-Tlahuizcalpantecuhtli that predominate in Tollan are not usually to be ascribed to the early period.

In résumé, then, the Tolteca-Chichimecas were mainly Nahua speakers who came to Tollan via Tulancingo from Marginal Mesoamerica, following an uncertain route. They were not necessarily a very homogeneous body, as their somewhat generic appellation makes fairly clear. Their numbers may have included several disparate elements, of varying cultural attainments and ethnic allegiances. As Sahagún specifically states, they were returning, having previously gone forth into the wilds at the end of the Classic period. They appear to have brought with them from the northwest their red-on-buff and Blanco Levantado pottery, but, as the very nature of such wares suggests, their cultural attainments were at the time modest.

Concerning the Nonoalcas, who came to Tollan from an easterly direction, information is more abundant. As already emphasized, they were to constitute the intellectual elite; they arrived from an area to which the *tlamatinime*, or wise men, are reported to have dispersed after the dissolution of Teotihuacán, bearing off with them the written codices and the ancient lore. Possibly to be included among the Nonoalcas of Tollan was a band of Amantecas, the traditional feather workers, who were to appear not only in Tollan but later in Tenochtitlan, to which Seler thought that they had been brought by force. These Amantecas are ever present as a kind of connecting link between one culture and its successor. Jiménez Moreno considers that they came originally from Teotihuacán, a suggestion which Piña Chan supports.[65]

The true meaning of the place name "Nonoalco" presents many problems. In practice "Nonoalca" is often thought to have implied those who spoke Nahuatl differently or even poorly, though even this is not certain. Such a notion apparently became also applicable to the manner in which other languages were spoken; for instance, the Itzas were referred to as *U nunil ah itza* (*nunil* is an apparent corruption of Nonoalca), meaning "those who speak our language imperfectly."[66]

But as with "Tollan" and "Toltec," one should seek first the etymology of the place Nonoalco rather than that of the Nonoalca people. The more currently accepted meaning of "Nonoalco," proposed by Seler, is "where the language changes," stemming from the Nahuatl word *nontli*, meaning "dumb." This interpretation, for Seler, follows the same principle which led the Russians and other Slavs to call Germany *Njemetzija* (the land of the dumb), not because the Germans could not speak at all but because their language was different.[67]

Lehmann follows Seler in translating "Nonoalco" as "foreign land."[68] This general notion as to its meaning has been accepted by leading investigators, including Jiménez Moreno. Ruz also, looking at the problem from the Maya end, calls "Nonoalco" "the land where the languages change."[69]

Such an interpretation, however, has not met with universal acceptance. Garibay points out that the adjective *nontli* would produce the toponym "Nononco" or "Nonpan." For this author, "Nonoalco" derives from *onoc*, meaning "to be stretched out," or thus to be established in a place, or living there. Siméon translates this verb as "*etre couché, étendu, allongé,*" meaning "to lie down" as much as "to be stretched out," and thus implicitly to settle. For Garibay, the noun would be formed from the impersonal form, *onca*; from this would come *onoalli* or *neonoalli*, which by contraction from *onoalco* could become Nonoalco. Its meaning is thus simply "in the inhabited place." Incidentally, only Torquemada and Clavijero use the form "Onohualco" rather than "Nonohualco."[70]

Sullivan, however, suggests in personal communication that the particle *ne* is a reflexive pronoun for the impersonal or passive form of a transitive verb. *Onoc* as an intransitive verb could not be compounded with this reflexive particle *ne*. Therefore, Garibay's interpretation is not altogether satisfying from the purely etymological point of view, apart from its lack of any very positive direct meaning. Sullivan tentatively proposes that "Nonoalco" could be derived from the adverb *nononcua*, meaning "separately" or "independently"; from this could perhaps be formed a noun *nononcualli*; with the locative suffix *co*, such a substantive would in turn give the place name Nononcualco. In Nahuatl, *n*'s tend to be lost; Nononcualco might have become first Nonocualco and in course of time Nonohualco (Nonocualco is very clumsy to pronounce). Accordingly, given the meaning of "separately" for *nononcua*, Nonoalco becomes "the place of separateness." Sullivan tentatively offers such an interpretation as etymologically sound, though not necessarily semantically correct, inasmuch as the two Nahuatl dictionaries extant lack many words. I myself would add, however, that such a derivation, implying "separateness" rather than mere "settlement," does make very much the better sense of the two. Admittedly Seler's rendering of people who are "dumb," or "speechless," has rather the same implication, but its etymology is unsatisfactory, as explained.

In actual fact, the Nonoalcas were and remained a separate people. As already noted, they did not in Tollan come to form one single entity with the Tolteca-Chichimecas, and at its fall departed alone and separately to a separate destination.

Having dealt with the question of etymology, one must now ask: just where was this Nonoalco of Mexican and Mayan fable? At least on this point agreement is more general. Nonoalco was on the coast of the Gulf of Mexico, probably occupying the region of Tabasco and neighboring territories. To quote Torquemada, "the Lands of Onohualco, which are situated by the sea, and are those which today we call Yucatán, Tabasco and Campeche; the natives in pre-Christian times called them Onohualco."

Ixtlilxóchitl associates Nonoalco with southeast Veracruz and refers to *coatzaqualcas*, *nonoalcas*, *xicalancas*. He is in all probability referring here not to the town of Coatzacoalcos but to the sixteenth-century province, which stretched as far westward as the River Papaloapan.[71] Clavijero writes of "towards Onohualco and Yucatán."[72] The *Memorial Breve* uses the phrase "Huehuetlapallan Nonoalco."[73] As already explained, Huehuetlapallan almost certainly lay in the same easterly direction. In the dirge from the *Cantares* on Quetzalcoatl's flight from Tollan, Nonoalco is linked to Xicalanco.[74] In Durán it is stated that Axayácatl sent invitations to a ceremony to the "*Nonohualcas, cempoaltecas y quiahuiztecas*."[75] Quiahuiztlan, on the Gulf Coast, had of course not yet been absorbed by the Aztec Empire.

One may already note in this last reference that, like other appellations, Nonoalco tended to develop a different sense in distinct epochs. In this latter context, it is not merely the Tabasco region but the whole Gulf Coast, though any tendency to ascribe wider territories to the Nonoalcas may derive from some confusion between these and the Olmeca-Xicallancas. The former probably to a certain extent shared common origins with the latter, and Kirchhoff was almost certainly right in associating the two. However, the part is not equal to the whole, and a certain separate identity is usually conceded to the Nonoalcas; for instance, Motolinía's list of the sons of Iztac Mixcoatl and Ilancue included both Nonoalcatl and Olmecatl Xicalancatl.[76]

Modern investigators have generally accepted as correct the identification of Nonoalco with the Tabasco region. In this Seler, Lehmann, and Jiménez Moreno concur.[77] Borhegyi, writing of the Pipils, locates the Nonoalcas as living near the Laguna de Términos, where they constituted a very complex ethnic group composed of Gulf Coast Huaxteca-Mayas and Tajinized migrants from Teotihuacán.[78]

From the Maya land one finds confirmation of the above contentions concerning Nonoalco and certain Nonoalca connections with the Olmeca-Xicallancas. In the *Anales de los Cakchiqueles* (Recinos), the latter arrive at a place called Tepeu Oliman, where they meet warriors of the Nonoalcats and Xulpils, who lived on an island near the seacoast.[79] Krickeberg identifies this Tepeu Oliman with the land of the rising sun.[80] Scholes and Roys, Thompson, and Ruz all associate Nonoalco with Tabasco and southwest Campeche.[81]

But like the Olmeca-Xicallancas, the Nonoalcas are at times associated with almost the whole Gulf Coast. Chimalpain writes of the arrival in 7 Tecpatl of a group of Nonoalca affiliation who called themselves "people of Panohuayan, or Pánuco."[82]

The true ethnic affinities of the Nonoalcas are rather hard to trace; in Tollan they stand out as par excellence the *Kulturvolk*, the bearers of the most prized arts and skills of Mesoamerica and the guardians of its ancient lore. On the other hand, as already emphasized, they appear to be linked with the Olmeca-Xicallancas, who as a general category show few signs of comparable attainments.

The same problems tend to arise if one studies the situation of the Nonoalcas in the Teotitlán del Camino region, where they took refuge after the fall of Tollan; this migration is reported principally in the *Historia Tolteca-Chichimeca*, but also according to the *Historia de los Mexicanos* Ce Acatl himself led a migration from Tollan to Cozcatlán, situated in this area. In addition, the *Anales de Cuauhtitlán* confirm the existence of a place called Nonoalco in the Cozcatlán-Tehuacán region.[83]

Taking his clue from the language of their ultimate refuge, Jiménez Moreno describes the Nonoalcas as "Mazateca Popoloca, partially Nahuatized."[84] In another context he modifies his qualifying adjective and calls them "recently Nahuatized."[85] He further suggests that they spoke Nahuatl in the same manner as the Pipil-Nicaraos.[86]

One certainly would not deny the possibility of Mazatec linguistic affiliations, where the Nonoalcas are concerned; however, the possibility should not be overlooked that at least part of such a composite group of migrants might have been speakers of a Mayoid language. As will be seen in the next chapter, not only did Chontal prevail in the Tabasco area at the time of the Conquest, interpersed with Nahuatl, but Mayan cultural influences had been actively present there during the Late Maya Classic period, that is to say, in the era preceding the Nonoalca departure.

One might moreover question whether the situation of the Nonoalcas was essentially parallel to that of the Pipil-Nicaraos. A form of Nahuatl must surely have been the principal, rather than the auxiliary, language of this group when they migrated, since otherwise they would surely have abandoned its use altogether in the linguistically alien surroundings of Nicaragua.

As to the Nonoalcas being Nahuatized, it would seem that this process had been all but completed by the time of their departure from Tollan, but not surely when they arrived there. Centuries later they presumably constituted the Nahuatl-speaking element in their final habitat, where both this and languages of the Mazateca-Popoloca group were spoken. But as to their being of Mazateca-Popoloca origin, it is more than possible but much harder to demonstrate. Their departure to a Mazateca-Popoloca-speaking area after the Toltec debacle proves little. It is, however, fair to add that the Olmeca-Xicallancas, to whom the Nonoalcas were to some extent related, display certain Popoloca affinities, as already explained. It should also be mentioned that Jiménez Moreno finds additional reasons for associating the Nonoalcas with the Mazateca-Popolocas; for instance, one is the view that both the former and the latter are connected with the Olmeca-Xicallancas. It must be confessed, however, that the Nonoalcas seem rather overcivilized to rank as pure Popoloca, even if they apparently descended to a somewhat lower cultural level in their new home, after leaving Tollan. In addition, it must be added that not all the Nonoalcas went to the Teotitlán area. Some, as we shall see, went to Chalco, and others may have remained behind in the Valley of Mexico. It would seem illogical to think that Culhuacán later became the spiritual leader of that region without some admixture of Nonoalca blood and talent.

Whereas the Nonoalcas' place of origin, the Tabasco region, is relatively easy to identify, their linguistic and ethnic affiliations are much harder to determine. They certainly constituted a rather special group and possibly owed their unique qualities to a rich blend of different genes, combining in their blood the ancient heritage of Teotihuacán and El Tajín with an admixture of Mixtec, Mazateca-Popoloca, and even Maya elements.

Paddock indeed asks if these Nonoalca refugees from Tollan's troubles were not simply Mixtecs returning to their native land.[87] But one must strongly doubt that they were pure Mixtecs, though it has to be remembered that in later times pockets of Mixtec speakers still lived in the Gulf Coast area between Mixtlan and Cozamaloapan. One also cannot overlook Sahagún's reference to Olmeca-Uixtotins who became the Anauaca Mixtecas, thus connecting the Mixtecs with the Gulf Coast.[88]

Whatever language the Nonoalcas spoke when they arrived at Tollan, they certainly appear to have used Nahuatl when they left, to witness, "*La Lengua Mexicana Nonoalca*" found by the Spaniards in part of their new homeland.[89] Presumably they drove the original inhabitants into the hills, where, according to the *Relaciones Geográficas*, languages of the Mazateca-Popoloca group continued to be spoken. In this region Nahuatl constituted the language of the ruling classes, while the peasants spoke these other tongues.[90]

And finally one should again mention what are ostensibly latter-day Nonoalcas. Chimalpain writes of the Nonoalca Teotlixcas-Tlacochcalcas, who came from Tlapallan, crossed the sea, and eventually became the inhabitants of Tlamanalco, near Chalco.[91] According to the *Memorial Breve* by the same author, those Nonoalca Teotlixcas came out of Huehuetlapallan only *after* the fall of Tollan; this however may be due to some chronological misunderstanding on his part. They are probably part of the last wave of Nonoalcas to arrive in Tollan. Chimalpain goes out of his way to stress that the Nonoalca Teotlixcas were very civilized, undoubtedly related to the other Nonoalcas, all of whom constituted a true *Kulturvolk* and whose roots derived from the Mesoamerican Classic efflorescence.

Naturally, just as the English and Spaniards transposed the names of cities to the New World, a series of new "Nonoalcos" sprang up in Central Mexico, adjacent to Tollan Xicocotitlan in the Valley of Mexico. One of these seems to have been a part of Tollan itself; a verse from one of the *Cantares* tells how Quetzalcoatl left his ruined temples in Tollan Nonoalco, or possibly Tollan *and* Nonoalco.[92] And apart from the Nonoalco situated in Tlatelolco in later times, the *Historia Tolteca-Chichimeca* also mentions a Nonoalco near Cuauhtitlan.[93] Kirchhoff also identifies a place of that name to the west of Tollan Xicocotitlan.[94]

Thus, the frequent occurrence of the name Nonoalco in Central Mexico might easily lead to the suggestion that the Nonoalcas really derived from one of these and were really just another Central Mesoamerican group of wanderers who eventually reached Tollan. One might even discount Melgarejo's identification of the place names on their route and discard Ixtlilóchitl's whole story as garbled and therefore unreliable. But one is still faced with the question: how then did Toltec culture, whatever its limitations, develop? Assuming that Tollan was not simply a spiritual colony of Xochicalco (itself Maya-influenced), then surely elements from the Gulf Coast must have been added; otherwise the Toltecs would have remained mere marginal Mesoamericans. Thus, if the Nonoalcas had not provided an element of inspiration, one is forced to presuppose the existence of yet another migratory element in Tollan that fulfilled this role.

Latter-day Nonoalcas were not confined to one area and included Tímal, described as "the Nonoalca," who arrived from Tollan as conqueror, capturing, among other places, Cuauhnáhuac.[95] The Anónimo Mexicano also mentions a Timatzin, who founded Nonohuatícpac.[96] These post-Tollan Nonoalcas seem also to be associated in the *Cantares* with the Tepanecs: "Come ye and hear the man of Nonoalco, the Tepanec."[97]

Because of their later date, such people called Nonoalcas and cities called Nonoalco reflect only an echo of the original people who came to Tollan at its inception, perhaps followed by others toward its end. Most, but possibly not all, of the former repaired to the Tehuacán-Teotitlán area, whereas the latter apparently went to Chalco Tlalmanalco. All of these became thoroughly Nahuatized. Their original language may have been one of the Mazateca-Popoloca group, spoken in the area to which many finally emigrated. Alternatively, it might have been a Mayoid tongue. Neither contention can be proved today. Their high cultural attainments are suggestive of earlier ties with

Teotihuacán, with perhaps an added tincture of Mixtec blood. It was largely through the practice of their skills and the manifestation of their genius that the words "Tollan" and "Toltec" eventually became synonymous with refinement and splendor.

Questions of Chronology

Serious attempts have been made to calculate the foundation date of Tollan based not on archaeological evidence but on the written sources. The most current solution places the inception of the Toltec era in A.D. 908. This is derived from the date of I Tecpatl given in the *Anales de Cuauhtitlán*, originally taken as A.D. 752, but to which three calendar cycles, or 156 years, are now added, to give the year 908.[98]

Unfortunately, such reckonings encounter serious objections. Kirchhoff, in his chronological studies, emphasized that the written sources cannot provide adequate data for Tollan's inception or early period.

On examination, the impression is confirmed that the available written dates for early and middle Tollan are mainly mythical. As can be seen in Appendix B, which is devoted to rulers lists and their chronology, the *Anales de Cuauhtitlán* and Torquemada give dates supposedly of its early rulers, each with a reign of exactly fifty-two years, or one calendar cycle. Such symmetrical figures are hard to take literally; moreover, in Appendix B it is demonstrated that they refer mainly to rulers of Culhuacán, not Tollan.

But if the dates for rulers are not acceptable, as being mainly conventional rather than real, then by the same token no valid reason can exist for sustaining the accuracy of those variously offered for Tollan's foundation. To show that these are basically ritual rather than factual, one need only cite Ixtlilxóchitl, who solemnly lists four principal events of the early Toltec migration as occurring successively in the years I Acatl, I Tecpatl, I Calli, and I Tochtli.[99] That important happenings should really follow one another at precise intervals of thirteen years is an assumption as improbable as the acceptance of a fifty-two-year cycle for the reign of each ruler.

Mesoamericans had a penchant toward symmetry as much as accuracy. As I have fully explained in another work, an almost uncanny proportion of major events are reported as occurring in the year I Tecpatl—for instance, the beginning of the Toltec migration, the establishment of Tollan or its dynasty, the fall of Tollan, the commencement of the Mexica journey from Aztlan, the foundation of Tenochtitlan (2 Calli is one year after 1 Tecpatl), and the accession of its first Tlatoani. Second only in popularity as the years given for important happenings come 1 Calli, 1 Tochtli, and 1 Acatl. I have even gone so far as to suggest that for the above-mentioned accession of Acamapichtli, a special year count was created, beginning with 1 Tecpatl.[100] Thus, it is difficult not to believe that dates such as 1 Tecpatl, given for early Toltec events, are ritual rather than actual, and one prefers to abstain from the task of laboriously seeking to adjust them to our own Christian calendar! They were surely not historical, since they had been previously adjusted to comply with the commencement of thirteen- and fifty-two-year periods of the Mesoamerican reckoning.

Jiménez Moreno and others tend also to date the early Tollan on the supposition that Ce Acatl-Topiltzin was born, somewhat naturally, in the year I Acatl, and that this was the equivalent of A.D. 935 in what Jiménez Moreno has named the Mixtec year count rather than in the Mexica count. According to this version, Ce Acatl became ruler of Tollan after a brief career of conquest, and the *Anales de Cuauhtitlán* give 5 Acatl for his accession to the throne; this, in the Mixtec calendar, would be the equivalent of A.D. 965. But in Appendix B these dates are explained rather differently and related to Tollan's end.

Quite apart from doubts already expressed as to whether early Toltec dates are real or ritual, even if one accepted their authenticity, it would still be quite impossible to give a Christian year equivalent. An early 1 Acatl could quite as well be A.D. 987, 883, or 831, instead of 935, by a process of adding or substracting fifty-two years or multiples thereof. Nor does one know to which of the various Mesoamerican year counts this date belongs, which in turn makes it harder still to relate it to any particular Christian year. In point of fact, in such sources as the *Anales de Cuauhtitlán*, Ixtlilxóchitl, and Chimalpain, a number of different counts are employed, as we have illustrated in detail in the above-mentioned work. Only when one has a whole series of dates can a workable pattern be evolved on a comparative basis. Then by listing different alternatives given for the same event may one reconstruct native chronology and demonstrate to which count—e.g., Mexica, Texcocan, Cuitlahua, and so on—a certain date belongs. But for the inception of Tollan one would be working in a void; one does not have comparative dates sufficient even to speculate as to which native year count was used, nor could it be said with any confidence to which particular cycle of that year count the date in question belongs.

One is faced thus with a somewhat isolated I Tecpatl without the necessary abundance of other dates which can be used for cross checking, as can be done for instance for the accession of Acamapichtli or the foundation of Tenochtitlan. This I Tecpatl therefore can be the equivalent not only of A.D. 883, 935, or 987, if assumed to belong to the Mixtec year count, but it could equally be 887, 915, 939, 967, and so on, if assumed instead to belong to only two other of many other year counts that are now commonly accepted to exist. Only when one possesses enough alternatives can one draw up a full chart and arrive at reasonable probabilities.

It may be worth adding that certain other dates are given for this early period, but not sufficient for making a comparative table. For instance, one finds I Calli for the origin of the Toltecs, as well as for the building of Tollan.[101] Both Torquemada and Ixlilxóchitl report 7 Acatl for the year of the foundation of Tollan, but again, 7 Acatl like 1 Tecpatl is just another ritual date, traditionally linked to the mythology of Quetzalcoatl.

One becomes engulfed in even greater contradictions if one is bold enough to take the chroniclers' estimates of Tollan's total life span and then use these to calculate the year of its foundation. For the duration of Tollan or of Toltec power, one finds estimates ranging anywhere from an upper limit of 572 years[102] through a middle range of 468 years,[103] or 342 years,[104] to a minimum of 169 years.[105]

It is therefore surely wiser to abandon the attempt and concentrate one's efforts upon making rational calculations for the last rulers and for the end of Tollan, as Appendix B attempts to do; for these, dates are more plenteous and seemingly historic in nature rather than merely ritual or traditional.

For Tollan's beginning, one is accordingly left with only the lamps of archaeology to light his way, and even these as yet burn dimly in this respect.

That pottery recalling Teotihuacán IV should have continued to be used at that time, as demonstrated by its discovery in Tula Chico, is not altogether surprising. Having been found in association with Coyotlatelco, it must surely be contemporary with the earlier phases of that style.

The earliest definitely known phase of localized occupation in Tollan is therefore post-Metepec, and corresponds more closely to the end of Oztotícpac or to the transition from Oztotícpac to Xometla, since in Oztotícpac only a kind of proto-Coyotlatelco is found. That Teotihuacanoid pottery, and even a few truly Metepec sherds, should be present after the end of Metepec (about 700 A.D.) may constitute one of many examples of delayed diffusion or of the survival of a previous style already abandoned in its core area. Mesoamericanists sometimes make the mistake of assuming that just because a given pottery ceases to be made in its place of origin, a strict edict forbids its manufacture from that date onward throughout the length and breadth of the land; the dangers of such a notion have been more clearly illustrated in Old World archaeology.

Alternatively, Matos suggests that the Metepec sherds *might* have been brought to Tula Chico from the small Teotihuacán site to the north of Tollan and used in the foundations of a building. The whole problem is at present *sub judice* and awaits further clarification. Proof may one day be forthcoming that Tula Chico indeed existed during Teotihuacán IV, but such a settlement would have been on a small scale and its discovery would not alter the basic conclusion that Tollan only began to assume a certain importance after the fall of Teotihuacán.

Chadwick, whose bolder interpretation of data from the written sources one may be less ready to accept, quotes certain archaeological evidence equally suggestive of an earlier foundation date for Tollan than the more orthodox version.[106] He cites Andrews' radiocarbon dates of Puuc type, or pre-Toltec styles, at Chichén giving A.D. 600, 610, and 780, all ± 70. He also mentions a date of 860 ± 100 for the period when Chichén was already strongly influenced by Tollan itself. This reading presumably refers to Xipe and Tláloc *censarios* in the Cave of Bolonkanche on the outskirts of Chichén. However, both these deities are to be found over vast stretches of Mesoamerica and it seems questionable to insist that they denote a Toltec presence at the time. Chadwick in addition mentions indications given by Bernal that Monte Albán IV might be contemporary with Tollan and further cites a number of radiocarbon dates which indicate strongly that Monte Albán IV began in about A.D. 700. These dates must however be treated with caution, since it is by no means certain whether they relate to Monte Albán IV or III A.[107]

It should perhaps be added that what Bernal actually states is that Monte Albán IV begins with the appearance of Toltec elements "in the broadest sense."[108] These could of course be of the same type as the "Mexican" influences present in the Puuc period in Yucatán, and therefore not exactly contemporary with Tollan itself.

Admittedly, the evidence quoted above is somewhat tenuous and scanty, but there is at present not much more upon which one can base even tentative chronological conclusions.

Let us therefore be clear upon one thing: one cannot yet know exactly when Tollan was founded. But my suggestion that the full Tula-Mazapan horizon begins in mid-ninth century at least would lengthen the existence of Tollan as a major center to a full three hundred years. Previous calculations have tended to suggest that its total life span was nearer to two centuries; such a period would seem rather insufficient to allow for Tollan first to be founded, to grow to maturity as a city, to develop into an empire, and finally to decline toward partial collapse.

Against this contention might be put forward the spectacular achievements of Tenochtitlan in less than two centuries. But it must be remembered first that the Aztecs were able to accelerate their rise to power by taking over an already-existing empire, that of the Tepanecs. Second, no positive decline or decadence had set in during the time spanned by their history; it was simply cut off in mid stream by the Spaniards. Whatever might have occurred, the normal life span of Tenochtitlan must surely have exceeded two centuries, and probably would have been much longer.

Concluding Points

Throughout this chapter, evidence has been considered concerning the two migratory groups that are seen as converging upon Tulancingo and Tollan at the time of the latter's foundation. In addition, the Tolteca-Chichimecas, who were the first to arrive at Tollan, may have included some Otomí elements; one does not really know whether the Otomís were there before the Toltecs, whether they arrived together, or whether the Otomís came toward the end. At all events, it was they who occupied or reoccupied the region after the fall of the city. Tollan Xicocotitlan may therefore have housed what was more a triethnic rather than just a biethnic blend. The Otomís, as Sahagún explains, were of very varied cultural attainments, depending upon their geographical location. It is therefore hard to say what, if anything, they would have contributed to the final fusion of different tribes in this case.

Of the provenance of this eastward-moving group, the Tolteca-Chichimecas, I have been able to trace certain archaeological evidence in the form of pottery used in Marginal Mesoamerica in Classic times and then apparently brought to Tollan, where its manufacture continued in the Postclassic era. After sifting the sources, one is left only with a single passage of Sahagún authentically referring to these people. One cannot know why the early Tolteca-Chichimecas moved from marginal Mesoamerica when they did; their travels may spring from a new time of trouble in the northwest. The frontier of Mesoamerica was already tending to recede in the Early Postclassic period, as the area of civilized settlement diminished in those parts. In general terms, pressures probably developed on the Mesoamerican border, generated by Teochichimec nomads. These in their turn would have impelled the semicivilized inhabitants of the zone to migrate in a southeasterly direction; one of such movements brought the Tolteca-Chichimecas to the Teotlalpan and the Valley of Mexico.

It is not altogether surprising that one should possess more archaeological evidence of these people than of the westward-moving Nonoalcas; the latter probably constituted a less numerous elite, whereas the Tolteca-Chichimecas formed the bulk of the combined population. It is natural that the written sources refer more to the Nonoalcas, who, if fewer in number, were certainly more literate; they were thus likely to keep written records, even if these were later destroyed, to survive mainly as oral sagas. The Nonoalcas surely provided the intellectual leadership of Tollan's population, as Torquemada and others imply. In Tollan, they presumably contributed the brains, and the Tolteca-Chichimecas the brawn.

These Nonoalcas, coming originally from the general region of Tabasco, probably inherited, together with the mysterious Amantecas, some of the cultural traits of the *tlamatinime* who, according to Sahagún, went eastward at the fall of Teotihuacán. One of the Nonoalca leaders seems to have been a Ce Acatl or Topiltzin, perhaps even bearing the name or title of Quetzalcoatl and being in some special way associated with that god as priest or priest-ruler.

As in cultural matters, so in questions of religion, Nonoalca norms probably initially tended to prevail over those of the less sophisticated Tolteca-Chichimecas. In this respect one may perhaps discern three stages. First, the Nonoalcas brought from Tabasco a relatively peaceable form of Quetzalcoatl as Morning Star, a symbol of such deep significance in the Maya area; this cult was already well established in the Altiplano, particularly in Xochicalco, and through contact with the Huaxteca had been gradually enriched by the Ehécatl aspect of Quetzalcoatl as God of Wind. However, on contact with the Tolteca-Chichimecas, the latter attributes of the god tended to become rather muted, even if certain wind symbols, such as sections of shells, are present in Tollan. On the other hand, Quetzalcoatl as Morning Star took on a new significance, becoming merged with the northern Hunting God, Mixcoatl, and thus assuming a much more martial aspect in Tollan as not merely the Morning Star but the warrior of the Dawn, a blending of Tlahuizcalpantecuhtli and Mixcoatl, two deities who had borrowed each other's plumes and become very similar in outward form.

Contact between the two ethnic groups was perhaps established when the Tolteca-Chichimecas had reached Tulancingo and the Nonoalcas were established for a time in the Huaxteca. Accounts vary as to how long the Tolteca-Chichimecas stayed in Tulancingo and the Nonoalcas in the Huaxteca. Their sojourn may have lasted for quite a considerable period, sufficient for the latter to have become partly "Huaxtecized" and above all long enough for them to have adopted as their own the fully fledged cult of the new Quetzalcoatl.

It would seem probable that the Tolteca-Chichimecas came to

occupy the general region of the Teotlalpan, including the Tollan area, and even the Valley of Mexico; from there they could have fanned out as far as Tulancingo, a much older site than Tollan, to which all sources say that they went first. Tulancingo might even have constituted their original capital in the period immediately following their eastward trek.

Probably at about the same time the Nonoalcas reached the Huaxteca; thus they and the Tolteca-Chichimecas would in effect have settled in contiguous areas and become neighbors.

Such moves would have taken place at a time when Xochicalco and El Tajín were already tending to decline, leaving a kind of power vacuum. At this moment, as has constantly been emphasized, Cholula was playing a rather muted role between its two periods of greatness; in the Valley of Mexico such places as Azcapotzalco and Culhuacán had already existed for some time.

As a rather speculative explanation of what happened, it might be suggested that the Nonoalcas had problems with other peoples of the coast, including the Huaxtecs, with whom they enjoyed a certain cultural affinity. Or, alternatively, they may have been the victims of pressure exercized by wilder peoples situated beyond the Pánuco region. Ixtlilxóchitl hints as much when he states that the "Toltecs," when they were in Xiuhcoac (lying in the direction of Pánuco and Tampico), were harassed by their Chichimec rivals, whose territory lay very close.[109] Sahagún even writes of the "Huaxteca Chichimecas," but in fact a clear distinction should be drawn between the civilized Huaxtecs and their more barbarous northern neighbors. A kind of double pressure may have been exerted, as often occurs; the Chichimecs might have harassed the Huaxtecs, who in turn reacted upon the Nonoalcas, at least temporarily established in the Pánuco region. The latter then tended to move westward, at a time when the Tolteca-Chichimecas had occupied Tulancingo, having first settled in the Teotlalpan and perhaps formed some kind of settlement in the future Tollan. A natural partnership would thus have developed between the two peoples, already known to each other through trading relations. The superior talents of the Nonoalcas would have been in demand throughout the whole territory then occupied by Tolteca-Chichimeca elements, and not merely at its fringe in Tulancingo.

Tollan Xicocotitlan, on the face of it rather far removed from the center of gravity of Mesoamerica, offered a more favorable site as the capital for this new amalgamation of peoples because of its greater distance from the borders of the Huaxteca, at this time a more constant source of danger. It was only later, when the frontier of Mesoamerica further disintegrated, that the tribes situated to the northwest became a real menace, and Tollan itself came into the line of fire.

5. The Mayan March

A POINT has now been reached where, before discussing Tollan's middle period, or apogee, one must first consider its most spectacular quest: the penetration into the farthest confines of Mesoamerica, in the remote peninsula of Yucatán. By this extraordinary feat, links were forged between these two extremities that made a reality of the greatest legend of native history, the departure of Ce Acatl-Topiltzin-Quetzalcoatl into the mists of Tlillan Tlapallan.

Tlillan Tlapallan

All evidence suggests that the incursion stems from the early Tollan period, if not before. It may therefore be convenient to treat this great enterprise of the Toltecs separately, before considering the general development of their power and its extension in other directions, and to examine once and for all the living enigma of the Tollan-Chichén association.

Yucatán was thus linked with Central Mesoamerica only once in its history. The Aztecs confined themselves to commercial contacts and never imposed their will upon the area. In fact, the Maya lowlands had always remained a world somewhat apart, influenced but never dominated by the forces of the altiplano.

The peninsula had perhaps a special lure for the Toltecs, as had Oaxaca for the Aztecs when it became the scene of some of their earliest imperial triumphs under Moctezuma I. The appeal of Yucatán was not unaccountable; after all, Tlillan Tlapallan was conceived as the final destination of the Toltec Topiltzin-Quetzalcoatl, whose other name, Acatl, in part symbolized the east; moreover, in his role as the planet Venus, the east was in a sense also the land of his birth or rising. It was thus for the Toltecs a land of mystery and magic; on the other hand it was by no means, as we shall see, terra incognita. The advent of Kukulcan merely fortified bonds already in part established.

Seler's inference that Tlillan Tlapallan means "the Maya land," because that is par excellence the place of provenance of written codices using the colors red and black, seems to rest on slender foundations. It could by the same token be argued that Tlillan Tlapallan would be the place of warriors, because they painted themselves red or red and black. Equally it could be the place of the ball game, and Seler himself draws attention to the contrast between the red and black sectors of the ritual ball court.

A more likely solution would be that Tlillan Tlapallan simply signifies the east, the place where the red of the newly risen sun emerges out of the surrounding darkness; this surely is a more logical and direct explanation. The probable correctness of this assumption is demonstrated by a passage in the *Título C'oyoi*: ". . . then there at Amak'tan, the name of the mountain, the red place [Cakibal in Quiché] . . . when it dawned, they were occupied . . . shouting, when the great star came out."[1] One here finds a clear association of dawn and red, and Cakibal, the equivalent of Tlapallan in Nahuatl, is clearly identified as both the red place and the place where they witness the dawn and the rise of the Morning Star. Moreover, Chimalpain associated Tlapallan with Teotlixco, in this context identifiable as the east.

Quite apart from denoting his final destination, these two colors seem to have had a special over-all significance for Quetzalcoatl; after Cópil, the nephew of Huitzilopochtli, had been killed by the Mexicas, Cuauhtlequetzqui is instructed to cast away his heart at a point in the lagoon where Quetzalcoatl rested when he departed from there: "Of his [Quetzalcoatl's] seats, one is red and the other is black."[2] It was of course here that Tenochtitlan was later founded.

Thus Quetzalcoatl, the Morning Star, is the lord of the red and the black, that is to say, the east. By inference, this may of course become the Maya land in general or Yucatán, even if this is not its specific meaning.

By one of those paradoxes which confront the Mesoamerican investigator, as Ce Acatl-Topiltzin, Quetzalcoatl is linked with the east in an additional sense and with the color white, Acatl being associated in various codices not only with east but with white.

Notwithstanding the dictates of such hallowed legends binding Quetzalcoatl of Tollan to Tlillan Tlapallan, the distant east, it is nevertheless extraordinary that such close bonds could have been forged not only in legend but in actual fact between the two extremes of Early Postclassic Mesoamerica. It is easy to forget the distance which separates Tollan from Chichén Itza and which amounts to some thousand miles by the modern road. This is a very long journey on foot; most travelers would gladly forego the attractions of present-day Yucatán if they had to walk a thousand miles to get there.

But in spite of their limited means of transport, pre-Columbian peoples were remarkable for their ability to conquer distance, and comparable feats of mobility had been performed before. For instance, Michael Coe writes of the Olmecs' "colonial" monuments in places ranging from Chalcatzingo in the state of Morelos to Las Victorias in El Salvador.[3] An even more outstanding example is offered by the Esperanza phase of Kaminaljuyu, the site lying in the periphery of the modern city of Guatemala and described by the same author as a cultural satellite of Teotihuacán. Whether such similarities in Kaminaljuyu were attributable to actual military occupation, as the same writer himself proposes, is indeed hard to assess; they are, however, so striking as to lead other authorities, including Millon, to accept the possibility of some physical presence there of people from Teotihuacán, even if only for a limited period. Though they perhaps fall into a somewhat different category, one should also bear in mind the strong Teotihuacán influences in Tikal, including a pyramid with talud and tableros. Forms very reminiscent of that center appear also in Becan.

Last but not least, one might recall the Aztec colony sent to occupy the city of Oaxaca, and their conquest of distant Soconusco; of these, documentary evidence is ample, even if physical remains of their presence are comparatively meager. The trek to Chiapas required a prodigious military effort, the troops being spurred toward their goal by the pitiless Ahuítzotl. Accounts of this expedition duly stress the difficulties of such distant operations in Mesoamerica and make no secret of the attitude of the soldiery, who complained that they had gone far enough and demanded extra booty as a reward for their trials.[4] Such reports of the conquest of Soconusco certainly illustrate the problems of long-range campaigning in Mesoamerica; in my opinion such distant Aztec conquests might have proved very difficult to maintain.[5]

It need hardly be emphasized that it is not my intention to rewrite in one chapter the history of Postclassic Yucatán; on the contrary, only phases and aspects will be examined that directly concern relations between Tollan and Chichén. Some comments will also be included on the vexing problem of the origins of Toltec-Maya style and culture. One can hardly attempt more in this work, and indeed to do so would be superfluous; certain other historical territory where I have ventured may be comparatively virgin, but where Yucatán is concerned, one need only refer the reader to the work of Thompson, Scholes and Roys, and others duly quoted in the text.

Since datable indications of the emergence of a fully fledged Quetzalcoatl, or Kukulcan, cult in the area are primarily to be sought in certain documents, and since their factual information is in other respects rather circumscribed, the previous order will be reversed, and the written evidence will be studied first. Questions related to archaeology and to architectural styles will then be examined, passing finally to the establishment of a tentative chronology.

"The Quetzal shall come"

According to the second series of Katun prophesies in the *Chilam Balam of Chumayel*, Katun 4 Ahau is associated with the coming to Chichén of Quetzalcoatl-Kukulcan: "Katun 4 Ahau . . . is established at Chichén Itza. The settlement of the Itza shall take place [there]. The Quetzal shall come, the green bird shall come . . . Kukulcan shall come with them for the second time. [It is] the word of god, the Itza shall come."[6]

In the first series of such prophesies, that for Katun 4 Ahau is more imprecise, lacking direct reference to Kukulcan or to the Itza: "There shall arrive the quetzal . . . there shall arrive Christ."[7] The quetzal is an obvious reference to Kukulcan, also representing the establishment of a new cult.

The form of words has a certain interest in itself; the arrival of Kukulcan is actually compared with that of Christ. No one thought that Jesus actually visited Yucatán; therefore, by the same token, it might be reasonable to suppose that the coming of Kukulcan is also figurative. The actual arrival in person of a religious leader or prophet of that name is therefore surely not implied, but simply the introduction into the area of an already established cult, centered upon that deity.

The whole significance of such "prophesies" resides in the fact that they constitute a form of recording history. Future Katuns were expected to be repetitions of their past equivalents, and what had already happened before in a given Katun was expected to recur when one of the same number returned. Thus prophesies of what would occur in a future Katun 4 Ahau automatically presuppose that these events had already taken place in a previous 4 Ahau. Accordingly, the *Chilam Balam of Maní*, not content with "prophesying" the arrival of the Spaniards, also "foretells" that of the French, naturally after the event had taken place.[8] One imagines that the French in question would have been Huguenot pirates who raided the coast of Yucatán in about 1570. Some were captured in a Maya village and hanged in Mérida, while others appeared before the Inquisition in Mexico in 1574.[9] The reference in the *Chilam Balam of Chumayel* of the *second* coming of Kukulcan emphasizes this concept of cyclical repetition of happenings.

History and prophesy are thus inextricable and share the same mysteries; at the beginning of Part II of the *Chilam Balam of Maní*, preceding a very obscure mention of the return of Kukulcan, occurs a description of the manner in which the Chilam Balam (jaguar prophet) himself received the prophesy. Alone in his room, he lay motionless and prostrate, sunk in a deep trance.

Further allusions in written sources to the coming of Quetzalcoatl are not numerous; Landa mentions a lord called Kukulcan who ruled in Chichén. He confuses the situation by saying that he also founded Mayapan (which of course occurred later) and then returned to Central Mexico via Champoton.[10] No doubt this is only one example of the confusion of two or more different individuals, all bearing this name or title.

As evidence of the migration of the Itzas (but not of Kukulcan), Thompson also mentions the well-known Valladolid lawsuit of 1618. Witnesses, recalling traditions obviously well established, talked of groups who had come to Chichén from Central Mexico. The leader of the group that settled at Chichén was called Cupul.[11] This might be a Mayanized version of Cópil, a significant name in later legends concerning the Mexicas.

The informants of Landa were unsure whether Kukulcan originally arrived before or after the Itzas at Chichén. However, basing his conclusions upon the association of Katun 8 Ahau with the arrival of the first wave of Itzas, according to the *Chilam Balam of Chumayel*, Thompson is confident that they came in about A.D. 918 and that Kukulcan (or what one might prefer to think of as simply the main Toltec group) followed in about 980.[12] The Katun 4 Ahau corresponding to their arrival, according to the Goodman-Martínez-Thompson correlation, runs from 968 to 987.

In agreement with Scholes and Roys, Thompson considers that the Itzas came to Chichén from Cozumel; thus they would have arrived from the east, whereas the Toltec intruders later came from the west. He believes the Itzas to have been of Chontal Maya stock and generally refers to the latter as Putuns, a name assumed by at least part of this whole group. Among the detailed evidence which Thompson gives for his assertions, one may cite: the known domination of Cozumel by the Putuns; murals in the Temple of the Warriors in Chichén depicting seaborne invaders, easily associated with the Putuns, the principal seafarers of the Caribbean shores of the Maya area; specific mention of the invaders of Chichén as Putuns in the song of the seizure of Chichén Itza; the close association in the *Chilam Balam* of the Iztas with Chakanputun, the great Putun center.[13]

Putun, or Chontal, is of course a language of the Maya family, being quite closely related to the Chol dialect spoken around Palenque. The similarity between Chontal-Putun and Yucatec may be compared to that prevailing between Portuguese and Spanish. "Chontal" is a name of Nahua origin, meaning simply "foreigner"; as a generic term it is incidentally also applied to quite different peoples in Oaxaca and Nicaragua, whose languages are unrelated to the Chontal of Tabasco.

Thus, notwithstanding a certain affinity with previous occupants, the Itzas were themselves comparatively recent immigrants into Yucatán, just as the Toltecs were. In the eternal flux and reflux of Mesoamerican ethnic groups, they seem merely to have been the first of the two to arrive.

They were commonly referred to as *U Uunil* or *Ah Nunob*, meaning "those who do not know the language of the land" or thus "those who speak it imperfectly." Accordingly, as strangers, or foreigners, they present a certain parallel to the Nonoalcas of Tollan; it will be recalled that "place of separateness" was tentatively proposed as the true etymology of "Nonoalco." It may also be of interest to note that in Colonial Maya inscriptions, the Itzas were called *Dzul*, meaning "foreigners," i.e., those who spoke the local language poorly or differently.[14]

At the time of the Spanish Conquest, Chontal territory included most of coastal Tabasco and part of southwestern Campeche. By that time the Chontalpa (the river delta area of Tabasco) was strongly infiltrated by Nahua speakers. Not only was the chief Putun town known as Potonchan (in Nahuatl "the home of the Putuns"), but no less than eleven out of fourteen known place names were of Nahua origin. Such was the influence of these Nahua-speaking towns on the autochthonous population that Nahuatl had become almost a second language.[15]

Of course linguistic situations could change with relative rapidity in Mesoamerica, and it is difficult to affirm when such a process of infiltration first began. It will, however, be recalled from Chapter 3 how "Mexican" influences penetrated part of the Maya region in the Puuc-Chenes period and even before; moreover, it is very possible that the Itzas were themselves already influenced by Nahua culture before reaching Chichén. Their leader when they conquered this place is called in the *Chilam Balam* Mizcit Ahau; Thompson thinks this Mizcit is of Nahua derivation and might refer to the mesquite bush; alternatively, it could quite possibly be a corrupt version of Mixcoatl (Ahau in this context simply means "leader").

As to the Toltec group associated with Kukulcan, their subsequent arrival may be inferred from cryptic references in the *Chilam Balam* and Landa, but one is told nothing of their route. Thompson suggests that they probably came first to the territory at the bottom of the Gulf of Mexico occupied by Putuns, but already subjected to strong Nahuatizing influences. Perhaps they were accompanied to their final destination in Chichén by a second group of Putun-Itzas, people who had possible connections both with the Nahua west and the Maya east. The particular religious cult of the Toltecs and its accompanying symbolism found subsequent expression in the monuments of the new Chichén.

Putun Power

Following the development of Chichén, both Scholes and Roys on the one hand and Thompson on the other postulate a kind of Putun empire, centered partly on this new capital and occupying much of the territory of Yucatán.

Thompson thinks that the Putuns, of whom the Itzas constituted a part, controlled an extensive area, probably with two capitals in Chakanputun and Chichén Itza, with Potonchan or some other center of the Chontalpa constituting a third (Chakanputun has disappeared, and Thompson does not identify it with present-day Champoton). Scholes and Roys tend to stress the primacy of Chichén itself and quote the *Relaciones de Yucatán* as telling how the lords of the province paid tribute to Chichén: "At one time all this land was under the dominion of one lord, when the ancient city of Chichén Itza was in its prime, to whom all the lords of this province were tributaries. And even from without the province, from Mexico, Guatemala, Chiapas and other provinces, they sent presents in token of peace and friendship."[16]

The Maya chronicles, moreover, make it clear that the Itzas, when they conquered Chichén and Cozumel, did not relinquish their old territory; Thompson even suggests that Nonoalco may have been partly under their control.[17] Thus a strip of land already under Putun domination, stretching from Nonoalco itself in Tabasco through Campeche as far as the east coast of Yucatán, would have furthered any Toltec penetration into the region.

Thompson quotes evidence pointing to Putun expansion not only eastward to Cozumel and Chetumal but also southward toward Yaxchilan on the Upper Usumacinta and beyond to Seibal. Murals at Santa Rita, Belize, which must have been close to the ancient site of Chetumal, exhibit a mixture of Mexican and Maya traits, characteristic of Putun culture.

Thompson envisages a possible Putun penetration, perhaps of short duration, as far inland as Seibal in the Late Classic Maya period. The later stelae in that center depict people with strikingly non-Classic features; at Altar de los Sacrificios in the same area huge quantities of Fine Orange (essentially Y type) and Fine Gray pottery overlay all major constructions, including the latest dated monument, Stela 15, with inscription 9.17.0.0.0. (Goodman-Martínez-Thompson A.D. 771).[18] Both Fine Orange and Fine Gray are thought to have originated somewhere at the bottom of the Gulf of Mexico. Berlin considered that Fine Orange Type Z, closely associated with Puuc, originally came from Jonuta in the Usumacinta Valley, to judge by the vast amount of sherds found there.[19] Fine Orange Z is, incidentally, considered by Brainerd to be the oldest of its variety. Fine Orange Y is found in considerable quantities in Uaxactún, associated with Tepeu 3.[20] It would seem that more clues as to the chronological relation between Puuc and Late Classic Maya periods might eventually be sought in further studies of the different types of Fine Orange, prior to Fine Orange X, contemporary with Toltec Chichén.

Since the Putuns, or Chontal Mayas, were par excellence expansionist and aggressive traders, Thompson finds it not unreasonable to suppose that it was they who carried these initial "Mexican" influences both into the interior and eastward to the farthest regions of Yucatán. They quite possibly developed such qualities as a result of an early injection of blood and culture from the altiplano; the bearers of the latter influences, which spread their tentacles in various directions in the Late Classic period, seem to have been of a Nahua-Maya hybrid

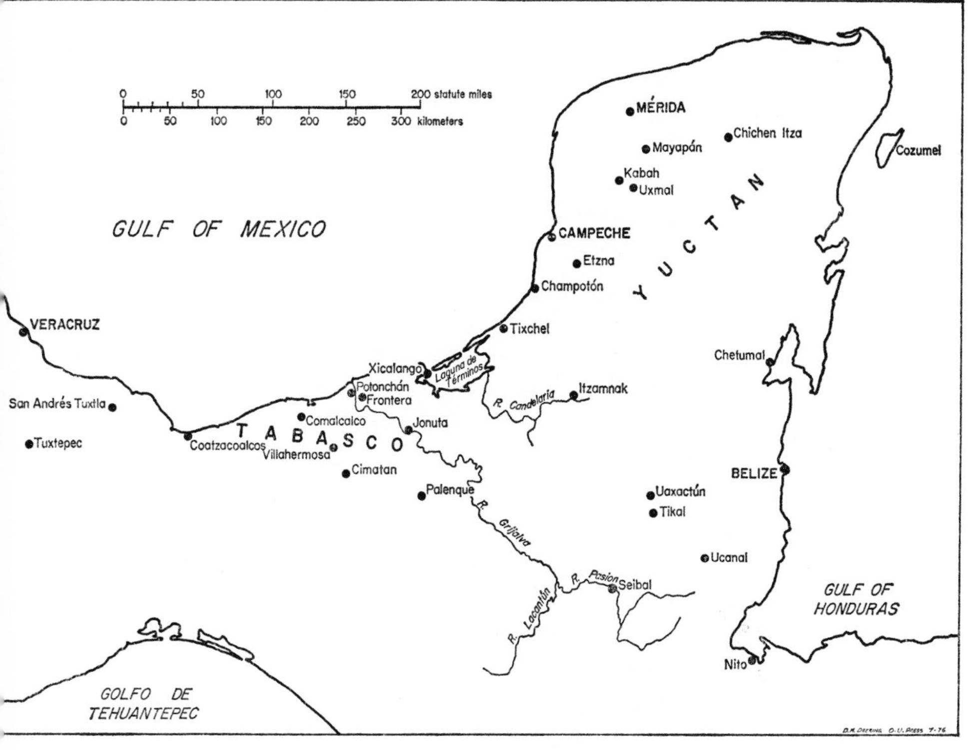

The Maya and their Neighbors

nature. Thus Thompson, who for many years opposed the term "new empire," at last saw it emerging as a reality.

The same author is at pains to emphasize the importance of seamanship as a vehicle for Putun expansion. He not only cites evidence of the arrival of the Putun invaders by sea, but stresses that water transport was then as now the natural method of conveyance in the region of the Grijalva-Usumacinta delta. Outstanding as well for their commercial pre-eminence, their maritime skills obviously gave the Putuns great mobility, enabling them to penetrate to the La Pasión River and beyond to Ucanal, thus establishing themselves on the east coast of Yucatán. In another context, Thompson points out that the circum-Yucatán trade was much in the hands of Acalan (Nahuatl for "place of canoes") and of other Chontal groups who were indeed the Phoenicians of Mesoamerica, by comparison with the landlubber Nahuas.[21]

As a pointer to the importance of sea travel, it is significant that markets in pre-Hispanic Yucatán are reported only on the coast, obviously as embarkation points for the export to Tabasco and Highland Mexico of a limited range of luxury items.[22] As an example of the far-reaching trade network of Postclassic Yucatán, one may cite the discovery in Chichén of gold and other metal objects from Panama, as well as of a pottery pipe probably coming from Michoacán.

The peninsula itself was in a sense as much an entrepôt as a production center. It possessed none of those traditional Mesoamerican status symbols such as quetzal feathers, turquoise, jade, and gold; its main products were wax, honey, and salt, and it was famous for its cotton textiles; slaves, at least in Aztec times, were exchanged with Tabasco for cacao.

Though Sanders questions whether the region developed a true *pochteca* class, comparable with that of Central Mesoamerica, it would seem in actual fact that merchants not only enjoyed a certain pre-eminence, as has already been noted, but were sometimes even to be found in control of the whole community. Herrera says that in Acalan, the most important merchant would be elected ruler; its capital, Itzamnak, at the time of the Conquest was divided into four quarters, each headed by its own chief: the over-all ruler was the leading merchant; his brother, incidentally, governed the Acalan quarter at Nito, a distant center on the Río Dulce in Guatemala.[23]

It has always been my contention that in Classic Mesoamerica considerations of commerce tended to outweigh the urge to political control or military conquest as effecting the relations between the different cultures. Only with the coming of the Postclassic period is a certain change discernible, as trade became progressively more subordinated to the military designs of the rulers. With this in mind, it would seem more likely that any original Chontal-Putun expansion, which apparently began in the Late Classic era, was primarily a vehicle of commerce rather than conquest. However, the Toltecs rather than the Itzas were the ultimate protagonists of the new Postclassic spirit, and with their subsequent coming to Chichén this situation may have changed;

the fearsome features and martial array of the intruders are still there for all to see, depicted on every monument.

It would therefore seem likely that the trading area in which the Putun-Itzas dominated would have become a prey to more militarist tendencies; within such an empire, as it probably became, the military cast of Chichén itself would have become increasingly preponderant over the chiefs of other capitals or confederates such as Potonchan, where we lack evidence of Toltec lords and masters. Thus an original Putun confederation of city-states would have become, under Toltec pressure, an empire centered upon Chichén.

More Quetzalcoatls

No study of "Mexican" intrusions into the Maya area would be complete without at least mentioning the rich written sources of Highland Guatemala, even if their relation to our subject is not always a direct one.

In these sagas, as recorded particularly in the *Popol Vuh* and the *Anales de los Cakchiqueles*, claims of Toltec descent are regularly made, and mention is frequent of rulers bearing variants of the name Quetzalcoatl. For instance, both the above-mentioned sources refer to the presence of a ruler called Nacxit, i.e., Nacxitl, a name which is synonymous with Quetzalcoatl in Central Mesoamerica, as well as in the Maya area.[24] In particular, the *Popol Vuh* speaks of Gucumatz (guk = quetzal in Quiché), referring to Tepeu and Gucumatz as wise and learned rulers who were the progenitors of the tribe.[25] Tepeu is of course only another version of Totepeuh ("our conqueror" in Nahuatl), often associated with Topiltzin-Quetzalcoatl in Nahuatl lore, commonly as one of various names for his father.

In addition, in the *Anales de los Cakchiqueles*, when the different tribes came across the sea to Tulán Zuiva in the east, they were ruled by Gagavitz and Zactecauh. In another creator legend, Zipacna, son of the ruler Vucub Caquix, kills four hundred men with the aid of the ants, a story closely parallel to certain Quetzalcoatl legends of the Altiplano.

In the *Popol Vuh*, reference also occurs to Venus worship; as the tribes journeyed from Tulán Zuiva, they rejoiced to see the star that came out before the sun.[26] A Gucumatz is later mentioned, coupled with the name Cotuhá; as joint rulers they founded the fifth generation of Quiché kings. Their doings are described in some detail, and we find mention again of a Nacxit, who was ruler of the east.

Similarly, in *Los Títulos de la Casa Ixquin Nehaib, Señores del Territorio de Otzoya* the names Tepeu-Gucumatz and Gucumatz-Cotuhé occur as leaders.[27] In the *Historia de Guatemala* by Francisco Antonio Fuentes y Guzmán, Jiutemal, son of a great monarch, Acxopil, became leader of the Cakchiquels.[28] As W. Lehmann points out, this Jiutemal is surely the same as the Ihuitimalli who, in the *Toltec Elegy*, leaves Tollan Nonoalco and goes to Xicalango and Zacanco.[29] Ihuitimalli in its turn is either just another appellation of Topiltzin-Quetzalcoatl or more probably that of a companion in his journey to Tlillan Tlapallan or even a coruler in Tollan. (*See* Appendix B.)

Such multiple references to Quetzalcoatl under a variety of names both as legend and leader are accompanied by mention of Tulán or Tulán Zuiva as the place of origin of the migrant tribes, who themselves of course claimed Toltec descent. The question of Tulán Zuiva has been discussed at some length in Chapter 2; the conclusion was reached that this place was probably to be sought on the Laguna de Términos or nearby; also, the possible existence was noted of two Tuláns, one lying on the Laguna or at least in Tabasco, and the other being Chichén itself. The mention by the *Anales de los Cakchiqueles* of four Tuláns underscores the mystical or mythical element inherent in these accounts. At the same time I was reluctant to accept the likelihood that Tulán Zuiva could be physically equated with Tollan Xicocotitlan, as opposed to Chichén, to which, according to certain accounts, the tribal leaders of the region went to render homage and to bring gifts. Those concerned were not Nahua speakers, even if they used names originally deriving from Nahuatl. Stories of maritime crossings in an easterly direction might refer to their legendary progenitors, but surely not to the migrants themselves, unless a much shorter sea journey was involved, perhaps simply from Tabasco to Chichén, which they visited before departing for their final destination in Guatemala.

As already emphasized, the *Anales de los Cakchiqueles* frequently refer to Tulán Zuiva as lying in the east, across the sea, and the *Popol*

Vuh also implies that it lay toward the east; this in itself surely excludes the possibility that Tollan Xicocotitlan is intended. Admittedly, the *Chilam Balam* says that Holtun Zuiva (the port of Zuiva) lay in the west. However, such an assertion only serves to fix even more surely the location of the original Zuiva, usually coupled with the name Tulán, as lying in eastern Tabasco or southwestern Campeche. Such a location would indeed lie westward as far as the Itzas of Chichén were concerned; on the contrary, for the Quichés and Cakchiquels, as they came eastward through Nonoalco, or Olimán, the land of rubber, situated around the Grijalva delta, it would be farther to their east.

When Olmeca-Xicallanca and Nonoalca origins were discussed, it was already noted that "Gucumatz" appears in the *Popol Vuh* as god of the Gulf Coast; he is not only designated as "Ah Toltecat" but also as "Ah h' ol," i.e., "the Lord of Rubber," or in general terms "the Olmec."[30] The same source writes of Tepeu Olimán, and in the *Anales de los Caḱchiqueles* enemy tribes are encountered who are known as Nonoalcas and Xulpits and who lived on the seashore.[31] One is thus left in no doubt that these people passed through the region of coastal Tabasco, Nonoalco or Olimán; and at precisely this point in their story they refer to Tulán Zuiva as lying in the east. Accordingly, from the Tabascan melting pot of Mesoamerica, there emerged not only the westward-moving Nonoalcas who went to Tollan Xicocotitlan and the eastward-moving Itzas who left for Chichén but also these southward-moving immigrants into Highland Guatemala. Toltec influences could perhaps have reached Guatemala via the Putun trading post at Nite near the modern Puerto Barrios. Alternatively, it is just possible that the migrants into Guatemala might have followed in part the route of the Itzas and of those migrant Toltecs who reached Chichén; it was perhaps from the latter that they would have learned to speak of Tulán and have come even to claim Toltec descent for their own rulers, who then adopted titles such as Gucumatz, Gacavitz, and so on, as well as other names with the same associations, such as Nacxit. Even after settling in their final abode, the Cakchiquels and Quichés would send their messages and gifts to the great Lord Nacxit, probably residing in Chichén. Robert Carmack gives detailed reasons for believing that they came from the southern Gulf region around Tabasco; among their traditional places of provenance, apart from Oloman and Nonoualcat, Coatzacam is mentioned, presumably to be identified with Coatzacoalcos.[32]

As Carmack also points out, while in contrast to Chichén certain "Mexican" features are present in the art and architecture of Highland Guatemala during the Early Postclassic period, specifically diagnostic Toltec features such as serpent columns, chacmools, Coyotlatelco and Mazapan pottery, murals with prowling jaguars, coyotes, and eagles are missing.[33]

Scholes and Roys point to the lack of any lasting changes in Maya language or culture as a result of Toltec influence, and it is therefore unlikely that the Toltecs were present in more than limited numbers or that they brought their women with them.[34] Under such circumstances, it would seem uncertain that these invaders of Chichén would have possessed the numerical strength to infiltrate the other tribes; physical rule by Toltec overlords of the Quichés and Cakchiquels, as opposed to domination of the Itzas, would thus seem very questionable.

In Chichén itself we face a Toltec presence that is too prevalent to deny. The Guatemalan tribes, however, surely acquired a veneer not of pure Toltec culture coming direct from Tollan Xicocotitlan but of this Toltec-Maya civilization, taken from the great Chichén, the Tollan or Tulán of the east—in a sense, a kind of New Jerusalem. After embracing the cult of Quetzalcoatl-Kukulcan, it was to be expected that the rulers should also assume his name in some form or other and that their subjects should claim to be of Toltec descent.

Their chronicles plainly demonstrate that they also assimilated the martial spirit of the Postclassic era; more emphasis should be placed upon the warlike prowess of these neo-Quetzalcoatls in marked contrast to the more sacerdotal qualities sometimes attributed to the Topiltzin or Quetzalcoatl of Tollan Xicocotitlan. Their position may perhaps be compared to latter-day Arab kings who bore the name of the Prophet Mohammed, but whose office was more that of a secular than a religious leader. The prestige conferred by the adoption of names deriving from a traditionally powerful or important people is a world-wide phenomenon; one may even recall the example of the prime minister of the Tonga Islands in the nineteenth century, who changed his name and took that of the British prime minister, Sir Robert Peel.

One feels, in short, that the proliferation of provincial Tuláns and Quetzalcoatls in Highland Guatemalan legend bears witness not so much to a further extension of Toltec domination as to the magnetic prestige of Toltec religious, political, and social norms, reflected outward from their great retransmission center of Chichén. To these the Guatemalan tribes were fully exposed and thus became general votaries of Quetzalcoatl-Kukulcan, but without direct subjection to his original Toltec protagonists.

The Land in Between

In Chapter 3 attention has already been drawn to the presence of Mesoamerican influences in the Maya land, well before the initiation of Toltec Chichén. In particular, certain traits were mentioned characteristic of the altiplano and found in such Puuc sites as Seibal and Kabah; the man-bird-serpent concept for example was at this time already present among the Mayas. Moreover, Mayan cultural interchange in this pre-Toltec period was not confined to Central Mexico; the Puuc and Río Bec cultures seem to present Classic Maya elements combined not only with those of Central Mesoamerica but also with traits introduced from Veracruz; such motifs appear for instance at Oxkintok and Etzna.[35]

Thompson points out that the center where the Puuc complex originally developed has not been found; he suggests that it perhaps lay in southwestern Campeche.[36] If this were the case, the Tabasco and adjacent areas, later to become the linchpin between Tollan and Yucatán, already occupied a key position as a focus of cultural diffusion; clearly the region is pivotal to our problems.

Documentary evidence contained in the chronicles of Yucatán and Highland Guatemala has already been quoted to this effect. One encounters Nonoalco and Olimán, whose Tabascan associations have already been demonstrated at some length. In earlier times the region already flourished as a kind of cultural melting pot; it was there that the *tlamatinime* repaired, as the old order of Teotihuacán collapsed; from there the Nonoalcas and Itzas emerged to conquer new worlds.

Tabasco itself was blessed by two principal assets: its abundant production of cacao and its favored situation for trans-Mesoamerican commerce. These advantages reinforced its links both with Central Mesoamerica and with Yucatán. Cacao was after all Mesoamerica's main substitute for a proper coinage (though the problems of depending upon nature rather than the government printing press as the provider of currency must have been considerable); cacao was therefore a crop of inestimable importance, for the growing of which the Tabascan climate was ideally suited. Moreover, the whole Quetzalcoatl legend was not unassociated with this product, and Sahagún even tells us that he cultivated it in Tollan Xicocotitlan.

Regarding trade relations, one's knowledge of course mainly derives from the Tabascan situation in the Late Postclassic period. In trade, as in other matters, the Aztecs may have merely elaborated an already established pattern; however, certain evidence will be cited which may suggest somewhat different orientations for Tabasco in the early Postclassic period to those prevailing later.

First, however, as a supplement to Aztec documentary evidence, what physical clues do we possess regarding transit or settlement in the period which immediately concerns us? Unhappily, it must be admitted that the area, so rich in Teotihuacán remains, offers but meager traces of what followed or preceded this period. There is on the one hand no evidence of Preclassic or even Early Classic culture in the region of the lower Grijalva, though Preclassic remains are found on its middle and upper reaches. (La Venta lay well to the west, on the border of Tabasco and Veracruz.) However, the late Teotihuacán culture is very well represented. As Coe points out, "that the southern Veracruz-Tabasco area had an occupation as provincially Teotihuacán as that of Kaminaljuyu is generally not realized."[37]

Sanders describes the vast proportions of the site of Comalcalco, situated between Villahermosa and the Caribbean coast; it appears to belong basically to the Late Classic Maya era, subsequent of course to Teotihuacán. This center has all the attributes of Maya civilization, with brick architecture, dated monuments, and stucco modeling on the walls; its settlement pattern is comparatively similar to that of such Maya centers as Tikal and Uaxactún. The author goes so far as to suggest that this might have been the capital of a fairly large and compact state during the Late Classic Maya period, including much of the region now known as the Chontalpa.[38] Other important sites are also mentioned, such as Tierra Nueva, also of the same period; it has a large plaza, numerous pyramids, and a small ball court, but lacks the specific links of Comalcalco with the typical Classic Maya style. Postclassic remains are, however, not totally lacking in the area, and sites mainly of that period are to be found in the Chontalpa, such as Sigero, which seems to have acted as a ceremonial center for a population scattered over several square miles of neighboring territory.[39]

Heinrich Berlin made a survey of the region, also yielding rather negative results from the point of view of the Early Postclassic period. On the Isla del Carmen he found Fine Orange Type Z (contemporary with Puuc), but not Type X, so abundant in Toltec Chichén.[40] The same situation prevailed on the banks of the Usumacinta, from its mouth at Frontera as far upstream as Emiliano Zapata.[41] The Early Postclassic period, probably coeval with the time of Toltec expansion, is only lightly represented, though the author does mention some Fine Orange Type X and Tohil Plumbate found at Tecolpan. More in evidence was material from the later Cintla period, which continued until the arrival of the Spaniards. Berlin thus concurs with Sanders in suggesting that at the time of Fine Orange Z (i.e., the Puuc period), Tabascan trade was oriented more toward the southeast, and intimate commercial links were maintained with the Late Classic Maya world; only in later times did the preponderance of commerce shift toward the west, with the importation of metal from Oaxaca and other parts of Central Mesoamerica and of green obsidian from the Valley of Mexico. In general terms, both Toltec and contemporary traits were found by Berlin to be but lightly represented in Tabasco, and little evidence was uncovered that the Toltecs had ever settled there for sufficient time to leave their mark on local culture.

Michael Coe, so rightly insistent upon the previous massive Teotihuacán presence, also finds only scattered information on a Toltec horizon in southern Veracruz and Tabasco. In the Tuxtla mountains, lying on the natural land route between this province and Central Mesoamerica, Late Teotihuacán cultural influences abounded in the Metacapan I phase; however, the succeeding Metacapan II yielded only fragmentary indications of a Toltec presence, such as one incense burner and one Tláloc figure.[42] Coe adds that no Aztec or Aztecoid material was found.

Like Berlin and Sanders, Coe sees the southern Veracruz-Tabascan region as adopting an entirely different alignment in Late Classic Maya times, following the fall of Teotihuacán, but of course before the rise of Tollan Xicocotitlan. There exists in that intermediate period a kind of Mayoid "superculture," a Gulf Coast horizon, which links all peoples of the area with coastal Campeche, itself lying at the time under the Mayan cultural shadow. Curiously enough, such influences are confined mainly to mold-made figurines and polychrome ceramics; the outstanding Maya traits, such as the construction of stone masonry temples (Tabasco of course has little building stone) and the erection of dated stone monuments, are absent.[43]

Alberto Ruz, moreover, seems to perceive closer links in the Early Postclassic period between Yucatán and the Gulf Coast of Veracruz than Yucatán and Tabasco; the first two were marked by the presence of Fine Orange Type X. He draws attention to Brainerd's opinion that the Fine Orange X of Chichén was actually made in Central Veracruz.[44]

However, in the Laguna de Términos area Ruz did succeed in locating somewhat more concrete evidence of Toltec-period occupation. In his view, this territory, lying just to the east of Tabasco, was occupied by the Itzas from the end of the seventh century to the middle of the tenth, when they moved toward Chichén. Among other sites, he investigated mounds situated eight miles southeast of a hacienda known today as Xicalango, at the eastern end of a peninsula bearing the same name, lying opposite Ciudad del Carmen (the actual site of the ancient Xicalango has very possibly disappeared through coastal erosion). At that place, he found in the upper strata pottery which seemed to be related to the Fine Orange X of Chichén. In Los Guariches, on Isla del Carmen, he found much Fine Orange Z, as well as some that was similar to Type X. In addition, in Tichchel and other sites lying farther to the northeast, on the Campeche coast, and therefore nearer to Chichén itself, much material similar to the Fine Orange X of the Chichén was located in the upper layers.[45]

Reverting now to the documentary sources, these bear ample witness to the importance of the Tabascan commercial centers at the time of the Conquest. Three cities were then predominant: Xicalango, Potonchan, and Cimatan, itself lying well inland from Potonchan. In the latter center the people spoke Chontal, but Xicalango and Cimatan were at least in part Nahua speaking. Cimatan was important because it was the first of the three places which merchants from the altiplano encountered; farther to the west, Coatzacoalcos was also visited.[46] This latter province appears to have been a linguistic Tower of Babel, and according to its *Relación Geográfica*, it included speakers of Nahuatl, Popoloca, Mixtec, and Zapotec.

Sahagún's informants underline the significance of Aztec trade with Yucatán and Highland Guatemala, saying that it lay within the special preserve of the *tlatoani*, Ahuítzotl. Not all merchants were privileged to proceed beyond Tuxtepec to "Anahuac Xicalango," but only those of certain cities, including of course Tenochtitlan itself. They took gold there, including crowns for the rulers, cotton capes, and large quantities of goods fashioned from obsidian, designed for the use of commoners, or *macehuales*.[47]

Our source tells how these merchants would meet the lords of Cimatan, Xicalango, and Coatzacoalcos, both they and their trading partners being girt for war. In return for what the traders brought, the local rulers would offer large round green stones like tomatoes, and other types of green stones, together with pyrite, shells, feathers, and skins. These products obviously did not derive in the main from Tabasco; the actual place of origin of the green stones which the Aztecs purchased is still unknown. Because of the presence of Nahua-speaking colonies, it has been suggested that the Aztecs actually conquered the region, but this would seem most unlikely, since Sahagún refers to the "enemy land" which they passed en route, a term commonly accorded to areas still independent of the empire. Ahuítzotl, having expressed reluctance to absorb Guatemala, may indeed have preferred to leave southeastern Veracruz and Tabasco free of tribute, as an independent buffer area which could serve as a trade link between the empire and Highland Guatemala, together with parts of Chiapas that remained unconquered.

So much for the conditions in Late Postclassic times. Such information is not entirely conclusive, bearing in mind once more the dangers of retrospective deductions and of ready assumptions that what held good for A.D. 1519 was automatically valid for, say, 919. One really cannot adopt the attitude of the Mayan Chilans and assume that history was a kind of revolving wheel, providing an endless repetition of the same occurrences and processes at set intervals. However, in the particular instance under discussion, archaeological evidence does suggest that the situation prevailing in Tabasco at the time of the Conquest was not exactly new, but had been building up over the centuries. The earlier presence of Nahua speakers in the region is suggested not only by the Toltec flavor of Chichén itself but by the infiltration of altiplano influences some time before this development. It is even possible that, as Berlin suggests, the Teotihuacán presence in southern Veracruz and Tabasco provides the mysterious link binding Teotihuacán to Highland Guatemala.

Indeed, if the presence of Nahua speakers in the sixteenth century is to be taken as an added pointer to earlier altiplano infiltrations, then by the same token the presence of Maya speakers at this moment must also be taken into account. In the north of Tabasco, in the sixteenth century, Chontal was mainly spoken; some Zoque speakers were to be found inland. This Late Classic predominance of Mayoid languages, taken together with the physical presence of corresponding cultural influences in the seventh to ninth centuries in such sites as Comalcalco, may serve to reinforce suspicions that the Nonoalcas themselves may at least have included Mayoid elements; in going to Chichén in the Toltec period, they were perhaps only rejoining their "own people."

What must be freely admitted is the rather weak archaeological evidence of a Toltec presence in the general area under discussion; the same is of course amply true where the Aztecs are concerned. Nevertheless, the Tabasco region had been for some time past the crossroads where two worlds met; the western extremity of the area first became something of a spiritual offshoot of Teotihuacán; then, with the passing of that civilization, the cultural wind veered. The remainder of the region now felt the strong impact of the still-surviving Late Classic Maya culture, but without suffering full absorption, though it was mainly inhabited by Maya-speaking Chontals.

From this catalyst of diverse Mesoamerican cultural currents were to emerge both the westward-moving Nonoalcas and the eastward-bound Itzas; the latter, though basically Mayan, were thus partly Nahuatized, while the former, destined to become Toltecs, were perhaps not uninfluenced by Mayan civilization. At all events, Maya traits certainly made their mark in Xochicalco, a site from which certain features of Tollan derive.

Rather curiously, during the great Toltec-Maya efflorescence that followed these movements, Tabasco seems to manifest few clear influences from either direction and lapses instead into something of a cultural vacuum. Possibly, once the Nahua and Maya traditions had become merged in Chichén and elsewhere, the Tabascan link had for the present served its purpose. Having previously constituted a kind of haven where the migrant tribes could settle, it now became more of an area of transit, assuming a more limited role as a connecting corridor between distant Tollan and Chichén. If any Toltecs settled there, they would presumably have been few in number, contenting themselves with local wares, and leaving no marked traces of their own civilization, so little in evidence there.

Moreover, it must be borne in mind—as will later be seen—that the population of Tollan Xicocotitlan and of the surrounding region was modest in size by comparison with that of the Valley of Mexico in Aztec times, or for that matter with Teotihuacán at its apogee. Assuming that the propensity existed to import wares from Yucatán, or more particularly from Highland Guatemala, the required volume of quetzal feathers, green stones, and the like would surely have been limited compared with the inexhaustible appetite which the sprawling metropolis of Tenochtitlan-Tlatelolco and its lakeside satellite cities later developed for such luxuries.

And finally, as we shall discover, it must not be taken for granted that the original relationship between Tollan and Chichén was primarily commercial. Its preservation may not therefore have required, as in the days of Ahuítzotl, the presence of a cohort of Nahua-speaking intermediaries living in staging posts along the route. Furthermore, it is not beyond the bounds of possibility that with Putun help some of the Yucatán trade went by sea and bypassed Tabasco. If the landlubbing Toltecs from the altiplano were strangers to this medium of transport, Putun maritime skills would have been readily available for the purpose.

If on the other hand the Toltecs came by land, one must still ask what route they followed. Possibly the easiest means of approach was that followed by the merchants of Ahuítzotl, which then lay through the great merchant center of Tuxtepec, in the northeast corner of the state of Oaxaca; from there it led by an inland route to the Laguna de Términos area, without crossing coastal Tabasco at all. Thompson has suggested the existence of a possible staging post of importance between Yucatán and Tollan; perhaps this should be sought in the vicinity of Tuxtepec, rather than on the Gulf Coast.

The problem of possible transit areas between Tollan and Chichén has not been clarified; it possesses however a certain significance. The question still arises as to whether there existed a kind of continuous and contiguous Toltec domain, comparable with that of the Aztecs, stretching from the metropolis as far as Chiapas, or whether the Toltec presence in Yucatán was more of an isolated colonizing venture. If the latter, it might perhaps more recall the implantation of French culture in Egypt following Napoleon's expedition, which did not involve the domination of intervening territories.

Sister Cities

In examining the Toltec-Maya relationship, one has been able so far to discover certain common origins, but no well-defined connecting route between the two. After discussing such initial problems, the true essence of the resulting civilization remains to be considered.

It has already been stressed that the Kaminaljuyu-Teotihuacán connection offers a comparable example of Mesoamerican mobility, and thus in a sense the phenomenon was not altogether new. But in our case the Teotihuacán-Kaminaljuyu relationship is almost reversed; it is no longer the Central Mesoamerican metropolis but its distant counterpart that displays the fullest physical manifestations of an ostensibly common culture.

Fortunately, the almost uncanny stylistic and cultural parallels between Tollan Xicocotitlan and Chichén have already been so fully described that they require no further exposition. To name only a few similarities, in both centers one finds friezes of warriors, processions of jaguars, chacmools, caryatids, and butterfly pectorals, together with common architectural features such as halls filled with rows of columns, stairways with sculptured serpent balustrades, and columns formed by serpent bodies.

Of equal significance, the over-all theme of the two sites is strictly comparable, quite apart from the details; both are imbued with a spirit of austerity, scarcely native to Yucatán and forming a stark contrast to earlier Maya styles; they are moreover marked by the ubiquitous presence not only of plumed serpents but of fearsome warriors, Toltec in dress and profile.

To such familiar traits, it may be worth adding a further point of comparison, arising from comparatively recent investigations. The ball court that occupies the west side of the main plaza in Tollan reproduces almost exactly, albeit in plainer and less decorated form, the principal characteristics of the Great Court of Chichén.

1. Both courts occupy the west side of their respective plazas. (The previously excavated ball court in Tollan, lying to the north of the Temple of Tlahuizcalpantecuhtli, recalls more those of Monte Albán and Xochicalco.)

2. They share the same north-south orientation.

3. They offer an identical profile of sloping court and upright wall.

4. Each has an imposing main stairway to the west side.

5. Their arms at each end have the same low walls.

6. Both have a *tzompantli* on the east side.

7. Their scale is comparable; the Tollan court is the second largest known after Chichén, measuring 116 meters from north to south.

It may thus be seen that these two buildings present parallels even closer than those of most other linked structures in each site, of which various examples exist.

The great similarities apparent in art and architecture briefly mentioned above have never been at issue. Nevertheless, marked controversy has arisen in recent years over the obvious question of the origins of the admittedly common style and spirit; are they to be sought in Tollan, in Chichén, or did they mainly derive from third parties?

The relevant arguments have been plainly expounded, notably by George Kubler and Alberto Ruz. These may be less familiar than the general repertoire of features common to the two sites and thus perhaps merit more discussion, since they are fundamental to our theme and basic to the provenance of Toltec civilization.

Kubler sees Chichén as representing a renaissance of the Classic Maya era; for him this site is no mere receptor but the creator of a new style in architecture, painting, and sculpture.[48] He points out, writing in 1961, that until the present time investigators generally assumed that the Toltecs had dominated the Chichén scene in every way; the proof lay visible for all to see, in the form of Toltec-type warrior friezes, chacmools, non-Maya deities, atlantean columns, and so on.

Kubler bases his assertions upon probable influences in the reverse direction and particularly on the fact that, while Tollan has revealed traces of the second and third phases of the Toltec-Maya style, as manifest in Chichén, it lacks the first phase. He gives examples of the three Toltec-Chichén periods:

Early. The Caracol and the substructure of the Castillo.

Middle. The Temple of the Chacmool (i.e., the substructure of the Temple of the Warriors) and the Castillo.

Late. The Ball Court, Mercado, Tzompantli, and Temple of the Warriors.

He points out that buildings in Tollan that have obvious counterparts in Chichén, such as the North Temple and its colonnade, correspond to Chichén structures that are definitely of the late period (in this case the Temple of the Warriors). One might add that his contention is amply reinforced by the above-mentioned excavation of the ball court at Tollan, so strikingly parallel to that of Chichén, and generally also accepted as belonging to the late period, even if it was not built all at one time.

Reverting to earlier Chichén buildings, Kubler writes that the Caracol, which he and others assign more to the Puuc period, has profiles recalling that style rather than the Toltec. The substructure of the Castillo, which Thompson tentatively regards as more attributable to Petén styles, also has Puuc and even Río Bec associations. The Caracol seems to be the earliest manifestation of the cult of Quetzalcoatl in Chichén; the concept may be Mexican, but the techniques are definitely Maya. Thompson incidentally does not regard the substructure of the Castillo and the early Caracol as in any sense non-Maya. The early Castillo he tends to attribute to the Putuns; in the case of the Caracol, he suggests that only certain additions are Toltec; the cornices, masonry, and stone lintels are pure Maya, together with the marks and hieroglyphic texts.[49]

Kubler freely accepts that certain traits present in Chichén emanate from Tollan Xicocotitlan, such as circular temples, plumed serpents, and other elements of the Quetzalcoatl cult; however, he also lists Chichén features not present in Tollan, such as narrative relief sculpture with presentation of landscapes. Moreover, the jaguar, frequently to be found in Chichén, has antecedents in Maya forms, as encountered for instance in Tikal. Atlantids, as Thompson had suggested, might be representations of the bacabs who held up the heavens at the four cardinal points, such as those on the pre-Toltec Iglesia façade; columns formed of serpent bodies could well derive from effigy columns in the Puuc region, principally at Oxkintok; the decapitation rites depicted in the Great Ball Court are to be seen in El Tajín. Frankly, it would seem that the somewhat pot-bellied figure in Oxkintok wearing feather dress constitutes a rather uncertain predecessor to the plumed-serpent columns; Thompson thinks the figure might derive from the Tuxtlas region of Veracruz.

In general terms, therefore, for Kubler the formative stages of the Toltec period of Chichén are to be found only in Chichén itself, and not in Tollan. In no respect does he deny the Toltec irruption, nor the establishment of Toltec influence; he insists however that such foreign intruders were leaders who brought ideas and concepts rather than artisans who brought objects. Eventually they acquired a new form of art from their Mayan subjects, producing "Mexican ideas with Maya forms."

A seemingly fundamental part of Kubler's theme is the acceptance of the Spinden Long Count correlation, producing Maya dates 260 years earlier than Goodman-Martínez-Thompson. He suggests that the validity of this calculation is upheld by radiocarbon dating—surely a rather uncertain contention. He points out that this dating system leaves an interlude of some three hundred years (from about A.D. 600 to 900) between the end of the Maya Classic and the Maya Toltec periods. Such an interval would allow time for Maya art to be gradually transformed from Classic into Florescent (as Andrews terms the

Puuc-Río Bec period), and then into Modified Florescent, i.e., the Toltec-Maya style.

In short, he sees Chichén as a revival of the great traditions of Mesoamerican antiquity and above all as a renaissance of Classic Mayan art. If Chichén may be compared to Rome, then for him Tollan Xicocotitlan is more to be likened to a frontier garrison station on the extreme edge of the civilized world, at whose very gates the uncouth barbarians wandered; it had taken its art forms only from the middle and late phases of the development of the great eastern metropolis.

Counter arguments to Kubler's thesis are put forward by Ruz Lhuiller.[50] But just as the former readily acknowledges the presence of some Toltec traits in Chichén, so Ruz fully agrees that certain Toltec-Maya elements stem from the Mayan tradition, as for example human heads emerging from the serpent's mouth, which abound in Classic Maya art. Such figures are to be found in both Tollan and Chichén, symbolizing Quetzalcoatl-Kukulcan as man-bird-serpent.

Ruz, however, argues that certain so-called non-Toltec aspects of early Chichén Modified Florescent are really Toltec. Kubler, for instance, describes the substructure of the Castillo as pre-Toltec, but it contains a procession of jaguars. This animal is not traditional to Yucatán, though admittedly not unknown in Classic Maya art in general; accordingly, it was more probably introduced by the Toltecs. Equally, Ruz cannot accept the plumed serpent as a Mayan element; few examples are to be found, in marked contrast to those of Teotihuacán, and it would definitely appear to be a product of the altiplano. The round edifice of the Caracol represents a concept that is not Mayan, though of frequent occurrence in the Huaxteca. The builders merely applied their own roofing technique to the structure, and a locally inspired ornamentation, such as the large masks that form part of the Yucatán tradition.

In opposition to Kubler, Ruz insists that the serpent columns in Chichén do not resemble those of the Puuc and Río Bec; the latter are not made in this form, which thus has no antecedents among the Mayas.

The representations of eagles and jaguars eating hearts constitute another typically Toltec element; Ruz insists that they do not derive from those of Bonampak, Piedras Negras, and Yaxchilan. In contrast to the sculpture of these sites, in Chichén hundreds of figures are depicted; here there is no tendency to glorify one individual, a point on which Proskouriakoff places great emphasis where Classic stelae are concerned. The Chichén frescoes depict typical Toltecs, with blunt noses and lacking cranial deformation. A blue bird is often fastened to the front of the head, and they always have blue necklaces; they wear a *tezcacuitlapilli* on their backs and the *atlatl* is their weapon.

Ruz concedes that certain antecedents of the atlantids might be sought in Xcolhoc and Oxkintok, but those of Chichén and Tollan Xicocotitlan are so different from these that, even if the concept is not Toltec, the more rigid sculptural technique appears to be so. He admits the presence of additional non-Toltec elements in Chichén, such as the stone facing of walls, the vault, and Chac masks, and he accepts the likelihood of the penetration into northern Yucatán in a previous age of other ideas emanating from Teotihuacán, Oaxaca, and the Petén.

In general terms, Ruz sees the Toltecs as bringing to Chichén elements of the altiplano, of which some may go back as far as Teotihuacán and which were not therefore necessarily Toltec innovations—for instance, the deviation of 17 degrees east of astronomic north in the orientation of the buildings, as well as the talud-tablero complex; also the round temples evidently derived from the Huaxteca. As specifically Toltec, he proposes such elements as the great halls filled with columns at the foot of certain temples, as well as balustrades formed of intertwined serpents or processions of eagles and jaguars. The Modified Florescent, or Toltec, era in Chichén may indeed represent a continuation of the Puuc culture, but markedly altered and transformed by Toltec influence and by the elements which marked its diffusion.

Ruz does not accept Kubler's thesis that Chichén represents a renaissance of Classic Maya art, or that its cultural role is that of creator rather than receiver. Nor on the other hand does he go to the opposite extreme of agreeing with Acosta that this center is simply an integral part of Toltec culture. The relations between Tollan and Chichén are of a more complex nature.

The situation cannot be explained by simply suggesting that Chichén belongs purely to Toltec or Tollan solely to Mayan culture. Our knowledge of the processes involved is surely very partial. It is difficult to say exactly up to what point Chichén is a prolongation of

Maya culture, resulting from an amalgamation of Classic Maya, Teotihuacán, and Zapotec elements. It is equally difficult to measure to what degree it stems from Toltec influences, in their turn stemming from the traditions of Teotihuacán and impregnated with influences from other contemporary cultures: the Mixtec (viz., the scrolls of the Tollan *coatepantli*), Huaxtec (El Corral), and even Maya, through the medium of Xochicalco. Moreover, one should not overlook the southern Veracruz influences transmitted by the Putuns to Yucatán, notably a phallic cult and eroticism, which Thompson thinks seeped into Campeche and Yucatán somewhat earlier than the Putun conquest of Chichén. Numerous movements of flux and reflux continually occurred that affected the development of Mesoamerican civilizations, producing in the process of time varied cultural interractions with which we are only partially famiilar.

The two facets have thus been summarized of a problem which, at first sight, might seem to constitute a mere digression. In actual fact, however, it is germane to our theme; the Tollan-Chichén efflorescence is an outstanding feature of its whole period, and its true nature must be weighed in assessing the full Toltec achievement.

It is easy to suppose at first sight that one is faced with two diametrically opposed viewpoints, the one seeing Tollan as a mere copy of Chichén and the other emphasizing the reverse. However, on closer examination one discovers common ground between the two hypotheses almost as extensive as the areas in which they differ.

Both Kubler and Ruz accept the fact of Toltec irruption into Yucatán, leading to political domination and to the imposition on the inhabitants of a different spiritual outlook and a revived religious cult. Both discuss the presence in Chichén of certain non-Maya traits, such as round temples, plumed serpents, and jaguars depicted in profile. Both equally recognize the existence in that site of typically Maya elements, such as vaults and Chac masks, that salient characteristic of Puuc and related styles. They are also in agreement that certain non-Maya concepts in Chichén have pre-Toltec antecedents, as for example the talud-tablero complex and the orientation of buildings east of north. Kubler goes so far as to admit "the arrogant affirmation of foreign customs" in sculptural details; Ruz in his turn accepts Kubler's contention that the intruding Toltecs came unaccompanied by artisans and agrees that Maya artists probably often followed verbal instructions given by their Toltec masters.

But notwithstanding much ground in common, marked differences are apparent between the two viewpoints, first as to the provenance of certain artistic elements, such as chacmools, atlantids, and serpentiform columns. At the same time, a more fundamental divergence of opinion emerges, as to whether Chichén was the creator and Tollan the receptor, or vice versa, and as to how far, if at all, Chichén represents a continuance or renaissance of the Classic Maya tradition.

As regards the first point at issue, the origins of decorative elements are hard to determine conclusively. One is bound to admit that, in addition to Ruz, leading Maya scholars such as Thompson and Proskouriakoff tend to regard Modified Florescent Chichén as non-Maya in essence. However, the arguments could be prolonged indefinitely without reaching sure conclusions; one need only take the chacmool as an example of the difficulties that beset any search for true origins. This rather odd art form, relatively more abundant in Chichén and Tollan than elsewhere, seems to possess few limitations either in time or space. Bernal even suggests that the famous Olmec head of San Lorenzo might possibly have possessed a body in the reclining position and could therefore conceivably have constituted an embryonic predecessor of the chacmool.[51] Seler illustrates a jaguar from Teotihuacán that also recalls in certain measure the chacmool.[52] At the opposite end of the time scale, apart from those of Chichén and Tollan Xicocotitlan, various examples have been discovered in Tenochtitlan.[53]

As to the spacial extension of this art form, it has been found in places as distant as El Salvador and Nicaragua.[54] One even occurs (in jaguar form) in Costa Rica.[55] On the other hand, chacmool coyotes have been reported from the lake region of Michoacán.[56] Possible jaguar antecedents make one suspect that the origins of the chacmool may be very remote; the atlantids are surely an ancient art form, not only preceding the Toltecs but even the Classic Mayas, occurring in the Olmec altar of Potrero Nuevo. Thus from only few examples the hazards become apparent of pinpointing in time and space the origins of these elements common to Chichén and Tollan.

Concerning the second and fundamental problem, who created and who received the Toltec-Maya norms, Ruz rightly stresses the confusing flux and reflux of peoples and ideas involved; however, he goes so far as to concede that, while certain Central Mesoamerican patterns were imposed upon the Maya culture, its foundations remained unaltered.[57] On the whole, the Mayas surely displayed a tendency to receive and absorb influences rather than to transmit them; as Meggers points out, they were essentially nonexpansive.[58] Maya traits are discernible in other areas, notably Xochicalco, where a whole series of unmistakably Maya elements are visible, quite apart from the famous reliefs. One does not, however, really denote the true presence there of a Maya culture.

Another notable example of the penetration of Maya influences into the central Altiplano came to light very recently; in September, 1975, a construction was accidentally discovered in Cacaxtla, Tlaxcala, which seems to be a palace and which contains several frescoes in good condition. They present a strange mixture of Teotihuacán and Maya traits, which might very tentatively be dated to early Tepeuh. One fresco portrays a human figure with Mayan facial features and carrying a Mayan-type staff of office, while the surrounding shells and serpents are painted in a style more akin to Teotihuacán; the drawing includes a glyph that is similar to those of Xochicalco.

Possibly the whole discussion could be enriched, if not resolved, by concentrating upon historic as well as stylistic trends. Certain basic questions might thus be first posed: who were the inhabitants of Tollan Xicocotitlan and of Chichén Itza respectively, and where did they come from? Hence, to what influences would each in the natural course of events have been subjected?

It has already been noted that the intellectual leaders of Tollan were clearly not the ruder elements coming from the northwest but rather the Nonoalcas, closely to be associated with Tabasco. Also in this chapter, attention has been called to this very region as the home of the parent stock of the Itzas, who went from there to Chichén; the resulting culture therefore sprang from a joining of Nahuatized Nonoalcas and Mayan Itzas; the two had previously been neighbors in a region unquestionably subject to both Nahua and Mayoid penetration. Historically, therefore, the Nonoalcas and the Itzas had much in common, even before they developed common art forms.

Not only did the Puuc-Chenes-Río Bec complex already display traces of altiplano influence, but the Nonoalcas hailed from a region to which the *tlamatinime* of Teotihuacán had probably fled, according to Sahagún. The already-cited accounts of the Nonoalca journey from there to Tollan Xicocotitlan involved a sojourn in the Huaxtec part of the Gulf Coast and in Tulancingo, a place where strong Teotihuacán influences had prevailed; these migrants also, as may be seen in Tollan, enjoyed close contacts with Xochicalco, so rich in Maya traits.

In general, one is left with certain main impressions of the general problem. First as to chronology: this aspect of the question is naturally important and will be further investigated in the following section of this chapter. Briefly, Thompson's view now seems generally acceptable, to the effect that the full Toltec influence was brought to bear on Chichén in about A.D. 980; it would have then continued in both cities until the late eleventh or early twelfth century. This accords with Proskouriakoff, who dates the Toltec incursion as first occurring somewhere between 10.3.0.0.0. (A.D. 889) and 10.10.0.0.0 (A.D. 1027). On the basis of such calculations, Tollan and Chichén may have begun more or less independently one of another, but after their initial phases their great periods of expansion would more or less coincide.

It is necessary to bear in mind another point not altogether alien to our theme; Chichén was probably older than Tollan, becoming a leading center well before the Toltec Chichén period began. Bartels, for instance, calls attention to the importance of Late Classic inscriptions in Chichén.[59] Conversely, in its post-Toltec phase, Chichén reverted to purely Maya norms, but of a decadent nature. Structures were crude and jerry-built, and of course difficult to date.[60]

Kubler regards the acceptance of the Spinden Maya calendar correlation as fundamental to his views; it would not, however, seem inconsistent to reject Spinden's calculations but to accept certain aspects of Kubler's hypothesis. He maintains that Puuc, or Florescent Maya, culture was a posterior development to Late Classic Maya, or Tepeuh, just as Chichén Modified Florescent, or Toltec, by the same token grew out of Puuc. He implies that the Goodman-Martínez-Thompson correlation would make the Classic Maya period overlap Toltec Chichén, but that is surely not exactly the case. According to the latter system of date correlation, Puuc and Tepeuh are indeed largely contemporary, though the latter ends slightly before the former. However, Chichén Modified Florescent could have developed just as well from a Pure Florescent, or Puuc, that was more or less *contemporary* with Tepeuh, as from a Puuc that followed after Tepeuh, as Spinden maintained. One merely has to be prepared to accept the contention that Mesoamerican cultural developments do not necessarily follow one another in orderly and precise fashion, and that considerable overlap may occur.

Secondly, one is struck by the stress universally laid by investigators, whatever their divergences, on the widespread presence of influences neither strictly Maya nor Toltec, whether in Tollan or Chichén. Thus in a sense Maya Toltec forms to quite a considerable extent were originally neither Maya nor Toltec! The column, as Ruz emphasizes, does not appear to originate in the Maya area (nor in Tollan) but in Oaxaca.[61] The first excavated ball court in Tollan seemingly owes its inspiration to Monte Albán and Xochicalco. Moreover, certain elements encountered in both centers, such as the orientation of buildings and even the whole man-bird-serpent concept, go back to Teotihuacán itself. Piña Chan particularly stresses the cultural debt which the later Chichén owes to the general area of El Tajín, the Huaxteca, and Central Veracruz; for instance, the ball-court reliefs show players with Tajín-style palms and yokes as well as similar decapitation rites. The whole decorative motif of garlands and intertwining vegetation belongs to a style deriving from Central Veracruz, further developed on the coast of Guatemala.[62]

The ball-court reliefs in Chichén constitute a good example of elements that plainly could not have emanated from Tollan Xicocotitlan. These follow a pattern established in El Tajín and Bilbao, involving not only decapitation but a rich plant iconography (in Chichén and Bilbao mainly consisting of flowering vines and in El Tajín of magueys). All three sites presumably derived such rites from earlier times, since decapitated heads of ball players are already illustrated in Dainzu in Oaxaca in the Late Preclassic period.[63] As already stated, the death cult as manifest in El Tajín probably had its influence on the development of Postclassic culture in general. Gulf Coast influence is also present in Tollan, and Acosta draws attention to certain reliefs in that site also that recall those of El Tajín.[64]

The decapitation rite associated with the ball game and with vegetal fertility is described in the *Popol Vuh.* The brothers Hun Hunapu and Vucub Hunahpu lose a ball game to the ruler of the Underworld. They are sacrificed and the head of Hun Hunapu is placed on a tree. Immediately this tree is covered with fruit. Esther Pasztory actually suggests on the basis of such evidence that the ball game itself may have been a ritual to speed the onset of the rainy season; in this drama the ball player, as representing the sun, was sacrificed on the ball court.

Thompson also calls attention to Huaxtec traits in Chichén; in addition to the presence of round buildings, he notes in a mural of the Temple of Warriors the depicting of round beehive huts at its base, also a Huaxtec feature, even if the whole scene is more probably intended to depict a village somewhere on the Tabasco-Campeche coast and illustrates a force of warriors sailing by this place.[65]

Thirdly, one cannot help considering that in the final analysis certain over-all considerations, historical as much as architectonic, must be paramount and that matters cannot be explained uniquely by seeking the provenance of certain stylistic details, so hard to determine at all events. It is seldom disputed that, regardless of its artistic affiliations, the *spirit* that inspired the Toltec-Chichén efflorescence came from Central Mesoamerica. Moreover, comparing the principal monuments of the later Chichén with, say, those of Uxmal, the difference in feeling that animates the two periods is arresting. In the florid façades of Chenes and even Puuc, one positively senses the Maya heritage; by contrast, Toltec Chichén is markedly "Nordic." Its geometric proportion and harsher outlines seem almost alien to the Maya land and are more reminiscent of highland zones and colder climes.

Noticeable in addition is the profound change of concept that accompanies this development; Toltec Maya architecture is concerned with interior as well as outer space, and thus departs from established Maya patterns, implying quite different social and religious traditions. Moreover, the shared tendency in both Tollan and Chichén toward a quick and even shoddy finish serves to demonstrate that interest was focused on over-all grandeur rather than upon patient execution. The general notion was thus preponderant over the actual elements used in its realization.

With the approach of the Postclassic era, a new martial spirit was abroad in Mesoamerica, but its full impact only struck the Maya area with the advent of the Toltecs. More bellicose tendencies manifest toward the end of the Classic Maya era, for instance in Bonampak, hardly measure up to the harsher norms of Toltec Chichén, with its ubiquitous warriors and grinning skulls. A good example of the marked cultural change is the actual presence in Toltec Chichén of the gruesome *tzompantli*, a typical Postclassic feature. It is true that in Tollan itself only the *tzompantli* platform has been discovered—identifiable by its identical location with reference to the principal ball court, as in Chichén.[66]

Thus, neither in a historical nor moral sense can we see Chichén as the creator rather than the receiver of the spirit of the new age and of the standards which it engendered; those were of pre-eminently Central Mesoamerican origin. Paradoxically, however, most of what Chichén acquired was not necessarily "made in Tollan," but was an amalgam of different traditions, brought to fruition over the centuries. By the same token, granted that its central motivation seems alien to Maya traditions, one cannot see in Toltec Chichén simply a renaissance of Maya culture. That word surely implies a kind of resuscitation of older art forms in new guise, inspired by local or native traditions rather than by notions seemingly imported from elsewhere, as one finds in Chichén.

On the other hand, in the purely technical sense, even if the Toltecs provided the new inspiration, it does not automatically follow that it was they who gave it tangible artistic form. One is thus faced with a fundamentally unusual situation, where one city, Chichén, is apparently the spiritual offspring of another, but then utterly outpaces its mentor in artistic achievement.

Perhaps one might seek a parallel in the case of Byzantium; although that city was conceived as a second Rome, in practice it had a two-fold source of inspiration: on the one hand the classical norms of Hellenistic culture, also present in Rome itself and still abundantly alive in the great cities of the Christian East, such as Alexandria,

Antioch, and Ephesus; and on the other, the Oriental tradition, deriving from the old Iranian or Semitic East, which had assumed new vigor following its contact with Sassanid Persia. In Byzantium this dualism of two opposing influences, eastern and western, was to endure as a permanent feature.

One may even find parallels in the actual stylistic development. The simpler representation of Christian heroes gives way in Byzantium to more complex compositions, showing groups rather than individuals. Precisely the same difference distinguishes Toltec Chichén from the Classic Maya. Thus, out of the blending of two cultural influences, Byzantium developed an art style of a new and exquisite delicacy, reflecting the full fervor of the Christian cult which the region had adopted; this was then actually transported back to Italy and made manifest in Ravenna and later in Norman Sicily. Such an efflorescence surely occurred because Byzantium was located in an area with a longer and deeper tradition of artistic creation than Rome itself, and lay adjacent to other great cities of the East and not too distant from certain Asiatic centers.

Similarly, it would seem that, whatever its over-all inspiration, Toltec Chichén architecture and art owe their refinement to the aesthetic achievements and skills of the surrounding region and are in that sense an indigenous style, though based on notions and attitudes imparted mainly from Tollan. On the one hand, the artistic achievement of Chichén is extremely rich and varied. On the other, one cannot deny Tollan's relative inferiority in this respect, notwithstanding a certain lavishness of scale. One has only to examine the two ball courts to see that the edifice occupying the west side of the principal plaza of Tollan is a pale if not baleful reflection of its Chichén counterpart (admittedly the Tollan court has not been improved by shoddy Aztec additions). The same is true of the Chichén Mercado, of which a small and inferior replica is to be found in Tollan.

We therefore consider it much more probable that certain Tollan structures were modeled on those of Chichén, rather than the reverse. Cases are surely few and far between where art critics and historians can assert that of two replicas of a work of art, it is the smaller and inferior of these that is the original. In the western world, in the relatively rare instances where copies have been made of older buildings, it is those later versions whose dimensions and execution fall short of the first model. It defies the imagination to recall a known and documented case where a building or statue made in imitation of another actually surpassed its original. To suggest therefore that structures of Tollan Xicocotitlan were the prototypes, from which certain of those of Chichén were merely copied, or at best derived, is to advance an unlikely hypothesis.

Moreover, Kubler's chronological arguments, as affecting the development of such styles, would appear valid. He is plainly justified in stating that the known buildings in Tollan recalling Chichén are late rather than early. Since it was seemingly a new foundation, the early Tollan, like the original Tenochtitlan, was probably a modest affair, perhaps mainly of adobe, as was already customary farther to the north. It would have hardly constituted a model for others to copy, least of all the sophisticated Mayas.

Acosta fully conceded the impossibility of recognizing any real evolution of style in the art of Tollan. He further opines that the tendency toward exuberant decoration is a later development.[67] This most certainly would not be true of Yucatán. Moreover, we have previously pointed out that Tollan architecture is more or less all of a pattern, and one is confronted today with what is in essence the final version of the site; admittedly the pyramid of Tlahuizcalpantecuhtli now visible is the penultimate superposition, but even that must be of relatively late construction.

In contrast, Chichén is conspicuous for its chronological depth and is rich in substructures, overlaid by later buildings; it has moreover a long pre-Toltec past. Thompson is surely correct in suggesting that the inner Castillo coincides with the early Toltec Maya phase (Kubler also consigns it to his early period). But what occurs in Tollan resembles not this inner structure but the outer one; one can hardly escape the fact that, irrespective of its origins, the formative stages leading to the ultimate buildings are manifest in Chichén, but not in Tollan.

To sum up, I cannot on the one hand go so far as to agree that from the spiritual or historical point of view Toltec Chichén, or Modified Florescent, represents the true continuation of the Classic Maya tradition. I do not see Chichén as a true creator, since it first absorbs the spirit of a new age conceived elsewhere and introduced by the Toltecs, in their turn influenced by notions and styles from previous eras. Such Toltec contributions were then blended in Yucatán with certain local traditions. Out of this amalgam grew Toltec-Maya art, inspired thus from outside but then confected in Chichén.

Unlike the Toltec-Chichimecas, or even the Nonoalcas, who came from an artistically somewhat marginal region, the Mayas of Chichén possessed a rich cultural heritage as artificers and architects. By their skill and ingenuity they were able to bring such a blend of norms and traditions to early visual fruition in such grandiose projects as the Great Ball Court, the Temple of Warriors, and the Castillo. This is something which the Toltecs would never have been able to accomplish unaided. Such artistic achievements, by the same process of flux and reflux, were then relayed back to Tollan, where some were faithfully, if rather inadequately, copied. The original Toltec spiritual inspiration was now made manifest in Tollan in solid stone, as the city itself became the architectural or artistic reflection of its own brilliant offspring, contemporary Chichén.

Chronological Questions

Various aspects of the Tollan-Chichén question have now been examined and it has been seen that, regardless of which of the two provided the initial inspiration, everything points to the contemporaneity of the two centers. The relative lateness of common artistic manifestations is of historic importance, since this indicates a long continuity of contact rather than merely an early connection which later lost its vigor.

It is hard to seek in Chichén itself exact confirmation of more general chronological contentions. The association of Maya dates with Toltec style is rare; even in the Puuc period, while glyphic inscriptions continued, the glyphs themselves are neither familiar nor translatable. The last recorded Long Count date in Chichén itself is 10.2.9.1.9.; in the Short Count, this falls in Katun 1 Ahau.

Thus, for any positive guidance to Chichén chronology, one is obliged to fall back on the katun prophecies of the *Chilam Balam*, which, of course, refer only to the Short Count. The assigning of corresponding years in our own calendar to Short Count dates involves the same problem of correlation as for the Long Count, that is to say, Short Count calculations also depend on the basic question of whether the year A.D. 1539 coincides with 11.16.0.0.0., in accordance with Goodman-Martínez-Thompson, or with 12.9.0.0.0., as in the Spinden version, or is alternately equivalent to some different and intermediate year.

It has already been mentioned that the *Chilam Balam of Chumayel* connects the first appearance in Chichén of the Itzas with Katun 8 Ahau (928–48). It has equally been stressed that whatever happened in a given katun was expected to recur when the same number returned 256 years later; hence, such vaticinations became equivalent to recorded facts. The arrival of Kukulcan, as well as of certain Itzas (presumably an additional group), remain associated with Katun 4 Ahau, but the question still remains as to its correct Christian equivalent.

Before Tollan had been more extensively excavated, controversy arose about whether, on the basis of the Goodman-Martínez-Thompson correlation, Katun 4 Ahau corresponded to the years A.D. 967–87 or to those of the next katun of that number, 1224–44. Beyer particularly favored the latter interpretation. But since then, following further archaeological investigation showing the Mazapan of Tollan and the Fine Orange X of Chichén to be more or less contemporary, opinion has increasingly favored 967–87 as the Katun 4 Ahau associated with the coming of Kukulcan. Thompson actually proposes the year 987 for his arrival; this calculation is based on the conversion to our calendar of the year 1 Tecpatl, when he reportedly left Tollan, on the basis of Jiménez Moreno's Mixtec year count. It has already been explained that we cannot regard such early Toltec I Tecpatl dates as anything more than mythical; therefore, while accepting Thompson's general contention regarding the correct equivalent of the Katun 4 Ahau in question, it does not seem possible to determine the actual year of the event. Roys, rejecting the implications of a report (dated 1581) that the followers of Kukulcan took possession eight hundred years before, places the incursion in about 940.[68]

As to the first arrival of the Itzas at Chichén, the actual date for the coming of "our enemies," as the Mayas termed them, is given as 2

Akbal I Yaxkin in the *Chilam Balam of Chumayel*. As Thompson points out, the first recurrence of this date (which occurs every fifty-two years) after the last lintel of the Classic Long Count was carved in 10.2.9.1.9., is April 26, 918, and the next 2 Akbal I Yaxkin would occur in 970. He favors the former of the two dates and suggests that they arrived about 918.

As for the date of the fall of Toltec Chichén, evidence suggests it may have survived Xicocotitlan, but probably for not much more than one generation. As will be explained in more detail in the next chapter, Fine Orange Type X and Plumbate approximately span the duration of this period in both sites. Moreover, since it is the late Chichén and the late Tollan periods which present such close stylistic similarities, they must have been roughly contemporary. Regardless of which site created the original version of various monuments, it would be difficult to argue that one city would imitate the art forms of another only *after* the latter had already become a prey to alien invaders.

According to the second chronicle of *Chumayel*, the depopulation of Chichén Itza consequent upon the invasion of Hunac Ceel, ruler of Mayapan, occurred thirteen katuns, or 256 years, after its original occupation by the Itzas. Logically, this should imply a date falling between 1222 and 1244. Morley places this happening one katun later, suggesting that the destruction of Toltec Chichén took place in Katun 2 Ahau (1244–63).[69] With these dates Ruz more or less concurs, suggesting the first half of the thirteenth century for the occurrence. Of course, such disaster did not involve total abandonment, any more than in the case of Tollan. As will later be stressed, it seems very possible that Toltec power had already passed its peak many decades before this; it may be that Hunac Ceel merely delivered the *coup de grâce* to what was already a declining polity.

Any consideration of chronological questions might seem incomplete without mentioning the hypothesis of E. Wyllys Andrews. Paradoxically enough, he more or less accepts Thompson's Chichén dating while rejecting the Goodman-Martínez-Thompson correlation and embracing that of Spinden. He suggests that the Modified Florescent (i.e., Toltec) period in Chichén lasted from A.D. 900 to 1150, following a 250-year period spanned by Puuc, and so on, after the earlier fall of the Classic Maya period, as propounded by Spinden.[70]

Indeed, if any modification were to be made to the chronology of the coming of the Itzas and of Kukulcan, it would seem preferable to advance the figure rather than the reverse. Radiocarbon dates are not as yet conclusive, but may nevertheless act as a pointer in this respect. One date is given for Toltec Chichén of 870 A.D. ± 100.[71] In addition, we have figures of 799 ± 70 and 819 ± 100 for the Castillo, presumably for the inner structure.[72]

It would seem as if the Goodman-Martínez-Thompson equivalent of Katun 4 Ahau A.D. 967–87, as given above, represents the latest rather than the earliest likely date for the inception of the Toltec period. To suggest their coming in a previous 4 Ahau, falling 256 years earlier, would clearly involve going to an opposite extreme. It must, however, not be forgotten that the so-called arrival of Kukulcan is only the final or culminating act in the long-drawn-out process of penetration from the Altiplano.

What Might Have Happened

Certain principal aspects of this trans-Mesoamerican cultural marriage have now been examined. The linkage resulted in the appearance of certain virtually identical forms in two places a thousand miles apart. But it still remains to ask ourselves in terms of history what actually happened, and how did such remote partners even come to combine? One may now tentatively propose the following stages in the processes involved.

1. During the Teotihuacán period, a gradual infiltration of its culture into southern Veracruz and part of Tabasco took place, reaching its climax in the later Teotihuacán phases. Such penetration is most apparent in sites in the Tuxtla Mountains in southern Veracruz. After the fall of Teotihuacán, during the predominantly Puuc period in Campeche and Yucatán as well as in certain Late Classic Maya sites farther inland, "Mexican," or non-Maya, influences became manifest in ways already outlined; this development may not have been entirely unassociated with the reported departure eastward of the wise men from Teotihuacán. In this same period, Tabasco increasingly became a Mayan cultural province, as the great site of Comalcalco bears witness;

this is essentially Mayan with no specifically non-Maya traits. One thus encounters not only an eastward but a westward flow of new trends.

2. Probably during the early ninth century, or perhaps before, some Nonoalcas went off from Tabasco in a northwesterly direction; after a long migratory journey they reached first the Huaxteca, and then Tulancingo. In this area they joined forces with the Tolteca-Chichimecas, and Tollan Xicocotitlan became their joint capital. It is not unlikely that other moves of Nonoalcas and related peoples took place at this time, not only westward but also southeastward, as one of many waves of Pipil incursions into Central America.

At a somewhat later date a Putun group, later to be called the Itzas, occupying territory situated not far to the east of Nonoalco and beyond the Grijalva delta, departed in the opposite direction and occupied Chichén. Conceivably this displacement (and also that of the Nonoalcas) was not a once-and-for-all affair, but consisted of several waves of migrants, moving at different times from Tabasco to Yucatán. An innate tendency may have persisted for peoples to move between these two areas; Landa reports that at a much later date auxiliaries were brought from Tabasco to the Cocom ruler in Mayapan.

3. In what was reportedly Katun 8 Ahau, as part of this process of flux and reflux some Toltecs, presumably partly of Nonoalca stock, came back from Tollan to Nonoalco in Tabasco; for some reason they did not remain there, but continued their journey in an easterly direction until they reached what was now Chichén Itza. As Thompson suggests, they may have been accompanied there by a further migrant wave of Chontal Itzas from Tabasco. The long trek from Tollan to Chichén was less unaccountable than might appear at first; it was not unnatural that the Nonoalcas of Tollan should maintain contacts with their previous abode in Tabasco, which in those days must still have struck vivid chords in the memory of people now faced with the much bleaker surroundings of Tollan. Nor was it surprising that if some of their former neighbors, the Chontal Itzas, had moved off to Chichén, any Nonoalcas returning to Tabasco should be tempted to follow them and share the fruits of their Yucatán venture. The Nonoalcas, as already noted, were nothing if not mobile and adaptable.

From the many illustrations of Toltec-type warriors in Chichén, so un-Maya in profile, it would appear that the newcomers arrived not purely as traders but as conquerors, who imposed their will upon the local inhabitants. Since Sahagún tells us that the Aztec merchants went armed to the teeth to Xicalango, it might be argued that the Toltecs also went as armed traders. It is hardly likely, however, that portraits of mere merchants would have predominated to such a degree in the great monuments of Chichén. In some cases a military conquest is indeed implied, since battle scenes are depicted in which a distinction is drawn between Toltecs and Mayas, the former clearly emerging victorious.

From the many illustrations in murals and reliefs of plumed serpents and of Quetzalcoatl, it becomes equally evident that the new influx marked the final hegemony of religious trends that had already seeped into the area, though not of Maya origin.

The invaders accordingly came armed both with the sword and the book; the resulting change was basically even more fundamental than in the altiplano, where the old gods continued and the new ones had deeper local roots; in Yucatán very marked modifications in the pantheon seem to have occurred as compared with Classic times.

In a sense the intruders were colonists, and Wauchope even suggests that they may have alienated the local people by their very strangeness.[73] Such remarks may apply in particular to the Toltec-Chichimecas, numerically probably the stronger element in Tollan; the Nonoalcas might have been less alien and perhaps more familiar with Maya customs and even language. The newcomers seem to have remained somewhat apart from the rest of the population, as can be seen by the separate and distinctive way in which they are depicted. They certainly left very little long-term imprint on the local tongue and none on the race. When finally conquered in 1697, the Itzas were occupying various islands in Lake Petén, of which Tayasal, the site of present-day Flores, was the most important. Not only was their language pure Yucatec of a somewhat archaic kind, but the few Nahua names among them bore about the same proportion to Maya appellations as in Yucatán; they possessed very few traits that could definitely be defined as "Mexican." The Toltecs thus seem to have imported general concepts and attitudes rather than a definite pattern of living;[74] moreover, it was not until the later efflorescence of Mayapan that urbanism in any sense spread from the Altiplano to Yucatán.

The intruders can hardly therefore have been very numerous and were probably unaccompanied by their womenfolk.

Roys indeed insists that a Maya aristocracy continued to exist in Yucatán during the Toltec period.[75] Perhaps their situation was not unlike that of the Indian nobility in the early days of the Spanish Conquest. And, like the Spaniards, the new overlords had the advantage of superior or new weapons, in this instance the atlatl and dart; the Mayas themselves seemingly continued to rely on spear and battle-ax. Tozzer describes in detail such differences between the costume of the altatl-bearing Toltecs and the spear-carrying Mayas, as depicted in Chichén.[76]

4. Following these initial migrations to and fro, empires gradually formed around the nuclei constituted by Chichén and Tollan Xicocotitlan. One is not concerned at this point with Tollan, to be discussed in the following chapter. Apart from other evidence of Itza expansion, the overtly militarist spirit evident in Chichén art surely implies at least the achievement of regional conquests; indeed, certain sources actually refer to tribute and gifts offered to the rulers of Chichén.

5. As a simultaneous development to such presumed conquests, art forms were developed using elements which later became common to both centers. These were accompanied by concepts not previously present among the Mayas, such as the use of exterior space and the portrayal of groups as well as individuals. This new inspiration came mainly from the Toltecs, who had already absorbed other cultural influences; on the other hand, the actual development of the new style was more attributable to Maya skill in execution. When thus fully developed on partly alien soil, such forms were then reflected back in perfected shape to their original source in Tollan, rather as a ray of light may be magnified by a reflecting mirror and retransmitted in the reverse direction. As the continuing cultural identity demonstrates, during several centuries these contacts were maintained over a vast intermediate territory. Much of this was inhabited by people of Olmeca-Xicallanca stock, extending from Cholula to the Gulf Coast of Veracruz. These people enjoyed certain ethnic ties with the Nonoalcas; no doubt their mutual relations were not unconnected with trade.

6. Finally, in the late twelfth or early thirteenth century, both

centers went into a decline as they suffered outside attack, though neither ceased to exist altogether. This process will be studied in more detail where Tollan is concerned.

Two points deserve further comment. First is the part played by any human Quetzalcoatl-Kukulcan. It is hardly necessary to re-emphasize our previous contention that, if any historic personage had existed as a kind of heroic precursor to the new Quetzalcoatl cult, he would have lived centuries before the Tollan-Chichén era. Logically, therefore, if an actual man called Quetzalcoatl, Topiltzin, Nacxitl, or Kukulcan had led any Toltec irruption into Yucatán, he would have been the upholder of an already-formed tradition and the incumbent of an established office.

It is considered that when the *Chilam Balam* tells of the coming of Kukulcan, it refers less to one individual than to the general arrival of Toltecs and the full diffusion of the cult of the god Quetzalcoatl, already present in incipient form. Possibly, of course, the first group was led by a man who had actually assumed the title of Quetzalcoatl or Kukulcan, arising from the presence in Tollan of a succession of leaders bearing that name or title.

What is unacceptable to me is the likelihood that any great man-hero called Quetzalcoatl first established himself in Tollan and then quixotically abandoned his own creation in its early stages, fleeing from there to Chichén, where he then erected buildings recalling in style his former capital. It must again be stressed that most of what is now visible in Tollan that recalls Chichén belongs to its end, rather than to the early period. We have, moreover, already questioned the validity of the stories concerning a first ruler of Tollan who left in the relatively early stages, accompanied by part of the population.

If an actual Quetzalcoatl really led the eastward migration, he would have been only one of a long line of such titleholders in Tollan; more probably, he might have adopted the appellation in his capacity as leader of the new Tollan in the east. Landa tells us of another Kukulcan who founded Mayapan, and leaders called Kukulcan or Gucumatz positively abounded in Highland Guatemala. In the Maya area, far from being a mere name, it seems to have become a kind of designation applied to rulers, like the original name Caesar, both in Imperial

Rome and thereafter. Its assumption of course reinforced claims to Toltec descent.

Secondly, one may briefly recapitulate the part played in these occurrences by the general region of southeastern Veracruz, Tabasco, and southern Campeche. That verdant land in some ways represents an earthly Tlalocan; as a nurturing ground of many tribes, it played a part parallel to that of Chicomoztoc in the northwestern marches of Mesoamerica; like Chicomoztoc itself, it was even on occasion referred to as Quinehuan, the place of rising up or starting out.[77] In the pre-Colonial era the role of the region was pivotal, at times as a principal place of settlement, at others as a transit and trading area, serving to link the Altiplano with Chiapas and the Highlands of Guatemala. It had attracted to itself many cultural trends, both Teotihuacán and Maya, and became a kind of germinating plot "where people changed language," and from where both the Nonoalcas and the Itzas emerged.

Evidences, however, of Toltec occupation of the area are few and far between. As will shortly be seen, the inhabitants of Tollan were far less numerous than those of the Aztec capital and could not be expected to plant colonies everywhere. If they did so at Chichén, it was not essential to do likewise in Tabasco, still possibly inhabited in part by their Nonoalca kith and kin.

In general terms, the whole Toltec-Chichén epic demonstrates the new spirit manifest in the Mesoamerican world and above all the Toltecs' own will to conquer.

If one takes Adams' definition of pristine and secondary states, it was Chichén which in reality played the latter role, while Tollan Xicocotitlan represented a development *sui generis* and could therefore indeed be called pristine.[78] Nevertheless, this original relationship became partly reversed, and Chichén may be regarded, artistically speaking, as a creator in its own right as much as a receiver.

Chichén was the outward manifestation, transported to the Maya scene, of the new Postclassic trends, markedly at variance with the more static theocratic regime that probably still partly prevailed among the Mayas of the Puuc period. As such, it witnessed the inception of a new situation. It may reasonably be suggested that in previous ages, particularly in the Maya area, warlike operations were subject to considerations of trade rather than the reverse, and that the norm was the independent city-state, existing side by side with others of its kind. On the other hand, in the Postclassic period, a process began whereby commerce gradually became subordinated to military dictates and to the acquisition of tribute-paying territories. This development was to culminate in Central Mesoamerica in the Aztec achievement; on the other hand, in unconquered Yucatán, it led merely to local and suicidal warfare between would-be collectors of tribute in the last pre-Hispanic period.

6. Toltec Apogee: The Home Base

We must now retrace our steps from distant Chichén to Tollan proper in order to examine its structure and strength when standing at the apex of its power, say from A.D. 1000 to 1100. It will be explained in Chapter 8 that Tollan's decline probably set in after that date; thus the city enjoyed a period of supremacy that was probably short, but none the less significant.

One is witnessing, indeed, the first endeavor since Teotihuacán to re-establish a supreme authority in Central Mesoamerica, whether of a spiritual, commercial, or military nature. After Tollan, two further such attempts were to follow: the short-lived Tepanec experiment in empire building, and the great Aztec expansion, also cut short in its very prime.

Compared with the relative longevity of Teotihuacán, its three successors were fated to die young, for different and unrelated reasons. The first of these, Tollan Xicocotitlan, probably succumbed mainly to pressure exercised by semibarbarians; the Tepanecs fell victim to revolt from within; the Aztec Empire was overwhelmed by invasion from another world.

How Many Toltecs?

The Toltec attempt to reconstruct order out of chaos was in many respects the most remarkable, simply because it was the first, following a period of cultural collapse in that part of Mexico. As we have seen, the early inhabitants of Tollan looked out on a changed world; many ancient gods and customs survived, but other familiar landmarks had vanished and basic norms were altered. To understand this new situation and to assess Tollan's significance, one must first consider the city's internal structure, population, institutions, and commerce. Only thereafter, in the following chapter, can the question be examined of a putative Toltec empire, in relation to areas possibly subjugated and to others lying probably beyond its grasp.

The problem of how many Tollans might have existed has been studied at some length. In turn it becomes necessary to ask how many Toltecs there were, referring in this context to the inhabitants of Tollan Xicocotitlan itself.

While extensive excavations had previously been effected by Acosta, they were largely confined to the area of the principal ceremonial center. Only recently has attention become focused more on the city as a whole and the very basic question of Tollan's total area and population been examined; much indeed still remains to be done before information on settlement plans and general layout can compare with that now available for Teotihuacán. Renewed explorations, involving excavation of house remains in the northeast portion of the city as well as a survey of the whole populated area of Tollan, was initiated by the University of Missouri Archaeological Project in 1970, headed by Richard Diehl. Comprehensive work of this nature is now also being carried out by the Instituto Nacional de Antropología e Historia, under the direction of Eduardo Matos. The specific matters under investigation are germane to the problem of Toltec internal organization; but, arising out of this, they equally affect the nature of the empire which the Toltecs could perhaps have controlled.

The Tollan of the Tula-Mazapan horizon occupied a considerable part of the natural limestone ridge that overlooks the modern town of Tula de Allende, situated in the river valley below. (*See* Map 3.) The ancient city covered most of this ridge, constituting a kind of L-shape, that ran for some two kilometers in an east-west direction, and for a farther kilometer from north to south.[1]

It is not at present known whether any sizable proportion of the population lived in the valleys on either side of the high ground, including the area covered by the modern town. Signs exist of pre-Hispanic occupation; for instance, the *parroquia*, dating from the sixteenth century, rests on what appear to be ancient foundations, and other mounds are visible in the river valley in the area overlooked by Tula Chico.

The only tentative published estimate for Tula's population is that of James Stoutamire of the Missouri expedition. Taking the area of the urban zone, excluding the El Salitre marsh, as covering approximately thirteen square kilometers, he tentatively proposes a maximum figure for Tollan's population of 65,000. He points out that Sanders suggests a density of 2,500 to 5,000 inhabitants for what he calls the High Density Compact Village in modern Highland Mexico, and takes the higher of these two figures. Millon's estimate of 125,000 for Teotihuacán's twenty square kilometers suggests a density of 6,250 per square kilometer. Stoutamire, however, states that the evidence is fairly strong that Tollan's population was less dense than that of Teotihuacán.[2] Matos agrees on the over-all area covered by the city, but tends toward a somewhat more conservative population figure of about 37,000, though he accepts the possibility that it could have reached 50,000.

Wynn backs up the possible comparison between the density of population in Teotihuacán and Tollan by the example of his Unit 3 in the latter site, situated in the vicinity of El Corral. It occupies 179 square meters, of which 133 were roofed in. Since almost no Coyotlatelco or Aztec II sherds were found and pottery was virtually all Mazapan, it may be concluded that the dwelling unit belongs exclusively to Tollan's middle, or great, period. Wynn concludes that eighteen to twenty people at a time may have occupied this structure, based on an average of two per room in a house that probably contained two nuclear families, with an additional structure built on to suffice for another two families. This would accord with Borah and Cook's estimate of 4.5 persons per nuclear family.[3] One thus reaches a total of nine people in a two-family unit, or eighteen in all, including those in the additional structure.[4]

Certain observations may be added to these admittedly very tentative figures. On the one hand, this is stated to be an upper-class house, and the author agrees that for people of higher status, space tended to be used more generously. Wynn mentions that in a lower-class tenement occupying the same space, as many as sixty people could have lived.[5] The difference in density is thus very substantial.

On the other hand, population is seldom uniformly distributed, and one must take into account decreasing density toward the periphery of the city, only partly included in the above survey, which might act as a counterbalancing factor. This tendency may of course in its turn be compensated not only by a possible occupancy of unknown proportions in the river valley but also by the likely presence of peasant abodes made of perishable materials on the city outskirts. It is known that in Aztec times land cultivators tended to be housed in such structures on the edge of a town, though this hardly applied in Tenochtitlan itself, surrounded by water. As will later be seen, the apparent absence of a large rural population in the immediate vicinity reinforces the possibilities of peasant housing on the city's edge.

It should also be mentioned that Millon has tended to revise upward his estimates for Teotihuacán. He proposes a probable figure for the Xolalpan phase of 125,000 (i.e., over 6,000 per square kilometer), but states that the population *could* have even reached 200,000.[6] Of course Calnek's tentative estimate of a maximum of 250,000 for Tenochtitlan gives a density of more like 17,000 per square kilometer, but no one has so far proposed a comparable degree of urbanization for Tollan.[7]

Nevertheless, the inhabited area on the ridge is impressively large; thus, bearing in mind the different factors already mentioned, one might expect a tendency to revise upward any early estimates of population. Even so, the total would surely still fall far short of that of Teotihuacán, let alone of Tenochtitlan. On the other hand, it would much exceed that of Tikal, for which Sanders suggests 10,000 to 20,000.[8]

In the first place, one must not take for granted the presence of a vast population wherever one finds large and imposing buildings, as Tikal aptly demonstrates. In ancient societies, a considerable proportion of the people were almost inactive for up to five months of the year and therefore readily available for construction work. Attention has already been called to Kaplan's insistence that in Mesoamerica public-works building usually took place in discontinuous stages and by accretions over a long stretch of time.[9] Thus a limited labor force working over an extended period could have completed the buildings of any given Mesoamerican site; Tollan Xicocotitlan, while impressive, is of course by no means the biggest.

However, over and above its relatively large extent, perhaps the most significant pointer which might suggest a comparatively high figure for Tollan arises from information concerning its early colonial population; from this, certain deductions may be drawn.

The considerable importance of Tollan in Aztec times should always be borne in mind—a factor to which the close ties binding the royal houses of Tollan and Tenochtitlan bear constant witness. Rather oddly, Tollan is not mentioned in the *Matrícula de Tributos*, and it has been suggested by Robert Barlow that, because of its special and sanctified status, it may have been exempt from tribute. Alternatively, as Feldman suggests, it might conceivably have been a direct tributary of the Tenochca *tlatoani*. Xilotepec is the provincial center from the tributary point of view, and possibly had become the commercial capital of the region, rather as Miacatlán had earlier assumed the economic headship of the Xochicalco area. The *Codex Osuna* incidentally mentions Tula as one of the eight *tlahtocayotl* under Tlacopan, the junior member of the Aztec Triple Alliance, a further indication of its continued significance. It seems to have been a leading provincial center, as much as or more so than Xilotepec, even if the latter headed the tribute list from which Tula is conspicuous by its absence. When the *Codex Osuna* speaks of Tula, it may of course be referring to a Tula-Xilotepec rather than a separate Tollan community.

Diehl emphasizes that during its apogee, the area of ancient Tollan was much more continuously occupied than in Aztec times (indicated by Aztec III and IV pottery), even if the population was perhaps less concentrated. The latest investigations of the INAH also confirm the finding of Aztec III and IV in part only of the earlier Toltec city. The impression is clearly gained that Tollan, as capital of its own empire, was inhabited by more people than in later centuries, when it was reduced to the status of an Aztec provincial capital.

Thus the probable population in 1519, at the close of this period, would provide pertinent clues as to figures for imperial Tollan. Sanders gives the estimated population of the city in 1568 as 14,593; for Tula province he quotes for the same date 67,367. The population of the City of Mexico in that year he gives as 52,000.[10] The *Suma de Visitas* mentions the existence in the city of Tula of 2,072 houses and 7,800 married men.[11] As such, it is larger than most comparable centers; Toluca, for instance, then had only 1,602 houses. It is furthermore of interest that as late as the 1570's Tula was sufficiently large to provide for the founding of a barrio in Xochimilco, rather recalling the pre-Conquest *calpulli* foundations.[12] The City of México incidentally in 1570 had 30,000 tributaries, that is to say, under five times that of Tula at the same moment.

It is estimated that by 1570 numbers had fallen to one fifth of those of 1519 in many areas. However, one might in this case presuppose a somewhat less drastic decline and base one's calculations on data given for the Teotihuacán Valley, another high and arid area and therefore somewhat comparable. Sanders calculates that the latter possessed 50,000 inhabitants in the late 1560's, 75,000 in 1548, 100,000–125,000 in 1530, and 135,000 in 1519.[13] A comparable fall would suggest a figure of approximately 40,000 for the city of Tula in 1519, based on some 14,593 in 1568, as proposed above.

It has already been stressed that the Aztec city was very far from occupying the whole site of the earlier Tollan; therefore, even allowing for a greater degree of urbanization in the Late Postclassic period and an increased density in occupied areas, it becomes hard to propose that the population was actually greater in 1519 than in 1100; it is much more likely to have been appreciably smaller. Admittedly, the *rural* population of the Teotlalpan may well have augmented in Aztec times; with the advent of more elaborate irrigation techniques, the ratio of country dwellers to urban inhabitants may have risen in areas suited to hydraulic schemes. As will later be noted, the number of sites in the country surrounding Tollan actually increased in the later pre-Hispanic period, as indeed did the rural population living in the Valley of Teotihuacán. Thus Stoutamire's tentative estimate of 65,000 for Tollan's population is not altogether unreasonable, since it is about 60 per cent higher than our suggested figure for 1519.

Turning now to the surrounding district, various figures are also available for the early Colonial period. Concerning the whole area of the Teotlalpan, Sherburne F. Cook observes that the population in 1565 was 190,632.[14] Sanders, as already mentioned, quotes a figure of 67,367 for the Tula province in 1568; this, however, covers a much smaller area, totaling 1,451 square kilometers, or embracing, say, the area within a radius of 20 kilometers around Tula itself. Zantwijk estimates a total of 45,000 inhabitants in 1568 for the Tula military district, one of the four into which the home territory of Tlacopan was divided and which in Zantwijk's map embraces a strip of territory about 20 kilometers wide, stretching from Tula in the south up to and beyond Ixmiquilpan in the north. He considers that the same area would have possessed about 300,000 inhabitants in 1519.[15] Incidentally, by using Zantwijk's multiplier of over five to one for converting 1570 populations into those of 1519, a much larger number would be reached for the *city* of Tula in 1519 than was proposed above.

Of these different figures, one of the more pertinent is that for the Tula province given by Sanders; the *Codex of Otlazpan* incidentally mentions as the pueblos of this province in 1746 Tepeji del Río, Tepetitlan, Nextlalpan, Iztlapa, Tultengo, and Xicapotla. Such a territory might be described as the inner heartland, comparable to the Central Valley of Mexico, from which the Aztecs drew their main strength. (The distance from Tepeji to Tula as the crow flies is only marginally less than that dividing Tenochtitlan from Texcoco.) Using the same multiplier as we applied in the case of the city itself, a population of 67,000 in 1569 for the Tula province would give an approximate total of 180,000 in 1519. As will be recalled, the calculation for the *city* was based on comparative figures for those living in the Valley of Teotihuacán, but Sanders' charts of decline between 1520 and 1568 for Tepoztlan, as well as for a much larger surrounding area, do not differ greatly from this pattern; in these two cases the population at the time of the Conquest was at least three times greater than fifty years later. We have used 2.7 as a multiplier, and therefore our suggested figures for 1519 may err on the conservative side.

If one takes the whole of the Teotlalpan, as opposed to the Tula province, the total population is naturally very much higher. Using the 1568 figure of 190,632 as a basis, the number of inhabitants rises to over 500,000 in 1519. But the Teotlalpan is relatively large in extent; for instance, the distance from Tula to Ixmiquilpan is comparable not to that from Tenochtitlan to Texcoco but to Cuernavaca or Toluca; the latter was of course only conquered by the Aztecs in the reign of Axayácatl. The Teotlalpan is thus not really to the Toltecs the equivalent of what the Central Valley of Mexico was to the Aztecs, but is more to be compared to the latter area, with the adjoining valleys of Morelos and Toluca added to it. It is the population of 180,000 for the inner province surrounding Tula that is perhaps more relevant, as constituting the Toltec heartland. This figure is what may more aptly be compared with that of the lakeside region, studded with teeming cities, that constituted for Tenochtitlan a kind of core area; this veritable conurbation served the Mexicas as a basis for internal trade, produced food for the metropolis, paid taxes, and most important of all, provided the manpower for unceasing war. It is hard to see how the Aztecs could have dominated their empire without drawing on this whole population, which Gibson suggests to have been as high as 1,500,000 in 1519.

But whereas the population of Tollan itself was probably larger when it stood at its apogee than in Aztec times, one suspects, as already stated, that the immediately surrounding territory was more densely settled in 1519. The region in question would correspond in part with that which Feldman describes as "maize irrigation," in connection with the tribute which it paid to the Aztecs. It seems probable that irrigation had been intensified in the Late Postclassic period.

Highly significant with regard to the Toltec heartland is the report of Guadalupe Mastache, who made a survey covering a radius of fifteen to twenty kilometers around Tula, stretching as far as Tezontepec in the north and Tepeji del Río in the south and covering a total of 106 archaeological sites. She located three sites belonging to the Preclassic and fourteen to the Classic horizon, situated in general near rivers or some form of water; in the latter, pottery belonging to Teotihuacán II, III, and IV was found; no place was very large, and six yielded only sherds.

The number of located sites for the Postclassic period increased considerably, and forty-eight containing Tula-Mazapan pottery were found, mainly also near water. Most of these were merely small villages, and in only four cases was it possible to identify any kind of ceremonial center. Mastache very tentatively suggests that in none of these would the total population have exceeded 1,000, and stresses that Tollan Xicocotitlan is the *only* major place in its immediate vicinity—again a totally different situation to that later prevailing around Tenochtitlan.[16]

What is most significant is that in the Late Postclassic period the number of sites increased, and a larger proportion of the total possessed ceremonial centers. Diehl also mentions intensified Aztec rural occupation, as discovered by a preliminary regional survey undertaken by the Missouri expedition. For instance, in Tepatepec, as well as farther afield in Actopan, Cobean found Aztec remains to be far more in evidence than those of the Toltec horizon; the same is true of Ajacuba, which can boast of an Aztec settlement of large but undetermined size located near the modern town. Structures include pyramids and an I-shaped ball court; occupational debris covers the hillsides and surrounding valley floor. There may have been a nucleated settlement there with an area in excess of one square kilometer. On the other hand, the major occupation of Tepeji del Río spans the whole Postclassic period; even Preclassic sherds have been found.[17] The site possesses two small ceremonial centers.[18] Ixmiquilpan and Mixquiahuala also have traces of both Toltec and Aztec occupation. At the former, both Mazapan and Aztec ceramics were found on a mesa between two and four kilometers north of the present town. The remains of Mixquiahuala are mainly Aztec, but a small Toltec site was also found on a hillside above the Tula River four kilometers to the west of the modern pueblo.[19]

These initial surveys thus reinforce the feeling that, in contrast to Tollan itself, the population of the surrounding region probably reached its maximum in the Late Postclassic period. If that of the province of Tula in 1519 was in the vicinity of 180,000 (including of course the city), one may question whether it much exceeded 120,000 in 1100, and of this figure well over half probably lived in the city itself.

In this respect, the settlement plan of the Tollan region appears more as a carry-over from Teotihuacán than as a foretaste of the future Tenochtitlan. As Barbara Price points out, Teotihuacán seems to have virtually depopulated its own hinterland; she notes that of 135,000 people living in the Teotihuacán valley in Classic times, 85,000 to

100,000 inhabited the city itself. (It will of course be recalled that Millon has since tended to increase his estimates of the city population). Price mentions that the Lower Valley of Teotihuacán—today and probably already in Classic times perennially irrigated and considered as the choicest agricultural land in the valley—contains little rural settlement contemporary with the apogee of the city. She therefore naturally and probably rightly concludes that farming was carried out by the inhabitants of the city itself. Such a supposition should not be taken to imply that Tollan possessed no full-time artisans. Diehl considers that the two large obsidian workshops that he discovered employed specialists who did little or no farming.[20]

Now what Mastache found in the vicinity of Tula, particularly along the river valley, may not be identical in form to the Teotihuacán settlement plan in that certain rural sites of limited size were found, but the picture is surely similar. Thus one notes the apparent absence in the area surrounding the city of a population remotely recalling that of the Central Valley of Mexico in Aztec times, and which the metropolis of Tenochtitlan could exploit to the maximum as cannon fodder, for the purpose of conquering a pan-Mesoamerican empire. It is this absence of such human resources that will later lead us to question whether Tollan could physically conquer and hold a comparable extension of territory.

Contrasting Landscapes

From patterns of settlement, one must now pass to those of subsistence, in order to study Tollan's economic strength, and to ask the basic question: how did its inhabitants feed themselves? Were their local resources sufficient for the purpose, or must they perforce have depended on tribute for necessities as well as luxuries?

Retrospective deductions possess their limitations for solving demographic problems; however, they may be more valid for estimating agricultural resources, since there is little evidence of a marked local climatic variation from Classic to Postclassic period; this point will also be treated in Chapter 8, concerning possible causes of the fall of Tollan. To take one relevant example, José Luis Lorenzo insists that the paleoclimas of Central Mexico do not seem to have undergone any radical change in the past two thousand years, and the fluctuations in lake levels are not very marked.[21] It must be added that the Teotlalpan was perhaps somewhat marginal to this area; however, in the Teotlalpan as a whole, precipitation, humidity, and *absolute* aridity have probably not altered within the past millennium; on the other hand, *ecological* aridity has increased, even though the transition has not been perceptible to contemporaries.[22]

However, even if no great over-all changes occurred, early examples of environmental abuse probably accompanied the creation of the main Mesoamerican centers and resulted in localized ecological deterioration. As Sherburne Cook points out, it can hardly be a coincidence that such cities as Teotihuacán and Mitla are located in what is now parched and almost desert country. Sites initially so arid would surely not have been selected in preference to more inviting localities. Local changes almost certainly did occur, such as deforestation around Teotihuacán caused by the excessive burning of wood. Concerning Tollan, Cook actually writes of an area lying half a mile east of the center of the city, apparently a valley bottom with a deep mature soil profile, of which the upper part seems to have been removed in Toltec times.[23] Nevertheless, it must be admitted that, outside the River Tula valley, the Toltecs did not have much to spoil. The soil on the high ground is, and probably was, arid and poor; Cook considers that that region was almost uninhabited before the population increase under the Toltecs; small quantities of Teotihuacán sherds since located there hardly serve to invalidate the suggestion. Regarding the Teotlalpan as a whole, Cobean, quoting Cook, suggests that extensive soil erosion did occur because of deforestation of the hillsides and excessive cultivation of the valleys. This of course probably occurred more in the Late Postclassic period, when the rural population had increased.

As Sanders and Price emphasize, in the Tula region itself sedentary agriculture is at best precarious.[24] One might add that this has probably not radically changed since earlier times, even if the situation may have suffered further deterioration. Today the peasants still plant scattered crops, but the yield is minimal and they are apt to fail entirely. The vegetation is basically xerophytic, consisting principally of mesquite bushes, nopal, and maguey cactus, with a very light grass cover, more suited for small herds of goats and sheep than for crop cultivation; since the Conquest, the pirul tree has spread with great rapidity throughout the area, but from the strictly economic point of view, it is little more than a weed. Admittedly, certain archaeological evidence exists of earlier terracing in the surrounding high ground in order to increase yields, but it is not extensive. Surface artifacts found there include an unusually high number of chert scrapers, which Diehl suspects to be maguey rasps.

Accordingly, in view of the very evident barrenness of the outlying areas, the key to the problem of Toltec subsistence patterns must lie in the possibilities of contemporary irrigation along the banks of the River Tula. Nowadays the general region of Tula outside this fertile zone, while not totally barren, is almost more reminiscent of, say, coastal Perú, with its desert-like open stretches interspersed with rich and verdant river valleys, where superabundant cultivation results from irrigation. In this it differs much from the Valley of Mexico, where the contrast between the irrigated and nonirrigated areas is considerably less stark. Indeed, such is the disparity today between the rich valley of the River Tula and the poor hilltops that the very air one breathes seems different; below it smells cool and refreshing while above it blows hot and dusty.

Bearing in mind the obvious difficulties of feeding the people without some irrigation (much of the river valley would not be automatically verdant during most of the year) and in view of this extraordinary transformation that human skill has since effected, it is barely conceivable that Tollan itself did not have some recourse to hydraulic systems. It is hard to imagine that the inhabitants of this new and thriving metropolis should have stood idly by, watching the abundant waters of the river flow across their arid acres on their untrammeled way to the sea. Moreover, we would agree with Armillas when he maintains that the principal Mesoamerican civilizations could not have developed by sole dependence on slash-and-burn agricultural techniques; this is surely truer of Tollan than of any other.

Today the River Tula still possesses a very ample flow, sufficient to provide for a great number of reservoirs and irrigation schemes on an ever increasing scale, and the irrigated area, particularly between Tula and Ixmiquilpan, is already very extensive. Obviously, before such developments took place, the volume of water reaching Tula must have

Temple of Tlahuizcalpantecuhtli, Tula.

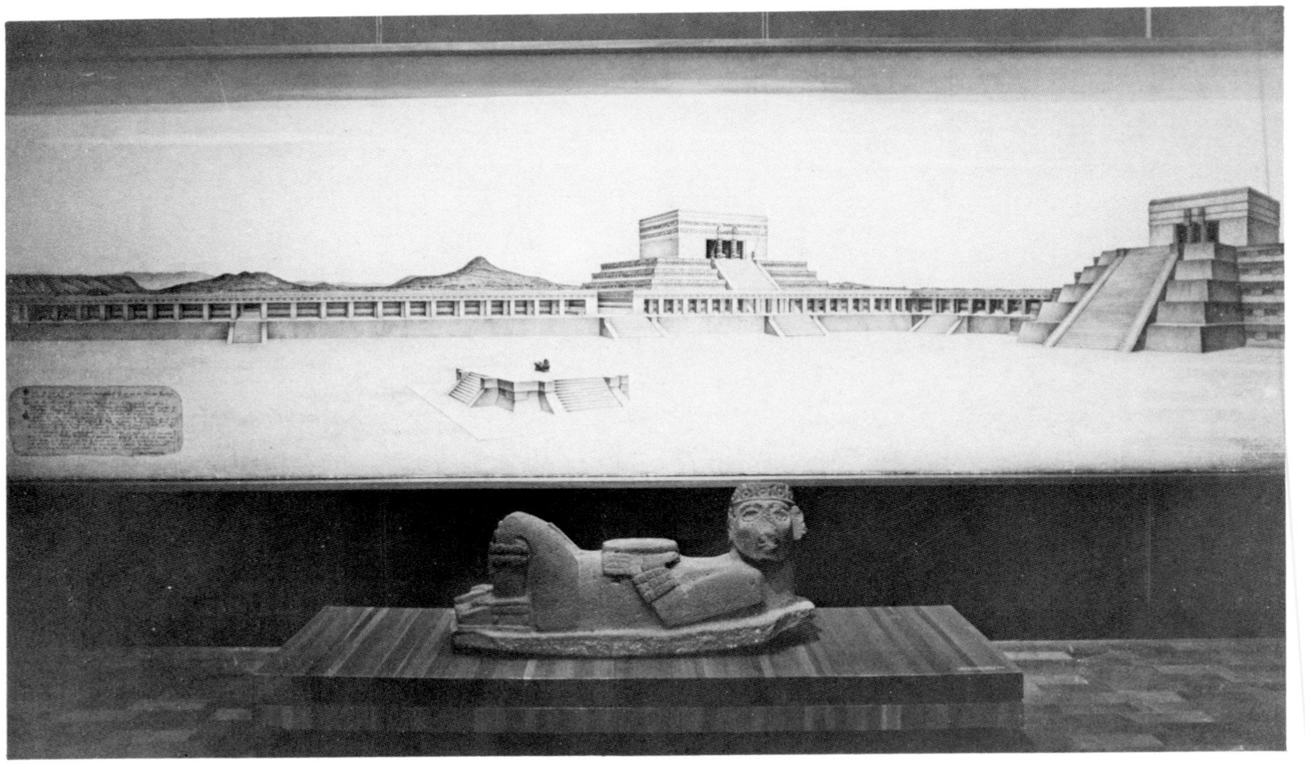

Model reconstruction of the central plaza of Tula with Chacmool in the foreground, Museo Nacional de Antropologia.

Coatepantli, Tula.

Coatepantli with Jaguars and Coyotes eating human hearts, Tula.

Wall of Serpents and Skulls (Coatepantli), Tula.

Atlantids, Tula.

Chacmool, Tula.

Jaguar, Tula Museum.

Incensario, Tula Museum.

Jaguar from Tula standing on hind feet, Museo Nacional de Antropologia.

Eagle frieze, Chichén Itza.

Plumbate figure from the state of Hidalgo, Museo Nacional de Antropologia.

Stone of the Four Glyphs. At the top are the Nahua glyphs 10 Acatl and 4 Tochtli, and below them are two Zapotec glyphs. Museo Nacional de Antropologia.

Jaguar Standard Bearer, Museo Nacional de Antropologia.

Early Postclassic Tlaloc figure, Museo Nacional de Antropologia.

Coyotlatelco style vessel, Museo Nacional de Antropologia.

Stela 3 from Xochicalco, Museo Nacional de Antropologia.

Colonnade of the Temple of the Warriors, Chichén Itza.

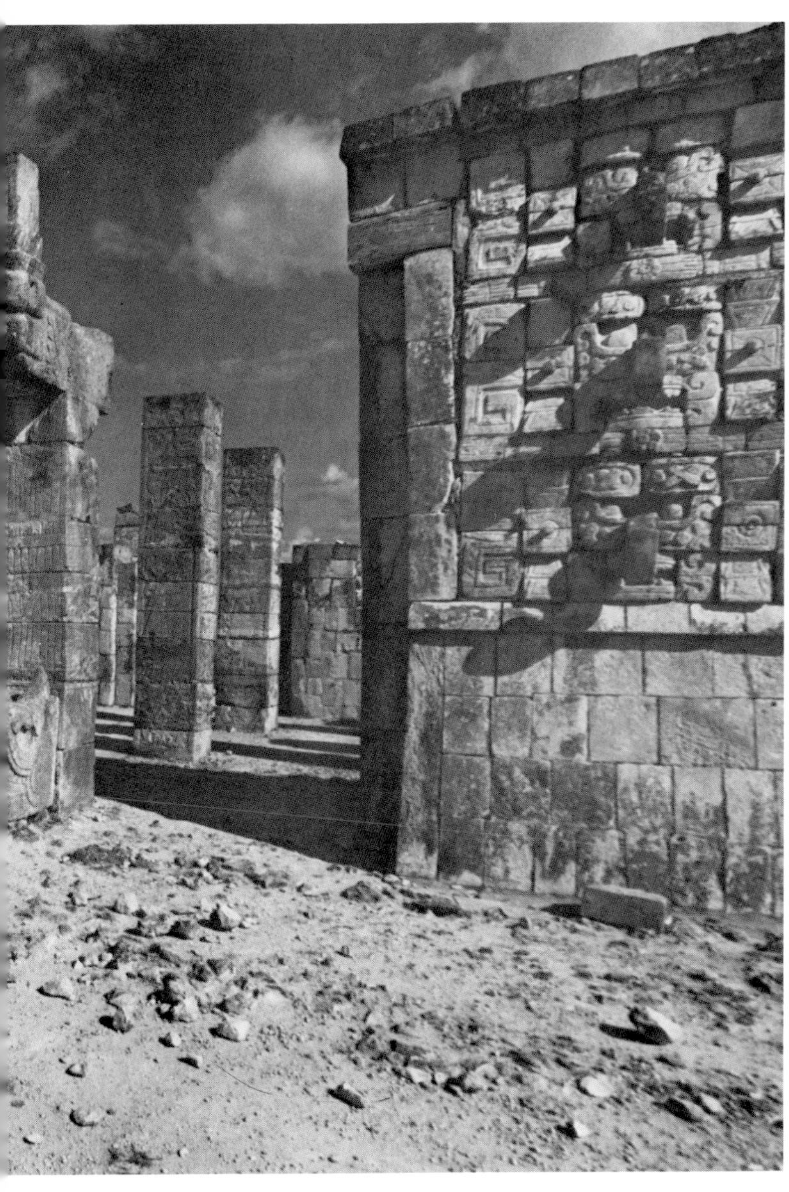

The Temple of the Warriors, Chichén Itza.

The Temple of the Niches, El Tajin.

The Caracol, Chichén Itza.

The Great Ball Court, Chichén Itza.

Base of the Skull Rack, Chichén Itza.

Atlantids, Chichén Itza.

Atlantid figure from Tula, Museo Nacional de Antropologia.

been considerably greater. Even in relatively barren years, a certain flow is still maintained, even if it diminishes in the dry season; according to the *Relación de Tequisquiac*, this seasonal variation was equally perceptible in early Colonial times.[25]

It may be added that a kind of natural or automatic irrigation does take place at one point; the area contiguous to the river and lying just below Tula Chico becomes regularly flooded by the high water in the rainy season. Before the river was extensively dammed, this natural inundation would probably have occurred on a greater scale. Surely it required only a further step in the same direction to ensure that such flooding was put to more permanent and controlled use in Toltec times. Incidentally, something not dissimilar seems to have occurred in the case of Teotihuacán. Bernal points to an area marginal to the shore of the Lake of Xochimilco that today becomes flooded in summer and dries up in winter; the long narrow strip in question offers the possibility of much better crops than can be obtained with no irrigation.[26] Sanders and Price also call attention to other phenomena of this type and mention indirect evidence of perennial irrigation of the Lower Teotihuacán Valley in former times, based on springs and floodwater.[27]

Notwithstanding some rudimentary indications of canals recently discovered below Tula Chico, it has not yet proved possible to detect extensive signs of Early Postclassic irrigation in Tollan, let alone to define its intensity, though one might perhaps add that in certain other cases aerial photography has served to reveal prehistoric hydraulic patterns; the matter is of course complicated in Tollan's case by the presence of the modern town in the valley. In addition, as Diehl points out, writers have occasionally mentioned the possibility of Chinampa agriculture in the swampy area known as El Salitre. However, intensive survey has failed to produce evidence of aboriginal occupation; today the soil and ground water are so saline that only a few specialized grasses can grow. The swamps may have been a source of fish and small aquatic products, but the use of this area for Chinampa cultivation seems most unlikely.[28]

The practice of irrigation in the Teotlalpan in Aztec times is amply demonstrated. The *Relacion de Tequisquiac* mentions extensive schemes five leagues distant from Tequisquiac itself; the River

Tula flowed by many large pueblos and its waters would nourish extensive fields of maize and vegetables.[29] The soil of the valley is of course itself fertile, in contrast to the barren hills above. This basic richness may partly be due to the fact that from Tlahuililpa to Tula the river valley is the moribund remnant of a once solid oak forest. Thus any well-directed attempt at irrigation will bring the land to full fruition and produce copious crops.[30] The *Suma de Visitas*, incidentally, mentions oaks in connection with Apaxco, where none are visible today.

Under such circumstances, it becomes hardly conceivable that the sophisticated Toltecs should have been content to depend for their existence on a semiarid waste, intersected by an abundant but untapped river. Even had they wished to do so, the feat would surely have proved impossible. Compelled to scratch a living in this rudimentary manner, the city could not have reached such proportions, let alone developed the resources and the surplus manpower necessary to conquer any kind of empire.

Indeed, had the Toltecs been totally unversed in the arts of irrigation, why would they ever have developed their capital in a zone so dependent upon such techniques? One may suspect that the Nonoalcas had already become familiar during their travels with certain hydraulic systems and that it was only after their coalescence with the Tolteca-Chichimecas, less versed in science, that Tollan grew from village to metropolis.

Moreover, what might otherwise rank as mere speculation concerning Toltec irrigation is indirectly backed by written evidence. The *Crónica Mexicayotl* tells how the itinerant Mexicas reached Tollan after its debacle, perhaps in the late twelfth century. The account relates that these Mexicas built for themselves elaborate dams and created a kind of artificial lake. It is highly improbable that a mere migrant tribe should have accomplished such feats of engineering, as has already been stressed in Chapter 1. If such dams and lake ever existed in those times—the account almost brings to mind those which are visible today on approaching Tula—they would surely have been constructed by the Toltecs themselves and not by mere squatters in their ruined capital. The story of their destruction, supposedly on the orders of Huitzilopochtli, is surely just another of the many anachronisms which abound in the sources; such devastation, together with the reported disappearance of the lacustrine fauna and flora, might have constituted a natural accompaniment to Tollan's own disasters. It is not entirely impossible that the Mexicas, or perhaps some other marauding tribe, might have *destroyed* Tollan's waterworks; however, they certainly could not have *built* them at that early stage in their development.

The whole problem of hydraulic systems in pre-Hispanic times is somewhat complex; even the Aztec pattern is not altogether clear. In many instances archaeology provides only uncertain clues. If, however, one can be sure that some form of irrigation existed in Mesoamerica prior to Tollan Xicocotitlan, then it becomes not only probable but almost certain that the Toltecs would have availed themselves of such already existent skills.

Evidence of rudimentary systems are available even for Preclassic times. Signs are detectible of an earth dam below the Purron and Abejas caves during the Santa María phase of Tehuacán (900–200 B.C.). A dam of stone and rocks with a dry-laid masonry facing was built across the stream, probably 100 to 150 meters in length, 6 meters wide, and 2.8 meters high; within a few decades it was greatly enlarged to become a major structure, capable of impounding some six hundred to seven hundred thousand cubic meters of water.[31] Since these important discoveries of McNeish, an ever increasing volume of evidence has become available as to relatively early irrigation schemes. As Angel Palerm points out, it is sometimes now even suggested that these were to be associated with the very beginnings of agriculture in Mesoamerica.[32]

In the case of Teotihuacán, apparent canal systems have been detected. However, the evidence, while plentiful, is not absolutely conclusive. Sanders and Price insist that no direct proof exists of irrigation in that site, though Sanders in another publication does say that certain techniques were probably known in the Early Classic period, in the form of terraces provided with floodwater canals.[33] Armillas and Palerm mention apparent traces of a small system, including a masonry structure constituting a dam 530 meters long.[34] Drewitt writes of a canal reaching the northwest edge of the main city, coming from the eastern part of the valley.[35] Mooser insists upon the existence of a canal system visible from air photographs.[36] Lorenzo also mentions the apparent existence of a canal cutting the Street of the Dead at right angles.[37] In addition, the famous Tláloc mural in Tepantitla depicts something resembling a spring or a canal.

Thus, where Tollan Xicocotitlan is concerned, if for certain reasons one cannot yet prove the presence of extensive hydraulic systems, the evidence of their existence in previous cultures is extremely strong. This reinforces the probability that Tollan itself employed some kind of artificial irrigation.

This question is fundamental to the city's whole history and development. Passages in certain written sources suggest that its downfall was partly due to famine, but one should be wary of too literal an interpretation of such accounts; according to our present information, the population of the city does not seem to have exceeded 60,000 to 70,000 and the immediate vicinity was not then thickly settled. As also previously mentioned, Sanders maintains that the section of the Teotihuacán Valley that he surveyed (excluding the Upper Valley) could have supplied maize for about 110,000 to 120,000 people, with the help of pre-Colombian irrigation techniques.[38] But it should not be forgotten that the Tula River possessed a much greater flow of water and that food was required for a smaller population.

Thus one cannot help surmising that, of the great Mesoamerican centers, Tollan Xicocotitlan was among the least susceptible to the vagaries of climatic variation; at the most a limited area of irrigated land would surely have fed the inhabitants of Tollan and the surrounding districts, taking Sanders' estimate that under such conditions one hectare would feed seven persons.[39] Of course, it might be argued that if such assumptions are correct, Tollan would have been even more vulnerable on another count and would have lain at the mercy of any invaders who systematically destroyed its dams; however, this is hardly what the written sources say when they speak of droughts and other climatic catastrophes.

The presence of a major hydraulic system would in its turn have made for inner cohesion and thus influenced the political organization of the city. Sanders and Price are probably correct in suggesting that, while a variety of methods of irrigation were apparently practiced in different parts of Mesoamerica, political power even then would have been closely related to hydraulic agriculture; as evidence, they cite a parallel case occurring in Nigeria.[40]

The City in Its Prime

Having so far in this chapter discussed problems of ecology and plans of settlement, one must now examine the layout of the city itself in its middle, or peak, period, during what might be termed the Golden Century of Tollan, from about A.D. 1000 to 1100. It has already been noted that what we see today are essentially the remains of its later structures, some of which conform closely to corresponding buildings in Chichén in style and in certain cases in their detailed plan; substructures are found under many of Tollan's final edifices.

The difficulty of establishing clear and distinct periods in Tollan, in terms of architectural and ceramic styles, has not yet been surmounted. This is in part due to the somewhat unchanging nature of Mazapan, which spans the greater part of Tollan's known history and which it has not yet been possible to divide into distinct phases, though Diehl feels it may become possible. It is of course true that an early-Mazapan stage does appear, when Coyotlatelco tends to predominate, and perhaps also a tentative late-Mazapan phase, when Aztec II makes its appearance; Cobean reports the latter as present in the same levels as Mazapan in Missouri Unit 05.

The principal ceremonial center, thoroughly explored and described by Acosta, requires little additional description. Presumably it was initiated later than Tula Chico, since it has yielded no sherds recalling Teotihuacán IV. However, the main center seems to have enjoyed a relatively long life span, since the Temple of Tlahuizcalpantecuhtli reveals the presence of six superpositions and even continued to be used in Aztec times.

As may clearly be observed in Map 3, Tollan can really boast of three very distinct ceremonial centers, the principal one mentioned above, and two more known as Tula Chico and the Plaza Charnay. Both the latter are clearly identifiable, each with its plaza surrounded by fairly large structures. In all, six ball courts have been found, of which three are in Tula Chico.[41] It might be tempting to speculate whether a fourth ceremonial center could have existed in the valley (the division into four parts is suggested for Teotihuacán by archaeological evidence and for Tenochtitlan by certain written accounts). Sahagún in his descriptions of Tollan Xicocotitlan—that admittedly have a rather apocryphal ring—writes of the presence of palaces situated at the side of the river; moreover, it will be shown in Chapter 8 that the sources' information is sometimes suggestive of the presence in Tollan of four rulers, each of whom might conceivably have had his own ceremonial center, or *tecpan*. Though no sure evidence to that effect exists, the ancient title of Atempanecatl (Lord of the Water's Edge) or Atecpanecatl (Lord of the Water Palace), mentioned in connection with Tollan (*see* Chapters 4 and 7) might conceivably have originated in that city, where water, in the form of a swift-flowing river, is very much in evidence.

The whole built-up area, as defined in Map 3, was undoubtedly in use during Tollan's apogee, and Mazapan was then universally present in the different centers. In the residential sectors a pottery is frequently found called Brush-on-Orange (*Anaranjado a Brochazos*), a name coined by Acosta and used by Matos, though Diehl tends to include this ware within the general definition of Mazapan. The discovery of Teotihuacanoid pottery in Tula Chico in the lowest level, and the predominance there of Coyotlatelco over Mazapan, surely gives the impression that this was one of the first parts of the city to be constructed (the El Corral structures, of later date, are probably related to the Tula Chico complex). Incidentally, a very small site also yielding Teotihuacán sherds was found by the INAH group on the high ground to the north of Tollan. However, such discoveries do not deter us from insisting once more that if a very early Tollan Xicocotitlan, contemporary with Teotihuacán, really existed, it has not yet been discovered. Teotihuacanoid pottery located in Tula Chico *in association with Coyotlatelco* cannot be contemporary with the Teotihuacán IV period in Teotihuacán itself, since in that site the two wares are *not* found together and the earliest Coyotlatelco, or Proto-Coyotlatelco, belongs to the subsequent Oztotícpac phase, when the city was almost deserted and the Teotihuacán IV style had fallen into disuse. It cannot always be a correct assumption that, at the very moment that production of a given type of pottery was discontinued in its place of origin, the same or similar styles ceased to be used in remoter centers. More-

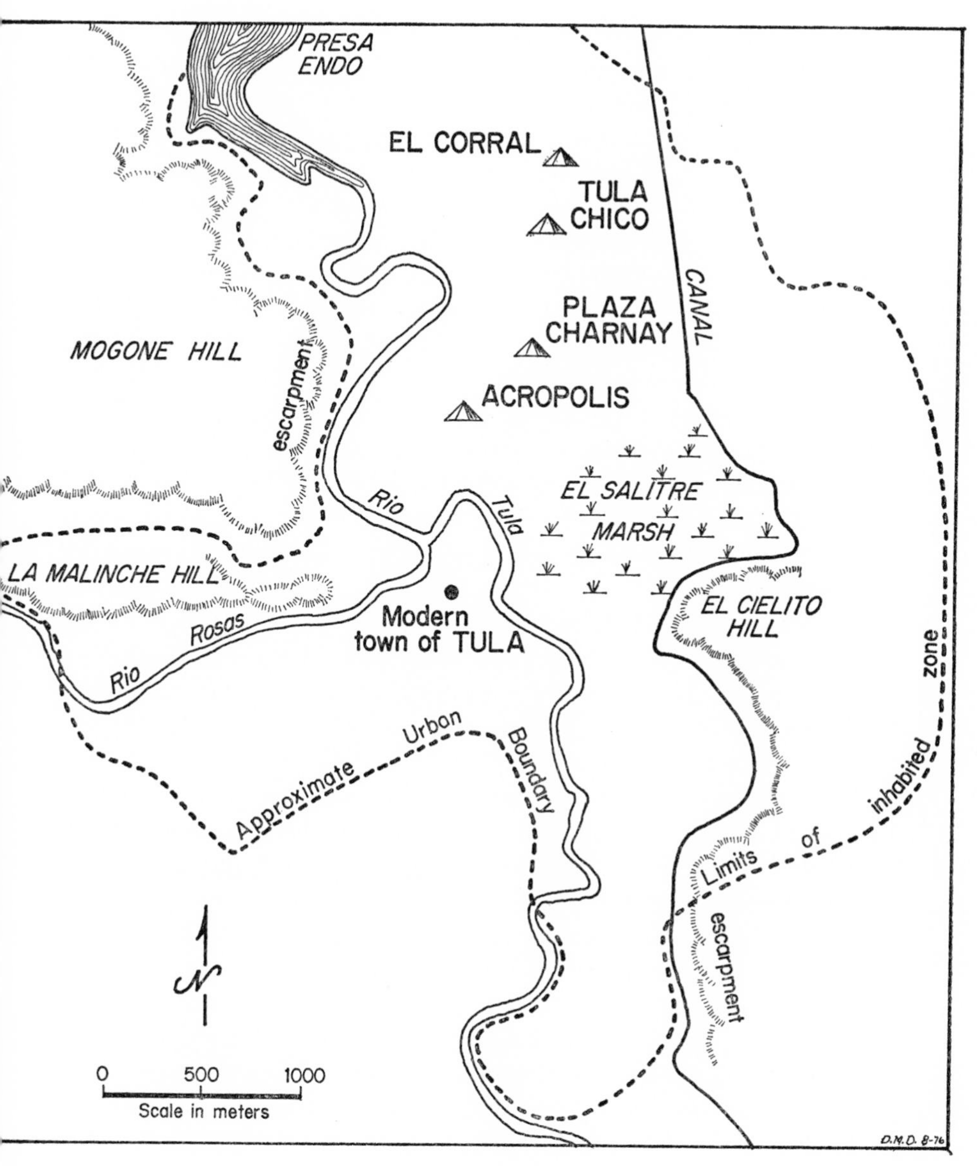

Tollan Xicocotitlan

over, the fact that pottery recalling the Cholulteca I of Xicotécatl was found in Tula Chico also tends to place the inception of that site in the post-Teotihuacán period.

It is important to note that Tollan appears to have lacked extensive man-made defenses and to have relied on its natural strategic strength to ward off attack. No surrounding ramparts have been located, apart from sloping structures around the main ceremonial center, where terraced walls fifteen to eighteen meters high have been found on the north and west sides of the precinct. Major streets and thoroughfares have not so far been identified; Diehl, as mentioned, suspects that the population density, while much greater than in Tikal and Chichén Itza, was somewhat less than in Teotihuacán.[42] Similarly, it has not so far been possible to delineate barrios, or distinct sectors, where different types of craftsmen might have lived and worked. Moreover, the city seems to have followed the lie of the land, rather than to have possessed any kind of symmetrical layout. The main marketplace has not been identified.

Regarding its material resources, Diehl draws attention to two obsidian-processing locations and to the probable existence of others. He considers that most of the construction stone was of local origin. Pottery clay and ceramic workshops have not been pinpointed.

Diehl mentions that the spindle whorl has been found in every house that he excavated, though not in quantities great enough to indicate an actual household specialization. The abundance of this article is nonetheless sufficient to suggest that both the spinning of thread and cloth manufacture must have been important to the economy of Tollan. Among other skilled occupations whose presence may be assumed are nopal cultivators, maguey growers, and pulque processors; industrial specialists must have included experts in mining as well as the working of obsidian, perhaps the making of flint and ground stone tools, in addition to ceramists, construction experts, stone carvers, and carpenters.[43] Since most of the shells found in Tollan are of local freshwater varieties, craftsmen skilled in working this material may also have been present.

The general impression gained is that of a very large inhabited zone, mainly, but perhaps not solely, situated on the high ridge, well provided with important buildings and impressive ceremonial centers, and surrounded by a very extensive residential district. One may well wonder what purpose was served by extending the city over such a large area if the soil and climate of the high ground was so poorly suited for garden and small-holding cultivation, in marked contrast to Tenochtitlan, where spaces left between the houses constituted Chinampas and were thus abundantly prolific, even if the bulk of the people's food came from outside the urban area. Moreover, Diehl's excavations tended to indicate that gardens were not cultivated in the city. One may therefore again be permitted to express a suspicion that Tollan's population was possibly a little more concentrated than has yet been suggested.

At all events, irrespective of its exact demographic density, there is no disputing the urban layout of the city, as opposed to sites that are more exclusively ceremonial centers, as for instance were those of the Maya area before Mayapan, or for that matter as was Xochicalco. Of course urbanism is not necessarily in itself a measure of civilization, and tended to become characteristic of highland Mesoamerica, when the lowlands still clung to the more traditional and dispersed patterns of settlement.

Trade and Commerce

In Chapter 3 it was suggested that in earlier times, and indeed until the Late Classic period, relations between the different peoples of Mesoamerica were based on considerations of commerce more than of conquest. In the Early Postclassic period, notwithstanding an increasing lust for war, the urge to trade had not abated, to witness the relatively universal presence of Plumbate wares and the wide distribution of Fine Orange. At times commercial interchange even burst the bounds of Mesoamerica, as illustrated by the presence of Panamanian gold in the Cenote of Chichén.

But one must nevertheless ask: granted the continued and vital importance of commerce in the Early Postclassic period, what exact part did Tollan Xicocotitlan play in this Pan-Mesoamerican trading community. From the available evidence it must be confessed, perhaps not without surprise, that its role appears to have been rather restricted.

Of the two great tradewares of the period, Fine Orange X and

Plumbate, the latter was the more omnipresent; however, the former also enjoyed a very wide distribution. Basically, Fine Orange is to be regarded more as a coastal ware; Fine Orange X extends over the whole area of south and central Veracruz, and from there into Yucatán and Guatemala, where it also constitutes an important horizon marker; it may have actually been manufactured in central Veracruz. Type Z, the earliest Fine Orange (contemporary with Puuc), had, however, penetrated from the coast as far inland as Xochicalco, and Type X was even found in Texmelincan in the state of Guerrero. Fine Orange is really the product of two traditions, those of Veracruz and Central Mexico, and it has already been noted that it enjoys fairly close links with Aztec I, indicating the sharing of a certain common tradition. It was thus a fairly universal ware; apart from the standard types, kindred varieties were made in places farther afield, as in the case of Sula Fine Orange of Honduras.[44] But, strangest of all to relate, not one single sherd of Fine Orange has appeared in Tollan.

Turning to Plumbate, that other hallmark of the Early Postclassic period, the later variety, Tohil, was certainly the most important tradeware of its epoch, found in places stretching from Tepic, beyond Guadalajara, to Nicaragua; it is likewise located in areas as widely dispersed as the state of Hidalgo, Guerrero, Chiapas, Guatemala, El Salvador, Honduras, and Yucatán, to name only a few.

As in the case of Thin Orange, of Classic times, and possibly that of Fine Orange, a relative uniformity of production tended to indicate a single place of manufacture; Shook and others have proposed Soconusco, near the Guatemalan border, where Plumbate sites abound (e.g., huge quantities have been found at Tajumulco). Many effigy vases illustrate "Mexican" rather than Maya gods, particularly Tláloc.[45] It is, however, nowadays commonly considered that even if the clay came from one place of origin or one region, it was not exported solely as a finished product, but also as a raw material, for the purpose of local manufacture in different places.[46] This does not alter the fact that both Plumbate and Fine Orange seem each to have derived from a single center.

It may be worth adding that, at least for Plumbate, a few chronological clues do exist. San Juan Plumbate, the earlier version, appears to have lasted some two hundred years, from about A.D. 700 to 900. In the site of Izapa, Thomas Lee found that in the Remanso phase, dated by radiocarbon as starting in about A.D. 900, Tohil Plumbate already predominates; it appears to continue in that site until about A.D. 1100 or perhaps later.[47]

Again, while Tohil Plumbate stands out by common consent as the all-present marker of its age, what of its presence in Tollan itself? The answer is that finds of Plumbate are scattered, though unlike Fine Orange it is not wholly absent. Acosta states that barely one sherd in one thousand of what he found was Plumbate.[48] Matos even puts the figure as one in five thousand.[49] Diehl, on the other hand, did locate a larger proportion in the area which he investigated; he unearthed in all one thousand Plumbate sherds and five complete vessels.[50] It should be added that, however limited its proportion of the total sherds, Plumbate does seem to occur at all levels except the uppermost.

When one seeks for metal or precious stones in Tollan, the picture is equally blank. Acosta discovered only one jade plaque, which he thought to derive from Monte Albán. And, notwithstanding Sahagún's evidently anachronistic insistence on Toltec metalworking skills, no metal at all has been found, except for copper objects associated with the later Aztec III and IV pottery.

Taking as a basis the very wide distribution of Mazapan and Mazapan-type pottery, one might conceivably argue that Tollan Xicocotitlan, as the ostensible fountainhead of this popular product, was consequently itself a great trading emporium. But it has already been demonstrated that in all possibility Mazapan has antecedents outside Tollan; moreover, it rather lacks refinement, as one can well observe from the figurines in the Tula Museum. It cannot be classed as a luxury product, emanating from one district and borne from there on the backs of slaves from one center to another, over the length and breadth of Mesoamerica. On the contrary, it is clearly a style, or a fashion, and not strictly speaking a ware, and was probably produced locally in many places. Thus, in this respect, Tollan does not appear as a center of distribution but merely as a city sharing the same style with other cities near and far.

However, this picture, while negative, may not be altogether complete. Notwithstanding the relative rarity in the site of certain hallmarks of the early Postclassic period, Diehl finds evidence that Tollan at least participated in several long-distance trade networks. He identified pottery from Nicaragua and Costa Rica (Papagayo), as well as sherds thought to be from Campeche and the south coast of Guatemala.[51] A variety of Gulf Coast sherds from the University of Missouri excavations, including ceramics from central and northern Veracruz, have also been tentatively identified. On the other hand, Cholula ceramics are conspicuous by their absence.[52] In addition, several types of Pacific shells have been located, probably deriving from the southern Sinaloa-Nayarit coast; only one type of Caribbean shell has so far been found.[53] Recent investigations have yielded much additional data on imports into Tollan, but the question of the exports from the city that served to pay for imports is at present very poorly understood. Tribute probably played its part in achieving the Toltec balance of payments.

Written sources offer indirect hints concerning the trading activities of Tollan. Sahagún associates it with the Amantecas, saying that the Toltecs "arrived in Amantlan, right in Tula."[54] The Amantecas were considered by Seler to have come from Teotihuacán, though Krickeberg believed that they originated in the Mixteca or in the general region of the Gulf Coast. But whatever their remoter antecedents, they later came to be associated not exclusively with featherwork but also with the trading *pochteca* in general.

An additional if tenuous link between Tollan and commercial enterprise may be sought in the connection between the merchants and Quetzalcoatl, par excellence the god of Tollan and later of Cholula, which became in the Late Postclassic period both a trading center and a sacred city. The *Codex Ramírez* actually mentions a merchant feast in honor of Quetzalcoatl.[55] The principal god of merchants in Aztec times, Yacatecuhtli, probably has ancient antecedents, and Séjourné notes his presence in Zacuala, Teotihuacán. Acosta Saignes suggests that Yacatecuhtli may originally have been a manifestation of Quetzalcoatl rather than of Tezcatlipoca, as has more usually been proposed.[56] Sahagún in addition refers to the richest merchants as *acxoteca*, and Jiménez Moreno suggests the possibility of some connection between this appellation and an archaic form of *ixcitl* (foot), from which seemingly derives Nacxitl, a common name for Quetzalcoatl.

Other links, direct or indirect, exist between Quetzalcoatl and merchants. Among the Nicaraos, Mixcoa (Mixcoatl), as the father figure so intimately bound with the Topiltzin legend, was patron deity of merchants. Tezozómoc moreover refers to Ce Acatl-Topiltzin as "Ynacxitl, the god of the itinerary I Reed."[57] Such an expression (in Spanish *caminador*) more usually applies to trade than to war.

Notwithstanding such rather slender indications to the contrary, it is hard to escape the conclusion that the Toltecs, while undoubtedly traders like nearly all Mesoamericans, were not at the very hub of the over-all commercial network of their time, as was Teotihuacán and later Tenochtitlan, but operated rather on the periphery. Not only did Fine Orange never reach Tollan, but one feels that where Plumbate is concerned, the city stood somewhat at the end of the line and did not constitute a focal point of distribution. One must also bear in mind that probably a certain portion of the goods that Tollan received derived from tribute rather than from trade.

One readily appreciates that, on the one hand, in Early Postclassic Mesoamerica commercial activity had lost none of its intensity. At the same time, however, one gains the impression that this teeming trade was not centered upon Tollan, even if it participated actively—notwithstanding Sanders' insistence that he finds numerous *pochteca* sculptured on the stone slabs of Tollan.[58] One does not of course really know how this commerce was conducted. Bernal asks for instance whether Plumbate was borne to El Salvador by one set of merchants covering the whole distance or redistributed successively from one center to another along the route.[59] The possibility that in certain cases the clay rather than the finished product was transported does not affect the essence of the question. To point to the rather patchy distribution of Plumbate in Tollan and to insist at the same time that this was the main trading center of its time would surely be difficult. In Xochicalco, for instance, undoubtedly an important center of commerce in its heyday, the typical tradewares of the time have been found in reasonable abundance, including a number of jade plaques, together with Fine Orange Type Z.

Nor would it be any more correct to suggest that Cholula in the Early Postclassic period was the focal point of Mesoamerican commerce. Its apparently limited significance at this moment in its long history has already been stressed. References to Cholula in the *Cantares* as a great merchant city almost surely refer to the Late Postclassic period, when the Cholula polychrome of the time became a deluxe article of trade.

Friedrich Katz has insisted upon the basically coastal associations of the *pochteca* merchants.[60] In support of this hypothesis he cites a whole series of traits which they exhibit, originally mentioned by Kirchhoff. It would seem very possible that in Toltec times the whole trading complex of Mesoamerica lay more in the hands of people from the coastal regions or from the warm lands in general. Even in the Aztec period—notwithstanding the commercial pre-eminence of Tenochtitlan-Tlatelolco, endowed by military supremacy with a virtual trading monopoly over vast areas—considerable emphasis is placed on Tuxtepec as a great center and rallying point for merchants, who traveled from there to "Anahuac," i.e., to the various different coastal regions; it should always be borne in mind that the more prized luxury wares came from the *tierra caliente*, or the more tropical areas.

As against this, one might with some reason insist that Teotihuacán, lying far inland, was obviously the supreme trading emporium of its era. However, one cannot be sure that the actual *pochteca* of later times existed there, even if it might be logical to suppose that in some form they were present. But it could perhaps be argued that, irrespective of where the goods came from, the widespread commerce emanating from Teotihuacán was carried out by peoples more native to the coast than to the Altiplano—just as in the Middle Ages it was the Venetians who carried sugar and spices from the East to England and even acted as carriers of English wool to Flemish weavers, at a time when England and Holland were not yet maritime nations; we have always insisted that Teotihuacán was plainly "Gulf orientated." Whatever economic pre-eminence the city may have enjoyed in its time, with its fall the commercial center of gravity could well have returned to the coastal Gulf regions, to which the Wise Men of Teotihuacán repaired at its time of trouble, and, furthermore, it remained centered there in Toltec times.

The empire of Tollan was short-lived and not necessarily very far-flung, as will be seen. Possibly neither its life span nor its extent were sufficient to enable the city to wrest the commercial supremacy of Mesoamerica from the coastal peoples, to whom it may traditionally have belonged. It is significant that while one source mentions Amantlan in connection with Tollan, no actual reference to the *pochteca* is made, where that city is concerned. Thus, whereas Tollan before its decline extended its military hegemony over at least parts of Central Mesoamerica, it was perhaps not able to establish a corresponding commercial predominance, such as might have been attained if its sway had been more prolonged. Moreover, questions of demography, discussed above, must also be taken into consideration; the manpower at Tollan's disposal seems to have been rather limited for the purpose of controlling a vast empire, whether military or commercial.

The Internal Order

Certain aspects of the Toltec home base have so far been discussed in this chapter, for which our information has been mainly derived from the findings of archaeology; on such matters as settlement plans, population, and even trade, the written sources tell almost nothing. However, it is upon the latter that one must rely principally for any clues as to patterns of government. In this respect one must first ask: was the government secular or theocratic? Was kingship individual or plural, and what part in affairs of state was played by a man, or by a succession of men, bearing the title of Topiltzin or Quetzalcoatl?

In general terms, it may be fair to assume that Tollan Xicocotitlan enjoyed strong and reasonably stable rule at the height of its power, just as did Tenochtitlan or Azcapotzalco; this surely constitutes a precondition for conquest on any scale. In another work we have insisted upon the many-sided genius of the Mexicas not only in war but in the arts of government; there is no reason to suppose that in this domain the Toltecs fell so far short of their ultimate successors.[61]

An additional factor making for cohesion may have been present in Tollan's case; from what has already been stated, it may be concluded to have been in part at least a "hydraulic state," or the nearest approach to this condition in Mesoamerica, since one cannot envisage how the city could have grown and prospered without irrigation. And clearly any polity which depends for its existence on some form of collective control over river waters cannot dispense with a reasonably high degree of political centralization. Of course one must not go to the opposite extreme and fall into the trap of regarding this in itself as assuring a state of superdevelopment; it is merely a pointer in that direction. Gordon Childe has pointed out that public works are an unreliable index of the social and political integration of a society. David Kaplan in this respect quotes the example of ancient Ceylon, with its waterworks and irrigation on an important scale, but without any initial evidence of a correspondingly complex bureaucratic organization.

When one asks what kind of government presided over the destinies of Tollan, an immediate paradox arises. On the one hand ample evidence has already been quoted as to the transformation of Mesoamerica from a comparatively pacific society to one that was starkly militaristic; the process of change had already begun in late Teotihuacán times, becoming even more evident in the Epiclassic interlude and in the Late Classic Maya era.

But normally one might expect such tendencies to go accompanied by a general transfer of rule from the temple to the palace. To take Mesopotamia—often the closest Old World parallel to Mesoamerican development—in Sumerian times each city-state was ruled by the *patesi*, or "tenant farmer" of the principal local god, who stood at the head of the civil administration and whose office was renewed annually. However, after the Babylonian period which followed, the economic strength, and hence the political importance of the temple, shrank. The ensuing era then witnessed the rise of the palace organization, headed by the king, notwithstanding the fame and glamor of the later temples of Mesopotamia. This process went accompanied by a progressive militarism of the state.[62]

However, in Tollan less conclusive evidence is forthcoming that secularization went hand in hand with militarism, or that with the advent of the latter, the palace immediately took over from the temple. As Armillas has rightly insisted, following the decline of Teotihuacán and the emergence of more war-oriented polities, new social forces were indeed made manifest, but at the same time governmental structure seems mainly to have adhered to already established patterns.[63]

As this author points out, the whole prevalence of Quetzalcoatl-Kukulcan during the initial historic period presents something of a contradiction, or even a return to previous norms. Changes seem to have been more social than governmental, and up to a point the outer fabric of the old order survived the shattering blows it had suffered, even if the reality was somewhat different. Taking again a Babylonian example to illustrate what may have occurred in Mesoamerica: while this trend toward centralization and militarism was developing in Mesopotamia, new figures began to emerge, either from the ranks of the temple personnel or independently, who had less regard for the old priestly prerogatives.[64] In other words, these new leaders could still play the part of a priest, but their outlook was increasingly secular. Julian Steward also draws attention to the predominance of priest-warriors, usually under the supremacy of a divine monarch, in that intermediate stage in the development of human societies, which he calls the age of "cyclical conquests."[65] Steward's definition of the age so designated is interesting and in many ways applicable to Tollan, involving, as Steward suggests, "the emergence of large scale military expansion, the extension of political and economic domination over large areas or empires, a strong tendency toward urbanization, and the construction of fortifications. In the social structure, priest-warriors constituted the ruling groups, usually under a divine monarch, whose importance is revealed in elaborate status burial. Social classes now tend to become frozen into hereditary classes . . . gods of war become prominent in the pantheon of deities." Admittedly one knows nothing about status burial in Tollan, but it certainly already existed under the Tepanecs, as demonstrated by Ixtlilxóchitl's description of Tezozómoc's funeral; moreover, the relief in the North Temple of the Great Ball Court of Chichén Itza is somewhat suggestive in this respect. Certainly Quetzalcoatl, originally perhaps a relatively peaceful deity, in his personification as Tlahuizelpantecuhtli, the warrior of the Dawn, had in effect become in part a god of war.

The apparently unusual phenomenon of partly theocratic rule ostensibly continuing during a period of increased centralization and militarism is not therefore necessarily an isolated one. The evidence for the prevalence of such a state of affairs in Tollan is certainly plentiful. To take only one source, the *Anales de Cuauhtitlán* call Quetzalcoatl both priest and king.[66] Though enjoying certain clearly temporal functions, he is also addressed as "my son and priest, Ce Acatl Quetzalcoatl."[67] Quauhtli, who established himself as Quetzalcoatl's substitute and likeness, is a *tlenamacac*, or *sahumador*, and therefore also of priestly rank.[68]

Sahagún is equally at pains to stress the sacerdotal role of Topiltzin-Quetzalcoatl, whereas the *Memorial Breve* of Chimalpain and the *Historia de los Mexicanos* on the contrary treat him as a temporal ruler. Notwithstanding, Topiltzin-Quetzalcoatl, according to most accounts, is not merely a king, but also a priest and the personification of a god.

Similar examples of priest-rulers may also be sought in the Maya area. During the capture of Chichén by Hunac Ceel of Mayapan, it is stated that the second priest, Chable, was ruler. The Mayas' commander, Uxmal Chac, was also formerly their priest.[69] At the same time, the military as well as sacerdotal significance of the Quetzalcoatl-Kukulcan-Gucumatz concept is not in doubt. The chronicles of Highland Guatemala never cease to write of Gucumatz as predominantly a military ruler and conqueror. Where Tollan Xicocotitlan is concerned, Ixtlilxóchitl gives descriptions of battles fought in person by the last Topiltzin.

It has on occasion been suggested by Kirchhoff and others that in Tollan a clear division of powers persisted; Topiltzin Quetzalcoatl would thus fulfill a priestly role, while the temporal sway was held by other rulers. However, in Chapter 7 the whole question of the relationship between Topiltzin and Huemac will be examined in some detail, and evidence will be offered that questions the existence of any such division of powers. I basically consider that Sahagún's insistence on the separate roles of Quetzalcoatl as priest and Huemac as king derives from certain misunderstandings and is not well supported by other sources; if the latter concede priestly powers to Topiltzin, they insist that he was also a civil ruler. It is indeed hard to avoid the conclusion that he was both priest *and* king; this is precisely how the *Memorial Breve* describes the role of his successor, Nauhyotl.[70]

Indeed, as Sir James Frazer pointed out, nothing is more natural than to find priest-rulers in earlier or less-developed societies. In Sparta, where dual kingship prevailed, one king held the priesthood of Zeus Lacedaemon and the other of the Heavenly Zeus; Cambodia was ruled until very recently by men regarded as divine.

It may also be dangerous to interpret too literally reports suggesting that Topiltzin-Quetzalcoatl was a kind of aesthetic recluse, cloistered in a Mesoamerican version of the proverbial ivory tower and spending his days brooding on the evils of human sacrifice, which he sought (vainly) to extirpate. Admittedly, examples exist elsewhere of secluded rulers. The king of Dahomey was prohibited from beholding the sea. And to the west of this territory, among the Ewe-speaking peoples, the king, who was at the same time high priest, could not be approached by his subjects; he was only allowed to leave his dwelling at night, and none but his counterpart, or representative, the "visible king," together with three elders, could converse with him, and then exclusively with their backs turned. Similarly, the fetish king of Benin, now part of modern Nigeria, could not leave his palace.

But where Topiltzin-Quetzalcoatl is concerned, one suspects that his reported aversion to human sacrifice, together with permanent as opposed to periodical celibacy and abstention from intoxicating beverages, were mere embellishments added by the chroniclers in order to satisfy European notions of proper priestly behavior. Surely in Tollan the circumstances are different; one is dealing with an empire, albeit of limited proportions, and with a man called to a higher destiny than the direction of a mere tribe. *In theory*, the representative on earth of the leading deity may have been expected to live as a recluse, and perhaps such norms for rulers were inherited from earlier and more peaceful times. One may cite later accounts of how Moctezuma I, par excellence a conqueror and administrator, ordained that the *tlatoani* should never be seen in public, except on very special occasions.

However, in practice the exigencies of empire must have drawn out from his gilded cage any would-be hermit who sought to rule Tollan, and he would have been forced to participate in the direction of a complex political system. A secluded tyrant may possibly maintain his sway over a small city-state, but empires simply cannot be conquered and defended by a recluse, and in such instances practical needs must invariably triumph over the mere dictates of religious custom. A great ruler may become divine but he can hardly remain invisible; after all, there was nothing incompatible in Egypt between the established and complete divinity of the king and his role as an active monarch and even a commander of armies.

It may thus be fair to deduce that the government of Tollan, devolving partly but not wholly upon a human ruler holding the title of Topiltzin-Quetzalcoatl, was a blend of the secular and the theocratic; it would perhaps represent a kind of half-way house in that respect between Teotihuacán on the one hand and Tenochtitlan on the other; in the latter instance, notwithstanding Moctezuma I's ordinances, only certain sacerdotal vestiges can still be discerned in the office of *tlatoani*.

At this stage it becomes necessary once again to refer to the important contribution of López Austin to the whole question of priest-rulers or man-gods, not always one and the same thing. We certainly accept the concept of a deified or semidivine ruler as applicable to Mesoamerica, perhaps well illustrated by I Death, seemingly both god and man in the Mixtec codices. In the *Codex Nuthall*, for instance, I Death, usually figuring as a god, is at times illustrated as a man and a great ruler; on other occasions in the same codex he appears as a god.[71] Even the famous Eight Deer himself, though portrayed as a man, sometimes appears in the presence of clearly mythical or divine figures, such as a jaguar seated on a mountaintop. Caso connects I Death with the Sun and also with Tezcatlipoca; in the *Codex Colombino* he appears alternatively as a deity and as an old man, apparently head of a confederation of city-states.[72]

In his work on the subject, López Austin naturally cites Topiltzin-Quetzalcoatl of Tollan as foremost among man-gods. He rightly insists that not only Quetzalcoatl, but Topiltzin, is also the name of a deity, as Sahagún makes clear in the *Primeros Memoriales*. In general terms, we are in full agreement that to a certain degree his status is divine as well as human; Topiltzin-Quetzalcoatl was more than a mere ruler invested with priestly functions. Concerning the latter category, one may recall that Moctezuma II, Ahuítzotl, and Tízoc are all specifically stated to have been priests before becoming *tlatoani*, in itself an office with sacerdotal undertones; however, these surely could not rank as man-gods, on a par with Topiltzin.

López Austin, however, goes further in regard to the latter, and suggests that the holder of the title Topiltzin-Quetzalcoatl may have actually been expected to live out in person the legendary life of the god, whose powers and attributes he was believed to acquire. Thus he would have been beholden physically to enact the god's traditional and final journey to Tlillan Tlapallan, where he died, to be resurrected as the Morning Star. López Austin even questions whether, as certain sources state, the Topiltzin of the day might not in actual fact have reigned fifty-two years—a full calendar cycle—and whether, if he died before this, a surrogate did not then complete his preordained period of rule.

Here again one is compelled to differ, since it is felt that, even if such was the position in theory, the pressure exercised by affairs of state would have made such a system impossible in practice. Admittedly, as already mentioned, descriptions exist of Topiltzin-Quetzalcoatl as a cloistered recluse, but the actual account in the *Anales de Cuauhtitlán* giving details of his secluded abode, which included such exotic trappings as mats studded with precious stones, makes it clear that such stories are somewhat allegorical.[73]

It must be admitted that such unseen sovereigns did exist in other parts of the world, and that examples are even forthcoming of rulers who held sway for a fixed term, though not for so long as fifty-two years. For instance, the king of Calicut on the Malibar Coast enjoyed but a twelve-year reign; the kings of Ethiopia in ancient times were put to death if they displayed any physical flaws—something that might in a strange way be related to the legend of how the last Topiltzin-Quetzalcoatl was filled with horror when presented with a mirror in which he saw for the first time his own facial defects.

It has already been stressed that a distinction constantly has to be maintained between the heavenly and earthly Tollan. It would seem that Topiltzin-Quetzalcoatl is likewise portrayed on two different planes, on the one hand the eternal and ethereal hero and on the other the human ruler who governed Tollan, perhaps alone, but more probably with other rulers, as will shortly be seen. One must think not in terms of a single and unified Topiltzin-Quetzalcoatl but of several concepts concentrated in one being or succession of beings; not only does one encounter the contrasting notions of god and mortal, but in addition the tired old man, the bold warrior, and even the little child. In the region of Acaponata, according to Seler, the people actually revered a god in the form of a little child known as Teopiltzintli; *pilli* has the meaning of "son" and thus even "child," in addition to that of "prince."[74]

One need not deny the possibility of attributing divine qualities to an active sovereign, as already illustrated by the example of the Egyptian pharaohs. But it is almost impossible to envisage the exercise of supreme power by a being dedicated to an other-worldly life and reigning for a fixed span. Such conditions would surely have been enforceable only in a relatively primitive community. Tollan could not have mastered its neighbors and become a ruling power while laboring under such handicaps. López Austin even goes so far as to question whether Tollan, to comply with such magico-religious norms and with the Quetzalcoatl legend, was not destined to stage a kind of collapse over and over again at fixed intervals and then begin a new existence.[75] But empires are built by those who are ready to cast off impediments imposed by preordained religious dictates and who give prior consideration to strength and continuity in political and military institutions. By the same token, the acquisition of empire usually results from the more practical course of first trampling on the weakest adversaries and following thereafter the line of least resistance in choosing the victims of one's career of conquest. Thus it will later become apparent that we are also unable to accept in toto Kirchhoff's somewhat parallel scheme of a Toltec empire constructed on symmetrical lines to the north, south, east, and west of Tollan.

Such ritualistic notions might conceivably have formed part and parcel of early Mesoamerican statecraft, but it would seem unlikely that they prevailed in Teotihuacán, let alone in Tollan Xicocotitlan. No doubt in theory the head of the Roman Church should always have lived in a manner exactly modeled on that of Our Lord; but leaving aside earlier and more overt examples of papal departure from such norms, it is manifestly impossible to direct a world-wide organization with financial and political as well as religious responsibilities and at the same time to lead an existence that precisely follows the pattern set by the Good Shepherd himself.

López Austin cites other Mesoamerican examples of secluded governors; for instance, in one case in Guatemala, the high priest, at times also acting as supreme ruler, remained separated from his subjects for months on end and spoke to no one. He was restricted to a diet of dry maize and some fruit and might not consume anything that had been touched by fire. His dwelling (in contrast to the bejeweled abode attributed to Quetzalcoatl) was a small hut on the mountainside, made of green leaves, where he passed his time engaged in autosacrifice.[76]

But surely this illustrates one principal point: if such a man was truly the temporal ruler of his people, which seems a little hard to envisage, he presided over a tribe of very limited importance. It would hardly have been in a favorable position to impose its will upon others if its ruler, no ferocious warrior leading his armies into battle, remained immured in a hovel for months on end, wasting away on a starvation diet. One may well ask what would have happened to the Aztec Empire if Ahuítzotl, instead of being the mighty commander that he was, had settled himself down in a secluded grass hut?

The next problem that requires examination is the prevalence of single or plural rule in Tollan. Most if not all the evidence points to the latter situation, which probably in the main prevailed in Mesoamerica until the Late Postclassic period. Single rulership seems then to have been adopted by the Tepanecs and Acolhuas from the Chichimecs and handed on in modified form to the Mexicas.

Examples exist of plural kingship from other parts of Mesoamerica in Toltec times, if not in Chichén itself, where Kukulcan tends to be mentioned alone. For instance, the *Anales de los Cakchiqueles* tell of tribes governed by Gagavitz, in conjunction with another ruler, usually Zactecauh. Gucumatz is to be found in the *Popol Vuh* coupled with Tepeu or Cotuhé. A four-captain military system later became common to Nahua peoples on the Pacific Coast of Guatemala.[77]

When one examines the case of Tollan itself, evidence of plural kingship is manifold, as explained more fully in Appendix B; the possible chronologies of several apparently contemporary rulers is given in there. It is also explained in detail how the lists of Toltec rulers given by Torquemada and the *Anales de Cuauhtitlán* are based on certain misapprehensions, because of the preconceived notion of the chronicler or recorder that kingship had to be single; Table B shows clearly that the true situation was rather different. In Appendix B as also in Chapter 8, it is shown that when sources mention various companions in flight of the last Topiltzin-Quetzalcoatl, at times also named as his rivals, such individuals are in point of fact more probably comonarchs, often three in number.

Certain evidence of the simultaneous presence in Tollan of more than one ruler may briefly here be cited. The *Anales de Cuauhtitlán* imply that Quetzalcoatl and Quauhtli were probably contemporary.[78] The *Leyenda de los Soles* names four princes who jointly succeeded to Topiltzin's throne.[79] The *Memorial Breve* not only mentions a kind of Triple Alliance that controlled the Toltec empire but also writes of the presence of two or more simultaneous rulers in Tollan itself; for instance, Totepeuh made his son Huemac king during his own lifetime; in addition he gave kingly rank to Nauhyotzin Opochtli.[80] Also in the immediate post-Tollan period, the same source mentions Huetzin and Nonohualcatl as contemporary rulers of Culhuacán.[81] Ixtlilxóchitl writes of a kind of triple rule in Tollan consisting of Topiltzin, Cuauhtli, and Maxtlatzin.[82] The Anónimo Mexicano also mentions the joint exercise of royal power with reference to Tollan.[83]

If such evidence were not in itself sufficient to convince, the probable presence in Tollan of more than one *señor* is reinforced by the existence of plural government in various "Toltec" states in the Valley of Mexico after Tollan's decline. In particular Culhuacán, its temporal heir and one-time confederate, seems to have had four rulers, as the *Historia de los Mexicanos* and other sources make clear.[84] As we have been at pains to emphasize in another work, certain other cities in the Valley of Mexico that claimed Toltec descendance had several kings; Xochimilco for instance possessed three and Cuitláhuac, four. It was not unusual for city-states to have four rulers, though one probably acted as a kind of *primus inter pares*, as apparently occurred later in Tlaxcala.[85]

Quite possibly Tollan may have been divided into four quarters, as in the case of other cities, but no archaeological evidence exists as to any creation of four symmetrical portions. Three principal ceremonial centers are discernible, and the possibility was very tentatively put forward of the existence of a fourth near the River Tula, where Sahagún mentions fabulous buildings.

In considering the general political and social pattern that might have prevailed in Tollan, one is forced into the realm of pure speculation and reduced to playing the well-tried but hazardous game of drawing retrospective deductions from knowledge of conditions prevailing several centuries later.

One can only suppose that a militaristic state would have possessed a nobility dedicated mainly to war, but perhaps accompanied, as in Tenochtitlan, by a purely military caste, standing somewhat lower in the social scale and deriving its status as much from martial valor as from hereditary right. In this respect, evidence exists of the presence of eagles and ocelots, the emblems of the leading military order of later times. Having already discussed the religious aura that surrounded the monarchy, it becomes almost superfluous to suggest that the role of the priesthood in general must have been significant. Similarly, it is logical to presuppose the existence of freemen, or *macehuales*, merchants, craftsmen, and even slaves—all essentially part and parcel of the Mesoamerican social scene. It would further seem probable that, as in Tenochtitlan and elsewhere, conquest increased the power of the nobility and the military caste and caused wealth to be concentrated in ever fewer hands. The receipt of tribute in large quantities, mainly of a sumptuary nature, not only strengthens and enriches the ruler, but also favors those upper classes who form his battle elite and to whom he accordingly distributes the choicest spoils of war.

To seek to probe further into the totally unknown and to draw more inferences concerning, say, the nature of clans, or *calpullis*, in Tollan and their possible role would be to indulge in mere guesswork. Possibly archaeology may one day reveal more clearly the administrative layout and divisions of the city and may furnish evidence of separate barrios dedicated to traders, artisans, and other categories of citizens, thus providing a basis for assessing the social structure of Tollan.

In conclusion, it may again be stressed that reasonable evidence exists of plural rule in Tollan. Indications are also offered by the sources of a regime part secular and part theocratic. In this respect Tollan may have represented an intermediate stage between the governments of Teotihuacán and of Tenochtitlan. It seems, moreover, probable that a series of holders of the title Topiltzin-Quetzalcoatl played a leading part in the collective ordering of the state, even if their precise role is not absolutely clear.

7. Toltec Apogee: Subjects and Neighbors

Numerous references survive naming the Toltecs as universal rulers before Aztec times. For instance, the *Relación de la Genealogía* states that all the earth recognized the king of Tollan as lord.[1] But it is hard for the historian to penetrate the mists of time and to evaluate such claims; one cannot easily assess what territory the Toltecs controlled or how they ruled it.

Possible Partners

It must again be stressed that we possess no contemporary documents on Toltec history; one is dependent upon what the Aztecs relate. And if the latter re-edited their own history, as Sahagún actually states, by the same token they could scarcely present an unvarnished tale of their Toltec forebears.

Moreover, the caution voiced in Chapter 1 remains essentially valid. Whatever norms may be appropriate to define the extent of Toltec rule, one method must remain excluded; it will serve no purpose to designate as "Toltec empire" sites whose monuments generally recall those of Tollan or areas whose pottery remotely resembles Mazapan. One may again call to mind the bizarre conclusions that might have been reached had one lacked written records of Aztec conquests and employed such criteria to define their domains.

Likewise, it should again be recalled that Mazapan is not a tradeware, emanating from one center, but a style, easily spread from one region to another, unrestricted by political boundaries. As already mentioned, the Mazapan of Tollan even differs somewhat from the "wavy-line" variety found at certain other sites.

On the other hand, one should not go to the opposite extreme and ignore completely the evidence of architectural forms. In particular, in special instances which transcend mere similarity and amount to a virtual identity, these may signify much, as in the case of Kaminaljuyu and later of Chichén; here one is surely dealing not with a generalized diffusion of style to various independent peoples but with a series of monuments in two places, remote one from another, whose inspiration and detail clearly derive from one single source.

The archaeologist is ever faced with severe limitations in seeking the boundaries of fallen empires, in cases where he cannot hope to uncover contemporary texts in stone or papyrus. However, it must be admitted that where the Toltecs are concerned, even the written evidence deriving from later ages is also scanty. In most of the relevant documents, little more than passing references occur as to possible bounds of empire; as examples, one may cite Ixtlilxóchitl's mention of Toltec palaces in Toluca, or a report by the *Anales de Cuauhtitlán* of campaigns undertaken in Morelos, which may or may not refer to a Toltec leader.

Two sources provide somewhat more positive information on the subject: the *Historia Tolteca-Chichimeca* and the *Memorial Breve* of Chimalpain. It may be preferable to examine the latter first, since its observations are reasonably clear and to the point. Alone among the surviving documents, the *Memorial Breve* mentions the existence of three realms—Tollan, Culhuacán, and Otompan—which exercised a joint sway lasting for 191 years.[2] At the end of this period the alliance fell asunder; only Culhuacán survived as a ruling power, while the scepter of Tollan passed to Coatlichan (i.e., to the Aculhuas) and that of Otompan to Azcapotzalco (i.e., to the Tepanecs). The source thus in effect implies a continuing series of triple alliances extending from

Toltec to Aztec times, of which the partnership of Tenochtitlan, Tlacopan, and Texcoco was only the last. Tenochtitlan was to become the self-proclaimed heir to Culhuacán, whereas the power of Azcapotzalco passed, in rather attenuated form, to Tlacopan, also a Tepanec city; the Aculhua scepter was later transferred from Coatlichan to Texcoco.

Concerning territory which the earliest of these alliances might have controlled, the *Memorial Breve* names only certain cities that were vassals of Culhuacán, ostensibly in Toltec times: Xochimilco, Cuitláhuac, Mízquic, Coyoacan, Ocuilan, and Malinalco. It may be noted that the first three are mentioned in various sources as also conquered by Tenochtitlan's first *tlatoani*, Acampichtli, who also fought wars against Culhuacán. The joint reference to Xochimilco, Cuitláhuac, and Mízquic is somewhat natural, as their inhabitants, together with those of Culhuacán, are invariably grouped together in later historical accounts as the peoples of the Chinampas. Moreover, Ocuilan and Malinalco were reportedly conquered by the second Tenochca *tlatoani*, Huitzilíhuitl, and their inclusion in the *Memorial Breve* list of Toltec subjects is therefore not without significance. It is perhaps not unnatural that, having reportedly "conquered" Culhuacán, under Tepanac auspices, even before Acamapichtli's reign, the Mexicas should then proceed to attack places in the Valley of Toluca such as Ocuilan and Malinalco, associated long before with Culhuacán.

The fact that this particular report of a Toltec triple alliance is given prominence only in the *Memorial Breve* does not necessarily detract from its accuracy. It is reasonable to question whether Tollan was populous enough to control singlehandedly an empire of any size; moreover, the suggested line of succession from one triple alliance to another contains a certain logic. The Tepanecs have Matlatzinca associations and thus become the natural heirs of Otompan, since the Otomís and the Matlatzincas are ethnically linked. Indeed, it seems more reasonable to suppose that Tollan would have tended to join forces with allied or confederate cities rather than the reverse; such combinations for the purpose of conquering "empires" may have been the established norm in Mesoamerica well before the Aztecs, and it is hard to see how extensive dominions could otherwise have been subjected, since the manpower and resources of one single city-state, the basic Mesoamerican unit of government, would hardly have sufficed for the purpose.

The geographical distance dividing these three putative Toltec partners might at first sight seem surprising; however, it must not be supposed that, simply because Tenochtitlan, Tlacopan, and Texcoco lay in relatively close proximity one to another, the same norms were automatically applicable in the case of every triple alliance. In some respects, a wider distribution of provincial capitals would have facilitated territorial control; the enormous distance that separated both Tenochtitlan and Texcoco from much of the Aztec Empire was a potential source of weakness, and it has even been seriously suggested that the Aztecs might eventually have been forced to establish some kind of additional capital, farther to the southeast, in order to tighten their grip on those far-flung and rebellious domains.

In respect of possible Toltec alliances, the *Anales de Cuauhtitlán* also report that authority resided in Tollan itself, Cahuacan, Cuauhchinanco, Cuauhnáhuac, and Huaxtepec. This account then gives the same version as the *Memorial Breve*, to the effect that the seat of power was then transferred to Azcapotzalco, Culhuacán, and Coatlichan, and finally to Tenochtitlan, Tlacopan, and Texcoco.[3] Cahuacan lies on the northern edge of the Valley of Mexico; one might question whether the Cuauhchinanco in question is a homonym rather than the place now called Huauchinango, situated beyond Tulancingo, though this area will later be discussed separately; reference will also be made to the mention of Cuauhnáhuac (Cuernavaca) and Huaxtepec when discussing possible Toltec control over the Valley of Morelos. Sufficient let it be at this point to say that the two reports, those of Chimalpain and of the *Anales de Cuauhtitlán*, are not as contradictory as might at first sight appear; it would obviously be most probable that any Toltec domination of the Huaxtepec-Cuauhnáhuac area would have involved *ipso facto* some kind of association with Culhuacán, as suggested by the *Memorial Breve*. Also, from the Valley of Mexico, if not from Tollan Xicocotitlan, Otumba lies in the direction of Tulancingo, while Huauchinango is situated beyond it. Thus, in effect, both reports suggest that Tollan had partners situated first in Culhuacán or, alternatively, beyond this in the Valley of Morelos and secondly in Otumba or beyond it in Huauchinango.

Archaeological evidence supports certain contentions of the *Memorial Breve*. Notwithstanding a previous tendency to insist that the Culhuacán situated in the Valley of Mexico was not contemporary with Tollan, but was founded much later, the city was apparently the prime producer of Aztec I, a pottery clearly inseparable from the Tula-Mazapan horizon. In addition, remains of the Teotihuacán era are present in Culhuacán.

As already mentioned, the city played a leading role during the period of Tollan's decline; it even seems, as will later be explained in much more detail, that the famous Mixcoatl and his son Topiltzin first ruled in Culhuacán, and that the latter only subsequently came to govern Tollan. The sources make much of another Culhuacán, or Teoculhuacan, situated in the remoter regions of the northwest. It probably had indeed once existed as an inhabited place, but, in association with Chicomoztoc, it came to assume a semilegendary status; other earthly counterparts bearing the same name existed, and glyphs of curved mountains representing the name Culhuacán or its equivalent are even to be found in Mixtec codices.

It thus seems reasonably safe to assume that the Culhuacán situated in the Valley of Mexico was in existence during the apogee of Tollan Xicocotitlan and that it was already an important center, itself producing one of the principal potteries of the Tula-Mazapan horizon. Subsequently it was to survive as the chief temporal heir of Tollan, providing refuge for part of its population and a throne for one of its reigning dynasties.

One may therefore suggest that the account of the *Memorial Breve*, while not strictly proven, appears reasonably well-founded. Though written much later than the parallel version of the *Anales de Cuauhtitlán*, in this respect it would appear to be the more accurate, for reasons which will become apparent. It is hard for instance to see how a Toltec empire could have dominated Morelos without the Culhuacán region, which controlled the normal approaches from Tollan. In general terms, it might be logical to suppose that Culhuacán, which became the seat of Tollan's fallen dynasty, would have been a partner in rule during most of its period of power. One may doubt whether Tollan could have claimed any true dominion over central

Mexico without some hold over the pivotal Valley of Mexico, on which the Teotlalpan bordered.

Of course, it may be argued that the differences of location between Aztec I on the one hand and Aztec II and Mazapan on the other represent a kind of ceramic frontier, separating the northern and southern sectors of the Valley of Mexico, and that such a dividing line constituted the limits of Toltec power, with Culhuacán lying beyond and to the south. Jiménez Moreno tends to favor this viewpoint. But surely no rule can be cited that obliges political partners to use the same pottery. Tenochtitlan and Texcoco had their distinct styles, more disparate than Aztec I and II; there exists no special reason why Culhuacán and Tollan should not have been closely associated without standardizing their artistic designs. Aztec I and II, as well as Mazapan, are styles rather than commercial wares and tended to prevail in different regions; Aztec II is also present in Culhuacán, though it does not appear to have originated there.

The version of the *Memorial Breve* raises a further problem. Kirchhoff, among others, questioned whether the Otompan concerned is really the present-day Otumba, lying to the northeast of Teotihuacán. The name, meaning "place of Otomís," could obviously be applied to a whole variety of localities. Thus the mention by the *Memorial Breve* of Otompan in this context has at times been regarded as merely figurative, serving to indicate the presence of Otomí elements among the peoples of Tollan, or at most the sharing of power by some unspecified Otomí city or province.

It may, however, be stressed that the town of Otumba is mentioned in various documents as a relatively important place in late pre-Hispanic times. For instance, Motolinía states that the Otomís descended from Otomitl, sixth son of Iztac Mixcoatl and, like his other brothers, the progenitor of a tribe; the author adds that the three main Otomí centers were Tula, Xilotepec, and Otumba.[4] Thus, at least by that time, Otumba was represented as a principal "place of Otomís." It is also mentioned by Sahagún as one of the twelve places whose merchants had a permanent place of residence in the great trading center of Tuxtepec.[5] In the "Mapa Quinatzin," an Otompan (in this context surely Otumba) figures in the famous drawing which depicts Teotihuacán itself, accompanied by the glyph of Tollan.[6] We are told how, in actual Toltec times, Nahuyotl, Topiltzin's successor, went from Tollan to Otumba when Tollan met with disaster. In the subsequent period of Tepanec domination, Techotlalatzin, ruler of Texcoco, gave land in the province of Otompan to refugees from Xaltocan, after their defeat by the Tepanecs.[7] The city also played an important part in the Tepanec war against Texcoco.

Other evidence exists as to the relevant importance of Otumba at the time of the Conquest. Sherburne Cook cites documents for the period 1560–70 showing that even after the drastic reduction in native population that had occurred, it still had 23,635 inhabitants at that time.[8] At the end of the decade, in 1570, it possessed 6,472 tribute payers, suggesting a population of some 18,000.[9]

The possible presence of Otomí partners within the Toltec polity would not in itself be at all surprising; the Otomís were later left as the main occupants of the Tollan region, though some Nahua speakers remained, and it is often suggested that they also played a leading role in the overthrow of Teotihuacán. Otumba itself is situated so near to that center, that, if it was indeed a principal Toltec confederate, that would in a sense represent simply the continued exercise of power from one traditional location.

It might have occurred that *initially*, as related by many sources, Tollan's principal partner was Tulancingo, a very fountainhead of Toltec tradition. Perhaps, given the proximity of that city to the hostile Huaxtecs, whose influence at one time even extended into the Tulancingo region, the center of gravity tended to move westward to Otumba. Moreover, the distance that divides Tula from Otumba is much less than that from Tula to Tulancingo, which might also have proved rather remote for the maintenance of an effective partnership.

Subjects and Confederates

Turning now to the *Historia Tolteca-Chichimeca*, our other major source of information on such topics, at its very beginning a list is given of twenty peoples that are ostensibly Toltec subjects or allies. As will become readily apparent, their true status vis-à-vis Tollan is unclear, and this passage has proved itself a veritable puzzle. The Nahuatl text runs as follows:

Yzcate yn ialtepepouan yn tolteca
yn imacicayan cattca yn ueycan tollan
centecpantli yn altepetli
yn ima yn icxi mochiuhticac yn toltecatli
yn iyapo yn itepepo cattca
zan oncan xixinque yn ueycan tollan
ynic quittlatlamaceuito yn imaltepeuh

After this follows a list of the twenty peoples concerned, whose identity will later be discussed. These have usually been taken as implying places as much as peoples; for instance, though the text lists the Tochpaneca, this has been taken as indicating more precisely the town of Tochpan.

Krickeberg translates the text as follows:

These are the pueblos belonging to the Toltecs.
Which formed the entirety [Gesamtheit] *of the great pueblo of Tollan.*
Twenty cities.
Which were the hands and feet of the Toltecs [*i.e., subordinate members*].
Which were the pueblos belonging to the Toltecs.
In this same place they separated, in the great pueblo of Tollan,
To occupy their own pueblos.[10]

The translation of Heinrich Berlin and Sylvia Rendón differs somewhat:

These are the nations who were allies of the Toltecs in the Great Tollan.
Twenty were the inhabited places which formed its hands and feet.
The waters, the mountains were of the Toltec.
Only when the great Tollan dispersed, did they obtain their kingdoms.[11]

Luis Reyes, in a new translation, first suggests that the *Nahuatl* "yn tolteca yn imacicayan" is a misreading of the original manuscript and that the correct version should be "yn tolteca yn imacicayo." Having made this modification, or correction, he then translates the text:

These are the peoples of the Toltecs,
Who were their complement there in the great Tollan.
Twenty cities formed their hands and feet,
Their waters and their mountains were similar [semejante],
Then in the great Tollan they separated in order to merit [merecer]
their own pueblos.[12]

It is the first three rather than the last four lines of the Nahuatl text, as transcribed above, for which a true meaning is hardest to attain. As to the last four lines, the three translations agree in presenting the twenty pueblos as "hands and feet" of Tollan, that is to say, part of its main body. All three make clear that, having been situated in or near the great Tollan, the twenty subsequently dispersed and founded their own pueblos or principalities. (Clearly the plural verb *xixinque* means that it was the pueblos who "separated" or "dispersed," rather than Tollan itself, as in the Berlin version.) It also seems reasonable when Reyes states in his version that the pueblos and Tollan shared the same mountains and the same water; the Berlin translation makes it appear that the mountains and the water belonged to Tollan, not to the twenty pueblos. But Reyes insists that the suffix *po* signifies or implies equality rather than subordination; thus the mountains and the water did not necessarily belong to the one or to the other, but were shared.

Turning now to the first three lines of the text: Reyes insists that *ialtepepouan* implies (as also containing *po*) that these people were of the same standing as Tollan, and not therefore subjects. The true nature of the relationship, however, lies in the word *imacicayo*, which derives from *aci*, "to arrive" or "to reach"; Reyes for this expression gives the rendering of "complement." As supporting evidence for this, he refers to a passage of the *Ordenanzas de Cuauhtinchan* in which the *regidores* are described as the *imacica* of the governor and the mayor; in this latter case he finds that "complement" is the most appropriate translation.[13] He calls attention to the occurrence of the same word later in the *Historia Tolteca-Chichimeca*, used this time to describe the relationship between the Chichimecs coming from Chicomoztoc and the Tolteca-Chichimecas of Cholula. In this instance a position of subordination cannot be implied, since it was the Chichimecs who came to deliver the Tolteca-Chichimecas from oppression at the hands of the Olmeca-Xicallancas. Reyes is, however, prepared to concede that in yet another subsequent passage, when *imacica* is also used to describe the relationship between the Tolteca-Chichimecas on the one hand and the Xochimilcas and Ayapancas, in this case only it indeed involves a degree of subordination. But we would consider that even in this instance equality, not subjection, is implied, since the Xochimilcas are not rebels, but simply enemies whom the Tolteca-Chichimecas defeat.[14] Reference here is surely to the more recent settlers of Xochimilco, not to its pristine inhabitants.

Sullivan sees *imacica* as literally "those who arrive," and therefore by implication people who are possibly called in and settle round the edge, or periphery, of Tollan. She thus does tend to read into the expression a certain degree of subjection, rather than a relationship of pure equality.[15]

We would, however, tend to suggest that Berlin's rendering of "allies" or more particularly Reyes' of "complement" are not unacceptable; Krickeberg's *Gesamtheit*, or "entirety," conforms with this notion, but not his implication that the twenty pueblos *belonged* to Tollan. It is worthy of note that the word *imacica* is also used on several occasions in the early part of the *Historia Tolteca-Chichimeca* to describe the relationship prevailing between the Tolteca-Chichimecas and the Nonoalcas. These two principal elements of the Toltec polity, as already demonstrated at length, clearly appear as equals, and indeed complemented one another, since each contributed different and special qualities to the Toltec community.

Therefore, to sum up our conclusions on this difficult but vital passage, it would seem first that the twenty pueblos (*ialtepepouan*) were more equals than subordinates of Tollan, even if they looked up to the metropolis as something collectively greater than themselves; secondly, that they constituted a vital part of the Toltec body politic as its "hands and feet" (*yn ima yn icxi*); thirdly, that they formed one Toltec community, actually sharing the same territory (*yn iyapo yn itepepo*); and finally, that they eventually separated and founded other pueblos, or cities, which presumably took their names from their respective tribes. It is not clear when this happened, since *xixinque* (separated) is indubitably governed by the pueblos rather than by Tollan, which is singular. It does not therefore necessarily signify, as in the Berlin version, that this occurred when Tollan fell and its people were dispersed.

As to the twenty pueblos themselves, Krickeberg was among the first to seek their correct identity; he deduced first that these names, ostensibly of *peoples*, really referred to *places*, and second that the latter lay mainly on the Gulf Coast. Hence a picture was formed of a very large Toltec empire, for which these twenty names constituted one of the principal pieces of evidence.[16]

The first group of five names—Pantecatli, Itzcuintzocatli, Tlematepeua, Tezcatepeua, and Tlequaztepeua—Krickeberg related to places in the Huaxteca, mainly by identifying Pantlan (derived from Pantecatli) with Pánuco.

The second group of five—Tecollotepeua, Tochpaneca, Cenpoalteca, Cuetlaxteca, and Cozcateca—he placed somewhat farther to the south, where four could be identified as still existing on or near the coast (Tecolutla, Tuxpan, Cempoala, and Cotaxtla), as well as Cozcatlan farther inland.

The third group—Nonoalca, Cuitlapiltzinca, Aztateca, Tzanatepeua, and Tetetzíncatli—he placed tentatively in Tabasco, due to the mention of the Nonoalcas.

And finally the fourth group—Teuxilcatli, Çacanca, Cuixcoca, Quauhchichinolca, and Chiuhnauhteca—he sought on the route between Tollan and Tabasco, because of the mention in the *Leyenda de los Soles* of Cuixcoc and Zacanco as places visited by Topiltzin-Quetzalcoatl on his way to Tlillan Tlapallan.

Kirchhoff, who also concentrated upon this problem, agreed with Krickeberg that the names really referred to places rather than peoples. He examined the question in detail and arrived at totally different conclusions.[17]

Kirchhoff first draws attention to the dedication of Mesoamericans to the cult of numbers and symmetry; from this he deduces that the names had some kind of additional or special significance connected with the cardinal points—north, south, east, west—and also center. He points out that the division into categories of five in the text is arbitrary, and he redivided them (converted from peoples into pueblos) into five groups of four names; these, by means of certain topographical identifications, he situates as follows with respect to Tollan itself:

Central group. Cuetlaxtlan, Cozcatlan, Nonoalco, Cuitlapiltzinco. A Nonoalco exists a short distance to the west of Tollan, but the other three names cannot be identified in this region.

East group. Tezcatepec, Tecolotepec, Tochpan, Cempoallan. Discounting Krickeberg's coastal identifications, Kirchhoff points to a Zempoala situated between Tula and Tulancingo; there are also two Tezcatepecs near the latter city. A Tuspan existed in the sixteenth century to the south of Tula, but he rejects this identification, because, according to his symmetrical scheme of things, the Tochpan in question must perforce be the northernmost of this eastern group of cities. (It should perhaps be explained that Kirchhoff's pattern of orientation also to a considerable extent orders the cities in such a way that they could form a reasonably logical line of march to Tollan, and then back to Cholula, as described in the *Historia Tolteca-Chichimeca.*)

North group. Pantlan, Itzcuintzonco, Tlematepec, Tlequaztepec. None identifiable in this particular area, to the north of Tollan.

West group. Aztatlan, Tzanatepec, Tetetzinco, Teuhxilco. Of these Kirchhoff could identify only Aztatlan, as being the original home of the Mexicas, situated in his view near San Isidro Culiacán, in the state of Guanajuato.

South group. Zacanco, Cuixcoc, Quauhchichinolco, Chiuhnauhtlan. All four were identified as situated in the Valley of Toluca. Cuixcoc is Cuixcocingo mentioned in a document of 1578. Several Zacangos exist in the area. Chiuhnauhtecatl was formerly the name of the volcano now called the Nevada de Toluca. Quauhchichinolco is the modern Cuachichinola.

One may well ask what more can be made of this conundrum, involving such conflicting views. In the first place, one must clear one's thoughts as to what these names really signify. Were they indeed far-off cities, subject to a vast Toltec empire, as Krickeberg proposes? Or were they subject cities of Tollan, but less far-distant, as Kirchhoff suggests? Or, alternatively, were they simply peoples or tribes forming part of the central Toltec polity, who only *later* formed their own cities, as the passage in question tends literally to indicate. Both Krickeberg and Kirchhoff seem to have taken for granted that these were subject cities of Tollan, but the text does not go this far; in my analysis, the conclusion was reached that their status was rather one of relative equality with Tollan and that they were even *part* of the great Tollan, rather than subjected to its remote rule.

On the one hand, if places, not people, are concerned, we tend to agree with Kirchhoff on their greater proximity to Tollan and indeed would locate them much nearer still. On the other hand, his symmetrical layout is a little hard to accept *in toto*; just as empires could not be conquered by a cloistered recluse, as already stressed, so also they could not be acquired in such a meticulously neat fashion, obeying the rigorous dictates of a ritually prescribed pattern. It may be true, as Levi-Strauss has pointed out, that in certain cases villages and even cities may be based on a formal or magic plan; it might even be added that the Inca Empire was collectively known as Tahuantinsuyo, meaning "the four Quarters." But what may be applied to a village cannot hold good for an empire, and it would be hard indeed to devise an imperial domain less symmetrical in geographical form than that of the Incas. As we have already insisted, conquerors tend to follow the line of least resistance or the path which offers the greatest material rewards; they do not, and could not in practice, accumulate their domains in a kind of chessboard manner. There was, after all, nothing remotely symmetrical in the sequence of Aztec conquests, as we know them. Moreover, it must frankly be stated that Kirchhoff's system, while appropriately identifying the four names of his southern group, is less successful where the others are concerned, and for the northern group not one place can be found on any map.

In contrast to the findings of Krickeberg and Kirchhoff, we would in very general terms regard the names in question as basically referring to *peoples*, as the text itself states; these tribes were somehow connected with the Toltecs and, far from originally constituting outposts of empire, had established villages or settlements relatively near to Tollan; perhaps originally some had even inhabited barrios of the city itself. Many of their names also occur as places on the Tolteca-Chichimeca line of march to Cholula, as described in subsequent passages of the *Historia Tolteca-Chichimeca*; this Kirchhoff has been at pains to emphasize. As such, they can hardly be associated initially with the Gulf Coast.

For the purpose of possible identification, one may return to the text's original grouping in series of five names and comment as follows:

Group I. Pantécatl, Itzcuitóncatl, Tlematepehua, Tlequaztepehua, Tezcatepehua. Pantécatl, deriving from Pantlan or Panotlan, is unlikely to refer to Pánuco. One finds in a later passage a Panotlan situated on the original route of the Tolteca-Chichimecas from Tollan to Cholula, mentioned in the same paragraph as a Quiahuiztlan, as well as a Xilotepec;[18] from the context, one doubts if this refers to Jilotepec, southwest of Tula. Tlematepec and Tlequaztepec are listed among the places visited by the Tolteca-Chichimecas and the Chichimecs on their return route from Chicomoztoc to Cholula; in this instance they are grouped together with Mazatepec and Nenétepec.

In Appendix A, the conclusion is reached that these two places (among the first also to be visited by Mixcoatl) are situated to the northeast of Tollan. Nenétepec is probably the same as Tepenene, which exists today to the southeast of Actopan. A Texcatepec also is still to be found to the northeast of Tula in the direction of Ixmiquilpan. It would thus seem likely that the whole group is to be sought to the northeast of Tollan and situated not too far from the city itself.

Group II. Tecollotepehua, Tochpaneca, Cenpoalteca, Cuetlaxteca, Cozcateca. The *Historia Tolteca-Chichimeca* also mentions a Cuetlaxtlan and a Cozcatlan lying on the line of march to Cholula, and occurring in the same paragraph as Tollan itself and Nonoalco.[19] Following this, the travelers proceeded first to Cuauhnáhuac (possibly a homonym for a place lying in the Valley of Mexico), and then to Chapultepec and Amecameca. In view of the mention of two names of this second group of five names in the same sentence with Tollan itself and Nonoalco, it would seem that these peoples were centered around Tollan (Kirchhoff located a Nonoalco just to the west of the city). What is hardly conceivable is that localities on the Gulf of Mexico are intended in this particular context.

Group III. Nonoalca, Cuitlapiltzinca, Aztateca, Tzanatepehua, Tetetzíncatl. Aztatlan and Tzanatépec are also cited in the *Historia Tolteca-Chichimeca* as among the very first places to be visited by the Chichimecs after leaving Chicomoztoc on their way to Cholula.[20] It might therefore be reasonable to suppose that they lay to the northwest or west of Tollan, where Chicomoztoc is generally to be sought.

Group IV. Teuhxílcatl, Zacanca, Cuixcoca, Quauhchichinolca, Chiuhnauhteca. Kirchhoff's identification of four of these places as situated in the Valley of Toluca is very convincing; the fifth, Teuxílco, cannot be located on the map. But while Kirchhoff's discovery of these four names in the same area could hardly be a pure coincidence, one wonders whether homonyms might not originally have existed much nearer to Tollan, before these people moved collectively to more distant homes in the Valley of Toluca.

In general terms, the four groups seem to follow a reasonably logical order. Group I appears to lie northeast of Tollan, Group II around the city itself, Group III to the west, and Group IV to the south. It seems likely therefore that they lay relatively near to Tollan, and certainly not on the Gulf Coast, however plausible such an identification might seem at first sight.

A tendency exists in Mesoamerica, to which Carlos Navarrete has called attention, for not merely one but a whole series of names belonging to a given region to be subsequently repeated elsewhere. This may have been due to joint migrations from one territory to another of the inhabitants of a cluster of neighboring villages. It thus seems most possible that the Tochpan, Cempoallan, and Tecolotlan on the Gulf Coast derived from earlier places of that name situated in the same area of central Mexico. One is specifically informed, for instance, that Toltec refugees went to Cempoallan, as well as to Quiahuiztlan. The *Historia Tolteca-Chichimeca* is literally filled with names of seemingly distant localities, as one knows them today; however, from the context in which they are mentioned, they can only be homonyms of such places, unless one is to suppose, for instance, that the Tolteca-Chichimecas included the Gulf Coast in their itinerary to Cholula. Many of the present-day townships in question probably acquired their names after the Toltec diaspora, which gave rise to genuine and perhaps also to spurious claims to Toltec descent.

One may thus infer that, insofar as the twenty names at the beginning of the *Historia Tolteca-Chichimeca* refer to place names at all, then, with the possible exception of Group IV, they are to be sought in or near Tollan itself. It is significant that the Cozcatecas (of Group II) are named in the same document as among the peoples who eventually emigrated from Tollan with the Nonoalcas, and the relevant passage implies that, like the latter, the Cozcatecas were also inhabitants of Tollan itself; later of course they founded Cozcatlan in the Teotitlan region. One can identify no Cozcatlan near Tollan today, though the place is mentioned in the *Historia Tolteca-Chichimeca* immediately following Nonoalco and Tollan itself.

One must really go back to what the text *says*, rather than to what it omits—something of which it is easy to lose sight. The twenty names are given as those of peoples, not places; far from being distant and subject cities, they are described in words implying equality with Tollan and suggesting that they were vital members of the Toltec body corporate; as sharing the same mountains and waters, they must have been situated nearby. One cannot help feeling that this was the original situation. Only later, as the text also specifically states, they dispersed and founded their own pueblos, perhaps in many cases those that today bear the names in question.

One is apt at times to seek tidiness in Mesoamerican systems of government; however, one often discerns rather a lack of symmetry, whatever the theoretical penchant towards magical numbers. One does not even know for sure that these twenty names constitute a complete list, and whether others were omitted by accident or design. Similarly, it may be incorrect automatically to assume that all those listed form a single category; their situations may have been different one from another. It is quite possible, for instance, that some names belong to peoples actually settled in barrios in Tollan and who only at its fall went off to found places of the same name on the Gulf Coast and elsewhere. At the same time, others may refer to tribes who, at a much later date, moved out and formed pueblos, such as Texcatepec, in the surrounding country. Some of these may conceivably have gone so far afield as the Valley of Toluca before the fall of Tollan, though it will later be seen that any evidence of Toltec domination of this region is rather inconclusive.

It is thus considered in general terms that this list, whether it refers to twenty places or peoples, concerns the heartland of the Toltec domains, rather than any far-flung possessions. It may be worth recalling that Chalco was reported by Chimalpain as being the "father and mother" of twenty-five cities. Surely no one would suggest that these unnamed places were situated, say, on the Gulf Coast; the passage clearly implies that they constituted a central nucleus. The *Anales de Cuauhtitlán* state that Tollan itself was the leader of twenty cities or villages.[21] But this particular passage refers to the time of the Conquest, when any physical control that Tollan might have exercised would have been confined more to its own vicinity.

Bounds of Empire

Having considered certain more generalized statements occurring mainly in the *Memorial Breve* and the *Historia Tolteca-Chichimeca*, one must now examine the appropriate regions one by one, in order to seek, if at all possible, the outlines of a Toltec empire, or at least some system of alliances and dependencies.

VALLEY OF MEXICO

It will be recalled that mention was made of Culhuacán in the *Memorial Breve* as a Toltec confederate. As to its evident significance at the time, one need only recall once more the abundant presence of Aztec I in Culhuacán itself, and later, Aztec II; the former belongs essentially to the Tula-Mazapan horizon, while the latter was still extensively used at the moment of Tollan's decline.

Kirchhoff has insisted that the Culhuacán contemporary with Tollan's apogee to which the sources refer is not the place of that name in the southern part of the Valley of Mexico, but the older Teoculhuacán, lying to the west of Tollan; in particular, he cites the *Anales de Cuauhtitlán* and the *Relación de la Genealogía* as stating that the later Culhuacán was founded long after Tollan. However, in Chapter 8 and in Appendix B, while I accept most of Kirchhoff's views concerning the end of Tollan, reasons are given for believing that the Culhuacán so closely linked to Tollan in the *Memorial Breve* is indeed the city in the Valley of Mexico. Not only does archaeology demonstrate its relatively early creation, but the existence of inseparable ties that bound its dynasties to those of Tollan will later be stressed.

The old Teoculhuacán is clearly both a legendary and a real place, just as was Huehtlapallan or even Chicomoztoc, with which it is closely associated by certain sources. As already suggested, it often serves more as a kind of other-worldly counterpart to the Culhuacán of the Valley of Mexico, with which we are primarily concerned in Toltec times. It plays rather the same role in Toltec history as Tulán in that of the Quiches and Cakchiquels.

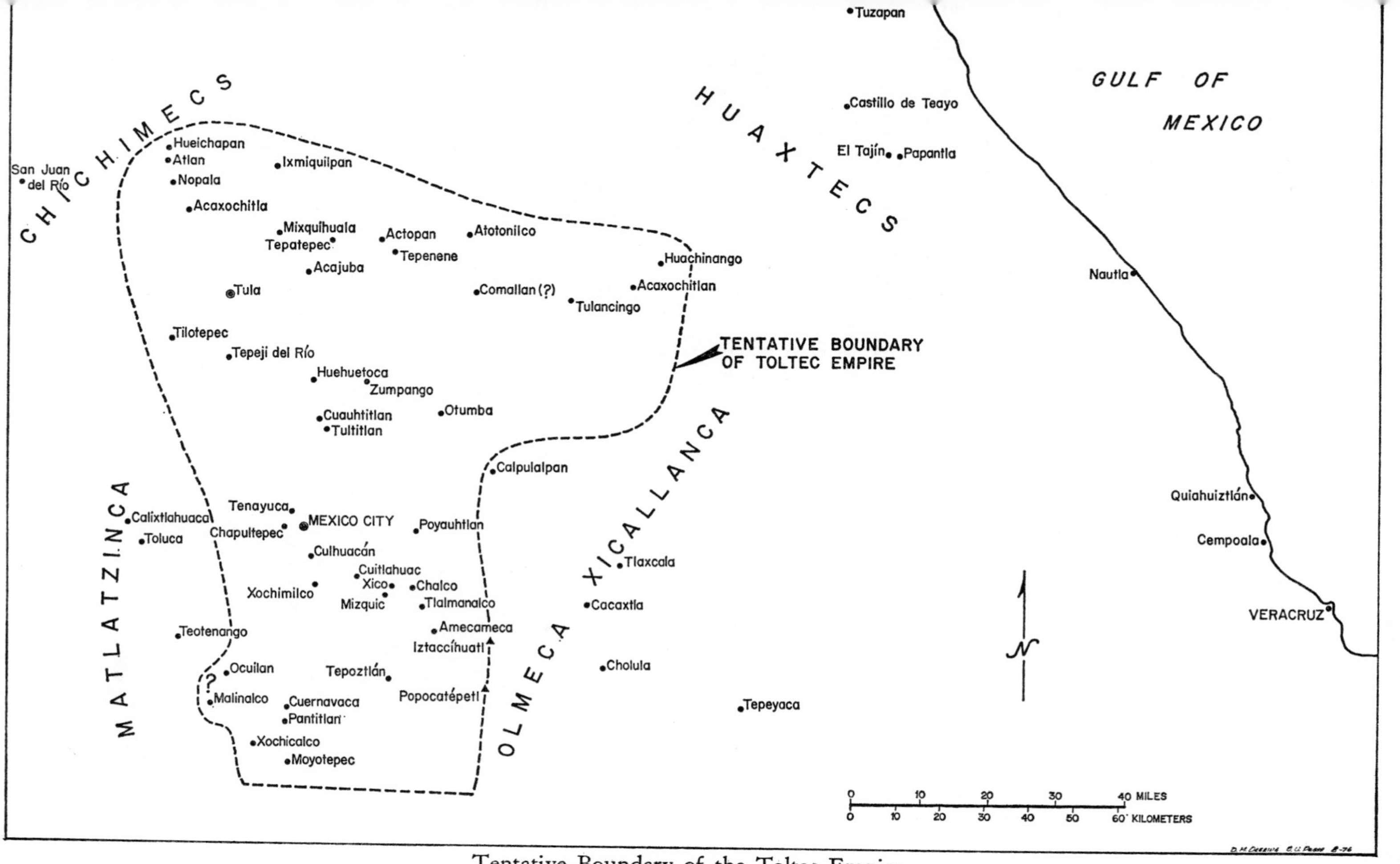

Tentative Boundary of the Toltec Empire

Moreover, from any map one may see that if Tollan could not dominate the area in which Culhuacán is situated, that is to say, the inner Valley of Mexico, its territory would have barely exceeded an arid strip to the north stretching from Tollan itself as far as, say, Tulancingo and scarcely even deserving the name of empire.

While Toltec power in the Valley of Mexico was seemingly based upon Culhuacán, mentioned in various accounts, and which served as its chief bastion or partner, certain evidence exists of connections with other places in the vicinity. Attention has already been drawn to the ties binding the peoples of Culhuacán with those of Cuitláhuac, Mízquic, and Xochimilco, in later times described collectively as the people of the Chinampas. In another work, I have examined the whole question of the affinities linking the Toltecs, Chalcas, and Culhuas.[22] Alfonso Caso drew attention to the presence of archaeological remains of the Tula-Mazapan horizon both in Xico and Chalco.[23] Incidentally, the Aztec I found in Chalco to which Caso presumably is referring is slightly different to that of Culhuacán.[24] George O'Neill goes so far as to name Chalco as a focal point in the distribution of Aztec I, and in addition points to associations between this city and Cholula during the Aztec I-Mazapan horizon. Close contacts naturally tended to link the eastern part of the Valley of Mexico and the western portion of the Puebla-Tlaxcala Valley, and Cholula polychrome was later to appear in Chalco, bearing a marked resemblance to that of Chalco itself.

Concerning other parts of the Valley of Mexico, Chapultepec is also named as an ultimate place of Toltec refuge, quite apart from its prominence in the legend of Huemac.[25] Farther to the east, at the extremity of the area under discussion, Texcoco as well as Chalco is mentioned in connection with the Toltec diaspora.[26] As an additional link with Texcoco, whose historic role was modest until later times, it may be added that the *Tlaillotlaque* who came there in the reign of Quinatzin were of "Toltec" lineage.[27] Incidentally, these people had first gone to Chalco.

Tenayuca also has Toltec associations. In the first place, it was an abundant source of Aztec II pottery, which was also to appear in Tollan; the possible significance of this phenomenon is discussed in Chapter 8 in connection with the fall of Tollan. A report even exists that Topiltzin-Quetzalcoatl went first to Tenayuca rather than to

Culhuacán or Cholula, when he departed from Tollan. Tenayuca moreover is another place whose history goes back well beyond its traditional inception and which seemingly rests on Toltec foundations.[28]

Finally, one should mention the Cuauhtitlán area, including Zumpango and Tultitlán, that border on the Teotlalpan. The latter, as its name implies, is mentioned as specifically Toltec.[29]

THE VALLEY OF MORELOS

It would seem preferable to deal with the Valley of Morelos immediately following the Valley of Mexico, because of a certain innate tendency for those who dominate the latter to seek also to control the former. The Valley of Morelos offers relatively close and easy access to the products of the warmer lands, especially cotton, not available at the higher altitudes; the Mexicas, when still under Tepanec tutelage, were drawn there as early as the reign of the second Tenochca *tlatoani*, who married the daughter of the ruler of Cuauhnáhuac.[30]

One cannot of course maintain that whoever dominated the Valley of Mexico automatically penetrated into that of Morelos; however, the urge to do so remained strong, and it seems improbable that it would have been absent in Toltec times. Culhuacán itself is situated very near, as the crow flies, to this region, even if separated by a mountain barrier. And indeed, at least in the Late Postclassic period, certain ties joined the peoples on both sides of the Sierra, and a special relationship seems to have existed between the Xochimilcas and the Tlalhuicas of Tepoztlán.[31]

It cannot be said that one possesses much more than indirect pointers to a Toltec-Culhua domination of Morelos. Ixtlilxóchitl, for one, mentions Toltec buildings and palaces in Cuauhnáhuac;[32] in another context he mentions markets held there in Toltec times.[33] He also states that Topiltzin in his final war against his adversaries had two armies, one stationed in Tultitlán and the other in the land of the Tlalhuicas.[34] By this Morelos is clearly indicated, even if the Tlalhuicas themselves had not yet settled there. The *Anales de Tlatelolco* tell how the conqueror Tímal, a Nonoalca, conquered Cuauhnáhuac; from there he went on to occupy Chalco.[35] A Tímal is also mentioned in the *Historia Tolteca-Chichimeca* as one of the leaders of the Nonoalcas on their southward migration from Tollan.

Of greater significance is the reference in the *Anales de Cuauhtitlán*, mentioned above, to Tollan's association with Huaxtepec and Cuauhnáhuac.[36] However, as explained, I feel that as in the case of Cuauhchinanco, mentioned in the same context, these two places represent more probably the limits of Toltec expansion rather than its principal allies or confederates, as Culhuacán would have been.

It is also important to mention that toward the end of the *Anales de Cuauhtitlán*, recounted among events of the reign of Moctezuma II, is a report of an Iztac Mixcoatl, who made a series of conquests, some of which Jiménez Moreno and Florencia Muller have been able to identify as situated in the state of Morelos. Apparently the first part of this narrative consists of one of these flashbacks to earlier times that occur so frequently in Mesoamerican sources. This is made clear by the mention of Comallan (or rather Comaltecas) and Tecama (Tecoma); these places are named in various other reports of the deeds of the Mixcoatl of Toltec times. (*See* Appendix A, Table A.) But after this passage names are given for his sons that in no way correspond with the other accounts (Topiltzin is not mentioned), and shortly thereafter Moctezuma I is introduced into the story as being the father-in-law of one of his descendants. One of the sons of this Mixcoatl, Quetzalteuctli, "founded" the four barrios of Cuitláhuac. His successor at one remove was Quetzalmazatzin, stated by the text to have been a contemporary of Itzcoatl of Tenochtitlan. It is only after this interpolation that we again return to the feats of Iztac Mixcoatl, and places are now mentioned, such as Moyotepec and Pantitlan, that have been identified in Morelos.[37] But, in the first place, the account is very confused, with happenings of Toltec times interpolated between events that took place a few years before the Conquest; and secondly, as stressed in Chapter 4, the story of Iztac Mixcoatl belongs to the end of Tollan, not its beginning. At best, therefore, if my views are correct, this passage in the *Anales de Cuauhtitlán* could be taken only as an additional pointer toward some earlier Toltec occupation of the Valley of Morelos; assuming, as proposed, that an invading Mixcoatl took Culhuacán in late Toltec times, he would have also tended to take possession of other places already under Toltec domination, like Morelos, in preference to breaking new ground in areas that had never fallen within the Toltec sphere of influence.

It has already been explained that I also find it hard to associate the whole Tepoztecatl legend with the story of Topiltzin. However, at least in later times, Macuilxochitl and Xochiquetzal, deities linked with Quetzalcoatl, were greatly venerated in the Valley of Morelos. Also, Tepoztecatl was one of the gods of the Amantecas, who had apparently formed part of the population of Tollan. Tepoztlán undoubtedly existed at the time, and Aztec I pottery is to be found there.[38]

Looking toward the other extremity of Morelos and to the early rather than late Toltec period, it should not be forgotten that Xochicalco is in many respects Tollan's most direct predecessor. Notwithstanding the presence of some Mazapan in Xochicalco, Litvak insists that as Tollan rose to power the city was already in the process of being reduced to a place of minor importance, while Miacatlán was becoming the principal center of the region.[39] There was, however, a very marked carry-over of architectural traits from Xochicalco to Tollan.

Litvak in particular calls attention to the similarity between the North Ball Court of Tollan and that of Xochicalco, though rightly stressing that the former city was hardly built when the latter was already reduced to relative insignificance; he questions whether the Tollan ball court might not belong to an early phase in that site. However, I have already reached the conclusion, with reference to connections between Tollan and Chichén, that the surviving buildings of the former tend to belong to its later period, and would thus regard the Tollan ball court as representing the continuity of a tradition rather than as being a near-contemporary imitation of that of Xochicalco. Forms recalling Xochicalco could have prevailed in Tollan, just as did the Palladian styles in England long after its original efflorescence in Italy.

At all events, irrespective of the method of transference of such common traits, their very existence serves to reinforce notions as to close and early connections between Tollan and this part of the Valley of Morelos; these probably continued after Miacatlán had partly assumed the former status of Xochicalco. Litvak also draws attention to possible links during this period between the Valley of Morelos and the Matlatzinca zone via Cacahuamilpa.[40] He also mentions similarities between Orange B pottery, typical of Xochicalco, and Cholulteca II, though presumably the latter would postdate the former.

THE EASTERN BORDER

We now turn to the region lying to the east of Tollan and northeast of the Valley of Mexico, which may well have been at one time under Toltec control. Within such an area one might perhaps include the towns of Actopan, Atotonilco el Grande, Tulancingo, and Acaxochitlán; from the latter its boundary would possibly follow a line running southwest along the present Hidalgo-Puebla border (pre-Hispanic limits often continued into later times) and from there in a westerly direction to include Otumba but exclude Calpulalpan and the Puebla-Tlaxcala Valley. Farther to the south, a Toltec border would logically follow the line of the Sierra Nevada, thus including Chalco and Amecameca within the area controlled.

Tulancingo is mentioned by various sources in connection with early Toltec history, and there is no need to re-emphasize its major role in Tollan's formative stages as a likely link between the Nonoalcas coming from the Huaxteca and the Tolteca-Chichimecas from marginal Mesoamerica. Archaeological remains in Tulancingo are more in evidence for the Teotihuacán period; Sahagún mentions "Toltec" structures in that place, but one does not know to what particular Toltecs he may be referring. Bernal emphasizes that the Tulancingo region constituted part of the home territory of Teotihuacán, where the culture of the period in question is exclusively derived from that center, without the continued presence of distinctive local influences. Later, together with other places mentioned above, it formed part of the region described by Ixtlilxóchitl on various occasions as constituting a kind of domestic patrimony of the rulers of Texcoco.

One would nevertheless agree with Jiménez Moreno and others in seeing a certain Huaxtec encroachment in this direction; as a result, whatever its initial significance, Tulancingo itself may have become somewhat peripheral to any latter-day Toltec empire. Even if never actually occupied by Huaxtecs, it would at least have been situated rather near to the frontier area.

It seems very possible, if not probable, that the Toltecs would have controlled the area outlined above. It is in fact one that always tended to be dominated by any conquerors of central Mexico, whether Toltec, Tepanec, or Aztec. Apart from any other significance it may possess, it forms a natural gateway to important parts of the coast. Unless the Toltecs had indeed occupied this territory, it is hard to see how they could have enjoyed such apparently close contacts with the Huaxteca, as reported by several sources.

Very possibly Otumba, rather than Tulancingo, came to be the principal center of the region in Toltec times; in view of its proximity to Teotihuacán, this in itself would have provided a measure of continuity from former days.

THE NORTHWESTERN FRONTIER

The most intangible question of all must now be examined: what control, if any, did Tollan exercise over the marginal lands that lay to the northwest, and what was the possible extension of its rule in that direction?

It is unnecessary to re-emphasize the state of relative flux that had prevailed in this region ever since the Late Classic period. It has also already been stressed that, notwithstanding the instability of the Mesoamerican frontier in that direction since late Teotihuacán times, a kind of corridor still existed that fed Mesoamerican influences into areas as remote as the Aztatlan complex in Sinaloa; Isabel Kelly considers this in general terms to be contemporary with Mazapan. Sinaloa Red-rimmed ware indeed recalls Coyotlatelco, though also present in the area are traits emanating from the Puebla-Tlaxcala Valley, which Ekholm attributes to the Early Postclassic period, since they were absent in the previous Chametla complex.

It may be added that "Mexican" influences penetrated far beyond this; in the Museo Nacional de Antropología, a copper disk from Casas Grandes in Chihuahua may be seen, which represents four stylized serpents. But an almost identical mosaic disk from Chichén is also to be found there. In turn, these closely resemble those worn by the Atlantids of Tollan Xicocotitlan. Even farther afield, in the American Southwest, one discovers such emblems as a horned and feathered serpent; in the Anasazi phases Pueblo II and early Pueblo III, from, say, A.D. 1000 to 1100, copper balls, also of Mesoamerican origins, have been located.[41]

Some doubts remain as to how these various central Mexican traits were introduced into such distant areas and by whom. Charles Kelley and Ellen Abbott note the presence of a strong wave of Mesoamerican ceremonialism introduced by new colonists through diffusional processes; this had occurred already in the Alta Vista phase of the Chalchihuites culture, probably in about A.D. 350, at the height of the Classic period.[42] The same authors mention that such influences continued in the Las Joyas phase, from about A.D. 800 to 1000; the "new" Quetzalcoatl is now found represented on pottery as the Morning and Evening Star. By this time, however, Mesoamerican influences were generally on the wane in Zacatecas and Durango, as already explained.

To account for Toltec-period cultural penetration of this area, Charles Kelley in another context mentions Edwin F. Ferdon's hypothesis regarding the possible infiltration of an organized Mesoamerican trading group, or *pochteca*, as far as the Southwestern United States—or, alternatively, the entry into the region of a small group of "militaristic Toltec nobles," displaced from Central Mesoamerica at the fall of Tollan.[43] Once more, one hesitates to accept deductions of an historical nature drawn from the presence of artifacts; in this respect one may mention Braniff's insistence that in the Early Postclassic phase in San Luis Potosí, Toltec influence does not appear to derive from military overlords, but rather appears as improvised and incidental, in contrast with the stronger imprint of the Late Classic culture.[44]

One would incline to the view that cultural traits, and even works of art such as copper disks, could well be introduced by the simple process of progressive diffusion from one center to another, without further historical implications. Doubts have already been expressed as to the attainment by Tollan of any true pre-eminence as a center of trade and commerce. Concerning the final diaspora, the sources mention so many destinations for Toltec refugees that the whole population of Tollan could barely have provided a respectable quota for each, without adding any more. While of course accepting a possible Central Mesoamerican physical presence in Kaminaljuyu and Chichén, it is hard to envisage *pochteca*, whether from Teotihuacán or Tollan Xicocotitlan, marching to the far north, which offered little that would have tempted their clients.

It is somewhat natural for both religious cults and art styles to overstep their immediate bounds and spread from one center to others less highly developed; items such as copper bells can easily be passed along the line from one trading post to another. One feels that this spread of goods and beliefs was a long-drawn-out process, and in some ways a natural one.

On the crucial question of the northern limits of Toltec power and influence, archaeology tells little, and one again enters the realm of pure speculation. It is really impossible to do more than offer a personal opinion, since the worship of Quetzalcoatl, the copying of Mazapan styles, and the acquisition of Mesoamerican trophies in themselves offer no scientific proof of any physical intervention by the Toltecs.

It is possible that the early Tolteca-Chichimecas enjoyed continued links with the remoter regions of marginal Mesoamerica, from where they had come; such associations might even help to explain the siting of their capital in a northwesterly direction from the Valley of Mexico. But, as a purely personal opinion, I would propose that, by the time Tollan attained the zenith of its power, its zone of domination was unlikely to have stretched much beyond the Teotlalpan; that is to say, it would have ended at a very limited distance to the northwest of Tollan itself. One might perhaps envisage a frontier with Ixmiquilpan as its most northerly point, from there running southwest, to include places that also marked the limits of Aztec expansion, such as Timilpan, Acaxochitlán, Nopala, Atlán, and Hueichiapan. (*See* Map 4.) At the very most, one might as an alternative propose a line approximately following the Río San Juan, thus including as Toltec territory a somewhat larger zone stretching up to the vicinity of San Juan del Río. Admittedly, in one of the few sites to be investigated to the west of this, called El Pueblito and situated near Querétaro, Mazapan pottery has been found, as well as a chacmool, but the possibility of Toltec domination of the area can really be neither proved nor disproved.

It is difficult to depart from the view that from irrigated lands bordering the River Tula the Toltecs would have obtained all the maize, beans, and other local products that their economy could have required, and that the whole impetus of their expansive urges would have been directed in precisely the opposite direction, not in search of surplus maize and beans but of feathers, turquoise, and jade. Even if Tollan was not literally built of such materials, as the more apocryphal accounts suggest, its inhabitants were not necessarily averse to acquiring them. The northern marches, poor at the best of times, simply would not have offered the kind of things that the Toltecs were likely to seek. Moreover, in general terms, Braniff tends to see these areas as then populated partly by settled and partly by nomadic peoples; as such, they would have been very difficult to control, and the Toltecs, like their Aztec successors, might have preferred to leave them to their own devices. Later, as will be seen, a movement in the reverse direction probably occurred, when some of the latter penetrated Toltec territory.

THE VALLEY OF TOLUCA

It has been found preferable to leave this region to the last, among those surrounding the Toltec heartland of the Teotlalpan; it is in reality most problematical and hard to place definitely within or without any putative Toltec empire. Evidence as to a possible Toltec presence is very conflicting, though certain factors suggest at least the existence of fairly intimate ties.

One may leave aside for the moment any analogies between the sites of Tollan and Teotenango and first seek for evidence of cultural interchange rather than of political domination. In this respect, one may point to the close relationship between Tula-Mazapan pottery and that of the Matlatzincas, as emphasized by Acosta.[45] García Payón also emphasizes the resemblances between the two pottery styles. However, Matlatzinca contacts were naturally not confined to the area of Tollan or the inner Valley of Mexico; García Payón mentions that their pottery was also found in Mazapan itself, near to Teotihuacán.[46] Florencia Muller writes of the relationship between the ceramic styles of the Valley of Toluca and Cholula.[47] She also mentions cultural links between the Valleys of Toluca and Morelos, with particular reference to Xochicalco and Teotenango, whose buildings present certain similarities.

Noguera and Piña Chan also write of analogies in form and decoration between Matlatzinca and Tlalhuica Laqueur, the latter corresponding to the pre-Aztec period.[48] Even in Seler's time, certain connections were noted between Xochicalco and the Ocuiltecas of Tenango and Tenancingo.[49]

When one turns to the written sources, four places immediately come to mind that are named together among the twenty Toltec confederates of the *Historia Tolteca-Chichimeca*: Cuixcoc, Zacanco, Chiuhnauhtecatl, and Quauhchichinolco. It will be recalled that Kirchhoff identified these as probably situated in the Valley of Toluca. It may also be mentioned that Ixtlilxóchitl affirms that the Toltecs built palaces in Toluca, as well as in Cuauhnáhuac.[50] It has already been noted that the *Memorial Breve* refers to the domination of Ocuilan and Malinalco by Culhuacán, allied to the Toltecs; Sahagún actually equates the Ocuiltecas with the "Toloque," i.e., Matlatzincas, and says that their language is very similar.[51]

Chimalpain is par excellence the source that associates the Valley of Toluca, or more specifically Teotenango, with Tollan. He actually makes mention of a structure in Teotenango which he calls "the Pyramid of the Toltecs"; he describes it as resembling a hill and as situated beside the water, in which grew great rushes.[52] It was called Chiconcoac, after the serpent who guarded it; the place was also called Tzacualtitlan Teotenanco (nearby the Pyramid); following the migration there of the Teotenancas, this name was transferred to Amecameca, which became Tzacualtitlan Teotenanco Amaquemecan.[53]

As to possible links between Teotenango and Tollan, Chimalpain further states that the former was settled by Teochichimecs, who remained there for two or three centuries and had wars with Tollan. The contemporaries of Acxitl-Quetzalcoatl were the great-grandsons of the original founders of the city. The description which this source gives of the place of worship of the god of Teotenango, Nauhyotecuhtli, as being replete with edifices studded with precious stones, is very reminiscent of Sahagún's account of Tollan. So grandiose were these monuments that Quetzalcoatl of Tollan actually envied the kingdom of Nauhyotecuhtli and often tried to destroy his city.

Chimalpain also tells us of people who migrated to Tollan from Teotenango: the Nonoalca Tlacochcalcas, who came from Tlapallan, that is to say, the east, and who also were known as the Teotlixcas (the people from the place facing the sun).[54] These migrants eventually reached Tollan, but only after first sojourning in Teotenango, among other places which they visited. They reportedly spent only twenty years in Tollan, but such a period may be interpreted somewhat figuratively; they are said to have been among the first arrivals there and therefore may in fact have been a kind of breakaway group from Teotenango. It is interesting to speculate as to whether some of Nonoalcas discussed in Chapter 4 might not have visited or sojourned in Teotenango. It is not inconceivable that, apart from those other Nonoalcas who according to Ixtlilxóchitl went from Tlapallan to Pánuco and from there to Tollan, a further Nonoalca group went to Teotenango, which probably began to flourish before Tollan, and then only later joined their kinsmen in Tollan itself.

One must now return to certain archaeological aspects of the problem and ask whether the recently uncovered remains of Teotenango serve to confirm or deny Chimalpain's contentions. It should first be stressed that the site is extremely imposing. It is protected on one side by a great wall; on the three others, the abrupt slope of the mountain gives strong natural protection, and added reinforcement is provided by artificial containing walls. Seen from afar, the protective girdle of stone indeed has an almost divine aspect, justifying its name of "place of the divine wall." (It also of course means "place of the great wall," *teo* having the double meaning of "great" and "divine.") The area of the ancient city is considerably larger than that of the modern town of twelve thousand inhabitants that lies below it, but whose layout is perhaps more concentrated.

As to the chronology of Teotenango, Piña Chan, in describing the site, suggests that it was founded about A.D. 700, since in the lowest levels pottery somewhat recalling Coyotlatelco was located, combined with other sherds displaying late Teotihuacán influences. The cornice and tablero form of its architecture also recalls very late Teotihuacán, as found, for instance, in Calpulalpan; its style is also related to that of Xochicalco. Certain vessels from Teotenango certainly recall Late Teotihuacán, though with the distinctive red patches typical of all Matlatzinca wares.[55]

In the following period, which Piña Chan dates from about A.D. 1000 to 1400, pottery of Matlatzinca type is present from the beginning, and thereafter the true Matlatzinca style develops. In the Late Postclassic period, Aztec superstructures are to be found (partly in the ball court, as in Tollan), and Aztec III pottery also makes its appearance.

Its relatively long life span as a leading center is an interesting feature of the site. It would seem that it began to be a place of some consequence before Tollan, where signs of late Teotihuacán influences are less prominent and have so far come to light only in Tula Chico. Teotenango survived until the Conquest as a fairly major center without any apparent interruption. It is a more imposing site than any other known rival to Tollan, situated in regions not too remote from the latter and flourishing during the Tula-Mazapan horizon.

Piña Chan is of the opinion that nothing truly Toltec is to be found in Teotenango, as opposed to identifiable Aztec remains in later times; he is accordingly of the opinion that it was not conquered by the former.[56]

I myself, as repeatedly emphasized, take perhaps an overcautious view regarding the use of archaeological evidence to define the bounds of empire. One would readily agree that the presence of any Coyotlatelco or Mazapan influences prove nothing in that respect; Aztec I and Cholulteca II have much in common with Mazapan, but no one suggests that all the territory where these wares abound formed part of one political unit. But it is surely open to question whether the absence of truly Toltec remains in itself proves that the Toltecs never occupied the area. The relative lack of Aztec III and IV pottery over large areas certainly conquered by the Triple Alliance has already been stressed. The presence of Aztec traits in Teotenango (as well as in Tollan) may be somewhat fortuitous, since in many other conquered places they left no traces.

At the same time, however, Teotenango appears so formidable that one cannot doubt its capacity to resist attack; it must have been well able to stand up to any rival, including Tollan, against which, according to Chimalpain, wars were indeed fought. Moreover, subsequent history affirms that the Matlatzincas were a tough people; they fought tenaciously against the Aztec armies and very nearly succeeded in killing the *tlatoani*, Axayácatl, who only escaped from their ambush by a hair's breadth.

The exact significance of the Nonoalca Teotlixcas, who according to the same source, went from Teotenango to Tollan, is not easy to explain. It may, however, be reasonable to suppose that in the early days a group of migrants connected with the Nonoalcas did indeed first go to Teotenango, already a thriving center, and then proceeded to Tollan, in order to join forces with their Nonoalca compatriots, by then well established in that place. Such migrants would have established a connecting link between the two centers.

It further seems possible that in a later period the Tepanecs, of mainly Matlatzinca affiliations, were linked with the declining Toltec empire, before they themselves settled in the Valley of Mexico and became in their turn the leading power. This could indicate that another movement of people from the Valley of Toluca into Toltec territory, this time the Tepanecs, had occurred. Alternatively, part of the Valley of Toluca could have been subjected to Toltec rule, thus incidentally causing these Tepanecs, of Matlatzinca origin, to become partly Nahuatized before they reached the Valley of Mexico.

So far the case of Teotenango has been mainly considered. But it must not be forgotten that during the Toltec horizon and before, it was far from being the only significant site in the Valley of Toluca, where places such as Malinalco and Calixtlahuaca flourished. Both these sites can boast of Teotihuacán pottery, III as well as IV, and Calixtlahuaca particularly might have served as a kind of connecting link between Xochicalco and an incipient Tollan Xicocotitlan. Like Teotenango, the two sites had pottery recalling Coyotlatelco, but not true Mazapan; during this phase they shared the early Matlatzinca style. The Valley of Toluca was thus in Toltec times a region well provided with cities and enjoying a distinctive culture of its own; its pottery goes back at least to Teotihuacán III, apart from certain remains of Preclassic occupation. Thus, for very many centuries, until the Aztec conquest, it constituted an important center of power.

The whole question of Toltec intrusion into this area remains somewhat open. Archaeology on the one hand does not provide evidence of Toltec conquest of Teotenango or other sites. Chimalpain, the chronicler who mainly treats the matter, does not do so either, though he specifically names Culhuacán and Otompan as Toltec confederates. The latter could conceivably be identified as merely a region inhabited by Otomís (such as the Valley of Toluca), rather than the

Otumba near Teotihuacán, but such an assumption has been shown to be dubious. Chimalpain also mentions Ocuilan and Malinalco, though never Teotenango, as possessions of Culhuacán—to which they of course lay very much nearer than to Tollan itself.

One is also left with Kirchhoff's identification of the last four names in the *Historia Tolteca-Chichimeca* list of twenty Toltec dependencies or allies, as lying in the Valley of Toluca; these include Cuixcoc, coupled by Chimalpain in one context with Teotenango. But it has already been stressed that, where such names occur, one may at times be dealing with a whole series of homonyms; one cannot be sure that, like the remainder of these twenty places or peoples, they were not originally situated very near to Tollan itself, "sharing the same waters and mountains," as the text relates, and that only when Tollan collapsed did they repair to remoter pastures.

A basis is therefore lacking for affirming with any assurance that the Toltecs dominated the Valley of Toluca. At best, they might have conquered a part and established there a Toltec zone of influence. One must therefore leave this part of our inquiry on a note of interrogation. As a purely personal opinion, one may suggest that as a place girt with natural defenses, guarded by warlike peoples, and situated at some distance from Tollan itself, Teotenango would have proved a very hard nut to crack. In such a martial age, the likelihood of hostilities between the two foremost centers of Central Mesoamerica is self-evident, and wars are actually reported by Chimalpain. In view of its closer proximity to Teotenango, Culhuacán, not Tollan, may have borne the brunt of any fighting and have thus at least claimed, if not conquered, Malinalco and Ocuilan; this corner of the Toluca Valley seems to have become a traditional Culhua patrimony, to which the Mexicas were to lay early claims.

All the territories bordering on the Teotlalpan and its adjacent regions have now been examined, and it has been concluded that, with the exception of the northwestern marches and the area just discussed, they probably lay in some degree of subjection to Tollan; to be specific, in the latter category one would principally include the Valley of Mexico, the Tulancingo-Actopan area, and the Valley of Morelos.

But before finalizing our study and drawing even a tentative map, certain more remote areas also require investigation. These in my opinion were *not* subject to Tollan; however, in certain cases clues will be uncovered as to some kind of relationship or interconnection.

Friends and Neighbors

In turning now to such Toltec neighbors as they probably failed to conquer, one's attention is automatically focused upon the Puebla-Tlaxcala Valley. Jiménez Moreno has persistently and rightly drawn attention to its key position throughout the history of Mesoamerica, and stressed the need to dominate this fertile region, in addition to the Valley of Mexico, as a precondition to any secure mastery of Mexico as a whole. He sees it as a weakness of the Toltecs (and the Aztecs) that neither fully succeeded in this quest.

THE PUEBLA-TLAXCALA VALLEY

Both Jiménez Moreno and Kirchhoff go further, being equally at pains to stress the major role played by the Puebla-Tlaxcala Valley in the history of Toltec times. Kirchhoff in particular sees Cholula as a great Mesoamerican metropolis during this era, during which it was of course occupied by the Olmeca-Xicallancas; he suggests that it thus enjoyed an unbroken tradition from first to last as a great Mesoamerican center of power. Jiménez Moreno regards the Olmeca-Xicallancas as one of the Toltecs' most potent rivals and as a major cause of their ultimate downfall.

But, while paying full regard to the views of such eminent investigators, one is still bound to ask: where is the archaeological or written evidence that supports such a hypothesis? If archaeology offers unsure guidance as to actual areas of domination, it can at least tell us whether, in a specific period, a given center was important or otherwise. And already in Chapter 3 the significance of Cholula has been somewhat discounted, at least during the first period of Tollan's period of power. Reports of investigations have already been cited that show that during the Cholulteca I phase (corresponding perhaps only to the very deepest strata in Tollan, as located in Tula Chico), Cholula was virtually abandoned. During Cholulteca II, more or less contemporary with Tula-Mazapan and Aztec I, a revival took place, but on a very limited scale. After the site had been reduced to its minimum proportions in Cholulteca I, with the advent of Cholulteca II the center began to grow again, but in different directions, and Muller is at pains to insist that this revival was initially a modest one.

It is thus now suggested by the available evidence that the true second efflorescence of Cholula did not correspond to Tula-Mazapan at all, but took place during the ensuing Cholulteca III, now known to mark the commencement of Cholula polychrome, and contemporary rather with the period subsequent to the collapse of Tollan Xicocotitlan. Significantly, however, Teotihuacán staged a modest revival during its Xometla phase, and constructions exist along both sides of the Street of the Dead that correspond to Tula-Mazapan, even though they are often described as "Aztec."

When, on the other hand, one turns to the written documents, the version of the *Historia Tolteca-Chichimeca* comes first to mind. But this source, which relates the story of the occupation of Cholula by a group of Tolteca–Chichimecas from Tollan, does nothing to suggest that the latter had any initial difficulty in occupying the city; only after some years did they encounter resistance from the local inhabitants and find themselves in trouble. This opposition to their rule might well have come from the surrounding provinces, rather than from the urban population of Cholula.

Torquemada also relates that, when the Teochichimec conquerors of Tlaxcala in post-Toltec times climbed the Hill of Tláloc, they surveyed the Puebla Valley and found that it was not intensely populated; the writer adds that the Olmeca-Xicallancas, who were then still in occupation there, were not settled in the territory in a very concentrated fashion.[57] Moreover, it would seem that they inhabited a number of different places of limited size and almost equal importance, since he mentions various localities in this connection, and only finally Cholula as one of these.

It may be added that both Torquemada and Ixtlilxóchitl write of visits by Quetzalcoatl (not in this context called Topiltzin) to Cholula, as if it were then an important center; it will, however, be shown in the following chapter that such references probably concern an earlier Cholula and an earlier Quetzalcoatl, not even the first, let alone the last, ruler of Tollan. Doubts have already been expressed in Chapter 3 concerning the quite widely accepted occupation of a still thriving

Cholula by the Olmeca-Xicallancas in about A.D. 800; it was then explained that, according to my interpretation of Sahagún, they were *already* in that region and had been there for some time. It was moreover found difficult to connect with Cholula the migrants to Nicoya, described by Torquemada as assailed by an Olmeca-Xicallanca force.

Thus, while one by no means denies the over-all significance of the Puebla-Tlaxcala Valley at that time, the evidence raises doubts as to whether Cholula itself in Toltec times could possibly have constituted the mighty metropolis that it had once been and was to become again in the Late Postclassic period. Nevertheless, this does not mean that the territory as a whole was not actively involved in the trade and politics of the period; one detects, for instance, the continuance of connections with the Gulf Coast through the presence in Cholula of Fine Orange of the Isla de Sacrificios.[58] Links with the Valley of Mexico also are apparent through the ample presence of Aztec I in Cholula; Cholulan influences in the Aztatlan complex in Sinaloa have already been mentioned.

On the other hand, the known constructions in the original ceremonial center of Cholula corresponding to the Tula-Mazapan horizon are on an extremely modest scale, though rather more extensive remains have been located in the vicinity of the city; the decline may have affected the center of Cholula more than its immediate surroundings. If anything, more positive traces of this Olmeca-Xicallanca phase are identified by Armillas in Cacaxtla in the state of Tlaxcala.[59] However, apart from this one center, García Cook, who has extensively investigated the Tlaxcala area, finds no imposing contemporary sites, but only big villages covering several square kilometers, and considers that occupation was at a fairly low level of intensity during later Teotihuacán as well as Toltec times.[60] Armillas incidentally cites Muñoz Camargo as mentioning a place where the Olmecs of the region had their principal center and which he identifies with Cacaxtla, a fortified place with enormous artificial ditches and terraces. The site of Tepetícpac was also fairly extensive during the Tula-Mazapan horizon.

One may thus envisage a certain limited resuscitation of Cholula during the Tula-Mazapan horizon, but not on a scale approaching, for instance, the revival of Tollan Xicocotitlan under the Aztecs. Still less did the Early Postclassic Cholula remotely attain Tollan's proportions as a city when at the height of its power. As already explained, I regard Olmeca-Xicallanca as rather a generic term; in this it is perhaps not unlike the designation of Chichimec, used to describe a whole range of peoples of an intermediate and at times low cultural level. As such, one can only with difficulty conceive of these Olmecs as building a great metropolis or as conquering a powerful empire, able to rival that of the Toltecs; one sees them more as somewhat widely dispersed settlers, occupying a number of centers; of these none, even Cholula, was at that time very large.

Possibly, therefore, there existed a fairly extensive area, including the Puebla-Tlaxcala Valley and stretching perhaps as far as the Gulf Coast, inhabited mainly by Olmeca-Xicallancas and forming less of a rival empire than a no man's land, lying between the Toltec domains and the coastal peoples. It thus also separated Tollan from its sister city of Chichén.

By the end of the Tula-Mazapan period, Cholula may have already experienced a more marked revival; it will be explained in Chapter 8 that the Tolteca-Chichimecas perhaps occupied the city some two generations before Tollan's collapse. (They took thirty-eight years to travel from Tollan to Cholula, according to the account of the *Historia Tolteca-Chichimeca*!) Therefore, it is really only partly true to say that the Toltecs never conquered the Puebla-Tlaxcala Valley; a breakaway, or fugitive, group did without too much difficulty take Cholula at a moment clearly preceding Tollan's collapse. The Olmeca-Xicallancas, moreover, were still in occupation of Tlaxcala when the future Tlaxcalans arrived, as described by Torquemada and Muñoz Camargo. Any Tolteca-Chichimeca takeover of the region was thus seemingly partial, and the Olmec withdrawal gradual.

Reports indeed survive that Topiltzin and even Huemac, his rival, went to Cholula when Tollan fell. It may be that Cholula was by then once more becoming important, or alternatively, this may be perhaps just another anachronism, reflecting either Cholula's subsequent efflorescence as the seat of Quetzalcoatl or its former greatness as a contemporary of Teotihuacán.

THE GULF COAST

This region has often been regarded as a Toltec preserve, due in part to the association by Krickeberg of the famous list of twenty cities or peoples with the Gulf Coast, where places bearing certain of these names still exist. Added to this, the Toltec connection with Yucatán suggests the possibility of Toltec occupation of localities situated on the most obvious route, a notion reinforced by references to visits by Topiltzin-Quetzalcoatl to Quiahuiztlan and Coatzacoalcos, on his final journey to Tollan Tlapallan.

As to any archaeological evidence of a Toltec presence on the Gulf Coast, García Payón draws attention principally to Castillo de Teayo rather than to El Tajín, which had by then already declined in importance. Cultural influences had of course previously flowed in the opposite direction, and Acosta found in Tollan Xicocotitlan reliefs recalling those of El Tajín. García Payón sees strong stylistic resemblances between the pyramid of Castillo de Teayo on the one hand and those of Tollan and Calixtlahuaca on the other; Mazapan-type pottery was found there, together with Pánuco V and VI.[61] Castillo de Teayo might be considered as belonging to the latter part of the Tula-Mazapan horizon, since it also in some respects recalls Tenayuca, though lacking the characteristic double stairway.

García Payón also mentions Tuzapan, lying to the southwest of Tuxpan, and calls it a principal Toltec center (i.e., contemporary with the Tula-Mazapan horizon); its earliest pottery bears a certain relationship to Mazapan, Coyotlatelco, and Aztec I. He also writes of the "fortified cities" of Tuzapan, Tenampulco, and Cacahuatenco; he in particular believes that Tuzapan was actually founded by Toltecs, to judge by its location and architecture as well as its pottery; he even speculates on the possibility that Tuxpan housed a Toltec garrison.[62]

Seler incidentally had written long ago of Castillo de Teayo and drawn attention to the presence of figures of Mixcoatl and Tezcatlipoca.[63] He also identifies there the God I Death, so prominent in Mixtec codices; he illustrates reliefs in stone of a jaguar that is very similar to those of Tollan.

Farther to the south of these places, the site of Zempoala also deserves mention. Its great period is to be situated more in the Late Postclassic era, but David Kelley refers to Zempoala I and II as phases related to Mazapan, Aztec I, and the corresponding horizon in Chichén.[64]

Looking in the opposite direction, that is to say, farther northward toward the Huaxteca, Du Solier writes of a site, Cuatlamayan, whose last period of occupation corresponds perfectly with Aztec I.[65] The more typical Huaxtec pottery of the Toltec horizon, Pánuco V, discovered by Ekholm in Las Flores, Tampico, does not, however, show marked stylistic resemblances to that of Tollan, and only very generalized points of similarity are manifest. No objects imported from Tollan were found; by the same token, Huaxtec goods are absent in Tollan.[66] Even the architecture of Pánuco V does not much resemble Toltec styles, though parallels may be sought between Tollan's El Corral and the many Huaxtec round buildings.

Admittedly, information on the Huaxtecs is somewhat scarce, and few excavations have been carried out since those of Ekholm. However, material signs of close contact between Tollan and this region are rather conspicuous by their absence, notwithstanding mentions of interrelationship in the written source, to be dealt with in the following chapter. It might be considered that the Huaxteca constituted Tollan's natural outlet to the coast and to its coveted tropical products, in view of the greater distance separating that city from central and southern Veracruz. It might further be argued in this connection that El Tajín would have barred the route to lands lying south of the Huaxteca; however, bearing in mind the tendency to push dates for El Tajín's apogee further back in time, one must regard the latter as more a predecessor than a contemporary of Tollan; the same is also true of Xochicalco.

Relevant archaeological evidence concerning the coastal regions has thus briefly been cited. One finds little in it to prove a Toltec presence or even extensive influence. Castillo de Teayo is indeed a fairly imposing site, corresponding at least in part to the Tula-Mazapan horizon, as do other lesser ones of the coastal region. But there is nothing in all this remotely suggesting a Toltec conquest, let alone garrisons, as García Payón has proposed. In another work I have expressed the strongest doubts as to whether the Aztecs actually maintained standing forces in such places; if they did, the Spaniards certainly never found them.[67]

Written information implying a Toltec presence is also nebulous; mentions of a reported Huaxtec intervention during Tollan's final period will be discussed later. In addition to this, Ixtlilxóchitl writes of wars between Topiltzin and the rulers of coastal provinces, described as coming from "Quiahuiztlanxalmaloyan." This, however, far from proving Toltec control of the area, tends to suggest the opposite. In this respect, too, the correctness of Krickeberg's identification of many of the *Historia Tolteca-Chichimeca* list of twenty cities as lying in these regions has already been questioned.

Reports also exist not merely of Topiltzin himself but of Toltec refugees fleeing to the coast. Ixtlilxóchitl mentions groups of people of Toltec descent established in Tuxpan, Tuzapan, Xiuhcoac, and Xicotepec.[68] But "Toltec" in this sense is a very general term and probably merely denotes Nahua speakers, who are still present in the area today. It is hard to say when they arrived here and elsewhere—whether before, during, or after the great period of Tollan. They may even be confused at times with certain followers of Mixcoatl, who did not remain in the Valley of Mexico nor in the Puebla-Tlaxcala Valley, but who proceeded farther eastward and, according to Muñoz Camargo, settled in such places as Tuzapan, Tonatiuhco, Papantla, and Nauhtla.[69]

Finally, Lawrence Feldman should be mentioned as one of very few investigators who in the recent past have formulated views on such matters. He insists that central Veracruz was too far distant to come under the aegis of Tollan; on the other hand, he considers that the Huaxteca actually did at one time form part of the Toltec domain.[70] He offers the following grounds for his reasoning:

1. Certain names of the *Historia Tolteca-Chichimeca* list of twenty cities can be found in the Huaxteca.

2. Sahagún, Ixtlilxóchitl, and the *Anales de Cuauhtitlán* refer to interrelations between the Huaxteca and Tollan.

3. The Huaxtec language is rich in Nahuatl loan words; since Feldman thinks it unlikely that these derive from Teotihuacán or Aztec occupation, then logically they must stem from Toltec influence.

4. Tollan displays Huaxtec architectural traits, such as round temples.

In addition, Feldman mentions the known sea trade in salt in early Colonial times between the Huaxtec coast and Yucatán; he suggests that the area could therefore have constituted a point of departure for Toltec seaborne transport to Yucatán.

The question of the twenty cities has already been covered, and it must again be emphasized that certain of these names are also identifiable elsewhere. Moreover, it is difficult to regard the presence of Nahuatl loan words in the Huaxtec language as in any way proving actual conquest or occupation, in Toltec or at any other time. The Japanese language, for instance, was rich in English loan words long before the American occupation of 1945. As to architectural similarities, they really amount to little more than the presence of one round temple, El Corral, in Tollan; attention has already been drawn to the general lack of stylistic parallels between that city and the Huaxteca.

As to a certain interrelation mentioned in three sources, both the accounts of Ixtlilxóchitl and the *Anales de Cuauhtitlán* imply hostilities between Tollan and the Huaxteca, rather than a state of subordination of one to the other. Such references certainly indicate that both peoples were very conscious of each other's existence and suggest a measure of rivalry or even enmity. Moreover, in Chapter 4, it was stressed that the Nonoalcas probably came to Tollan from the Huaxtec coast, and therefore the relationship between them and the Huaxtecs would have been of long standing. One would, however, rather tend to agree with Jiménez Moreno that the latter were rivals of the Toltecs more than subjects.

One may thus go so far as to note certain associations between Tollan and the general region of the Gulf Coast, from the Huaxteca in the north to the southern limit of Veracruz and even beyond into Tabasco. One must never overlook that somehow or other the Toltecs maintained unbroken links with Chichén, which apparently survived until the end. This fact alone would tend to militate against any strong Toltec interest in, say, the Huaxtecs; whether they were to proceed to Chichén by sea or by land, this area lies very far removed from the direct routes. Southern Veracruz, however, constituted a potential steppingstone to the magic and mythical land of Tlillan Tlapallan, and as such would have a certain appeal for the Toltecs, for whom this concept remained so vivid. But one really finds it a little hard to believe that for such notable landlubbers as the Toltecs, sea travel played a conspicuous part in maintaining the connection, except in the last stages of the journey, when the Putun could have participated. As suggested in Chapter 5, the principal route between central Mexico and Tabasco might conceivably have led inland through Tuxtepec, the great merchant center of later times. As an alternative, however, one should not discount entirely the possible existence of one or more intermediate staging posts on the Gulf Coast, perhaps even including some kind of colony or settlement, such as the Aztec merchants founded at Tuxtepec; Quiahuiztlan, for instance, is mentioned as a place visited by Topiltzin-Quetzalcoatl on his way to Tlillan Tlapallan. But if such a Toltec stronghold indeed existed, it has not so far been discovered by the archaeologist, and its very existence must therefore be regarded as highly conjectural, though not impossible.

Notwithstanding a certain lack of archaeological evidence in Tollan itself, trade relations with parts of the coast must presumably have been important; luxury products from this region and beyond would have constituted indispensable status symbols for any Toltec nobility, to distinguish their attire from that of the common people; indeed, jade, turquoise, and the like are visible adornments of Toltec warriors depicted in reliefs and murals. One therefore tends to envisage the Toltecs as customers rather than conquerors of the coastal lands, obtaining goods that were perhaps traded by merchants who themselves came from the coast. Given more time, Tollan might have made coastal conquests, but the evidence that these had already been effected is present neither in written accounts nor in archaeological finds.

THE VALLEY OF OAXACA

Concerning the general area of the southeast, embracing the modern states of Oaxaca and Chiapas, the possibility of Toltec domination of part of this region has at times been suggested, and Jiménez Moreno's map of a putative Toltec empire includes certain areas in this direction. Pockets of Nahua speakers in Pochutla and Huatulco on the Pacific Coast and signs of Toltecoid remains, for instance in San Pedro Tototepec, have been cited as evidence. But Nahua dialects are to be found even today as far away as El Salvador, which no one suggests to have fallen under Toltec rule.

Moreover, archaeological evidence that might serve to connect the region with Tollan is patchy, and one could hardly suggest that one Toltecoid statue in Tototepec constitutes proof of conquest. One may also cite the location in Texmelincan, Guerrero of stone carvings depicting personages somewhat reminiscent of Toltec warriors.[71] These, however, are accompanied by numerals seemingly composed of bars as well as dots. Although these are also occasionally present in Tollan, García Payón associates these carvings more with Xochicalco. Moreover, Mayan influences are also present in Texmelincan. Tula-Mazapan remains are conspicuously absent from the Valley of Oaxaca; Fine Orange and Plumbate have been discovered there, associated with Monte Albán IV pottery of the corresponding period, but no Mazapan. Admittedly, the Mixteca Alta does present certain traits, such as flat figurines, remotely reminiscent of Tula-Mazapan; but even the Tehuacán area, later to become the principal refuge of the Nonoalcas, is more notable for Teotihuacán than for Toltec influences.[72] Bernal sees the Mixteca Alta as acting in this period more as a cultural barrier than a connecting link, though he mentions that Mixtec Creamware vaguely recalls Coyotlatelco.[73]

By way of contrast, it is fair to add that Tollan presents a few features apparently emanating from Monte Albán; for instance, its glyphs are similar to those of the Zapotecs.[74] Tenth-century Mixtec signs are also closely linked with those of central Mexico, and the bearers of the years—House, Rabbit, Reed, and Flint—are the same.

One may insist once more that the presence or absence of Tula-Mazapan traits in itself is inconclusive in defining patterns of dominance. In this respect, however, one may add that the Aztecs at least left some trace of their known presence, and burials containing Aztec III pottery were found in Coixtlahuaca.[75]

Apart from the presence of Nahua speakers in Huatulco and Pochutla, seen by Jiménez Moreno as denoting possible Toltec influences, certain other investigators have pointed to signs of a Toltec presence. Barbro Dahlgren also says that the Mixtec area was closely connected with the Toltecs.[76] She denotes many common traits, but possibly deriving from the period prior to Tollan's apogee. She cites as examples the use in both regions of a calendar name for each person followed by another appellation, but this is surely too widespread a Mesoamerican custom to prove very much; the same may be said of the shared cult of Quetzalcoatl, to which she also draws attention.

Of course, certain traditions exist among the Mixtecs to the effect that they came to the Mixteca Alta from the northwest, and these are mentioned in particular by Burgoa.[77] Paddock even sees early urban Cholula as a kind of Mixtec capital, and Sahagún refers to "Olmeca Uixtotin Mixteca." Moreover, it should not be forgotten that possibly somewhere in this region the future Puebla-Mixteca style was germinating during the Tollan period. In this connection, Paddock calls attention to the Huajapan area, where the Nuiñe style vaguely foreshadows this later period.[78]

Torquemada in addition tells how people went from Cholula to Oaxaca, and the *Anales de Cuauhtitlán* relate that a nucleus of migrants left Tollan for Coixtlahuaca. But, even if accurate, such reports of refugees from Tollan do nothing to make this region into a Toltec province. Ixtlilxóchitl also writes, as explained, of Huatulco in connection with early Toltec wanderings; the likelihood of error in such references has been pointed out in Chapter 4. The same writer mentions the presence of Toltecs in Tehuantepec and Tototepec.[79] But these were surely people who merely *claimed* Toltec ancestry and who, if they came from Tollan at all, did so after its collapse. It seems to have become a fashion for pockets of Nahua speakers in very diverse parts of Mesoamerica to proclaim their Toltec descent!

Spinden also has previously postulated a Toltec conquest of the Mixteca; he moreover identified the tule glyph of the *Codex Bodley* with Cholula. But in Chapter 2, the whole question of Mixtec glyphs representing tules was discussed, and the views of Elizabeth Smith accepted, to the effect that these had nothing to do with Tollan Xicocotitlan and referred to places within the Mixteca. As will be recalled, Caso insisted that, according to his reading of such codices, the Mixtec principalities were subject to some superior power of a political or religious nature.[80] He went so far as to consider that in the post-Tollan period their rulers went to be consecrated somewhere outside the Mixteca, perhaps in Cholula; however, he never expressed any real certainty as to the presence of these "foreign" allegiances during the Tollan period, which is what concerns us now. Caso moreover draws attention to codigal references to the famous ruler Eight Deer as crossing the sea and emphasizes the far-flung nature of his achievements. But the latter-day Mixtecs seem to have been confirmed landlubbers, hardly any more given to seaborne adventure than the Aztecs, or for that matter the Toltecs. This report would thus appear to be just another example, to be added to those already cited in Chapter 2, of legendary or mythical sea crossings occurring in earlier Mesoamerican history. For my part, I remain content with Smith's findings as to the Mixtec tule glyphs and her identification of two *local* Tulancingos in this connection; it is not therefore considered necessary to look outside the Mixteca for the places to which these signs refer.

In general terms, therefore, any evidence as to Toltec occupation of the region is rather scarce, whether on archaeological or linguistic grounds. One cannot moreover accept as a likely indication of this mentions of Toltec migrations to places in Oaxaca, let alone any identification of Mixtec codigal glyphs as denoting Tollan.

It is of course perfectly possible that, just as in Highland Guatemala, so in the Mixteca the concept of Tollan, or Tulán, came to play a significant part in the local mythology, as indicating more a legendary place of origin. Thus, even if Tollan Xicocotitlan was too remote to persist in peoples' minds as a living metropolis, it could still figure in the local version of the universal place-of-origin saga. Chicomoztoc, or at least the seven caves, appear in the *Rollo Selden*.[81] Caso also identifies a curved mountain (the glyph of Culhuacán) as appearing in several codices; both Chicomoztoc and Teoculhuacan often figure in the accounts of the early beginnings of peoples. Incidentally, an Aztatlan is even to be found in Oaxaca.[82]

Thus it would seem not entirely illogical to question whether at least certain Mixtec tule signs might not somehow be related to a place which would have been regarded in Mixtec legends as a general place of origin of the Mixtec tribes, just as Apoala was conceived as that of their gods. This would in no way indicate that such peoples had really come from Tollan, any more than did the Quichés or Cakchiquels. For the Mixtecs, as for the latter, the name Tollan could have become more a place of fable, a kind of original Garden of Eden, for which local counterparts also existed.

It has to be admitted that the Mixtecs, unlike the Cakchiquels, have no known legends of having originally come from any Tollan, or Tulán, apart from certain isolated claims of Toltec origins. Any such a hypothesis rests therefore on rather slender foundations and can be advanced only in very tentative form. Moreover, notwithstanding the use of such names as Gucumatz and references to Tulán, the tribes of Highland Guatemala seem to have fallen only indirectly under Toltec influence, having taken their culture and certain traditions from Toltec Chichén rather than from Tollan, and having thus themselves become Toltecized rather than Toltec.

What Kind of Empire?

In the course of two chapters we have studied Tollan's general significance when it stood at the height of its power. Its possible population, basic means of subsistence, and government were considered, as well as potential zones of domination region by region. It is therefore appropriate to ask what deductions may now be drawn from such a survey, though an over-all summing-up of the Toltec achievement must await my final conclusions, given at the end of this work. At this stage, a few suppositions may be put forward.

It is worth repeating that Tollan Xicocotitlan represented the first true attempt since the end of Teotihuacán to reconstruct an urban society in Central Mesoamerica with a widespread zone of influence or control. As such, its size and scope exceeds those of such Epiclassic centers as Xochicalco and El Tajín.

On the other hand, in population it fell short of that of Teotihuacán, let alone of the future Aztec capital. In many ways, Tollan's settlement pattern recalls more that of Teotihuacán; in both cases part of the agricultural population may have been housed within the city boundaries rather than in the surrounding countryside. In this, these capitals both differ from Tenochtitlan, which not only possessed a larger urban population, but was also surrounded by other thriving cities. Thus, for Tollan, one may well be dealing with a figure in the region of a mere 120,000 for the core area; on the other hand, the Valley of Mexico, adjacent to Tenochtitlan, may have had as many as 1,500,000 inhabitants at the moment of the Conquest.[83]

Thus it becomes apparent that the Toltecs probably lacked the necessary manpower to conquer and dominate vast tracts of Mesoamerica, as often suggested. A population of, say, 120,000, or even double this figure, would not remotely provide men of military age in numbers sufficient for such purposes, after allowing for the major groups of noncombatants: slaves, craftsmen, the old, the young, and the physically unfit. Admittedly, it could be argued that other areas also contained a smaller population in the Early Postclassic period and could thus have been conquered by proportionately smaller forces. However, the available archaeological evidence does not suggest the occurrence of a subsequent population explosion, for instance in the Mixteca area, comparable to that which the Valley of Mexico underwent in the Late Postclassic period. Moreover, the Mixtec codices bear witness to the existence in Toltec times of a whole number of thriving communities.

It must also be remembered in this respect that the Aztecs, who were clearly forced at times to conduct more than one military campaign at a time, did not rely solely on the subject cities of the Valley of Mexico for the necessary cannon fodder; in addition they employed on certain expeditions forces recruited in the Valley of Toluca, once conquered, as well as in Morelos. Of course, if, as proposed, Culhuacán was Tollan's active partner, additional manpower could have been drawn from the Valley of Mexico to swell the Toltec ranks, but it seems unlikely that it then possessed a population comparable with that of Aztec times, when such strong evidence exists of a great increase.

Moreover, one is basically considering a Toltec, not a Culhua, empire; while one may accept Culhuacán as a possible partner in a coalition, one must nevertheless suppose that Tollan, like Tenochtitlan, was its leading military member.

Admittedly, a great deal can be achieved with small numbers; King Henry V, for instance, set out to win the Battle of Agincourt with a force of only six thousand. But even if one can win battles with tiny forces, it is difficult to hold large territories in subjection, even if they are sparsely populated, and to mount continuous punitive expeditions for the purpose. This the Aztecs were continually forced to do, for lack of a better system of maintaining their sway and of collecting their tribute; probably compaigns of this kind actually mentioned by the historical sources represent a bare fraction of the total, which must have constituted a perpetual manpower drain. There exists no reason to suppose that the Toltecs had evolved a better system of control; they surely must also have faced similar rebellions in conquered regions, unless they were fairly restricted in extent. Most of the known uprisings in the Aztec domains occurred in relatively remote areas.

Moreover, supposing that the Toltecs had conquered a vast territory, including, say, parts of Guerrero and Oaxaca, as well as the Gulf Coast, the quantity of tribute gathered would have been totally out of proportion to the maximum requirements of its population. Not only were Tenochtitlan's inhabitants much more numerous, but, as Calnek is at pains to point out, a considerable proportion of these may now be considered to have belonged to specialized trades and therefore lacked the possibility to provide for their own personal necessities.[84] Even so, the Aztec population could scarcely absorb such items as the 123,400 cotton mantas received annually in tribute, which were forbidden the common people. Had Tollan really conquered as many far-flung provinces as did the Aztecs, on a simple per capita calculation, its people would have been literally swamped in tribute, and the streets of the city might truly have been paved in gold, as some of the more imaginative accounts suggest!

Furthermore, it must be remembered that the Toltecs had started more or less from scratch. There are no indications that they, like the Aztecs, took over an already existing and expanding empire. The time factor therefore becomes significant, as affecting the possibilities of unlimited conquest.

The Aztec Empire, of which we know much more, may offer an inadequate basis of comparison for Tollan, but it is hard to find a more suitable yardstick. There would seem, however, to have existed important differences between the two:

First, the Toltec domain was probably much smaller.

Second, its government in many ways represented a transitional stage between the presumed theocracy of former times and the almost despotic power of a sole temporal ruler, as encountered by the Spaniards in Tenochtitlan. This was probably a fairly recent development in the latter city.

Third, Tollan does not seem to have dominated Mesoamerican commerce in its time and appears even to have played a somewhat peripheral role in this respect.

Fourth, Tollan to a certain degree represented the continuation of the Teotihuacán "one city" settlement plan, as opposed to the conurbation that surrounded Tenochtitlan, whose inhabitants, notwithstanding their chinampas, relied mainly on others to produce their food.

One may in fact detect a certain imbalance inherent in Tollan's power structure. Not only was the capital located rather near the edge of its domains, a situation also applicable to Tenochtitlan, but if it failed to dominate the commercial scene, it remained peripheral in two senses. As already emphasized, it seems very possible that after the fall of Teotihuacán the center of gravity with respect to trade tended to revert to the coastal regions, with which the *pochteca* seem to be inherently linked. It thus seems uncertain whether Tollan possessed the underlying economic strength indispensable for long-term domination of territory, whether in Mesoamerica or in the world of today.

It would appear in general terms that the Toltecs achieved a military supremacy within a somewhat limited area, and also that some kind of colonies were established, particularly in Chichén. In this it is felt that Tollan's power structure differed from that of Teotihuacán, based, as we believe, less on military than on commercial and religious pre-eminence, though possibly also reinforced by certain "colonies," such as Kaminaljuyu. These more peaceful forms of penetration would require less supporting manpower than is necessary for military conquest, as undertaken by Tenochtitlan and probably, over a smaller area, by Tollan.

It finally fell to Tenochtitlan to gain what might be called the triple crown: to achieve predominance both in war and in trade and at the same time to establish an even closer control over a few key areas by means of certain colonies or settlements, such as those of Oaxaca and Alahuiztlan.

It remains to seek to define, even in the most hesitant fashion, the actual limits of Toltec domination. Based upon my deductions, a tentative outline is offered in Map 4. To recapitulate briefly such conclusions, it is considered that the Toltec heartland included the whole Teotlalpan, stretching as far north as Ixmiquilpan; however, a very limited territory to the west of Tollan is included within its boundaries. Concerning the Valley of Mexico, it has been cogently argued that Culhuacán's relationship to Tollan was very close, probably amounting to some form of partnership.

To this core area of the Teotlalpan and the inner Valley of Mexico may be added, for reasons already explained, the Valley of Morelos to the south and to the northeast an area centered upon Otumba and reaching beyond Tulancingo to the limits of the Huaxteca. Possibly at this time the Toltec zone of influence also embraced a part of the Valley of Toluca, but it is considered most uncertain that Teotenango itself ever became a subject city.

Apart from the Huaxteca, which I exclude, Feldman would also add the Metztitlan area to Toltec territory, while subtracting the Valley of Morelos. He bases these assertions partly on place names associable with Tollan; however, it is equally true that the Metztitlan region possesses places with names reminiscent of the Olmeca-Xicallancas of the Cholula area; I have even suggested in another work that the region may have been actually occupied by Olmeca-Xicallancas until the Late Postclassic period.[85] Metztitlan would moreover have been hard to subdue, as the Aztecs learned to their bitter cost, and would have contributed little to the Toltec economy in return for the military effort required.

To these areas mentioned above should be added some kind of colony in Yucatán that probably existed for the greater part of Tollan's own life span as a great power. A possibility exists, but remains unproven, that some further type of colony or settlement existed on the Gulf Coast. Finally, while discounting any domination of the Mixteca, some special relationship should not be entirely excluded with the Tehuacán area, to which the Nonoalcas repaired at Tollan's fall; this region stood astride the way to Tuxtepec, the inland route to Tabasco, later so much used by the Aztec merchants.

Finally, though I lend no support to such a thesis, it could conceivably be asserted that reports of even limited Toltec conquests owed more to legend than to fact; if no Toltec empire had existed, as we believe it did, then the Aztecs would have perforce invented it in order to legitimize their own, though Aztec accounts lay more emphasis on the intellectual than the military attainments of their forerunners. Moreover, it should be borne in mind that the control exercised over any area of domination may have been loose, and the quantities of tribute therefore limited. It is just conceivable that it amounted to little more than a confederation of several towns, which in Mesopotamia constituted the first kind of successor to the single city-state.

While reluctant ever to accept one single source as gospel truth, one cannot help feeling that the *Memorial Breve* comes nearest to the mark when it describes the Toltec empire as based upon an alliance of Tollan, Culhuacán, and Otumba, and which also controlled certain other territories. This is precisely the kind of area which one might have expected Tollan to dominate, and both the *Memorial Breve* and the *Anales de Cuauhtitlán* convincingly mention a continuing tradition of triple alliance, stretching from Tollan through Azcapotzalco to Tenochtitlan. For the Valley of Morelos, if this is to be included within subject territory, Culhuacán offers a natural springboard; the *Anales de Cuauhtitlán* imply domination by mention of Huaxtepec and Cuauhnáhuac.

Finally, one must perhaps recognize the possibility in certain cases of religious as well as military motivations for extension of control. The proselytizing of the new Quetzalcoatl is not to be discounted, and in Chichén and elsewhere subjection may have been partly to the god, of whose worship Tollan had become the center. The Indian penetration of Indonesia was after all religious as much as political (Hinduism still survives in Bali). Gordon Childe insists that the presence of megalithic remains in regions remote from Spain and Portugal resulted from subjugation to a common cult rather than from conquest.[86]

But as far as any historical conclusions can be reached concerning the Toltecs, their penetration of certain areas would seem to be reasonably well established by the written sources as much as or more than by archaeology. From the very nature of their culture it is more probable than otherwise that such dominion was mainly military, involving payment of tribute; for the general significance of such an achievement, the reader must await my final conclusions.

8. Doom and Disaster

We now reach the culminating episodes of the glory of Tollan. These constitute the very fabric of Aztec ancestral legend, passed faithfully from one *calmecac* generation to another. As tales of defeat and disaster, they are full of sound and fury, but to the historian, they may at times appear to be signifying nothing.

One may, however, discern a connecting link between the different accounts; like other national or tribal sagas, they are rich in moral implications intended to warn or uplift the young. As such, they may begin with stories of ruin, occasioned by sin and shortcoming, but often end on a note of redemption.

The Beginning of the End

Elements both human and divine joined forces to keep alive the legend of Topiltzin. Just as Aeneas, after Troy's downfall, snatched triumph from the jaws of defeat to become the fabled progenitor of the Romans, destined to rule the earth, so Topiltzin-Quetzalcoatl, following the Toltec debacle, lives on both as the newly risen Morning Star and as human ancestor to the *tlatoanis* of imperial Tenochtitlan.

Like the fall of Troy, Tollan's finale is filled with pathos; but to extract a historical or factual core from such accounts forms the most intractable part of our long and often baffling study. Archaeological evidence throws little light on this particular Toltec phase; the documentary information, on the other hand, is most ample, embracing not only descriptions of Tollan's decline but also certain passages which ostensibly refer to earlier periods.

The sources inevitably tend to contradict one another. In addition, each version presents a blend of myth and history in varying proportions. In order to separate the two, one must distinguish between accounts of what really occurred in Tollan Xicocotitlan and those sagas inherited from a yet remoter past and simply added for good measure to the tale of Tollan.

A further word may prove useful on how the surviving sources probably came into being; an understanding of such problems may serve as an aid to their correct interpretation. As an example, we may take the *Popol Vuh*. Robert Carmack states that it was presumably written by Quiché lords, originally from Utatlán, between 1554 and 1558. He is inclined to believe that most of the document had some representation in aboriginal codices which the authors once possessed. Because they were well educated in Quiché culture and were directly descended from the ruling houses of Utatlán, it is reasonable to assume that they had seen and listened to recitations from the great book of the council, which was frequently consulted in aboriginal times by the lords of state.[1] The author makes precisely the same point with regard to the *Annals of the Cakchiquels*.[2]

There is really no reason to believe that the Spanish and Nahuatl sources of central Mexico were not made up in much the same way; they probably consisted of fragments of original codices supplemented by the rich store of oral tradition that still existed, itself based at least in part on original painted manuscripts. But both these oral traditions and the codical remains were probably more fragmentary than the original and more complete "great book." Hence, particularly where Tollan Xicocotitlan is concerned, surviving accounts at times tend to present different aspects of the over-all historical panorama; one tells one part of the story and the next another. Sometimes the same episode is told in different ways; often versions whose origins are ostensibly diverse turn out on inspection to possess a common derivation. For instance, where the end of Tollan is concerned, the accounts of Sahagún and the *Anales of Cuauhtitlán*, so different in other respects, have much in common and appear to derive from the same source, whether oral or originally written. Moreover, the various reports of such events often differ greatly because of the particular viewpoint from which they are written. The *Anales de Cuauhtitlán* and Sahagún are inbued with magico-religious elements; on the other hand, the later versions of Chimalpain's *Memorial Breve* and of Ixtlilxóchitl recount events in a more factual manner.

Not only do descriptions of Tollan's end far exceed in length all that we possess of its earlier history, but the agony itself was much more prolonged than is usually appreciated. In actual fact, few empires or civilizations have been suddenly eclipsed; usually a gradual process of senescence and decline is discernible. To such a rule Tenochtitlan offers the outstanding exception, but under circumstances that were entirely special. Moreover, Tollan Xicocotitlan continued to exist as a city after its fall from greatness; overcome by every disaster, it may have changed masters, but it never exactly fell.

At this point, we must therefore seek to penetrate a jungle of contradictory statements. After due consideration, the salient facts have a habit of falling into place even if conclusions are at no point put forward as the only possible solution to the puzzle.

So confused is the picture at first sight, and so dependent the interpretation on matters of rather intricate detail, that it has seemed preferable where kings and their chronology are concerned to relegate to Appendix B the discussion of the more obscure details, giving in the text of this chapter only the results of the investigation and the broad reasoning that lies behind them. In particular, the identity of the different rulers is confused by a tendency to mention the same personage under several names, as though several separate individuals were concerned. Appendix B constitutes a tentative effort to unravel this tangled web.

After dealing with the archaeological evidence, the findings from my chronological studies will first be mentioned. The story of Mixcoatl, who eventually became ruler in Culhuacán, will next be treated, together with the early years of his son, Ce Acatl-Topiltzin. Finally, we shall come to the great disasters which befell Tollan. These derive partly from the internal struggle between the Nonoalcas and the

Tolteca-Chichimecas, personalized into a quarrel between Topiltzin and Huemac. Then the external threats to Tollan will be examined, before drawing certain final conclusions.

Incomplete Evidence

Before becoming enmeshed in the tangled web of the sources, one may first tackle the least complex aspect of the problem—the information which archaeology at present offers on this stage of Tollan's history. Unfortunately, it is neither very detailed nor conclusive.

Leaving for later consideration the question of chronology, evidence exists that at a certain point in the city's decline, part at least of the principal ceremonial center succumbed to violent destruction. As Acosta states, one is dealing with a city which was razed by a great fire and then underwent relentless pillage. On all sides were found remains of carbon, ash, and half-burned wood.[3] Visible today in what is known as the Palacio Quemado (Burnt Palace) are adobe blocks turned to brick by burning.

Everything seemed to suggest to Acosta that this destruction was wrought by people who were the makers of Aztec II pottery, of which large quantities were located above the level of Toltec floors and the rubble of the structures. It was also found in the residential zone excavated by the Missouri mission; in Building 3 of the Ceremonial Center remains were found of an edifice whose materials were not taken away elsewhere. Acosta reports that little effort to reconstruct had been made and that the new occupants had simply taken possession and then repaired some Toltec buildings. Obviously, sacking had been continuous since that date; the destruction was on such a scale that only a limited part of what was once Tollan can be made visible today.[4] From the available evidence, it can be deduced that further spoliation of certain buildings was effected in Aztec times.[5]

It may be pertinent to add that, notwithstanding such information concerning the Main Plaza, more recent excavations tend to suggest that the residential areas did not undergo the same fate; no evidence of their sudden destruction is to be found. After the damage inflicted upon the great ceremonial center of Teotihuacán, life seems to have continued in the surrounding residential districts for a century or more; the same may well have occurred in Tollan, though the domestic pottery used by the Toltecs in such areas seems rather hard to date precisely.

The possible identity of the users of Aztec II, mentioned by Acosta, is clearly important, and this point will be dealt with later. At this stage it may merely be observed that they were not necessarily themselves responsible for the destruction inflicted, but may have simply been present in Tollan after that date, perhaps in the role of victims as much as victors. Although in one instance Aztec II sherds were found in the same level as Mazapan, Diehl tends to regard this as a case of mixed materials from two different periods and to consider that during the Aztec II phase in Tollan, Mazapan was no longer used. Aztec II is closely associated with the northern part of the Valley of Mexico and with Tenayuca in particular. Concerning its origins, it naturally forms part of the "Aztec" complex (originally nothing to do with the Aztecs themselves) which Franco regards as forming a continuous tradition from beginning to end.[6] Thus, in the opinion of the leading student of this pottery, it is unlikely that Aztec II owes its origins to people radically different from the creators of Aztec I. The Mexicas, who are principally associated with Aztec III, after all regarded themselves as the spiritual heirs of the Culhuas, users of Aztec II and very possibly the initiators of Aztec I.

Aztec I is not found in Tollan, though it displays certain unmistakable Toltec traits, such as zoomorph supports identical to those of Tula Mazapan.[7] Rather puzzlingly, Aztec II is found in abundance in Tenayuca in association with Coyotlatelco, a pottery that tends to predate Mazapan, beginning and ending somewhat earlier. The presence in Tenayuca of Aztec I alongside Coyotlatelco suggests that the latter might be almost contemporary with Aztec I, as Muller has suggested. On the other hand, Franco insists that Aztec II came later and was basically developed out of Aztec I, and illustrates geographically the process of change. Griffin and Espejo also write of a series of gradual modifications leading from one to the other. They incidentally state that they do not see Aztec II as being of Chichimec origin, a significant point where Tollan is concerned.[8]

It would seem very possible that both points of view are in a sense correct. Aztec I, as pointed out in Chapter 4, belongs fully to the

Mazapan horizon and is likely to be contemporary with that pottery, thus originating in about A.D. 900. There is no reason why Aztec II could not have developed out of Aztec I without the latter coming to an immediate end. Perhaps one should not draw conclusions too absolute from the apparent contemporaneity of Aztec II and Coyotlatelco in Tenayuca (Aztec III was also found in that site by Moedano in conjunction with Coyotlatelco). However, evidence on the whole suggests that the life span of Aztec II was fairly long; it might have started in Tenayuca in about A.D. 1000 as an offshoot of Aztec I, already present in Culhuacán for at least a century (Tenayuca was also in existence in Toltec times, although it was less prominent than later as the Chichimec capital), and continued until, say, 1350, after the foundation of Tenochtitlan and long after the disappearance of Aztec I.

Aztec I and II would have thus existed side by side from, say, A.D. 1000 until about 1100–50, when the former probably came to an end. It is surely not unreasonable to suggest that they could have been partly contemporary, since they enjoy such a different distribution pattern; Aztec II occurs mainly in the northern part of the Valley of Mexico, in Tenayuca and Azcapotzalco and in places farther to the north and west of this, such as Calixtlahuaca (and Tollan), though small quantities were also found in Teopanzolco, in Cuernavaca.[9] On the other hand, Aztec I, abundant in Culhuacán, when found outside the Valley of Mexico has been located more in an easterly direction, toward the Gulf Coast, in places such as Cholula, Tulancingo, and even El Tajín. Aztec II eventually superseded Aztec I in Culhuacán itself, but this change could have been delayed till nearer the time of Tollan's fall and need not necessarily have occurred at the moment when Aztec II was first introduced in Tenayuca. As will be explained, it seems that the Aztec II which spread to Tollan in its declining period was brought from Culhuacán and Tenayuca.

To complete the ceramic picture, it may be added that Aztec III and IV are also found in Tollan in the uppermost strata, indicating an important Aztec presence. The signs of this have become increasingly apparent in the more recent excavations, though it is not present in Huapalcalco, outside the main area of the city, nor in Tula Chico. As we have seen, the area of the Tula-Mazapan city is very extensive, and it would not be surpprising if the Aztecs failed to settle the whole area.

They, incidentally, made additions, of a not very aesthetic quality, to certain structures, including the ball court on the west side of the Great Plaza. The Late Postclassic occupation presents many problems and the almost total abandonment of the city at the end of the Early Postclassic period, as suggested by the written sources, is not yet archaeologically identifiable.

Thus, the whole period of Tollan's greatness is marked by the continued if monotonous production of Mazapan pottery and figurines, accompanied by Coyotlatelco in the earlier phases; in addition, domestic wares such as Brush-on-Orange were used. In spite of its links with Mazapan, Aztec I, centered on Culhuacán, never itself penetrated to Tollan. Notwithstanding the ties that bound them, these two great centers each continued for a long time to prefer its own pottery, and apparently spurned that of the other.

Then, as troubles befell Tollan, suddenly Aztec II is found, a pottery already well established in the Tenayuca area. The question therefore obviously arises: who introduced this Aztec II to Tollan? It could hardly have been brought by Chichimecs coming directly from the northwest. Alternative explanations exist, which will be discussed later, concerning peoples who went first to the Valley of Mexico and then *returned* to Tollan.

Chronological Problems

We now come to consider the written sources, offering for this period a voluminous supply of legend and a rather more exiguous residue of fact. Among the latter element may be included a number of dates given for rulers of Tollan and Culhuacán; it would seem necessary to examine these first and seek to establish some kind of chronological framework, without which the remainder of the discussion would tend to be somewhat amorphous and even meaningless.

The whole question of native dates and year counts is a tortuous and tiring study, even if it offers certain satisfactions to those bold enough to seek solutions to its riddles. The basic problem lies in the manifold discrepancies between the dates to be found in different sources. Not only will each source often give a different year for a specific happening, but even within the text of any one such document several dates for the same event may often be inserted. As a good example, one may take the accession of the first *tlatoani* of Tenochtitlan, Acamapichtli; in my work on the early Mexicas, no less than eight alternative native dates for this event were listed, given by the different sources.

Up until very recently it had been assumed that all native dates belonged to the official Tenochca year count, which of course equates the year I Acatl with A.D. 1519, when Cortés arrived. Thus even such eminent scholars as Walter Lehmann translated native dates into their Christian counterpart by assuming that in all cases this Tenochca count provided the appropriate instrument.

But such a hypothesis is tenable only if one assumes that all except one of the eight different native dates given for the accession of Acamapichtli are mistaken, since this event could only take place once. Consequently, it has now come to be widely recognized that a number of different year counts were in use at the same time; only by this means can the constant discrepancies be explained. In effect, if one source says that Acamapichtli died in 2 Acatl, another in 7 Acatl, and a third in 10 Tochtli, then this simply means that the same year was differently named and numbered in each of these texts.

Certain evidence, not altogether conclusive, exists to suggest that these divergences can best be explained by the probability that the year began with a different twenty-day month in various places. For instance, if Sahagún implies that the year in Tenochtitlan began with the month Atlcahualco, and supposing the people of Tehuantepec began their own year on the first day of the succeeding month, Tlacaxipehualiztli—i.e., twenty days later—then a given year known in Tenochtitlan as I Calli would be called 8 Calli in Tehuantepec, since this is the day that follows precisely twenty days after I Calli. Such a supposition, as an explanation of differences, presupposes that only the numeral, but not the actual name or glyph of a specific year, would change from one year count to another, since the interval between the start of the year in the different calendars would always amount to multiples of twenty days, or the length of one month. Thus, if a year is 7 Tochtli in one place, then it may be 1, 2, or 13 Tochtli in centers using other counts, but never 1 or 2 Tecpatl. On this point, Kirchhoff expressed additional doubts, in view of the existence of so many divergent dates even within the same source, where the glyph as well as the number of a given event may vary; for instance, Chimalpain gives both 5 Acatl and I Tecpatl for the accession of Acamapichtli.

This may be partly explained by the fact that the years in various counts, starting in different months, could not coincide exactly. Thus, for instance, 5 Acatl in one calendar might have coincided partly with I Tecpatl in another, but partly also with 13 Acatl, which always must precede I Tecpatl in any count.

When one comes to deal with Toltec problems, difficulties multiply; available dates naturally contradict each other, but they are often few in number. To prove decisively the use of a given year count in any particular case, one must identify at least several dates as belonging to it and as making sense only if attributed to that particular count. For early Mexica dates, this proved relatively easy, but for these remoter Toltec times, one often possesses only one or two dates for an occurrence—for instance, I Acatl and 2 Acatl for the year of Topiltzin's death. Faced with this problem, I found it more practicable to start my study at the end of the story, not the beginning, and then work backward. Using better-known data as a basis, by taking the reigns of the later Culhuacán rulers, falling well outside the period covered by this book, it was possible to establish likely dates for these, in part contemporary one with another. In turn, they could be linked to a figure that is fairly positively identifiable, i.e., A.D. 1319, the date of the arrival of the Mexicas in Culhuacán at the outset of their captivity. Thus, through this date a definite connection was established between my smaller Toltec date charts given in Appendix B and the much larger and more elaborate table that it had previously been possible to contrive for early Mexica dates after their arrival in the Valley of Mexico, in respect to year counts. (*See* Appendix B, Davies, *Los Mexica.*)

The rather tedious and involved reasoning that supports these contentions has been set out in Appendix B and its accompanying charts. The following are the salient conclusions:

1. It was found that four distinct year counts could be identified as in use for these later Culhua rulers; confined to one or two counts, they would make little sense. But in going back from this point through the different identifiable reigns to Mixcoatl and Topiltzin, it was found that precisely the same four counts could be identified for

these earlier dates. This discovery considerably augmented the possibility that my methods were valid.

2. A more surprising fact then emerged. All lists of rulers given for both Tollan and Culhuacán were first tabulated in the Appendix, but it soon became clear that the two most important accounts in view of their richness in dates, those of the *Anales de Cuauhtitlán* and the *Memorial Breve*, did not really offer continuous lists at all, as ostensibly they pretended to do, but mere repetitions several times over of the *same* list, common to *both* sources! To illustrate this point, those described as the rulers of Tollan in the *Anales de Cuauhtitlán* were marked as list A, while the earlier rulers of Culhuacán in the same source were denominated list B. The *Memorial Breve* list of rulers attributed to Culhuacán was then also divided into two consecutive portions, the first called list C and the second list D. Setting these four date lists side by side, it can clearly be seen from the sovereigns' *dates* and in part from their names that the lists offer such remarkable similarities as to virtually exclude the possibility of mere coincidence. In Appendix B, the odds against such an assumption's being incorrect are calculated at several thousand to one.

No source, whether the two above-mentioned, or Torquemada, or the *Relación de la Genealogía*, really leaves us in any doubt that the majority of these names, apart from Topiltzin and Huemac, are really rulers of Culhuacán rather than of Tollan. Thus our common king list, repeated several times over with certain variations, is really a list of monarchs of Culhuacán, not Tollan; Topiltzin and Huemac are the only exceptions. Accordingly, working backward from the later Culhua reigns coinciding with the arrival of the better-documented Mexicas, it was possible to reconstruct a tentative chronology which ended with Achitómetl and Coxcox of Culhuacán and began with Mixcoatl and Topiltzin.

From these calculations, it can be seen that in dealing with such remote times it is the *dates* of rulers which count more than the *names*. For instance, for what I have called "reign 6" in my comparative chart in Appendix B, three of four lists coincide in giving a ruler as reigning from I Calli or 2 Tochtli until his death in 9 Tochtli. With fifty-two years to choose from, the odds against such similarities arising from pure coincidence amount literally to several multiples of fifty-two or many thousands to one. However, each list gives a different name for this ruler, though the dates coincide in each case. Not only does it thus become clear, as we know already, that such rulers were known by a variety of names (as was Topiltzin), but sometimes sources appear to mistakenly omit one name from their list or occasionally to add an extra one (probably treating as separate reigns two names of the same ruler); as a consequence, the other names on the same list then move up or down one rung on the chronological ladder and are associated with what are really the dates of their predecessor or successor.

In short, bearing in mind certain cautions, it has been deduced that Coxcoxtli probably reigned in Culhuacán from 1309 to 1329, while Achitometl reigned, partly simultaneously, from 1295 to 1321. Thus, as reported in various sources, they were both reigning when the Mexicas arrived, according to my reckoning in 1319. Admittedly, according to these calculations the two reigns do not continue until the departure from Culhuacán of the Mexicas, as some sources insist, but then there were almost certainly two rulers called Achitómetl.

Working back from these dates (*see* Appendix B), one arrives at the following:

Dynasty A

Mixcoatl/Totepeuh/Mazatzin	A.D.1122–50	(in Culhuacán)
Ce Acatl Topiltzin	1153–75	(in Tollan)

These are followed by five rulers of Culhuacán before Coxcoxtli and Achitómetl.

Dynasty B (in Tollan)

Chalchiuhtlanetzin/Chalchiuhtonac	7 Acatl to 7 Acatl (unidentifiable and ritual dates)
Tlilquechachuac/Tlachinoltzin	7 Acatl to 7 Acatl (unidentifiable and ritual dates)
Tlaltecatl/Huetzin	7 Acatl to 7 Acatl (unidentifiable and ritual dates)
Huemac	1169–78

Lamentably, these are the only dates that one may regard as authentic for Tollan's rulers. For its early and middle periods, no genuine names or dates survive. As in the *Anales de Cuauhtitlán*, clearly the lists of Torquemada and Ixtlilxóchitl also apply mainly to Culhua rulers and coincide with lists of the latter given in Appendix B.

The Stage Is Set: Mixcoatl and Topiltzin

In Chapter 4 we mentioned the famous Mixcoatl and his son, Ce Acatl-Topiltzin, to make clear that their story did not belong to the rise of Tollan but to its fall. At last a point has been reached where, after a very long wait in the wings, these two characters may now enter the Toltec stage, as the drama draws to its close.

Differing versions of their exploits are set out in tabular form in Appendix A, while their tentative chronology is established in Appendix B, on the lines already indicated. As may be seen from Appendix A, Mixcoatl appears as the leader of a group of Teochichimecs coming from a northwesterly direction, in the wake of the Tolteca-Chichimecas who went to Cholula. His son, Topiltzin, was born in or near Culhuacán.

It should first be stated once more that the true significance of some of the incidents of the story of Mixcoatl, as outlined in Table A and Appendix A, escape us, just as the meaning of certain mythical episodes attending the actual fall of Tollan seem to lack historical content. For instance, it is difficult to give a factual interpretation to the shooting of Itzpapálotl, and the descent of the two-headed deer. (*See* Appendix A, notes 4 and 8.) The deer is, of course, not only an emblem of Mixcoatl as God of Hunting; it has already been demonstrated that one of the actual names of the Mixcoatl in question was Mazatl, or Mazatzin (i.e., deer). Itzpapálotl as the second leading Chichimec deity is an associate of Mixcoatl, and it seems that some kind of sacrifice of victims dressed as Itzpapálotl is implied, and therefore also some form of warfare, but more one can hardly say.

Notwithstanding their similarity, it would seem as if two different episodes are involved. As already explained, the first, the shooting with arrows of Itzpapálotl, refers seemingly to encounters with other Chichimecs during Mixcoatl's journey to the Valley of Mexico; on the other hand, the incident of the two-headed deer, a symbol that occurs in various contexts, such as in the *Codex Borbonicus* or on a flute to be seen in the Mitla museum, is surely more concerned with the occupation of Culhuacán and neighboring cities by Mixcoatl. The deer, to be associated not only with Mixcoatl himself but with fire as well as hunting, is closely linked with these places in more respects than one. (*See*

Appendix A, note 8.) The relationship of the deer with hunting, and therefore by implication with Mixcoatl, is geographically fairly widespread; among the Tzetzals and Kekchis, the deer's head is linked with hunting rites. Maya hunting gods have similar associations—for instance, Ceh Lak, one of these deities, means "Deer Pottery Idol."

However, whatever obscurities the Mixcoatl saga may offer, it can easily be seen from Appendix A and the accompanying table that its history is part of the *end* of Tollan; if any doubts still remain, they may surely be resolved by considering the chronological aspects of the question, already outlined in this chapter and discussed in more detail in Appendix B.

As Kirchhoff has insisted in his work on the subject, any hypothesis to the effect that these two personages belong to the foundation period of Tollan relies basically on one or perhaps two sources out of a considerable number of accounts.[10] As he duly points out, the *Relación de la Genealogía* states that Topiltzin, son of Totepeuh (i.e., Mixcoatl) was the first ruler of Tollan, and adds that Huemac only succeeded him as the next ruler after an interval of ninety-seven years, counting since the time when the former had repaired to Tlillan Tlapallan. The parallel version of this story in the *Historia de los Mexicanos* offers similar information, to the effect that Topiltzin was the first ruler and that he went to Tlillan Tlapallan, but omits mention of the ninety-seven-year time gap and merely states that Tollan was without a ruler for nine years. This account continues in the very next paragraph with the story of the arrival of the Mexicas upon the scene, implying that Tollan had already fallen. In addition to these versions, the *Leyenda de los Soles* implies that Topiltzin had been ruler of Tollan before going to Tlillan Tlapallan; but the so-called "initial conquests" described by this source and analyzed in Appendix A, note 12, also lead finally to Tlillan Tlapallan, the ultimate destination of the last Topiltzin-Quetzalcoatl!

Even a cursory study of Appendix A, where the Mixcoatl saga is set out incident by incident, puts things in a rather different perspective. One first sees a close similitude between the *Relación de la Genealogía*, the *Origen de los Mexicanos*, the *Historia de los Mexicanos*, the *Leyenda de los Soles*, and the *Anales de Cuauhtitlán*; these accounts in turn exhibit irrefutable parallels with Muñóz Camargo's version. To judge by the people and places mentioned, one is undeniably dealing with the same narrative, obviously belonging in each case to the same moment in history.

To recapitulate what was already said in Chapter 4, one may take two simple examples. Not only are Camaxtli-Mixcoatl-Totepeuh and Ce Acatl-Topiltzin-Quetzalcoatl universally present, but Xiuhnel and Mimich are also to be found in four out of seven versions mentioned above, including of course that of Muñóz Camargo. As to places visited by Mixcoatl, Mazatepec occurs in both the *Anales de Cuauhtitlán* and Muñóz Camargo as the first to be reached; Comallan is common to the *Leyenda de los Soles* and Muñóz Camargo; Culhuacán (or Teoculhuacán or Huitznahuac) appears in five out of seven accounts, including again Muñóz Camargo. Similarly, the incident of the killing of Itzpapálotl is shared by the *Anales de Cuauhtitlán*, the *Leyenda de los Soles*, and Muñóz Camargo.

Over and above this, the version of Muñóz Camargo unquestionably runs parallel with the *Historia Tolteca-Chichimeca*; one has only to consider the names of the leaders involved. (*See* Appendix A, note 13.) No one has ever even suggested that the latter source can possibly refer to anything but the later part of Tollan's history. It might be added that the whole Mixcoatl saga, particularly as related by Muñóz Camargo, finds a counterpart in certain accounts of Torquemada. These tell of Teochichimecs, as he specifically calls them, who came ostensibly from the distant northwest, passing by Xilotepec, Tepotzotlán, and Cuauhtitlán, and settled in "the plains of Poyauhtlán." Their god was Camaxtli, and they had disputes with the people of Culhuacán. They ended by founding Tlaxcala, as did the Teochichimecs of Mixcoatl, according to Muñóz Camargo. Xolotl is also mentioned, but that would appear to be a mistaken reference or to refer to another and less-well-known leader of that name, which is also in some ways a title.[11]

The sequel to the story, both in Muñóz Camargo and in Torquemada's parallel account, is thus the founding of Tlaxcala, whereas in the *Historia Tolteca-Chichimeca* it is the re-establishment of Cholula under the Tolteca-Chichimecas. In these accounts, the story of Mixcoatl and his associates and the sequel to it form part of an unbroken narrative.

In all the other above-mentioned sources, which have been tabulated in Appendix A, the common series of episodes concerning Mixcoatl is followed by developments that are plainly post-Tollan. In the *Anales de Cuauhtitlán*, after the fall of Tollan itself, references occur to the main dynasty of Culhuacán; in the *Leyenda de los Soles* the Mixcoatl saga is followed by the story of the final fall of Tollan, in the *Historia de los Mexicanos* by the arrival of the Mexicas and in the *Relación de la Genealogía* by events in Culhuacán.

It is surely almost impossible to maintain that the various accounts listed in Table A are anything but differing versions of the same series of events. They may end differently, but near their beginning all relate the exodus of the Chichimecs from a northwesterly direction toward the Valley of Mexico and the Puebla-Tlaxcala Valley. In all but the *Historia Tolteca-Chichimeca*, Mixcoatl, under different names, is their leader; the latter source is of course concerned with those who went to Cholula, not Culhuacán, and Mixcoatl is merely mentioned incidentally, but not as the principal protagonist.

One may ask how several of these versions came to stress that Ce Acatl-Topiltzin was the first Toltec ruler; but it has already been explained that this is nothing but an interpolation referring to an earlier Topiltzin-Quetzalcoatl, whose existence I fully recognize and indeed have emphasized. The point has been made repeatedly in this work that, while much of the material of the written accounts is historically valid, the order in which it occurs is often quite incorrect. As explained, the flashback in question, so typical of Mesoamerican documents, seemingly concerns one of the Nonoalca leaders who came initially from Pánuco to Tulancingo and Tollan and who bore a name which survives in different but corrupted versions of Ce Acatl, e.g., Tzacat.

Jiménez Moreno, the leading and original proponent of the view that sees Topiltzin as first, not last, ruler of Tollan, agrees that the versions listed in Table A are plainly related. The difference between his interpretation, on the one hand, and that of Kirchhoff and myself on the other, is really that Jiménez Moreno regards the references in the *Relación de la Geneaología* and other sources to Topiltzin as first ruler as the key to his true place in history. According to this view, the other accounts would in their initial sector merely be telling the same tale of the same period, i.e., the beginning of Tollan, and in certain cases would be misinterpreting it, so that it appears to belong to the end of Tollan instead of its beginning. This Jiménez Moreno considers to be particularly true of the Muñóz Camargo version of the Mixcoatl saga, interspersed among events belonging patently to Tollan's final phase represents, and which he believes, a kind of grafting of earlier events on the later ones. On the other hand, I regard the story of Topiltzin as first ruler as an early interpolation into accounts of later events.

Admittedly, everything in history is open to more than one interpretation. But the fact remains that the accounts of Muñóz Camargo and the *Historia Tolteca-Chichimeca* are solely concerned, as far as their authors are concerned, with later events in Tollan, and form in this respect a coherent and, in the case of Muñóz Camargo, a continuous story.

On the other hand, the accounts which name Topiltzin as first, not last, ruler (in themselves a very distinct minority) are composite stories which profess to recount events from the beginning *and* the end of Tollan and pass rapidly from one to the other. It is surely much more likely that in these one event should be merely misplaced, transferred from the latter to the former, than for Muñóz Camargo and the *Historia Tolteca-Chichimeca* to introduce into their story episodes from a period with which they do not themselves pretend to be concerned at all. It may all in the final analysis be a matter of opinion, but we find it very hard to see the two latter sources being so mistaken, since in the Muñóz Camargo story of Mixcoatl, too many people and places are involved that coincide with those listed in the *Historia Tolteca-Chichimeca* for any possibility of coincidence to arise. But in the *Historia Tolteca-Chichimeca*, such personages constitute a few among a much larger number of names listed together who indisputably belong to the latter Tollan period.

Moreover, as is made clear in Chart I, one simply cannot deny that in many versions Topiltzin is closely associated with Huemac, who equally undeniably belongs to Tollan's end. In addition, a tentative but clear chronology for Topiltzin and Mixcoatl is given in Appendix B in support of my point of view.

These similar interpolations in several sources evidently emanate from one earlier document which had confused, as is so easy, the pre- and post-Tollan Ce Acatls and had introduced elements from the doings of the first into the longer story of the last.

The *Historia Tolteca-Chichimeca* is the only source which makes clear in this connection the distinction between the Tolteca-Chichimecas and the Teochichimecs, or true Chichimecs; but since so many of the same personages are mentioned by Muñóz Camargo, it becomes clear that those of his account, including Mixcoatl himself, are also some form of Teochichimecs. It would seem not altogether unlikely that Mixcoatl and his band were of Otomí stock. Sahagún includes Otomís within the category of Teochichimecs, and Torquemada specifically states that the Chichimecs who took possession of Tlaxcala were Otomís. These, as can be seen in greater detail in Appendix A, were part of the same general expedition as Mixcoatl. Moreover, Muñóz Camargo writes of the Tepanec Cocotzin who adopted the title of Mixcoatecuhtli; the Tepanecs themselves definitely had Otomí affiliations.[12]

But it may also then be asked: if Mixcoatl was a mere Chichimec chief, and his son half Chichimec and half Culhua, why do history and legend attach so much importance to this pair? In reality, Mixcoatl's clearly Chichimec characteristics in no way detract from his importance. One may balk at a Chichimec ruler of Tollan or of Culhuacán, but it may be worth recalling that Maximinus, who became Roman emperor in A.D. 235, centuries before Rome's fall, was a Thracian shepherd, son of a Goth and an Alan woman, and hence a thorough barbarian by descent.

Mixcoatl and Topiltzin, having as will be seen established a new and leading dynasty in Culhuacán, came to constitute the very fountainhead of Aztec dynastic legend. The knowledge at our disposal has accordingly reached us through the filter of Mexica interpretation and concerns those very people who were ostensibly their heroic ancestors; as such they are naturally to be identified with gods, since, like most ancient peoples, the Mexicas expected their primeval forebears to be divine or semidivine. The transference from the human to the divine condition was a relatively easy step in Mesoamerica, where one is concerned with rulers or priests who, as an integral part of their office, on occasion wore the dress and insignia of the gods and might even play the role of the deity, in certain instances actually converting themselves into their protecting *nahual*. This not only applies in the case of Tezcatlipoca but also to human bearers of the name Quetzalcoatl or its equivalent; the *Popol Vuh* writes of a Gucumatz, a Quiché ruler who for seven days changed himself into an eagle and for seven days into a jaguar. It is moreover worth bearing in mind that not only are Quetzalcoatl and Mixcoatl the names of gods as well as men, but their other respective appellations, such as Nacxitl and Totepeuh (our conqueror), are also divine titles more than mere appellations. The two even at times become confused, as when the *Historia Tolteca-Chichimeca* writes of Nacxitl Tepeuhqui. To seek the purely human designations of such personages, one has to recall such names as Meconetl, which Ixtlilxóchitl attributes to Ce Acatl-Topiltzin, or Mazatl, whom we consider to be identical with Mixcoatl. (*See* Appendix B.)

But one still must ask what actually happened at the time of the Mixcoatl saga, toward the closing period of Tollan. On the basis of more detailed reasoning set out in Appendix A, one may in general terms deduce the following:

1. The Tolteca-Chichimecas left Tollan some time before its final period of disaster.

2. Mixcoatl and his group formed part of the Chichimec rescue operation, following the appeal for help from the Tolteca-Chichimecas in Cholula.

3. Mixcoatl in actual fact broke away from this expedition and occupied the Culhuacán region. His son Topiltzin eventually went back to Tollan and became ruler of that city.

First, as regards the Tolteca-Chichimecas, it would seem that they left Tollan well before the final disasters, when it was still a comparatively powerful if declining polity. They may perhaps be likened more to the earlier pioneers who had previously occupied Chichén than to a mere group of refugees; one must not forget that they were strong enough initially to take possession of Cholula for themselves.

Such a suggestion may seem at first sight startling; however, Kirchhoff was among the first to insist that Mixcoatl and Topiltzin belonged to the end of Tollan and to associate them with the Teochichimecs who were "fetched" by the Tolteca-Chichimecas, already established in Cholula.[13] But the inescapable consequence of such reasoning, though not apparently clearly drawn by Kirchhoff himself, is that the Tolteca-Chichimecas must have left Tollan well before the final disaster involving Ce Acatl-Topiltzin. According to his interpretation of the chronology of Mixcoatl and Topiltzin, which appears to be correct, the time interval between the initial departure of the Tolteca-Chichimecas from Tollan and Topiltzin's eventual flight must have exceeded in duration the whole lifetime of the latter. Topiltzin after all was only *born* in the Huitznahuac region, long after the Tolteca-Chichimecas had left Tollan for Cholula, at the time when the Teochichimec rescue operation was already under way. The Tolteca-Chichimecas themselves are reported to have spent thirty-eight years en route from Tollan to Cholula.

As explained above, in order to allow for Topiltzin's life and rule in Tollan, the Tolteca-Chichimecas may be clearly seen to have left the city well before its final collapse. Therefore, the true beginning of the story seemingly comes on page 75, with the departure of these Tolteca-Chichimecas for Cholula. They really constitute an initial wave of emigrants from Tollan; others were to follow, but some time later, when the final disasters occurred. These first migrants to Cholula left in 2 Tochtli, to which the editor, Berlin, gives the Christian year equivalent of A.D. 1130; I would tentatively propose a Christian equivalent of 1122, or 2 Tochtli in our Chalca year count.

It would seem indeed probable that even if the empire was still at this time more or less a going concern, its territory was already being overrun by Teochichimecs of various kinds, with some of whom the migrants to Cholula evidently enjoyed close contacts. Doubting the future stability of Tollan, disturbed by incipient internal quarrels, or simply seeking newer and more verdant pastures, these Tolteca-Chichimecas, perhaps not unaccompanied by Nonoalcas, went and took Cholula. After six years, according to the account, they found themselves in trouble, possibly owing to their small numbers, and sought Chichimec help. It may well be that at this point Tollan was in a stage of its history not dissimilar to Teotihuacán IV, when the great ceremonial center had already suffered major destruction, while life continued in the surrounding areas and the majority of the population still remained. It is not impossible, as already suggested, that the principal ceremonial center of Tollan had already suffered the destruction described by Acosta and that, though the empire had not yet dissolved, the site was already soon to be occupied by users of Aztec II, which for a period succeeded Mazapan.

This general interpretation of events surely makes greater sense than a more literal reading of the *Historia Tolteca-Chichimeca.* It has always seemed odd if not impossible that *after* the fall of Tollan one group of hapless refugees should have been able to go and take Cholula, the strength of which Jiménez Moreno and others have been at pains to emphasize as constituting a positive menace to Tollan at the height of its power and glory; they have even proposed Olmeca-Xicallanca pressure, exercised from the Puebla-Tlaxcala Valley, as a contributory cause of the downfall of the Toltec empire.

In this as in other aspects, the decline of Tollan finds parallels in that of Rome; cities and empires do not fall, any more than they are built, in a day. Two centuries before its collapse, Rome underwent a severe and prolonged crisis of Gothic attacks, which were eventually repulsed by the heroic efforts of successive emperors, Claudius II, Aurelian, and Probus. Much nearer the final end, in A.D. 376, eighty thousand Visigoths who had been defeated by a newer enemy were actually allowed to settle in imperial territory across the Danube. They then became rebellious and slew the Emperor Valens in the Battle of Adrianople; however, it was not until a generation later, in 410, that Alaric the Bold actually sacked Rome itself. Similarly, it is considered probable that before they became rulers of Egypt, some at least of the Hyksos had lived for several generations among the people they were to conquer; the final invaders were thus preceded by kindred bands.

One may easily see a similar threat of infiltration looming over Tollan. At least a generation before the collapse, and possibly much earlier, numerous Chichimecs, perhaps part-civilized, might be envisaged as penetrating a frontier much less well defined and defended than the Danube and the Rhine, and as gradually infiltrating the empire, serving first as loyal subjects and only later turning rebel. This would have occurred at a time when the general area was in a state of ferment, as the frontier of Mesoamerica receded.

The Chichimecs who rushed to the rescue of the Toltecs in

Cholula, seemingly as friends rather than enemies, might then be likened to the Visigoths who crossed the Danube thirty-four years before the sacking of Rome. As a result of such official encouragement, the Teochichimecs seem to have literally come pouring in, even if their motives were not always as altruistic as one is led to suppose. Seven tribes in all are mentioned. Kirchhoff suggests that they were in part Otomí; certainly Sahagún confirms that some of the latter were of a relatively low cultural level. At all events, the newcomers were not Nahua speakers, as frequent mention is made of the use of interpreters. If they were indeed Otomís, this would explain the subsequent occupation of the Tollan region by the latter.

Apart from Cholula, the Chinampa region of the Valley of Mexico was one of the invaders' main objectives; both Muñóz Camargo and the *Historia Tolteca-Chichimeca* also mention Poyauhtlán, situated to the southwest of Tepetlaoztoc.[14] After the composite group had reached Amecameca, the route given by the latter source is so confused as to seem to Kirchhoff totally inexplicable. He therefore suggests that the two main bodies split one from another in Poyauhtlán, one going north to Tepetlaoztoc, and the other south to Amecameca. But even this more logical suggestion is difficult to plot on the map, and to judge by the different places mentioned, situated in various directions, it would seem more likely that, after visiting Amecameca, the respective tribes dispersed, ranging far and wide; some went to such places as Poyauhtlán, and others to Xico, Tlalmanalco, and Cholula; they would thus have occupied a general region between the Valley of Mexico and Cholula itself.

Of the incursive Chichimecs, the two most important bodies would seem to be, first, those who went on from Poyauhtlán-Amecameca to Cholula, and secondly, those who stayed behind and then moved in a *reverse* direction toward the Chinampa region of the valley; these are the subjects of the Mixcoatl saga. Ce Acatl and his followers eventually constituted a kind of subgroup of this contingent, which apparently went back to Tollan, where according to most reports he became ruler. It might be worth adding that it is by no means certain that Mixcoatl himself did not lend a helping hand in the subjection of Cholula. Among those mentioned together with Mixcoatl by Muñóz Camargo are Hueytapatli and Xicallan, appellations which are mentioned by the *Historia Tolteca-Chichimeca* as among the Chichimec leaders who actually occupied Cholula.[15]

Accordingly, to sum up, the following might be proposed with regard to Mixcoatl. He and his followers were part of a larger grouping of Chichimecs who decided to proceed in the direction of the Valley of Mexico and Puebla-Tlaxcala, ostensibly to "rescue" the Tolteca-Chichimecas who were embattled in Cholula. Having apparently given Tollan itself a fairly wide berth, to judge by their route, Mixcoatl and his followers seem, according to Muñóz Camargo, to have based themselves on Poyauhtlán, while others went on to Cholula. Other accounts mention only Culhuacán or places in the Valley of Mexico and omit Poyauhtlán.

En route, Mixcoatl had fought engagements in places located to the north of the Valley of Mexico. (*See* Appendix A, note 4.) On his arrival, he finally married Chimalma, also deified as Coatlicue, Quilaztli, and so on. (*See* note 9.) Ce Acatl-Topiltzin, whose chronology has already been discussed, apparently became a kind of coruler with his father Mixcoatl, and made various conquests or reconquests based upon Culhuacán. (*See* note 12.) To such triumphs, as will later be explained in greater detail, are tacked on the names of localities that really form part of the classic Toltec diaspora, reported to include places as widely dispersed as the Mixteca, coastal Veracruz, and Yucatán, the final destination of the legendary Topiltzin. Again, as in so many instances, fact and myth become merged. Ultimately, following Mixcoatl's death, Topiltzin managed to make himself ruler of Tollan as well as Culhuacán, holding power until the moment he was overtaken by disaster and forced to flee.

Such conclusions have been reached with the aid of my reconstruction of events in Appendix A. They are, however, amply borne out by another source, the *Memorial Breve*, which gives reasonably down-to-earth information and which in this particular context tells an independent story. Among other things, it states plainly and categorically that Totepeuh was ruler of Culhuacán and Topiltzin of Tollan. The fact that this account, probably erroneously, also describes Totepeuh as father of Huemac rather than of Topiltzin hardly nullifies its general validity. The salient achievement of the latter was to make himself also ruler of Tollan, Culhuacán's partner. Tollan may be considered to have still been at this time the senior member of any coalition of cities that ruled the Toltec empire. Topiltzin seems to have taken over the headship of the dynasty, ethnic group, or *calpulli*, whose leader traditionally claimed the title and the politico-religious role of Quetzalcoatl ("Topiltzin" may be taken as part of the same title). It is also interesting to note in this connection that the *Memorial Breve* bears out our contention by suggesting that Ce Acatl was not really born in Tollan but had been brought there.[16] It might fairly be said that accounts of Topiltzin's accession to power, irrespective of whether they imply that he belongs to late or early Tollan, concur in suggesting that he came from outside and was not a native of the city. In effect, Topiltzin was to become the standard-bearer of the Tolteca-Chichimecas, though not disassociated from the Nonoalcas, as will later be seen. As part Teochichimec and part Toltec from Culhuacán, his assumption of power represented an injection of new blood, and he was able to provide a momentary infusion of vitality to an already declining Tollan. Of course, it is just possible that the last ruler of Tollan was yet another Ce Acatl-Topiltzin, and not the one named as son of Mixcoatl. However, this is hardly likely, in view of the joint prominence given by so many sources to Mixcoatl and his son. Topiltzin may have been a usurper in Tollan, but he was an important one, both in his deeds and downfall.

His nemesis was Huemac, representing the older Toltec traditions, the conflict between them forming part of the general confrontation of Nonoalcas and Tolteca-Chichimecas, which will constitute the subject of the next section of this chapter. The fact that Topiltzin came from outside and had different affiliations may help to explain the rift that occurred.

It may seem surprising that he returned to Tollan at all, but, apart from the lure of a Toltec throne, it must be borne in mind that other Chichimecs must have been present in the region in force, as is demonstrated by the account of their being called upon by the Tolteca-Chichimecas, already embattled in Cholula. Moreover, Culhuacán itself, though to become ostensibly the remaining Toltec bulwark in a Chichimec world, itself clearly contained Chichimec elements and became progressively Chichimecized, to use Barlow's phrase. One of the dynasties of Culhuacán was later headed by Huetzin, who was part Acolhua and whose real home was Coatlichán.[17]

A very pertinent point in this respect is the discovery by Acosta of large quantities of Aztec II pottery above the main Toltec strata in Tollan. The notion that this style might have been introduced by Chichimecs who came directly from a northwesterly direction and who ravaged the ceremonial center has always seemed hard to accept. Just why and how should such Chichimecs have introduced this pottery, essentially a product of the Valley of Mexico? Surely only people who had actually resided in that area could have done so, and my interpretation of events thus provides a more adequate and appropriate explanation; logically, Aztec II would have been brought to Tollan by people who had established themselves in the Valley of Mexico and then had gone back there. This, quite independently of the Aztec II problem, is precisely the career which we have already proposed for Topiltzin and his followers.

By the time they arrived in Tollan, the ceremonial center had very possibly already suffered extensive damage; Toltec buildings would have been then reused by Topiltzin and his followers from Culhuacán, and Aztec II would thus occur above their floor level, in accordance with Acosta's information. In this respect, it may be of interest that the *Histoyre du Mechique* actually tells of Topiltzin's withdrawing initially to Tenayuca after his final departure from Tollan. Aztec II has also been denominated "Pyramid pottery," referring to the Pyramid of Tenayuca, where it abounds; thus Topiltzin's connection with that place might not seem altogether fortuitous.

End of an Empire

We have so far dealt with the career of Mixcoatl and the youth of his son Topiltzin, together with the Tolteca-Chichimeca migration to Cholula. With the establishment of Topiltzin in Tollan, we are now reaching the final episodes in the story of its fall from greatness. One tends always to employ the term "fall," but really it is more loss of power; as a city Tollan may have suffered a period of eclipse but never seems to have actually ceased to exist. Unlike Teotihuacán, it was still an important center of population in Aztec times. It may have been subject to great calamities at the end of the Early Postclassic period, but this in itself does not necessarily involve total abandonment, as suggested by certain sources. Somewhat in conformity with Toynbee's interpretation of history, the decline of Tollan seems to have resulted from a combination of internal and external pressures, caused by the enemy within and the enemy without. We will deal initially with the internal fissures; first the personal aspect, the Huemac-Topiltzin feud, will be examined, and then the more general antagonism between Nonoalcas and Tolteca-Chichimecas will be studied.

The conflict between Quetzalcoatl and Huemac, reported in various sources, might be classed as one of the great antagonisms of history, and, like others, the real happenings are obscured by the mists of time. From its legendary quality, embracing both human action and divine intervention, it almost recalls the Trojan saga of Hector and Achilles; in each case, both protagonists were ultimately destroyed.

There is one point which requires prior clarification: the Topiltzin-Quetzalcoatl story contains two episodes involving individual conflicts; his first enemy is Atempanecatl in Culhuacán, and the second, Huemac in Tollan. In Table A and note 11 of Appendix A, more detailed comments may be found concerning Topiltzin's killing of Atempanecatl. The latter is usually described as one of the four hundred Mimixcoas, whose death he managed to survive; he is also named as brother or brother-in-law of Mixcoatl. Atempanecatl and his confederates, according to most versions, had actually killed Mixcoatl before being in turn destroyed by his son Topiltzin.

This episode is often confused with the subsequent rivalry of Topiltzin and Huemac. The confusion arises mainly from the mention in the *Anales de Cuauhtitlán* of "Huemac, whose name as sovereign ruler was Atecpanecatl."[18] As explained in Chapter 4, Atecpanecatl and Atempanecatl tend to be used indiscriminately for the same person. But the passage in question makes it clear that one is concerned, as in many instances, more with a title than a proper name; Atempan was, among other things, an original barrio of Aztlan, and it may be recalled that the great Tlacaélel, brother of Moctezuma I, was frequently referred to as Atempanecatl or Atecpanecatl. Topiltzin's conflicts with Atempanecatl and with Huemac are really fundamentally dissimilar; he triumphantly revenges himself on Atempanecatl, his father's murderer, but on the other hand is usually balked, if not defeated, by Huemac. Moreover, the first conflict invariably occurs in the Huitznahuac-Culhuacán area, while the second is always situated in Tollan. Referring now to the Topiltzin-Huemac duel, with the aid of my chronological study, given in outline and in more detail in Appendix B, the following sequence of events is proposed after Mixcoatl's death.

1. Ce Acatl-Topiltzin succeeded his father as head of a new dynasty in Culhuacán; from there he returned to Tollan, where he reigned from 1153 to 1175. He managed to abrogate the title and office belonging probably to a succession of Quetzalcoatls, perhaps forming an actual dynasty; one does not know whether his other title of Topiltzin derives from Tollan or Culhuacán. He may be assumed to have built or rebuilt parts of Tollan and conquered or reconquered certain tributory provinces that had begun to fall away from the metropolis.

2. During this period, the outstanding personality among the heads of traditional dynasties of Tollan was Huemac, whom we calculate to have ruled from 1169 or 1170 to 1178 (he probably also possessed other names, since, like Quetzalcoatl, Huemac itself became akin to a divine title). He was thus at least in part a contemporary of Topiltzin, even if, according to my reconstruction, he acceded to his throne slightly later.

We now come to the hardest part of the Quetzalcoatl-Huemac problem, involving the discrepancies between the various sources, which may seem at first sight so complex as to be utterly unfathomable. The question is treated at some length by Kirchhoff, with whom I concur regarding Topiltzin and Huemac as virtually contemporary.[19]

In this case, as in others, it has seemed preferable, when confronted by contradictions of this nature, to employ the same method of horizontal comparison. Chart I sets out in summarized form what the various sources say about the relationship between Huemac and Topiltzin (*see* column A), together with their respective versions of divine interventions or religious conflicts involving Tezcatlipoca (*see* column B); to this has been added what each says about the final end

CHART I: HUEMAC AND TOPILTZIN

Source	*Relation of Huemac to Topiltzin*	*Fate of Topiltzin-Quetzalcoatl*	*Fate of Huemac*	*Mention of Tezcatlipoca or of religious conflict in general*
Anales de Cuauhtitlán	Surrogate and substitute (p. 12). Married "Coacueye," also described as Quetzalcoatl's mother (p. 14).	Died in Culhuacán in 2 Acatl (p. 8). Died in 1 Acatl (p. 8). Went to Tlapallan and was burnt (p. 11).	Killed himself in Cincalco (p. 15).	Tezcatlipoca tempted Quetzalcoatl, who got drunk (pp. 9–10) Tezcatlipoca mocked and deceived Huemac (p. 12). Yaotl (=Tezcatlipoca) instigates war between Toltecs (p. 14).
Leyenda de los Soles	Successor of Topiltzin-Quetzalcoatl (plus three other kings) (p. 125).	Arrived in Tlapallan in 1 Acatl (p. 125).	Fled to Cincalco (p. 124).	Huemac in conflict with the *tlaloque*, with whom he played pelota (p. 126).
Historia de los Mexicanos		Left for Tlapallan ("towards Honduras") (p. 217).		Tezcatlipoca tempted Ce Acatl and told him his house was ready in Honduras.
Relación de la Genealogía	Successor, after interval of 97 years (p. 243).	Went to Tlapallan (p. 243).	Hanged himself in Chapultepec (p. 244).	Tezcatlipoca and Huitzilopochtli incited Topiltzin to perform human sacrifice (p. 243).
Muñoz Camargo, *Historia de Tlaxcala*	Huemac went in search of Quetzalcoatl, already in Cholula (p. 5).			
Histoyre du Mechique	Tezcatlipoca, not Huemac, was Quetzalcoatl's enemy in Tollan. Robbed his mirror (p. 36).	Fled to Tenayuca, then to Cholula and Cempoala (p. 37).	Huemac took his people to Culhuacán (p. 37).	Tezcatlipoca robbed Quetzalcoatl's mirror in Tollan (p. 36).

Obras Históricas	Quetzalcoatl (I, p. 20). Huemac was necromancer who foretold Topiltzin's troubles (pp. 47–48).	appeared via Coatzacoalcos (I, p.20). Entered Xico (p. 54). Went to Tlapallan (I, pp. 55, 67, 73).		Toltec troubles (I, p. 38). Huemac was his confederate.
Chimalpain, *Memorial Breve*	Huemac also called Topiltzin (p. 7). Tuemac son of Totepeuh (p. 8). Topiltzin-Acxitl succeeded Huemac, but generally implied to be contemporary.	Went to Poctlan and Tlapallan (p. 11). Fled, pursued by Huemac (p. 13).	Disappeared in Cincalco (p. 13).	
Torquemada, *Monarquía Indiana*	Huemac was Topiltzin's successor (p. 254).	Went to Cholula (p. 255). Much later went to Onohualco, Tabasco, Campeche (p. 256).	Pursued Quetzalcoatl to Cholula (p. 256).	Tezcatlipoca and Huemac were adversaries of Quetzalcoatl in Cholula (p. 255).
Anales Toltecas			Fled to Cincalco and was killed in Oztotepan (pp. 13–14).	
Veytia, *Historia Antigua de México*	Huemac was father of Totepeuh. Totepeuh succeeded by Nacaxoc (Topiltzin?) (I, p. 173).	Took refuge in cave in Xico, then went to Huehuetlapallan (I, pp. 208–10).		
Sahagún, *Florentine Codex*	Huemac and Quetzalcoatl contemporaries; Huemac was ruler, and Quetzalcoatl priest (Bk. III).	Went to Tlapallan and set off in serpent raft (Bk. III, Ch. 13, 14).		Huitzilopochtli Titlahuacan and Tlacahuepan tempted Quetzalcoatl *and* Huemac. Huemac got drunk.
Clavijero, *Historia Antigua de México*	Huemac was astrologer who predicted Tollan's disasters (p. 50).	Died after 20 years' rule in Tollan (p. 52).		Huemac gave his daughter to Titlahuacan (= Tezcatlipoca) (Bk. III, Ch. 4, 5).

of both Topiltzin and Huemac and of places to which the Toltecs dispersed (columns C, D, and E).

From this table it may first be perceived that the great majority of those who mention both Topiltzin-Quetzalcoatl and Huemac, including the *Anales de Cuauhtitlán*, *Leyenda de los Soles*, Muñóz Camargo, *Memorial Breve*, Torquemada, and Sahagún, treat them as virtual contemporaries, whether as simultaneous incumbents of different offices or as immediate successors one of the other; Ixtlilxóchitl even treats the two as one person. In the opposite sense, a discordant note is struck only by the *Relación de la Genealogía* and its parallel version, the *Origen de los Mexicanos*, which maintain the posture that Huemac succeeded Ce Acatl-Topiltzin, but only after an interval of 97 years. By allowing for a total reign by Huemac of 62 years, the source then implies an interval of 159 years separating the departure from Tollan of Ce Acatl and that of Huemac. Also in disagreement, but in a different sense, is Veytia, who calls Huemac the father of Totepeuh, who in turn was succeeded by "Nacaxoc," who may be taken to be Topiltzin. This version might possibly result from some confusion between the older Huetzin, who seems to have preceded Totepeuh, and Huemac.

The two major writers on the topic, Kirchhoff and Jiménez Moreno, have both tended to diverge from what might be termed the majority view of the written sources. This in itself is a perfectly justifiable procedure, and we have already cautioned against the dangers of simply counting heads in order to build a hypothesis. Often, they may on closer examination be found to all emerge like the heads of the Hydra from the same body, in this instance an original basic account common to all.

Jiménez Moreno, on the one hand, adopts the viewpoint of the *Relación de la Genealogía* as regards Huemac.[20] Having associated Topiltzin-Quetzalcoatl with the beginnings of Tollan, he locates Huemac at its finale, accepting the suggested interval of a century and a half between their two ends. Kirchhoff, on the other hand, relies mainly on Sahagún's version and regards Huemac as a contemporary of Topiltzin rather than successor, as in certain other accounts. For Sahagún and consequently for Kirchhoff, they are coetaneous, but hold different offices; Topiltzin is a priest, while Huemac is a temporal ruler.

I myself cannot fully concur in either version. Let us first consider the views of Jiménez Moreno. His interpretation depends on his other assumption regarding this Topiltzin, son of Mixcoatl, being Tollan's first ruler, a hypothesis concerning which I have already expressed my objections, while readily accepting another Ce Acatl or Quetzalcoatl among the early Toltec leaders. If any reader is still not satisfied with the evidence cited in Appendix A and Appendix B, let him turn to the evidence of the sources concerning Topiltzin and Huemac, as given in Chart I accompanying this chapter.

The *Relación de la Genealogía* alone proposes a long time interval between Huemac and Quetzalcoatl. If the account is taken literally, Topiltzin's downfall resulted from his resistance to the introduction of human sacrifice in Tollan. That particular story is repeated in different forms in other versions; but the tale must surely be allegorical, if not spurious, since Mesoamericans knew plenty about human offerings well before Tollan. It is difficult to say how this oft-repeated legend of Topiltzin's opposition to sacrifice arose; such assertions have a highly apocryphal ring and may even have been inserted into the record for the benefit of the Spaniards in order to bestow a measure of respectability on at least one Mesoamerican deity—as it so happened, the one who had originally been identified with Cortés. As Litvak rightly remarks, Quetzalcoatl sometimes displays the characteristics of a medieval saint.[21]

At the end of its brief description of events, the *Relación de la Genealogía* finally says, "He [Ce Acatl] was exiled from the land and went away to territories said to be called Tlapallan, though it is not known where they lay. He took away with him the people of Culhua, and all the officials [*oficiales*]."[22] After this, Tollan was without a ruler for ninety-seven years, until the advent of Huemac.

Quite apart from the objections already expressed, it is highly improbable from the historical point of view that disasters of this kind should befall an incipient seat of empire, the very founder fleeing in disgrace, still less that he could take away with him a considerable proportion of the people, leaving behind a depopulated Tollan without a ruler, but which somehow contrived nonetheless to become the center of an empire. Even more unlikely does it seem that, coming as a mere refugee who had been driven from his capital in disgrace, the same individual could have occupied Chichén, as has been also suggested as part of the same interpretation of events, and then implanted Toltec ways and Toltec styles in that place. It has moreover already been emphasized that in any case architectural similarities with Chichén coincide with later rather than initial Tollan buildings.

It may be worth adding that the parallel account that occurs in the *Historia de los Mexicanos*, after similar remarks to the effect that Topiltzin was Tollan's first ruler—as previously explained, an obvious interpolation—clearly implies that his departure to Tlapallan marks the end of Tollan. Despite the mention of a successor after nine years' interlude (instead of ninety-seven), the account states that he took away with him *all* the *macehuales*, or freemen, something that really could not happen except in the wake of utter disaster.

Referring now to Kirchhoff's hypothesis, he discusses the many alternative versions and finally accepts Sahagún's contention that Topiltzin was a priest and Huemac a lay ruler. Sahagún relates at length the priestly penances of Quetzalcoatl and his many different temptations by Tezcatlipoca; in the same account, Huemac is plainly a temporal ruler, is referred to as "*tlatoani*," is married, and has a daughter. Quetzalcoatl, apparently celibate, is addressed as "*tlacatl*" (lord), and the Toltecs are called his vassals (*imacehualhuan*). The *Historia de los Mexicanos* supports Sahagún in stating that he was celibate, but Ixtlilxóchitl and others make frequent reference to his offspring, whom they name; such are the confusions with which we are confronted!

One cannot help feeling, however, that the distinction between kingly and priestly functions may be somewhat unreal where Tollan and the respective roles of Quetzalcoatl and Huemac are concerned, and that Sahagún's contention to that effect, drawn from legends familiar to his informers, amounts to an oversimplification. The *Anales de Cuauhtitlán* state that Quetzalcoatl was both priest *and* ruler, or "rey," though the latter title is made to apply more to the original, or pre-Tollan, Quetzalcoatl. The same source calls Huemac the "substitute" of Quetzalcoatl, and thus ascribes to him also a kind of dual role as priest and king, surely the more likely situation.

In the first place, it has already been made clear in Chapter 6 that, at least in practice, any office that embodied the title of Topiltzin or Quetzalcoatl had become mainly secular, whatever its remoter origins. There is, of course, nothing incompatible in the functions of priest and king, as one may observe from the history of ancient Egypt. Moreover, one need not go back to ancient Egypt, or for that matter to Teotihuacán, to seek examples of theocratic government or the fusing of ecclesiastical and temporal functions. The Vatican continued to exercise temporal power until 1870, with a government also possessing secular ministers and with its own general staff and armed forces. It was only Napoleon who abolished prince-bishoprics such as Wurzburg and Munster.

In the broad context of world history, Dumézil draws attention to the indivisible links between kingship and priesthood in India and Rome, which he compares in his study of the common Indo-European heritage. He points out that the Sanskrit *raj* and *magan* (king) correspond to the Italo-Celtic form to be found in the Latin *rex*, Gaulish *rix*, and so on. The connection between the Indo-Iranian word for priest, *brahman*, and the Latin *flamen* has for a long time been accepted by etymologists. In effect, as the author points out, one must not consider separately the case of the *rex-raj* and that of the *flamen-brahman*. In Rome, as in India, the two types of sacred personage who bore these names had a special relationship and formed in certain respects a couple.[23]

The historian Livy actually states that the *flamen dialis* was the substitute on a religious plane of the early kings of Rome; "substitute" is the very word used to describe the relationship between Huemac and Quetzalcoatl in the *Anales de Cuauhtitlán*. Dumézil, incidentally, also points out that the *flamen dialis* used the royal seal and the royal robe. One thus sees that both in Asia and Europe a close interconnection between kingly and priestly roles was more the rule than the exception. Seen in this light, the argument as to whether Topiltzin was a ruler or a priest becomes somewhat irrelevant.

Reverting to Mesoamerican problems, it should not be forgotten that even in Tenochtitlan the *tlatoani* was regarded as *in iyollo altepetl* (the heart of the city), and it was considered that through his mouth the god actually spoke; according to Sahagún, the newly elected ruler was told that he was no longer considered as a mere man, because he embodied the person and image of the deity.[24] In Tenochtitlan, the monarchy had most probably been further secularized since the days of Tollan Xicocotitlan; in that place the ruler surely had even more overtly priestly functions than in the Aztec capital. Thus any head of dynasty, whether Huemac, Topiltzin, or any other, would in a sense have been both priest and king. Thompson quotes ample evidence that in Yucatán at the time of the Conquest a similar situation prevailed. For instance, the *halach uinic*, or chief ruler, of Loche would only speak to the first Christians to arrive after a thin mantle had been stretched between them and his person to act as a kind of barrier. The Motul dictionary makes it clear that the *halach uinic*, like the Aztec ruler, had both secular and religious functions. It actually translates the term as "bishop, oidor [judge of the highest judicial court], governor, provincial head of a religious order."[25]

In reality, Topiltzin and Huemac are human rulers who are also converted into celestial beings, or rather men cast partly in a divine role and subsequently deified in different forms. Too much play, however, should not be made on that account upon any distinction between Topiltzin as the name of a man and Quetzalcoatl as that of a god. According to Sahagún's *Primeros Memoriales*, Topiltzin *is* the god Quetzalcoatl, creator of the earth, sky, and sun.[26] And, just as the human Ce Acatl-Topiltzin is also at times called simply Quetzalcoatl, like the deity, so also Huemac in certain aspects becomes a divinity, closely to be linked with Tezcatlipoca. Huemac later assumes the kingship of the Underworld, and it is he to whom Moctezuma II turns in his dire plight; to avoid confrontation with Cortés, the latter actually contemplated an escape to the Cave of Cincalco, where the original Huemac of Tollan hanged himself, but where he was still thought to reign in Moctezuma's time. Thus the final destination, where the earthly Huemac met his end, has divine connotations just as much as Tlillan Tlapallan, to which the human Topiltzin reportedly repaired. Cincalco is sometimes described as a grim and fearful place, sometimes as a kind of paradise, or Tlalocan. Huemac himself, as lord of underground caves, also recalls Tepeyollotl; as the latter's name implies (heart of the mountain), he is a deity of the interior of the earth and of caves, and is thus in turn closely linked with Tezcatlipoca.

The *Anales de Cuauhtitlán* not only states that Huemac became the substitute of Quetzalcoatl (*ipetlapan icpalpan*), but a further phrase is added, attributing to him also the role of surrogate (*ye yehuatl conmixiptlayoti Quetzalcoatl anmochihuaco in Tollan*).[27] Such statements suggest that the one in fact came to occupy the same office as the other, in this context seemingly that of priest and ruler. At the same time it is almost implied that in a sense they were also fellow deities, in the same way that Huitzilopochtli is described during the early part of the Mexica migration as the "image" of the god Tetzahuitl; *ixiptlatl* (i.e., "image" or "representative") possesses the same root as *conmixtliptlayoti*, quoted above with reference to the relationship between Quetzalcoatl and Huemac.

On the other hand, one has also to bear in mind the account of the *Memorial Breve*, which in one passage implies that Topiltzin-Quetzalcoatl actually was the successor of Huemac, and in another gives the more orthodox story of Huemac pursuing Topiltzin out of Tollan. But in its first version, placing Huemac before Topiltzin, the source perhaps tends to confuse the two, since Huemac himself is also referred to as "Tepiltzin."

The various statements as to the relationship between the two in different sources may perhaps be reconciled as follows:

1. Topiltzin-Quetzalcoatl and Huemac were near contemporaries. They simply belonged to different dynasties, Topiltzin having assumed the authority and functions of one ruling house, whereas Huemac had succeeded to the headship of another, already long established.

2. To this may now be added a second conclusion. A conflict arose between them, and Huemac succeeded in expelling Topiltzin from Tollan. But by this time the situation had so far deteriorated that Huemac himself was in turn driven out and met a violent end in Cincalco, near Chapultepec. Thus at one stage after the expulsion of Topiltzin, Huemac may in effect have been his successor and surrogate as well as his contemporary, since he could then have become the senior ruler of perhaps a total of four, a position which possibly bestowed upon its incumbent the title of Quetzalcoatl (hence the identification of one with the other in certain accounts). In Tollan as in Culhuacán,

rulers belonging to different dynasties would have succeeded to their respective thrones at different dates, their reigns overlapping. As I have emphasized in another study, one of the various *señores* of Culhuacán probably assumed a leading role at any given moment as a kind of *primus inter pares.*[28] The same situation clearly prevailed in Tlaxcala at the time of the Conquest.[29]

This somewhat confused situation between these two virtual contemporaries then became a fundamental part of Mesoamerican legend, and both protagonists, from being rulers and priests, became deities, Topiltzin as the Morning Star and Huemac as King of the Underworld. Thus, true to the deep-rooted Mesoamerican principle of duality, the original internal conflicts attending the fate of Tollan reach us as the story of two human beings, but at times the accounts are transferred to a divine plane and become part of the eternal duel between the gods Quetzalcoatl and Tezcatlipoca, as creators and destroyers of successive worlds. Tezcatlipoca thus alternates with Huemac as the tempter and destructive genius of Quetzalcoatl, in an epic in which the human element is inextricably interwoven with the divine.

Topiltzin, Huemac, and the Rival Ethnic Factions

Up to this point, the personal relationship between Topiltzin-Quetzalcoatl and Huemac has been examined in order to decide whether or not they were contemporary and whether they occupied identical or different offices. Having reached certain conclusions on such matters, one must now turn to the political issues and ask from what factions in Tollan each drew his support and whether ethnic differences were involved in such dissensions. After examining these sociopolitical questions, it will then be necessary to return to the basic elements of the Topiltzin-Huemac feud and examine its possible religious implications in terms of support for rival deities.

Most accounts concur in mentioning internal dissention in Tollan. However, whereas the *Historia Tolteca-Chichimeca* ascribes this to a quarrel between the two ethnic elements, the Nonoalcas and the Tolteca-Chichimecas, other versions tend to put the conflict on the semidivine plane, often involving Tezcatlipoca as well as Huemac, as the opponent of Topiltzin. This factor has led investigators to interpret the internal struggle as a kind of religious schism in the heart of the doomed empire.

Before discussing such divine antagonisms, we will first take up the more material differences between the Nonoalcas and the Tolteca-Chichimecas. Evidence on the subject is in the main limited to the *Historia Tolteca-Chichimeca* and a related source, the *Anales Toltecas*, but it is very much to the point. It brings to light not only the distinction between the two ethnic elements, not clarified in other accounts, but also emphasizes that, far from merging, they continued as separate entities, mutually hostile. The source states that in yet another year I Tecpatl, the Nonoalcas and the Tolteca-Chichimecas arrived at Tollan Xicocotitlan; after an initial period of accord, in the year I Calli they quarreled.[30] Thus, as in other versions, the beginning and the end of Tollan become automatically confused, since the arrivals and departures mentioned are really separated by several centuries.

The account of the dispute mentions Huemac and also cites divine intervention on the part of Tezcatlipoca as a possible cause of the ethnic rift. The meaning is not absolutely clear, since the Toltecs, i.e., Tolteca-Chichimecas, are described first as coming into conflict with Huemac and then with the Nonoalcas; it is accordingly more logical to assume that Huemac himself is to be identified with the latter and not with the Tolteca-Chichimecas, since both the Nonoalcas and Huemac are portrayed as objects of the latter's wrath. The Nonoalcas are several times described as the "settlers" or "complement" of the Toltecs. The corresponding Nahuatl word is *imacica*, a verbal noun deriving from *aci*, "to arrive" or "to reach." Thus, they are in effect "the arrived ones," or those who settle.

The whole significance of this word *imacica* has been discussed in Chapter 6. The Nahuatl text now in question reads, "*Yequincocohua in nonoalca in tolteca imacica in huemac. Quitoa in icxicoatl in quetzaleuéhuac* . . . ." This may be translated, "The Nonoalcas became angry with the Toltecs, the settlers (*imacica*) of Huemac. Icxicoatl and Quetzaleuéhuac said . . . ." At first sight it seemed odd to describe the Toltecs as "settlers" of Huemac, since in other contexts *imacica* is used to describe the relationship of one people to another, not of a people to an individual; I therefore suggested that the full stop after "Huemac" was misplaced and that it should have come between *imacica* and *huemac*. The text would then have read, "The Nonoalcas, the settlers of the Toltecs, became angry. Icxicoatl and Quetzaleuéhuac told Huemac . . . ." However, Reyes insists that this would not be grammatical and that in such a rendering not *quitoa* but *quimilhuia* would have to be used.[31]

With the original punctuation, one is left with a text in which the Toltecs, i.e., the Tolteca-Chichimecas, indubitably appear to be described as the settlers of Huemac, in other words, those who came to Huemac (*aci* = to arrive). On this count alone, the Tolteca-Chichimecas cannot be identifiable with Huemac, but are different, and hence by inference Huemac must himself be a Nonoalca, if he is not a Tolteca-Chichimeca. The term *imacica* is applied at times also to the Nonoalcas, to describe their relationship to the Tolteca-Chichimecas. But in this and other cases already discussed, the word draws a distinction between two disparate elements and on no occasion implies a state of identity.

Huemac seems in effect to be a Nonoalca, though the matter is admittedly open to different interpretations; one is next told how he asks the Nonoalcas, that is to say, apparently his own people, to provide him with a wife with exceptionally wide hips; she is produced, but he rejects her, since her hips do not have the required measurement of four handbreadths. But like so many other embellishments of similar nature, this is not just a homely incident in the life of Huemac, as we might like to think, but an apocryphal tale, also occurring in other situations, and whose true meaning escapes us. In the *Chilam Balam* occurs the story of a Maya lord who requests that a woman be brought to him with hips seven handbreadths wide. The possession of unusually wide hips is a recognized physiological condition the religious significance of which goes back to remote times, as one can see from many figurines of Tlatilco.

This generously proportioned female requested by Huemac seems at all events to have been the woman of discord, since the two Tolteca-Chichimeca leaders mentioned her as the cause of the quarrel between themselves and the Nonoalcas. Both the former and the latter were now prepared to agree that Huemac, the promoter of their dissension, should be killed. He consequently fled to the inside of the cave of Cincalco; according to this version, he was taken outside and killed with arrows.

The story then describes the subsequent journey into exile of the Nonoalcas, under Xelhua and other leaders, and their arrival in the Cozcatlán-Tehuacán regions.

In seeking to clarify the *Historia Tolteca-Chichimeca* account, confusion arises over the order in which events occur. It has already been explained that the departure of the Tolteca-Chichimecas to Cholula seems to have been an initial move, affecting only some of the group, and that the event really precedes the conflict of the Nonoalcas with the (remaining) Tolteca-Chichimecas and the final breakup of Toltec power. The correct order for the happenings described should surely be:

1. The initial migration of some Tolteca-Chichimecas to Cholula under Icxicoatl and Quetzaleuéhuac, recounted on pages 75–86 of the Heinrich Berlin edition.

2. The fetching of the Teochichimecs to aid them in Cholula, involving the migration, among others, of Mixcoatl-Totepeuh, father of the last Ce Acatl-Topiltzin (pages 86–102).

3. The subsequent quarrel between the remaining Tolteca-Chichimecas of Tollan and the Nonoalcas, occurring probably some years later (pages 68–70). Huemac is mentioned in this account, as has been seen, but not Topiltzin. In his place as Huemac's rival occur two leaders, Icxicoatl and Quetzalteuéhuac; I believe that this is just another of those confusing transpositions of names from one set of occurrences to another and that the real protagonist of the dispute with Huemac is Topiltzin, rather than these other two, already long since departed for Cholula. Their migration to that place, moreover, bears all the marks of an early breakaway rather than of a final collapse, not only for the reasons already given but because no ruler is involved as leader. Other accounts invariably speak of an actual monarch who led the people out of Tollan when the final disasters occurred, whether Topiltzin himself, Nauhyotl, or some other.

4. The departure of the Nonoalcas (pages 70–75).

5. The final collapse and the general exodus in different directions

as described by various sources, but only indirectly by the *Historia Tolteca-Chichimeca*, when it refers to the ethnic rift. Huemac really belongs to the very last act of the drama, and to accept him as included in the first is only possible if we envisage the existence of a second Huemac, who also went to Cincalco.

If Huemac is indeed to be associated with the Nonoalcas, then his antagonist Topiltzin must logically be a partisan of the Tolteca-Chichimecas, now at variance with the former. This in a sense constitutes a reversal of the original situation, whereby the deity Quetzalcoatl was more probably introduced by the Nonoalcas, coming from the direction of the Huaxteca. If, however, the last Topiltzin-Quetzalcoatl did occupy the office of principal ruler, then it might be natural that he should become associated with the Tolteca-Chichimeca majority.

One cannot help suspecting that the quarrel in Tollan may have arisen because, notwithstanding Topiltzin's apparent association with the Tolteca-Chichimecas, other rulers in addition to Huemac were more to be identified with the Nonoalcas, who, albeit a minority faction, may have continued to maintain a certain cultural and political ascendancy. However, while accepting that the Nonoalcas were probably in the minority, one can hardly go so far as to agree with César Olivé and Beatriz Barba that they were actually a *depressed* minority and that it is impossible that different peoples could have lived in free association in Tollan and yet preserved their separate identities.[32]

The *Historia Tolteca-Chichimeca* on several occasions mentions among the specifically Nonoalca leaders who left Tollan together Cuauhtzin and Timaltzin. A Tímal is to be found in the *Anales de Tlatelolco*, described as a conqueror who occupied Cuernavaca, mentioned by the *Historia Tolteca-Chichimeca* as lying on the Nonoalca route to their new home. Confusingly enough, Tezozómoc also mentions Tímal as one of three companions who accompanied Quetzalcoatl to Tlapallan.[33] In *Una Elegia Tolteca*, Lehmann lists Ihuitimal (probably the same person as Tímal) as another companion in flight, but his departure is mourned in such fashion that it might almost be implied that he was Topiltzin himself. On the other hand, the *Anales de Cuauhtitlán* report an Ihuitimal who succeeds Totepeuh, father of Quetzalcoatl, as ruler.[34]

Quauhtli (the same as Cuauhtzin) is also mentioned in the *Anales de Cuauhtitlán* as succeeding to Quetzalcoatl's throne and as apparently preceding Huemac as ruler;[35] he is later referred to as a companion of the god Tezcatlipoca, left behind when Tollan fell, and therefore presumably hostile to Topiltzin. Ixtlilxóchitl also writes of a Cuauhtzin who was Topiltzin's coruler and, according to this version, a loyal supporter.[36] The other coruler, according to the same author, was Maxtlatzin; the *Anales de Cuauhtitlán* also mention a Maxtla as a kind of collaborator of Quetzalcoatl. A Matlacxochitl is also mentioned by this source as successor to Quetzalcoatl, while Tezozómoc lists him as a companion in flight. Both the *Memorial Breve* and the *Histoyre du Mechique* also refer to him as ruling after Topiltzin.

From all this it may be deduced that the names of Topiltzin's corulers, successors, and companions in flight appear to be totally confused one with another; precisely the same people are mentioned, sometimes cast in one role and sometimes in another. But to judge by the majority of the sources, one is left with the feeling, at least in the case of Ihuitimal and Cuauhtli, that they were really rulers rather than mere companions; furthermore, in view of the clear and repeated insistence of the *Historia Tolteca-Chichimeca* on their Nonoalca identity, one may suspect that they may not have been wholly loyal to Topiltzin, notwithstanding what Ixtlilxóchitl says on the subject.

Huemac and Quetzalcoatl, the Religious Rift

So much for the political and ethnic antagonisms which attended Tollan's fall; we now come to the religious aspects of the dissensions that were involved.

In accounts of the fall of Tollan, Tezcatlipoca is variously mentioned in addition to Huemac as provoking discord, and thus a certain identification occurs of the man Huemac with the god Tezcatlipoca. It would seem not inaccurate to assume in very general terms that the Nonoalcas had become followers of Tezcatlipoca as their principal deity, and the Tolteca-Chichimecas of Quetzalcoatl. This is apparent in the subsequent pre-eminence of the latter in Cholula, to which many Tolteca-Chichimecas had repaired.

But generalizations on Mesoamerican religious topics are risky at the best of times and can seldom be carried to their logical conclusion. Any attempt in this direction usually ends up where it started, after taking a full circle. Identification of one god with a particular faction or people may turn out at best to be a half-truth; for instance, the Tolteca-Chichimecas, when they arrived in Cholula, continually called upon Tezcatlipoca, not Quetzalcoatl, to help them and console them in their misery. Moreover, it would seem more likely to be the Tolteca-Chichimecas from the northwest, rather than the Nonoalcas, who originally introduced Tezcatlipoca into Tollan.

Secondly, if one seeks to discern a kind of religious schism between supporters of two Mesoamerican deities, he may run into serious troubles. It may be finally discovered that each of the two contending gods displays many attributes of his supposed protagonist and is at the same time his image and his enemy; our schism thus ends as a deadly fight between two components of the same godhead.

The Topiltzin-Huemac antagonism derives from many sources and to a certain extent gives force to the identification of the man Huemac with the god Tezcatlipoca, just as Topiltzin by his very name is to be associated with Quetzalcoatl. For instance, Ixtlilxóchitl on different occasions refers to both Tezcatlipoca and Huemac as "sorcerers"; this is precisely the role, among others, which Sahagún ascribes to Tezcatlipoca Tlacahuepan, whom he refers to as "sorcerer." Torquemada also writes of "Tezcatlipoca, Huemac," as if they were almost identical. Huemac as King of the Underworld, and Tezcatlipoca, Lord of the Night Sky, are both also to be linked with the powers of darkness, quite apart from their common association with Tepeyollotl, already mentioned.

But like other generalizations, this cannot be taken as absolute. In the *Anales de Cuauhtitlán*, for instance, it is Huemac, not Topiltzin, who is himself the victim of Tezcatlipoca's machinations. In the *Leyenda de los Soles*, Huemac is also the victim of divine intervention, this time on the part of the *Tlaloque*.

It is curious to note this tendency for the struggle between two divinities to reproduce itself in so many diverse circumstances and civilizations. In most of the ancient Indo-European mythologies, the notion of sovereignty is projected at a cosmic level not by a single god but by two opposing and complementary deities. One of the two supreme beings is an all-powerful magician, violent, inspired, and often very terrible; the other is a kind or perfect purveyor of justice, well ordered, calm, and benevolent. Such is the Hindu couple, Varuna and Mitra, or the Scandinavian Odhinn and Tyr. An essential feature of this duality is that one of the two protagonists had lost one eye or both, and the other one or both hands.[37] It is remarkable how many features of this cosmic struggle are represented in the Quetzalcoatl-Tezcatlipoca drama. The descriptions of the two opposing deities fit remarkably the respective characteristics of Quetzalcoatl and Tezcatlipoca. Tezcatlipoca is indeed a magician and he has lost a foot (this kind of weakness also occurs in Greco-Roman mythology, as for instance in the case of Oedipus, who had trouble with his legs). All that lacks is for Quetzalcoatl to be missing an eye. This coincidence seems to underscore a certain indivisibility in world mythology. To quote Lévi-Strauss, "Without postulating the existence of some ancient and unproven link between the Old and New Worlds, I was able to show that the use of an astronomical coding imposed such strict limitations on mythic thought that it was understandable, on a purely formal level, that the myths of the Old and New World should, in certain circumstances, reproduce each other either directly or by inversion."[38]

The evidence of the sources tends to bear out Jiménez Moreno's contention that the cult of Tezcatlipoca, together with that of Huaxtec gods such as Tlazolteotl and even Xipe, was on the increase in latter-day Tollan. Archaeological evidence cannot provide very sure guidance on such subjects; sculptural representation tends to give prominence to older rather than newer gods. One may, for instance, observe in Mexico's National Museum of Anthropology that its fine and seemingly representative collection of Aztec sculpture contains not one single statue of either Huitzilopochtli or Tezcatlipoca, notwithstanding their pre-eminence in Tenochtitlan. A process had perhaps already been initiated in Tollan which was to culminate in Aztec times with the elevation of Tezcatlipoca to the all-powerful Tloque Nahuaque, whereas Quetzalcoatl came more to be identified with the wind, apart from his special role as supreme deity of Cholula. Sahagún refers to

Tezcatlipoca as a "young god."[39] His development in the Postclassic period may in a sense be a new departure, but here again paradox enters the field, and, as in so many other instances, one finds that the new has deep roots in the old.

Far from being a mere sky god, arriving late upon the scene from the outer marches of Mesoamerica, Tezcatlipoca displays a certain universality in both time and space. Jiménez Moreno sees the deity as sharing a common jaguar heritage with Tláloc;[40] his basic identification with this animal is indeed not in doubt. For instance, his close associate, Tepeyollotl, is a jaguar god. Tezcatlipoca thus personifies the oldest divine emblem to be found among the higher civilizations of Mesoamerica, linked with the basic elements of earth and fertility; he is even reported as having invented fire and thus becomes implicitly connected with another very old deity, Xiuhtecuhtli.[41] It may be interesting to note that in South America similar associations exist. Lévi-Strauss reports that in Ge myths, the jaguar appears as master of fire.[42]

Admittedly, the Tezcatlipoca complex is absent from the Oaxaca region, but certain reflections of the god are detectable among the Classic Mayas. Seler provides evidence of this in three illustrations. The first depicts the figure of Tezcatlipoca pierced by a spear, taken from the *Codex Borgia*; the second shows a jaguar in an identical pose, transfixed by a spear in precisely the same way; the third reproduces an exactly parallel illustration taken from the *Dresden Codex*, also of a jaguar in like attitude and with body pierced in the same manner.[43]

Tezcatlipoca was just as versatile as Quetzalcoatl and could undergo a bewildering variety of metamorphoses, appearing in many different forms. Nicholson discusses the Tezcatlipoca "complex," consisting of a number of deities originally independent but later merged into this one god, though that perhaps occurred partly in post-Tollan times. Among these deities he names Itztli, Tepeyollotl, Tecciztecatl, Meztli, Chalchiuhtolin, and Omecatl; he emphasizes the role of Tezcatlipoca as the archsorcerer, related to darkness.[44] Jiménez Moreno in addition calls attention to the god's links with Iztlacoliuhqui, Xochipilli, Piltzintecuhtli, and Macuilxóchitl.[45] As Seler points out, the last three deities are very closely related one to another.[46] Sahagún furthermore gives a series of alternative names for Tezcatlipoca: Titlahuacan,

Moiocoiatzin, Yaotzin, Necoc Iaiotl, and even Nezahualpilli.[47] Sahagún says that he was also referred to as Cuexcochtzin.

In addition, underlining the more ancient origins of the Tezcatlipoca concept, León-Portilla points out that, according to Sahagún's prayers to the gods in his Book VI, Tezcatlipoca and Tezcatlanextia (the double mirror which enveloped all things with darkness by night and illumined them by day) constituted a two-fold title for the creator god Ometeotl in the remotest times of Nahuatl culture.[48]

Giving added emphasis to his multifarious qualities as deity, Tezcatlipoca as sorcerer is able to undergo metamorphoses, a not uncommon talent among ancient deities. For instance, the Egyptian god Thoth would appear in a number of different manifestations, whether as moon, baboon, or ibis. Tezcatlipoca could change himself into another god, as in the significant passage in the *Historia de los Mexicanos* which tells us how he abandoned his own name and changed himself into Mixcoatl.[49] The same source, incidentally, describes Tezcatlipoca and Quetzalcoatl as brothers.

Not only is the human Mixcoatl father of Topiltzin-Quetzalcoatl, but the god Mixcoatl is also in many respects closely linked with Tlahuizcalpantecuhtli. In this context it may be interesting to note that Thompson sees the Maya gods of the planet Venus as actually usurping the patronage of game and hunting, the immediate province of Mixcoatl.[50] It may seem bewildering that on the one hand a kind of eternal conflict is discernible between Tezcatlipoca and Quetzalcoatl; Caso in particular calls attention to their alternate creation and destruction of successive worlds, thus personifying the struggle between light and darkness. But at the same time, in accordance with Mesoamerican notions of duality, they appear in certain ways as identical. As Seler puts it, they are sometimes companions and sometimes opposites;[51] for him the two gods constitute a kind of divine pair. A similar situation prevails in some respects with the human Huemac and Topiltzin, often enemies but sometimes portrayed as virtually one person. As depicted in the *Codex Vaticanus A*, Quetzalcoatl and Totec, i.e., the Red Tezcatlipoca, act as companions and are referred to as "the two masters of penitence;" both, incidentally, wear conical Huaxtec caps.[52] One of the two chief priests of Tenochtitlan was called "Quetzalcoatl, or by another name Totec."[53]

The two gods even tend to wear each others' adornments and share the same appellations. For instance, one finds Tezcatlipoca wearing an Ehécatl mask, characteristic of the God of Wind;[54] Quetzalcoatl appears with the dress of Xipe.[55] In one passage, Sahagún calls Topiltzin-Quetzalcoatl "Tloque Nahuaque," a title more usually applied to Tezcatlipoca.[56] In the same text, Yaotl, i.e., Tezcatlipoca, is named Yohualli Ehécatl, precisely the title the *Historia de los Mexicanos* uses for Quetzalcoatl.[57] Sahagún also by implication associates Quetzalcoatl with Yohualli Ehécatl, as the god that inspired the *tlamatinime* who left Teotihuacan at the end on their eastward journey. In fact this title, meaning "the Night and the Wind," could be taken as a kind of common denominator of the principal aspects of both gods and amply illustrates their partial identity.

It may thus be seen that Tezcatlipoca, far from being an entirely new god, has deep roots in the remote past and is at the same time inextricably linked with Quetzalcoatl himself. Under such circumstances, it is difficult to see the people of Tollan divided into two opposing factions, each supporting one god and opposing the other, since the deities themselves had so much in common. Accordingly, it seems that any identification of the Nonoalcas with Tezcatlipoca and of Quetzalcoatl with the Tolteca-Chichimecas, notwithstanding the implications of the *Historia Tolteca-Chichimeca*, can possess only a very limited validity.

On the one hand, worship of Xipe, the Red Tezcatlipoca, seems to have been strong in the Coxcatlán area, to which the fugitive Nonoalcas repaired. The *Historia de los Mexicanos* also mentions a Tlacaxipehualiztli ceremony dedicated to Xipe in that place, and Itzapal Totec was one of the chief gods of Teotitlán, according to its *Relación Geográfica*. In addition, one is told that the Nonoalca Tlaochcalca worshiped Tlatlauhqui (Red) Tezcatlipoca.[58]

But if Tezcatlipoca has associations with the Nonoalcas, he is also revered by the Tolteca-Chichimecas. Not only does he advise and console them in Cholula, but even at the very beginning, when the "Toltecs"—i.e., the Tolteca-Chichimecas—left Culhuacán (Teoculhuacán in this context), they brought out their god "Centeotl, son of Piltzintecuhtli."[59] The latter is certainly closely related to Tezcatlipoca, who as Yaotl is called by Sahagún "*in tloque nahuaque, in piltzintli.*"[60]

However, in general terms one may accept as valid a certain increase in the worship of Tezcatlipoca in the latter days of Tollan, though not exclusively at the expense of Quetzalcoatl, whose influence clearly remained very strong. This is illustrated in the leading part played by Topiltzin-Quetzalcoatl at the end of Tollan and the strong survival of his cult in Cholula, the spiritual heir of Tollan. One may also envisage a certain limited identification at this particular time of the Tolteca-Chichimecas with Quetzalcoatl and of the Nonoalcas with Tezcatlipoca. But such a linkage cannot be total, any more than the distinction between the respective deities is absolute.

In view of these rather blurred religious outlines, which defy any attempt at simplification, the Nonoalca conflict with the Tolteca-Chichimecas, in itself only one aspect of the disintegration of Toltec power, must surely be regarded mainly as political or ethnic rather than religious. Schisms of a religious nature are a somewhat European concept, all too familiar to students of the history of that continent; they imply that in adopting one cult, one must automatically be opposed to the other. But among the people of Mesoamerica and other polytheistic communities, such intolerance was conspicuous by its absence; the Mexicas merely superimposed Huitzilopochtli upon the gods of conquered peoples, without any intention of suppressing the latter. The capacity of the Mesoamerican pantheon to absorb additional gods was virtually limitless, and the introduction of a new deity did not normally provoke resentment or resistance in the adherents of the old; the one was simply added to the other. The notion of Tollan Xicocotitlan as rent by religious schism would not therefore conform to any known Mesoamerican pattern.

Reasons for the Nonoalcas and the Tolteca-Chichimecas actually colliding are hard to extract from any surviving sources, with their overlay of myth and their emphasis on divine intervention. It seems as if, for reasons unknown, the two disparate elements of Tollan never really merged into a single identity; perhaps they were intrinsically too diverse. They had come to Tollan from the opposite ends of Mesoamerica; on the other hand, the latter-day Nahuas and the Chichimecs who were to mingle in the Valley of Mexico in the succeeding period both came from a northwesterly direction. Possibly, as the Tolteca-Chichimecas became themselves more sophisticated, they no longer needed Nonoalca skills and might have resented patronizing attitudes or airs of superiority on the part of the Nonoalcas. More important still, perhaps the incumbents of the principal ruling dynasties of Tollan continued to be mainly Nonoalca, a notion for which certain evidence has already been cited. Such dynastic forces might have deliberately stirred up strife between the two factions to further their own ends. In view of the failing by two ethnic groups to fully merge, times of dire stress would automatically bring old resentments to the fore. The nature of such stresses, particularly in the form of external pressures, will shortly be examined.

Topiltzin and Huemac: the Final Count

Before studying other probable factors contributing to the downfall of Tollan, such as Huaxtec or Chichimec intervention, it may be preferable to complete our examination of internal dissensions and to comment upon the final act of the personal drama between Topiltzin and Huemac.

Even when one considers the more apparently meaningless episodes and anecdotes involved, one begins to see that even they often possess at least some significance of an allegorical or symbolic nature. This is particularly true where any association with mountains is concerned. Not only in Mesoamerica did they have religious connotation; one need look no further than the Book of Exodus to find the example of Mount Sinai, from which proceeded the voice of the trumpet, three days after Moses had descended carrying the Ten Commandments. Also from Tzatzitepetl, as the name implies, human cries or shouting were to be heard, and it is here that we are told that laws were made. Even the mysterious miniature figure whom Tezcatlipoca-Tlacahuepan made to dance in his hand in Tollan has certain implications of a more general nature; not only from the Fiji Islands but also from Malaysia come reports of beliefs that the soul took the form of a manikin of minute proportions. Perhaps, metaphorically, Tezcatlipoca was playing with the soul of his victims. Nor should it be forgotten that leading Maya personages were often illustrated bearing manikin scepters; also, gods appear in Mixtec codices holding tiny men.

But from much of the semimythical material, particularly that of

Sahagún, only limited factual data may be derived, whether concerning Tollan or Topiltzin-Quetzalcoatl himself. As López Austin points out, the many stories of Topiltzin and the end of Tollan include elements that simply defy any precise explanation, such as his attempts to slide down mountains in a seated position during his flight.[61] These are among many episodes to which it is hard to attach a historical significance and on which it is therefore pointless to dwell, even if they constitute an ample proportion of the total available material.

But not only is it often difficult to connect certain of these myths with a historical occurrence; alternatively, even when the narrative does seem to contain a kernel of truth, this factual portion may be related to events of a previous period of history rather than the one in question. For instance, the story in the *Anales de Cuauhtitlán* of Topiltzin-Quetzalcoatl's inebriation after drinking five cups of pulque is precisely the tale told by Sahagún's informants, not of Quetzalcoatl, but of the Huaxtec leader who lived in the period following the fall of Teotihuacán, before Tollan was even founded. Of course the original toper, if he ever existed in real life, was perhaps not the Huaxtec leader of relatively early date, but some personage of a yet remoter epoch. It is not inconceivable that a story of this kind could have originated in Preclassic times and then been passed on from era to era.

After discounting certain inexplicable items, one remains with the general impression that the stories of Tollan's disasters contain at least three distinct elements, involving different legends which became confused and combined in the sources. The first is that of the internal and external conflicts that beset Tollan, often personified into a general quarrel between Topiltzin-Quetzalcoatl and a human Huemac, sometimes abetted by a divine Tezcatlipoca. The second concerns the flight of Topiltzin to Tlillan Tlapallan, and his deification as the Morning Star, which really constitutes quite a different event from his actions in Tollan itself. The third, also after Tollan's fall, is the story of Huemac, later to become King of the Underworld, recounted only briefly. These may have been taught as separate sagas in the *Calmecac*, but have reached us usually merged and mangled into one rather amorphous whole. Sahagún gives us part of all three, as also does the *Anales de Cuauhtitlán* in shorter form. The *Memorial Breve* contains fewer allegorical embellishments, but duly mentions the internal quarrel, as well as the flight of both Topiltzin and Huemac. The *Historia Tolteca-Chichimeca*, on the other hand, mentions only Huemac, but also writes of the internal quarrel between Nonoalcas and Tolteca-Chichimecas. Ixtlilxóchitl concerns himself mainly with the external attack upon Tollan, then ruled by Topiltzin, adding brief mention of his flight and referring to Huemac merely as an incidental necromancer.

However contradictory these accounts, it might be said that they at least unite in presenting a general panorama of decrepitude, moral decadence, and vanity as responsible for the disasters that befell Tollan. Topiltzin neglects his priestly penances and becomes inebriated or commits carnal sin. Huemac's daughter marries the sorcerer Titlahuacan, after he has displayed himself in the market place naked and without *maxtatl* (usually considered as a Huaxtec trait, though Mixcoatl is also occasionally depicted in the codices without this garment). Topiltzin sees himself as looking old and worn in the mirror which he is given. Huemac plays pelota with the *tlaloques* and insists on taking his winnings in the form of green stones and quetzal feathers, rather than in maize, thus preferring vain baubles to sustenance for his people. One may even add the peculiar tale of the stinking corpse that no force can remove. All these stories have a faintly moralizing note, and their content reeks of decay and dissolution; Tollan had become the permissive society. The emphasis on decadence as well as disaster might perhaps be explained as constituting an essential and integral part of the Aztecs' own legendary history, based upon a superhuman Toltec past that perforce had to disintegrate. As Lévi-Strauss writes, "The emergence of order, whether it be natural or cultural, always results from the disintegration of a higher order, only the remnants of which are retained by humanity."[62]

But a further significant deduction might be drawn from certain versions: not only is one faced with a general picture of discord, but the opponents of Topiltzin or of Huemac are often three in number. One may recall the three demons of Sahagún's description who corrupt Quetzalcoatl; three tempters are named by the *Anales de Cuauhtitlán*; Topiltzin has three adversaries in Ixtlilxóchitl's account. This might all serve to reinforce previous suggestions concerning the presence of three other ruling dynasties, perhaps mainly of Nonoalca affiliations, in

Tollan; these may be represented in symbolic form by the three opponents or tempters of Topiltzin.

As regards what actually occurred, the possible nature of the dynastic conflict involving Topiltzin and Huemac has already been studied, and it only remains to comment upon their respective fates. That of Huemac presents fewer problems; no less than six sources state that he met his end in Cincalco (or Chapultepec). All except the *Historia Tolteca-Chichimeca*, which does not mention Topiltzin, say that Huemac's violent end, usually described as hanging, occurred only after Topiltzin's flight.

Accounts of what occurred to the latter are more varied. Apart from the "orthodox" story of his flight to Tlillan Tlapallan, the *Anales de Cuauhtitlán* say simply that he died in Culhuacán; only as an afterthought, the legend of the flight to Tlillan Tlapallan is added. The *Histoyre du Mechique* states that he first fled to Tenayuca. Ixtlilxóchitl gives the standard account of his flight to Tlapallan, but most significantly adds that many people say that he never went there at all, but remained in Xico![63]

This is surely a much more likely ending for the historic Topiltzin, the last, or penultimate, ruler of Tollan; it has already been deduced that he originally came from Culhuacán, and when disaster befell Tollan, what could be more logical than his return to his home base in the Valley of Mexico, whether Culhuacán itself, Tenayuca, or Xico? Culhuacán survived as the bulwark of Toltec power in the succeeding age, and it would have been natural that he should have gone back there; it would in fact have been his obvious course of action after failing to maintain his sway in Tollan, now beset with disaster. As explained in Appendix B, his progeny apparently ruled in Culhuacán, as members of the dynasty which he and his father had founded.

The Tlillan Tlapallan flight frankly bears all the marks of a legend tacked on to the life of a historical personage, just as one may find in the Bible or in Greek antiquity. The perpetual problem in Toltec history lies in the separation of fact from myth, and the eastward flight would seem to be an obvious instance of the latter. At some point in the account, history ends and legend begins, unless one is really to believe that the planet Venus was actually formed from his body and had not previously existed! The account cannot thus be *wholly* historical. From the purely practical point of view, at this moment of dissolution in Tollan, Chichén was probably also failing, and it is doubtful that secure communications between the two would have remained open; a Topiltzin-Quetzalcoatl determined to act out his full role in the original saga by actually going to die in Tlillan Tlapallan might have found it physically impossible to reach this destination without meeting a much less glorious fate on the way.

Of course Tlillan Tlapallan, as explained, is open to a different interpretation, and it could conceivably be maintained that the journey to Tlapallan is merely symbolic of dying at dawn, when black and red meet on the horizon. But whether at dawn or at any other time, we believe that the last Topiltzin is more likely to have died in the Valley of Mexico, as some accounts indeed suggest, rather than in the Maya land.

By way of detail, various localities are named on the supposed eastward route of Topiltzin, such as Cempoala, Quiahuiztlan, Coatzacoalcos, and Campeche; even Cozcatlán, the Nonoalca refuge, is mentioned. But these places, mainly on the Gulf Coast, refer surely to the Toltec diaspora in general rather than to the journey of one person. Certain accounts also attribute to the fleeing Topiltzin a prolonged stay in Cholula; these, however, appear to arise from confusion with yet another legend concerning a much earlier Quetzalcoatl, who visited that place in pre-Tollan times. In particular, Ixtlilxóchitl tells how a Quetzalcoatl, whose name he sometimes links with Huemac, came direct from Yucatán to Cholula at an early date, before the destruction of its Great Pyramid, in an era which the author describes as the Third World, and which he states to have preceded the Fourth, or Toltec, World.[64] In this context he writes of "Quetzalcoatl," whereas in his description of the end of Tollan he always refers to "Topiltzin." The story concerning Cholula was apparently recorded in relatively early post-Hispanic times by Olmos, and was also repeated by Mendieta, who also writes of a Quetzalcoatl who came from Yucatán to Cholula and then returned, without any mention of his visiting Tollan at all.[65]

It may again be emphasized that any true life story of Topiltzin had to be remolded in a form appropriate to offer inspiration to successive generations of Aztec schoolboys. It should also be borne in mind that Topiltzin actually was made to constitute a kind of legendary progenitor of the Mexica monarchs; Tízoc, for instance, is reminded on his succession that he has inherited the royal seat of the god Quetzalcoatl, the great Topiltzin.[66]

A prosaic decline and death hardly constitute the stuff on which such epic stories are constructed. But if a disaster can be unfolded in a tragic or dramatic setting, followed by a kind of resuscitation, like the Phoenix who rises from the flames, it may then act more as an inspiration than a warning. It may therefore again be observed that, like Aeneas, who turned the defeat of Troy into a victory by becoming the connecting link between the Romans and the past glories of Trojan and Greek civilization, so Topiltzin, after meeting every imaginable disaster and even breaking every sacred vow, ends in triumph, resurrected as the Morning Star, visible to all. Whether Topiltzin really did fulfill his legendary destiny by departing to the east is a much more open question, but Toltec history reaches us through the Aztecs, and in their rather contrived version of events such an ending was indispensible.

The Enemy Without: Huaxtecs and Chichimecs

So far, in discussing the fate of Tollan, emphasis has been placed first upon the general internal antagonisms between Nonoalcas and Tolteca-Chichimecas, and secondly on the duality of Topiltzin-Huemac, in both its political and its religious setting; one has therefore dealt with persons and events concerning which fact and myth are closely interwoven, but it has nonetheless been possible to draw certain conclusions of a historical nature about the forces which debilitated Tollan.

Excessive prominence may seem to have been given in this account to this rather personal side of Tollan's downfall; however, it is upon such internal dramas that the sources tend to concentrate, and other aspects are mentioned so much more briefly that it is hard to consider them in the same detail. But disaster is seldom attributable to one single cause, and one should generally seek to identify both the external and the internal foe. Before doing so, one must ask whether other more impersonal and prosaic factors did not also lie at the root of

Tollan's troubles in the form of physical and ecological phenomena, as well as outside enemies.

In the case of Teotihuacán, S. F. Cook does point to evidence of soil deterioration and less efficient food production as contributory causes of decline.[67] Recently, moreover, a tendency has developed to envisage the possibility of a certain climatic change in Teotihuacán in the form of a minor climatic cycling. It has been suggested that periods of high occupation of the Teotihuacán Valley and of high lake level have tended to be related. Curiously enough, in this particular region, after a possible decline, more favorable conditions seem to have been gradually returning at the end of the Toltec period.[68]

Certain sources such as Ixtlilxóchitl and even the *Anales de Cuauhtitlán* do mention crop failure, resulting from such adverse factors as frosts, and even famine, as well as internal conflict and war, as contributing to the troubles of Tollan. On the other hand, Palerm and Wolf do not favor the likelihood of any violent climatic changes at this time.[69]

In this connection, Armillas does suggest that Chichimec movements may have been triggered by environmental deterioration at that time occurring much farther away in the sensitive border zone between savannah and steppe climates. Data from the Southwest of the United States and from the eastern margin of the Great Plains support this ecological hypothesis, since it would seem that the North American arid zone was expanding in all directions between the twelfth and fifteenth century.[70] The same may be said of the climate of southern Tamaulipas; McNeish reports that in the La Salta phase, which he describes as continuing until about A.D. 1000, the climate was more humid than today; in the succeeding Los Angeles phase, however, it was already nearly as in present times.[71]

From the archaeological point of view, evidence does exist of the steady erosion of the northwest frontier of Mesoamerica, but this is a process which dates from early, not late, Toltec times, beginning even in the Late Classic period. At that time, Teotihuacán's cultural influences stretched as far as Chametla in Sinaloa. Since the process of cultural withdrawal was gradual, Tollan Xicocotitlan at the beginning would not have been unduly exposed to Chichimec attack, since a wide belt of territory separated the Toltecs from the less civilized peoples farther away; had this not been so, their capital would presumably have originally been built elsewhere. However, by the twelfth century, and very possibly before, this buffer zone had been drastically narrowed, and Chichimec territory, with little or no settled culture detectable by the archaeologist, reached as far as the approximate line of the rivers Pánuco, Lerma, Santiago, and Culiacán.

As already explained, the situation in Zacatecas and Durango was deteriorating at a relatively early date. Charles Kelley places the Vesuvio phase of the Suchil branch of the Chalchihuites culture, predominant in the region, as running from about A.D. 500 to 950 (Suchil itself is located about eighty kilometers southeast of the city of Durango). Kelley also gives the same approximate date for the termination of the ceremonial center of Alta Vista.[72] The actual number of Vesuvio sites declined after about A.D. 800. Eventually, "Mexican" influences disappeared, leaving only certain "colonies" which survived until about 1350 in northwestern Durango.

As regards the great site of La Quemada, ceramically related but not actually forming part of the Chalchihuites culture, information is not very conclusive, but radiocarbon dates range about the A.D. 1000 mark. As Kelley remarks, it is a veritable fortress, and its nature and situation suggest that it was constructed and organized especially to defend the northern frontier and in particular to block the passage of the Chichimecs down the open valley of the River Malpaso-Jerez.[73]

Farther to the southeast, and therefore nearer to Tollan, Braniff mentions a late Carabino phase in the Comonfort region (between San Miguel de Allende and Celaya) that is definitely Toltec in nature, though lacking Coyotlatelco pottery; it is comparatively separate from previous phases. Also, late Cóporo (in northwestern Guanajuato) not only contains Tula Water-colored, but also Plumbate, placing this phase equally in the Early Postclassic period.

Braniff emphasizes that neither in Guanajuato nor in the Altiplano area of San Luis Potosí are there any indications of occupation by pre-Hispanic peoples after the Early Postclassic period.[74] She states, moreover, that in marginal Mesoamerica in general, in the Early Postclassic period (i.e., from A.D. 900 to 1200), settlements already had become thinner. Little evidence seems to exist to prove matters one way or the other; however, one cannot help feeling that La Quemada may have fallen not at the very end of the Early Postclassic period but nearer A.D. 1000. Furthermore, one may suggest that Mesoamerican civilization (as opposed to mere nomad occupation) in the Guanajuato region did not long outlive such a collapse, and that the process of withdrawal to the very gates of Tollan was already fully in motion long before that city's downfall. This would coincide with Kelley's tentative date for the ending of the Chalchihuites culture, beyond which La Quemada itself is hardly likely long to have survived.

Needless to say, such developments, if my estimate of their time of occurrence is correct, would have brought about a radical change in Tollan's situation; it would have thus now found itself near to the very limits of Mesoamerica; from being the latter's main contemporary source of strength and stability, it would have itself become highly exposed to infiltration by warlike and wandering people.

Lying admittedly beyond this area, the Aztatlan complex was still flourishing, and the peak period of florescence in Sinaloa appears to belong to the centuries after A.D. 1000.[75] Certain elements of the Guasave phase undoubtedly recall the Puebla-Mixtec complex, but links with the rest of Mesoamerica, notwithstanding the above-mentioned surviving "colonies" in northwestern Durango, must have been at the best of times fragile.

When one comes to examine the written sources, he discovers cryptic references to famine and drought in Tollan, as well as civil strife. Ixtlilxóchitl writes of hunger and pestilence, frosts and drought.[76] The *Anales de Cuauhtitlán* mention famine; Vetancurt speaks of bad harvests.[77] A similar interpretation may perhaps be placed upon the account in the *Leyenda de los Soles* about how Huemac rejected the green maize offered by the *tlaloques*.[78] Torquemada adds a detail to the effect that a four-year hunger began after Topiltzin had reigned for four years.[79]

However, it must be borne in mind that such phrases are part and parcel of what might be called the standard Mesoamerican formula for describing periods of disaster, accompanied by the almost conventional accounts of dreadful omens that struck terror into rulers and ruled alike. A series of bad harvests may well have occurred, of the kind described in much greater detail in connection with the great hunger of 1451–55 under Moctezuma I (also a four-year period). This disaster made a deep impact on the incipient Aztec Empire and limited its immediate war potential, even imposing a kind of truce on operations against Chalco, likewise afflicted. However, notwithstanding the suffering caused, such events could not prove fatal to a healthy and expanding polity, but only to an empire already far advanced on the road to disintegration, for other and independent reasons.

Moreover, such accounts of ecological disasters befalling Tollan, apart from their somewhat stereotyped nature, ring false for another reason. It has already been explained that Tollan probably depended on the water provided by the River Tula rather than on seasonal rain, scanty at the best of times. Even in years of low rainfall, the flow of this copious stream, whose waters would in those times have sped almost untapped to the Tollan region, could hardly have fallen to a level insufficient for the cultivated area required to feed its population. In addition, the city could probably have obtained food supplies from the Valley of Mexico, far less densely inhabited than in Aztec times and therefore itself less liable to crop insufficiency, while already richly endowed with lagoon products. Furthermore, considering Tollan's apparent connections with the Gulf Coast, it would surely have been open to the Toltecs to obtain supplies from this well-watered area, as did the Aztecs during their famine (at a time when their armies had not yet conquered the coastal region).

Accordingly, on the one hand, it would not seem that Tollan itself was particularly vulnerable either to ecological change or to sudden adversities caused by drought. On the other hand, one may well agree that climatic changes much farther to the north, which triggered Chichimec movements, may have been an important adverse factor; certain evidence exists that these changes took place.

The disintegration of the northern frontier of Mesoamerica is archaeologically demonstrable. But it only in part coincides with the end of Tollan Xicocotitlan; it was a long-drawn-out procedure, just as the ecological process which may have driven the Chichimecs southward was also a gradual development. One may suspect that, as the Mesoamerican presence in Guanajuato weakened (and possibly had already disappeared), Tollan came under considerable pressure from that direction. Once more, the parallel with Rome may be valid, as did barbarians in the later centuries of Rome's rule, so Chichimecs may have been penetrating for some time into areas under Toltec control, originally as friends and allies, but tending to turn upon their masters in times of trouble and to demand excessive ransom in return for quiescence. Such intruders might have included the Tepanecs and Acolhuas, the main protagonists of the succeeding historical phase, and even the Mexicas. The Tepanecs probably originally spoke Otomí, the tongue which mainly survived in the region of Tollan.

Kirchhoff has rightly stressed the likelihood that Chichimec adversaries of Tollan were partly civilized and therefore were already in a sense ex-Chichimecs. One must remember that there was no natural barrier to protect Tollan from such peoples, in the form either of large rivers or high mountains. The Romans, with vast armies in later times standing guard on great rivers such as the Rhine and Danube, might be able to protect the frontiers of empire for two hundred years. But the situation of Tollan would have been very different; standing armies of any sort were not apparently the rule in Mesoamerica and I have argued in some detail that even the Aztecs had no real standing force.[80] In any case, the more limited population of the Teotlalpan could hardly have provided adequate manpower for this. Moreover, unlike the more stabilized situation which faced the Aztecs, in late Toltec times the different tribes were already on the move; the balance of the Toltec system of rule would have been upset, not necessarily by incursions of barbarians, but simply by the confusion caused by the migrations of displaced peoples, whether nomad or semicivilized. Such perils were probably more difficult to control than the constant menace of a rival empire, the Tarascans, on the Aztec northwestern boundary. At the time of the Conquest, a fairly hard-and-fast frontier divided settled peoples from nomads, and the Aztecs did not normally seek to penetrate nomad areas. On the other hand, as Braniff emphasizes, the frontier of A.D. 1000 or 1100 was a soft, or fluid, frontier, as well as being ill defined. It was only the Spaniards who created settled colonies in the marginal areas.

One may indeed note from the *Relaciones Geográficas* the great importance that the Aztecs attached to the frontier regions; there exist numerous accounts of border peoples being specially favored and exempted from tribute, except in the form of military service and the provision of supplies to forts, presumably manned by themselves.

Against a frontier that had perhaps become more stable, even if never without its dangers, the Aztec system of defense seems to have relied upon buffer tributaries, reinforced when necessary by expeditions from the center. Moreover, Tenochtitlan itself was very far from being in the line of fire, as Tollan may have been eventually.

On the other hand, when we come to examine the possibility of external attack on Tollan led by civilized powers, the evidence which the sources offer is more substantial. In the *Anales de Cuauhtitlán* we find: "8 Tochtli. In this year there were many omens in Tollan. Also in this year the she-devils arrived called *Ixcuinanme.* So say the old men. They tell how they came out of Cuextlan [the Huaxteca]; and in the place called Cuextecatlichocayan [where the Huaxtec wept], they spoke with their captives, which they took in Cuextlan, and assure that they spoke thus: 'Now we are going to Tollan: surely we shall arrive at that land and shall celebrate the feast; until now there has never been there sacrificial shooting with arrows, and we shall initiate the custom.' . . . 9 Acatl. In this year the *Ixcuinanme* arrived in Tollan: they arrived with their captives, and killed two with arrows. The demons were she-devils; their husbands were their Huaxtec captives. Here for the first time sacrifice by shooting with arrows began."[81]

Krickeberg, incidentally, explains the relationship existing between Tlazolteotl and the Ixcuinans, and how the former is thus also to be identified with this passage.[82] The suggestion that the Huaxtecs introduced sacrifice by shooting with arrows is rather obscure; Xipe, who is also to be associated with this rite, existed long before Tollan. The *Anales de Cuauhtitlán* add that Yaotl (i.e., Tezcatlipoca) introduced the practice of flaying, the principal Xipe rite. Tezcatlipoca is also referred to in this context as Tohueyo, a term normally used for Huaxtecs.* Moreover he appears in the marketplace without *maxtatl,*

* The expression "*tohueyo,*" used by Sahagún as applying to Huaxtecs, has sometimes been taken to signify "our neighbors," and thus cited as evidence of Huaxtec proximity to the Toltecs (or Aztecs). The relevant Sahagún passage calls the Huaxtecs "*tohueyo, quitzoznequi tohuampo.*" *Tohueyo,* according to Molina and Simeón, means "stranger" and *tohuampo* normally signifies "relative," or "kin." Thus, according to the above rendering of *tohueyo,* the phrase might be taken to mean people who were physically far away, but none the less in some manner related. Jiménez Moreno points out that *huentli* means "offering," and that *tohueyo* would therefore simply come to mean "our offerings." It

a Huaxtec trait. The account in the *Anales de Cuauhtitlán* also refers to the Toltecs as fighting with people from a place called Nextlalpan; these however were probably near neighbors rather than distant enemies, and this particular reference therefore more concerns an internal conflict, just as in the case of Coatepec, whose inhabitants, according to Sahagún, also fought against the embattled Toltecs.

Although Xipe had existed long before, he was originally in essence a Huaxtec god, and mentions of this deity, as well as the Ixcuinans in this text, may indeed imply some form of Huaxtec intervention against Tollan in its period of crisis; Jiménez Moreno even goes so far as to see the Toltecs giving up their own gods in desperation for Huaxtec deities, such as Xipe and Tlazolteotl, both implicitly or actually mentioned in the accounts. Since, however, Quetzalcoatl himself has very close Huaxtec ties, and even Mixcoatl exhibits certain distinctly Huaxtec traits, it would surely be almost a question of the Toltecs exchanging one set of Huaxtec gods for another.

It is undoubtedly true, as Jiménez Moreno has always stressed, that Huaxtec influence stretched farther west than in later times. Guy Stresser Péan writes that at the beginning of the Colonial period the Huaxtec language was still spoken in inland villages of the Sierra Madre, notably in the region of Tamasopo, Tanlacu, and Tancoyol.[83] He also writes of Huaxtecs in the northeastern part of the state of Querétaro. Meade in addition provides a map of the ancient Huaxteca that includes the northeast corners of both Hidalgo and Querétaro; he mentions that Huaxtec pottery has been found in Tuzapan and Tulancingo.[84] A certain relationship persisted between the Huaxtecs and those who dominated Central America after the fall of Tollan; the Chichimec ruler Xólotl married Tomiyauh, described as Lady of Tamiahua and Tampico.[85]

One must now turn to Ixtlilxóchitl, whose account is much more historical in form and content than those of the *Anales de Cuauhtitlán* and Sahagún; he in effect divides Topiltzin-Quetzalcoatl into two people: first "Quetzalcoatl," apparently concerned with Cholula in

may well be that this was the correct meaning as far as the Toltecs were concerned, and that Molina gave a later significance, which simply developed out of the fact that offerings, i.e., people whom one sacrificed, normally were strangers rather than compatriots.

pre-Toltec days. The second personage, referred to as "Topiltzin," is connected with the fall of Tollan. This source consistently depicts "foreign" intervention as the principal cause of its downfall.[86] Topiltzin succeeded to his throne and was immediately threatened by three *señores* who claimed his kingdom, who had come from two hundred leagues distant, from the region of the Pacific Coast, or "la Mar del Sur."[87] They are later referred to by name as Coanacotzin, Huetzin, and Mixtiotzin.[88] Xalixco is mentioned in connection with them, but later in the text reference is made to "*Xalixco en Quiahuiztlanxalmolan*" and also to the arrival of the three *señores* in question from "*las provincias de la mar del Norte.*"[89] This suggests that, as I previously insisted, the association of the Pacific littoral with such happenings is an embellishment of Ixtlilxóchitl, who thought in terms of the present-day Jalisco, and that in reality one is dealing with a Gulf Coast homonym. Such an interpretation is also more in keeping with other accounts of events, stressing Huaxtec intervention.

Faced with such problems, Topiltzin called on his loyal vassals, including two called Cuauhtzin and Maxtlatzin, who are stated to have possessed many cities and provinces; later they are described as kings, who had become in effect corulers. The *Anales de Cuauhtitlán* also write of a Cuauhtli, a priest who was apparently a kind of temporary successor of Quetzalcoatl, equally mentioned as a contemporary of Huemac and companion of Yaotl (Tezcatlipoca). Maxtla also occurs in the same source as a collaborator of Quetzalcoatl.

According to Ixtlilxóchitl, the Toltecs first yielded to carnal temptation, originally foreseen by Huemac, mentioned somewhat casually, and then encouraged by Tezcatlipoca in person. All kinds of disasters followed, including plagues, drought, and famine; at the same time the three rivals of Topiltzin became increasingly aggressive and occupied certain of his tributary provinces, although he sent them propitiatory gifts.

They were however not to be appeased, and in the year I Acatl came to Tollan with a great army; Topiltzin persuaded them to agree to a ten-year truce, but at its expiration in 10 Tecpatl they duly returned; it will thus be seen that Ixtlilxóchitl gives I Acatl for the virtual beginning of Tollan's disasters rather than as the date for their ending, coinciding with the death of Topiltzin. The latter now put two armies into the field, one in the Tlalhuica province (the present-day state of Morelos) and the other in the vicinity of Tultitlán (near Cuauhtitlán).

After a struggle lasting three years, Topiltzin was defeated; some Toltecs fled to Tultitlán, where Topiltzin himself was residing. He sent away his sons Pochotl and Xilotzin, and a terrible battle ensued, in which not only did Topiltzin himself join the fray, but his father and even his wives and other womenfolk took part.

The personage referred to as his father seems in fact to be one of his confederate rulers. Ixtlilxóchitl several times names Topiltzin's father as Tecpancaltzin or Iztaccaltzin; the latter of these is listed by the same author as Topiltzin's predecessor as ruler, while the former is given in one passage as his successor. In yet another context, Ixtlilxóchitl calls Iztaccaltzin one of Topiltzin's confederate rulers, along with Maxtla; from this one might infer that Iztaccaltzin=Tecpancaltzin=Cuauhtli, usually described as Maxtla's confederate. But Torquemada says that Tecpancaltzin is the same person as Quetzalcoatl, while the Anónimo Mexicano insists that he is the father of Pochotl and Xilotzin, usually known to us as Topiltzin's sons; such are the confusions of Toltec king lists. Perhaps the most likely guess, but not a sure one by any means, is that Tecpancaltzin-Iztaccaltzin is not really Topiltzin himself, let alone his father, but just two more of the many names given for his several companions or corulers.

In the year I Tecpatl, Topiltzin's resistance to his rivals collapsed, and he fled toward Tollan itself, accompanied again by the faithful Quauhtli and Maxtla; he hid in a cave in Xico, near Chalco; a further battle ensued, and one of his sons, Xilotzin, was captured, while the other, Pochotl, escaped.

After this triumph, the three enemy rulers sacked Topiltzin's temple and palaces and returned to their own land. This destruction could conceivably correspond to that which Acosta has described as occurring to the building in Tollan known as the "burned Palace"; I have however already expressed the opinion that the damage discovered by Acosta had occurred some time before this. After the disaster, Topiltzin, according to Ixtlilxóchitl's account, emerged from Xico, and after more wanderings went as predestined, to Tlapallan, where he lived for thirty years, dying at the legendary age of 104, i.e., the sum of two year cycles. Ixtlilxóchitl adds that some people say that he is still in Xico, and never went to Tlapallan, a passage to the importance of which attention has already been drawn.

Clearly one cannot on this occasion, or for that matter on many other occasions, take literally *all* that Ixtlilxóchitl relates; for instance, he gives for the casualties resulting from the three kings' offensive a figure approximately equaling the combined losses of France and England in World War I. However, his account seems nonetheless to be fundamentally historical, where others are mainly mythical. In general terms, one may deduce from what Ixtlilxóchitl relates:

1. The existence of three or four rulers in Tollan, as suggested in other versions.
2. The likelihood of certain internal dissensions, caused by vassals whom Topiltzin appeased and made into corulers. The chronicler insists on their loyalty, but other accounts make this seem less certain.
3. Tollan Xicocotitlan, when ruled by Topiltzin, was attacked and defeated by peoples coming from the Gulf Coast, an assertion of which we also find echoes in other versions.

It is difficult to assess with any assurance the respective parts played in Tollan's fall by Chichimecs or ex-Chichimecs from the northwest, on the one hand, and these coastal peoples, very possibly Huaxtecs, as mentioned in the *Anales de Cuauhtitlán* and described more specifically as aggressors by Ixtlilxóchitl.

But one has to bear in mind that according to the available evidence these Huaxtecs consisted of a number of separate principalities and thus hardly constituted one major power. As such, their nuisance value might have been very considerable, but it seems questionable that their attacks could have been the principal cause of the collapse of Tollan; they might rather have been a contributory factor which helped to deliver the *coup de grâce* to Topiltzin, when the end was near.

One tends to envisage the continued incursion of Chichimecs as taking place over a longish period and involving a number of tribes; as such, it would have constituted a more fundamental menace. It has already been stressed that any notion that semibarbarous peoples were no match for the more sedentary empires in Mesoamerica is patently mistaken. On the contrary, wars between civilized states only rarely result in the extinction of one of the adversaries. Usually some kind of understanding or treaty is reached in the end; often it is in the interest of the victor not simply to plunder the vanquished, but rather to prop him up, lest the whole social and economic order collapses and the former is engulfed in the total collapse of the latter.

On the contrary, barbarian hordes have no such axes to grind and are usually merely out for spoils; they may even profit from the collapse of a civilization. They have nothing to lose and stand to gain by simply overrunning the territories of settled peoples and possessing themselves of their property, even if the rewards they reap are diminished by a general economic decline.

The Final Count

Having discussed ecological and archaeological evidence concerning Tollan's last phase, as well as the historical content of the rather diffuse written accounts, we have now reached the point where one may perhaps draw certain conclusions.

Before doing so, the events that followed the disaster should first be mentioned, but only very briefly, as properly belonging to another volume, which will develop this theme in detail; the present volume ends, strictly speaking, with the fall of Tollan.

There is no need to retell here the story of the dispersal of the Nonoalcas. As related by the *Historia Tolteca-Chichimeca*, under various leaders headed by Xelhua, they departed for the Cozcatlán-Teotitlán-Tehuacán area, after settling Huaquechula, Izúcar, and other places on their route. The *Historia de los Mexicanos* also mentions Tochimilco as being ruled by a *señor* who came from Tollan; in some ways, being called Izcocutl and being married to a lady called Chimalma, he recalls Mixcoatl himself. The reported Nonoalca influx may have been only one of several Nahua-speaking migrations to the region; the *Relación de Papalotícpac* reports a Cuicateca tradition in Papalotícpac to the effect that the first inhabitants came from Amecameca.

The rest of the inhabitants of Tollan spread in many directions, except for a certain element who may have stayed behind, quite apart from those Otomís who now settled or who merely continued to inhabit the place.

Apart from the Toltecs' previous colonization of Cholula, which was to bear such notable fruit in the Late Postclassic period, the diaspora was concentrated above all upon Culhuacán and the surrounding area. Many of these neighboring cities boasted of Toltec antecedents, particularly Xochimilco, Cuitláhuac, and Mízquic.[90] Even Chalco may be included; Tlotzin later lived in Chalco "among Chalcas and Toltecs."[91] As explained in greater detail in Appendix B, the dynasty founded by Mixcoatl and Topiltzin continued to rule in Culhuacán, notwithstanding a rather confused interregnum between Topiltzin's reign and that of Nauhyotzin.

In addition, Toltecs are reported to have dispersed in many other directions. Ixtlilxóchitl mentions Xiuhcoac (toward the Huaxteca), Guatemala, Tehuantepec, Tototepec (on the coast of Oaxaca), Tecolutla (on the Gulf Coast), and Campeche.[92] Torquemada writes of Quetzalcoatl having sent his people to "Oaxaca and all the Mixteca Baja"; the *Anales de Cuauhtitlán* speak of Toltecs who went to Coixtlahuaca. Several other sources mention migrations to the Gulf Coast; e.g., the *Histoyre du Mechique* says that Quetzalcoatl himself went to Cempoala. Such reports might perhaps serve to reinforce my very tentative suggestions concerning some kind of Toltec colony on that coast, which apparently became a receiving area for fugitives.

But apart from the Tehuacán region, Cholula, Culhuacán and its neighbors, and possibly the Gulf Coast, reported Toltec migration to other places should perhaps not be taken too literally. Some accounts may have been written into the record to reinforce later and less certain claims to Toltec descent or may simply derive from the presence of Nahuatl speakers, present as a consequence of earlier Pipil migrations. For instance, notwithstanding the presence of some Toltec-type remains in Tototepec, the coast of Oaxaca remains a doubtful candidate as a receiving center for fugitive Toltecs. Swadesh points out that in the Nahua-speaking enclave of Pochutla, about 70 per cent of the words coincide with those of the more standard Nahuatl of Central Mexico. In terms of glottochronology, this would imply a period of separation of as much as fourteen centuries.[93]

The reported presence of "Toltecs" in certain other areas may arise from the attainment of a high level of artistic refinement, the term "Toltec" being then taken in its later sense as indicating a skilled artisan rather than a previous inhabitant of Tollan.

At all events, those unfortunate Toltecs who had joined their friends in the Valley of Mexico were not left to enjoy their new situation in peace. In 12 Acatl, possibly A.D. 1201, Xólotl and his Chichimecs appeared. He was far from being the wild barbarian formally depicted in codices, and he soon established his capital in Tenayuca, a former Toltec habitat. These Chichimecs were not prepared to leave Culhuacán to its own devices; one is told that in 9 Tecpatl, possibly A.D. 1249, Xólotl's son Nopaltzin killed Nauhyotl, then ruler of Culhuacán and sometimes described as Topiltzin's grandson.[94] But even after the ephemeral Chichimec power had subsided, Culhuacán still survived as an important entity during the following period styled by Caso as that of the "independent principalities" until finally overcome by the Tepanecs and their Mexica vassals. But, however significant Culhuacán's role after Tollan's fall, it could hardly claim to still rule an "empire" in any real sense of the word, and there is no evidence of its controlling territory outside the Valley of Mexico.

In outlining the events attending the decline of Tollan, certain inconsistencies in the record remain ever present in one's thoughts. How could the Tolteca-Chichimecas have taken over Cholula at a time when they themselves were refugees from a stricken city? How could the outside assailants of Tollan, supposedly Chichimecs from the northwest or Huaxtecs from the east, have introduced Aztec II pottery, seemingly native to the Valley of Mexico? And how could Tollan's fall have resulted from a kind of religious schism between followers of Topiltzin-Quetzalcoatl and Huemac-Tezcatlipoca, when such a concept is itself alien to Mesoamerican notions?

My interpretation of events may have many defects and leave many gaps unfilled; some of my contentions may be arguable. However, among other things, it does seek to explain or reconcile such points of paradox.

To sum up the conclusions of this chapter, one would first propose that the power and the glory of Tollan, like that of Teotihuacán, probably declined over a longish period. This is of course archaeologically demonstrable where Teotihuacán is concerned; a major if localized disaster occurred at the end of Phase III, and the subsequent phase IV was marked by a diminution in Teotihuacán's sphere of cultural influence, even if life continued in many respects unaltered in much of the great city. In a certain sense, one finds an archaeological parallel in Tollan. The end of Mazapan pottery appears to coincide with localized damage affecting the main ceremonial center; a period when Aztec II was substituted then followed, introduced, as explained, from the Valley of Mexico, possibly from Culhuacán itself. Archaeological investigations have so far revealed the presence of this pottery only in the main plaza and in certain areas; possibly until the great dispersal others sectors continued to be inhabited by people who still used Brush-on Orange as their domestic ware.

It still remains for the archaeologists to determine what happened in Tollan-Xicocotitlan between the end of Mazapan (to which Brush-on Orange is of course related) and the introduction of Aztec III in Aztec times; the extent and duration of the Aztec II occupation requires much clarification. One may hope that the reported abandonment of the city in the interval between its great period and its subsequent existence under the Aztecs may be confirmed or denied. It is not yet really clear whether an interval ensued between the use of Aztec II and III in Tollan. At present there is perhaps a tendency to suggest that scientific evidence for even a temporary abandonment of Tollan is rather lacking.

Acosta has expounded with clarity certain ceramic problems, but his explanation that the users of Aztec II actually destroyed the ceremonial center rests on less sure ground; no one after all suggests that the users of Teotihuacán IV themselves ravaged the center of that city—though admittedly the links between Mazapan and Aztec II are less direct than those uniting Teotihuacán III and IV.

If one accepts, as proposed above, that disaster finally befell Tollan in 1175 or thereabouts, then it might be considered that the ceremonial center was seriously damaged some time before that date. Notwithstanding Ixtlilxóchitl's account of invasion from the east in the very last phase, it has been suggested that more probably the assailants were people of Chichimec origin, already resident within Toltec territory. Following this initial attack on the ceremonial center, the users of

Aztec II came in, either with Topiltzin or perhaps before, and settled themselves in part of Tollan, where Mazapan ceased to be used and was replaced by Aztec II; even after the final catastrophe at the end of this interlude, Aztec II perhaps continued to be used for some time in certain areas of a city that now housed a somewhat reduced population consisting of former inhabitants who stayed behind and including certain Otomí elements. Much later, in Aztec times, the city again expanded, as demonstrated by the discovery of Aztec III over a fairly wide area, including the Plaza Charnay but excluding Tula Chico.

Thus, at this stage in our knowledge, it is perhaps fair to propose that Tollan, after its so-called "fall," suffered a reduction in population but not a total eclipse. Stories of the dramatic fate of the preceding civilization became, as already stressed, part of the legendary stock in trade of the Aztecs, just as had occurred with other ancient peoples.

Briefly, therefore, the following course of events is proposed:

1. Tollan had become increasingly exposed on its northwestern flank as the frontier of Mesoamerica receded; such a process continued for decades, if not for the best part of a century. During this phase Tollan itself was attacked and the ceremonial center suffered considerable damage. As occurred in Teotihuacán at the end of Phase III, certain elements then departed eastward, perhaps in A.D. 1122 or even before. These occupied part of the territory of the relatively weak Olmeca-Xicallancas, including Cholula; they were subsequently counterattacked.

2. By this time some Chichimecs, no longer necessarily nomad, were probably settled within the frontiers of empire, not unlike the Goths who had become established behind the Danube in late Roman times. Some of these, ostensibly loyal to Tollan, were "invited" to lend a helping hand to the hard-pressed Tolteca-Chichimecas of Cholula. Scenting the possibility of rich rewards to be derived from the fertile Puebla-Tlaxcala Valley, a true promised land in comparison with their own bleaker surroundings, they made massive incursions in that direction. They did not all go to Cholula, but dispersed to different destinations. One group, led by Mixcoatl-Totepeuh, whose personal name was probably Mazatzin, went and occupied Poyauhtlan, as well as Culhuacán, Tenayuca, and other parts of the Valley of Mexico.

3. In perhaps A.D. 1166, the correct equivalent of 5 Calli, some of these people, under the leadership of Mixcoatl's son Topiltzin, returned upon their tracks, and Topiltzin succeeded in making himself the principal ruler of Tollan, assuming the title of Quetzalcoatl. A phase of revival and resuscitation ensued in Tollan; however, its duration proved to be short, as an internal conflict burst out between Ce Acatl-Topiltzin and the members of the "establishment" of Tollan, led by Huemac, who had meanwhile succeeded to the headship of one of the ruling dynasties and was probably himself a Nonoalca. The situation was further aggravated by continued Chichimec pressure from the northwest as additional groups moved in, as well as by incursions by peoples based upon the Gulf Coast, including the Huaxtecs, who fell upon the ailing polity. Both Topiltzin and his rival Huemac fell victim to such stresses, and the former was driven out and retired, probably not to Tlillan Tlapallan, as legend required, but to the Valley of Mexico, following the dictates of expediency. Huemac followed and also met his end in that area.

4. Toltec power then finally collapsed—I suggest in 1175 or, in any case, not later than 1179. A major proportion of the population then left the city; the Nonoalcas retired to the Tehuacán-Teotitlán region, and certain other Toltecs to different destinations, as described above. A phantom ruler, named by the *Anales de Cuauhtitlán* and the *Memorial Breve* as Matlacxochitl, may have continued to reign in Tollan, but even if the city survived in somewhat reduced form under this ruler, its empire had surely succumbed.

5. Culhuacán continued to play its part as a center of limited Toltec power. Tollan-Xicocotitlan itself also survived as an inhabited place, as more Otomís moved in. Later, it again increased in size, becoming invested with a certain aura of sanctity under the Aztec Empire.

Such an account of the fate of Tollan may seem pedestrian, by comparison with the poignant surviving elegies relating stories of ghastly portents, mephistopholean temptations, departures on serpent rafts, and final apotheosis in planetal form. These, one cannot, alas! treat as part of history.

Each part of the story, as related by the sources, tends to present a dual aspect: first, the factual or historical basis, and then superimposed, the religious or mythical overlay, more apt for the uplift of future generations. Mixcoatl and Topiltzin-Quetzalcoatl, human beings also endowed with more ordinary names, become immortalized and were famed as gods; the strictly human conflict between Huemac and Topiltzin is thus elevated to a divine plane, as a struggle between the gods Quetzalcoatl and Tezcatlipoca, re-echoing their primordial and eternal strife, reflected in the creation of the successive worlds of Mesoamerica. The two human beings Huemac and Topiltzin are then finally assigned mythical endings in legendary places.

Actual events connected with Tollan's end may have occurred on a less sublime level than the sagas relate. The city was not built in a day, nor did it fall so quickly. Compared to its relatively limited total life span, the agony of Toltec decline may have been relatively prolonged.

But if the story is involved, its import is nonetheless dramatic. Tollan Xicocotitlan had kept alight the lamps of civilization for two centuries and had reunited the central nucleus of Mesoamerica after a period of divided influences following the fall of Teotihuacán. Centrifugal forces were now again to predominate in the epoch of the separate principalities, which divided Tollan's rule from that of Tenochtitlan. Tollan's fall indeed left a gaping power vacuum; friction was rife and power was shared between warring city-states.

Two more centuries were to elapse before first the Tepanecs and then the Aztecs were to begin anew the reunifying process. The Toltec achievement was notable, but like many human endeavors, relatively short-lived. However, great traditions remained, again to become fully manifest in the ecumenical empire of the Aztecs, who were proud to call themselves Culhuas and to claim the Toltec heritage as their own.

Just as, in the realm of the imagination, a resurrected Topiltzin-Quetzalcoatl shone to eternity as the Morning Star, so too in the world of human action the glory that was Tollan lived on as a vital force.

9. Some Conclusions

Our study of Toltec fact and fable is now almost complete, and it may be useful to end by reviewing conclusions already reached and by seeking to draw a few more.

Archaeological research has made sufficient strides to offer far more guidance to present-day investigators than to those of, say, half a century ago. At the same time it would be useless to deny that its contribution to Toltec problems is still hedged by limitations, including the absence of well-defined periods in architecture and pottery and the lingering uncertainties on the vital question of Tollan's population. Equally lacking as yet is enough detailed material evidence of what might have occurred at the close of Tollan's period of greatness and during the ensuing interlude before it became an Aztec city. The sources talk of total abandonment at the time, but the archaeological verdict still remains open.

In dealing with the written documents, we have also been confronted with ever-present lacunae; information is almost entirely lacking on Tollan's middle period, between its rise and fall. Furthermore, for its subsequent time of troubles many accounts survive, but they often contradict one another hopelessly. In such instances one is faced with several kinds of problems: first, that of one basic narrative related differently in each document, as in the case of the Mixcoatl saga;

secondly, the opposite tendency to fuse into one garbled whole several originally different stories, as in the reports concerning Huemac; and thirdly, an ever increasing awareness as one studies such records that the order in which incidents occur is often incorrect.

It is not now my intention to revert once more to the chronological problems of the Mixcoatl saga; but whatever the individual historian's point of view, by common consent *some* kind of interpolation has been made into certain accounts. Either episodes relating to the early Tula have been grafted on to reports of its end, or the reverse has occurred, since the apparent discrepancies can be explained in no other manner. As a result, it must be generally conceded that two distinct eras are at times treated as one. Our task therefore is not only to determine whether certain reports are in themselves factual, but to decide to which part of Toltec history they really belong.

As has been amply demonstrated, the picture is further confused by the tendency to present Tollan simultaneously on two levels, the human and the divine, the worldly and the ethereal. To the Aztecs it was thus both an earthly city, not so far distant from Tenochtitlan itself, and also a mythical place of wonder, originally replete with structures encrusted with jade or even covered with feathers. Exactly in the same manner, in the Middle Ages men could think simultaneously not only of the Jerusalem of this world that had been the object of a number of crusades, but also of the heavenly Jerusalem, the bride of Christ, with its gates of pearl and its ramparts made of jewels.

In disentangling as best one can the one from the other, and in adding to this interpretation of the sources the increasing volume of available archaeological information, it has proved possible to arrive at a coherent if tentative reconstruction, in particular concerning three points mentioned at the very beginning of our studies.

1. Quite apart from the heavenly Tollan, its earthly counterpart is based upon the general concept of *toltecayotl*, and should be envisaged at three levels: the primordial Toltecs of Teotihuacán, the inventors of all wisdom and the very creators of the arts and sciences (most of which of course possess earlier origins); the Early Postclassic Toltecs of Tollan Xicocotitlan, the founders of an incipient empire at the dawn of a new age of militarist conquests; and finally the Late Postclassic

Toltecs of Cholula and elsewhere, now become great artists and craftsmen and the epitome of all that is most delicate and refined in Mesoamerica.

2. An empire was indeed conquered by the Early Postclassic Toltecs of Tollan Xicocotitlan. It was, however, of more modest proportions than has at times been suggested, because of certain limitations which will again be summarized below. An attempt has been made in Chapter 7 to offer tentative boundaries for such a domain.

3. It has been seen that the appellation of "Quetzalcoatl" and even of "Topiltzin" grew to be a title more than an individual name. If there was not a continuous succession of persons who held that office, then at least there were several in the course of Toltec history. Previous arguments as to whether a Topiltzin was present at the foundation of Tollan or at its fall thus appear in somewhat altered perspective, and the controversy loses some of its force.

The complex question of the birth, or creation, of new deities has also been considered. Nothing can be proved, but one cannot altogether discard the possibility that in the case of the "new" Quetzalcoatl, but not necessarily of other gods, the very personalized legend may have owed its inspiration to the life story of a human hero. It has been argued in this work that if such a person indeed existed, then he is much more likely to have belonged to the period of Teotihuacán III, with its cataclysmic ending, than to Teotihuacán IV or later. Individuals named Topiltzin or Quetzalcoatl who lived after this era were thus basically priests or rulers, dedicated to an already dominant deity.

At all events, there is no denying the significance of this new or more personalized Quetzalcoatl, as graven on stone in Xochicalco, Tollan Xicocotitlan, and above all in Chichén. The extraordinary feat of Tollan in forming an apparent colony in Chichén may be partly due to some kind of religious proselytism, a feature not universally present among other Mesoamerican conquerors.

The complex problem of Tula-Chichén has also been examined; in broad outline it was concluded that if Chichén produced the craftsmanship, based on a long tradition of aesthetic achievement, it was due to Toltec notions that the spark was ignited that led to the new, or modified, style. The Toltecs may have borne to Chichén a new

Weltanschauung, together with certain broad architectural percepts, such as the great colonnades. In the Maya land these were then brought to fruition in forms that served to embellish Tollan as well as Chichén.

It has further been seen that in my opinion the Postclassic period in certain respects represents a radical departure from the more pacific or theocratic concepts of the Classic period, even if many gods, institutions, and customs were retained, the prevailing spirit is altered.

But changes do not occur overnight; they are perforce piecemeal and gradual, even if the final outcome or end product differs radically from the original or previous form. The religion of the Middle Ages had already been adopted in the time of the Late Roman Empire, and the basic type of social organization, feudalism, was already present in embryonic form in the great Roman estates into which the smaller farms had long since been merged. One cannot however suggest as a consequence that the Middle Ages, once their true genius developed, were nothing but a reflection of the later stages of the Classic, or ancient, world.

It may equally be argued that the seeds of the Mesoamerican Postclassic period were already sown in Teotithuacán, and that therefore Tollan represented no radical departure from already established norms. Moreover, it may be quite reasonable to suggest that the transition from Classic to Postclassic culture was never completed in Tollan Xicocotitlan, which represented in some respects an interim solution. On the one hand one finds there the full embodiment of the new spirit of militarism that was now abroad; in this it may justly be maintained that Mesoamerica was conforming, not to any rigid evolutionary laws, but at least to certain tendencies inherent among higher civilizations both of the Old World and the New. But just as in Mesopotamia the power of the temple only gradually gave way to that of the palace, so in Tollan we have observed that all signs of theocratic rule were not extinguished; moreover, collective or plural kingship may have persisted in forms reminiscent of Teotihuacán rather than of the single despotism more characteristic of Tepanec, Acolhua, and eventually Mexica rule.

Certain factors may help to explain any limitations to Toltec power; as a contributory element one may first cite this evidence for the continued presence of plural rule, ill-suited to the exigencies of the new age of militarism and conquest. Secondly, one faces an apparent failure of Tollan to establish a massive economic base as the leading commercial center of its day; it may be all very well to exact tribute as a means of securing abundance and surplus, but the evidence of Sahagún's Ninth Book and of the other sources show clearly that trade and tribute went hand in hand, and that the Aztec achievement was securely based on both these means of acquiring riches. Thirdly, to this one may add a certain lack of unity, a rock on which Tollan seems finally to have foundered; the two ethnic elements, which never wholly fused, went their own separate ways at the moment of final collapse.

As what may be termed a loose hydraulic state, relying on the ample flow of the River Tula, Tollan possessed the advantage of a secure ecological base for its economy. Notwithstanding this, its population never perhaps grew to proportions sufficient for conquest on a truly pan-Mesoamerican scale. Estimates tend to vary, but the true figure was at all events surely much smaller than that of Tenochtitlan. But possibly the real difference between the two lies more in the ability of the latter to draw upon the abundant military manpower of the whole Valley of Mexico, including a constellation of lakeside cities, that so impressed the Spaniards when they first beheld them. We have noted the presence near Tula of contemporary sites of limited proportions, apart from Tollan itself, but in mere population the Toltec Teotlalpan cannot remotely be compared with the Late Postclassic Valley of Mexico. Moreover even these abundant manpower resources were not sufficient in themselves to enable the Aztecs to establish control over a substantial part of Mesoamerica; the written sources bear ample witness to the recruitment of levies from the Valley of Toluca and the Valley of Morelos to swell the conquerors' ranks.

Accordingly, in its settlement plan, with a large urban center, but a relatively limited nearby rural population, Tollan also adhered more to the pattern of Teotihuacán than to that of Tenochtitlan. In certain respects our study of Tollan illustrates that the terms "Classic" and "Postclassic," which now form such an integral part of Mesoamerican terminology, may at times serve to mislead as much as to enlighten. Like most definitions, the distinction in question often appears too absolute. One would readily agree that between the apogee of Teotihuacán on the one hand and that of Tenochtitlan on the other, very great differences are discernible from many points of view. It may also be accepted that the fully developed spirit of militarism, already apparent in Tollan, led inevitably to further modifications of Mesoamerican patterns, which only later became manifest in Tenochtitlan, rather than in Tollan itself, and that such developments were the end product of processes already at work in Tollan.

That may all be very true, but it does not alter the fact that one tends thus to see Tollan as representing not the fully developed Postclassic domain, as embodied in the Aztec Empire, but a halfway house between Teotihuacán and Tenochtitlan. Admittedly, in Tollan militarism, usually taken as the principal characteristic that distinguishes the Postclassic from the Classic period, was not merely present but all-pervading. On the other hand, evidence is lacking of certain elements that were fundamental to the Aztec pattern of pan-Mesoamerican domination in the Late Postclassic period. Among these may again be cited the concentration of power in the hands of one ruler; a commercial pre-eminence used as an instrument of conquest; and a teeming population as a source of manpower in regions surrounding the metropolis. As representing the historic stage of universal conquest, one may thus detect a fairly marked difference between the Late Postclassic era and all that preceded it in Mesoamerica. To my way of thinking, the Early Postclassic period constitutes if anything an earlier stage on the road to ecumenical empire, perhaps conforming to that part of the process which Steward defines as "cyclical" or "regional" conquests.

The geographical location of Tollan also may have constituted a limiting factor, not for any lack of local natural resources but for its exposed situation vis-à-vis potential enemies. It may indeed be that the early Tollan faced greater dangers from its eastern neighbors; but if, as has been suggested on the basis of existing evidence, the northwestern frontier of Mesoamerica was already crumbling long before Tollan's own decline, then the latter must have become keenly exposed to infiltration and attack along an ill-defined border; the Toltecs, unlike the Chinese, constructed no Great Wall to ward off desert nomads and barbarians. Under such circumstances it is not unnatural that the center of gravity tended to shift back to the central part of the Valley of Mexico, which could later afford to treat the Teotlalpan as a kind of buffer zone against the encroaching nomad frontier.

It has at times been argued that mere nomad or seminomad Chichimecs could not have provoked the ruin of such a powerful polity as Tollan Xicocotitlan, notwithstanding a certain readiness by investigators to agree that Teotihuacán had previously fallen victim to Otomís and other less-developed peoples coming from the north.

But in other known cases this is precisely what did happen. History abounds in examples of how empires succumbed, not in wars against civilized adversaries, but to attacks of predatory nomads or desert barbarians. To quote only two examples: Egypt, as already mentioned, had fallen prey at the end of the Middle Kingdom to the incursions of the Hyksos; similarly, Palestine suffered a great nomad invasion in the last centuries of the second millennium B.C. that completely blotted out the preceding urban civilization.

It seems likely that internal dissensions, as in the subsequent instance of the Tepanec Empire, played a major part in the dissolution of Tollan. But as far as the enemy from without is concerned, the city was very possibly under constant pressure from a northwesterly direction long before its collapse. Its adversaries would have not been pure nomads, but rather "ex-Chichimecs," already quite well advanced on the road to civilization.

I have been at pains to insist that Tollan's decline may have been a gradual process. Empires tend to crumble fairly slowly; to the historian, examining the problem in retrospect, the signs of decay are usually apparent long before the end. Just as, over a period of centuries, barbarians penetrated Rome's imperial frontiers and even settled within its borders, so also, in the case of Tollan, its "soft" frontier on the Chichimec side became liable to infiltration.

An indication that the main foe was Chichimec rather than Huaxtec lies in the fact that it was the former, not the latter, who penetrated into the Valley of Mexico and beyond in the immediate post-Tollan era. In the final analysis, Tollan possessed too little unity, too few people, and insufficient wealth to withstand their incursions in the long run, even if it had offered a gallant resistance in the short.

This first attempt to reconstruct order in Central Mesoamerica after the Classic collapse was in itself a great achievement, even if the structure was never completed. It was left to the Aztecs, apt pupils of their Tepanec preceptors, to complete the task. Based upon the legacy of Tollan and inspired by the legends of its heroes, they were able to outpace their predecessors. With their destinies controlled by a more unitary monarchy and their war machine buttressed by an all-embracing and subservient commerce, they were able to realize the dream of universal conquest that may have eluded their hallowed forebears.

Appendix A: The Mixcoatl Saga

In this appendix is given in tabular, or horizontal, form the account of a story which I prefer to call the Mixcoatl saga. It concerns a leader of a Chichimec group called Mixcoatl (or Camaxtli or Totepeuh); together with a son called Topiltzin (or Ce Acatl or Quetzalcoatl), he ostensibly made conquests in the Valley of Mexico and beyond, having approached the area from a northwesterly direction.

References to his story occur in one form or another in seven sources. In addition, Torquemada's continuous narrative concerning Teochichimecs who settled for a time in Poyauhtlan, before founding Tlaxcala, presents certain parallels with the above-mentioned saga. But, since it omits some of the main incidents, it is not included in our table.

Because in many cases, as for instance the *Anales de Cuauhtitlán*, the saga occurs at the beginning of the document in question and contains certain references to a first ruler of Tollan and to early Toltecs, it has often been taken as generally constituting an account of Tollan's inception. This anomaly has been fully explained in Chapter 4, which concerns that period.

What is done in this appendix is to show, by a process of association, that the saga is more probably concerned with the end of Tollan, with only certain interpolations relating to the beginning.

The most conclusive part of the discussion is Table A itself, which illustrates the matter graphically. The notes are added by way of amplification; for the reader's convenience, in order to be able to consult both notes and table together, the former are placed first, before the table.

TABLE A: T

Episode	*Anales de Cuauhtitlán*	*Leyenda de los Soles*	*Historia de los Mexic*
1. Description of migrants and of their customs.	p. 4. Chichimecs without houses. Dressed in skins. Ate wild fruits, used arrows. p. 6. Emphasis on shooting, associated with directional colors. Shot jaguar.	p. 123. Emphasis on shooting of arrows of different colors. Shot jaguars.	p. 217. Chichimecs. A dicted to drunkenr
2. Place of departure or origin.	Chicomoztoc.		p. 219. Culhuacán.
3. Mention of Mixcoatl-Camaxtli, etc., as leader.	p. 1. Mixcoaxocóyotl (Mixcoatl the younger), Iztacmixcoatl, and also Mixcoatl.	p. 122–23. Mixcoatl mentioned as one of the five who fought the Mimixcoas.	p. 217. Camasale.
4. Places visited en route, in common between the sources.	p. 3. Mazatepec. p. 4. Macuexhuacan. p. 14. Cuauhnene Teoconpan.	p. 124. Comallan Teconma.	
5. Shooting or burning of Itzpapálotl.	p. 3. Itzpapálotl shot with arrows and burnt.	p. 124. Burning of Itzpapálotl.	
6. Killing of the Mimixcoas.	p. 3. Itzpapálotl ate the 400 Mimixcoas.	p. 123. Mixcoatl and four companions destroyed the 400 Mimixcoas.	p. 215. Tezcatlipoca (= Mixcoatl, *see* p 214) created 400 m and 5 women. The 400 men all died a 4 years.
7. Mention of Xiuhnel and Mimich.	p. 5. Xiuhnel became ruler of Cuauhtitlán when Mixcoamazatzin was made ruler of Tollan.	p. 123–24. Xiuhnel and Mimich pursued the two-headed deer.	p. 217. Camaxtli, Xiuhnel, and Mimi sole survivors of the 400 Chichimecs.
8. Pursuit of the two-headed deer.		p. 123. The two-headed deer descended and was pursued by Xiuhnel and Mimich.	p. 217. A two-headed deer fell down (fro heaven?). It becam Camaxtli's war emblem.
9. Parents of Ce Acatl-Topiltzin-Quetzalcoatl.	p. 7. Father, Totepeuh. p. 7. Mother, Chimaman. p. 10. Mother, Coacueye (Coatlicue).	p. 124. Father, Mixcoatl; mother, Chimalma. Was nurtured by Quilaztli and Cihuacoatl.	p. 217. Father, Cama: Mother, one of five women who surviv when the 400 Chic mecs were killed.
10. Birthplace of Ce Acatl-Topiltzin.		p. 124. Huitznáhuac.	p. 217. Cuitláhuac me tioned in previous p graph to that descr ing his birth.

XCOATL SAGA

ción de la ealogía	*Origen de los Mexicanos*	*Histoyre du Mechique*	*Muñoz Camargo, Historia de Tlaxcala*	*Historia Tolteca-Chichimeca*
41. Dressed in kins. Ate wild uits and ani- als. Much use f bow and rrow.	p. 257. Dressed in skins, etc. Use of bow and arrow.		p. 44. Called Chichimecas. Married only one wife.	p. 95. Described as Chichimecs, etc., as distinct from Tolteca-Chichimecas.
41. eoculhuacán.	p. 259. Teoculhuacán.			Chicomoztoc.
42. Leader, otehéb Totepeuh).	p. 261. Leader in Teoculhuacán was Totepev.	p. 35. Various mentions of Mixcoatl.	p. 40. Mixcoatl Camaxtli. p. 44. Mixcoatl one of 4 leaders.	p. 95. Mixcoatl included in list of Chichimec leaders who left Chicomoztoc.
			p. 39. Mazatepec. p. 40. Tepenene (Nenetepec?). Comayan (fighting took place). p. 45. Poyauhtlan. p. 40. Mimich killed Itzpapálotl with arrows in Tepenene.	p. 97. Mazatepec, Nenetepec, Comalla, Macuexhuacan, Tecaman, Poyauhtlan.
			p. 40. Xiuhnel left by Chichimecs in province of Mazatepec. p. 40. Mimich killed Itzpapálotl.	p. 95. Michia in list of Chichimec leaders. (*See* note 7.)
42. Father, otehéb Totepeuh).	p. 261. Father, Totepev.	p. 35. Father, Camaxtli; mother, Chimalma.	p. 40. Father, Mixcoatl Camaxtli. Mother, Coatlicue.	
42. Culhuacán.	p. 259. Culhuacán.	Nichatlanco.	p. 42. Province of Teohuitznáhuac.	

11. Killing of Atempanecatl.		p. 125. Ce Acatl killed his uncle Apanécatl, together with the latter's confederates Colton and Cuilton.	
12. Conquests of Ce Acatl-Topiltzin.		p. 124–25. Xihuacan, Ayotlan, Chalco, Xico, Cuixcoc, Çacanco, Tzonmolco, Tzapotlan, Acallan, Tlapallan.	p. 217. He became a g warrior.
13. Other leaders mentioned.	p. 6. Quahuícol. Nequametl. p. 7. Ihuitimal (= Tímal?). p. 12. Cuauhtli.	p. 124–25. Nequametl as one of four successors to Ce Acatl-Topiltzin as ruler of Tula.	
14. Arrival of Ce Acatl-Topiltzin at Tulancingo.	p. 7. Quetzalcoatl arrived in 2 Tochtli at Tulancingo from Pánuco.		
15. Ce Acatl-Topiltzin becomes ruler of Tollan.	p. 7. Quetzalcoatl became ruler of Tollan in 5 Calli.		p. 217. Ce Acatl was first ruler of Tollan
16. Immediate sequel to the Mixcoatl saga in each source.	p. 8. Legend of Quetzalcoatl's drunkenness and eventual flight to Tlillan Tlapallan.	p. 125. End of Tollan under Huemac.	p. 217. Ce Acatl led a all the *macehuales* (Tula. Went to Coz lán, Cholula, Cempoala, and Tlapalla

42. Topiltzin lled Atepanetl, his father's other-in-law.	p. 261. Topiltzin killed Apanécatl, his father's brother-in-law.			p. 95. Apanécatl mentioned, together with Cuitliz and Quauhtliztac, as being worshiped as gods.
			p. 45. Hueytlapatli, Pantzin, Cocoltzin. p. 42. Xicalan.	p. 95. Uetlapati, Cocoltzin. p. 100. Cocoltzin. p. 101. Xicallan. p. 72–3. Nequametl. p. 72. Timaltzin. p. 68–71. Cuauhtzin. p. 73. Pantzin.
43. Topiltzin rought his eople to Tulanngo.	p. 262. Topiltzin went to Tulancingo.	p. 35. Quetzalcoatl went to Tulancingo.	p. 41. Quetzalcoatl reported to have arrived at Tulancingo from Pánuco.	
43. Implies at Topiltzin as ruler of ollan.	p. 262. Some say Topiltzin was first ruler of Tollan, others not.		p. 41. Quetzalcoatl "had his house" in Tollan.	
43. Topiltzin ok away the ulhua people. ollan ended nder Huemac.	p. 262. The end of Tollan under Huemac.		p. 45. Story continued with Chichimecs who founded Tlaxcala.	p. 99–102. Story continued with the reconquest of Cholula with Chichimec help.

Notes to Table A

The numbers below correspond with the numbers assigned to incidents in Table A.

1. DESCRIPTION OF THE MIGRANTS

The *Anales de Cuauhtitlán* describe them as dressed in skins, eating wild fruits and even roots. Their children were carried in a kind of net, a typical Chichimec trait, illustrated by Sahagún. Considerable emphasis is placed in the *Anales de Cuauhtitlán* and the *Leyenda de los Soles* on their hunting activities and their continual use of bows and arrows. Muñóz Camargo confines himself to describing their family life; a man married one wife only, a trait often listed as a Chichimec characteristic in other accounts.

The *Relación de la Genealogía* also portrays the people in question as apparently pure Chichimec, before their departure from Teoculhuacán; they had no cotton, dressed in skins, and so on. This account, like Muñóz Camargo, mentions their matrimonial fidelity and stresses the use of bows and arrows. These Chichimecs joined forces, but seemingly in Culhuacán in the Valley of Mexico rather than their remote Teoculhuacán, with other groups of a far higher cultural level, who possessed a nobility, permanent buildings, and the like. The parallel account of the *Origen de los Mexicanos* gives the same data. As a god, moreover, Mixcoatl has essentially Chichimec traits. As Caso points out, he is represented in the Mixtec codices as armed with bow and arrow, whereas the other gods carry the *atlatl*. Quetzalcoatl himself, in the version of the *Histoyre du Mechique*, hides in a hole and comes out armed with bow and arrow. Beyer insists that Mixcoatl is a Chichimec god. Incidentally, he is often represented as wearing no *maxtatl*, surely a Huaxtec as well as a Chichimec trait.

In general, therefore, the typical traits of Teochichimecs are described. Their way of life is quite distinct from that of the Tolteca-Chichimecas as usually related, or for that matter from that of the early Mexicas, who from the start of their migration planted crops and erected buildings of a kind.

2. PLACE OF DEPARTURE

The *Anales de Cuauhtitlán* and Muñóz Camargo give Chicomoztoc as the place of departure, the *Historia de los Mexicanos* mentions Culhuacán, while the *Relación de la Genealogía* and the *Origen de los Mexicanos* speak of Teoculhuacán; this remote Teoculhuacán becomes quickly confused with the Culhuacán in the Valley of Mexico. The *Historia Tolteca-Chichimeca* describes how the Tolteca-Chichimecas under Icxicouatl and Quetzalteueyac went to Chicomoztoc to fetch the Chichimecs and bring them to Cholula.

Teoculhuacán, like Chicomoztoc, has many legendary connotations, and its possible location has given rise to much discussion. In certain sources, e.g., the *Memorial Breve*, the two are virtually synonymous or at least situated very close together. Both figure traditionally as points of departure for a whole host of migrants to Central Mesoamerica from a northwesterly direction, including of course the Mexicas.

3. THE LEADER

Mixcoatl in some form or another is mentioned in every single account, and in most he figures as the chief personage, or leader, of the migration.

In the *Anales de Cuauhtitlán*, this leader is called initially Iztac Mixcoatl or Mixcoacoyotl, as well as plain Mixcoatl. The Mixcoamatzin subsequently referred to in this source as inaugurating the dynasty of Tollan is in our opinion intended as the same person; the latter was in fact not the first ruler of Tollan, but the founder of a new (Chichimec) dynasty in Culhuacán and Tollan; this is clarified from the chronological point of view in Appendix B. Mixcoatl is also referred to in this part of the *Anales* as a "*diablo*," thus underlining the tendency throughout to confuse gods and men.

Mixcoatl is included in the account of the *Historia de los Mexicanos* and is more usually called Camaxtli; however, in the related versions of the *Relación de la Genealogía* and the *Origen de los Mexicanos*, Topiltzin's father and the ruler of the "Culhuas" is not Mixcoatl but Totepeuh. Jiménez Moreno has already suggested that they are one and the same person; our discussion on rulers in Appendix B confirms this point. The *Anales de Cuauhtitlán*, moreover, while naming Mixcoatl as the Chichimec leader, also give Totepeuh, not Mixcoatl, as the father of Topiltzin. Thus opinions are somewhat equally divided between Mixcoatl and Totepeuh as the name of Topiltzin's father.

4. PLACES VISITED EN ROUTE TO THE VALLEY OF MEXICO, COMMON TO SEVERAL SOURCES

Various names are cited, particularly in the detailed route of the *Historia Tolteca-Chichimeca*. Table A confines itself to those in common between the various sources, in order to illustrate their interconnection in this respect.

In both the *Anales de Cuauhtitlán* and in Muñóz Camargo, the Chichimecs first visit Mazatepec, after leaving Chicomoztoc. This place is also mentioned in the *Historia Tolteca-Chichimeca.* (For identification of many place names in this source, see Kirchhoff's map in his prologue to the Heinrich Berlin edition.) In the *Anales de Cuauhtitlán*, the action of this part of the story takes place in the Cuauhtitlán area; Huehuetocan is mentioned and Macuexhuacan, which in another passage in the same document implicitly lies near to Cuauhtitlán.

As Kirchhoff pointed out, comparing the *Leyenda de los Soles*, the *Historia Tolteca-Chichimeca*, and Muñóz Camargo, the following places as can be seen from Table A are mentioned in at least two of the three sources as lying on the Chichimec route: Mazatepec, Nenetépec (Tepenene?), and Comalla (or Comallan); Tecama and Teconma may also be the same. In addition, the *Anales de Cuauhtitlán* also included Mazatepec and, in a somewhat different context, refer to Teoconpan and Cuauhnene (Nenetépec?).

There is a rancho called Mazatepec in the Municipio of Zempoala, Hidalgo; however, perhaps a more likely identification is that of Jiménez Moreno, who equates Mazatepec with the modern Tefani, to the southwest of Actopan. T'öfani in Otomí means "The Hill of the Deer" as does Mazatepec in Nauhuatl. Jiménez Moreno also locates Comallan on the border of the States of Mexico and Hidalgo, to the southeast of Pachuca. In addition, there does exist a S. Pedro Cuamatla, a hacienda in the Municipio of Cuauhtitlán; the location fits but the root is not of course identical. Tepenene still exists to the southeast of Actopan and some way northeast of Tula, and there also is still to be found a Tecompa, a rancho of the municipality of Tultepec, just to the southeast of Cuauhtitlán, which may well be the Teconma, or Teocompan, mentioned in the texts. Alternatively, these might be the same as Tecama, a place which continues to exist to the southeast of Tepenene on the road from Actopan to Pachuca.

In the *Leyenda de los Soles* it is actually stated that Mixcoatl fought a battle in Comallan, but other sources merely mention that his followers passed through there. In certain accounts the journey seems to end in Huitznahuac or Teohuitznahuac, given as the birthplace of Ce Acatl-Topiltzin-Quetzalcoatl. These latter locations will be discussed under this heading.

5 & 6. THE SHOOTING WITH ARROWS OF ITZPAPÁLOTL, DIRECTIONAL COLORS, AND SO ON

This rather singular incident occurs in the *Anales de Cuauhtitlán* and Muñóz Camargo. In the former source, the Chichimecs at the beginning of their journey fall under the power of Itzpapálotl, who eats the four hundred Mimixcoas. Iztac Mixcoatl shoots Itzpapálotl with arrows and kills her; she is then burnt. Thus begins the calendar.

In the *Leyenda de los Soles*, Itzpapálotl is simply burnt, and from her ashes spring multicolored flints. Mixcoatl then bears the white flint on his journey as his own deity, Itzpapálotl. In Muñóz Camargo she is killed by arrows by Mimich, another semidivine leader. (*See* below.)

As Seler emphasized, Itzpapálotl is of course par excellence the Chichimec goddess, just as Mixcoatl is the Chichimec god. There are even certain common traits between the adornments of the two deities. Shooting with arrows is partly a Chichimec form of human sacrifice, though not confined to these people, as it was also used for victims of Xipe Totec, among others.

Apparently some form of human sacrifice is intended by this story—possibly the offering of victims to Itzpapálotl, who were dressed as the goddess herself. Perhaps these were captives taken in the fighting which took place on the journey, e.g., in Comallan, to which we have already referred. (Itzpapálotl occasionally figures in the codices as a masculine deity.)

Killing the god or goddess might at first sight appear strange, but it is really a common Mesoamerican notion, since, in general terms, sacrificial victims became identified with the god before death, and therefore in a sense the god or goddess *was* killed.

Apart from the ritual immolation of Itzpapálotl, the *Anales de Cuauhtitlán* mentions the shooting of the serpent, the jaguar, the rabbit, and the deer; shooting toward the east, the animals thus hunted are described as green in color, to the north they are white, to the west yellow, and to the south red. The same incident is mentioned in another passage; these same animals, each with the same respective directional colors, are referred to as gods. And indeed, all these four creatures have close associations with different deities.

The directional shooting of arrows seems to have been a widespread symbolic gesture. Thus one hears that on his accession an omukama of Bunyoro in western Uganda would ceremoniously "shoot the nations" by firing arrows to the four points of the compass.

The *Leyenda de los Soles* also refers to the killing of a jaguar. When this source tells of the slaying of Itzpapálotl, out of her ashes sprout the above-mentioned flints of green, white, red, and black, again obviously directional colors, if slightly different on this occasion. The connection with sacrifice, presumably human, is again in this source made clear by reference to giving nourishment to the sun, an expression also occurring in other accounts. Perhaps these "animals" who were shot were really warriors in animal guise, caught and sacrificed. A similar expression is found in the *Historia de los Mexicanos* (page 216), which actually refers to eagles and also mentions the giving of hearts to the sun to eat.

In the *Leyenda de los Soles* (page 123) the names of Mixcoatl's three brothers and one sister are given; in the *Historia de los Mexicanos,* what are presumably the same four men and one woman are mentioned, but this time as the children of Mixcoatl. In both accounts they take refuge in a tree, and in both they become intoxicated. These two versions of the incident thus clearly emanate from the same common source. The *Leyenda de los Soles* gives the names as Apantecuctli, Cuetlachcihuatl, Tlotepe, and Quauhtliconcuauh. The *Historia Tolteca-Chichimeca* has a curious reference to Apanecatl, Cuitliz, and Quauhtliztac, who were revered as gods. The two sets of names are perhaps too similar for a mere coincidence.

7. XIUHNEL AND MIMICH

These two semidivine or mythical beings are mentioned in almost all accounts. In the *Anales de Cuauhtitlán* they are called Chichimec rulers, along with Mixcoatl; Xiuhnel in this source becomes ruler of Cuauhtitlán. In the *Leyenda de los Soles* they figure as chasing the two-headed deer. (*See* note 8.) In the *Historia de los Mexicanos,* Xiuhnel, Mimich, and Mixcoatl-Camaxtli were the only survivors of an encounter with the four hundred Chichimecs (or Mixcoas). In Muñóz Camargo, as in the *Anales de Cuauhtitlán,* Xiuhnel is left behind in the early part of the journey, this time in Mazatepec; according to this version, Mimich kills Itzpapálotl. There is no Xiuhnel in the *Historia Tolteca-Chichimeca,* but a Michia occurs among a long list of Chichimec leaders who came out of Chicomoztoc. Michia seems to be a probable corruption of Michin, deriving from the same root as Mimich.

8. THE TWO-HEADED DEER

This peculiar incident occurs in different forms in the *Leyenda de los Soles* and the *Historia de los Mexicanos* only. As previously mentioned, the *Anales de Cuauhtitlán* refers to the hunting of deer in more general terms.

In the *Leyenda de los Soles,* after the passage cited above, where the four brothers and one sister kill the four hundred Mimixcoas, we are told of the descent (from the sky) of two deer, each having two heads. Xiuhnel and Mimich pursue them; the deer are then converted into women. Xiuhnel sleeps with one and then eats her; the other is pursued by Mimich, who shoots arrows at her.

In the *Historia de los Mexicanos* one deer with two heads descends; Mixcoatl Camaxtli instructs the people of Cuitláhuac to take it as their god. He himself uses it as an emblem in his war with neighbors. In a subsequent passage, the same source explains that Quilaztli, also described as the deity of Xochimilco, was the deer of Mixcoatl.

Quilaztli is clearly another name for Cihuacoatl; the latter is described in the *Cihuacoatl icuic* as the deer of Culhuacán (Seller, II, 1050). Cihuacoatl was the goddess of Culhuacán. Torquemada, incidentally, describes Quilaztli, whom he equates with Cihuacoatl, as the sister of Mixcoatl and Mimich, to whom she appeared as an eagle. Xiuhnel and Mimich are also themselves in another context referred to as being deer, i.e., probably dressed in deer costume.

In fact, Quilaztli seems to be a kind of hybrid such as we often find in Mesoamerican mythology—in this case part deer and part bird. Besides possessing the form of a deer, she descends from the sky, perches in a tree, and is also mentioned as being dressed in feathers.

The deer is of course a very important Indian symbol. It is generally connected with sun, fire, sky beings, and shamans. As Peter Furst points out, among the Huicholes it is the shaman's spirit helper and companion; certain gods are deer and vice versa.

As to the two-headed version of the animal, in the *Codex Borbonicus* (Plate 21) Oxomoco and Cipactonal are figures surmounted by two deer heads. A fragment of a palace mural in Mitla also depicts a two-headed deer. Seler draws attention to the mention in the *Anales de Cuauhtitlán* of Xiuhnel as priest of the God of Fire. He points out that the deer was connected with fire. The two-headed deer appears for Seler to have some connection with Quaxolotl, the two-headed deity in turn connected with Xantico, the fire goddess of Xochimilco. Lehmann says that Quahxolotl and Xantico are the same.

The whole apparent association therefore of the deer, and more specifically the two-headed deer in this context, is with fire in the first place, and secondly with the Culhuacán region, not only Culhuacán itself but equally the neighboring and ethnically related cities of Cuitláhuac and Xochimilco, the patron deity of the latter being actually the Goddess of Fire.

The deer is also connected with Mixcoatl; in a passage concerning the Mexica migration, the *Historia de los Mexicanos* refers to "the mantle and the deerskin of Mixcoatl." The *Codex Borgia* actually depicts a white-headed and white-bearded god wearing a deer-head mask; Seler explains in his commentary that this is Iztac Mixcoatl, or the old Mixcoatl, white being symbolic of cloud. Seler also illustrates a Teotihuacán vessel with a portrait of a bearded god in a deer-head mask (V, 581). One wonders if the older Iztac Mixcoatl has a longer past, even if Mixcoatl as deity of the Chichimecs is perhaps rightly described as a fairly "new" god. But Iztac Mixcoatl is surely merely a variant of Mixcoatl, and not to be differentiated. Many other references occur to Iztac Mixcoatl, e.g., in Motolinía. A "white," or "old," version of several other gods is on record, such as Iztaccenteotl and Iztacchalchiuhtlicue. Motolinía's Iztac Mixcoatl is a kind of father figure who engenders the future generations of men, who descend from his sons, compared by the author with the sons of Noah.

Jiménez Moreno takes this as further evidence that Mixcoatl and so on are pre- and not post-Tollan. But it has to be noted that the actual sons in question include Tenoch, progenitor of the Mexicas, a basically post-Toltec people. Moreover, one of the sons is Xelhua, and Motolinía relates how he peopled Cozcatlán, Tehuacán, and so on, a story that indisputably belongs to the Toltec diaspora. Nor would we indeed dispute the possibility of a human Mixcoatl having existed at the inception of Tollan, just as we have discovered another human Topiltzin, or Ce Acatl, belonging probably to that period; the Mixcoatl-Topiltzin combination is a tradition or concept just as much as a historic fact, and as such transferable from one era to another.

Seler states that Cihuacoatl is also the equivalent of Itzpapálotl. If that were always so, then the deer incident and the shooting of Itzpapálotl would be one and the same occurrence. Moreover, in Muñóz Camargo, Mimich is described as killing Itzpapálotl, while in the *Leyenda de los Soles* he shoots one of the two-headed deer. Similarly, in one account Mixcoatl takes as his personal deity the white flint that sprang from the ashes of Itzpapálotl, and in another he adopts the two-headed deer.

However, the shooting of Itzpapálotl is specifically connected with places such as Tepenene and Mazatepec, lying on the Chichimec route to the Valley of Mexico, and may refer to encounters with other tribes during the journey. The two-headed-deer incident, on the other hand, is more related to the region of Culhuacán and would seem to imply the conquest of places in that area. Mixcoatl is stated in the *Historia de los Mexicanos* to have married the ruler of that place. Unlike Itzpapálotl, par excellence the Chichimec goddess, encountered in the open country, Cihuacoatl is the goddess of more urban peoples and is particularly connected with the Chinampa region of Culhuacán.

9. THE PARENTS OF CE ACATL-TOPILTZIN-QUETZALCOATL

In the *Anales de Cuauhtitlán*, Topiltzin's father is Totepeuh and his mother "Chimaman." In another context in the same *Anales*, Quetzalcoatl speaks of his mother as Coatlicue. It has already been pointed out that

Totepeuh and Mixcoatl are the same person. Also, Coatlicue is to be identified with Cihuacoatl; Sahagún, incidentally, calls Coatlicue the wife of Mixcoatl (1 : 204). Chimalma in turn is basically another personification of Cihuacoatl, as also is Quilaztli. Motolinía refers to Chimalma as "a mother of the peoples"; as a kind of mother figure, she also figures among the guardians of Huitzilopochtli during the Mexica migration.

In the *Leyenda de los Soles*, Mixcoatl is Topiltzin's father and Chimalma his mother; they meet in Huitznahuac. Mixcoatl shoots Chimalma with arrows four times. She dies after Topiltzin is born, and he is brought up by Quilaztli and Cihuaccatl, a somewhat confused story, since the two latter are really the same person as Chimalma. What is interesting about this version is the mention of shooting with arrows; it seems somehow to be connected with the shooting of the two-headed deer; both seem to represent the conquest of the Culhuacán region by Mixcoatl and his forces.

I have already mentioned the reference in the *Cihuacoatl icuic* to the "deer of Culhuacán." This connection between the goddess and the city is confirmed by the version of Muñóz Camargo; it states that in Teohuitznahuac, in the province of Culhuacán, Mixcoatl's Chichimecs "wanted to shoot with arrows and kill a lady called Coatlicue, but they did not shoot her and rather made friends with her and Mixcoatl Camaxtli took her as his wife, and of him Quetzalcoatl was born." This again is a reference to the occupation of the Culhuacán region and again a mention of Coatlicue as Quetzalcoatl's mother. The *Origen de los Mexicanos* and the *Relación de la Genealogía* simply mention Totepeuh as Topiltzin's father.

The legendary or divine nature of Topiltzin-Quetzalcoatl's reported parentage hardly needs stressing. There is no reason, however, to suppose that Totepeuh Mixcoatecuhtli was not originally a human being, even if he later became confused with the god Mixcoatl. The same applies to Topiltzin's mother, not a Chichimec, but a native and probably a princess of the region where he was born, and where Coatlicue/Cihuacoatl, with whom she came to be identified, was specially revered under a number of different names.

10. QUETZALCOATL'S BIRTHPLACE

The *Leyenda de los Soles* and Muñóz Camargo say that he was born in Huitznahuac or Teohuitznahuac. (For probable location, *see* note 12.) In the *Historia de los Mexicanos* it is clear that he was born in the Valley of Mexico (Cuitláhuac is mentioned just previously to this event).

The only alternative version is given in the *Histoyre du Mechique*, which says that Quetzalcoatl was born in Nichatlanco, possibly a corruption of Michatlauhco. The place is not identifiable.

11. THE KILLING OF ATEMPANECATL

In the *Leyenda de los Soles* the four hundred Mixcoas are described as uncles of Ce Acatl and by implication brothers of his father Mixcoatl Camaxtli. Also specifically named as his uncles are Apanecatl, Colton, and Cuilton. In this version, these three killed Mixcoatl and in turn Ce Acatl killed them all.

This story is repeated in different forms by other sources. The *Relación de la Genealogía* and the *Origen de los Mexicanos* refer to the killing of "Atepanecate" by Topiltzin; they are described as brothers-in-law. The *Historia de los Mexicanos* refers to Mixcoatl as being killed by his own sons, not brothers.

Investigators have tended to associate this incident with a probably different story, the rivalry of Topiltzin and Huemac, which is referred to in much detail in many sources. But the killing of Atempanecatl seems to be a separate and previous incident, which took place in the Culhuacán area; the struggle between Huemac and Topiltzin is situated invariably in Tollan. Mention in the *Anales de Cuauhtitlán* of Atecpanecatl as a title of the ruler Huemac has led to the former being taken for the same person as Huemac. But Atecpanecatl is a traditional title, also, incidentally, used much later by the great Tlacaélel. The whole question of Huemac, including his dates, is discussed in Appendix B and Chapter 8.

12. THE CONQUESTS OF CE ACATL TOPILTZIN

Apart from a single mention in the *Historia de los Mexicanos* of how Ce Acatl began to make war, this story is confined to the *Leyenda de los Soles*. It has often been taken as a kind of preliminary conquest of empire by the early Toltecs, ranging from Guerrero to the Mixteca. I find it impossible to interpret the relative passage in the *Leyenda de los Soles* in this way. Not only do I see these conquests as occurring at the end of the period of Tollan's greatness, but as being of much more limited scope. The idea that a young Ce Acatl should have ranged far and wide conquering an area not subdued by the Aztecs before the reign of Ahuítzotl, and that he should have done this before he even became ruler in Tollan or possessed a properly established capital as a base, seems hard to accept.

First, in the *Leyenda de los Soles*, Ce Acatl is born in Huitznahuac (Teohuitznahuac in other sources). Kirchhoff has placed this near Texcoco, and in effect there exists a barrio of this name in the village of Chiauhtla, four kilometers to the north of Texcoco. It should also be remembered that in the reign of Techotlalatzin, immigrants came from the Cerro de la Estrella near Culhuacán to Texcoco, some of whom were called Huitznahuacas and who gave their name to a barrio in Texcoco (Ixtlilxóchitl 11:74). One cannot help therefore suspecting that in early Toltec times the name Huitznahuac is more to be associated with Culhuacán, the place from which these people later emigrated, than with Texcoco, to which they went. The *Historia de los Mexicanos* describes Huitznahuac as situated in the province of Culhuacán.

Muñóz Camargo recounts how Mixcoatl and his Chichimecs who arrived in the Valley of Mexico also went and established themselves in Poyauhtlan, or Poyauhtitlan, as he also calls it. Kirchhoff places this on his map in the *Historia Tolteca-Chichimeca* to the southwest of Tepetlaoztoc and north of Amecameca. On the 1:500,000 survey map, a Pautitlan is still to be found just to the southwest of the existing lake of Texcoco.

The point of departure for Ce Acatl's conquests is ostensibly Huitznahuac. The list is given with identifications where possible and grouped into what appear to be the correct categories:

Xihuacan. This, the first place mentioned after Huitznahuac, cannot today be identified. There is indeed a Xihuacan on the coast of Guerrero to which reference is made in the *Suma de Visitas*. Seler and Jiménez Moreno have favored this as the Xihuacan in question; to me the likelihood of that being correct seems remote. Jiménez Moreno links this excursion with a possible conquest of Pochutla on the coast of Oaxaca (Pochtlan is mentioned as a conquest of Mixcoatl between his fighting in Huehuetocan and his conquering Huitznahuac). Pochotlan, or Pochutla, is admittedly the same root as Pochtlan, but it is a very common name; e.g., there is a Poxtla near Ayapango, northwest of Amecameca. Mixcoatl's conquests, already discussed in note 4, are in the main identifiable as places in the vicinity of and to the north of the Valley of Mexico.

Ayotlan/Chalco/Xico. There is also an Ayotla on the coast of Guerrero. However, there is a place of that name in the municipality of Ixtapaluca, near Chalco and Xico, and this would clearly seem to be the correct identification, in view of the context. Chalco and Xico themselves need no identification, and these three names clearly form a composite group of nearby centers.

Cuixcoc/Zacanco. Cuixcoc is not identifiable on the map. A place of that name is mentioned by Chimalpain in conjunction with Temimilolco and Teotenango. Kirchhoff, equating it with a Cuixcocingo in a Colonial document, places it west of Teotenango (today Tenango del Valle) (*Toltekenreich*, 254). Jiménez Moreno identifies Cuixcoc as lying southeast of Teloloapan. But there is a village of Zacango in the municipality of Villa Guerrero, southwest of Tenango del Valle, as well as an hacienda in the municipality of Calimaya in the same district. I therefore identify Cuixcoc and Zacanco as more probably both situated in the Valley of Toluca and not too far from Culhuacán.

Tzonmolco/Mazatzongo. Jiménez Moreno identifies Mazatzongo as lying near Teotitlán del Valle; there is also a Tzomolco to the west of Teotitlán. I therefore identify these two places as lying in this region, which is identified with the final place of refuge of the Nonoalcas.

Tzapotlan. A frequent name which could therefore be almost anywhere. There is one near Cempoala on the coast of Veracruz. There is also a barrio of Atenco, in the state of Mexico, of that name, as well as a barrio of Tulancingo. However, since one is at this stage seemingly concerned with the story of the flight of Quetzalcoatl to Tlillan Tlapallan, I would favor the Gulf Coast identification; there are other reports of his visiting Quiahuiztlan on the way to Tlillan Tlapallan.

Acallan/Tlapallan. Traditional destinations of Ce Acatl-Topiltzin when he fled eastward. It may be noted that the last three groups of "conquests" mentioned correspond exactly to the places to which, at the end of Tollan, Ce Acatl took away all the *macehuales* of Tula, according to the *Historia de los Mexicanos*, namely, the "province of Cempoala, Cozcatlán, and Tonalá."

13. OTHER PERSONAGES MENTIONED IN CONNECTION WITH MIXCOATL AND TOPILTZIN

Recognizably similar names tend to recur and repeat themselves in different sources, apart from Mixcoatl, Xiuhnel, and Mimich, already mentioned as occuring in the majority.

Reference has also already been made to similarity in names between Mixcoatl's fellow warriors against the Mimixcoas in the *Leyenda de los Soles* and another series of Chichimec leaders mentioned in the *Historia Tolteca-Chichimeca*.

Above all, Muñóz Camargo, whose account is on the whole linked closely to certain incidents in that of the *Leyenda de los Soles*, on the other hand gives many names which coincide with those of the *Historia Tolteca-Chichimeca*, as Kirchhoff has already pointed out. Muñóz Camargo tells how Mixcoatl and his Chichimecs first arrived in Poyauhtlan, and subsequently Ce Acatl-Quetzalcoatl was born in Teohuitznahuac. Thus the visit to Poyauhtlan and the conquest of Teohuitznahuac form part of one story.

The names given by Muñóz Camargo as those of leaders associated with Mixcoatl in Poyauhtlan are Huetlapatli, Pantzin, and Cocoltzin, plus a woman called Xonecuilinam. But in the *Historia Tolteca-Chichimeca*, among the long list of Chichimec leaders who come out of Chicomoztoc, not only does Mixcoatl figure, but also included are a Uetlapati and a Cocoltzin (page 95). A Pantzin is mentioned in another context (page 100). Xicalan, referred to by Muñóz Camargo as offering great festivities to honor the birth of Quetzalcoatl, figures in the *Historia Tolteca-Chichimeca* in another list of Chichimec leaders who actually reached Cholula (page 101).

The sequel of their doings in the Valley of Mexico, in which the Chichimecs of Mixcoatl eventually leave Poyauhtlan, according to the story of Muñóz Camargo, follow closely the pattern of the *Historia Tolteca-Chichimeca*; even Icxicohuatl and Quetzalteueyac, who figure so prominently in the latter source, also figure in the former.

14 & 15. THE ARRIVAL OF TOPILTZIN-QUETZALCOATL AT TULANCINGO AND HIS ELEVATION TO THE THRONE OF TOLLAN

It is considered that this is a pre-Tollan interpolation in a post-Tollan story. This matter is fully discussed in Chapter 4, dealing with the beginnings of Tollan. The reference in the *Historia de los Mexicanos* and other sources to Topiltzin becoming first ruler of Tollan is rather obscure, since after this statement one passes immediately to events related to the end of the city.

All sources except the *Leyenda de los Soles* and the *Historia Tolteca-Chichimeca* (which lacks this interpolation) mention the arrival of Quetzalcoatl at Tulancingo. The *Anales de Cuauhtitlán* say that he came from Pánuco, and Muñóz Camargo also gives a report to that effect, as does Torquemada.

In Chapter 4 it is fully explained why it is considered that such a person did exist—totally distinct from Topiltzin, son of Mixcoatl—and was one of several collective leaders of the Nonoalcas who came from the Huaxteca to Tollan via Tulancingo.

16. THE IMMEDIATE SEQUEL TO THE MIXCOATL SAGA

Most accounts—namely, the *Anales de Cuauhtitlán*, the *Leyenda de los Soles*, the *Historia de los Mexicanos* and related sources—continue the story by dealing with the traditional account of the end of Tollan, the temptation of Quetzalcoatl by Huemac, his drunkenness, and so on. Only Muñóz Camargo and the *Historia Tolteca-Chichimeca* continue to devote themselves to Chichimec events, the one in Tlaxcala and the other in Cholula. The first-mentioned sources, after dealing with the end of Tollan, the flight to Tlillan Tlapallan, and so on, turn to the story of the dynasty founded by Ce Acatl-Topiltzin in Tollan and Culhuacán, of which more is told in Chapter 8 and Appendix B.

Appendix B: Problems of Chronology

THE PROBLEMS which one faces where Tollan's chronology is concerned are most difficult to resolve, because of the relative scarcity of data and its contradictory nature. One can do little more than set out the available information and make of it the best sense possible, with a view to establishing at least a tentative chronological system. It must however be emphasized that any attempted solution is beset with severe limitations, since, as will become apparent, in this initial period of recorded Mesoamerican history the sources at times clearly tend to confuse the dates and even the name of one ruler with that of others. One gets the inescapable impression that the same or similar dates for a ruler's reign are repeated many times over and on each occasion applied to a different personage.

Methods of Approach

In approaching the subject, I have worked on the following principles. First, I believe that several calendar counts must be involved in Toltec dates. That is to say, if one report states that Topiltzin died in the year 1 Acatl, and another gives the year as 2 Acatl, this does not mean that one of the two dates is mistaken, but that it belongs to a different year count. This point has already been fully explained. Secondly, whereas one at least possesses enough dates to form a coherent scheme where the end of Tollan is concerned, it is considered that little can be learned from single dates available for its inception, such as the inevitable 1 Tecpatl for the establishment of Tollan and its monarchy. As also already stressed, it is really impossible to make sense of isolated dates, since there is no means, other than pure guesswork, of deciding to which cycle or year count they belong. It must again be emphasized that one needs to possess a reasonable number of alternative dates for a given period in order to establish a coherent chronological pattern. One cannot, for instance, demonstrate conclusively that the 1 Acatl and 2 Acatl mentioned above do in fact represent the same year in different calendar counts unless one has several parallel cases of this nature to prove the point in tabular form.

Moreover, one really has to treat these 1 Tecpatl dates (and on occasion those of 1 Calli, 1 Tochtli, and 1 Acatl) as being as much ritual as historical. Hardly an important event comes to mind that one or more sources do not describe as occurring in the year 1 Tecpatl. To quote a few examples: in that year Huitzilopochtli was born, the Toltecs left Huetlapallan, the Toltecs reached Tollan, the Toltecs left Tollan, and the Aztecs left Aztlan; the first Toltec ruler ascended his throne in that year, as well as the first *tlatoani* of Tenochtitlan, the first ruler of Cuauhtitlán, and the first *señor* of Chalco! Thus for Tollan's early chronology one must rely on archaeological rather than documentary evidence.

My third proposition is that, in view of these early uncertainties, the only practical method of approach to Tollan's later chronology is to start at the other end and work backward. To do this involves establishing dates for certain rulers of Culhuacán, whose reigns coincided with the arrival of the Mexicas upon the scene, and to which dates a Christian-year equivalent can consequently be assigned with more confidence. But these Culhua kings also descend in a direct line from the last rulers of Tollan; thus, if one can define the length of their respective reigns, one may then tentatively calculate backward and arrive at a figure for Mixcoatl and Topiltzin, during the closing years of Tollan. This may not be an ideal method of approach, but until archaeologists or historians can offer a better one, it is put forward as the best available. Frankly, however, it has not been possible to endow it with the solidity of our previous findings on early Mexica history, which offers infinitely more dates for the purpose of cross checking.

Reordering the lists

It is necessary first to list the dates given for the rulers of Tollan and Culhuacán by the various sources.

Anales de Cuauhtitlán

Rulers of Tollan	Accession	Death
Mixcoamazatzin	1 Tecpatl	1 Calli
Huetzin	1 Calli	2 Tochtli
Totepeuh	2 Tochtli	6 Acatl
Ihuitimal	6 Acatl	?
Quetzalcoatl	5 Calli	2 Acatl (died in Culhuacán) or 1 Acatl (went to Tlillan Tlapallan)
Matlaxcóxhitl	1 Acatl	10 Tochtli
Nauhyotzin	10 Tochtli	12 Calli
Matlaccoatzin	12 Calli	1 Calli
Tlilcoatzin	1 Calli	9 Tochtli
Huemac (plus Quauhtli?)	9 Tochtli	7 Tochtli (or 1 Tochtli)

Rulers of Culhuacán	Accession	Death
Nauhyotzin	1 Tecpatl ?	9 Tecpatl
Cuauhtexpetlatzin	9 Tecpatl	1 Calli
Huetzin	1 Calli	9 Tochtli
Nonohualcatzin	9 Tochtli	4 Acatl
Achitómetl	4 Acatl	5 Calli
Cuauhitónal	5 Calli	6 Acatl
Mazatzin	6 Acatl	3 Tochtli
Quetzaltzin	3 Tochtli	3 Acatl
Chalchiuhtlatónac	3 Acatl	7 Tecpatl
Cuauhtlixtli	7 Tecpatl	1 Acatl
Yohuallatlatónac	1 Acatl	11 Calli
Tziuhtecatzin	11 Calli	11 Tochtli
Xihuiltemoctzin	11 Tochtli	3 Tecpatl
Coxcoxteuctli	3 Tecpatl	1 Tecpatl
Acamapichtli	1 Tecpatl	?
Nauhyotzin	2 Calli	12 Calli

Chimalpain, *Memorial Breve*

Rulers of Tollan	Accession	Death
Topiltzin-Quetzalcoatl	8 Calli	5 Calli
Huemac	5 Calli	1 Acatl
Matlacxóchitl	1 Acatl ?	?

Rulers of Culhuacán		
Tepiltzin-Nauhyotzin (first ruler of Culhuacán)	5 Calli	3 Acatl

Nonohualcatl	3 Acatl	3 Calli
Yohuallatonac	3 Calli	10 Tecpatl
Quetzalacxoyatzin	10 Tecpatl	7 Calli
Chalchiuhtlatonac	7 Calli	13 Calli
Totepeuh	13 Calli	2 Tochtl
Nauhyotzin (called Nauhyotzin II)	2 Tochtli	9 Tecpatl
Quauhtexpetlatzin	9 Tecpatl	1 Calli
Nonohualcatl and Huetzin	2 Tochtli	9 Tochtli
Achitómetl	10 Acatl	4 Acatl
Cuauhtlatonac	5 Tecpatl	5 Calli
Mallatzin	6 Tochtli	7 Tecpatl
Chalchiuhtlatonac	3 Acatl	13 Calli
Quauhtlix	13 Calli	7 Tecpatl
Yohuallatónac	7 Tecpatl	1 Tecpatl

Chimalpain, *Relaciones*

Rulers of Culhuacán	Accession	Death
Nauhyotzin	5 Calli or 11 Acatl	9 Tecpatl
Cuauhtlix	?	7 Tecpatl
Yohuallatónac	7 Tecpatl	1 Acatl
Tziuhtecatl	?	11 Calli
Xihuitltemoc	11 Calli or 7 Tecpatl	10 Calli or 11 Calli
Coxcoxtli	9 Tecpatl or 10 Calli	10 Acatl
Achitómetl	13 Tecpatl	11 Acatl

Ixtlilxóchitl, *Obras Históricas*

Rulers of Tollan, according to *Relaciones Históricas* (Vol. 1)	Accession	Death
Chalchiuhtlanetzin-Chalchiuhtonac	7 Acatl	7 Acatl
Tlilquechahuac-Tlachiholtzin-Ixtlilquechahuac	7 Acatl	7 Acatl
Tlaltecatl-Huetzin	7 Acatl	6 Tochtli
Totepeuh	6 Tochtli	5 Calli
Nacaxoc or Mitl	5 Calli	5 Calli
Tlacomihua	5 Calli	11 Acatl
Xiuhquentzin	11 Acatl	2 Acatl
Iztaccaltzin	2 Acatl	2 Acatl
Topiltzin	2 Acatl	1 Tecpatl?

Rulers of Tollan, according to *Historia Tolteca-Chichimeca* (Vol. II)	Accession	Death
Chalchiuhtlanetzin-Chalchiuhtonac	7 Acatl	7 Acatl
Tlilquechahuac-Tlachinoltzin	7 Acatl	6 Tochtli
Huetzin	6 Tochtli	6 Tochtli
Totepeuh	6 Tochtli	5 Calli
Nacazxoch	5 Calli	5 Calli
Tlacomihua	5 Calli	11 Acatl
Xiuhquentzin	11 Acatl	2 Acatl
Iztaccaltzin	2 Acatl	2 Acatl
Topiltzin	2 Acatl	?

The last two lists above are to a certain extent a condensation of different data that Ixtlilxóchitl gives several times over but which more or less coincide. As may be seen, the dates are largely "ritual," i.e., composing reigns each of exactly fifty-two years, to correspond with a calendar cycle. It seems very possible that the last rulers are really all one and the same person, with the exception of Xiuhquentzin, a "queen" who reigned four years and seems to have fulfilled the task of completing part of the fifty-two-year cycle. Nacaxoc and Mitl are at times classed together; Nacazxoch and Tlacomihua in two different versions both succeed Totepeuh; Tlacomihua is stated to be the same as "Acatl"—i.e., Ce Acatl? Iztaccaltzin, as already explained, is also a confederate ruler of Topiltzin, according to Ixtlilxóchitl.

However, a few of these dates may be useful as confirmation for data from other sources.

Torquemada Rulers of Tollan (I, 37)	
Chalchiuhtlanetzin	7 Acatl to 7 Acatl
Ixtlilquechahuac	7 Acatl to 7 Acatl
Huetzin	
Totepeuh	
Nacazxoc	
Mitl plus "queen" Xiuhquentzin	
Tecpancaltzin (also called Topiltzin)	
From his son Pochotl the rulers of Culhuacán were descended (also according to Ixtlilxóchitl).	

Rulers of Tollan (I, 254)
Totepeuh
Topil
Huemac

Rulers of Culhuacán
Nauhyotzin
Quauhtexpetlatl
Huetzin Nonohualcatl
Achitómetl
Quauhtonal, plus Mazatzin
Quetzal
Chalchiuhtlatonac
Quauhtlix
Yohuallatónac.
Xiuhtecatl
Xiuhtemoctzin
Coxcoxtzin

The first list of Tollan rulers (p. 37) is almost identical with Ixtlilxóchitl's lists. The second version of Tollan's rulers (p. 254) consists of those mentioned in the *Memorial Breve*, but without dates. The list of rulers of Culhuacán also follows very closely the *Memorial Breve*.

Relación de la Genealogía and *Origen de los Mexicanos*

Rulers of Tollan
Topiltzin
Huemac

Rulers of Culhuacán
Totepeuh
Nahuinci (Nauhyotzin)
Cuauhtexpetlatzin
Huetzin
Nonohualcatl
Achitómetl
Cuauhtonal
Cuezan
Cuauhtlix
Yohualtonac
Xiuhtecatzin

This list follows very closely the Torquemada list, in turn very similar to that of the *Memorial Breve.*

At first sight, these lists must seem bewildering, if not totally meaningless. On closer examination, however, one discovers certain interesting if unexpected facts. To illustrate these, let us (at this stage in arbitrary fashion) denominate the list of rulers of Tollan given by the *Anales de Cuauhtitlán* as List A, and the first five rulers of Culhuacán mentioned by the same source as List B. Then let us call the few rulers of Tollan given in the *Memorial Breve* together with its earlier rulers of Culhuacán List C, and finally label as List D the next six rulers of Culhuacán according to the *Memorial Breve*, starting with the second Nauhyotzin and ending with Chalchiutonac (the reasons for omitting Mallatzin will be explained later).

These may be set out side by side as follows; the division of the lists into numbered "reigns," another seemingly arbitrary procedure, will be explained fully later.

LIST A	LIST B	LIST C	LIST D
		Reign 1	
Mixcoamazatzin 1 Tecpatl-1 Calli Totepeuh 2 Tochtli-6 Acatl		Totepeuh 13 Calli-2 Tochtli	
		Reign 2	
a. Ihuitimal (Topiltzin?) 6 Acatl-? or 5 Calli-1 or 2 Acatl b. Huemac 9 Tochtli-7 Tochtli		a. Huemac 8 Calli-5 Calli b. Quetzalcoatl 5 Calli-1 Acatl	
		Reign 3	
Matlacxóchitl 1 Acatl-10 Tochtli			
		Reign 4	
Nauhyotzin 10 Tochtli-12 Calli	Nauhyotzin ?-9 Tecpatl	Nauhyotzin 5 Calli-	Nauhyotzin 2 Tochtli-9 Tecpatl
		Reign 5	
Matlacoatzin 12 Calli-1 Calli	Cuauhtexpetlatzin 9 Tecpatl-1 Calli	? -3 Acatl	Cuauhtexpetlatzin 9 Tecpatl-1 Calli

		Reign 6	
Tlilcoatzin 1 Calli-9 Tochtli	Huetzin 1 Calli-9 Tochtli	Nonohualcatl 3 Acatl-3 Calli	Nonoalcatl and Huetzin 2 Tochtli-9 Tochtli
		Reign 7	
Huemac (?) 9 Tochtli-7 Tochtli	Nonohualcatzin 9 Tochtli-4 Acatl	Yohualtonac 3 Calli-10 Tecpatl	Achitometl (?) 10 Acatl-4 Acatl
		Reign 8	
	a. Achitometl 4 Acatl-5 Calli b. Cuauhitonal 5 Calli-6 Acatl	Quetzalxoyatzin 10 Tecpatl-7 Calli Chalchiuhtlatonac 7 Calli-13 Calli	Cuauhtlatonac 5 Tecpatl-5 Calli Chalchiuhtlatonac 3 Acatl-13 Calli

From this reordering emerges a striking fact: on the face of it the two sources which give an ostensibly intelligible and credible chronology provide different information. The *Anales de Cuauhtitlán* give a list of the rulers of Tollan, followed by subsequent information, spread over many paragraphs, on those of Culhuacán. The *Memorial Breve*, on the other hand, mentions only the dates of the last Tollan rulers, Huemac and Topiltzin, and then provides a long list of the *señores* of Culhuacán, spread over the earlier part of the work.

Thus in each case one has certain, if divergent, information on Totepeuh, Topiltzin, and Huemac. So far, so good. But when one next examines what follows—i.e., in List A the *Anales de Cuauhtitlán's* version of rulers of Tollan *subsequent* to Topiltzin, in List B the earlier rulers of Culhuacán according to the same source—and if he then compares these with List C and List D (the earlier and later rulers of Culhuacán, according to the *Memorial Breve*), he finds that in fact he is dealing not with four lists but with one only! In other words, the same list is repeated twice over in the *Anales de Cuauhtitlán*, once as referring to rulers of Tollan and once to those of Culhuacán; the *Memorial Breve* also gives the same list twice over, once as the successors of Nauhyotzin I of Culhuacán and once as the successors of the person it erroneously styles Nauhyotzin II, who is really the same as Nauhyotzin I (a point to which Kirchhoff had already drawn attention).

In discussing this question further, it is important first to clarify certain problems which concern our study.

1. While several year counts are surely involved, accounting for certain discrepancies in the four lists, so many dates coincide in all of them that it

is clear that these at least belong to the same year count. Thus, to simplify matters at this stage, we will assume that we are dealing only with this one calendar, and the probable use of others will be left to later discussion.

2. In dates given for Mesoamerican rulers' reigns, even in later times, when the data is infinitely more exact, it is common to find discrepancies of one, two, three, and even more years in the dates given in different sources for the same ruler. To quote a good example, Ixtlilxóchitl states that Moctezuma II ascended the throne in 9 Calli, Chimalpain gives 10 Tochtli, and Torquemada, 11 Acatl. For Moctezuma I, the spread of dates is even wider. In another context I have tried to offer possible explanations as to how this phenomenon occurred, even for dates which fell within the living memory of the earlier chroniclers.

In our present context, it is most important to stress that, if twenty years before the Conquest such discrepancies could occur, then in dealing with this remote and confusing Toltec chronology they are likely to be much larger. If the date of accession of a ruler is given in one source as 4 Acatl and in another as 7 Tochtli (three years later), it is most probable that we are in fact dealing with the same person. Even if the difference is a great as from, say, 5 Calli to 10 Tochtli (five years) as in the case of two Nauhyotzins, the same proposition is still likely to hold good. A five-year variation over three centuries is proportionally small in comparison with a difference of two years for an event occurring a few decades before it was recorded in its present form.

3. In dealing with rulers so remote in history, it is the dates which count more than the names, for the purpose of identification. To take the simplest examples, Topiltzin is also known as Ce Acatl, Quetzalcoatl, Meconetzin, and, as already noted, probably also as Tecpancaltzin and Tlacomihua. Similarly, Mixcoatl is known as Camaxtli and Totepeuh and perhaps, as I have suggested, Mazatzin. One source will call a given personage by one name while a second document will give him another.

Therefore, regardless of *names*, which are used indiscriminately and confusedly, if in two lists the *dates* tend to coincide, we are probably dealing with the same person. It is on this basis that the personages in lists A, B, C, and D have been assigned to reigns numbered 1, 2, 3, and so on, even if the names are not the same in each list.

One may now return to the four lists and specify in more detail the many points which they possess in common and offer the following proposition:

1. From Nauhyotzin onward, List C = List D. (i.e., the *Memorial Breve* repeats the same list of Culhua rulers twice over).

Both lists start with a Nauhyotzin (called Nauhyotzin II in List D). In List D, this Nauhyotzin is succeeded directly, and in List C at one remove, by a Nonohoalcatl, and the two Nonohoalcatls start their reigns virtually simultaneously (3 Acatl in List C and 2 Tochtli in List D). In each list this Nonohoalcatl is in turn succeeded at several removes by a Cahlchiuhtonac, who in both cases dies in 13 Calli.

It should at this stage be explained that in List C, as mentioned, Nonohoalcatl is given as the direct successor of Nauhyotzin, whereas in List D, Cuauhtexpetlatzin reigns between the two. But since other sources, such as Torquemada and the *Relación de la Genealogía*, also give a Cuauhtexpetlatzin as first successor of Nauyhotzin, it is fair to assume that in List C this ruler has been omitted and that the dates given for Nauhyotzin are really those of the latter *and* his successor. In my chart he has therefore been assigned the spaces of reigns No. 3 and No. 4; the 3 Acatl with which the two reigns thus listed ends is only two years distant from the 1 Calli of the three other lists.

2. List B = List C = List D.

There is of course nothing revolutionary in saying that Lists B and C are the same, since both ostensibly concern the earlier rulers of Culhuacán. However, a glance at our chart will reveal that List B has just as much in common with List D as with List C, though List D, in theory, gives the *later* Culhua *señores*. This only serves to confirm our contention that Lists C and D are one and the same. For instance, Lists B and D both begin with a Nauhyotzin who dies in 9 Tecpatl. And, if this in itself is not sufficient proof, both these Nauhyotzins are succeeded by a Cuauhtexpetlatzin who reigns from 9 Tecpatl to 1 Calli. One really needs to take this argument no further.

3. List A = List B = List C = List D.

Here one comes to the crux of the matter, since List A, unlike the others, is stated to concern late rulers of Tollan, not Culhuacán. One is of course again referring to the second part of each list, starting with Nauhyotzin.

All lists start with a Nauhyotzin, though this in itself could be merely a coincidence. However, one cannot by the same token accept as pure chance that the first successor of Nauhyotzin A and Nauhyotzin B (and also Nauhyotzin D) dies in the same year, 1 Calli, even if he is named differently in each instance. Still less can it be a coincidence that the ruler subsequent to this first successor in each case dies in 9 Tochtli.

Assuming that the naming of the first ruler in each list as Nauhyotzin was correctly to be attributed to chance, then the odds against the successor of all of these dying in the same year would be exactly fifty-one to one (the total number of alternative year dates being fifty-two). Then, added to this chance of fifty-one to one, the odds against the next ruler in each case *also* dying in the same year could be 51 × 50 to 1, i.e., 2,550 to 1! This refers to similarities between *two* lists. If *three* lists are concerned, the odds become infinitely greater.

Moreover, this is not the end of the story. The third ruler after Nauhyotzin in List A dies in 7 Tochtli and in Lists B and D in 4 Acatl. But 7 Tochtli is only three years removed from 4 Acatl in the same year count, and it has already been explained that such differences of two or three years in recording rulers' dates are frequent even in later and much better-documented times. The similarity of the dates of death of these third-remove rulers after each Nauhyotzin increases to at least six figures the odds against such similarities amounting to mere chance, taking for this purpose only Lists A and B.

And if any doubts linger on this point, it may further be noted that Chimalpain, in his *Relaciones*, gives the dates ostensibly for the first Nauhyotzin of Culhuacán as 5 Calli to 9 Tecpatl, and also gives 11 Acatl for the accession of another Nauhyotzin—called this time Nauhyotecuhtli of Culhuacán—and 12 Calli as the year of his death. This 9 Tecpatl is the same date as he gives in his *Memorial Breve* for the death of the *second* Nauhyotzin, thus further cementing the links between Lists C and D. On the other hand, the date of 11 Acatl for the accession of this second Nauhyotzin (in theory that of List D) differs by only one year from that of the ruler of the same name in List A, and both die in the same year, 12 Calli. This would seem to prove beyond doubt the connection between List A and the remainder.

It may also be added that the Nauhyotzin of Culhuacán mentioned in the *Anales de Cuauhtitlán* also implicitly starts out originally from Tollan and proceeds to Culhuacán; the *Memorial Breve* also makes passing reference to a Nauhyotzin of *Tollan*, who succeeded in 8 Calli. Thus neither source draws in every instance a very sharp distinction between the Nauhyotzins of the two cities.

Therefore, in conclusion, I am led to the categoric assumption that, after Topiltzin, Huemac, and the shadowy Matlacxochitl, there *are* no true kings of Tollan listed in any source, but only kings of Culhuacán, mistakenly referred to in certain instances as belonging to Tollan. In view of my insistent contention that Topiltzin was the last, not the first, ruler of Tollan, this is hardly surprising.

Other Anomalies

In view of the many doubts that surround these dates and of the tendency to interpret too literally figures that reach us in such garbled form, it may be useful to list a few further anomalies and oddities concerning them, without seeking at this stage an explanation for this apparent borrowing of one ruler's dates by another.

For instance, Chalchiuhtlatonac, a late ruler of Culhuacán in the *Anales de Cuauhtitlán*, reigns from 3 Acatl to 7 Tecpatl; both the beginning and end of his reign thus differ by only one year from that of Totepeuh, father of Topiltzin (2 Tochtli to 6 Acatl). His successor reigns from 7 Tecpatl to 1 Acatl; 7 Tecpatl is the year of accession given by the same source for Ihuitimal, sometimes to be confused with Topiltzin, and 1 Acatl is the traditional year for the death of the latter.

Likewise, Mazatzin, another ruler of Culhuacán listed by the *Anales de Cuauhtitlán*, succeeds to his throne in 6 Tochtli, one year after 5 Calli, the most frequently cited accession date for Topiltzin, and dies in 2 Acatl, an alternative date given for the death of Topiltzin, in this instance stated to have occurred in *Culhuacán*!

It may of course be argued that if the later rulers of Tollan are in effect eliminated by becoming identified with Culhua rulers, as I have done, then the long list in the *Anales de Cuauhtitlán* of rulers of Cuauhtitlán itself remains in a kind of void, in the absence of equivalent and contemporary Toltec kings.

But, without going in this instance into such full detail, it must frankly be stated that this list of Cuauhtitlán rulers, as it stands, is also full of the strangest anomalies. For instance, Nequamexochtzin of Cuauhtitlán has virtually identical dates (11 Acatl to 12 Calli) as Nauhyotzin of Tollan of our List A (10 Tochtli to 12 Calli) *and* exactly the same dates as Nauhyotzin II of Culhuacán according to Chimalpain's *Relaciones*. This is another point that can only by a rare stretch of imagination amount to a coincidence.

Furthermore, Eztlaquencatzin of Cuauhtitlán reigns for exactly the same years as Ixtlilxóchitl's Xiuhquentzin of Tollan (11 Acatl to 2 Acatl)! Both Eztlaquencatzin and Teiztlacoatzin, another ruler of Cuauhtitlán, reign for fifty-seven years, another strange coincidence.

These are only a few of the oddities that one encounters, quite apart from the fact that the reigns of these Cuauhtitlán rulers are most unusually long, as compared with the average in Mesoamerica and elsewhere. Clearly some of these dates are confused with those of rulers of Tollan and/or Culhuacán already discussed, and in the main probably postdate rather than predate Topiltzin.

The Different Year Counts

So far it has been assumed that the years in our different king lists all belong to one year count. But, as already explained, it is clear that in Toltec as well as in later times, more than one year count was involved in the available chronologies. The problem is to find out exactly which of those later-known counts were used at that time, and to see how far any such identification may assist us in unraveling the confusions which confront us.

In such matters, there is really only one possible method of approach: one can only establish a valid system empirically, by trial and error, and then see how far it works in practice. If it makes reasonable sense, then it is probably correct. In making up my tables of year counts, various clues were at my disposal. First, the two dates of 1 and 2 Acatl in the *Anales de Cuauhtitlán* for the death of Topiltzin suggested that two counts were involved, in one of which 1 Acatl corresponded to 2 Acatl in the other. Added to this assumption, I found certain pointers to the effect that a third count was involved in certain instances when the above 1 Acatl was the equivalent not of 2 Acatl but of 3 Acatl. In addition, the use of yet a fourth count was suspected, partly from certain anomalies in Cuauhtitlán dates, in which 1 Acatl would become not 2 or 3 Acatl but 6 Acatl. It has been explained in Chapter 8 that between one year count and another, it is normally merely the *number* that changes for any given year, and not the glyph.

A Christian-year Equivalent

In order to link our list of Toltec and Culhua reigns to a Christian-year equivalent, it is now necessary to proceed to the last rulers of the list and then work backward. For at its end, that is, the reigns of Achitómetl, Chalchiuhtlatonac, and Coxcox, one is dealing with a period that is already historic from the chronological point of view, since it coincides with the presence of the Mexicas in Chapultepec, and their subsequent arrival in Culhuacán as fugitives.

At the moment when they reached Culhuacán, the sources mention a possible total of four rulers, and in particular two, Achitómetl and Coxcox, with whom they had various dealings.

It would seem that in point of fact, in our List D, by a transposition of names Achitómetl has "slipped" upward and occupies the space properly belonging to reign No. 7, not reign No. 8; this can be seen to be probable from the actual dates given for Achitómetl, which correspond more to those of reign No. 7 than to No. 8 in Lists A and B. By the same token, it is considered that Achitómetl really belongs to reign No. 8, in which we find another Achitómetl in List B; Achitómetl and Cuauhtlatonac are quite probably the same person. The dates for Cuauhtlatonac in List D correspond to those for Achitómetl in List B.

Similarly, one strongly suspects that Chalchiuhtlatonac, who seemingly follows Achitómetl, is the same as Coxcox, even though they are at times depicted separately in the same document. The date for the death of Chalchiuhtlatonac in Lists C and D (*Memorial Breve*) differs by only two years in the same count from that of Coxcox according to Chimalpain's *Relaciones*. Other similarities become apparent when the dates are set out in their probably different year counts, as we shall see.

Because the sources tend often to imply that Achitómetl and Coxcox were partly contemporary—the evidence of plural rulership in Culhuacán is considerable—the last two rulers under consideration have been grouped together as reign No. 8a and reign No. 8b. What now remains is to chart them in their apparent year counts and assign them a Christian-year equivalent.

In the main, it is considered that the count in which most of the dates in question are given is what Jiménez Moreno has designated "Texcocan" and which I, in my study of the early Mexicas, with its fairly elaborate chronological chart, have called "Texcoco-Culhua." It is in this count that the traditional date of 2 Calli for the foundation of Tenochtitlan coincides with the Christian year 1345 (not 1325, as believed correct until recently, using the official Tenochca count, which probably did not exist at the time). (*See* Davies, *Los Mexicas*, Appendix A.) This date for the foundation of Tenochtitlan has been previously shown to coincide with the same or similar Christian years in several other year counts. For the period with which we are now dealing, I do not possess the same plethora of data to prove the point, but nevertheless I believe that this Texcocan year count is the one in question, though it long preceded the rise to importance of Texcoco itself. This count comes in Column W of the following chart of the reigns of the kings of Culhuacan. Next, in Column X, comes a year count in which, e.g., the year 1 Acatl in Column W becomes 2 Acatl, 2 Tecpatl becomes the equivalent of 3 Tecpatl, and so on; this corresponds to the "Cuitláhuac" count of Jiménez Moreno. Thirdly, in Column Y has been inserted the "Culhua 1" count, also according to Jiménez Moreno's nomenclature, corresponding to what I in my previous work called "Anales de Cuauhtitlán VI" (a whole series of year counts are identifiable in that source). Fourthly and finally, in Column Z comes another year count in which, in general terms, if a year is 1 Acatl in Column W, or the Texcoco count, it will be 3 Acatl in Column Z, 2 Tecpatl will be the equivalent of 4 Tecpatl, and so on. For lack of a better name, and because it is used by Chimalpain, I have called this the Chalca count.

The accompanying chart is more or less self-explanatory. It can be seen that according to my calculations the reigns of Coxcox/Chalchiuhtlatonac and that of Achitómetl/Cuauhtlatonac coincide in part, as might be expected from what the sources actually say. The letters after the events listed refer to those of my original Lists A, B, C, and D. To these I have added a few more.

If we were to add yet a fifth year count, in which 1307, or 3 Acatl Texcocan (Column W) was the equivalent of 2 Acatl, this would explain the 2 Acatl date given for the accession of a Coxcox in the *Anales de Cuauhtitlán* and in the *Crónica Mexicayotl.* It would also give the equivalent of 1325 for the death of Quetzalxoyatzin in 7 Calli, suggesting that I am correct in taking this person to be the same as Achitómetl.

THE KINGS OF CULHUACÁN

Christian-year Equivalent.	W *Texcoco Count*	X *Cuitláhuac Count*	Y *Culhua I Count*	Z *Chalca Count*
1295	4 Acatl. Accession of Achitómetl (List B)	5 Acatl	9 Acatl	6 Acatl
1296	5 Tecpatl. Accession of Chalchiuhtlatonac (List D) ? = Achitómetl	6 Tecpatl	10 Tecpatl. Accession of Quetzalxoyatzin (List C) ? = Achitómetl	7 Tecpatl
1297	6 Calli	7 Calli	11 Calli	8 Calli
1305	I Calli	2 Calli	6 Calli	3 Calli
1306	2 Tochtli	3 Tochtli	7 Tochtli	4 Tochtli
1307	3 Acatl. Accession of Chalchiuhtlatonac (List D) ? = Coxcoxtli	4 Acatl. Accession of Coxcoxtli (Ixtlilxóchitl)	8 Acatl	5 Acatl
1308	4 Tecpatl	5 Tecpatl	9 Tecpatl. Accession of Coxcoxtli (Chimalpain, *Relaciones*)	6 Tecpatl
1309	5 Calli	6 Calli	10 Calli	7 Calli. Accession of Chalchiuhtlatonac (List C) ? = Coxcoxtli
1310	6 Tochtli	7 Tochtli	11 Tochtli	8 Tochtli

[illegible]	[illegible] Culhuacán (*Anales de Tlatelolco*)	[illegible]	[illegible]	[illegible]
1319	2 Acatl. Arrival of Mexica in Culhuacán (*Crónica Mexicayotl*)	3 Acatl	7 Acatl	4 Acatl
1320	3 Tecpatl	4 Tecpatl	8 Tecpatl. Mexica defeated in Chapultepec (*Anales de Cuauhtitlán*)	5 Tecpatl
1321	4 Calli	5 Calli. Death of Achitómetl (Lists B and D)	9 Calli	6 Calli
1322	5 Tochtli	6 Tochtli	10 Tochtli	7 Tochtli
1323	6 Acatl	7 Acatl	11 Acatl. Death of Achitómetl (Chimalpain, *Relaciones*)	8 Acatl
1324	7 Tecpatl	8 Tecpatl	12 Tecpatl	9 Tecpatl
1325	8 Calli	9 Calli	13 Calli. Death of Chalchiuhtlatonac (Lists C and D) ? = Coxcoxtli	10 Calli
1326	9 Tochtli	10 Tochtli	1 Tochtli	11 Tochtli
1327	10 Acatl. Death of Coxcoxtli (Chimalpain, *Relaciones* and *Crónica Mexicayotl*)	11 Acatl	2 Acatl	12 Acatl

On the other hand, the two dated for the death of Achitómetl coincide fairly well. The same can be said for the accession of Coxcox-Chalchiuhtlatonac and his death.

The key figure for the purpose of fixing these native dates in terms of our own calendar is that of the arrival of the Mexicas in Culhuacán. Two sources say that they spent twenty-five years in Culhuacán (*Crónica Mexicayotl*, page 54, and *Historia de los Mexicanos*, page 226); one source says that they spent twenty-one years (Clavijero, page 71). On the other hand, the traditional date for their leaving Chapultepec and arriving in captivity in Culhuacán (in the reigns of Coxcox and/or Achitómetl) is 2 Acatl (*Tira de la Peregrinación*, Chimalpain, *Crónica Mexicayotl*), or one year earlier, 1 Tochtli (*Anales de Tlatelolco*).

If this date is taken to belong to the Texcoco count, it would allow for a stay of twenty-four years in Culhuacán, or twenty-five years by the exclusive system of counting, and therefore seems perfectly correct. This is based upon the assumption, demonstrated in detail in my previous work, that Tenochtitlan was founded in 2 Calli, Texcoco count, i.e., A.D. 1345, a date in which Jiménez Moreno also concurs. It may be assumed that the Mexicas left Culhuacán two years before this, in 1343. Veytia says that they spent two years wandering after leaving Culhuacán; Chimalpain implies that they spent one or two years; the *Crónica Mexicayotl* says that they left Culhuacán in 13 Acatl, two years before 2 Calli. I therefore place the arrival of the Mexicas in Culhuacán in 2 Acatl, Texcoco count, that is to say, A.D. 1319. If one may accept this date, then he is in a position to give Christian equivalents to the other dates on the chart and use this as a basis for making a tentative king list, going back eventually to Topiltzin himself.

Moreover, a link-up has now been established between my charts and calculations for Tollan and Culhuacán, on the one hand, and the more imposing chronological edifice which the plethora of data enabled me to construct as a basis for early Mexica chronology (Davies, *Los Mexicas*, Appendix A, Table A). Thus a possible historical basis has been provided for the rather nebulous dates which the sources offer for Tollan's end; unfortunately, these cannot in turn be connected with its beginning.

Counting Backward

Accordingly, from my chart one may tentatively deduce that the reign of Achitómetl/Cuauhtlatonac began in 1295 or 1296 and continued until approximately 1322.

Returning now to our king lists, it may be suggested that reigns Nos. 5, 6, and 7, stretched from 9 Tecpatl to 4 Acatl in the same (Texcocan) year count, if one takes the most frequently repeated dates.

This then gives us a period for these three rulers, variously designated in the different lists, running from A.D. 1248 to 1295.

Next we come back to Nauhyotzin, whom I have already insisted to be one and the same person in the four lists. The dates of his death are alternatively given as 12 Calli (List A) and 9 Tecpatl (Lists B and D). But 12 Calli in the Chalca count is only one year different from 9 Tecpatl in the Texcocan count. By the same token, the 2 Tochtli date for Nauhyotl's accession, if taken to belong to the Cuitláhuac count, is only one year earlier than the 5 Calli for the same event in the Culhua 1 count, and four years earlier than 10 Tochtli (List A) if the latter is allocated to the Texcocan count.

Giving preference to the latter count for these dates, since it is the most frequently used, one may thus tentatively assign dates of 1210 (10 Tochtli) to 1248 (9 Tecpatl) for Nauhyotzin. His predecessor, Matlacxóchitl, according to the *Anales de Cuauhtitlán* reigned from 1 Acatl to 10 Tochtli, or, in the Texcocan count, 1175 to 1210. It must be admitted that the duration of such a reign is somewhat uncertain, since both Tezozómoc and the *Histoyre du Mechique* describe Matlacxóchitl as companion in flight, rather than successor, of Topiltzin. However, if he were to be eliminated altogether, the dates for Topiltzin's reign and for the collapse of Tula would fall rather later than one is led to expect.

Totepeuh, Topiltzin, and Huemac

We may now reverse our steps, having established a firmer basis in terms of the Christian equivalent of the year counts concerned, and consider the last rulers of Tollan. In our attempt at dating, we shall not of course include the "mythical" dates given by Ixtlilxóchitl of 7 Acatl to 7 Acatl for several reigns that precede Totepeuh.

Before considering Totepeuh himself, one important detail deserves to be mentioned: following our "List B" from the *Anales de Cuauhtitlán*, nine further names occur, which have not been listed. If this study were more directly concerned with the rulers of Culhuacán as such, it would be possible to categorize these and show that they also are virtually a repetition of the other lists. Among these nine names one finds a Mazatzin, specifically stated to have been ruler of Culhuacán when the Mexicas reached Chapultepec and said to have reigned from 6 Acatl to 7 Tochtli. In List D of the *Memorial Breve* one discovers a Mallatzin (i.e., Mazatzin), and Chimalpain in his third *Relación* also mentions a Mallatzin who reigned from 6 Tochtli to 7 Tecpatl.

In the first place, this Mazatzin is not often mentioned in the sources as a ruler of Culhuacán at that time; secondly, one could not help noticing that certain dates for his reign bear a remarkable resemblance to those given for Totepeuh. According to Chimalpain in two separate accounts, Mazatzin ascends the throne in 6 Tochtli, the same date as that given for Totepeuh by Ixtlilxóchitl; the *Memorial Breve* date of 2 Tochtli for his death only differs by three years in the same year count from 5 Calli given by Ixtlilxóchitl. Furthermore, Mixcoatl (i.e., Totepeuh) is also at the beginning of the *Anales de Cuauhtitlán* called Mixcoamazatzin; he dies in 1 Calli, or one year before Totepeuh, according to the *Memorial Breve* (List C). Thus one is left in little doubt that Totepeuh, Mazatzin, and Mixcoamazatzin are the same person. That he should have been inserted as a kind of odd-man-out in the wrong place in both the *Anales de Cuauhtitlán* and *Memorial Breve* lists of Culhuacán rulers is one of those inconsistencies that, when dealing with such remote dates, defy explanation.

In dealing with Totepeuh-Mazatzin, Topiltzin, and Huemac, it has been found that precisely the same four year counts appear valid and applicable as for the later rulers of Culhuacán already discussed. From the accompanying table, it can be seen that 6 Tochtli, Ixtlilxóchitl's date for the accession of Totepeuh, and the date for Mazatzin according to Chimalpain's two versions only differ by three years—if taken in the Chalca count—from 6 Acatl, the date which the *Anales de Cuauhtitlán* give for the accession of Mazatzin if the latter date is taken to belong to the Culhua I count. In the Cuitláhuac count, 13 Calli, the date in List C for the accession of Totepeuh, is only a further three years earlier, a fairly normal divergence for such remote dates.

The dates for the death of Totepeuh, 2 Tochtli in List C and 3 Tochtli for Mazatzin in the latter part of the *Anales de Cuauhtitlán* list, coincide exactly, when placed in the Texcoco and Cuitláhuac counts; most notably, the 1 Calli date given for the death of Mixcoamazatzin in the *Anales de Cuauhtitlán* falls only one year before this. Ixtlilxóchitl's date of 5 Calli for the death of Totepeuh is only three years later.

This same date of 5 Calli is given in two lists for the accession of Topiltzin; this of course refers to his reign in Tollan, whereas Totepeuh, according to most accounts, reigned in Culhuacán. Ixtlilxóchitl gives the same year for the accession of both Nacaxoch and Tlacomihua, perhaps other names for Topiltzin. For Topiltzin's death one has 1 Acatl, fairly obviously belonging to the Texcoco count, and 2 Acatl, the same year in the Cuitláhuac count.

THE CHRONOLOGY OF TOPILTZIN

Christian-year Equivalent	*Texcoco Count*	*Cuitláhuac Count*	*Culhua I Count*	*Chalca Count*
1121	12 Calli	13 Calli Accession Totepueh (List C)	4 Calli	1 Calli
1122	13 Tochtli	1 Tochtli	5 Tochtli	2 Tochtli
1123	1 Acatl	2 Acatl	6 Acatl Accession of Mazatzin (*Anales de Cuauhtitlán*)	3 Acatl
1124	2 Tecpatl	3 Tecpatl	7 Tecpatl	4 Tecpatl
1125	3 Calli	4 Calli	8 Calli	5 Calli
1126	4 Tochtli	5 Tochtli	9 Tochtli	6 Tochtli Accession Mazatzin (List D & Chimalpain, *Relaciones*) Accession Totepeuh (Ixtlilxóchitl)
⋮	⋮	⋮	⋮	⋮
1149	1 Calli Death Mixcoamazatzin (List A)	2 Calli	6 Calli	3 Calli
1150	2 Tochtli Death Totepeuh (List C)	3 Tochtli Death Mazatzin (*Anales de Cuauhtitlán*)	7 Tochtli	4 Tochtli
1151	3 Acatl	4 Acatl	8 Acatl	5 Acatl

	Death Totepeuh (Ixtlilxóchitl) Accession Ce Acatl Topiltzin (Lists A, B) Accession Nacaxoch (Ixtlilxóchitl) Accession Tlacomihua (Ixtlilxóchitl)			
1169	8 Calli Accession Huemac (List B)	9 Calli	13 Calli	10 Calli
1170	9 Tochtli Accession Huemac (List A)	10 Tochtli	1 Tochtli	11 Tochtli
1171	10 Acatl	11 Acatl	2 Acatl	12 Acatl
1172	11 Tecpatl	12 Tecpatl	3 Tecpatl	13 Tecpatl
1173	12 Calli	13 Calli	4 Calli	1 Calli
1174	13 Tochtli	1 Tochtli	5 Tochtli	2 Tochtli
1175	1 Acatl Death Topiltzin (List A)	2 Acatl Death Topiltzin (List A)	6 Acatl	3 Acatl
1176	2 Tecpatl	3 Tecpatl	7 Tecpatl	4 Tecpatl
1177	3 Calli	4 Calli	8 Calli	5 Calli Death Huemac (List B)
1178	4 Tochtli	5 Tochtli	9 Tochtli	6 Tochtli
1179	5 Acatl	6 Acatl	10 Acatl End of Tollan's rule (*Memorial Breve*)	7 Acatl

For Huemac's accession there are two dates in succeeding years, 8 Calli and 9 Tochtli, in the Texcoco count, and 5 Calli and 7 Tochtli for his death. The first 5 Calli, would seem to belong to the Chalca count: according to most accounts it may be inferred that he did not long outlive Topiltzin. Such dating of course allows only for a very short reign for this ruler; however in view of his abrupt falling-out with Topiltzin, and accounts of his violent end, this is not to be wondered at. In any case, these dates should perhaps be treated with caution, since, as already explained, they coincide almost exactly with those of a Culhua ruler, and thus might conceivably not apply to Huemac at all. Equally, Huemac is given as the successor at third remove of Nauhyotzin, another possible mistaken identity. Such discrepancies may account for the fact that the *Anales de Cuauhtitlán* date of 7 Tochtli for Huemac's death hardly fits into our chart.

Dynasty A	Dynasty B (all of Tollan)
	Chalchiuhtlanetzin/Chalchiuhtlatonac
	7 Acatl to 7 Acatl (ritual dates)
	Tlilquechahuac/Tlachinoltzin
In Tollan:	7 Acatl to 7 Acatl (ritual)
Mixcoatl/Totepeuh/Mazatzin	Tltltecatl/Huetzin
1122–50	7 Acatl to 6 Tochtli (ritual)
Ce Acatl-Topiltzin	Huemac 1169–78
1153–75	
Matlacxóchitl (in Tollan and Culhuacán)	
1175–1210	
In Culhuacán:	
Nauhyotzin	
1210–48	
Cuauhtexpetlatzin/Matlacoatzin	
1248–53	
Huetzin/Nonohualcatl	
1253–74	
Nonohualcatl/Quetzalxoyatzin	
1274–95	
Achitómetl	
1295–1321	

The Full List

Having established the Christian-year equivalent for the later rulers of Culhuacán, Achitómetl and Coxcox, and linked them as firmly as possible to my already existent table of Mexica dates, and having also worked out a chronology for Topiltzin based on native year counts, one is now in a position to link the two and suggest the following Christian-year equivalents for Totepeuh, Topiltzin, and Huemac, taking for the purpose mean averages where divergences of a few years exist between one version and another.

A problem arises in the gap between Topiltzin and Nauhyotzin, filled only by the rather shadowy Matlacxóchitl, listed by both the *Anales de Cuauhtitlán* and the *Memorial Breve* as reigning in Tollan. Some reports give Nauhyotl as virtually contemporary with Topiltzin's last years and as leading the Toltecs out of Tollan to Culhuacán. The *Relación de la Genealogía* states that Nauhyotzin reigned sixty years; if this were so, then his reign would have started some twenty years earlier, eliminating most of that of the unsubstantial Matlacxóchitl. Both this source and the virtually identical list of Torquemada for Culhua rulers give four monarchs as reigning between Topiltzin and Achitómetl. Tentatively, for reasons already given, I have inserted five. If anything, it could be argued that the time lag between Topiltzin and Achitómetl was shorter rather than longer than I have suggested. That, of course, would produce a later date for the fall of Tollan.

As regards the first part of Dynasty B of Tollan, before Huemac the most frequently used names of a few monarchs listed by Ixtlilxóchitl have been inserted. As already explained, these fifty-two-year reigns are regarded as deriving from dates that are purely ritual. They have been consigned to the same dynasty as Huemac, since it is considered that they derived from the older Tollan "establishment" rather than from the new blood injected by Topiltzin.

Dates of Disasters

For the various disasters that befell Tollan—plagues, famine, omens, and so on—one is again faced with a plethora of dates. However, unlike the actual accession or demise of a ruler, these are not in most cases very specific events that can properly be equated one with another as given in the different sources. As a possible exception, one might cite the 7 Tochtli given by Ixtlilxóchitl as a year of fearful omens and 8 Tochtli described in the same manner by the *Anales de Cuauhtitlán*. These dates, if taken as belonging to our Cuitláhuac and Chalca counts respectively, would give us in both instances the year of 1154, or that which followed Topiltzin's accession. But it must frankly be stated that such dates, relatively few in number and of uncertain implications, hardly form a basis for serious attempts at calendrical correlation; it would be possible to adapt them to almost any year-count system, to suit one's fancy. Even the date of Tollan's final breakup remains unclear. 1 Tecpatl dates are always suspect, as being applied to almost any happening in Mesoamerica; but the *Memorial Breve* also gives a date for the end of Tollan's rule of 10 Acatl; this, if taken to belong to the Culhua count, would fall in the year 1179, or just one year after the death of Huemac, a not illogical assumption. After the departure of both Topiltzin and Huemac, whatever phantom king might have reigned in Tollan, any surviving Toltec power had surely passed into the hands of Culhuacán.

Sahagún gives the year 1110 for Tollan's destruction. Adding one cycle of fifty-two years, plus a further twenty years (to convert to the Texcoco count from the Tenochca, in which Sahagún and others tended to calculate), one reaches 1182, or only three years from my date of 1179.

Notes and References

1. FACT AND LEGEND

1. Julian Steward, "Cultural causality and law," 2.
2. Robert McC. Adams, *The evolution of urban society*.
3. Francisco Clavijero, *Historia antigua de México*, 48.
4. J. Eric S. Thompson, *Maya history and religion*, xvi.
5. José García Payón, "La cerámica del Valle de Toluca," 238.
6. Michael Coe, "Archaeological synthesis of southern Veracruz and Tabasco," 700, 713.
7. John Paddock, "Mixtec ethnohistory and Monte Albán V," 88.
8. Miguel León-Portilla, "Ramírez de Fuenleal y las antigüedades mexicanas," 34.
9. Paul Kirchhoff, "Quetzalcoatl, Huemac y el fin de Tula."
10. Román Piña Chan, "Arqueología y tradición histórica, un testimonio de los informantes de Sahagún," 6–7.
11. David Clark, *Analytical archaeology*, 388.
12. Nigel Davies, *Los mexicas: primeros pasos hacia el imperio*, Appendix A.
13. Bronislaw Malinowski, *Magic, science and religion*, 146.
14. Georges Dumézil, *L'Héritage Indo-européen à Rome*, 116.
15. Robert McC. Adams, *The evolution of urban society*, 34.
16. Anónimo Mexicano, 117.
17. Fray Juan de Torquemada, *Monarquía indiana*, I, 42.
18. Domingo Francisco Chimalpain, *Relaciones originales*, 170.
19. Fray Bernardino de Sahagún, *Florentine codex*, Book X, 190.
20. Diego Muñoz Camargo, *Historia de Tlaxcala*, 10.
21. Chimalpain, *Relaciones*, 169.
22. Mariano Veytia, *Historia antigua de México*, I, 107.
23. Torquemada, *Monarquía*, I. 335.
24. Adrián Recinos, *Popol Vuh: las antiguas historias del quiché*, Part 3, 142.
25. Eduard Seler, *Gesammelte Abhandlungen*, II, 22.

2. TOLLAN AS NAME AND CONCEPT

1. E. O. James, *Myth and ritual in the ancient Near East*, 279.
2. U. Bahadir Alkin, *The ancient civilization of Anatolia*, 180.
3. Seler, *Gesammelte*, II, 56.
4. Richard Diehl, "Contemporary settlement and social organization," 358.
5. Mary Elizabeth Smith, *Picture writing from ancient southern Mexico*, Figs. 61, 62, 64, 65.
6. *Descripción de Cholula*, 159.
7. Agustín de Vetancurt, *Teatro Mexicano*, I, 235.
8. Seler, *Gesammelte*, II, 7.
9. Chimalpain, *Relaciones*, 134.
10. Wigberto Jiménez Moreno, "El problema de Tula," 3.
11. Daniel Brinton, *Were the Toltecs an historic nationality?* 241.
12. Seler, *Gesammelte*, II, 21–23.
13. S. Linné, *Mexican highland cultures*, 198.
14. *Ibid.*, 198.
15. *Codex of Cholula*, 276, 282.
16. *Ibid.*, 298.
17. *Historia Tolteca-Chichimeca*, 7.
18. *Codex Vaticano-Ríos*, Plate XIV.
19. Torquemada, *Monarquía*, I, 255.
20. Veytia, *Historia antigua de México*, I, 144.
21. Henry Frankfort, *Ancient Egyptian religion*, 112.
22. Alfonso Caso, "El complejo de Tula y las grandes culturas indígenas," 20.
23. *Ibid.*, 33.
24. George Vaillant, "A correlation of archaeological and historic sequences," 559.
25. Leonhard Schultze-Jena, *Alt-aztekische Gesänge*, 187.
26. *Ibid.*, 33.
27. Davies, *Los mexicas*, 25–30.
28. Chimalpain, *Relaciones*, 60.
29. Alfonso Caso, *Interpretación del Códice Bodley*, 59–60.
30. Alfonso Caso, *Interpretación del Códice Selden*, 25.
31. Smith, *Picture writing*, 70, 71.
32. *Ibid.*, 72.
33. Robert Chadwick, "Postclassic pottery of the central valleys," *passim*.
34. F. V. Scholes and R. L. Roys, *The Maya Chontal Indians of Acalan-Tixchel*, 2.
35. Robert Carmack, *Quichean civilization*, 273, 287.
36. *Ibid.*, 38.
37. Alfredo Barrera Vásquez and Sylvanus Morley, *The Maya chronicles*, 30.
38. Seler, *Gesammelte*, III, 576.
39. Walter Lehmann, *Una elegía tolteca*, 14.
40. Adrian Recinos, *Anales de los Cakchiqueles*, 48, 61.
41. Sahagún, *Florentine codex*, Book VII, 14.
42. Wigberto Jiménez Moreno, personal communication.
43. Thompson, *Maya history*, 23.
44. Ralph Roys, *Literary sources for the history of Mayapan*, 42.
45. Robert Carmack, *Toltec influence on the Postclassic culture history of Highland Guatemala*, 68.

46. Recinos, *Anales*, 170.
47. Seler, *Gesammelte*, III, 336.
48. Recinos, *Anales*, 48.
49. Recinos, *Popol Vuh*, 149.
50. Seler, *Gesammelte*, III, 644.
51. Sahagún, *Florentine codex*, Book III, 21.
52. *Anales de Cuauhtitlán*, 14.
53. Sahagún, *Florentine codex*, Book III, 21.
54. *Ibid.*, 23, 29.
55. *Anales de Cuauhtitlán*, 14.
56. *Historia de los Mexicanos por sus pinturas*, 22.
57. Chimalpain, *Relaciones*, 56.
58. Schultze-Jena, *Gesänge*, 201.
59. Rudolf van Zantwijk, "La estructura gubernamental del estado de Tlacopan," 145.
60. Torquemada, *Monarquía*, II, 52.
61. Fray Diego Durán, *Historia de las Indias de Nueva España*, II, 511.
62. Alvarado Tezozómoc, *Crónica Mexicayotl*, 87.
63. *Ibid.*, 151.
64. Laurette Séjourné, "Tula, la supuesta capital de los toltecas," 154.
65. Robert Chadwick, "Native pre-Aztec history of Central Mexico," 496–99.
66. *Ibid.*, 498.
67. Domingo Francisco Chimalpain, *Memorial Breve*, 164.
68. Séjourné, "Tula," 158.
69. Richard Diehl, *Preliminary report*, 49.
70. Miguel León-Portilla, *Los antiguos mexicanos a través de sus crónicas y cantares*.
71. Sahagún, *Florentine codex*, Book X, 166.
72. *Anales de Cuauhtitlán*, 8.
73. Tatiana Proskouriakoff, *A study of Classic Maya sculpture*, 172.
74. Earl Morris, *The Temple of Warriors at Chichén Itzá*, 40, 335.
75. Seler, *Gesammelte*, III, 331.
76. Fernando de Álva Ixtlilxóchitl, *Obras históricas*, I, 14–18.
77. Eulalia Guzmán, "Un manuscrito de la Colección Boturini," 90.
78. *Leyenda de los Soles*, 121.
79. Enrique Palacios, "Teotihuacán, los toltecas y Tula," 116.
80. Anton Kovar, "The physical and biological environment of the Basin of Mexico," 81.
81. The Book of Revelations, Chapter XXI.
82. Chimalpain, *Memorial Breve*, 50.
83. Schultze-Jena, *Gesänge*, 90.
84. Seler, *Gesammelte*, II, 980.
85. *Anales de Tlatelolco*, 35.
86. Henry Nicholson, "Topiltzin Quetzalcoatl of Tollan," 205.
87. Ixtlilxóchitl, *Obras históricas*, I, 50.
88. Wigberto Jiménez Moreno, "Síntesis de la historia precolonial del Valle de México," 223.
89. Recinos, *Popol Vuh*, 29.

90. Wigberto Jiménez Moreno, "Historia antigua de la zona tarasca," 151.
91. Ralph Roys, *The Chilam Balam of Chumayel*, 83.
92. Sahagún, *Florentine codex*, Book X, 187.
93. Paul Kirchhoff, "Das Toltekenreich und sein Untergang," 259.
94. Paul Kirchhoff, "El Valle Puebla-Tlaxcala," 20.
95. *Descripción de Cholula, passim.*
96. Durán, Historia, I, 61.
97. Davies, *Los mexicas*, 197.
98. Seler, *Gesammelte*, 675.
99. George Kubler, "La iconografía del arte de Teotihuacán," 70–71.
100. Michael Coe, "The Olmec style and its distribution," 754.
101. Ignacio Bernal, *El mundo olmeca*, 83.
102. Miguel Covarrubias, *Indian art of Mexico and Central America*, 63.
103. Román Piña Chan, "Los informantes de Sahagún," 75.
104. J. Eric S. Thompson, "Aquatic symbols common to various centers," 36.
105. Wigberto Jiménez Moreno, "Religión o religiones mesoamericanas?" 203.
106. Seler, *Gesammelte*, II, 979.
107. Thelma Sullivan, "Tláloc: a new etymological interpretation."
108. Pedro Armillas, "La serpiente emplumada, Quetzalcoatl y Tláloc," 175.
109. Wigberto Jiménez Moreno, "Síntesis de la historia pretolteca," 1071.
110. Enrique Florescano, "Tula-Teotihuacán, Quetzalcoatl y la Toltecayotl," 208.
111. Jiménez Moreno, "Religion," 203.
112. Seler, *Gesammelte*, I, 669.
113. Alfonso Caso, "Dioses y signos teotihuacanos," 273.
114. Sullivan, "Tláloc."
115. Seler, *Gesammelte*, II, 1071.
116. Hermann Beyer, *Obras completas*, I, 234.
117. Laurette Séjourné, *El universo de Quetzalcoatl*, 161.
118. Caso, "Dioses," 264.
119. *Ibid.*, 265.
120. Laurette Séjourné, *La arquitectura de Teotihuacán*, 18.
121. Miguel León-Portilla, "Quetzalcoatl; espiritualismo de México antiguo," 129.
122. Seler, *Gesammelte*, V, 491.
123. Jorge Acosta, *El Palacio de Quetzalpapálotl*, 35.
124. Agustín Caleti, "Mural painting in Central Mexico," Fig. 18.
125. George Kubler, "La evidencia intrínseca y la analogía etnológica," 18.
126. Kenneth Clark, *Civilization*, 90.
127. Jiménez Moreno, "Religion," 203.
128. James, *Myth and ritual*, 297.
129. Piña Chan, "Los informantes," 29.
130. César Sáenz "Tres estelas de Xochicalco," 46.
131. César Sáenz, *Quetzalcoatl*, 77.
132. César Sáenz, "Las estelas de Xochicalco," 79.
133. Sáenz, "Tres estelas," 42–43.
134. Pablo González Casanova, "El ciclo legendario del Tepoztecatl," 38.
135. Jaime Litvak King, "El Valle de Xochicalco," 255, 267.
136. Henry Nicholson, "The religious-ritual system of Late pre-Hispanic Central Mexico," 235.

137. Alfonso Caso, "Los lienzos mixtecos de Ihuitlán y Antonio de León," 258.
138. Alfonso Caso, "El primer embajador conocido en América," 287.
139. Alfonso Caso, "El Díos 1 Muerte," 40.
140. Silvia Garza de Gonzales, "La indumentaria de los dioses masculinos," 289–90.
141. Seler, *Gesammelte*, IV, 142.
142. Wilfrido du Solier, "Estudio arquitectónico de los edificios huaxtecos," 133.
143. David Kelley, "Quetzalcoatl and his coyote origins."
144. Piña Chan, "Los informantes," 80–81.
145. Alfredo López Austin, "Hombre Díos," 103.
146. Alfredo López Austin, personal communication.
147. Smith, *Picture writing*, 74, 124.

3. THE LAST DAYS OF TEOTIHUACÁN

1. Florencia Muller, "Secuencia cerámica de Teotihuacán," 37–42.
2. René Millon, "Cronología y periodificación," 10.
3. Ignacio Bernal, "Teotihuacán: nuevas fechas de radiocarbono y su posible significado."
4. Marta Foncerrada de Molina, "Fechas de radiocarbono en el área maya."
5. E. Wyllys Andrews, "Archaeology and prehistory in the northern Maya Lowlands," 288–91.
6. William Coe, "A summary of excavation and research at Tikal," 62.
7. Linton Satterthwaite, "Radiocarbon and Maya long count dating," 228.
8. Colin Renfew, "New configurations in Old World archaeology," 199.
9. *Ibid.*, 201.
10. H. T. Waterbolk, "Working with radiocarbon dates," 21.
11. Eskil Hultin, *The accuracy of radiocarbon dating*, 187.
12. Waterbolk, "Working," 23.
13. *Ibid.*, 27.
14. René Millon, Bruce Drewitt, and George Cowgill, *Urbanization at Teotihuacán*, 110; and Millon, "El Fin de Teotihuacán."
15. Millon, Drewitt, and Cowgill, *Urbanization at Teotihuacán*, 77E.
16. *Ibid.*, 82.
17. Thomas Charlton, "Contemporary agriculture in the Teotihuacán Valley," 321–23.
18. William Sanders, "The population of the Teotihuacán Valley," 442.
19. Sherburne Cook, "The interrelation of population, food supply and building," 50.
20. David Kaplan, *Men, monuments and political systems*, 403.
21. Stephan Borhegyi, "Archaeological synthesis of the Guatemalan Highlands," 38–39.
22. S. W. Miles, "Summary of preconquest ethnology," 282.
23. Steward, "Cultural causality," 8.
24. Jiménez Moreno, "Síntesis de la historia pretolteca," 1068.
25. James Bennyhoff, "Chronology and periodization," 22.
26. Carmen Cook de Leonard, "Algunos antecedentes sobre la cerámica tolteca," 39.
27. Florencia Muller, "La cerámica de Cholula," 131.

28. D. E. Drummond and Florencia Muller, "Classic to Postclassic in Highland Central Mexico."

29. Bennyhoff, "Chronology," 29.

30. Pedro Armillas, "Los olmeca xicallangas y los sitios arqueológicos del suroeste de Tlaxcala," 144.

31. Beatriz Braniff, "Secuencias arqueológicas en Guanajuato," 274.

32. Jorge Acosta, "El epílogo de Teotihuacán," 150–55.

33. Henry Nicholson, "The problem of the historical identity of the Cerro Portezuelo/San Antonio archaeological site."

34. Frederick Hicks and Henry Nicholson, "The transition from Classic to Postclassic," 503.

35. Román Piña Chan, "Un complejo Coyotlatelco en Coyocán," 147.

36. Sahagún, *Florentine codex*, Book X, 190.

37. *Ibid*., 190–91.

38. Gonzalo Fernández de Oviedo. *Historia general*, Book XLII, Chapter 2.

39. Wigberto Jiménez Moreno, "El enigma de los olmecas," 132.

40. *Suma de visitas*, 298.

41. Jorge Acosta, "El Altar 1," 102.

42. Sahagún, *Florentine codex*, Book X, 192.

43. Seler, *Gesammelte*, III, 228–29.

44. *Ibid*., 292.

45. Eduard Seler, *Codex Borgia*, I, 155.

46. Beyer, *Obras*, I, 39.

47. *Ibid*., 41.

48. Muñoz Camargo, *Historia*, 155.

49. Chimalpain, *Memorial Breve*, 84.

50. Seler, *Gesammelte*, III, 287.

51. *L'Histoyre du Mechique*, 27.

52. Lehmann, *Una elegía tolteca*, 6.

53. Seler, *Gesammelte*, II, 33.

54. Beyer, *Obras*, I, 40.

55. Seler, *Codex Borgia*, I, 235.

56. Seler, *Gesammelte*, II, 1034.

57. Jiménez Moreno, "El problema," 3.

58. Schultze-Jena, *Gesänge*, 72–73.

59. *Ibid*., 88–89.

60. Chimalpain, *Memorial Breve*, 84.

61. Angel Maria Garibay, *Veinte himnos sacros de los nahuas*, 158.

62. Seler, *Gesammelte*, II, 1032.

63. Chimalpain, *Memorial Breve*, 170.

64. Nicholson, "The religious-ritual system of Late pre-Hispanic Central Mexico," 229.

65. Muñoz Camargo, *Historia*, 52.

66. Sahagún, *Florentine codex*, Book X, 187–88.

67. Fray Toribio de Benavente Motolinía, *Memoriales*, 9.

68. Ixtlilxóchitl, *Obras*, II, 318.

69. Motolinía, *Memoriales*, 10.

70. *Papeles de Nueva España*, V, 264.

71. Recinos, *Anales de los Cakchiqueles*, 59–60.
72. Walter Krickeberg, *Los totonaca*, 135.
73. Seler, *Gesammelte*, II, 480.
74. *Ibid.*, IV, 21.
75. Krickeberg, *Los totonaca*, 157.
76. Wigberto Jiménez Moreno, "Relación entre los olmecas, los toltecas y los mayas," 21.
77. Nigel Davies, *Los señoríos independientes del imperio azteca*, 22.
78. *Ibid.*, 22–23.
79. F. V. Scholes and Dave Warren, "The Olmec region at Spanish contact," 784.
80. Jiménez Moreno, "Síntesis de la historia pretolteca," 1075.
81. Jiménez Moreno, "El enigma," 121.
82. Sahagún, *Florentine codex*, Book X, 208.
83. Ixtlilxóchitl, *Obras*, I, 19; II, 22.
84. Sahagún, *Florentine codex*, Book X, 192.
85. Seler, *Gesammelte*, II, 1020.
86. Sahagún, *Florentine codex*, Book X, 190.
87. Fray Bernardino de Sahagún, *Historia general de las cosas de Nueva España*, Book X, 208.
88. Pedro Armillas, "Condiciones ambientales y movimientos de pueblos," 311–12.
89. Drummond and Muller, "Classic to Postclassic."
90. *Ibid.*
91. *Ibid.*
92. Florencia Muller, *La extensión arqueológica de Cholula.*
93. Torquemada, *Monarquía*, I, 332.
94. Jiménez Moreno, "Historia antigua de la zona tarasca," 157.
95. Seler, *Gesammelte*, II, 1106.
96. *Ibid.*, II, 49–77.
97. Doris Stone, "La posición de los chorotegas," 127.
98. Walter Lehmann, *Zentralamerika*, II, 994.
99. Miguel León-Portilla, "Religión de los nicaraos."

4. THE APPROACH TO TOLLAN

1. Pedro Armillas, "Tecnología, formación socio-económica y religión," 19.
2. Gordon Willey, "Archaeological theories and interpretation: New World," 378.
3. Frankfort, "Ancient Egyptian religion," 86.
4. Lopez Austin, "Hombre Díos," 119.
5. Kubler, "La evidencia," 6.
6. Jorge Acosta, "Interpretación de algunos datos obtenidos en Tula," 83.
7. Jorge Acosta, "Los últimos descubrimientos arqueológicos en Tula," 56.
8. Jorge Acosta, "La cuarta y quinta temporada," 60.
9. Florencia Muller, "Costumbres funerarias del Valle de Tulancingo," 27.
10. Florencia Muller, "Tres objetos de piedra de Huapalcalco," 319–22.
11. E. F. Jacobs Müller, "El Valle de Tulancingo," 129.
12. Caleti, "Mural painting," 148.
13. Eduardo Noguera, *La cerámica arqueológica de Mesoamerica.*
14. Drummond and Muller, "Classic to Postclassic," 178.

15. Laurette Séjourné, *La arqueología del Valle de México*, 35–36.
16. George O'Neill, "Preliminary report," 48–50.
17. Ramón Piña Chan, personal communication.
18. Tatiana Proskouriakoff, "Sculpture and major arts of the Maya Lowlands," 488.
19. Proskouriakoff, *A study*, 162.
20. *Ibid.*, 170.
21. Thompson, *Maya history*, 10.
22. Ramón Piña Chan, "Algunas consideraciones sobre las pinturas de Mul-Chic, Yucatán," 74.
23. Jaime Litvak King, "Los patrones de cambio de estadio," 93.
24. Charles Kelley, "Archaeology of the Northern Frontier," 784.
25. *Ibid.*, 787.
26. Charles Kelley, "Mesoamerica and the southwestern United States," 100.
27. Charles Kelley, "Archaeology," 787.
28. Beatriz Braniff, "Estratigrafía en Villa Reyes."
29. *Ibid.*
30. Beatriz Braniff, personal communication.
31. Braniff, "Secuencias arqueológicas," 290.
32. *Ibid.*, 296.
33. Piña Chan, "Un complejo," 149.
34. García Payón, "La cerámica," 209.
35. César Sáenz, *Nuevas exploraciones y hallazgos en Xochicalco*, 11.
36. Acosta, "Interpretación," 92.
37. Séjourné, *La arqueología*, 49.
38. Alfred Tozzer, *Excavations of a site at Santiago, Ahuitzotla*, 53.
39. O'Neill, "Preliminary report," 47.
40. E. F. Jacobs Müller, La cerámica arqueológica de Tepoztlán, 126.
41. José García Payón, "La ciudad arqueológica de El Tajín.
42. Kirchhoff, *Das Toltekenreich*, 263.
43. Chimalpain, *Relaciones*, 62.
44. *Ibid.*, 46.
45. *Ibid.*, 47.
46. Chimalpain, *Memorial Breve*, 101.
47. José Luis Melgarejo, *La historia de Veracruz*, I, 48–50.
48. Davies, *Los señoríos*, 34–35.
49. Ixtlilxóchitl, *Obras*, II, 27–28.
50. Torquemada, *Monarquía*, III, 205.
51. *Ibid.*, 37.
52. *Ibid.*, 254–56.
53. Ixtlilxóchitl, *Obras*, I, 28.
54. Davies, *Los mexicas*, 57–58.
55. Sahagún, *Florentine codex*, Book X, 195.
56. Kirchhoff, "Quetzalcoatl, Huemac y el fin de Tula," 163–96.
57. *Anales de Cuauhtitlán*, 7.
58. Muñoz Camargo, *Historia*, 40–41.
59. Torquemada, *Monarquía*, I, 255.
60. Ixtlilxóchitl, *Obras*, I, 25.

61. Sahagún, *Florentine codex*, Book X, 197.
62. *Ibid.*, 173.
63. *Ibid.*, 171.
64. *Ibid.*, 175.
65. Piña Chan, "Algunas consideraciones," 70, 76.
66. Roys, *Chilam Balam*, 106; Roys, *The Maya katun prophesies*, 16–18.
67. Seler, *Gesammelte*, II, 1040–41.
68. Lehmann, *Elegía*, 13.
69. Alberto Ruz Lhuiller, "Presencia atlántica en Palenque," 458.
70. Torquemada, *Monarquía*, I, 256.
71. Ixtlilxóchitl, *Obras*, II, 318.
72. Clavijero, *Historia*, 51.
73. Chimalpain, *Memorial Breve*, 105.
74. Schultze-Jena, *Gesänge*, 139.
75. Durán, *Historia*, II, 275.
76. Motolinía, *Memoriales*, 9–12.
77. Seler, *Gesammelte*, III, 49; Lehmann, *Zentralamerika*, I, 986; Jiménez Moreno, "Síntesis de la historia pretolteca," 1077.
78. Borhegyi, "Archaeological synthesis," 53.
79. Recinos, *Anales*, 40.
80. Krickeberg, *Los totonaca*, 136.
81. Scholes and Roys, "The Maya," 2; Thompson, *Maya history*, 20; Ruz, "La costa de Campeche," 280.
82. Chimalpain, *Relaciones*, 173.
83. *Anales de Cuauhtitlán*, 15.
84. Jiménez Moreno, "Relación," 21.
85. Jiménez Moreno, "Síntesis de la historia precolonial," 224.
86. Wigberto Jiménez Moreno, "Los imperios prehispánicos," 193.
87. Paddock, "Mixtec ethnohistory."
88. Sahagún, *Florentine Codex*, Book X, 187.
89. Paul Kirchhoff, "Prólogo a la *Historia Tolteca-Chichimeca*," xxi.
90. Antoinette Nelken and Richard McNeish, *La Vallée de Tehuacán*, 1175.
91. Chimalpain, *Relaciones*, 169.
92. Schultze-Jena, *Gesänge*, 141.
93. *Historia Tolteca-Chichimeca*, 88.
94. Kirchhoff, "Das Toltekenreich," 253.
95. *Anales de Tlatelolco*, 35.
96. Anónimo Mexicano, 23.
97. Schultze-Jena, *Gesänge*, 225.
98. Jiménez Moreno, "Síntesis de la historia precolonial," 222.
99. Ixtlilxóchitl, *Obras*, I, 26–27.
100. Davies, *Los mexicas*, Appendix A.
101. *Anales de Cuauhtitlán*, 7.
102. Ixtlilxóchitl, *Obras*, II, 33.
103. *Ibid.*, I, 69–70.
104. Chimalpain, *Memorial Breve*, 12.
105. By calculation from dates in the *Anales de Cuauhtitlán* and the *Relación de la Genealogía*; *see also* Kirchhoff, "Quetzalcoatl," 193.

106. Chadwick, "Postclassic pottery," 230–32.
107. Ignacio Bernal, personal communication.
108. Ignacio Bernal, "Archaeological synthesis of Oaxaca," 806.
109. Ixtlilxóchitl, *Obras,* I, 30.

5. THE MAYAN MARCH

1. Carmack, *Quichean civilization,* 288.
2. Tezozómoc, *Crónica Mexicayotl,* 43.
3. Michael Coe, "Olmec style," 771.
4. Durán, *Historia,* II, 388–89.
5. Nigel Davies, *The Aztecs,* Chapter VII.
6. Roys, *Chilam Balam,* 161.
7. *Ibid.,* 139.
8. *Codex Pérez,* 141.
9. J. Eric S. Thompson, personal communication.
10. Fray Diego de Landa, *Relación,* 13.
11. Thompson, *Maya history,* 12.
12. *Ibid.,* 11.
13. *Ibid.,* 15.
14. Ralph Roys, "Native empires in Yucatán," 161.
15. Scholes and Roys, *The Maya Chontal,* 27.
16. *Relaciones de Yucatán,* I, 120.
17. Thompson, *Maya history,* 20.
18. Gordon Willey and A. L. Smith, *New discoveries at Altar de Sacrificios.*
19. H. Berlin, *Late pottery horizons of Tabasco,* 115.
20. Robert E. Smith, "The place of Fine Orange pottery," 151.
21. J. Eric S. Thompson, "Trade relations between the Maya Highlands and Lowlands," 245.
22. W. T. Sanders, "Cultural ecology of the Maya Lowlands," 234.
23. Ralph Roys, "Lowland Maya native society," 677.
24. Recinos, *Anales,* 67, 68; Recinos, *Popol Vuh,* 142, 169.
25. *Popol Vuh,* 23.
26. *Ibid.,* 121.
27. Adrián Recinos, *Crónicas indígenas de Guatemala,* 77, 81.
28. Antonio Fuentes y Guzmán, *Historia de Guatemala,* I, 20.
29. Lehmann, *Elegía,* 14.
30. Krickeberg, *Los totonacas,* 135.
31. Recinos, *Anales,* 60.
32. Carmack, *Toltec influence,* 60.
33. *Ibid.,* 60, 65.
34. Scholes and Roys, *The Maya Chontal,* 23.
35. Tatiana Proskouriakoff, "Scroll patterns of Veracruz," 396.
36. J. Eric S. Thompson, "Archaeological problems of the Lowland Maya," 134.
37. Michael Coe, "Archaeological synthesis," 700.
38. W. T. Sanders, "Cultural ecology and settlement patterns of the Gulf Coast," 554–56.
39. *Ibid.,* 554.

40. Berlin, *Late pottery*, 147.
41. *Ibid.*, 117.
42. Michael Coe, "Archaeological synthesis," 711.
43. *Ibid.*, 715.
44. Ruz, "Presencia atlántica," 457, 462.
45. Ruz, *La Costa de Campeche.*
46. Scholes and Roys, *The Maya Chontal*, 27–31.
47. Sahagún, *Florentine codex*, Book IX, 17–18.
48. George Kubler, "Chichén Itzá y Tula," 47–80.
49. J. Eric S. Thompson, personal communication.
50. Alberto Ruz Lhuiller, "Chichén Itza y Tula."
51. Bernal, *El mundo olmeca*, 87.
52. Seler, *Gesammelte*, V, 426.
53. Henry B. Nicholson, "Religion in pre-Hispanic Central Mexico," 415.
54. Francis B. Richardson, "Non-Maya monumental sculpture of Central America," 318–20.
55. *Ibid.*
56. Herbert J. Spinden, Chorotegan influences in western Mexico, 36.
57. Alberto Ruz Lhuiller, "Campeche en la arqueología maya," 90.
58. Betty J. Meggers, "Environmental limitations on the development of culture," 819.
59. Thomas S. Barthel, "Comentarios a las inscripciones clásicas tardías de Chichén-Itzá," 223.
60. Carl Ruppert, *Chichén-Itzá*, I.
61. Alberto Ruz Lhuiller, "Influencias mayas en las tierras altas y bajas," 234.
62. Piña Chan, "Los informantes," 92.
63. Esther Pasztory, "The historical and religious significance of the Middle Classic ballgame," 442.
64. Jorge Acosta, "La tercera temporada de exploraciones," 13.
65. Thompson, *Maya history*, 19.
66. Eduardo Matos, "El tzompantli en Mesoamérica," 115.
67. Acosta, "Interpretación," 80.
68. Roys, "Native empires," 153.
69. Barrera Vásquez and Morley, *Maya chronicles*, 36.
70. E. Wyllys Andrews, "Archaeology and prehistory in the Northern Maya Lowlands," 289.
71. *Ibid.*, 313.
72. Foncerrada de Molina, "Fechas de radiocarbono en el área maya."
73. Robert Wauchope, "Southern Mesoamerica," 330–86.
74. J. Eric S. Thompson, "The Itzá of Tayasal, Petén," 389–400.
75. Roys, "Native empires," 158.
76. Alfred Tozzer, *Chichén Itza and its cenote of sacrifice*, 172–73.
77. Chimalpain, *Relaciones*, 169.
78. Robert McC. Adams, *the evolution of urban society.*

6. TOLTEC APOGEE: PART I, THE HOME BASE

1. Jack T. Wynn, "Inferences from Toltec residential architecture," 3.

2. James Stoutamire, "Archaeological survey of the Tula urban zone," 25, 28.

3. Woodrow Borah and Sherburne Cook, *The population of Central Mexico in 1548.*

4. Wynn, "Inferences," 21.

5. *Ibid.*, 23–24.

6. Millon, Drewett, and Cowgill, "Urbanization," 8.

7. Edward Calnek, personal communication, shortly to be published.

8. W. T. Sanders, "Settlement patterns in Central Mexico," 32.

9. Kaplan, "Men, monuments," 401.

10. Sanders, "The population of the Teotihuacán Valley."

11. *Suma de Visitas*, 289.

12. Charles Gibson, *The Aztecs under Spanish rule*, 152.

13. Sanders, "The population," 438.

14. Sherburne Cook, *The historical demography and ecology of the Teotlalpan*, 12.

15. Zantwijk, "La estructura," 136–39.

16. Guadalupe Mastache, "Reconocimiento arqueológico de superficie en el área de Tula, Hgo."

17. Robert Cobean, "Archaeological survey of the Tula region," 17–19.

18. Diehl, *Preliminary report*, 41–42.

19. Cobean, "Archaeological survey," 17.

20. Barbara Price, "Population composition in pre-Hispanic Mesoamerican urban settlements," 265; and Diehl, "A summary of recent investigations at Tula."

21. José Luis Lorenzo, *Las zonas arqueológicas de los volcanes*, 52.

22. Cook, "The interrelation," 48.

23. Sherburne Cook, *Soil erosion and population in Central Mexico*, 45.

24. W. T. Sanders and Barbara Price, *Mesoamerica*, 33.

25. *Relación de Tequisquiac*, 300.

26. Ignacio Bernal, "Teotihuacán; Su prehistórica historia," 8.

27. Sanders and Price, *Mesoamerica*, 149.

28. Diehl, *Preliminary report*, 47.

29. *Relación de Tequisquiac*, 300.

30. Cook, *Historical demography*, 29.

31. Richard B. Woodbury, "Prehistoric water management systems," 346.

32. Angel Palerm, *Obras hidráulicas prehispánicas*, 13–14.

33. W. T. Sanders, "Life in a Classic village," 135–37.

34. Armillas, Palerm, and Wolf, "A small irrigation system," 396.

35. Bruce Drewitt, "Planeación de la antigua ciudad de Teotihuacán," 85.

36. Federico Mooser, "Geología, naturaleza y desarrollo," 36.

37. José Luis Lorenzo, "Clima y agricultura en Teotihuacán," 55.

38. Sanders, "The population," 442.

39. *Ibid.*, 440.

40. Sanders and Price, *Mesoamerica*, 150.

41. Eduardo Matos, personal communication.

42. *Diehl, Preliminary report*, 46.

43. *Ibid.*, 49.

44. John B. Glass, *Archaeological survey of Western Honduras*, 174.

45. Anna O. Shephard, *Plumbate: A Mesoamerican tradeware.*

46. Florencia Muller, personal communication.

47. Thomas Lee, personal communication.
48. Acosta, "Exploraciones," 188.
49. Eduardo Matos, personal communication.
50. Diehl, *Preliminary report*, 44.
51. *Ibid.*, 49.
52. Robert Cobean, "The ceramics of Tula," 74, 81.
53. Lawrence Feldman, personal communication.
54. Sahagún, *Historia*, III, 79.
55. *Codex Ramírez*, 158–59.
56. Miguel Acosta Saignes, *Los Pochteca*, 37.
57. Tezozómoc, *Crónica mexicana*, 523–24.
58. Sanders, "Settlement patterns in Central Mexico," 34.
59. Ignacio Bernal, "Archaeology and the written sources," 223.
60. Katz, *Situación social y económica de los aztecas*, 81–82.
61. Davies, *Los mexicas.*
62. Leo A. Oppenheim, *Ancient Mesopotamia*, 187.
63. Armillas, "Tecnología," 29.
64. Robert Adams, "Some hypotheses," 229.
65. Steward, "Cultural causality," 14.
66. *Anales de Cuauhtitlán*, 7.
67. *Ibid.*, 9.
68. *Ibid.*, 12.
69. Roys, *Chilam Balam of Chumayel*, 66–67.
70. Chimalpain, *Memorial Breve*, 83.
71. *Codex Nuttall*, 44, 55.
72. J. Cooper-Clark, *The story of Eight Deer*, 30.
73. *Anales de Cuauhtitlán*, 8.
74. Seler, *Gesammelte*, III, 375.
75. Alfredo López Austin, personal communication.
76. López Austin, "Hombre Díos," 106.
77. Miles, "Summary," 283.
78. *Anales de Cuauhtitlán*, 12.
79. *Leyenda de los Soles*, 125.
80. Chimalpain, *Memorial Breve*, 8.
81. *Ibid.*, 38.
82. Ixtlilxóchitl, *Obras*, I, 46.
83. Anónimo Mexicano, 116.
84. Davies, *Los mexicas*, 57.
85. Davies, *Los señoríos*, 101–102.

7. TOLTEC APOGEE: PART II, SUBJECTS AND NEIGHBORS

1. *Relación de la Genealogía*, 244.
2. Chimalpain, *Memorial Breve*, 14.
3. *Anales de Cuauhtitlán*, 63.
4. Motolinía, *Memoriales*, 12.
5. Sahagún, *Florentine Codex*, Book IX, 49.
6. "Mapa Quinatzin," 103.

7. Ixtlilxóchitl, *Obras*, II, 78.
8. Cook, *Soil erosion and population in Central Mexico*, 32.
9. Gibson, *The Aztecs under Spanish rule*, 137.
10. Krickeberg, *Los totonacas*, 119.
11. *Historia Tolteca-Chichimeca*, 68.
12. Luis Reyes, personal communication.
13. Luis Reyes, "Ordenanzas para el gobierno de Cuauhtinchan."
14. *Historia Tolteca-Chichimeca*, 159–61.
15. Thelma Sullivan, personal communication.
16. Krickeberg, *Los totonacas*, 119–20.
17. Kirchhoff, "Das Toltekenreich," 251–52.
18. *Historia Tolteca-Chichimeca*, 78.
19. *Ibid*., 98.
20. *Ibid*., 96.
21. *Anales de Cuauhtitlán*, 63.
22. Davies, *Los mexicas*, 25–26.
23. Alfonso Caso, "La época de los señoríos independientes," 149.
24. O'Neill, "Preliminary report," 48.
25. Ixtlilxóchitl, *Obras*, II, 37.
26. *Ibid*., 57.
27. *Ibid*., I, 123.
28. Caso, "Los señoríos," 149.
29. Ixtlilxóchitl, *Obras*, I, 86.
30. Tezozómoc, *Crónica Mexicayotl*, 91–95.
31. Davies, *Los mexicas*, 110.
32. Ixtlilxóchitl, *Obras*, I, 38.
33. *Ibid*., 57.
34. *Ibid*., 52.
35. *Anales de Tlatelolco*, 35.
36. *Anales de Cuauhtitlán*, 62.
37. Florencia Muller, *Historia antigua del Valle de Morelos*, 25–26.
38. Jacobs Muller, "La cerámica arqueológica."
39. Jaime Litvak, "Las relaciones externas," 68.
40. *Ibid*., 69.
41. Charles Kelley, "Mesoamerica," 105.
42. Charles Kelley and Ellen Abbott, "The cultural sequence on the North Central frontier of Mesoamerica," 325–44.
43. Charles Kelley, "Mesoamerica," 99.
44. Braniff, "Estratigrafía," 150.
45. Jorge Acosta, "Exploraciones en Tula, Hidalgo," 192.
46. García Payón, "La cerámica," 209, 230.
47. Florencia Muller, "Cerámica de la cuenca del Río Lerma," 50.
48. Eduardo Noguera and Ramón Piña Chan, "Estratigrafía de Teopanzolco," 156.
49. Seler, *Gesammelte*, II, 161.
50. Ixtlilxóchitl, *Obras*, I, 38.
51. Sahagún, *Florentine codex*, Book X, 183.
52. Chimalpain, *Relaciones*, 134.

53. *Ibid.*, 135.
54. *Ibid.*, 169.
55. Piña Chan, personal communication.
56. Piña Chan, personal communication.
57. Torquemada, *Monarquía*, I, 260.
58. Muller, "Cerámica de Cholula," 131.
59. Armillas, "Los olmecas-xicallangas," 137–43.
60. Angel García Cook, personal communication.
61. José García Payón, "Archaeology," 533.
62. *Ibid.*
63. Seler, *Gesammelte*, III, 445, 449.
64. David Kelley, "Historia prehispánica de Totonacapan," 310.
65. Du Solier, *La Huaxteca*, 150.
66. Richard Diehl, "Relations between Tula and the Huaxteca."
67. Nigel Davies, "The military organization of the Aztec Empire."
68. Ixtlilxóchitl, *Obras*, I, 37, 56, 89.
69. Muñoz Camargo, *Historia*, 45.
70. Laurence Feldman, personal communication.
71. José García Payón, "Estudio preliminar de la zona arqueológica de Texmelincan," 341–64.
72. Noguera, "Excavations at Tehuacán," 310.
73. Bernal, "Archaeological synthesis," 808.
74. Alfonso Caso, "El calendario mixteco," 488.
75. Ignacio Bernal, "Exploraciones en Coixtlahuaca, Oaxaca," 5.
76. Barbro Dahlgren, *La Mixteca*, 84.
77. José Antonio Gay, *Historia de Oaxaca*, I, 274–76; Ronald Spores, *The Mixtec kings and their people*, 61.
78. John Paddock, "Oaxaca in Ancient Mesoamerica," 176–82.
79. Torquemada, *Monarquía*, I, 86.
80. Caso, "El Díos I Muerte," 43.
81. Alfonso Caso, *Interpretación del Códice Gómez de Orozco*, 17.
82. Caso, "Los lienzos," 249.
83. Gibson, *The Aztecs*, 141.
84. Edward Calnek, "Settlement patterns and chinampa agriculture at Tenochtitlan."
85. Davies, *Los señoríos*, 22.
86. Gordon Childe, *The prehistory of European society*, 124.

8. DOOM AND DISASTER

1. Carmack, *Quichean civilization*, 25–27.
2. *Ibid.*, 49.
3. Acosta, "Interpretación," 75.
4. Acosta, "Los últimos," 59.
5. Jorge Acosta, personal communication.
6. José Luis Franco, "Comentarios sobre la decoración negra," 164.
7. Acosta, "Interpretación," 92.
8. James B. Griffin and Antonieta Espejo, "Alfarería correspondiente al último período de ocupación nahua," 141.

9. Noguera and Piña Chan, "Estratigrafía," 149.
10. Kirchhoff, "Quetzalcoatl."
11. Torquemada, *Monarquía*, I, 258–60.
12. Muñoz Camargo, *Historia*, 45.
13. Kirchhoff, "Prologo," xlix.
14. *Ibid.*, map opposite p. lxiv.
15. *Historia Tolteca-Chichimeca*, 101.
16. Chimalpain, *Memorial Breve*, 9.
17. *Ibid.*, 38.
18. *Anales de Cuauhtitlán*, 14.
19. Kirchhoff, "Quetzalcoatl."
20. Jiménez Moreno, "Los imperios prehispánicos en Mesoamérica," 191.
21. Jaime Litvak King, "La introducción posthispánica de elementos a las religiones prehispánicas," 27.
22. *Relación de la genealogía*, 243.
23. Dumézil, *L'héritage Indo-européen à Rome*, 21–22.
24. Sahagún, *Historia*, II, 95.
25. J. Eric S. Thompson, "Maya rulers of the Classic period," 55.
26. López Austin, "Hombre Díos," 77.
27. Walter Lehmann, *Die Geschichte*, 39.
28. Davies, *Los mexicas*, 58.
29. Davies, *Los señoríos*, 96–103.
30. *Historia Tolteca-Chichimeca*, 68.
31. Luis Reyes, personal communication.
32. César Olivé and Beatriz Barba, *Sobre la disintegración de las culturas*, 69.
33. Tezozómoc, *Crónica mexicana*, 514.
34. *Anales de Cuauhtitlán*, 7.
35. *Ibid.*, 12.
36. Ixtlilxóchitl, *Obras*, I, 46.
37. Dumézil, *L'héritage*, 159.
38. Claude Lévi-Strauss, *From honey to ashes*, 77.
39. Sahagún, *Florentine codex*, Book III, 49.
40. Jiménez Moreno, "Religión," 203.
41. *Historia de los Mexicanos*, 234.
42. Lévi-Strauss, *From honey to ashes*, 245.
43. Seler, *Gesammelte*, I, 652.
44. Nicholson, "The religious-ritual system," 231.
45. Jiménez Moreno, "Religión," 203.
46. Seler, *Gesammelte*, II, 499–500.
47. Sahagún, *Florentine codex*, Book III, 15.
48. León Portilla, *Aztec thought and culture*, 87.
49. *Historia de los Mexicanos*, 214–15.
50. Thompson, *Maya history*, 199.
51. Seler, *Gesammelte*, IV, 40.
52. *Codex Vaticanus A*, Plate XII.
53. Sahagún, *Historia*, I, 307–308.
54. *Ibid.*, 319.
55. Seler, *Gesammelte*, III, 339.

56. Josefina García Quintana, "El baño ritual entre los nahuas," 202.
57. *Historia de los Mexicanos*, 209.
58. Chimalpain, *Relaciones*, 164–65.
59. *Historia de los Mexicanos*, 219.
60. Sahagún, *Florentine codex*, Book III, 50.
61. Torquemada, *Monarquía*, II, 48.
62. Lévi-Strauss, *From honey to ashes*, 256.
63. Ixtlilxóchitl, *Obras*, I, 55.
64. *Ibid.*, 20.
65. Fray Jeronimo de Mendieta, *Historia eclesiástica indiana*, I, 99.
66. Durán, *Historia*, II, 302.
67. Cook, "The interrelation," 48.
68. Kovar, "The physical . . . environment," 81.
69. Angel Palerm and Eric Wolf, *Potencial ecológico y desarrollo cultural en Mesoamerica*, 4.
70. Pedro Armillas, "Northern Mesoamerica," 317.
71. Braniff, "Secuencias," 277.
72. Charles Kelley, "Archaeology," 777–78.
73. *Ibid.*, 773.
74. Braniff, "Secuencias," 281.
75. Betty Bell, "Archaeology of Nayarit, Jalisco, and Colima," 766.
76. Ixtlilxóchitl, *Obras*, I, 48, 473.
77. *Anales de Cuauhtitlán*, 13.
78. *Leyenda de los Soles*, 126.
79. Torquemada, *Monarquía*, I, 278.
80. Davies, "The military organization."
81. *Anales de Cuauhtitlán*, 13.
82. Krickeberg, *Los totonacas*, 156.
83. Guy Stresser Péan, "Les indiens huastèques," 217.
84. *Ibid.*, 298.
85. Ixtlilxóchitl, *Obras*, I, 82.
86. *Ibid.*, 46–56.
87. *Ibid.*, 46.
88. *Ibid.*, 70, 493.
89. *Ibid.*, 51.
90. Davies, *Los mexicas*, 26.
91. Ixtlilxóchitl, *Obras*, 11, 57.
92. *Ibid.*, 37, 56, 89.
93. M. Swadesh, 'Algunas fechas glotocronológicas."
94. Ixtlilxóchitl, *Obras*, I, 98.

ABBREVIATIONS USED IN BIBLIOGRAPHY

The following references are additional to normal usage:

A. Anthr.: *American Anthropologist.*
A. Antiq.: *American Antiquity.*
C.I.W.: Carnegie Institution of Washington.
E.C.M.: *Estudios de Cultura Maya.*
E.C.N.: *Estudios de Cultura Nahuatl.*
H.M.A.I.: *Handbook of the Middle American Indian.*
I.C.A.: *Proceedings, International Congress of Americanists.*
I.N.A.H.: Instituto Nacional de Antropología e Historia.
M.R.: *Mesa Redonda.*
R.M.E.A.: *Revista Mexicana de Estudios Antropológicos.*
R.M.E.H.: *Revista Mexicana de Estudios Históricos.*
U.N.A.M.: Universidad Nacional Autónoma de México.

Bibliography

Abbott, Ellen. *See* J. Charles Kelley and Ellen Abbott.

Acosta, Jorge

1940 "Exploraciones en Tula, Hidalgo," *R.M.E.A.*, Vol. IV, No. 3, pp. 172–94.

1941 "Los últimos descubrimientos arqueológicos en Tula, Hgo., 1941," *R.M.E.A.*, Vol. V, Nos. 2 and 3, pp. 239–48.

1944 "La tercera temporada de exploraciones en Tula, Hgo., 1942," *R.M.E.A.*, Vol. VI, No. 3, pp. 125–64.

1945 "La cuarta y quinta temporada de excavaciones en Tula, Hgo., 1943–44," *R.M.E.A.*, Vol. VII, Nos. 1, 2, and 3, pp. 23–64.

1956–57 "Interpretación de algunos datos obtenidos en Tula relativos a la época tolteca," *R.M.E.A.*, Vol. XIV, No. 2, pp. 75–110.

1957 "Resúmen de los informes de las exploraciones arqueológicas en Tula, Hgo. durante las novenas y décimas temporadas," *I.N.A.H. Anales*, Vol. IX, pp. 119–69.

1961 "La indumentaria de los cariátides de Tula," *Homenaje a Pablo Martínez del Río*, pp. 221–29. I.N.A.H., Mexico.

1964 *El Palacio de Quetzalpapálotl.* I.N.A.H., Mexico.

1966 "Una clasificación tentativa de los monumentos arqueológicos de Teotihuacán," XI *M.R.*, Vol. I, pp. 45–55.

1970 "El Altar 1," in *Proyecto Cholula*, pp. 93–103. I.N.A.H., Mexico.

1972 "El epílogo de Teotihuacán," XI *M.R.*, Vol. II, pp. 149–56.

Acosta Saignes, Miguel

1946 "Migraciones de los mexica," *Memorias de la Academia Mexicana de la Historia*, Vol. V, No. 2, pp. 177–87.

1948 *Los Pochteca; ubicación de los mercaderes en la estructura social tenochca.* Mexico.

Adams, Richard
1961 "Archaeological reconnaissance in the Chiapas Highlands," VIII *M.R.*, pp. 105–10.

Adams, Robert McC.
1956 "Some hypotheses on the development of early civilization," *A. Antiq.*, Vol. XXI, No. 3, pp. 227–32.
1966 *The evolution of urban society.* Aldine Publishing Company, Chicago.

Addhofer, Otto. *See* Codex Vindobonensis.

Alkin, U.Bahadir
The ancient civilization of Anatolia.

Anales de Cuauhtitlán
1945 In *Códice Chimalpopoca.* Edited and translated by Primo F. Velásquez. Imprenta Universitaria, Mexico. *See also* Walter Lehmann, 1938.

Anales de los Cakchiqueles. *See* Recinos, 1953.

Anales de Tlatelolco
1948 "A sequence of cultural development in Mesoamerica," in *A reappraisal* Robredo, Mexico.

Anales de Tula (1361–1521)
1949 In *Tlalocan*, Vol. III, No. 1., pp. 2–14.

Anales Toltecas
1949 Editorial Vargas Rea, Mexico.

Andrews, E. Wyllys
1965 "Archaeology and prehistory in the northern Maya Lowlands: an introduction," *H.M.A.I.*, Vol. II, pp. 288–330.

Anónimo Mexicano
1903 In *Anales del Museo Nacional de México, época I*, Vol. VII, pp. 115–32.

Armillas, Pedro
1946 "Los olmeca xicallangas y los sitios arqueológicos del suroeste de Tlaxcala," *R.M.E.A.*, Vol. VIII, Nos. 1, 2, and 3, pp. 137–45.
1947 "La serpiente emplumada, Quetzalcoatl y Tláloc," *Cuadernos Americanos*, Vol. VI, pp. 161–78.
1948 "A sequence of cultural development in Mesoamerica," in *A reappraisal of Peruvian archaeology.* Edited by Wendell C. Bennett. Menasha, Wis.
1948 "Arqueología del Occidente de Guerrero," IV *M.R.*, pp. 74–76.

1951 "Tecnología, formación socio-económica y religión en Mesoamérica," in *Selected Papers, XXIX I.C.A.* Chicago.

1964 "Condiciones ambientales y movimientos de pueblos en la frontera septentrional de Mesoamérica," in *Homenaje a Fernando Márquez Miranda.* Madrid.

1964 "Northern Mesoamerica," in *Prehistoric man in the New World.* University of Chicago Press, Chicago.

———, Angel Palerm, and Eric R. Wolf

1956 "A small irrigation system in the Valley of Teotihuacán," *A. Antiq.*, Vol. XXI, pp. 396–99.

———, and Robert C. West

1950 "Las chinampas de México, poesía y realidad de los 'jardínes flotantes'," *Cuadernos Americanos,* Vol. IX, pp. 165–82.

Barrera Vásquez, Alfredo, and Sylvanus Morley

1949 *The Maya Chronicles. C.I.W. Pub. 585.* Washington, D.C.

Barthel, Thomas S.

1964 "Comentarios a las inscripciones clásicas tardías de Chichén-Itzá," *E.C.M.*, Vol. IV, pp. 223–44.

Bell, Betty

1971 "Archaeology of Nayarit, Jalisco and Colima," *H.M.A.I.*, Vol. XI, pp. 694–753.

Bennyhoff, James A.

1966 "Chronology and periodization: continuity and change in the Teotihuacán ceramic tradition," XI *M.R.*, Vol. I, pp. 19–29.

Berlin, H.

1956 *Late pottery horizons of Tabasco, Mexico. C.I.W. Pub. 606.* Washington, D.C.

Bernal, Ignacio

1948 "Exploraciones en Coixtlahuaca, Oaxaca," *R.M.E.A.*, Vol. X, pp. 5–76.

1957 "Relación de Tequisquiac, Citlaltepec y Xilocingo." Commentary by Ignacio Bernal in Tlalocan, Vol. III, Number 4, pp. 289–308.

1962 "Archaeology and the written sources," *XXXIV I.C.A.* pp. 219–25.

1965 "Archaeological synthesis of Oaxaca," *H.M.A.I.*, Vol. III, Part 2, pp. 788–813.

1965 "Teotihuacán: nuevas fechas de radiocarbono y su posible significado," *Anales de Antropología,* Vol. II, pp. 27–35.

1966 "The Mixtecs in the archaeology of the Valley of Oaxaca," in *Ancient Oaxaca,* pp. 345–66. Edited by John Paddock. Stanford University Press, Stanford, Calif.

1966 "Teotihuacán: Capital de imperio?" *R.M.E.A.*, Vol. XX, pp. 95–110.
1967 "Teotihuacán: su prehistórica historia." Lecture in the Museo Nacional de Antropología. I.N.A.H., Mexico.
1968 *El mundo olmeca.* Editorial Porrua, Mexico.

Beyer, Hermann
1965 *Obras completas,* I. *México Antiguo,* Vol. X.

Bittmann Simons, Bente
1968 "The *Codex of Cholula* and its ancient barrios," *XXXVIII I.C.A.*, Vol. II, pp. 139–50.
See also Codex of Cholula.

Borah, Woodrow, and Sherburne F. Cook
1960 *The population of Central Mexico in 1548.* University of California Press, Berkeley and Los Angeles.

Borhegyi, Stephan F.
1965 "Archaeological synthesis of the Guatemalan Highlands," *H.M.A.I.*, Vol. II, pp. 3–58.
1965 "Settlement patterns of the Guatemalan Highlands," *H.M.A.I.*, Vol. II, pp. 59–75.
1967 "Una fecha de C–14 para la influencia teotihuacana en Guatemala," *E.C.M.*, Vol. VI, pp. 221–22.

Brand, Donald D.
1971 "Ethnohistoric synthesis of Western Mexico," *H.M.A.I.*, Vol. XI, pp. 619–32.

Braniff, Beatriz
1967 "Estratigrafía en Villa Reyes, San Luis Potosí." Mimeographed paper.
1972 "Secuencias arqueológicas en Guanajuato y la Cuenca de México: intento de correlación," XI *M.R.*, pp. 273–323.

Bray, Warwick
1970 "Land use, settlement patterns and politics in Prehispanic Middle America, a review," in *Man, settlement and urbanism.* Duckworth, London.

Brenner, Anita
1931 "The influence of technique on the decorative style in the domestic pottery of Culhuacán," *Contributions to Anthropology,* Vol. XIII.

Brinton, Daniel
1887 *Were the Toltecs an historic nationality?* McCatten, Philadelphia.

Butler, Mary
1962 "A pottery sequence from Alta Verapaz, Guatemala," in *The Maya and their neighbors.* D. Appleton-Century, New York.

Caleti, Agustín Villagra
1971 "Mural painting in Central Mexico," *H.M.A.I.*, Vol. X, pp. 135–56.

Calnek, Edward E.
1972 "Settlement patterns and chinampa agriculture at Tenochtitlan," *A. Antiq.*, Vol. XXXVII, pp. 104–15.

Cardos, Amalia
1959 *El comercio de los Mayas antiguos.* Acta Anthropológica, Mexico.

Carmack, Robert M.
1968 *Toltec influence on the Postclassic culture history of Highland Guatemala.* Middle American Research Institute, Tulane University, New Orleans.
1973 *Quichean civilization.* University of California Press, Berkeley and Los Angeles.

Carrasco Pizana, Pedro
1950 *Los otomíes.* Publications of the Institute of History, National University of Mexico, Mexico.

Caso, Alfonso
1928 "Los jeroglíficos de Tenayuca, México," *R.M.E.H.*, Vol. II, pp. 141–62.
1937 "Tenían los teotihuacanos conocimiento del tonalpohualli?" *México Antiguo*, Vol. IV, pp. 131–43.
1939 "Correlación de los años azteca y cristiano," *R.M.E.A.*, Vol. III, pp. 11–45.
1941 "El complejo de Tula y las grandes culturas indígenas de México," *R.M.E.A.*, Vol. V., pp. 85–95.
1941 "El problema de Tula," 1 *M.R. Boletín No. 1*, pp. 8–11.
1942 "El paraíso terrenal de Teotihuacán," *Cuadernos Americanos*, Vol. VI, pp. 127–36.
1949 "El Mapa de Teozacualco," *Cuadernos Americanos*, Vol. VIII, pp. 145–81.
1950 "Explicación del Reverso del Códice Vindobonensis," *Memorias del Colegio Nacional*, Vol. V, pp. 9–46.
1952 "Base para la sincronología Mixteca y Cristiana," *Memorias del Colegio Nacional*, Vol. VI, pp. 49–66.
1954 *Interpretación del Códice Gómez de Orozco.* Sociedad Mexicana de la Antropología, Mexico.
1956 "Los barrios antiguos de Tenochtitlan y Tlatelolco," *Memorias de la Academia Mexicana de la Historia*, Vol. XV, pp. 7–62.
1956 "El calendario mixteco," *Historia Mexicana*, Vol. V, pp. 481–97.
1958 "El primer embajador conocido en América," *Cuadernos Americanos*, Vol. XVII, pp. 285–93.
1958 "El Lienzo de Yolotepec," *Memorias del Colegio Nacional*, Vol. XIII, pp. 41–55.

1958 "Comentario del Códice Baranda," in *Miscelánea Paul Rivet*, pp. 373–89. México.

1959 "Glifos teotihuacanos," *R.M.E.A.* XV, pp. 51–70.

1960 "El Dios 1 Muerte," *Mitteilungen aus dem Museum für Völkerkunde und Vorgeschichte*, Vol. XXV, pp. 373–89.

1960 "Valor histórico de los códices mixtecos," *Cuadernos Americanos*, Vol. XIX, No. 2.

1960 *Interpretación del Códice Bodley 2858*. Sociedad Mexicana de Antropología, Mexico.

1961 "Los lienzos mixtecos de Ihuitlán y Antonio de León," in *Homenaje a Pablo Martínez del Río*, pp. 237–74. I.N.A.H., Mexico.

1961 "Nombres calendáricos de los dioses," *México Antiguo*, Vol. IX, pp. 77–100.

1964 "Los señores de Yanhuitlán," *XXXV I.C.A.*, Vol. I, pp. 437–48.

1964 *Interpretación del Códice Selden 3135*. Sociedad Mexicana de la Antropología, Mexico.

1966 *Interpretación del Códice Colombino*. Sociedad Mexicana de la Antropología, Mexico.

1966 "La época de los señoríos independientes," *R.M.E.A.*, Vol. XX, pp. 147–54.

1966 "Dioses y signos teotihuacanos," XI *M.R.*, Vol. I, pp. 249–79.

1967 *Los calendarios prehispánicos*. Instituto de Investigaciones Históricas, U.N.A.M., Mexico.

1968 "Religión o religiones mesoamericanas," *XXXVIII I.C.A.*, Vol. III, pp. 189–200.

Castillo, Victor M.

1969 "Caminos del mundo náhuatl," *E.C.N.*, Vol. VIII.

Castillo Tejero, Noemi

1972 "El uso de sistemas mecanizados en el manejo de fuentes históricas (el *Popol Vuh*)," XII *M.R.* pp. 335–43.

Ceballos Novelo, Roque J.

1935 *Antecedentes legendarios e históricos de Tenayuca*. Departamento de Monumentos Prehispánicos, Mexico.

Chadwick, Robert

1966 *The Olmeca-Xicallanca of Teotihuacán: a preliminary study. Mesoamerican Notes, Nos. 7–8.* University of the Americas, Mexico.

1971 "Postclassic pottery of the central valleys," *H.M.A.I.*, Vol. X, pp. 228–57.

1971 "Native pre-Aztec history of Central Mexico," *H.M.A.I.*, Vol. XI, pp. 474–505.

1971 "Archaeological synthesis of Michoacan and adjacent regions," *H.M.A.I.*, Vol. XI, pp. 657–93.

Charlton, Thomas

1970 "Contemporary agriculture in the Teotihuacán Valley," in *The Teotihuacán Valley Project, Final Report*, Vol. I, pp. 253–348. Pennsylvania State University, State University, Pa.

Chilam Balam of Chumayel. *See* Ralph Roys.

Childe, Gordon

1958 *The prehistory of European society*. Pelican, London.

Chimalpain Cuauhtlehuantzin, Domingo Francisco de San Anton Muñon

1958 *Das Memorial Breve acerca de la fundación de la ciudad de Culhuacán*. Translated by Walter Lehmann and Gerdt Kutscher. W. Kohlhammer Verlag, Stuttgart.

1963 *Die Relationen Chimalpains zur Geschichte Mexicos*, Teil I, *die Zeit bis zur Conquista*. Edited by Günter Zimmermann. Hamburg University, Hamburg.

1965 *Relaciones originales de Chalco-Amaquemecan*. Translated by Silvia Rendon. Fondo de Cultura Económica, Mexico.

Cholula. *See* Proyecto Cholula.

Clark, David

1968 *Analytical archaeology*. Methuen, London.

Clark, Kenneth

1969 *Civilization*. Harper and Row, New York.

Clavijero, Francisco Xavier

1964 *Historia antigua de México*. Editorial Porrua, Mexico.

Cobean, Robert

1973 "Archaeological survey of the Tula region." Mimeographed report on Tula expedition, 1970–72, pp. 11–21. University of Missouri, Columbia.

1973 "The ceramics of Tula." Report on Tula expedition, 1970–72, pp. 59–80. University of Missouri, Columbia.

Codex Becker I–II

1961 With commentary by Karl A. Nowotny. Akademische Druck- und Verlagsanstalt, Graz.

Codex Bodley. *See* Alfonso Caso, 1960.

Codex Borgia. *See* Eduard Seler, 1963.

Codex Nuttall

1902 With introduction by Celia Nuttall. Peabody Museum of American Archaeology and Ethnology, Cambridge, Mass.

Codex of Cholula
1968 With commentary by Bente Bittmann Simons. In *Tlalocan*, Vol. V, pp. 267–340.

Codex of Otlazpan
1967 With study by Bridget Leander. I.N.A.H., Mexico.

Codex of Tula
n.d. *Anales mexicanos del pueblo de Tezontepec*. Copy in the Library of the Museo Nacional de Antropología, Mexico.

Codex of Yanhuitlan
1940 Facsimile edition with preliminary study by Wigberto Jiménez Moreno and Salvador Mateos Higuera. Museo Nacional, Mexico.

Codex Osuna
1878 Manuel G. Hernández, Madrid.

Codex Pérez
1949 Translated from Maya into Spanish by Dr. E. Solís Alcalá. Imprenta Oriente, Mérida.

Codex Ramirez
1944 Editorial Leyenda, Mexico City.

Codex Selden II. *See* Alfonso, Caso, 1964.

Codex Sierra
1906 Museo Nacional de México, Mexico.

Codex Vaticano-Ríos
1900 Stabilmento Donesi, Rome.

Codex Vindobonensis Mexicanus I
1963 History and description by Otto Addhofer. Akademische Druck- und Verlagsanstalt, Graz.

Coe, Michael
1960 "Archaeological linkages with North and South America at La Victoria, Guatemala," *A. Anthr.* Vol. LXII, pp. 363–93.
1965 "Archaeological synthesis of southern Veracruz and Tabasco," *H.M.A.I.*, Vol. III, Part 2, pp. 679–715.
1965 "The Olmec style and its distribution," *H.M.A.I.*, Vol. III, Part 2, pp. 739–75.

Coe, William
1962 "A summary of excavation and research at Tikal, Guatemala," *E.C.M.*, Vol. III, pp. 40–64.

Cook, Sherburne F.

1947 "The interrelation of population, food supply and building in pre-Conquest Central Mexico," *A. Antiq.*, Vol. XIII, pp. 45–52.

1949 *Soil erosion and population in Central Mexico.* University of California Press, Berkeley and Los Angeles.

1949 *The historical demography and ecology of the Teotlalpan.* University of California Press, Berkeley and Los Angeles.

1960 *See* under Woodrow Borah.

———, and R. F. Heizer

1965 *The quantitive approach to the relation between popuplation and settlement size.* University of California Press, Berkeley and Los Angeles.

———, and Lesley Bird Simpson

1948 "The population of Mexico in the sixteenth century," *Ibero-Americana*, Vol. XXXI.

Cook de Leonard, Carmen

1956–57 "Algunos antecedentes sobre la cerámica tolteca," *R.M.E.A.*, Vol. XIV, No. 2, pp. 37–44.

———, and Ernesto V. Lemoine

1954–55 "Material para la geografía histórica de la región Chalco-Amecameca," *R.M.E.A.*, Vol. XIV, No. 1, pp. 289–96.

Cooper-Clark, J.

1912 *The story of Eight Deer in the Codex Colombino.* Taylor and Francis, London.

Covarrubias, Miguel

1957 *Indian art of Mexico and Central America.* A. A. Knopf, New York.

Dahlgren de Jordan, Barbro

1953 "Etnografía prehispánica de la costa del Golfo," *R.M.E.A.*, Vol. XIII, pp. 146–56.

1954 *La Mixteca: su cultura e historia prehispánicas.* Imprenta Universitaria, Mexico.

Dark, Philipp

1958 *Mixtec ethnohistory: A method of analysis of the codical art.* Oxford University Press.

Davies, Claude Nigel

1968 *Los señoríos independientes del imperio azteca.* I.N.A.H., Mexico.

1972 "The military organization of the Aztec Empire," *XL I.C.A.* (in press).

1973 *Los mexicas: primeros pasos hacia el imperio.* Instituto de Investigaciones Históricas, U.N.A.M., Mexico.

1973 *The Aztecs.* Macmillan, London.

Delgado, Agustin
1961 "La secuencia arqueológica en el Istmo de Tehuantepec," VIII *M.R.*, pp. 93–104.

Descripción de Cholula
Por Gabriel Rojas. *Relaciones históricas y estadísticas*, Vol. IX, pp. 363–83. Manuscript in Library of Museo Nacional de Antropología, Mexico.

Diehl, Richard
1971 *Preliminary report. University of Missouri archaeological project at Tula, 1970–1971 field seasons.* University of Missouri, Columbia.
1972 "Contemporary settlement and social organization," XI *M.R.*, Part 2, pp. 353–63.
1973 "Summary and conclusions." Mimeographed report on Tula expedition, 1970–72. University of Missouri, Columbia.
1973 "Relations between Tula and the Huaxteca," XIII *M.R.*
1974 "A summary of recent investigations at Tula." XLI I.C.A. (in press).

Drewitt, Bruce
1961 *See under* René Millon.
1966 "Planeación de la antigua ciudad de Teotihuacán," XI *M.R.*, pp. 79–94.
1972 *See under* René Millon.

Drummond, D. E., and Florencia Muller
1972 "Classic to Postclassic in Highland Central Mexico," *Science*, Vol. CLXXV, pp. 1208–15.

Dumézil, Georges
1949 *L'héritage Indo-européen à Rome.* Gallimard, Paris.

Durán, Fray Diego
1967 *Historia de las Indias de Nueva España.* 2 vols. Editorial Porrua, Mexico.

Du Solier, Wilfrido
1939 "Una representación pictórica de Quetzalcoatl en una cueva," *R.M.E.A.*, Vol. III, pp. 129–41.
1941 "Recopilación y conclusiones sobre los problemas arqueológicos de Tula, Hgo.," *R.M.E.A.*, Vol. V, pp. 185–92.
1943 "Conclusiones sobre el estudio Arqueologico de la Zona Huaxteca," in *El Norte de Mexico y el Sur de Los Estados Unidos*, pp. 148–52. Sociedad Mexicana de Antropologia. Mexico..
1945 "Estudio arquitectónico de los edificios huaxtecos," *Anales del I.N.A.H.*, Vol. 1, pp. 121–45.

Dutton, Bertha
1955 "Tula of the Toltecs," *El Palacio*, Vol. LXII, pp. 195–225.
1965 "Mesoamerican culture traits which appear in the American Southwest," *XXXV I.C.A.*, Vol. 1, pp. 481–91.

Ekholm, Gordon F.

1941 "Tula and northwestern Mexico," *R.M.E.A.*, Vol. V, Nos. 2 and 3, pp. 193–98.

1942 "Excavations at Guasave, Sinaloa, Mexico," *Anthropological Papers of the American Museum of Natural History*, Vol. XXXVIII, Part 2, pp. 23–139.

1944 "Excavations at Tampico and Pánuco in the Huaxteca," *Anthropological Papers of the American Museum of Natural History*, Vol. XXXVIII, Part V, pp. 319–509.

1962 "The archaeology of northern and western Mexico," in *The Maya and their neighbors*. D. Appleton-Century, New York.

Espejo, Antonieta

1944 "Algunas semejanzas entre Tenayuca y Tlatelolco," *Memorias de la Academia Mexicana de la Historia*, Vol. III, No. 4.

1947 *See under* J. B. Griffin.

Feldman, Lawrence H.

1972 "Tollan in Hidalgo. Native accounts of the Central Mexican Tolteca." A preliminary report for the archaeological project at Tula, Hidalgo, of the University of Missouri, Columbia.

Florentine Codex. *See* Fray Bernardino Sahagún, 1950–63.

Florescano, Enrique

1963 "Tula-Teotihuacán, Quetzalcoatl y la Toltecayotl," *Historia Mexicana*, Vol. XIII.

Foncerrada de Molina, Marta

1964 "Fechas de radiocarbono en el área maya," *E.C.M.*, Vol. IV, pp. 141–66.

Foster, George M.

1940 "Notes on the Popoloca of Veracruz," *Publications of the Instituto Panamericana de Geografía e Historia*, Vol. LI.

1951 "Some wider implications of the soul-loss illness among the Sierra Popoloca," *Homenaje a Alfonso Caso*, pp. 167–74.

Franco, José Luis

1945 "Comentarios sobre la decoración negra en la cerámica Azteca II," *R.M.E.A.*, Vol. VII, pp. 163–86.

1957 *Motivos decorativos en la cerámica azteca.* Museo Nacional de Antropología, serie científica, No. 5.

Frankfort, Henry

1948 *Ancient Egyptian religion.* Columbia University Press, New York.

Fuentes y Guzmán, Antonio

1882 *Historia de Guatemala ó Recordación Florida.* 2 vols. Luis Navarro, Madrid.

Gamio, Manuel
1912 "Arqueología de Azcapotzalco," *Cuadernos Americanos,* Vol. XIII, pp. 180–87.

García Payón, José
1940–41 "Estudio preliminar de la zona arqueológica de Texmelincan, Estado de Guerrero," *México antiguo,* Vol. V, pp. 341–64.
1941 "La cerámica del Valle de Toluca," *R.M.E.A.*, Vol. V, Nos. 2 and 3, pp. 209–38.
1951 "La Ciudad arqueológica de El Tajin," *Proceedings of Round Table Conference,* University of Veracruz, Jalapa.
1971 "Archaeology of Central Veracruz," *H.M.A.I.*, Vol. XI, pp. 505–43.

García Quintana, Josefina
1969 "El baño ritual entre los nahuas, según el *Códice Florentino,*" *E.C.N.*, Vol. VIII, pp. 189–214.

Garibay K., Angel María
1958 *Veinte himnos sacros de los nahuas.* U.N.A.M., Mexico.

Garza de Gonzalez, Silvia
1972 "La indumentaria de los dioses masculinos en el *Códice Borgia,*" XII *M.R.* pp. 287–92.

Gay, Fray José Antonio
1950 *Historia de Oaxaca.* Talleres V. Venero, Mexico.

Gibson, Charles
1964 *The Aztecs under Spanish rule.* Stanford University Press, Stanford, Calif.

Glass, John B.
1966 "Archaeological Survey of Western Honduras," *H.M.A.I.*, Vol. IV, pp. 157–79.

González Casanova, Pablo
1928 "El ciclo legendario del Tepoztecatl," *R.M.E.A.*, Vol. II, pp. 18–63.

Griffin, James B., and Antonieta Espejo
1947 "Alfarería correspondiente al último período de ocupación nahua del Valle de México," *Memorias de la Academia Mexicana de la Historia,* Vol. VI, pp. 131–47.

Guzmán, Eulalia
1938 "Un manuscrito de la Colección Boturini que trata de los antiguos señores de Teotihuacán," *Ethnos,* Vol. III, Nos. 4–5, pp. 89–103, Stockholm.

Haviland, William A.

1969 "A new population estimate for Tikal, Guatemala," *A. Antiq.*, Vol. XXXIV, pp. 429–34.

Healan, Dan M.

1973 "Residential architecture at Tula." Mimeographed report on Tula expedition, 1970–72, pp. 30–69. University of Missouri, Columbia.

Heizer, Robert F.

1960 "Agriculture and the theocratic state in Lowland Mesoamerica," *A. Antiq.*, Vol. XXVI, No. 2.

Hicks, Frederick, and H. B. Nicholson

1962 "The transition from Classic to Postclassic at Cerro Portezuelo, Valley of Mexico," *XXXV I.C.A.*, Vol. I, pp. 493–505.

Historia de los Mexicanos por Sus Pinturas

1941 In *Relaciones de Texcoco y de la Nueva España*, pp. 209–40. Editorial Chávez Hayhoe, Mexico.

Historia Tolteca-Chichimeca

1947 Translated from Nahuatl into Spanish by Heinrich Berlin and Silvia Rendon. Prologue by Paul Kirchhoff. Antigue Librería Robredo, Mexico.

Histoyre du Mechique

1905 Edited by Eduard Yonghue. *Journal de la Société des Américanistes de Paris*, Vol. II, pp. 1–41.

Howard, Agnes M. *See* Lister and Howard.

Huastecos, Totonacos y sus Vecinos

1953 Edited by Ignacio Bernal and Eusebio Dávalos Hurtado. Sociedad Mexicana de Antropología, México.

Hultin, Eskil

1972 *The accuracy of radiocarbon dating. Etnologiska Studiar No. 32*, Stockholm.

Ixtlilxóchitl, Fernando de Álva

1952 *Obras históricas.* 2 vols. Editora Nacional, Mexico.

Jacobs Müller, E. F.

1951 "Las cerámicas del horizonte Culturas Locales," in *Selected Papers, XXIX I.C.A.* University of Chicago Press, Chicago.

1956–57 "Azcapotzalco: estudio tipológico de su cerámica," *R.M.E.A.*, Vol. XIV, No. 2, pp. 25–32.

1956–57 "La cerámica arqueológica de Tepoztlán, *R.M.E.A.*, Vol. XIV, No. 2, pp. 125–28.

1956–57 "El Valle de Tulancingo," *R.M.E.A.*, Vol. XIV, No. 2, pp. 129–37.

James, E. O.
1958 *Myth and ritual in the ancient Near East.* Thames and Hudson, London.

Jennings, Jesse D.
1956 "The American Southwest. A problem in cultural isolation," in *Seminars in Archaeology*. Edited by Robert Wauchope. Salt Lake City, Utah.

———, and E. Norbeck
1964 "Northern Mesoamerica," in *Prehistoric Man in the New World.* University of Chicago Press, Chicago.

Jiménez Moreno, Wigberto
1940 *Estudio sobre el ambiente del Códice de Yanhuitlan.* Museo Nacional de Antropología e Historia, México.
1941 "El problema de Tula," I *M.R., Boletín No. 1*, pp. 2–8.
1941 "Tula y los toltecas según las fuentes históricas," *R.M.E.A.*, Vol. V, pp. 79–85.
1942 "Relación entre los olmecas, los toltecas y los mayas, según las tradiciones," II *M.R.*, pp. 19–25.
1942 "El enigma de los olmecas," *Cuadernos Americanos*, Vol. V, pp. 113–45.
1943 "Tribus e idiomas del Norte de México," III *M.R.*, pp. 121–33.
1948 "Historia antigua de la zona tarasca," IV *M.R.*, pp. 146–59.
1953 "Historia antigua de México." Mimeographed lecture notes. Escuela Nacional de Antropología e Historia, México.
1954–55 "Síntesis de la historia precolonial del Valle de México," *R.M.E.A.*, Vol. XIV, No. 1, pp. 219–36.
1959 "Síntesis de la historia pretolteca de Mesoamérica," in *Esplendor del México Antiguo*, Vol. II, pp. 1109–96. Centro de Investigaciones Antropológicas de México, Mexico.
1961 "Diferentes principios del año entre diversos pueblos y sus consecuencias para la cronología prehispánica," *México Antiguo*, Vol. IX, pp. 81–85.
1966 "Los imperios prehispánicos en Mesoamérica," *R.M.E.A.*, Vol. XX, pp. 179–95.
1968 "Religión o religiones mesoamericanas?" *XXXVIII I.C.A.* Vol. III, pp. 201–206.

Kaplan, David
1963 "Men, monuments and political systems," *Southwestern Journal of Anthropology*, Vol. XIX, pp. 397–410.

Katz, Friedrich
1966 *Situación social y económica de los aztecas durante los siglos XV y XVI.* Instituto de Investigaciones Históricas, U.N.A.M., Mexico.

Kelley, David H.
1953 "Historia prehispánica de Totonacapan," in *Huastecos, Totonacos y sus Vecinos*, pp. 303–10. Sociedad Mexicana de Antropología. Mexico.
1955 "Quetzalcoatl and his coyote origins," *México Antiguo*, Vol. VIII, pp. 397–416.
1965 "The birth of the gods at Palenque," *E.C.M.*, Vol. V, pp. 93–134.

Kelley, J. Charles
1956 "Settlement patterns in north-central Mexico," in *Prehistoric settlement plans in the New World*. Edited by Gordon R. Willey. Viking Fund Publications in Anthropology, New York.
1966 "Mesoamerica and the southwestern United States." *H.M.A.I.*, Vol. IV, pp. 95–111.
1972 "Archaeology of the northern frontier: Zacatecas and Durango," *H.M.A.I.*, Vol. XI, pp. 768–804.

———, and Ellen Abbott
1964 "The cultural sequence on the North Central frontier of Mesoamerica," *XXXVI I.C.A.*, Vol. I, pp. 325–44.

———, and Howard D. Winters
1960 "A revision of the archaeological sequence in Sinaloa," *A. Antiq.*, Vol. XXV, pp. 547–61.

Kelly, Isabel
1941 "The relationship between Tula and Sinaloa," *R.M.E.A.*, Vol. V, pp. 199–208.

Kirchhoff, Paul
1940 "Los pueblos de la Historia Tolteca-Chichimeca. Sus migraciones y parentescos." *R.M.E.A.*, Vol. IV, pp. 65–76.
1941 "El problema de Tula." I *M.R.*, *Boletín No. 2*, pp. 3–9.
1942 "Distribución de elementos culturales atribuidos a los olmecas de las tradiciones," II *M.R.*, pp. 25–28.
1947 "Prólogo a la *Historia Tolteca-Chichimeca*," in *Historia Tolteca-Chichimeca*, pp. 1–XVI. Antigua Librería Robredo, Mexico.
1948 "Etnografía antigua," IV *M.R.*, pp. 134–36.
1955 "Quetzalcoatl, Huemac y el fin de Tula," *Cuadernos Americanos*, Vol. XIV, pp. 169–96.
1955–56 "Calendarios tenochca, tlatelolca y otros," *R.M.E.A.*, Vol. XIV, No. 2, pp. 257–67.
1956–57 "Composición étnica y organización política de Chalco según las *Relaciones* de Chimalpain," *R.M.E.A.*, Vol. XIV, No. 2, pp. 297–99.
1959 "Las dos rutas de los Culhua entre Tula y Culhuacán," *Mitteilungen aus dem Museum für Völkerkunde in Hamburg*, Vol. XXV, pp. 78–80.

1961 "Das Toltekenreich und sein Untergang," *Saeculum*, Vol. XII, Heft 3, pp. 248–65.
1964 "La aportación de Chimalpain a la historia tolteca," *Anales de Antropología*, Vol. I, pp. 78–90. U.N.A.M., Mexico.
1967 "El Valle Puebla-Tlaxcala." Lecture in the Museo Nacional de Antropología. I.N.A.H., México.
1968 "Las 18 fiestas anuales en Mesoamérica. 6 fiestas simples y 6 fiestas dobles," *XXXVIII I.C.A.*, Vol. III, pp. 207–22.

Kovar, Anton
1970 "The physical and biological environment of the Basin of Mexico," in *The Teotihuacán Valley Project*, Vol. I, pp. 14–67. Pennsylvania State University, State University, Pa.

Krickeberg, Walter
1933 *Los totonacs: contribución a la etnografía histórica de la América Central.* Talleres Graficos del Museo Nacional de Arqueología, Etnografía e Historia, Mexico.

Kroeber, A. L.
1940 "Conclusions: the present status of Americanistic problems," in *The Maya and their neighbors*, pp. 460–90. D. Appleton-Century, New York.

Kubler, George
1961 "Chichén-Itzá y Tula," *E.C.M.*, Vol. I, pp. 47–80.
1972 "La evidencia intrínseca y la analogía etnológica en el estudio de las religiones Mesoamericanas," XII *M.R.*, pp. 1–25.
1972 "La iconografía del arte de Teotihuacán," XI *M.R.*, Vol. II, pp. 69–86.

Landa, Fray Diego de
1959 *Relación de las cosas de Yucatán.* Editorial Porrua, S.A., México.

Ledyard Smith, A.
1940 "The corbeled arch of the New World," in *The Maya and their neighbors*, pp. 202–21. D. Appleton-Century, New York.

Lehmann, Walter
1902 "Des peintures mixteco-zapothèques," *Journal de la Société des Américanistes de Paris*, Vol. II, No. 1.
1920 *Zentralamerika.* 2 vols. Verlag Dietrich Reimer, Berlin.
1938 *Die Geschichte der Königreiche von Culhuacan und Mexico.* W. Kohlhammer Verlag, Stuttgart.
1941 *Una elegía tolteca.* Publicaciones de la Sociedad Alejandro Humboldt, *Folleto No.* 2, Mexico.

Lemoine, Ernesto. *See* Carmen Cook de Leonard.
León-Portilla, Miguel

1959 "Quetzalcoatl: espiritualismo del México antiguo," *Cuadernos Americanos*, Vol. XVIII, pp. 127–39.
1961 *Los antiguos mexicanos a través de sus crónicas y cantares*. Fondo de Cultura Económica, Mexico.
1963 *Aztec thought and culture*. Translated by Jack Emory Davis. University of Oklahoma Press, Norman.
1965 "Los Huaxtecos, según los informantes de Sahagún," *E.C.N.*, Vol. V., pp. 15–30.
1968 *Quetzalcoatl*. Fondo de Cultura Económica, Mexico.
1969 "Ramírez de Fuenleal y las antigüedades mexicanas," *E.C.N.*, Vol. VIII, pp. 9–50.
1972 "Religión de los nicaraos. Análisis y comparación de tradiciones culturales nahuas," *E.C.M.*, Vol. X, pp. 11–112.

Lévi-Strauss, Claude
1958 *Antropología estructural*. Translated into Spanish from French by Eliseo Verón. Editorial Universitaria de Buenos Aires.
1973 *From honey to ashes*. Translated from the French by John and Doreen Weightman. Johnathan Cape, London.

Leyenda de los Soles
1945 In *Códice Chimalpopoca*. Edited and translated by Primo F. Velásquez. Imprenta Universitaria, Mexico.

Linné, S.
1934 *Archaeological researches at Teotihuacán*. The Ethnological Museum of Sweden, Stockholm.
1942 *Mexican highland cultures*. The Ethnological Museum of Sweden, Stockholm.

Lister, Robert H.
1971 "Archaeological synthesis of Guerrero," *H.M.A.I.*, Vol. XI, pp. 603–18.

———, and Agnes M. Howard
1955 "The Chalchihuites culture of Northwestern México," *A. Antiq.*, Vol. XXI, pp. 122–29.

Litvak King, Jaime
1970 "El Valle de Xochicalco. Formación y análisis de un modelo estadístico para la arqueología regional." Thesis in the Library of the Museo de Antropología, Mexico.
1972 "La introducción posthispánica de elementos a las religiones prehispánicas: un problema de aculturación retroactiva," XII *M.R.*, pp. 25–30.
1972 "Las relaciones externas de Xochicalco: una evaluación de su significado," in *Anales de Antropología*, Vol. IX. U.N.A.M., Mexico.
1973 "Los patrones de cambio de estadio en el Valle de Xochicalco," in *Anales de Antropología*, Vol. X. U.N.A.M., Mexico.

Lizardi Ramos, Cesar
1944 "El Chacmool mexicano," *Cuadernos Americanos,* Vol. III, pp. 137–48.

Longyear, John M., III
1944 *Arqueological investigations in El Salvador. Memoirs of the Peabody Museum of Archaeology and Ethnology.* Harvard University, Cambridge, Mass.
1966 "Archaeological survey of El Salvador," *H.M.A.I.,* Vol. IV, pp. 132–56.

López Austin, Alfredo
1972 "Hombre Díos. Religión y política en el mundo náhuatl." Mimeographed thesis, U.N.A.M., Mexico.

Lorenzo, José Luis
1957 *Las zonas arqueológicas de los volcanes Iztaccíhuatl y Popocatépetl.* I.N.A.H., Mexico.
1968 "Clima y agricultura en Teotihuacán," in *Materiales para la arqueología de Teotihuacán,* pp. 51–72. I.N.A.H., Mexico.

Lothrop, Samuel
1927 "Pottery types in El Salvador," in *Indian Notes,* Vol. I, No. 4. Museum of the American Indian, New York.
1939 "Cuatro antiguas culturas en Panamá," *XXVII I.C.A.,* Vol. I, pp. 205–209.
1966 "Archaeology of Lower Central America," *H.M.A.I.,* Vol. IV, pp. 180–208.

McNeish, Richard S.
1954 "An early archaeological site near Pánuco," *Transactions of the American Philosophical Society,* Vol. XLIV, No. 5, pp. 2–25.
1958 "Preliminary archaeological investigations in the Sierra de Tamaulipas," *Transactions of the American Philosophical Society,* Vol. XLVIII, Part 6.

MacWhite, Eoin
1956 "On the interpretation of archaeological evidence in historical and social terms," *A. Anthr.,* Vol. LVIII, pp. 3–25.

Mahler, Joy
1961 "Grave associations and ceramics in Veraguas, Panamá," in *Essays in Pre-Columbian art and archaeology,* pp. 218–28. Harvard University Press, Cambridge, Mass.

Malinowski, Bronislaw
1948 *Magic, science and religion, and other essays.* Doubleday, New York.

Mapa de Cuauhtinchan
1966 Edited by Zita Basich de Canessi. Facsimile edition, Mexico.

Mapa Quinatzin
1886 In *Anales del Museo Nacional de México*, Epoca I, Vol. III, pp. 304–20.

Margain, Carlos R.
1955 "La zona arqueológica de Tulancingo," *I.N.A.H. Anales*, Vol. VI, pp. 41–47.
1971 "Pre-Columbian architecture of Central Mexico," *H.M.A.I.*, Vol. X., pp. 45–92.

Marquina, Ignacio
1941 "Relaciones entre los monumentos del Norte de Yucatán y los del Centro de México," *R.M.E.A.*, Vol. V, Nos. 2 and 3, pp. 135–50.
1970 "La pirámide de Cholula," in *Proyecto Cholula*, pp. 31–46. I.N.A.H., Mexico.
1972 "Influencias de Teotihuacán en Cholula," XI *M.R.*, Vol. II, pp. 231–43.

Martinez del Rio, Pablo
1946 *Tlatelolco a través de los tiempos. No. 7. Memorias de la Academia Mexicana de la Historia*, Vol. V., No. 2. Mexico.

Mason, J. Alden
1962 "The native languages of Middle America," in *The Maya and their neighbors*, pp. 52–87. D. Appleton-Century, New York.

Mastache, Guadalupe
1973 "Reconocimiento Arqueológico de superficie en el área de Tula, Hgo," XIII *M.R.*

Matos Moctezuma, Eduardo
1972 "El tzompantli en Mesoamérica," XII *M.R.*, pp. 109–16.

Mayer-Oakes, William J.
1960 "A developmental concept of pre-Spanish urbanization in the Valley of Mexico," in *Middle Research Records*, Vol. II. Tulane University, New Orleans.

Meade, Joaquin
1953 "Historia prehispánica de la Huasteca," *R.M.E.A.*, Vol. XIII, Nos. 2 and 3, pp. 291–302.
1953 "Relaciones entre las Huastecas y las regiones al poniente," *R.M.E.A.*, Vol. XIII, Nos. 2 and 3, pp. 475–78.

Meggers, Betty J.
1954 "Environmental limitations on the development of culture," *A. Anthr.*, Vol. LVI, pp. 801–24.

Meighan, Clement W.
1971 "Archaeology of Sinaloa," *H.M.A.I.*, Vol. IX, pp. 754–67.

Melgarejo, V. José Luis
1947 *La historia de Veracruz.* 2 vols. Enríquez, Jalapa, Veracruz.

Mendieta, Fray Jeronimo de
1945 *Historia eclesiástica indiana.* 4 vols. Editorial Chávez Hayhoe, Mexico.

Meyer, Enrique
1939 "Noticia sobre los petroglífos de Tula, Hidalgo," *R.M.E.A.*, Vol. III, No. 2, pp. 122–28.

Miles, S. W.
1957 "The sixteenth-century Pokom Maya. A documentary analysis of social structure and archaeological setting," *Transactions of the American Philosophical Society*, Vol. XLVII, Part 4, pp. 733–81.
1965 "Summary of preconquest ethnology of the Guatemala-Chiapas Highlands and Pacific Slopes," *H.M.A.I.*, Vol. II, pp. 276–87.

Millon, René
1960 "The beginnings of Teotihuacán," *A. Antiq.*, Vol. XXVI, pp. 1–10.
1964 "The Teotihuacán mapping project," *A. Antiq.*, Vol. XXIX, pp. 345–53
1966 "Cronología y periodificación: datos estratigráficos sobre los períodos cerámicos y sus relaciones con la pintura mural," XI *M.R.*, Vol. I, pp. 1–18.
1966 "Extensión y población de la ciudad de Teotihuacán en sus diferentes períodos; un cálculo provisional," XI *M.R.*, Vol. I, pp. 57–78.
1966 "El problema de integración en la sociedad teotihuacana," XI *M.R.*, Vol. I, pp. 149–55.
1970 "Teotihuacán: Completion of map of giant ancient city in the Valley of Mexico," *Science*, Vol. CLXX, pp. 1077–82. "El fin de Teotihuacán." XLI I.C.A. (in press).

———, and Bruce Drewitt
1961 "Earlier structures within the Pyramid of the Sun at Teotihuacán," *A. Antiq.*, Vol. XXVI, pp. 371–80.

———, ———, and George Cowgill
1972 "Urbanization at Teotihuacán." Mimeographed version, to be published by University of Texas Press, Austin.

Moedano Koer, Hugo
1946 "Tollan." Professional thesis, Escuela Nacional de Antropología e Historia, Mexico.

Mooser, Federico
1968 "Geología, naturaleza y desarrollo del Valle de Teotihuacán," in *Materiales para la arqueología de Teotihuacán*, pp. 29–38. I.N.A.H., Mexico.

Morley, Sylvanus. *See* Alfredo Barrera Vásquez.

Morris, Earl H.

1931 *The Temple of Warriors at Chichén-Itzá, Yucatán.* 2 vols. *C.I.W. Pub. 406.* Washington, D.C.

Motolinía, Fray Toribio de Benavente

1941 *Historia de los indios de la Nueva España.* Editorial Chávez Hayhoe, Mexico.

1967 *Memoriales.* Published by Luis García Pimentel and reproduced in facsimile edition by Edmundo Aviña Levy, Guadalajara.

Muller, Florencia

1948 "La cerámica de la cuenca del Río Lerma." IV *M.R.*, pp. 50–54.

1949 *Historia antigua del Valle de Morelos.* Acta Antropológica, Imprenta Nuevo Mundo, Mexico.

1954 "Tres objetos de piedra de Huapalcalco, Estado de Hidalgo," in *Homenaje a Pablo Martínez del Río*, pp. 319–22. I.N.A.H., Mexico.

1963 "Costumbres funerarias del Valle de Tulancingo, Hidalgo," *R.M.E.A.*, Vol. XIX, pp. 27–36.

1966 "Instrumentos y armas," XI, *M.R.*, Vol. I, pp. 225–38.

1966 "Secuencia cerámica de Teotihuacán," XI *M.R.*, Vol. I, pp. 31–44.

1970 "La cerámica de Cholula," in *Proyecto Cholula*, pp. 129–42. I.N.A.H., Mexico.

1972 "Estudio iconográfico del mural de los bebedores de Cholula, Puebla," XII *M.R.*, pp. 141–46.

1972 *See under* Drummond and Muller.

1973 *La extensión arqueológica de Cholula a través del tiempo.* Fundación Alemana para la Investigación Científica, *Primer Simposio.* Puebla.

Muñoz Camargo, Diego

1947 *Historia de Tlaxcala, Mexico.* Publicaciones del Ateneo de Ciencias y Artes de México.

Navarrete, Carlos

1961 "Investigaciones arqueológicas acerca del problema chiapaneco," VIII *M.R.*, pp. 63–74.

Nelken-Terner, Antoinette, and Richard S. McNeish

1971 *La Vallée de Tehuacán (Mexique). 12,000 años de préhistoire. Annales*, No. 6, Librairie Armand Colin, Paris.

Nicholson, Henry B.

1955 "The temalacatl of Tehuacán," *México Antiguo*, Vol. VIII, pp. 95–134.

1957 "Topiltzin Quetzalcoatl of Tollan: a problem in Mesoamerican ethnohistory." Doctoral dissertation, Harvard University.

1958 "An Aztec monument dedicated to Tezcatlipoca," in *Miscelánea Paul Rivet*, Vol. I, pp. 593–607.

1961 "The use of the term 'Mixtec' in Mesoamerican archaeology," *A. Antiq.* Vol. XXVI, pp. 431–33.

1962 *See under* Hicks and Nicholson.

1968 "The religious-ritual system of Late pre-Hispanic Central Mexico," *XXXVIII I.C.A.*, Vol. III, pp. 223–38.

1971 "Major sculpture in pre-Hispanic Central Mexico," *H.M.A.I.*, Vol. X, pp. 92–134.

1972 "Religion in pre-Hispanic Central Mexico," *H.M.A.I.*, Vol. X, pp. 395–446.

1972 "The problem of the historical identity of the Cerro Portezuelo/San Antonio archaeological site," XI *M.R.*, Vol. II, pp. 157–200.

Noguera, Eduardo

1935 "La cerámica de Tenayuca y las excavaciones estratigráficas," in *Estudio arqueológico de la pirámide de Tenayuca.* Talleres Gráficos del Museo Nacional de Arqueología, Historia e Etnografía, Mexico.

1940 "Excavations at Tehuacán," in *The Maya and their neighbors*, pp. 306–19. D. Appleton-Century, New York.

1963 *La cerámica arqueológica de Mesoamérica.* U.N.A.M., Mexico.

———, and Ramón Piña Chan

1956–57 "Estratigrafía de Teopanzolco," *R.M.E.A.*, Vol. XIV, No. 2, pp. 167–91.

Nowotny, Karl A. *See* Codex Becker.

Olivé Negrete, Julio César

1958 *Estructura y dinámica de Mesoamérica. Acta Antropológica*, Epoca 2, Vol. I, No. 3.

———, and Beatriz Barba de Piña Chan

1957 *Sobre la disintegración de las culturas clásicas. Anales*, Vol. IX. I.N.A.H., Mexico.

O'Neill, George

1956–57 Preliminary report on stratigraphic excavation in the southern Valley of Mexico: Chalco-Xico," *R.M.E.A.*, Vol. XIV, No. 2, pp. 45–51.

Oppenheim, Leo A.

1964 *Ancient Mesopotamia.* Chicago University Press, Chicago.

Orcadiz, Roberto

1940 *Tulancingo y sus alrededores.* Mexico.

Orozco y Berra, Manuel

1960 *Historia antigua de la conquista de México*, 4 vols. Editorial Porrua, Mexico.

Oviedo y Valdes, Gonzalo Fernández de
1851–55 *Historia general y natural de las Indias, islas y tierra firme del Mar Océano.* Madrid.

Paddock, John
1966 "La idea del imperio aplicada a Mesoamérica," *R.M.E.A.*, Vol. XX, pp. 83–84.
1966 *Ancient Oaxaca: discoveries in Mexican archaeology and history.* Stanford University Press, Stanford, Calif.

Palacios, Enrique
1940 "El simbolismo del chacmool. Su interpretación," *R.M.E.A.*, Vol. IV, Nos. 1 and 2, pp. 43–56.
1941 "Teotihuacán, los toltecas y Tula," *R.M.E.A.*, Vol. V, Nos. 2 and 3, pp. 113–34.

Palerm, Angel
1952 *La civilización urbana. Historia Mexicana,* Vol. II, No. 2.
1955 *La secuencia de la evolución cultural en Mesoamérica.* Unión Panamericana, Vol. VI. No. 36. Washington, D.C.
1956 *See under* Pedro Armillas.
1973 *Obras hidráulicas prehispánicas.* I.N.A.H., Mexico.

———, and Eric R. Wolf
1954–55 "El desarrollo del área clave del Imperio Texcocano," *R.M.E.A.*, Vol. XIV, No. 1, pp. 337–50.
1958 *Potencial ecológico y desarrollo cultural en Mesoamerica.* Unión Panamericana. *Estudios Monográficos,* No. 3. Washington, D.C.

Papeles de Nueva España
1905–1906 Edited by Francisco del Paso y Troncoso. Second series, 9 vols. Sucesores de Rivadeneyra, Madrid.

Pasztory, Esther
1972 "The historical and religious significance of the Middle Classic ballgame," XII *M.R.*, pp. 441–56.
1972 "The gods of Teotihuacán: a synthetic approach in Teotihuacán iconography," *XL I.C.A.*, Vol. I, pp. 147–60.

Peterson, Frederick A.
1950 *Notes on Coatlichan ceramics. Mesoamerican Notes,* No. 1, pp. 29–33. Mexico.

Phillips, Philip. *See* Willey and Phillips.

Piña Chan, Román
1956–57 *See under* Eduardo Noguera.

1964 "Algunas consideraciones sobre las pinturas de Mul-Chic, Yucatán," *E.C.M.*, Vol. IV, pp. 63–78.

1967 *Un complejo Coyotlatelco en Coyocán. Anales de Antropología*, Vol. IV, pp. 141–60. Mexico.

1970 "Arqueología y tradición histórica, un testimonio de los informantes de Sahagún." Thesis, U.N.A.M.

1972 *Historia, arqueología y arte prehispánico.* Fondo de Cultura Económica, Septiembre 1971. Gobierno del Estado de México.

1972 *Historia, arqueología y arte prehispánico.* Fondo de Cultura Económica, Mexico.

Pomar, Juan Bautista

1941 *Relaciones de Texcoco y de la Nueva España.* Editorial Chávez Hayhoe, Mexico.

Popol Vuh. *See* Adrián Recinos.

Porter, Muriel

1948 "Pottery found at Chupicuaro, Guanajuato," IV *M.R.*, pp. 42–47.

Prehistoric Man in the New World

1964 Jesse Jennings and Edward Norbeck, eds. William Marsh—Rice University, Houston, Texas.

Price, Barbara J.

1968 *See* under William T. Sanders.

1972 "Population composition in pre-Hispanic Mesoamerican urban settlements. A problem in archaeological inference," *XXXIX I.C.A.*, Vol. II, pp. 257–70.

Proskouriakoff, Tatiana

1950 *A study of Classic Maya sculpture. C.I.W. Pub. 593.* Washington, D.C.

1953 "Scroll patterns (*entrelaces*) of Veracruz," *R.M.E.A.*, Vol. XIII, Nos. 2 and 3, pp. 389–401.

1960 "Historical implications of a pattern of dates at Piedras Negras, Guatemala," *A. Antiq.*, Vol. XXV, pp. 454–75.

1960 *Varieties of Classic Central Veracruz sculpture. C.I.W. Pub 606.* Washington, D.C.

1962 "Civic and religious structures of Mayapan," in *Mayapan, Yucatán, México. C.I.W. Pub. 619.* Washington, D.C.

1965 "Sculpture and major arts of the Maya Lowlands," *H.M.A.I.*, Vol. II, pp. 469–97.

Proyecto Cholula

1970 Ignacio Marquina, ed. I.N.A.H., México.

Recinos, Adrían

1947 *Popol Vuh: las antiguas historias del quiché.* Translated into Spanish by A. Recinos. Fondo de Cultura Económica, Mexico.

1948 *Anales de los Cakchiqueles.* Fondo de Cultura Económica, Mexico–Buenos Aires.

1954 *Prophecies of the Chilam Balam. C.I.W. Pub. 606, Contribution 57.* Washington, D.C.

1957 *Crónicas indígenas de Guatemala.* Imprenta Universitaria, Guatemala.

Relación de Atengo y Misquiahuala

1957 Vargas Rea, ed. México.

Relación de Culhuacán

1927 In *Relaciones históricas estadísticas.* Manuscript compiled by Joaquín García Icazbalceta and kept in the Library of the Museo Nacional de Antropología, México.

Relación de Cuzcatlan

1905–1906 In *Papeles de Nueva España,* Vol. V, pp. 46–54.

Relación de la Genealogía

1941 In *Relaciones de Texcoco y de las Nueva España,* pp. 240 ff.

Relación de Papaloticpac

1905–1906 *Papeles de Nueva España,* Vol. IV, pp. 88–93.

Relación de Teotitlan

1905–1906 In *Papeles de Nueva España,* Vol. IV, pp. 213–31.

Relación de Tepeji del Rio. *See* Codex of Otlozpan.

Relaciones de Yucatán

1898–1900 *Colección de documentos inéditos relativos al descubrimiento, conquista y organización de las antiguas posesiones españolas de ultramar.* Vols. XI and XIII. Madrid.

Renfew, Colin

1970 "New configurations in Old World archaeology," *World Archaeology,* Vol. II, No. 2.

Reyes García, Luis

1972 "Ordenanzas para el gobierno de Cuauhtinchan, año 1559," *E.C.N.,* Vol. X, pp. 245–314.

Richardson, Francis B.
1940 "Non-Maya monumental sculpture of Central America," *XXVII I.C.A.*, Vol. I, pp. 312–40.

Rojas, Gabriel. *See Descripción de Cholula.*

Rose, H. J.
1945 *A handbook of Greek mythology.* Methuen and Co., London.

Rovirosa, José N.
1888 *Nombres geográficos del Estado de Tabasco.* Secretaría de Fomento, Mexico.

Roys, Ralph L.
1933 *The book of Chilam Balam of Chumayel. C.I.W. Pub. 438*, Washington, D.C.
1948 *See under* F. V. Scholes.
1949 *The prophecies for the Maya tuns or years in the books of Chilam Balam of Tizimin and Mani. C.I.W. Pub. 585, Contribution 51.* Washington, D.C.
1949 *Guide to the Codex Pérez. C.I.W. Contributions to American Anthropology and History*, Vol. X, No. 49.
1954 *The Maya katun prophecies of the books of Chilam Balam.* Series I., *C.I.W. Pub. 606, Contribution 57.* Washington, D.C.
1962 *Literary sources for the history of Mayapan. C.I.W. Pub. 619.* Washington, D.C.
1965 "Lowland Maya native society at Spanish contact," *H.M.A.I.*, Vol. III, Part 2, pp. 659–78.
1966 "Native empires in Yucatán," *R.M.E.A.*, Vol. XX, pp. 155–78.

Ruppert, Carl
1952 *Chichén Itzá. Architectural notes and plans. C.I.W. Pub. 595.* Washington, D.C.

Ruz Lhuiller, Alberto
1945 *Campeche en la arqueología maya. Acta Antropológica*, Vol. I, Nos. 2 and 3. Mexico.
1953 "Presencia atlántica en Palenque," *R.M.E.A.*, Vol. XIII, Nos. 2 and 3, pp. 455–62.
1959 *La costa de Campeche en tiempos prehispánicos, prospección, cerámica y bosquejo histórico.* I.N.A.H., Mexico.
1962 "Chichén Itzá y Tula: Comentarios a un ensayo," *E.C.M.*, Vol. II, pp. 205–23.
1964 "Influencias mexicanas sobre los mayas," in *Desarrollo cultural de los mayas.* U.N.A.M., Mexico.
1964 "Influencias mayas en las tierras altas bajas del area maya," *XXXV I.C.A.*, Vol. I, pp. 225–43.

Sáenz, César A.

1963 "Exploraciones en la Pirámide de las Serpientes Emplumadas en Xochicalco," *R.M.E.A.*, Vol. XIX, pp. 7–26.

1961 "Tres estelas de Xochicalco," *R.M.E.A.*, Vol. XVII, pp. 39–65.

1962 *Quetzalcoatl.* I.N.A.H., Mexico.

1964 "Las estelas de Xochicalco," *XXXV I.C.A.*, Vol. II, pp. 69–84.

1964 *Ultimos descubrimientos en Xochicalco.* I.N.A.H., Mexico.

1967 *Nuevas exploraciones y hallazgos en Xochicalco, 1965–6.* I.N.A.H., Mexico.

Sahagún, Fray Bernardino de

1956 *Historia general de las cosas de Nueva España.* 4 vols. Editorial Porrua, Mexico.

1950–63 *Florentine Codex. General history of the things of New Spain.* Translated from Náhuatl into English by Charles E. Dibble and Arthur J. O. Anderson. 11 vols. The School of American Research and the University of Utah, Santa Fe, New Mexico.

Sanders, William T.

1962 "Cultural ecology of Nuclear Mesoamerica," *A. Antiq.*, Vol. LXIV, No. 1, pp. 34–44.

1962 "Cultural ecology of the Maya Lowlands, Part 1," *E.C.M.*, Vol. II, pp. 79–122.

1963 "Cultural ecology of the Maya Lowlands, Part II," *E.C.M.*, Vol. III, pp. 203–42.

1964 *The cultural ecology of the Teotihuacán Valley.* Department of Sociology and Anthropology, Pennsylvania State University, State University, Pa.

1966 "Life in a Classic village," XI *M.R.*, Vol. I, pp. 123–48.

1970 "The population of the Teotihuacán Valley, the basin of Mexico and the Central Mexican symbiotic region in the sixteenth century," in *The Teotihuacán Valley Project Final Report*, Vol. I, pp. 386–456. Pennsylvania State University, State University, Pa.

1971 "Settlement patterns in Central Mexico," *H.M.A.I.*, Vol. X., pp. 3–44.

1972 "Cultural ecology and settlement patterns of the Gulf Coast," *H.M.A.I.*, Vol. XI, pp. 543–57.

———, and Barbara J. Price

1968 *Mesoamerica. The evolution of a civilization.* Random House, New York.

Satterthwaite, Linton, Jr.

1942 "Opposed interpretation of dates and hieroglyphs at Chichén Itzá," *R.M.E.A.*, Vol. VI, Nos. 1 and 2, pp. 19–35.

1965 "Calendrics of the Maya Lowlands," *H.M.A.I.*, Vol. III, pp. 603–31.

1967 "Radiocarbon and Maya long count dating 'Structure 10,' Tikal," *R.M.E.A.*, Vol. XXI, pp. 225–50.

———, and William Coe
1961 *Inscriptions and other dating controls in the carved lintels at Tikal. Tikal Report No. 6.* Museum Monographs, University Museum. University of Pennsylvania, Philadelphia.

Schaller, P.
1924 "Notes on the Huaxtec Indians of San Luis Potosí," *México Antiguo*, Vol. II, pp. 129–40.

Scholes, F. V., and R. L. Roys
1948 *The Maya Chontal Indians of Acalan-Tixchel: a contribution to the history and ethnography of the Yucatán peninsula. C.I.W. Pub. 560.* Washington, D.C.

Scholes, F. V., and Dave Warren
1965 "The Olmec region at Spanish contact," *H.M.A.I.*, Vol. III, pp. 776–87.

Schultze-Jena, Leonhard
1957 *Alt-aztekische Gesänge.* W. Kohlhammer Verlag, Stuttgart.

Séjourné, Laurette
1954 "Tula, la supuesta capital de los toltecas," *Cuadernos Americanos.* Vol. LXXIII, No. 1, pp. 153–69.
1962 *El universo de Quetzalcoatl.* Fondo de Cultura Económica, Mexico.
1966 *La arquitectura de Teotihuacán.* Fondo de Cultura Económica, Mexico.
1970 *La arqueología del Valle de México.* I.N.A.H., Mexico.

Seler, Eduard
1960 *Gesammelte Abhandlungen zur Amerikanischen Sprach-und Altertumskunde.* 5 vols. Akademisch Druck Anstalt, Graz.
1963 *Codex Borgia*, with commentary by Eduard Seler. 3 vols. Fondo de Cultura Económica, Mexico.

Shaekel, Richard P.
1949 "Major commercial centers in Northern Peru," in *Selected Papers, XXIX I.C.A.* New York.

Shepard, Anna O.
1948 *Plumbate: A Mesoamerican trade ware. C.I.W. Pub. 573.* Washington, D.C.

Smith, A. L.
1962 "Residential and associated structures at Mayapan," in *Mayapan, Yucatán, México. C.I.W. Pub. 619.* Washington, D.C.

Smith, Mary Elizabeth
1973 *Picture writing from ancient southern Mexico.* Oklahoma University Press, Norman.

Smith, Robert E.

1958 "The place of Fine Orange pottery in Mesoamerican archaeology," *A. Antiq.* Vol. XXIV, pp. 151–60.

Spencer, Michael W.

1966 "Los talleres de obsidiana de Teotihuacán," XI *M.R.*, Vol. I, pp. 213–18.

Spinden, Herbert J.

1948 "Chorotegan influences in Western Mexico," III *M.R.*, pp. 311–19.

Spores, Ronald

1967 *The Mixtec kings and their people.* University of Oklahoma Press, Norman.

Stanislawski, Michael B.

1964 "Mesoamerican influences in Northeastern Arizona," *XXXVI I.C.A.*, Vol. I, pp. 309–19.

Steward, Julian

1948 "The Circum-Caribbean tribes: an introduction," in *Handbook of South American Indians*, Vol. IV, pp. 1–41.

1949 "Cultural causality and law: a trial formulation of the development of early civilizations," *A. Anthr.*, Vol. XLI, No. 1, pp. 1–27.

1953 "Evolution and process," in *Anthropology Today*, edited by A. L. Kroeber. University of Chicago Press, Chicago.

1955 *Theory of cultural change; the methodology of multilinear evolution.* University of Illinois Press, Urbana.

1955 *Teoría y práctica en el estudio de áreas. Manuales Técnicos No. 2.* Panamerican Union, Washington, D.C.

Stirling, Matthew W.

1965 "Monumental sculpture of Southern Veracruz and Tabasco," *H.M.A.I.*, Vol. III, pp. 716–38.

Stone, Doris

1946 "La posición de los chorotegas en la arqueología centroamericana," *R.M.E.A.*, Vol. VIII, Nos. 1, 2, and 3, pp. 121–31.

1959 "The eastern frontier of Mesoamerica," in *Mitteilungen*, Vol. XXV, pp. 118–21. Museum für Völkerkunde und Vorgeschichte, Hamburg.

Stoutamire, James

1973 "Archaeological survey of the Tula urban zone." Mimeographed report on Tula expedition, 1970–72, pp. 22–30. University of Missouri, Columbia.

Stresser Péan, Guy

1953 "Les indiens huastèques," *R.M.E.A.*, Vol. XIII, Nos. 2 and 3, pp. 213–34.

1953 "Les Nahuas du Sud de la Huasteca et l'ancienne extension méridional des Huaxtèques," *R.M.E.A.*, Vol. XIII, Nos. 2 and 3, pp. 287–90.

Sullivan, Thelma
1972 "Tláloc: a new etymological interpretation of the god's name and what it reveals of his essence and nature," *XL I.C.A.*

Suma de Visitas
1905–
1906 In *Papeles de Nueva España,* Vol. I. Sucesores de Rivadeneyra, Madrid.

Swadesh, M.
1954–55 "Algunas fechas glotocronológicas importantes para la prehistoria nahua," *R.M.E.A.*, Vol. XIV, No. 1, pp. 173–92.
1961 "Algunos reflejos lingüísticos de la prehistoria de Chiapas," VIII *M.R.*, pp. 145–60.

Tello, Fray Antonio
1891 *Libro segundo de la crónica miscelánea en que se trata de la conquista espiritual de la santa Provincia de Xalisco.* Imprenta de la República literaria de Guadalajara, Guadalajara.

Tezozómoc, Hernando Alvarado
1944 *Crónica mexicana.* Editorial Leyenda, Mexico.
1949 *Crónica Mexicayotl.* Instituto de Historia, U.N.A.M., Mexico.

Thompson, J. Eric S.
1939 "Las Ilamadas fachadas de Quetzalcoatl," *XXVI I.C.A.*, Vol. I, pp. 391–400.
1940 "Archaeological problems of the Lowland Maya," in *The Maya and their neighbors.* D. Appleton-Century, New York.
1941 "A coordination of the history of Chichén Itza with ceramic sequence in Central Mexico," *R.M.E.A.*, Vol. V, Nos. 2 and 3, pp. 97–111.
1942 "Representations of Tezcatlipoca at Chichén Itza," *XXVII I.C.A.*, Vol. I, pp. 391–400.
1943 *Pitfalls and stimuli in the interpretation of history through loan words. Publication No. 11*, Middle American Research Institute. Tulane University, New Orleans.
1951 "The Itzá of Tayasal, Petén" in *Homenaje al Dr. Alfonso Caso,* pp. 389–400. Mexico.
1951 "Aquatic symbols common to various centers of the Classic period in Mesoamerica," in *Selected Papers, XXIX I.C.A.* University of Chicago Press, Chicago.
1953 "Relaciones entre Veracruz y la región maya," *R.M.E.A.*, Vol. XIII, Nos. 2 and 3, pp. 447–54.
1962 "Trade relations between the Maya Highlands and Lowlands," *XXXV I.C.A.*, Vol. I, pp. 245–47.
1965 "Maya creation myths, Part I," *E.C.M.*, Vol. V, pp. 13–32.
1965 "Archaeological synthesis of the Maya Lowlands," *H.M.A.I.*, Vol. II, pp. 331–59.

1970 "Maya rulers of the Classic period and the divine right of kings," in *The iconography of Middle American sculpture*, pp. 52–71. The Metropolitan Museum of Art Centenary Symposium, New York.

1970 *Maya history and religion*. University of Oklahoma Press, Norman.

Thurber, Floyd and Valerie

1964 "Hieroglyphs Imix and Kan as non-calendrical symbols for the Maya creator couple," *E.C.M.*, Vol. IV, pp. 245–56.

Tibon, Gutierre

1967 El heroe tepozteco. Sicoanálisis de un mito universal," *Humanitas*, Vol. VIII, pp. 449–59.

Tolstoy, Paul

1958 "Surface survey of the northern Valley of Mexico," *Transactions of the American Philosophical Society*, Vol. XLVIII, Part 5.

Torquemada, Fray Juan de

1943–44 *Monarquía indiana*. 3 vols. Editorial Chávez Hayhoe, Mexico.

Tozzer, Alfred M.

1921 *Excavations of a site at Santiago, Ahuitzotla*. U.S. Government Printing Office, Washington, D.C.

1957 *Chichén Itza and its cenote of sacrifice. A comparative study of contemporaneous Maya and Toltec.*

Vaillant, C. George

1938 "A correlation of archaeological and historic sequences in the Valley of Mexico," *A. Anthr.*, Vol. XL, No. 4, pp. 535–73.

Vetancurt, Agustín de

1780–81 *Teatro mexicano*. 4 vols. Imprenta Escalante y Compañía, Mexico.

Veytia, Mariano

1944 *Historia antigua de México*. 2 vols., Editorial Leyenda, Mexico.

Warren, Bruce

1962 "A hypothetical reconstruction of Mayan origins," *XXXV I.C.A.*, Vol. I, pp. 289–305.

Waterbolk, H. T.

1971 "Working with radiocarbon dates," *Proceedings of the Prehistoric Society*, Vol. XXXVII, Part 2.

Wauchope, Robert

"Southern Mesoamerica," in *Prehistoric Man in the New World*.

Weiant, C. W.
1939 "Consideración preliminar sobre la cerámica de Tres Zapotes," *XXVII I.C.A.*, Vol. 11, pp. 97–112.
1943 *An introduction to the ceramics of Tres Zapotes.* Bureau of American Ethnology, *Bulletin No. 139*. Smithsonian Institution, Washington, D.C.
Weitlaner, R. J.
1941 "Los pueblos no-nahuas de la historia tolteca y el grupo lingüístico Macro Otomangue," *R.M.E.A.*, Vol. V, Nos. 2 and 3, pp. 249–69.

West, Robert C. *See* Armillas, Pedro.

Whitecotton, Joseph W.
1977 *The Zapotecs: Princes, Priests, and Peasants.* University of Oklahoma Press, Norman.

Whorf, B. L.
1943 *Loan words in Ancient Mexico.* Middle American Research Institute, *Publication No. 11.* Tulane University, New Orleans.

Willey, Gordon R.
1953 "Archaeological theories and interpretation: New World," in *Anthropology today*, pp. 361–85. Edited by A. L. Kroeber. University of Chicago Press, Chicago.
1956 "The structure of Ancient Maya society: evidence from the Southern Lowlands," *A. Anthr.*, Vol. LVIII, pp. 777–83.

———, and Philip Phillips
1958 *Method and theory in American archaeology.* University of Chicago Press, Chicago.

———, and A. L. Smith
1963 *New discoveries at Altar de Sacrificios, Guatemala.* Peabody Museum Papers, Vol. LIV, Cambridge, Mass.

Winters, Howard D. *See* J. Charles Kelley and Winters.

Wolf, Eric R. *See* Armillas, Palerm, and Wolf.

Woodbury, Richard B.
1966 "Prehistoric water management systems in the Tehuacán Valley, Mexico," *XXXVI I.C.A.*, Vol. I, pp. 345–47.

Wynn, Jack T.
1970 "Inferences from Toltec residential architecture." Mimeographed report, University of Missouri, Colombia.

Yadeun Angulo, Juan
1975 "El Estado y la Ciudad. El Caso de Tula Hidalgo." Thesis. Escuela Nacional de Antropología e Historia, Mexico.

Zantwijk, Rudolf A. M. van
1969 "La estructura gubernamental del estado de Tlacopan (1430–1520)," *E.C.N.*, Vol. VIII, pp. 123–56.

Index